Blood Libel

BLOOD LIBEL

On the Trail of an Antisemitic Myth

 MAGDA TETER

Harvard University Press
Cambridge, Massachusetts
London, England
2020

Copyright © 2020 by Magda Teter
All rights reserved
Printed in the United States of America

First printing

Library of Congress Cataloging-in-Publication Data
Names: Teter, Magda, author.
Title: Blood libel : on the trail of an antisemitic myth / Magda Teter.
Description: Cambridge, Massachusetts : Harvard University Press, 2020. |
Includes bibliographical references and index.
Identifiers: LCCN 2019029681 | ISBN 9780674240933 (hardcover)
Subjects: LCSH: Blood accusation—Europe—History. | Christianity and
antisemitism—Europe—History. | Anti-Jewish propaganda—Europe—History.
Classification: LCC BM585.2 .T48 2020 | DDC 305.892/404—dc23
LC record available at https://lccn.loc.gov/2019029681

In gratitude to

YOSEF HAYIM YERUSHALMI ז״ל
who introduced me to Isaac Cardoso and *Shevet Yehudah*

JEREMY ZWELLING
who gave me support when I needed it

JEANNETTE HOPKINS
who taught me all I know about writing and book publishing

STEPHEN FREEDMAN ז״ל
who brought me to Fordham and offered cheer and encouragement

CONTENTS

Illustrations	ix
Note on Places and Names	xi
Introduction	1
1. From Medieval Tales to the Challenge in Trent	14
2. The Death of Little Simon and the Trial of Jews in Trent	43
3. Echoes of Simon of Trent in European Culture	89
4. Blood Libels and Cultures of Knowledge in Early Modern Europe	152
5. Ashkenazi and Sephardic Jews Respond to Blood Libels	208
6. "Who Should One Believe, the Rabbis or the Doctors of the Church?"	236
7. "Jews Are Deemed Innocent in the Tribunals of Italy"	279
8. The "Enlightenment" Pope Benedict XIV and the Blood Accusation	300

9. Cardinal Ganganelli's Secret Report	323
10. Calculated Pragmatism and the Waning of Accusations	345
Epilogue: The Trail Continues	377
Notes	*387*
Archival and Printed Primary Sources	*493*
Acknowledgments	*515*
Index	*519*

ILLUSTRATIONS

Map 1	European sites of blood libel court cases.	xiii
Fig. 0.1	*Der Stürmer,* May 1, 1934, the ritual murder issue.	3
Fig. 0.2	A mural of Simon of Trent on Brückenturm in Frankfurt.	6
Fig. 0.3	Simon of Trent, late sixteenth-century painting, northern Italy.	8
Fig. 1.1	William of Norwich, from Hartmann Schedel, *Weltchronik* (1493).	16
Fig. 1.2	Simon of Trent, from Schedel, *Weltchronik* (1493).	17
Fig. 2.1	Pilgrims visiting the relics of Simon (1475).	45
Fig. 2.2	Tobias capturing Simon, *Hystorie von Simon zu Trient* published by Albert Kunne (1475).	66
Fig. 2.3	Simon's martyrdom with Simon held by Moses, Kunne chapbook.	67
Fig. 2.4	Simon as martyr, Kunne chapbook.	68
Fig. 2.5	Simon on the altar, Kunne chapbook.	69
Fig. 2.6	A 1475 broadsheet with Brunetta.	77
Fig. 3.1	Simon of Trent, pirated edition of Schedel's *Liber chronicarum* (Augsburg, 1497).	90
Fig. 3.2	Antonio Gesti, *Martirio di S. Simone di Trento* (1589).	115
Fig. 3.3	Michelangelo Mariani, *Il glorioso infante S. Simone* (1668).	126
Fig. 3.4	Passover seder, Kunne chapbook.	129

Fig. 3.5	Examination of Simon's body after its discovery, Kunne chapbook.	130
Fig. 3.6	Jews put to the flames, Kunne chapbook.	131
Fig. 3.7	Execution of the baptized Jews, Kunne chapbook.	132
Fig. 3.8	Jews conspiring to kidnap a child, with Christian symbols of fish and lamb, Kunne chapbook.	133
Fig. 3.9	Tobias ordered to kidnap a Christian child, from Tiberino published by Ginther Zainer in Augsburg (1475).	134
Fig. 3.10	Fresco on the site of Simon's house in Trent.	141
Fig. 3.11	"Tobias the Jew snatches the boy," a painting in Sandomierz, Poland.	144
Fig. 3.12	Simonine iconography of ritual murder, Sandomierz, Poland.	145
Fig. 3.13	"Raptus," from a painting "San Simonino da Trento" by Pietromartino Fiammingo di Anversa (1597).	146
Fig. 3.14	Northern European iconography stressing murder (1698).	150
Fig. 4.1	A Jew desecrating a crucifix, from Schedel, *Weltchronik*.	155
Fig. 4.2	Burning Jews, from Schedel, *Weltchronik*.	156
Fig. 4.3	Pages from Münster's *Cosmography* (1567).	159
Fig. 4.4	First printed illustrated Haggadah, by Thomas Murner (1512).	176
Fig. 6.1	S. Simonino da Trento, broadside by Giovanni Parone (1643–1730).	262
Fig. 8.1	Andreas of Rinn, early twentieth-century devotional card.	313
Fig. 10.1	A drawing of a body found near Tyczyn in 1766.	360
Fig. 11.1	Story of Simon of Trent in *Der Stürmer*, 1934.	381

NOTE ON PLACES AND NAMES

During the premodern period covered by this book, political boundaries changed, and some states known today did not exist. The Polish state, for example, transformed from a union of two independent states of the Polish Crown and the Grand Duchy of Lithuania into the Polish-Lithuanian Commonwealth. The terms "Poland" and "Poland-Lithuania" are sometimes used in the text to denote the Polish-Lithuanian Commonwealth, especially for sources in Polish, unless specific regions are pertinent. Italy as a single state did not exist; it comprised separate principalities, including the Papal States, Venetian Republic, Duchy of Milan, and others. But sources do use the term *Italia*, and in some cases the term *Italy* is used in the book. But political units that are particularly pertinent are referred to by their proper names.

Towns and cities are identified throughout according to the terminology of the period, unless an English equivalent exists. For example, present-day Vilnius in Lithuania appears as Wilno, and current-day Lviv in Ukraine is referred to as Lwów. But for Kraków, Trento, or Warszawa, for which English names exist, Cracow, Trent, and Warsaw are used. In the bibliography, the place names correspond to those in the publication itself, except for well-known places such as Rome, Venice, or Amsterdam.

Names appear the way they are shown in court records, often in Latinized form. For example, the Polish name Katarzyna is referred to as Caterina in court documents. The Latinized form, which is also easier for the English reader, is the version used in the book. Trent and other multilingual borderlands present a particular problem. When records exist in different languages—for example, in Latin, Italian, and German sources in Trent, where different versions of names appear—the name that corresponds to the language the person spoke is used. So, for example, the German-speaking Jew Engel, referred in Latin or Italian records as Angelus or Angelo, respectively, but in German contemporary sources as Engel, is named Engel in the book. The Trent trial was a German affair, in the German-speaking part of the town.

All translations within the text—from French, German, Hebrew, Italian, Latin, Polish, Russian, Spanish, and Yiddish—are mine, unless otherwise noted. If there exists a published English translation, usually that translation is used, unless otherwise noted. Early modern sources in English retain their spelling.

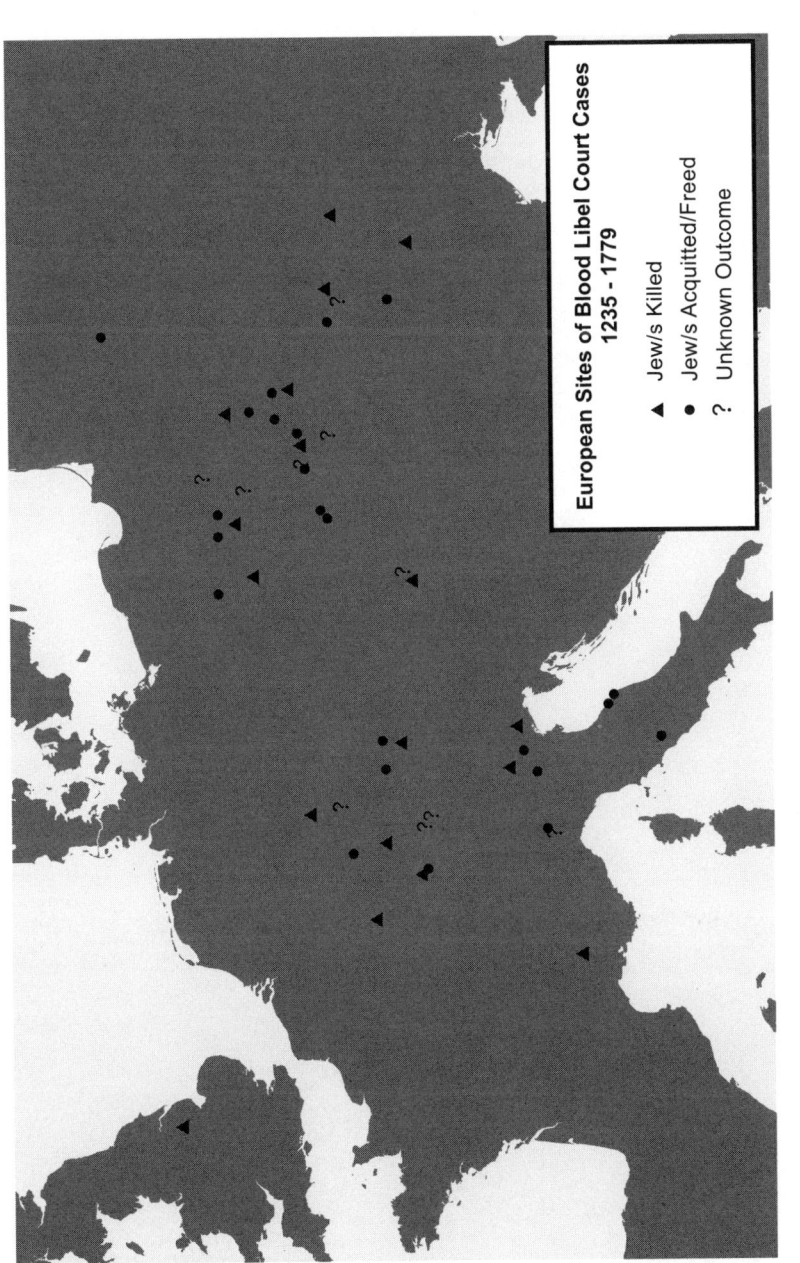

Sites where legal proceedings took place or legal evidence exists.
For more extensive maps see www.thebloodlibeltrail.org

Blood Libel

Introduction

IN 2014, the Anti-Defamation League appealed to Facebook to take down a page titled "Jewish Ritual Murder."[1] It took four years until the page was finally removed. Yet the interest in "Jewish ritual murder" has not been limited to online activity. In May 2015, members of the British Movement, a white supremacist group in the United Kingdom, gathered in the town of Lincoln to "revive a tradition of the English Middle Ages."[2] The group proceeded to the Lincoln Cathedral, where they wanted to honor "Little Hugh of Lincoln," a nine-year-old boy who died in 1255. Little Hugh's death was blamed on the Jews and became the first case in England to result in their execution, though it was not the first such accusation. A shrine devoted to Little Hugh was fashioned, and the story was included in contemporary chronicles and local ballads.[3] In the fourteenth century, the story entered popular works of literature, the most famous among them, Chaucer's "Prioress's Tale." Although Little Hugh of Lincoln was the focus of a site of popular devotion, he was never officially recognized as a saint by church authorities, either Catholic or, later, Anglican.

When they arrived at the cathedral in 2015, the group was confronted by a priest who informed them that Little Hugh of Lincoln was not a saint. In fact, since 1959, at a time when Europe was reckoning with the enormity of the Nazi destruction of Jews and beginning to reexamine Christian, anti-Jewish sentiments in culture and prayers, a plaque has hung at the site of Little Hugh's tomb.[4] It calls the accusations "trumped-up stories" and "fictions" that "cost many innocent Jews their lives" and includes a prayer: "Such stories do not redound to the credit of Christendom, and so we pray: Lord, forgive what we have been, amend what we are, and direct what we shall be."[5]

The neo-Nazi men in Lincoln rejected this rebuttal and gave their own counter-prayer, leaving offerings of flowers (symbolic red and white roses) at the burial site of Little Hugh of Lincoln: "We are here today in memory of Little Saint Hugh, who was murdered in the year 1255 by Jews, he was just 9 years old. Medieval historian Mathew Parris recorded the event. A Jew named Jopin confessed to the murder and implicated the wider Jewish community of the time in this crime, Jopin suggested that the killing of Hugh was a ritual religious sacrifice. The modern statement here is an abomination and an insult to the memory of Little Saint Hugh." Though the Lincoln Cathedral contains burial sites of two other venerated figures—Bishop Hugh of Lincoln, who died in 1200 and was officially canonized in 1220, and Bishop Edward King, who died in 1910—the group's targeting of the remnants of the shrine of Little Hugh of Lincoln reveals the enduring power and attraction of anti-Jewish elements of medieval history.[6]

Although other medieval anti-Jewish tales, including the desecration of the consecrated communion wafer and the poisoning of wells, have lost their power and appeal, the tale that Jews killed Christian children—known as the "ritual murder" or "blood libel"—survives, adapting to changing cultural and political climates. In the Middle East, the ritual murder iconography is a visual tool in anti-Israeli cartoons. In Europe the stories and sites associated with it are magnets for fascist and white supremacist groups, as suggested by the May 2015 encounter in Lincoln. The British Movement is not the only group embracing this narrow part of the medieval past in desiring to revive cults grounded in these anti-Jewish tales. In 2007, a group in Italy emerged, seeking to revive the cult of Simon of Trent, which had been abolished in 1965.[7] Simon's death in 1475 resulted in one of the most notorious persecutions of Jews, leaving a lasting literary, visual, and even legal legacy. In April 2019, a gunman entered a synagogue in Poway near San Diego, killing one and injuring several others. In his online manifesto, he invoked Simon of Trent saying, "You are not forgotten Simon of Trent, the horror that you and countless children have endured at the hands of the Jews will never be forgiven."[8]

The attraction of the blood libel legend for far right, fascist, and white supremacist groups has a longer history than its twenty-first-century revival. On May 1, 1934, the Nazi paper *Der Stürmer* published a special issue devoted to "Ritual Murder" (Fig. 0.1). The headline in big red letters screamed "A Jewish Plan to Murder Non-Jews Uncovered!" Below was an

FIG. 0.1 *Der Stürmer*, May 1, 1934, the *Ritualmord* issue.

image of Jews filling basins with blood of Christian children, with three crosses in the background. The caption read, "Throughout the millennia, the Jews, following the secret rite, shed human blood. The devil is still sitting on our necks today, it's up to you to pack the devil's brood." Stories and images of Jews killing Christians filled the rest of the issue, nearly twenty pages. Three more such issues would follow in 1937, 1939, and 1942. In 1942, the Italian Fascist publication *La difesa della razza* also devoted part of an issue to ritual murder and blood libels.[9]

For centuries, Jews and their defenders have been trying to discredit these tales, and yet they have proven impossible to root out. What sociologists call "confirmation bias," a term that gained particular currency after the 2016 US presidential elections, may prove useful in understanding why. In 2016 and thereafter, computer algorithms following our steps while we browse the Internet have created "echo chambers." These echo chambers make it easier for people to "seek out information that strengthen[s] their preferred narratives" and "reject information that undermine[s] it."[10] Alarmingly, social scientists have found that when exposed to false information that confirms readers' views, not only are readers more likely to accept and share it with others but also attempts to correct the falsehoods are either "ignored" or "reinforce the users' false beliefs." Social media and the speed with which information spreads today may exacerbate the phenomenon, but it is not something entirely new. The story of anti-Jewish accusations demonstrates that, in earlier centuries, false or distorted information was accepted if it fit already existing preconceptions and came from sources the audience knew and trusted. Otherwise, it was treated with disbelief and rejected.

Accusations that Jews killed Christian children emerged in the mid-twelfth century. The first such story—told years later—of the death of a twelve-year-old boy named William in 1144 in Norwich, England, typically marks the beginning. In their earliest form, the accusations, which scholars have called "ritual murder" or "ritual crucifixion," were linked to the reenactment of Jesus's suffering and death. But in the thirteenth century a new motif was added: Jews killed Christian children to obtain their blood, turning "ritual murder" into "blood libel" or "ritual cannibalism."[11] These stories drew on themes from Christian beliefs and practices, which made them more believable. The new blood accusations were quickly condemned by the highest church and secular authorities. Yet they persisted, despite condemnations and despite evidence to the contrary, remaining deeply ingrained in European culture and imagination even today.

But these were not only stories of blood. Real blood was spilled—Jews were tried and executed when a Christian child went missing or a body was found. These cases created a massive paper trail of letters, edicts, and laws, as well as a memory trail shaped by literature and art. *Blood Libel* reveals the processes of the making and diffusion of knowledge that made the accusations so difficult to eradicate. The book follows, literally, the paper trail these bloody affairs left in medieval and early modern Europe, pursuing sources from England to France, Germany to Poland, and Italy. Broadening the geographic and chronological lens reveals a Europe much more connected culturally and politically than previously considered.

This long paper trail crisscrosses the boundaries of states and regions traditionally studied in isolation and of religious communities, uncovering networks of lobbyists and courtiers, lawyers and scholars—Catholic, Protestant, and Jewish—seeking to engineer responses to the blood libels against Jews, through diplomatic interventions as well as secret and published writing. The paper trail follows the arguments, in defense of or against Jews, revealing what people read and saw. *Blood Libel* thus connects the dots scattered across Europe, highlighting distinct cultures of knowledge that shaped the varied responses to the anti-Jewish accusations and the outcomes of anti-Jewish trials.

Accusations that Jews killed Christian children—frequently thought to be a medieval phenomenon—declined in western Europe after the Reformation, but they emerged with new force in early modern eastern Europe, especially in Poland-Lithuania.[12] Still, as the numerous iconographic reminders and even occasional trials testify, even in the West the charges did not die out completely. The Protestant Reformation thus does not explain their decline. Frankfurt, for example, a Protestant city, displayed a mural of Simon of Trent in its tower bridge, or Brückenturm (Fig. 0.2). Neither was Catholicism entirely to blame. In Poland-Lithuania, for example, the outcomes of anti-Jewish accusations differed from that on the Italian peninsula, even though both regions were predominantly Catholic. Regional cultures of knowledge and structures of power provide a better explanation for these differences.

If the memory trail of anti-Jewish accusations began in twelfth-century England and France, with stories about murders inserted into monastic chronicles, the legal trail of arguments and precedents can be traced back to two thirteenth-century cases: in 1235 in Fulda in the Holy Roman Empire and in 1247 in Valréas in Provence. These two cases were also the first in which Jews were accused not just of killing Christian children as a ritual reenactment of Jesus's passion but also of using their blood. The persecution of Jews in Fulda resulted in the first official imperial denunciation of such accusations by Emperor Frederick II in 1236. The first papal admonitions came in 1247, following an appeal by Jewish leaders to Pope Innocent

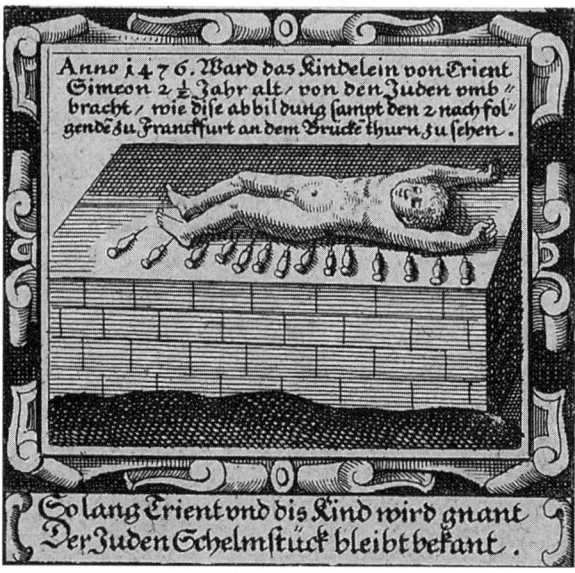

FIG. 0.2 A mural of Simon of Trent in its Brückenturm as represented in *Der Juden Badstub* broadside (fragment), ca. 1615. ©The Trustees of the British Museum. All rights reserved.

IV after a Christian girl was found dead in the town of Valréas and Jews were arrested, tortured, and then burned at the stake. The pope decisively denounced the persecution as the result of "the unpraiseworthy zeal" and "detestable cruelty" of Christians, "who covetous of their possessions or thirsting for their blood, despoil, torture, and kill [Jews] without legal judgment, contrary to the clemency of the Catholic religion."[13] During the following centuries, popes restated their protection of Jews against similar accusations, and this papal policy remained relatively stable, until the aftermath of a dramatic trial in Trent in 1475.

The death of a toddler named Simon, whose body was found in a canal under a Jewish house in Trent during the Easter-Passover season in March 1475, unleashed a chain of events that would eventually lead to the end of papal protection of Jews against blood accusations. The unusually lengthy and uniquely well-documented trial that followed Simon's death led to the arrest, torture, and execution of nearly all the male Jews of the tiny Jewish community of Trent and, by 1478, the conversion of its women and children, ultimately ending the Jewish presence in Trent for centuries. The affair became one of the most notorious blood libels, leaving behind not only a trail of blood, tears, and suffering but also the cult of "Little Simon," or Simonino, along with an unsurpassed documentary, literary, iconographic, and legal legacy. The existence and dissemination of Simon's story and cult helped further reinforce European Christians' belief that Jews murdered Christian children.

As R. Po-Chia Hsia has noted, the blood libel in Trent, a city at the foothills of the Alps, was "neither the first nor the last in the long series of anti-Jewish charges in European history," but it was pivotal and paradigmatic.[14] After Simon's body was recovered, the local prince-bishop, Johannes Hinderbach, wasted no time in instigating the trial, while seeking to create a pilgrimage site to venerate Little Simon. In response to Hinderbach's actions, Pope Sixtus IV set up a commission to investigate the bishop's claims, the legitimacy of the trial of the Jews, and the authenticity of alleged miracles said to have ensued. The pope faced a dilemma: on the one hand, since the thirteenth century popes had explicitly condemned similar accusations against Jews; on the other, Hinderbach's efforts promoted popular devotion and had the strong support of some high-profile clergy. In his communications with Hinderbach, the pope reminded the bishop of earlier papal statements about blood libels and threatened him with suspension. But after much pressure from Hinderbach's supporters and his massive public relations campaign, the pope partially relented, exculpating the bishop of wrongdoing but refraining to authorize the cult, and sternly prohibiting calling Simon *beatus,* or blessed. It took more than a century before another pope, Sixtus V, formally authorized the cult of Little Simon in 1588. But it was not the 1588 authorization of a regional cult that arguably had the most powerful and long-lasting consequences for the persistence of blood accusations against Jews. It was the earlier inclusion of Simon, in 1583 amidst the reforms of the Church, in the newly revised liturgical calendar *Martyrologium romanum,* which sparked a renewed interest in him, complicated his legal status in canon law, and spurred new works of art (Fig. 0.3).[15]

The events in Trent and their aftermath marked a departure from earlier medieval persecutions and trials of Jews accused of murdering Christian children. The impact of the earlier persecutions was mostly felt locally, only occasionally producing local shrines or more than a few lines in local chronicles. For example, the story of William of Norwich, whose mutilated body was found in 1144, led to a rise of a local cult, but it survived only in a few mentions in monastic chronicles and in one elaborate narrative of his "life and passion" written as a document advocating for his sainthood. This longer narrative, however, lay forgotten until the nineteenth century, when it was rediscovered and printed.[16] And though the story of William's death is thought to be the first case of the anti-Jewish accusation, its impact seems more limited than previously thought. True, medieval England appears to

FIG. 0.3 Simon of Trent, undated late–sixteenth-century painting by a northern Italian painter, painted soon after Simon was included in *Martyrologium romanum*, likely between 1583 and 1597. The boy has a halo, the sign of a saint, instead of rays typical of previous representations of Simon as *beatus*. Private collection.

have been the hotbed of accusations that Jews killed Christian children, and William's shrine was known there, but the continental stories, among them Simon of Trent, had a far more lasting impact in history, memory, and law.[17]

Even in Trent the earlier papal bulls protecting Jews were included in papal correspondence during the proceedings but were not recognized as applicable by the instigators of the trial. The Trent case was a turning point. If the medieval period was marked by papal condemnations of anti-Jewish accusations and by papal protection of Jews facing those charges, the legacy of Simon's case in Church law and Christian historical memory made such public papal protection of Jews difficult if not impossible. It is no coincidence that the last papal defense of Jews against such accusations was in 1540, before Simon's cult was officially sanctioned.

At the heart of the trial in Trent were not only anti-Jewish sentiments but also a clash between Rome and Trent: this clash went far beyond questions of the authenticity of miracles and the authorization of the cult of Simon, of authority and power, and of traditional practices and religious control. At its center were cultural and political differences between the Italian Rome and the Germanic Trent, differences that signaled subsequent trajectories in the history and memory of blood libels against Jews in Europe, soon to be divided by the Reformation.

It turned out that it mattered what people read. One cannot underestimate the role early printed books played in shaping regional epistemologies. Early printed works provided topics, vocabulary, and iconography that would create regional molds for thinking about Jews. Strikingly, the same works, with versions published in different regions in Latin and the vernaculars, varied depending on the place and language in which they were published.

Writers tended to read and respond to works published in their regions. In Italy and the German lands, Christian Hebraism meant that some Christians could read Jewish books. Though in each region the focus of interests and the reasons for studying Hebrew works differed, the knowledge gained by reading Jewish works was everywhere marshaled for polemical purposes, often to discredit Judaism and provide Christians with arguments against Jews. Still, with few exceptions, the exposure to Hebrew language and rabbinic literature provided enough knowledge of Jewish customs to counter, or at least mitigate, accusations against the Jews. According to these Christian polemical works, Jews may indeed curse Christians, they may even hate them, but they do not kill. This was not the case for Poland-Lithuania, where, like elsewhere, early vernacular books about Jews published in the region shaped subsequent literature for centuries to come. And although non-reading Christians might have learned about Jewish practices through personal interaction, sharing living space, and seeing them firsthand, what Christians in Poland knew about Jews from books was limited to explicitly anti-Jewish vernacular works by writers who had never studied Jewish texts and who were steeped in ignorance about Jewish literature, religion, and religious practices. It was the printed books, not personal contacts, that became accepted knowledge—knowledge that gradually had an impact on what happened in the courtroom.

Yet knowledge about Jews came not only from explicitly polemical, anti-Jewish works. Often, chronicles, cosmographies, and other books not devoted directly to Jews included stories about them, such as tales found in local chronicles, lore, or court records. Indeed, as early modern writers became interested in archival sources, trial records began to circulate in print, entering the paper trail of accessible "evidence" of Jewish "cruelties," as one Polish writer would title his book. Authoritative sources were difficult to dismiss; thus when the Bollandists, Jesuits in Antwerp renowned for their scholarly diligence, included in their *Acta Sanctorum,* or lives of the saints, several tales of purported child victims of Jews, the impact was incalculable. Who should Christians trust: the esteemed Christian scholars or the Jews and their defenders? Rumors and lore became "facts" once they entered reputable printed books.

Cultural differences, perhaps unsurprisingly, were also prominent among Ashkenazi and Sephardic Jews in their reactions to anti-Jewish accusations. With the exception of the earliest medieval accusations, which occurred in England and France, the majority of the accusations affected directly Ashkenazi Jews in northern and later in eastern Europe. The actions that Ashkenazi Jews took in the aftermath of accusations reflected their diplomatic skills and legal and political sophistication. But Sephardic Jews—who were not the direct victims of blood libel—were the ones to leave a literary mark on the subject. Jewish works touching on the subject of blood libels were certainly not as quantitatively impressive as the corpus of Christian anti-Jewish works, but they shine light onto Sephardic and Ashkenazi Jewish cultures. The rare Ashkenazi works were mostly Yiddish songs and short tales, deeply rooted in the Ashkenazi ethos of martyrdom, *kiddush ha-shem,* dating back to the Crusades. They told stories of innocent Jews falsely accused of horrific crimes, but able to withstand torture and dying a martyr's death. They affirmed the victims' fidelity to their God despite horrific suffering and persecution, while providing concrete models and values on how and why to withstand torture, and guidance on how to respond practically by organizing financial and political support in the face of similar accusations. The Sephardic responses, in contrast, had a polemical character, undermining the premises and logic of these anti-Jewish libels. The arguments and sources marshaled in these works played an important role in shaping legal arguments in defense of Jews in the eighteenth century. In fact, they created a chain of legal sources that would help shape even a famed report by Cardinal Lorenzo Ganganelli prepared in 1759 in the midst of a wave of violent anti-Jewish accusations in Poland.

For modern scholars, Cardinal Ganganelli's report became one of the most frequently cited documents in defense of Jews. It methodically undermined the arguments supporting blood libels against Jews, often turning to evidence from printed books and chronicles. Yet, Ganganelli's report still acknowledged as valid two stories of alleged child victims of Jews: Simon of Trent and Andreas of Rinn. Writing his report, Ganganelli had to navigate dangerous terrain. On the one hand, he knew that numerous popes had condemned such accusations and that much evidence against the charges existed as well. On the other hand, some popes, including Gregory XIII in 1583, Sixtus V in 1588, and Benedict XIV, Ganganelli's own boss, had sanctioned and reaffirmed popular shrines celebrating the alleged child victims Simon of Trent and Andreas of Rinn. Indeed, just a few years before Ganganelli finished his report, Pope Benedict XIV formally recognized the cult of Andreas of Rinn, near Innsbruck. Benedict's effective affirmation of anti-Jewish accusations has baffled scholars and tarnished the pope's reputation as "the Enlightenment pope," so admired for condemning slavery, installing a woman as a professor of sciences at the University of Bologna, and embracing science and the arts.[18] In his report, thus, Ganganelli had to strike a careful balance—at stake were profoundly consequential questions of papal authority and power.

Archival evidence, including hitherto unknown sources from the archives of the Holy Office of the Inquisition (now the Archive of the Congregation of the Doctrine of the Faith), shines light on the wrangling between the nuncio in Poland and papal officials in Rome; it shows that the Ganganelli report was explicitly prohibited from being made public. As a secret internal document, the report was thus never published by the Catholic Church and had little impact on the defense of Jews in late eighteenth-century Poland and even later.

The existence of the report was first mentioned in 1862 in the Italian Jewish journal *L'Educatore Israelita,* with the text published only in the 1880s, in the aftermath of a number of trials of Jews, including one in Tiszaeszlar, Hungary.[19] During the Beilis affair in 1911–1913, in which a Jewish man, Menachem Mendel Beilis, was accused of killing a Christian youth in Kiev, Baron Nathaniel Mayer Rothschild requested that the Vatican confirm the authenticity of the report's published version, as well as the authenticity of the 1247 bull by Innocent IV. The Vatican's secretary of state complied with his request. The authentication of these documents, not an insignificant action, was the closest Church officials in Rome came to condemning anew anti-Jewish accusations since the last papal bull defending Jews, issued in 1540. But the letter to Baron Rothschild was still a private letter, not an official statement.

The ambivalence of the popes and their emissaries about the official papal policies of protection of Jews against blood libels underlines the complexity of attitudes of the Catholic Church toward the accusations. It illuminates regional differences in the levels of intervention against such accusations or their tacit approval for political reasons, often revealing tensions between official policies and local popular piety.

Blood Libel spotlights the burden that history, tradition, and law have placed on individual and institutional actors. This burden was palpable when on October 28, 1965, Archbishop of Trent Alessandro Maria Gottardi published a "Notification concerning the Cult of Little Simon of Trent," effectively abolishing the cult of the boy.[20] The contrast between Gottardi's notification announcing the abolition and the cult's notorious beginnings in 1475 could not be starker. Gottardi's "Notification" was not a big public announcement. It did not explicitly state that the cult was abolished; instead, the announcement was opaquely cloaked in references to recent historical studies, canon law, and a document issued in 1963 by the prefect of the Congregation of the Rites, a body of the Roman Curia originally established in 1588 and responsible for supervision of the liturgy and the canonization of saints. Gottardi accepted "with reverence and gratitude the prudent decisions of the Holy See," noting with "great satisfaction the happy coincidence for which they appear to be entirely relevant to the spirit and the documents of the Second Vatican Council." He expressed his hope that "even this local circumstance" may "increase in all, as it should, mutual feelings and attitudes of respect, justice, and brotherhood." Printed in a diocesan monthly publication meant for official statements of the diocesan authorities, "The Notification" was thus effectively an internal document. And it is perhaps for that reason that the archbishop did not need to articulate explicitly what "decisions of the Holy See" he was referring to, but included only a shorthand reference to "the application of canon 1284 [of canon law]," without quoting it directly. Still, all this was enough to signal that the cult of Simon was to be abolished—canon 1284 of the 1917 code of canon law states that in case of impossibility to authenticate relics related to a cult, such relics should be removed from worship by the faithful.[21]

If the abolition of the cult seemed disappointingly restrained, it coincided, quite consciously, with a major event in the history of Jewish–Catholic relations. "The Declaration on the Relation of the Church to Non-Christian Religions 'Nostra Aetate,'" a landmark document of reconciliation between Jews and the Catholic Church, was proclaimed by Pope Paul VI at the Second Vatican Council on exactly the same day.[22] This synchrony and Gottardi's mention of "mutual" feelings of "respect, justice, and brotherhood" were clues signaling that the archbishop's undemonstrative announcement was of major significance.

And significant it was. "The Notification" did more than abolish a minor regional cult that was unsavory in a new era of improved Jewish–Catholic relations. Its significance was more profound, for not only had the veneration of Simon of Trent been sanctioned by popes but also the cult had come to have a surprisingly important place in the history of Church law. The story of Simon of Trent and its aftermath would ultimately play a key role in undermining centuries of papal policies and protection of Jews. It would muzzle Church authorities, with ramifications felt even in the twenty-first century.[23]

CHAPTER ONE

From Medieval Tales to the Challenge in Trent

After years of secretive preparation, Anton Koberger, a prominent printer from Nuremberg, finally published in 1493 the monumental Nuremberg Chronicle, *Liber chronicarum,* a chronicle of world history "from the beginning of the world to our own time by the highly learned Doctor Hartmann Schedel."[1] The publisher's advertisement announced that the book would "recount everything that has occurred in the passage of time. . . . Show the ages of the world, kingdoms in succession, all the cities that the world possesses . . . the acts of dukes and kings with those of scholars who reveal natural science and philosophy."[2] Koberger promised readers an unprecedented experience: "nothing has hitherto appeared that can guarantee scholars and all men of learning greater and deeper pleasure than the New Book of Chronicles with its pictures of famous men and cities." The delight was to be so great that readers would think they were "not reading a series of stories but looking at them with your own eyes." All these stories would seem "alive." The publisher knew that the book was like nothing ever published before, and he and the financial backers of the project, Sebald Schreyer and Sebastian Kammermaister, "the rich citizens of Nuremberg," eagerly sought to keep it secret until it was ready to be released.[3]

Among the hundreds of woodcuts of kings, popes, cities, and tales are several vivid images of Jews, some of the earliest visual representations of

Jews in print.[4] Indeed, the images—a Jew desecrating a crucifix, Jews burning at the stake (repeated three times), and two images representing Jews killing Christian children: for the year 1144, William "a boy crucified by perfidious Jews" (Fig. 1.1) and for 1475, "Blessed Simon of Trent" (Fig. 1.2)[5]—do bring to life the text alongside them. Unlike the rather generic images of kings and popes, these images of Jews and the select stories they accompanied are not plain or formulaic: they served to underscore the notion of Jews' enmity and hatred of Christianity, expressed through the desecration of objects venerated by Christians and the killing of Christian children.

The story of William, whose mutilated body was found near the English town of Norwich in 1144, is the first known tale accusing Jews of killing a Christian for ritual purposes.[6] In Norwich, however, there was no trial, and no blood of Jews was spilled. This was not the case in Trent, where the body of a toddler named Simon was found in March 1475, when Easter and Passover converged. Simon's death led to one of the most notorious and best-documented trials against Jews, to the proliferation of visual representations of the imagined deed, and, ultimately, to the undermining of the medieval protection of Jews against similar accusations. The stories of William of Norwich and Simon of Trent serve as bookends of the medieval accusations against Jews. The two are the most studied, but by no means the only ones that left an imprint on subsequent history.[7] In fact, the Nuremberg Chronicle mentions another story—that of Richard of Paris, also known as Richard of Pontoise, whose death according to medieval chroniclers, and the Nuremberg Chronicle itself, led King Philip of France to expel Jews from his kingdom.[8] And then there is the late thirteenth-century story of Werner of Oberwesel, whose cult spread through songs and poems along the Rhine Valley and in eastern France, without approval from Rome.[9] These cases shared a common thread: the attempt to create a cult of boy martyrs. In subsequent centuries, other tales would be added, and additional attempts to make dead children into saints would take place across Europe. But not all of those tales would have a long-lasting effect. Some would fade from memory altogether; others would be brought back to light only by modern scholars, attracting attention greater than historical reality would have merited. And still some of these accusations against Jews would create a trail of evidence that would serve not only the accusers but also the defenders of Jews for centuries. But, perhaps more important, the Middle Ages were marked not only by the beginning of the ritual murder and blood libel accusations, the rise of Christian narratives, and persistent beliefs about Jews killing Christian children but also by the most explicit defense of Jews by both secular and ecclesiastical authorities against these accusations.

FIG. 1.1 William of Norwich, Hartmann Schedel, *Nuremberg Chronicle, Weltchronik* (Nuremberg: Anton Koberger, 1493), CCXX verso.

FIG. 1.2 Simon of Trent, Hartmann Schedel, *Nuremberg Chronicle, Weltchronik* (Nuremberg: Anton Koberger, 1493), CCLIIII verso.

William of Norwich, A Broken Memory Trail

In the 1140s, around the time of the Second Crusade, a new rumor began to surface in Europe: Jews kill Christians. In 1144, during a bloody civil war in England, a twelve-year-old boy named William disappeared during the Easter season; his body was found on Good Friday by a forester in the Thorpe Wood near the town of Norwich, but was left there until Monday, after the holiday.[10] On that day, the forester returned to bury it on the spot. Miracles were said to have followed, and William's body was moved to the monks' cemetery, then to a new sarcophagus in the chapter house, and finally to the cathedral. The Jews of Norwich were never tried or harmed as a result of William's death, though rumors apparently circulated soon thereafter. The lack of immediate action in response to the boy's death suggests that it was not treated as a martyr's death and that Jews were not seriously implicated. But the story is shrouded in mystery, because no contemporary record of any investigation exists.

The earliest evidence is provided by brief mentions, sometimes limited to one sentence, of Jews crucifying a Christian boy in Norwich; they were found in monastic chronicles within Cistercian circles both in England and on the continent that can be dated to the late 1140s and early 1150s.[11] Some years after William's death, around 1150, a monk named Thomas of Monmouth arrived in Norwich. Soon he began to write an extensive narrative in which he blamed the Jews for William's death. Thomas's tale, by far the most detailed account of the story written, as he said, when the "memory of the murder had almost died out," was not completed until sometime between 1172 and 1174.[12]

Thomas, as John McCulloh has convincingly argued, did not invent the charge that Jews killed Christians. And though the Cistercian chronicles suggest the rumor had already been in circulation, Thomas's account, *The Life and Passion of William of Norwich*, is the first narrative of what Gavin Langmuir calls "ritual crucifixion," which frames the death of a Christian boy in the language and tropes paralleling the life and passion of Jesus.[13]

Thomas himself noted the novelty of the affair.[14] And this might not be surprising, given that the Jewish presence in Norwich was fairly new. Having arrived only after the Norman conquest, Jews were seen as foreigners allied with the invaders. Jeffrey Cohen has argued that the "Norman colonial context" is key to understanding both the Jews' presence in Norwich and the reactions to William's death.[15] But there is more. The Jews' recent arrival in Norwich and William's death also coincided with new forms of piety increasingly focused on the humanity of Christ and his true suffering during his passion.[16] In Thomas's detailed and riveting telling, William was a stand-in for all Christians, indeed, for Christ himself, whom Jews killed out of hatred.[17] In addressing the novelty of the claims, Thomas's book is also a treatise against doubt, with tropes connecting William to Christ, serving to reassure and quiet the doubters.

From the very beginning of Thomas's *Life and Passion,* the tone and the expectations to fit the story into the mold of Christ's passion are set. Describing the conception of William, Thomas alluded to Marian imagery: "The mercy of divine piety had him conceived in the womb of a mother ignorant of what she carried and caused a fragrant rose to grow little by little among the thorns."[18] The imagery of a fragrant rose signals both Marian associations, reinforcing the parallel between the births of Jesus and William, and William's anticipated martyrdom.

In medieval Christian theology, Mary was associated both with a lily and a rose and sometimes with a "rose garden" in which she bore Jesus.[19] The image of the rose, one of the most beautiful flowers because of its fragrance and color, but with thorns that can cause bleeding, proved powerful for Christian thinkers. "Just as a rose grows surrounded by thorns but remains free from their disfiguring influence," wrote Adrienne Nock Ambrose, summarizing a later devotional work from Germany, "Mary lived among sinful humanity while remaining free of sin."[20] The rose also came to symbolize martyrdom. For Honorius Augustodunensis, the author of popular devotional works, among them *Sigillum Beatae Mariae,* who lived in the first half of the twelfth century and was apparently a student of Anselm of Canterbury, "the rose signifies the martyrs" because "the rose excels all other flowers in redness."[21] Honorius then linked the rose as a symbol of Mary to the trope of martyrdom: "she saw the Son of God born of her so innocently tortured on the cross, she endured in her soul a torment greater by far than that of all the martyrs. Thus she was greater than a martyr, for they suffered in body, but she suffered in spirit, as it is said: 'And your own soul a sword shall pierce (Luke 2:35).'" That imagery of a rose would reappear in Thomas's work as one of the miracles signaling William's holiness: a rose bush blossomed in the midst of winter on William's grave, its blossoms lasting from Advent until Christmas.[22] Nor was the trope of the Advent accidental: Mary and the preparation for the birth of Jesus are at the center of celebrations during the season, and the trope of a rose blossoming in the middle of winter as a Marian miracle is used frequently in Christian devotion.[23]

Thomas then elaborated how the Jews chose William, "who was twelve at the time and innocent indeed," to be "mocked and sacrificed in disgrace of Lord's Passion."[24] William had frequented Jewish homes, but according to Thomas, Jews used a ruse to lure him to join them. Still, when his mother did not want to let the boy go before Easter, "the traitor," hired by Jews to bring William to them, "swore that he would not be without him for three days, not even for thirty pieces of silver," and offered the mother three shillings for the boy. When the boy was brought to the Jews, they received him "kindly, like an innocent lamb led to the slaughter." But soon he was "humiliated" and tortured. The description of the torture evoked explicit elements of the passion of Christ along with a mix of what seem to be contemporary methods of torture. Thomas wrote that when William was held, some Jews "inserted into his open mouth a torture instrument known in English as a teasel." They tied a knot to his temple and rope around his neck and chin. They then shaved the boy's head and "wounded it with an infinite number of thorn pricks and made him bleed miserably." While the boy was tortured, other Jews "sentenced him to be crucified," "in mockery of the Passion of the Cross," while saying, "Just as we have condemned Christ to a most shameful death, so we condemn a Christian, so that we punish both the Lord and his servant in the punishment of reproach; that which they ascribe to us we will inflict on them." "They then fastened him with chains to a post, pierced his left hand and left foot with a nail." Finally, to satisfy "their inborn hatred of the Christian name," they "pierced his left side up into his heart."

The parallels between Christ and William are even more explicit in a heavenly vision apparently experienced by a little girl, which shows William, sitting in the presence of Christ and of Mary the Virgin, dressed in a similar robe as Christ. A dove then announces him to be a martyr "killed by Jews in derision of the Lord's Passion," who "imitated Christ in the passion of death" and who therefore "deserved to be like Christ Himself in the honor of the purple robe."[25]

For all the noted similarities to Jesus and his passion, there were also differences. Perhaps in response to the criticism that the wounds and alleged method of killing did not resemble Christ's passion, Thomas claimed that the differences were meant to disguise the Jews' guilt, in hopes of shifting the blame onto Christians. Thomas took pains to assert repeatedly that no Christian would have done such a deed—a curious assertion given that England was experiencing a cruel civil war that left many people dead, some suffering tortures resembling those described by Thomas.[26]

In Thomas's telling, William's torturous death was needed to assure him of the title "the glorious boy and martyr of Christ . . . crowned with the blood of glorious martyrdom" who "achieved the kingdom of eternal glory, alive for eternity," his soul "exalted joyfully in heaven among the illustrious host of saints" and his body working "wonders gloriously on earth by the omnipotence of divine mercy."[27] Among those "wonders" were rays of light reaching William's head and an intact body exuding a "sweet smell" for a long time after his death.[28]

Thomas's *Life and Passion of William of Norwich* reads as an apologetic treatise rebutting doubts about William's martyrdom and saintly status.[29] And doubts abounded, from the troubling neglect of William's body after it was discovered to the alleged, and entirely implausible, conspiracy of silence protecting Jews and covering up their crime involving one Aelwerd, a rich Norwich man who was said to have encountered the Jews as they were trying to dispose of the body; the sheriff, John to whom Jews apparently confessed their crime and whom they then bribed into silence; and a Christian woman who worked as a servant in the Jews' house.

And then there was William himself, rather questionable material for a saint. He was an apprentice with a relatively common background, had no particular achievements, and was not known for his piety and devotion. In short, he did not do anything in his life to warrant sainthood.[30] But Thomas nonetheless asserted, "We are confident that the glorious martyr William lives [in heaven] among their holy communities, marked by a triple stole and counted among the illustrious. He deserves the badge of a triple stole, he who already had two stoles, that is of innocence and of virginity, so that he should claim the third, painted in red by the blood of the martyr."[31] He continued, "The boyhood and innocence of the blessed William saves and . . . the purity of his virginity commends." His wounds prove "that he was truly killed," and because he "was young and innocent with no previous sins," he did not deserve to be killed. The miracles that followed his death showed "that he ought to be called a saint, and indeed, he is." To those who claimed that "William was lacking in any merit after death, . . . who had been but a little poor boy, insignificant in life, . . . [whom] they held in contempt, because they knew him to have been a poor little ragged boy, working for his living as far as he could in the art of tanning," Thomas responded that "Christ himself was poor, not having a place to lay His head, and He called the poor—not the rich—to be His apostles; the weak, not the strong; the unlearned, not the worldly wise; innocent children, not those grown old in malice."[32]

But serious theological issues remained. Could childhood be "a reason to reject sanctification"? Could "a little, worthless, ragged, and poor boy" attain veneration? European Christian tradition had a few models of "Christ-like" adult saints, but in the tenth and eleventh centuries, as Paul A. Hayward has shown, the Anglo-Saxons developed a number of cults of boy saints, including those of St. Æthelberht and Æthelred of Ramsey, Æthelberht of Hereford, and Edward the Martyr.[33] Yet all these boys shared "an outstanding royal pedigree," were projected to assume royal status, and "strove to live as virgins."[34] This may be why Thomas's *Life and Passion of William of Norwich* highlights William's poverty and low status, as well as virginity. Thomas briefly mentioned the ancient child saints Pancras, Pantaleon, and Celsus.[35] And, importantly, during Thomas's life Christian theologians began to meditate on Jesus's adolescence. For example, Aelred of Rievaulx, an English Cistercian monk and an abbot since 1147, wrote an exegesis titled "Jesus at the Age of Twelve."[36]

But there was another precedent of venerated child martyrs to whom Thomas turned: the Holy Innocents, who "were not distinguished by the merits of a lifetime, but whom God's grace alone glorified."[37] The cult of the Holy Innocents, popular since the second century and based on the account from the Gospel of Matthew of the massacre ordered by King Herod of "the boys in Bethlehem and its vicinity who were two years old and under," would prove powerful in the justification of anti-Jewish accusations.[38] Given that Herod was seeking to kill Jesus, the Holy Innocents were thus killed in place of Jesus, much like the accusers claimed Jews did with the Christian boys: this argument was later used to justify the veneration of Simon of Trent and Andreas Oxner.[39] As Patricia Healy Wasilyw has argued, "The Holy Innocents were not only innocent victims; they were also innocent by proxy. The infant Jesus did not merit death any more than the children who died in his place."[40] The child "saints" who were said to have been killed by Jews were also seen as martyrs by proxy: they were not old enough to deserve sainthood and martyrdom, but were seen to have died at the hands of Jews in place of Jesus.

Indeed, the crown of the argument to justify William's saintly status was that—as Thomas forcefully claimed—he was killed by Jews. This is one of Thomas's most obvious innovations. But here too Thomas faced detractors who knew "someone to be killed cruelly, but since they are unsure by whom and why, they dare to say on that account that he is neither a saint nor a martyr."[41] To them Thomas responded by asserting that William "was surely slain by the Jews both because it is the custom of *dierum* [*paschalium*], and also by the nature of the torments, and by the sure signs of the wounds, too, as well as by the most truthful arguments we have from witnesses."

Thomas's fascinating and, sometimes, contradictory work grabbed scholars' attention and led them to overstate the historical importance of William of Norwich's story. Gavin Langmuir calls Thomas of Monmouth "an influential figure in the formation of Western culture,"[42] but not because he "alter[ed] the course of battles, politics, or the economy," or solved "philosophical or theological problems," or was "noteworthy for the holiness of his life or promotion of monastic office." He was influential because "he created a myth that affected Western mentality from the twelfth to the twentieth century, and caused, directly or indirectly, far more deaths than William's murderer could ever have dreamt of committing."

Still, even if some tropes appearing in Thomas's work did enter the vocabulary of subsequent anti-Jewish libels, they cannot necessarily be attributed to his work. As John McCulloh has shown, *The Life and Passion of William of Norwich* remained unknown until its discovery in the nineteenth century; in contrast to its value for modern scholars, its historical influence was limited.[43] More likely, the tropes found in it now seem familiar and influential because they were built on "language replete with typological and liturgical resonance," emphasizing "William's typological relationship to Christ."[44] Heather Blurton has persuasively argued that Thomas's opus must be understood "as a response to liturgical expression in the long twelfth century," because "it borrows consistently from the language of liturgy, especially in those moments when it is most at pains to make the case that William was truly a martyr and a saint."[45] In fact, Thomas's work not only borrows the language and tropes of liturgy for Lent and Easter but also reflects new developments in Christian liturgy at the time. According to Blurton, "twelfth-century liturgical change helped to shape the field of discourse within which the ritual murder accusation might emerge."[46] Among these liturgical tropes, she claims, was the newly developed *Planctus Mariae*, which focuses on Mary's grieving response to Christ's death, and liturgies for other feasts, including that of the Holy Innocents. Scholars claim that early in medieval Christianity the connection "between the Massacre of the Holy Innocents and the Crucifixion of Christ was made precisely through their shared representation of Jewish violence," and, as Teresa Tinkle has shown, "The exegetes from the eighth century to the thirteenth similarly read the scene [of the Massacre of the Innocents] as a narrative about Jewish anger and Christian suffering, wherein the Innocents witness to a violent Jewish hatred of Christ that begins with his birth and extends to the contemporary persecution of the saints."[47] Thomas's opus may thus be simply reflecting these liturgical developments more broadly, not inventing them. The reappearance of these tropes elsewhere in turn may speak more to the dissemination of the new cultural trends within Christianity than the power and influence of Thomas's narrative. His work, thus, appears to be an innovative synthesis of existing tropes and precedents of martyrdom, both adult and child; the suffering of Christ; and devotional trends and liturgy.[48]

The Making of a Saint

Thomas's narrative of William's "life and passion" was written to establish, promote, and justify a local cult, and as such, it shares much "with earlier Anglo-Saxon legends" of child saints, "murdered for political reason."[49]

When Thomas was writing, the criteria sufficient for making someone a saint were popular veneration and authorization by a local bishop, with the translation of the body from a burial site to a public space in a church or cathedral marking the formal recognition of sainthood.[50] And although evidentiary rules in canon law had begun to change already in the late eleventh century, ultimately also influencing procedures of canonization, no strict procedures for sainthood had been articulated until 1179, when Pope Alexander III issued the bull *Audivimus,* which affirmed the papal role in authorizing a cult. But even after Alexander III's intervention, as André Vauchez has argued, "for the papacy, the cult of saints remained and would long remain a marginal issue, essentially regulated by custom."[51]

The criteria for sainthood in Thomas's time were still vague and subject to abuse. Two canons issued in the fifth and eighth centuries guided the procedures, and they were included in Gratian's *Decretum,* composed at about the same time as Thomas arrived in Norwich in 1150.[52] He may have known about them, because his *Life and Passion of William of Norwich* seems to have addressed precisely the questions about the validity of sainthood raised by these two canons. The first, Canon Fifteen issued at the Fifth Council of Carthage in 401, addressed questionable places of veneration containing no bodies or relics of the martyrs. In such cases, the bishop was required to examine and destroy such improper sites, and in the case of a public outcry the bishop should admonish people not to venerate places that have no reliable historical connection to the martyrs.[53] According to E. W. Kemp, the canon put the onus on the bishop, "subject to the direction of the provincial synod."[54] The second canon came from the 813 Council of Mainz, which forbade the translation of the bodies of saints, "the principal outward sign of recognition of a saint," without the authorization of "the bishop and synod acting with the knowledge of the secular power." With the issuance of the bull *Audivimus* in 1179, the authorization for sainthood would begin to change; by the thirteenth century, when the bull was included in Pope Gregory IX's *Decretales,* the authority to recognize a saint lay with the pontiff himself.

In his work, Thomas went out of his way to address the issues of episcopal recognition of William and the translation of his body. Priest Godwin, William's uncle, went specifically to the synod to "present to the ears of the bishop and his fellow priests a mournful complaint the like of which was unheard of in present times" and to denounce the "affront recently committed against all Christians."[55] In his address, Godwin noted that William's body still had not been moved and was "still buried without Christian interment." Ultimately, the participants of the synod agreed with Godwin, but Bishop Everard wavered because "he feared to confront the king and his officials openly."⁵⁶ In the end the participants of the synod, especially Aimar, prior of St. Pancras, convinced the bishop "in favor of a cult." The bishop then "arranged to have the body of the most blessed boy brought to the cathedral and buried in the monks' cemetery." The translation of William's body implied the bishop's recognition of William as a saint.

Still, doubts remained. Perhaps an indication of these lingering doubts is the fact that William was buried in the monks' cemetery and not in the cathedral itself. Moreover, for their universal recognition, saints required papal approval.⁵⁷ Thomas seemed to have been aware of these debates and addressed them head-on. "Apart from the glorious Virgin Mother of God and John the Baptist and the Apostles," he wrote,

> It can be said of few saints that knowledge of them is widespread in all the lands where the religion of the Christian name flourishes. Truly, is it possible that all those whom Rome herself venerates, Gaul and Britain accept for worship too? . . . Is it true that the whole of Europe also is used to celebrate all those which Asia and Africa hold as famous? If it were so, or rather because it is firmly so, what sort of blame is incurred by those who celebrate with fitting veneration someone whom the Church does not know or worship universally? What they call presumption—to hold as a saint one who is not—we assert the same without a shadow of doubt and agree in attesting to it.⁵⁸

Thomas's *Life and Passion of William of Norwich* thus reflects the debates over who was, or even who could be, a saint and who conformed to the process of making a saint before the procedures became more formal and subject to Rome's approval.

Thomas's work had very limited direct impact. Even the diligent Bollandists, seventeenth-century Jesuits dedicated to preparing an annotated scholarly edition of the lives of saints, did not seem to know about this text.⁵⁹ Instead they were aware of several mentions of William in English chronicles and the shortened narrative by John of Tynemouth, which was heavily dependent on Matthew Paris, a thirteenth-century English chronicler and Benedictine monk at St. Albans Abbey, and which they attributed to John Capgrave, a fifteenth-century English chronicler and hagiographer.⁶⁰ John of Tynemouth's account, published in both English and Latin in 1516, was the first narrative about William to become known to the wider public. Until then only short entries, sometimes one-sentence long, found their way to printed chronicles.

The Bollandists were heavily dependent on printed works. Their *Acta Sanctorum* included several other tales from England and the continent of Jews killing Christian children, mostly those that inspired shrines to these children, or attempts to create new cults. Among those tales was that of Hugh of Lincoln, whose death in 1255 occasioned the first anti-Jewish accusation in England to produce an official response and sanction from the royal authorities, and the first to result in the execution of Jews there. The story was told in contemporary chronicles, including by Matthew Paris, and in an Anglo-Norman ballad. These texts, along with a shrine in Lincoln, guaranteed that Hugh's memory was preserved. Indeed, the story entered known works of literature, most famously Chaucer's "Prioress's Tale."[61] Little Hugh's story also became part of the Bollandists' *Acta Sanctorum* because, like that of William of Norwich, the narrative was included in John of Tynemouth's chronicle of England and was available to them in print.[62]

Twelfth-century England became a hotbed of stories of Jews killing Christian children.[63] And although Thomas of Monmouth's version may not have had much direct impact, the story of William's death and his local shrine were certainly known. It seems to have circulated within the network of Benedictine houses and likely influenced other such tales, among them that of Robert of Bury St. Edmunds, who died in 1181 and whose cult appears to have developed by the 1190s.[64] But with the possible exception of Robert of Bury, the stories of Jews killing Christian boys largely appeared only after the death of Hugh of Lincoln and the affair that followed, or, perhaps even after the expulsion of Jews from England in 1290. For example, Harold of Gloucester, said to have been "crucified" in 1168, and for that reason often listed chronologically listed right after William of Norwich, was first mentioned in the *Peterborough Chronicle*, written between 1273–1295; another, more elaborate version was included in the late fourteenth- to early fifteenth-century *Chronicle of the Monastery of St. Peter's*.[65] But in all but one of these cases, even if shrines to the purported child victims were actually, or were only sought to be, established, no Jewish blood was spilled. The only exception in England was the case of Hugh of Lincoln, whose death led to the intervention by King Henry III and the execution of nearly twenty Jews—a tragedy unprecedented, at least in England.[66] And although the story of Hugh of Lincoln would be included in Matthew Paris's chronicle and remembered in English literature, its impact, too, was limited beyond the isle—even though its memory would be preserved to the present day.

To be sure, England has an important place in the history of anti-Jewish accusations charging Jews with killing Christian children. The first shrines and narratives devoted to these dead children emerged there, often supported by monastic, especially Benedictine, networks.[67] Yet perhaps because of the expulsion of the Jews from England in 1290, the continued impact of the English accounts was blunted, the memory trail broken.[68] England's role in this history would reemerge in the era of print, when some of the boys were mentioned in European chronicles.

A far more lasting and influential documentary and memory trail would come from events, and sometimes even just lore, on the European continent. Indeed, even England's only case that resulted in judicial action against Jews—the death of Little Hugh of Lincoln in 1255—took place after the first trials of Jews had taken place on the continent.

A Continental Memory Trail

The tale that Jews crucified Christian children appears to have reached the continent long before the first Jews lost their lives on its account. The story of William of Norwich reached continental Europe as early as the 1140s, no doubt because of the Anglo-Norman connection. In the mid-twelfth century, certainly before Thomas of Monmouth wrote *Life and Passion of William of Norwich* and perhaps even before he arrived in Norwich, a notice of William's death had appeared in "a German martyrology" under April 17: *Apud Anglos Willehelmi pueri a Iudaeis crucifixi* ("a boy William was crucified by Jews in England").[69] But it was the Blois massacre of Jews in 1171 and the story of Richard of Pontoise, whose shrine was established in the Church of the Holy Innocents in Paris (hence he is often referred to as Richard of Paris), that left a more lasting mark in European chronicles and the Jewish memory trail.[70] The two events produced, for the first time, both Hebrew and Latin accounts.[71]

The French chronicler Rigord, writing after 1190, noted that King Philip Augustus "had heard" as a child from boys he knew that Jews in Paris had killed a Christian "in contempt of the Christian religion."[72] Scholars disagree when Richard of Pontoise died: some claim in the 1160s; others in the 1170s.[73] Richard's shrine in the Church of the Holy Innocents in Paris became the first continental shrine devoted to a child victim and mentioned in both Christian and Jewish sources. And yet, the full narrative of the "passion of Richard" was only produced by Robert Gaguin in 1498,[74] more than two decades after the death of Simon of Trent in 1475 and the ensuing multimedia campaign promoting Simon's shrine, and also just a few years after the publication of the Nuremberg Chronicle with its visual representation of William of Norwich and the elaborate woodcut of Simon of Trent. It was the narrative by Robert Gaguin to which the Bollandists turned.[75]

The rumors that Philip is said to have heard as a child were perhaps related to the Blois incident in 1171, in which more than thirty Jews were burned at the stake.[76] He would have been around six years old when that massacre is said to have happened. Although the event is just briefly mentioned in Christian chronicles, Hebrew sources in poetry and prose provide longer accounts, for the first time documenting the Jewish response to an accusation and to the execution of Jews.[77] These responses would provide long-lasting models for Jewish responses to other accusations.

According to the surviving sources, on Maundy Thursday in 1171, a Jew carrying untanned skins near the Loire River encountered a Christian man, a servant to a local lord. The man thought the Jew was carrying instead a body of a Christian child to be thrown into the river.[78] He denounced the Jew to his master, who informed the local Count Thibaut. The count in turn seized the opportunity to take advantage of the Jews, with whom he evidently had financial dealings through a relationship with an influential Jewish woman named Pucellina. In need of cash and embroiled in "rivalry with the crown," the count first sought an "exorbitant" ransom from the Jews and then condemned them to flames.[79] Despite the claims of chronicler Robert de Torigni, no body was ever found, and no Christian child was ever reported missing. Still, even though there was no *corpus delicti*, the first victims of the emerging anti-Jewish accusation lost their lives.[80] The massacre of Jews at Blois suggests the rapid dissemination of the tale that Jews killed Christian children.

The event shocked the Jewish community both because of the scale of persecution and because it was the first instance when "a secular ruler charged with their protection had persecuted the Jews and condemned them to death."[81] It produced, as Susan Einbinder has noted, "a new kind of martyr, the victim of judicial violence." The trauma was captured in Jewish liturgical poetry produced to memorialize the event. Seeking to make sense of this unprecedented catastrophe and to answer the question Jews seem to have faced in light of this suffering—Where is your God now?—the poems fashioned the victims of Blois as burning sacrifices of atonement for "the expiation for communal sins;" they were "burnt offerings" whose smell pleased God;[82] the "sacrificial lamb" that, according to Einbinder, "reaffirmed the covenant between God and Israel" and served as "the agent of this collective purification."[83] In that framing, the martyrs of Blois are said to have gone to the fire with joy "as if they were bringing a bride to a wedding canopy."[84] The tropes in these poems would mark Ashkenazi literary responses to suffering, and especially to anti-Jewish accusations, for centuries to come.[85] They promote the idea of martyrdom—the sanctification of God's name, or *kiddush ha-shem*.

The Hebrew prose accounts also contain motifs of burnt offering and martyrdom representing a communal sacrifice for the sins of "all Israel." The so-called "Orleans Letter," a carefully crafted morality tale, affirms the martyrs' faithfulness to God in light of unjust persecution, underscored not only by the unfounded accusations but also by the shaky justice system; it also warns Jews against behaviors that may cause persecution.[86] The thirty-one "angels" burned in Blois remained steadfast in their faith, "clinging to our God, the God of Israel"; they died believing, so the "letter" reassured, that their death "may serve as atonement [*kaparah*] for all our sins" and for the transgressions of the community. To commemorate the tragedy, a fast was established on the 20th of Sivan. According to Israel Yuval, "in the Franco-Ashkenazi world, Jewish martyrs filled the role that Jesus played in Christianity."[87]

The function of the "Orleans Letter" as a morality tale is evident in the structure of the text: only after the description of the suffering, martyrdom, and the steadfastness of the martyrs did the narrator describe the events that had led to their martyrdom. The author implied that the accusation was concocted to take revenge on a prominent Jewess, the unnamed Pucellina, who acted haughtily and "harmed" the local lord. To buttress Jewish leaders' concern with the perceived appearance of Jewish status, the text also described sumptuary laws.[88] (The role that Jews' behavior played in spurring such accusations would become a prominent feature in some early modern Sephardic sources, such as Shlomo ibn Verga's *Shevet Yehudah*.)

Examples included in the "Orleans Letter" served to highlight both the martyrdom of the Jews and the miscarriage of justice. For instance, two of the martyrs, both *kohanim* of priestly lineage, were delivered from the fire because the bonds around their hands were severed and their hands were freed. But instead of being allowed to live, as was the custom in the case of failed executions, "the enemy rose against them and smote them mightily."[89] In another vignette, a Catholic priest advised Count Thibaut to subject one of the Jews, R. Itzhak, to an ordeal by water, which is described in Hebrew sources in an inverted way: if the Jew floats, he is innocent; if he sinks, he is guilty. In the standard medieval ordeal, the guilty were expected—contrary to natural law—to float. An ordeal was *iudicium dei*, God's judgment, a miraculous intervention to reveal the truth when little evidence was available.[90] This unjust inversion of the ordeal was amplified in Hebrew by the inverted parallel pun: they "acquitted the wicked and condemned the innocent [*ve-hizdiku et ha-rash'im, ve hirshi'u et ha-zadikim*]."[91]

The inverted description of the ordeal, coupled with the description of a botched execution, was not accidental or merely "ironic."[92] It emphasized that what happened in Blois was clearly a miscarriage of justice, even by the standards of the law of the time. But the message of injustice was sharpened by the fact that Jews were exempted from ordeals by royal or imperial privileges, which the Jews surely would have known at the time.[93] Not only was the ordeal applied fraudulently but it should not have been applied to Jews at all—in Blois, justice failed. Thus the outrage was not just about the new libel (*davar sheker*), as Ephraim bar Jacob of Bonn called it some twenty years later, but also, perhaps even more alarmingly, about the fact that laws were not properly followed. An unreliable legal system was potentially more frightening than this new accusation.

Jews, understandably, relied on courts of justice wherever they lived, and their estimation of how just local laws were had an impact on how they perceived their neighbors. According to Jewish tradition, for non-Jews to be excluded from the category of "idolaters" and, thus, from the restriction such categorization imposed on Jewish–gentile interaction, they had to abide by the Noahide laws, which were said to have applied to humans before the revelation on Mount Sinai. One of the categories of Noahide laws concerned just laws with functioning courts of law.[94] Calling Christian laws "bad" therefore also had serious halakhic consequences for Jewish–Christian interaction.[95] It is perhaps for this reason that other accounts of the Blois affair stressed the king's outrage at miscarried justice, as if to reassure not only that faithfulness to God was important but also that, although in Blois "a secular authority defaulted on his legal responsibility to protect his Jews,"[96] Christian authorities more generally had not abandoned them and could still be relied on for support.

Indeed, the tone of the Hebrew prose accounts of Blois is surprisingly positive, conveying, as one of the "letters" phrased it, "good tidings [*basurah tovah*]" to the Jewish community.[97] When Jewish leaders went to see the king, who remains unnamed, he received them generously and asked the Jews to speak openly to him. The king then condemned Count Thibaut and promised to punish him "if he acted against the law," because even the ruler was frightened by what the count had done. Moreover, the king felt the obligation to protect the "bodies and property of the Jews" like a "pupil of the eye." These stated concerns that laws were broken in the persecution of Jews along with the assurances of the king's protection are striking in these Hebrew texts. They address precisely the novelty of the Blois incident and try to mollify the sense of threat and betrayal by those who were supposed to protect Jews. As if to amplify the message that Jews had not lost the protection of those in power, the Hebrew texts mention the king's willingness to issue charters of protection that were to be disseminated across his kingdom. This optimistic picture of the monarch's defense offered hope in moments of crisis and assurances that, after all, Jews had not been abandoned by either God or the Christian kings.

Indeed, in affirming their commitment to the safety of the Jews, secular rulers are also shown to have expressed disbelief about the charges. In one of the Hebrew accounts, the king is reported as saying that "there is no truth" to the accusation against Jews like the one in Pontoise, even though the child was made a "saint in Paris"—a reference to Richard of Pontoise, whose body was placed in the Church of the Holy Innocents in the Field in Paris.[98] The king then assured the Jews that in his kingdom they should not fear similar charges, even if the non-Jews (ha-goyim) find a body of "a non-Jew killed in the field or in a city." Another text adds an exchange with "Count Henry, the brother of the wicked [Thibaut]," in which Henry articulates, for the first time, an argument that there is nothing in Jewish law permitting them to kill non-Jews.

Scholars have debated whether these surviving epistolary narratives were indeed letters written immediately after the events in Blois to inform other Jewish communities about the accusations or whether they were written only in the thirteenth century or even later for other purposes.[99] The presence of the arguments defending Jews against the ritual murder accusation seems to point, as Kenneth Stow has argued, to a later, post–thirteenth-century dating, when both the Holy Roman Emperor and the pope, but admittedly not a French king, provided letters defending the Jews and condemning the blood accusations against them.[100] If, however, we were to accept the Hebrew letters as more or less contemporaneous to Blois, that would mean that these Hebrew texts captured the existence of the first, now lost, official royal defense of Jews against anti-Jewish accusations. But another clue suggests that the letters were indeed written much later. The letter, said to have been sent by "the leaders of Paris," notes that "now we cannot go there [Paris]," implying it was written after one of the expulsions of Jews from France, or at least after 1182, the first time Jews were expelled from the French domains.

Scholarly debates over the Hebrew accounts of Blois stem from the fact that some of these epistolary accounts come from manuscripts written as late as the fifteenth century. Two are appended to the end of Crusade chronicles—one by Shlomo bar Shimson in a manuscript relating other accounts of persecution and dated to 1453,[101] and another by Ephraim bar Jacob of Bonn—alongside other stories of Jewish persecutions in a collection that likely served a liturgical purpose of commemorating Jewish suffering.[102] Though the dates of these manuscripts have generated debates over their historical origins and significance, their precise chronology is not pertinent here, nor is it of crucial importance whether they describe what may have happened or just provide embellished accounts of the drama following the Blois affair, trying to fit the story into the liturgy commemorating Jewish suffering. What matters is that in retelling the story of Jewish martyrdom these accounts provide not simply reassurance and meaning for suffering but also a model for intercommunal communication and mobilization in the aftermath of anti-Jewish libels. They highlight the steps to be taken while seeking help from Christian authorities. Thus, even if, as Kenneth Stow has argued, these letters were in fact written or redacted a long time after the events, what they capture is a powerful story of Jewish martyrdom and communal responses. That very combination would become the core of early modern Ashkenazi songs and tales of anti-Jewish libels; the Sephardic works would lose the martyrological motif.

Fulda and Valréas—The Beginning of the Legal Trail

If the story of Blois began the memory trail in Jewish literature and martyrology in the aftermath of anti-Jewish libels, the legal trail started in the thirteenth century with two cases that generated the first reliable evidence of Christian authorities defending Jews from anti-Jewish accusations: Holy Roman Emperor Frederick II in 1236 following violence in Fulda in Hesse and Pope Innocent IV in 1247 in the aftermath of the death of a girl in Valréas in Provence.[103] Fulda and Valréas represent a new development in the history of anti-Jewish accusations. There, for the first time, not only were Jews said to kill Christian children but also to do so to obtain their blood. The Fulda accusation led to what seems to have been the first inquiry into Jewish religious practices ordered by Christian authorities, which resulted in the exculpation of Jews.

What is known about Fulda comes from the imperial decree, a *bulla aurea*, issued by Frederick II in July 1236, and from two monastic chronicles: *Annales erphordienses,* a Dominican chronicle covering 1220–1253 and written in Erfurt between the 1230s and sometime after 1253, and *Annales marbecenses,* a Cistercian chronicle compiled in the thirteenth century in Marbach.[104] Frederick II's imperial decree, a legal document, sets the legal framework and affirms imperial power in administering justice and giving protection to his subjects, but says little about what happened beyond mentioning "the murder of certain boys by Jews," which gave rise to a menacing new opinion about Jews' "clandestine crimes."[105] The chronicle, in contrast, captures the memory of the events.

For the year 1235, the Erfurt chronicle briefly mentions a story of eighteen Jews murdered in the village of Wolfesheim for killing a Christian.[106] The staggering number reportedly killed and the chronicler's enigmatic pronouncement—"for it seems that he who thirsts for blood, his blood shall be shed"—perhaps indicate more than a charge of simple murder. Though the reported incident may be evidence of the crusade-related unrest, the statement may also imply a connection to the new belief that Jews not only killed Christians but also desired their blood. Given the chronicle's textual context, it may set up a link between what is said to have happened in Wolfesheim and the incident in Fulda.

According to an account for the following year, on December 28, 1235 (5 Kal. Ianuarii), thirty-four Jewish men and women were killed in Fulda by Crusaders—"Christians marked with a cross"—because two of them "had killed miserably five sons of a certain miller, who lives outside of the city walls, and who, together with his wife, was attending church at the time."[107] They collected the boys' blood in waxed sacks and burned the house down, the chronicler claimed. After the crime was discovered and "confirmed" by the Jews' confession, they were punished "as mentioned above"—attacked by the Crusaders. The chronicler's note is confusing. On the one hand, it suggests an inquiry and the Jews' confession, which ultimately led to punishment. On the other, it implies extrajudicial mob violence by the Crusaders, a likely reference to the unstable political situation in the region during the Sixth Crusade, which targeted not just Muslims in the Holy Land but also heretics at home.[108]

The slightly later Cistercian chronicle of Marbach does not mention Wolfesheim, but it offers a more detailed account of Fulda that seems to corroborate the reports of mob violence against Jews.[109] It also refers to the blood motif and sows doubt about the emperor's role in the affair. According to the chronicle, citizens of Fulda killed "many Jews" after they "had slain some Christian boys in a certain mill in order to draw their blood for their own remedy." The bodies of the boys were taken to Hagenau, an imperial city about 100 miles away, and deposited in the imperial castle. More violence against Jews was then reported. "Unable to quell the violence that erupted there against Jews," the emperor called for an inquiry to confront the "popular rumor" that Jews needed Christian blood "for the day of preparation" [*in parasceve,* Passover]. The emperor was assured, so the chronicler says, that "if this turned out to be true, all the Jews of his empire would be destroyed," a language that mirrors that of the Hebrew accounts of Blois. But, the Marbach chronicler asserted, nothing certain came out of this inquiry and the emperor's serious intentions were quickly weakened, not least on account of Jewish bribes.[110]

The chronicler's claims contradict the imperial decree, which exculpates the Jews. He clearly did not accept either the conclusions of the imperial commission[111] or the resulting official decree. For the Marbach monk, there was no clear exoneration of the Jews, and whatever the result of the inquiry, it was determined by Jewish money. The *fama communis*—a term meaning public opinion, or rumors—about Jews and the Fulda murder was stronger than the 1236 imperial decree or later papal bulls condemning such anti-Jewish beliefs and accusations. Indeed, although valuable, neither the imperial decree nor the papal bulls defending Jews would prevent subsequent accusations and new tales about Jewish murders of Christian children from arising.

The imperial decree, while lacking in detail about what happened in Fulda, is unequivocal about what actions the emperor took and why, and what conclusions were reached. It was appended to and framed within the traditional protections of Jews as imperial subjects belonging to the imperial chamber, which had been granted to Jews in 1157 by Emperor Frederick I Barbarossa, and meant to affirm the emperor's protection of Jews and assert imperial authority over them.[112] This is exactly what the Hebrew accounts of Blois claimed had happened in France.

Given the events at Fulda and the subsequent attacks on Jews caused by hostile rumors, the emperor, in an effort to "elucidate the truth about this crime," decided to consult many notables, including princes, magnates, nobles, abbots, and other religious figures.[113] Because these men could not reach a consensus, the emperor then sought counsel from Jewish converts to Christianity, who, having rejected Judaism, were expected not to "keep quiet" about anything they found in Jewish books. He summoned converts who were "experts in Jewish law" to conduct a diligent study of the matter and find out the truth. Their findings were conclusive: Jews do not desire to consume human blood. Indeed, according to the laws of Moses and "Jewish decrees, called in Hebrew Talmud [Talmilloht]," they guard themselves from "pollution" by blood. Even those cultures for which animal blood was permitted, human blood was not. The emperor, with the support of the princes, thus pronounced "the Jews absolved of the grave crime," and prohibited anyone from launching such accusations against them, calling Jews the emperor's "kind and favorable servants." This imperial condemnation would enter the legal trail of defense against the blood libel accusations, and Jews were eager to have it registered in official records. In 1260, the decree was inscribed into the records of Worms, and in 1360 in Cologne. Though the emperor used the occasion to assert his authority, the fact that the decree would be marshaled in subsequent accusations underscores the limits of imperial protection of Jews and, as the Marbach chronicle manifests, casts doubt on the efficacy of even explicit condemnations of blood accusations.[114]

It is not clear whether Fulda was the first case in which the charge of the use of blood was levied. But this is how Pope Innocent IV understood it when he reissued the papal constitution *Sicut Iudaeis* on June 9, 1247.[115] Addressing "all faithful Christians," Innocent warned them not to "accuse

[Jews] of using human blood in their religious rites since in the Old Testament they are instructed not to use blood of any kind, let alone human blood. But since at Fulda and in several other places many Jews were killed because of such a suspicion, we, by the authority of these letters strictly forbid the recurrence of such a thing in the future."[116] The pope threatened excommunication and loss of honor for anyone who would oppose "the tenor of this decree," but qualified that "only those be fortified by this our protection who dare plot nothing against the Christian faith."

Innocent IV issued this version of *Sicut Iudaeis* in the aftermath of an incident in the Provencal village of Valréas, thirty-seven miles north of Avignon. On March 26, 1247, during Holy Week, a two-year-old girl named Meilla disappeared; her body was found the next morning in a nearby moat.[117] In a subsequent inquest witnesses claimed that her body "smelled good" and that miracles ensued after her body was moved to the local church.[118] No sooner had people started claiming that the girl had last been seen on the Jewish street than two Franciscan friars, Guillem Chaste and Azemar, began to investigate, although without authorization from the local authorities. They arrested three Jews—Benedig, Burcellas, and Durand—and apparently had them tortured. The three were held for seven days, until April 4, when they finally confessed to killing Meilla. On April 9, the lord of Valréas, Dragonet de Montauban, intervened in this unauthorized investigation, and ordered his own.

During this second inquest, whose summary was written by Petrus Bernardus, the lord's notary, Benedig implicated other Jews—Astrucus, Crescas, Burcellas, Lucius, and Durantus.[119] He also is reported to have said that after kidnapping Meilla they extracted her blood in a hidden place inside his house; fearful of discovery and further violence committed by local Christians (*propter tumultum et timorem populi*), they tried to dispose of any remnants. He also reportedly showed the knife with which the girl was wounded and the glass vessel in which the blood was to have been collected. "Of the blood," Benedig said, "they were to partake on the recent Holy Sabbath, and believed to be saved [by it]."[120] Not only that, they did this every year, especially in Spain, because of the great number of Jews there. And "when they cannot have a Christian they eat a Saracene [Muslim]."

The surviving record claims that Burcellas also said Meilla had been killed to obtain blood "for a sacrament" because in ancient time the great priest of the Temple "received the blood of a ram" and "sprinkled" it in a plaza before the Temple, according to the Law of Moses.[121] Another Jew, Lucius, apparently said that the infant and its blood would be "almost like a sacrifice": "almost" because without the Temple they could not make sacrifices. The blood was to be shared with other Jews, and the remains of "a

Christian or Jewish person" killed "in place of a ram" were to be burned "according to their law."[122] Lucius, invoking the Christian justification of Jewish exile, is reported to have said that the child was to be crucified in place of "the prophet called Jesus on whose account we are in captivity."

Another Jew, Durantus, denied killing Meilla. But when asked about what was supposedly done with her body, he reportedly claimed that it was to be crucified "on the holy Friday in opposition and affront to Jesus Christ."[123] When asked about the blood, he claimed Jews needed it for a procession similar to that done with "the blood of the ram in the old law." When subjected to torture, the men's confessions contradicted each other's. Some denied what was said; others changed their answers. In the end, many were burned at the stake, others murdered in the cruelest way, being "cut in two," with men castrated and women's breasts torn out; some, including children, were forced to be baptized.[124] Christians, for their part, sought to prove not just the Jews' guilt but also the miracles following the girl's death. But no cult seems to have emerged there.

Though Fulda seems to be the first place where the blood accusation emerged, the case in Valréas may offer its first detailed description and first claims connecting the death of a Christian child with "the law of Moses." This is why it was imperative for Jews to demonstrate that Jewish law did not include demands to use blood of any sort. Jews promptly turned to the pope to seek help and protection, who happened to be in Lyon, 105 miles north of Valréas. On May 28, 1247, Pope Innocent IV issued two letters to Archbishop Jean de Bernin, whose bishopric included the town of Valréas. The pope enjoined the bishop to "restore" status and liberty to the Jews and protect them against future persecution. Pope Innocent IV explicitly lay the blame for the violence in Valréas on Christians, "who covetous of their possessions or thirsting for their blood, despoil, torture, and kill them without legal judgment, contrary to the clemency of the Catholic religion, which allows them to dwell in the midst of its people and has decreed tolerance to their rites."[125] The pope objected to the process: Jews were "inhumanely burned [at the stake]," even though they "were not legally convicted, nor had they confessed," he wrote, contradicting the summary the notary had prepared. Such actions were not to be tolerated because "divine justice has never cast the Jewish people aside so completely that it reserves no remnant of them for salvation." Indeed, in his second letter to the archbishop, Innocent IV wrote,

> If the Christian religion were to give a careful heed and rightly analyze by the use of reason, how inhuman it is and how discordant with piety for it to afflict with many kinds of molestations, and to smite with all sorts of grave injuries, the remnant of the Jews, to whom, left as witnesses of his saving passion and

of His victorious death, the benignity of the Savior promised the favor of salvation, it would not only draw back its hands from harming them, but as a show of piety and solace of human kindness to those whom it holds, as it were, in tribute.[126]

In this letter, it seems that the pope consciously chose to use mild language in reference to Jews. In fact, in another context, in 1244, the same pope was not shy about referring to Judaism as the "impious perfidy of the Jews" and bemoaning that "our Redeemer has not removed the veil of blindness [from their hearts] because of the enormity of their crime."[127] But here this language was missing.

Based on a petition sent by the Jews, in the second letter, the pope offered more details about the injustice that took place in Valréas.[128] According to the pope, the Jews, accused of "having nailed to the cross a certain girl who had been found dead in a certain ditch," complained about the process. Though they "were not convicted, nor had they confessed nor had they even been accused by anyone," the Dragonet de Montauban

despoiled them of all their goods and cast them into a fearful prison, and without admitting the legitimate protestation and defense of their innocence, he cut some of them in two, others he burned at the stake, of others he castrated the men, and tore out the breasts of the women. He afflicted them with other diverse kinds of torture, until, as it is said, they confessed with their mouth what their conscience did not dictate, choosing to be killed in one moment of agony than to live and be afflicted with torments and tortures.

And then other lords, taking advantage of the crisis, also "threw into prison whatever Jews dwell in their lands and dominions, after having robbed these Jews of all their property." The pope expressed concern with the process that would be voiced in response to other blood accusations over the following centuries: "No one deserves punishment unless he has first committed a crime, nor should anyone be punished for the crime of another."

But in his first letters responding to what happened in Valréas, Innocent IV did not address the crux of the charge: that Jews murdered Christian children for cannibalistic purposes. This charge was only addressed later in the summer, in two separate statements on June 9 and July 5.[129] In the first, Innocent reissued the constitution *Sicut Iudaeis,* adding language that explicitly condemned what would become known as the "blood libel." He admonished Christians not to accuse Jews "of using human blood in their religious rites, since in the Old Testament they are instructed not to use blood of any kind, let alone human blood."[130] In his July 5 letter to the archbishops and bishops of Germany, the pope countered another kind of false accusation: that, during Passover, Jews "share the heart of a murdered child."¹³¹ He defended Jews, stating that "the Divine Scriptures pronounces the law 'Thou shalt not kill'" and asserting, somewhat mistakenly, that it was prohibited to Jews "to touch any dead body" while celebrating Passover.¹³² The bull was reissued again on August 18, 1247, this time addressed to the archbishop of Vienne, Jean de Bernin; a copy eventually found its way to Trent, as part of the dossier related to the trial of Jews there in 1475.¹³³

The narrative that emerged in Valréas seems to have been heavily influenced by the projection of Eucharistic practices and beliefs onto the Jews.¹³⁴ The blood, the records state, was said to have been extracted "to partake on the recent Holy Sabbath, and believed to be saved [by it]."¹³⁵ It was "a sacrament" consumed, like the Eucharist in the medieval period, every year. The blood, also like the Eucharist, was to be divided and shared among Jews. The victim, like Jesus in Christian theology, was a replacement for the Passover ram.¹³⁶ But, in contrast to Christian reverence for Jesus in the Eucharist during the Easter season, all this was to be done "in opposition and affront to Jesus Christ." What supposedly happened in Valréas was represented as a Eucharistic counternarrative.

But if the storyline was heavily influenced by the Eucharistic sacrament, it may have also reflected a new awareness of Jewish texts, which had been exposed only recently to Christian eyes. The events in Valréas took place just seven years after the "trial of the Talmud" in 1240.¹³⁷ And although the consumption of blood, as the pope affirmed, was prohibited according to the Bible, blood did play an important role in Temple sacrificial rituals discussed in the books of Exodus and Leviticus and elaborated in rabbinic literature.¹³⁸ In Exodus 29, the blood of a ram and a bull is used in the consecration of the High Priest. In Leviticus, and then in more detail in Mishnah *Yoma*, the high priest slaughters sacrificial animals—a bull or a goat—and collects their blood.¹³⁹ The Mishnah adds information about Temple topography and instruments: a basin into which the blood is collected and a description where it was sprinkled: "He [the High Priest] slaughtered it and collected its blood in a basin, and gave it to the one who would stir it on the fourth terrace of the sanctuary so that it would not congeal.... He took the blood from the one who was stirring it, went to the place where he had entered and stood at the place where he had stood, and sprinkled from [the bowl] once up and seven times down."¹⁴⁰ Blood, of course, also plays an important role in the Exodus story and thus in the Passover story: the Nile River turns into blood, and blood is sprinkled on the doors of the Israelites, saving their firstborn from the angel of death. Though biblical—both Hebrew and Christian—texts provided enough textual bases for inspiring charges of both ritual crucifixion and blood libels, in a new context of Jewish–Christian polemic and animosity in the High Middle Ages, it is not implausible that the interest in Jewish texts heightened the sensitivity to and awareness of other discussions of blood in Jewish texts.

Moreover, the idea of blood's restorative and curative power was also known among Jews and Christians. Pliny's *Historia naturalis,* as Efraim Shoham-Steiner has shown, contains a story of the king of Egypt bathing in blood to cure leprosy.[141] In the legend of Saint Sylvester, Emperor Constantine, affected by leprosy, is advised to bathe in blood, but chooses baptism instead.[142] And some Jewish midrashim tell a story of the pharaoh's affliction with leprosy and his demand for the blood of the infants of Hebrews.[143] Shoham-Steiner has demonstrated that, during the Middle Ages, this last story underwent changes from the earlier version in *Exodus Rabbah,* in which the infants are saved, to later versions influenced by the Christian context, in which the pharaoh slaughters the infants for their blood. In the Jewish stories it is never Jews who desire blood but the pharaoh. The Christian blood piety, which emerged in the late Middle Ages in northern Europe, certainly played into the imaginary Jewish desire for blood. As Caroline Bynum has noted, the geographic overlap between Christian blood piety and anti-Jewish blood accusations was not accidental.[144] The beliefs in the purifying or curative attributes of blood and Christian blood piety make the charges against Jews in Christian Europe less culturally discordant; they also underscore the role of belief in the dissemination of anti-Jewish libels, despite explicit biblical prohibitions against the consumption of blood and explicit prohibitions against bringing charges of blood libels against Jews, at least after Fulda and Valréas.

Although earlier cases provided nascent narratives—some forgotten for centuries—of ritual murder or of Jewish martyrdom in the wake of murder charges, the cases in Fulda and Valréas resulted in the first legal documents in defense of Jews: they thus represent the beginning of the trail of legal documents and arguments related to anti-Jewish accusations. They also, particularly the case from Valréas, provide some of the earliest and clearest evidence of Jewish efforts at diplomacy undertaken to defend Jews (that is, if one accepts the later dating of the Hebrew letters about Blois). Paradoxically, while defending Jews and debunking the accusations, the legal protections marshaled after Fulda and Valréas also inscribed the accusations for posterity. They offered not only evidence in favor of the Jews but also a historical source to those who wished to chronicle the Jewish "crimes" and expressed disbelief in papal and imperial protection, like the Marbach chronicler.[145]

Werner of Oberwesel—An Unapproved Popular Saint

Unlike in Norwich or Paris, in Fulda or Valréas no cult emerged as a result of the accusations.[146] It is unclear whether that was because of the quick intervention of both imperial and church authorities or a lack of interest on the part of local officials or, in the case of Valréas, because of the gender of the alleged victim. But when the body of an adolescent boy was found in the spring of 1287 near the town of Bacharach along the Rhine, a popular and, in contrast to the cult of William of Norwich, quite sustained cult of "S. Werner" developed in Bacharach and Oberwesel, spreading to France in the fourteenth century as "S. Vernier" or "S. Verny."[147] Contemporary local chronicles briefly mention Werner's death and name Jews as culprits.[148] According to one account, as the rumors about Werner's death at the hands of the Jews spread, violence against them claimed tens of lives and some Jews were arrested.[149] Soon Jewish representatives approached Emperor Rudolph II to seek justice and protection, apparently while offering monetary compensation. In response, the emperor imposed fines on the communities where Jews were attacked and requested assistance from the archbishop of Mainz who, as one chronicler recounted, preached against attacking Jews. The archbishop is said to have ordered that the body of Werner, whom "some Christians of simple spirit" venerated as "almost divine," should be "burned by flames and the ashes of his body scattered in the wind and dissipated into nothingness [*ad nihilum dissipari*]."[150] The chronicler added that a great number of Jews [*quingenti*], apparently armed, were present while the bishop was preaching, threatening to kill any Christian who would express opposition.[151] Despite opposition to the cult at the higher levels of both secular and Church authorities, which was explained by the Jews' detractors as a result of bribes, the cult of Werner—encouraged by the local clergy and spread through songs, poems, tales by performers and lower-rank preachers—attracted pilgrims; its canonical status, however, remained uncertain for centuries.[152]

Over the subsequent decades, indulgences were granted by local bishops to the Chapel of S. Cunibert in Bacharach, where the body of Werner was laid, and in 1428–1429, during wars against the Hussite heresy, a formal bid for canonization was forwarded to Rome at the request of the Elector Palatine, Duke of Bavaria, Louis III.[153] Still, despite the role papal legates played in the process and the political needs of the Church in fighting heresy, Pope Martin V, who had just a few years earlier reissued *Sicut Iudaeis*, including a clause condemning blood accusations, ignored the request, and did not follow through with the canonization, adding to the confusion about the status of "the good Werner."[154] In the end, Werner was popularly described as a "saint," but formally he has never become one.

In the post-Reformation era, Werner's relics were dispersed, with the effect of solidifying and expanding the cult into France. In 1548, Werner's finger turned up in Besançon, helping popularize the cult in Franche-Comté in eastern France.[155] But when the cult of "S. Vernier" spread to France, where no Jews were allowed to live after the end of the fourteenth century, its anti-Jewish character was lost until modern times.[156] Instead, in France, S. Vernier became a patron of winemakers, with ubiquitous iconography depicting the youth with sickle and grapes. Still, the Eucharistic blood connection appears to have been retained. According to Carolyn Bynum, "grapes and the winepress are traditional Eucharistic images."[157] In the seventeenth century, especially during the Thirty Years' War, Werner's remaining relics found their way to Belgium and Italy.[158]

If the explicit anti-Jewish meaning of the story was lost in France, it did not disappear in the German lands, perhaps because of the blood devotion among Christians and the continuous presence of Jews there. In 1578, Laurentius Surius, a Carthusian hagiographer from Cologne, inserted the story "Werner, a Boy Cruelly Killed by Impious Jews" into the second edition of his lives of saints. Surius's work was not the first to mention Werner. Some of the earliest printed editions of Jacques de Voragine's lives of saints, known as the Golden Legend, included the story as well, but it was not mentioned, for example, in Hartmann Schedel's Nuremberg Chronicle.[159] And in 1474, Werner Rolevinck, another Carthusian from Cologne, included a brief mention of Werner in his bestseller *Fasciculus temporum*, a chronicle of the world, which went through numerous editions even before 1500. If Rolevinck secured Werner a place in the history of the world, Surius's stature and the readability of his work meant that his lives of saints left an influential mark on early modern hagiographies.[160] The Bollandists used it as an important source for their own opus.[161]

The Bollandists did not shy away from the controversy surrounding Werner's status as a saint and discussed it directly: the 1665 volume of *Acta Sanctorum* for April illustrates the confusion surrounding his status, with various running heads: "B. Wernhero," "blessed Werner," and "S. Wernhero," a saint.[162] The Bollandists included a lengthy discussion of the cult, along with primary documents supporting it: more than forty pages were devoted to Werner in the *Acta Sanctorum* compared to only nine pages discussing the 1475 story of Simon of Trent.[163] These documents became proofs of the legitimacy of the cult and made Werner's story accessible to much broader audiences. It entered diocesan liturgical calendars, and in 1742 it was allowed to have an office in the diocese of Trier. Still, the cult itself remained localized and was never fully embraced by the Church.[164] Indeed, Pope Benedict XIV, arguably the most important legal scholar of canonization, referred to him as *beatus,* which Werner's nineteenth-century apologist Henri de Grèzes took to be a mistake caused by "either an error of the copyist" or inattention by the "distinguished author."[165]

But for all the popularity of Werner, or Venier, and the attention given to him by the Bollandists and other hagiographers, and even by historians who saw in Werner an important conflation of blood libels and host desecrations, his cult would not have much of an impact on the history of anti-Jewish accusations.[166] It may be because of its timing, with efforts to promote the cult limited to word of mouth and coinciding with strong imperial and papal protection of Jews, or because of the geographic direction in which the cult spread—to areas where Jews were not allowed to live, transforming Werner, as André Vauchez puts it, from "the martyr of the Jews" into "an innocent winemaker."[167] To be sure, Werner has a place in the history of anti-Jewish accusations—he was seen as a victim of the Jews by Christian hagiographers, Bishop Johannes Hinderbach of Trent, who was intimately involved in the trial of Jews there in 1475, had an interest in Werner, and his story has been discussed by historians of antisemitism.[168] But Werner's death, its aftermath, and the efforts to turn him into a martyr-saint are still part of the medieval story, in which Jews were able to rely on the known legal and political landscape shaped by medieval law. That landscape would change in the early modern era, when the story of Simon of Trent's death in 1475 and its aftermath would play a key role in reshaping the legal and political framework on which Jews had relied for protection. Although the cases of Fulda and Valréas left as their legacy new legal tools for Jews to use in their defense, the story of Simon of Trent would ultimately undermine their efficacy.

CHAPTER TWO

The Death of Little Simon and the Trial of Jews in Trent

During the Christian Holy Week of 1475, which started with Palm Sunday on March 19 and ended on Easter Sunday, March 26, rumors began circulating in Trent, a city at the foothills of the Alps, that Jews had killed a toddler named Simon. The boy disappeared on Thursday, March 23, while the tiny Jewish community of Trent was celebrating Passover, which had begun the evening before. Simon's body was discovered on Easter Sunday in a canal running under the house owned by a Jewish family. His death unleashed a chain of events that resulted in the destruction of Trent's tiny Jewish community and the creation of a cult of Little Simon, or Simonino as he would be called in Trent, with the relics of the boy's body at its center. But the impact of the events extended beyond Trent: they revealed fissures between German and Italian political and legal cultures and between the political and religious influence of the pope; in the long term, they also undermined centuries of papal policies and protection of Jews, effecting a policy transformation with ramifications extending beyond well into the twentieth century. Until the 1475 events in Trent, the medieval papal policy of condemning the persecution of Jews resulting from blood accusations had remained unchallenged. In fact, copies of the bulls by Innocent IV from 1247 and Gregory X from 1272 on behalf of Jews facing similar accusations are preserved in Trent among the massive amount of documents related to the affair.[1]

The story of Simon of Trent is probably one of the best-documented blood accusations, archivally and iconographically, with thousands of documents and hundreds of pieces of art, printed broadsheets, pamphlets, and books preserved in Trent, the Vatican, and other European archives (Fig. 2.1). Because of this volume of material, which allows scholars to mine it from different angles and approaches, it is also the most-studied blood accusation in premodern European history.[2] Yet, despite the unprecedented amount of historical evidence, we know relatively little about what happened in Trent in the spring of 1475 and the following months. And what is known comes primarily from sources created or preserved by Bishop Johannes Hinderbach, a preeminent player in the affair. Hinderbach and his allies shaped the public memory of Simon's death and the trial that ensued; they also shaped the historical records on which later scholars have relied. The records of the trial of Jews in Trent demonstrate, to use Jennifer Bishop's words, "the 'creative' nature of documentary records" that are "manipulated to serve particular ends."[3] The thousands of documents left by Hinderbach and his network of supporters reflect the extent to which they sought very self-consciously to promote their version of the story while suppressing or discrediting others. In fact, a close reading of the documents shows that the trial of Trent, the most notorious blood accusation in premodern European history, was also a fight over records and memory.[4]

That fight mattered. Bishop Hinderbach, who had a deep interest in saints and relics and had earlier been involved in a canonization process, knew how to fashion evidence used in assuring a saint's recognition.[5] He may have been surprised by the pushback he received in 1475 from Rome and elsewhere, but his knowledge of the canonization process played an important role in shaping the records of the trial, as well as the facts on the ground through the iconographic representations of Simon. Hinderbach understood that the validity of the cult of Little Simon was dependent on the validity of the trial proceedings and of the testimonies extracted there. Simon was a martyr only if it could be proven that Jews killed him. Ultimately, Hinderbach was correct; the records and the existing cult would become the foundation for a shift in papal policy of protecting Jews against blood accusations and for the official recognition of the cult of Simon. But Hinderbach would not live to see these results.

Records are not independent of power, and in Trent—a liminal place nestled between the spheres of influence of the Holy Roman Empire and the Italian princes and rulers, between the emperor and the pope, and between German and Italian cultures—the clash over records was also a clash over influence and power. Trent was part of the Holy Roman Empire, subject

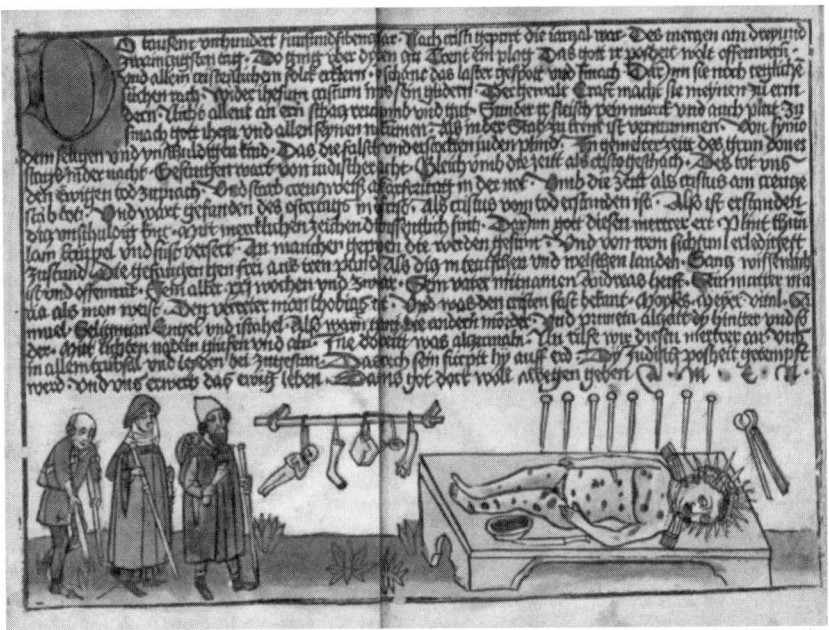

FIG. 2.1 German broadsheet showing pilgrims visiting the relics of Simon, in a position known as *victima*. Bound with the account of Matthia Tiberino. Bayerische StaatsBibliothek, Rar. 338.

to the rule of both the emperor and the duke of Tyrol, the latter residing in Innsbruck. In the fifteenth century, a complex relationship between the city of Trent and the duke of Tyrol was articulated in several agreements, according to which the bishop of Trent, a prince-bishop with governing powers, recognized the duke of Austria, who was then also a ruler of Tyrol, as his overlord (*unser gnediger herr*), promised loyalty, allowed the duke access to all castles and fortresses, and acknowledged the duke's right to appoint a city captain, who was to assist the bishop in secular matters.[6] The duke was obliged to defend the bishop and the church of Trent.

There was a personal element to Hinderbach's involvement as well. For Hinderbach, a German trained in Italy, the trial of the Jews came on the heels of a humiliating confrontation with the pope over his own election as bishop of Trent in August 1465. The pope had preferred an Italian and refused to accept Hinderbach's election until May 1466, and then only after Emperor Frederick III intervened.[7] The Trent trial, and especially the resulting clash with Rome, must have stirred up painful memories and raised questions of the legitimacy of Hinderbach's authority as bishop, similar to those that had surfaced in the aftermath of his election as bishop of Trent.

The trial of the Jews, though grounded in Christian anti-Jewish attitudes and beliefs, was thus about much more than Jews.

What Is Known—The Bare Facts of the First Days

After a toddler named Simon disappeared on the evening of Maundy Thursday, March 23, 1475, and the search by family and neighbors brought no results, his father reported his son's disappearance the next morning, Good Friday, to Bishop Hinderbach, fearing the boy may have drowned in a nearby canal.[8] The bishop ordered Giovanni de Salis, the *podestà* or chief magistrate, to coordinate the search. Rumors began circulating that Jews may have kidnapped the boy because, during that season, it was said, they "capture Christian children and kill them."[9] That same day, a city official named Dainessius was ordered to go with a notary to the house of Samuel, a prominent member of Trent's tiny Jewish community, and search for the boy. After searching Samuel's house in many places, the officials left empty-handed.

On the evening of Easter Sunday, March 26, a Jewish servant found the boy's body immersed in a canal running under Samuel's house. Jews immediately reported their discovery to the authorities, who performed a preliminary autopsy on the spot and ordered Simon's body moved to a hospital in the German Church of St. Peter's in Trent to be reexamined the next day.[10] Eight Jews were immediately arrested, among them the heads of the three Jewish families living in Trent: Samuel, Israel, and Tobias. The day after the autopsy, additional Jews were arrested, including visitors to Trent and servants in the existing Jewish households, along with Samuel's wife Brunetta, the only woman among the arrested. On March 31, the notarized recording of "miracles" allegedly performed by Simon began, and no time was wasted before the first narrative of the murder was composed.[11] On April 4, not even two weeks after the boy's disappearance, Giovanni Mattia Tiberino (Johannes Matthias Tiberinus), a physician at the court of Bishop Johannes Hinderbach of Trent, who had on March 27 examined the boy's body along with other physicians, issued a short address in Latin to the Senate of Brescia, his town of origin, reporting the story of Simon's death. Tiberino sent a copy also to Rafaele Zovenzoni, a poet from Bishop Hinderbach's circle who would play an important role in promoting the cult of Simon of Trent.[12] Tiberino's address, soon printed as short pamphlets in Italian, Latin, and German, would become the dominant version of the story.[13] But Tiberino's account was written many months before the trial ended and, more ominously, even before the first confessions were extracted under torture from the accused Jews. And yet, it was that early version, along with its follow-up updated on April 17, which would remain the primary voice about the Trent affair for centuries.

Tiberino's Narrative

Addressing the Senate of Brescia on April 4, 1475, Tiberino promised to write "about a most important event, such as no era—from the Lord's passion up to these times—has ever heard of": a horrible crime, perpetrated by Jews.[14] He wished to spread the word, so that Jews "may be eliminated from the whole Christian world" and the memory of them "utterly vanish from the land of the living." Jews, Tiberino wrote, not only "devour" Christian property through usury but also "feast on the living blood of our sons, afflicting them with terrible punishment in their synagogues, and cruelly slaughtering them in place of Christ."[15] Shifting attention to Trent, Tiberino introduced "three families of Jews headed by Tobias, Engel, and Samuel" and began to describe their "horrible crime."

Everything, according to Tiberino, began on March 21 with a gathering in the synagogue at Samuel's house, "during what the Christians call Holy Week." At that meeting, Engel said, "On this Day of Preparation, we have plenty of meat and fish. We lack only one thing."[16] Samuel asked, "What are you without?" and all understood that Engel meant a Christian child to serve as a sacrifice killed "in contempt of our lord Jesus Christ," with his "gore" used "in their unleavened loaves" so it may prevent "the powerful stench they exude."[17] According to Tiberino, they called "this their Iobel, that is Jubilee."

After much back and forth, it was decided that the deed was to take place in Samuel's house, and Tobias was given the task of finding a child.[18] He initially declined, saying he was "poor ... and had small sons," but others "coerced him with their curses." On Thursday night (March 23), Tobias went around the town and found Simon, a "handsome," "pretty," "kindly and compliant" boy, nearby. Tobias, "the betrayer," quickly grabbed Simon's "beautiful hand with his own rabid right hand," and when Simon began crying, he offered the boy "a silver coin" and "silenced him with coaxing talk"; he then took the child to Samuel's house. There, Samuel awaited "like a tiger eager for blood" and brought the boy inside where the rest of the Jews "howled over Christian blood." Tiberino then described, in gratuitously gross detail, Simon's supposedly torturous death; his circumcision by Moses, who "unsheathing a knife, pierced the infant's penis, and [then] seizing pincers began to tear apart his right jaw next to the chin, and placed the severed piece of flesh in a bowl that was there ready." Thereupon the Jews were able to collect the boy's "sacred blood." "Anyone who wished," Tiberino continued, "proceeded to cut out for himself a little bit of living flesh. All the main participants did this." If the boy made any noise, he was gagged and smothered. "After all this, Moses speedily lifted the infant's right shin and placing it on his lap, set about similarly ripping open with the same knife the outer portion of flesh lying between the tiny penis and the leg muscle, and, taking up the pincers again, proceeded to rend the living flesh with its living blood." The whole event ended with the symbolic crucifixion of "half-dead" Simon, with his "most holy arms" violently stretched "in place of the crucified [Christ]," while other Jews encouraged Samuel and Moses to stab the "holy body" with "hard needles." At the end, the Jews gathered to curse and blaspheme against Christ, while piercing Simon's body, muttering, as Tiberino reported, incomprehensible pseudo-Hebrew curses: *"tolle yesse mina, elle parachies elle parissen tegmalen,"* which he explained meant, "Let us butcher this boy just like Jesus, the Christian's God, who is nothing. Thus may our enemies be eternally confounded."[19]

Simon was killed, Tiberino claimed, in contempt of "our Lord Jesus Christ" and "to insult the Christian faith"; his killing underscored Jews' broader contempt for Christianity.[20] "By an everlasting statute," Tiberino wrote, Jews cursed daily against "the divine Eucharist and the Blessed ever Virgin Mary." Their book, called "the Thalmut," which they "prefer[ed] to the Books of Moses and the Prophets," contained blasphemies and tales; for example, that "God studies the Thalmut" and Jesus suffers "mighty torments in Hell." They cursed Christians in their prayers, Tiberino wrote, "men in Hebrew, women in the language, which they learned from their first years," and prayed for the destruction of their enemies and for the "uprooting of the wicked Christian kingdom." This relatively lengthy—for a short pamphlet—discussion of Jewish prayers and blasphemies helped Tiberino "contextualize" the motivations behind the killing of Simon and explain any misfortune afflicting Christians. "No wonder," he bemoaned as he addressed Christians directly, "if Christ should afflict us with wars, famine, thirst, hail, and frost," because "we suffer [Christ's] enemies to rule among us!" We Christians simply "cling on to his perpetual enemies, disdaining the inviolable faith." But in Trent, this was finally to change, Tiberino concluded, and the Jews, "from elders to minors" now in prison, would not be released without paying "the due penalties" for the crimes they committed.

Tiberino's provocative rhetoric was peppered with phrases referring to the Jews of Trent as "cruel," "most rabid," like "tigers eager for blood," and "howling with dry throats over Christian blood," sometimes singling out specific figures such as Moses, or Tobias, or Samuel. In committing these "horrible crimes," the Jews were juxtaposed to Simon, who was described as "glorious," "innocent," and in the German texts also "blessed."

Tiberino's violently inflected language and detailed description of Simon's suffering, written before the first Jews confessed under torture, certainly served to emphasize Jews' "cruelty" and their hatred of Christianity. His explanation for why Christians "suffer Christ's eternal enemies" in their midst alluded to Jewish political influence and the economic role they played in Christian society. "Listen, you rulers of peoples, to the unheard-of-crime, and watch over your peoples as faithful shepherds should! Let earth's denizens awake and see what snakes they are nurturing in their own bosom! The cruel Jews not only eat up Christian's property in their frenzied craving for interest payments, but, conspiring against our lives and for our destruction, they feast on the living blood of our sons, afflicting them with terrible punishments in their synagogues and cruelly slaughtering them in place of Christ."[21] The use of these phrases was meaningful; it harkened back to the language of the Brescia Council's earlier condemnations of Jewish usury.[22] The death of Simon in 1475 allowed Tiberino to renew calls not only for the Jews' expulsion from Trent but also, and much more ominously, the elimination "of this savage race from the whole Christian world" so that "the remembrance of them [may] utterly vanish from the land of the living."[23]

But when Tiberino wrote these words, the trial of the Jews was just beginning: nothing in the existing records suggests that Tiberino's writing was based on what he learned from testimonies of the arrested Jews. Tiberino's April 4 letter to the Brescia Senate demonstrates that the deck was stacked against the Jews from the very beginning. A powerful narrative was set down, miracles were being carefully recorded, and Bishop Hinderbach was quite eager to disseminate Tiberino's story.[24]

What May Have Been Known by April 4

When Simon's father Andreas reported his son's disappearance to the bishop, he appears not to have mentioned Jews; he thought the boy drowned in the canal.[25] Only when news spread across the town and the search under the auspices of the city government began in earnest did rumors start circulating that Jews might have kidnapped the boy. But when Samuel's house was searched on Good Friday (March 24), no body, nor even suspicious signs were discovered. Indeed, it seems that the Jews fully cooperated with the search, with Brunetta, Samuel's wife, providing tools as needed.[26]

On Sunday night, March 26, Jews discovered the body of a toddler dressed in a dark-gray garment and inexpensive shoes (*uno pari caligarum et sotularium*). Tobias reported the discovery to the authorities, and officials soon arrived to examine the body. After an initial autopsy it was deemed that the death must have occurred recently, since the body was still flexible, the skin pink, and blood still present and flowing.[27] Though the body was retrieved fully dressed, there were apparently wounds underneath the clothing, including on the tip of the boy's penis. Initial interviews with Samuel and Tobias about the discovery of the body apparently differed, but records of their content have not been preserved. Even though Samuel was first officially interrogated on March 31 and Tobias not until April 3, on the day the body was found—March 26—the decision was made to arrest eight Jews: Samuel, Tobias, Engel, and five others. They were arrested on the grounds that, as the official protocols from November 1475 state, the wounds on the boy's body emitted blood when Jews were present, a proof, it was believed, of Jews' culpability in the boy's death "because experience shows that wounds on the dead emit blood when a murderer stands near the corpse."[28]

The next day, on March 27, the body, now in the Church of St. Peter's, was identified as Simon's, and another autopsy was performed by two physicians, one of whom was Giovanni Mattia Tiberino of Brescia, the bishop's personal physician. During that second autopsy, the physicians agreed that the boy must have died recently, at the earliest on Saturday night—but as the trial progressed and a narrative set in, the time of death would change to fit better with the timeline of Christ's passion. Ten more Jews are arrested on that day, among them Brunetta.

The podestà de Salis wanted to follow up on the rumors of Jews killing Christian children during the Easter-Passover season, because such rumors provided legal grounds to open a trial against the Jews. It just so happened that a Jew who had converted to Catholicism, Giovanni da Feltre, was imprisoned at that time in Trent for another crime. De Salis, "wanting to get information whether it was true that Jews are used to killing Christian boys and taking their blood, as it is reported," interrogated the convert under oath.[29] The prisoner, Giovanni da Feltre, recalled what appeared to be a real case of blood libel from 1440, claiming that many years ago his father, who had decades ago lived in Landshut in "lower Germany" (Bavaria), had told him that that "some Jews" in his town had killed a Christian boy "to get his blood and use it." The authorities arrested all the town's Jews, except for those who, like his father, escaped. Those who were captured were burned at the stake, some forty-five Jews, "but it is not clear how the child was killed, nor by whom." Asked if he, when he was still a Jew, or his father had ever used such blood, Giovanni gave a response that, at least as recorded, is ambiguous: it focuses on a description of a ritual in the Passover seder when red wine is spilled to mark the ten plagues in Egypt; the first one is, of course, blood. Giovanni noted that his father "had received the blood and put it in his wine cup, in which there was wine, and from there he sprinkled it on the table, cursing the Christian faith."[30] Blood was also used, Giovanni seems to have said, in the making of the Passover bread, but he did not know how it was done.

It is unclear in what language Giovanni told this story. The testimony as it is preserved now is in a Latin summary, but that was surely not the language he used to testify. This linguistic distance makes it impossible to know what was actually said. It might be that Giovanni da Feltre simply recounted a story he had heard from his father about Jews accused of killing a Christian boy in Landschut in 1440. It is also possible that the convert of some years recalled fragments of memories about the Passover seder. It is possible that he described the spilling of wine, when the plagues, including the plague of blood, were mentioned. What was actually said in his testimony will remain unknown, but, importantly, the way it was recorded in the Latin trial records sent to Rome served to justify the legal procedures used in Trent in the aftermath of Simon's death by validating rumors that Jews committed such crimes.

From a legal point of view, that kind of validation was what the authorities needed to proceed with their investigation of Simon's death as murder by Jews. And it may be why Giovanni da Feltre's testimony was sought and included in the records, even though it did not meet the legal requirements for proper witnesses—honest, bona fide witnesses, not *infamis personae* like Giovanni da Feltre who was imprisoned for another crime.[31] In this light his testimony could not pass legal muster, but it served to justify proceeding against the Jews.

The following days were spent on interrogations of both Christians and Jews about what they heard or saw in the days following Simon's disappearance and about the circumstances surrounding the finding of the body. Between March 27 and April 4, seven Christians, including Giovanni da Feltre and another Jewish convert, Roper the Tailor, and nine Jewish men and women were examined. These early testimonies seem innocuous, and many shared similar details. On March 28, Anna, the wife of Samuel's son Israel, told the podestà de Salis that Seligman (known in the Latin records as Bonaventura), Samuel's cook, had discovered the body on Sunday evening when he was asked to fetch water from the canal under Samuel's house. He immediately notified Brunetta, Samuel's wife. That same day, March 28, Seligman was brought to the torture chamber to testify, where he said that when he saw something submerged in water he thought it was "some skin or entrails of an animal," which he had seen "many times in this canal" before. But when he notified his mistress of the find, she inquired if it might be the corpse of the boy.[32] The podestà wanted to know why Brunetta thought it might have been Simon's body, implying she was in on the murder. Seligman answered matter of factly that the authorities had already searched for the child in the house and in the canal.

Seligman then recounted that on that Sunday evening when he told Brunetta about the body, the Jewish men were in synagogue, which was in Samuel's house. He did not know what happened next because he stayed in the kitchen, but, he testified under torture, that that some Jews were worried "something bad" would befall them when Samuel's house was being searched by the podestà on Friday. They surely knew that vicious rumors were circulating around the town. And yet, until the body was found the Jews did not seem particularly troubled and continued with their celebration of Passover. When asked why Jews visiting Trent did not flee when Simon disappeared, Seligman responded that first they stayed because of the holidays, as the first two days of Passover were immediately followed by the Sabbath. Second, they did not flee on Sunday, because "they did not believe anything bad would come upon them."[33] Under torture the cook confirmed his testimony several times and was not interrogated again until April 10, almost a week after Tiberino had written his first version of Simon's story.

The testimonies of the other Jews corresponded to what Seligman the cook had said. Each person may have added personal details about what they specifically did, but their stories overlapped: the body was discovered in the canal running under Samuel's house on Sunday evening while the men were in the synagogue finishing their evening prayers. Brunetta informed them about the discovery, and they immediately notified the bishop of the gruesome find.[34]

Even the other Seligman (or Bonaventura, as he appears in the Latin records), son of Mayer (or Mohar), whose testimony under torture on March 28 provided some elements of confirmation for those claiming that Jews must have killed Simon, at first told the same story.[35] On Sunday, after the evening prayers, Seligman, Mayer's son, left the synagogue, which was in Samuel's house, and went to play cards with women at Tobias's house, staying there for about an hour. He then returned to Samuel's house, whereupon Tobias asked him to follow him and his servant Ioaff with a light to the cellar, where the canal was. Ioaff went down into the water and retrieved Simon's body. According to Seligman, Tobias then went to the castle to notify the authorities. The interrogators decided that Seligman "did not want to tell the truth" and ordered him tortured. Soon Seligman broke and changed his story. He said that on Saturday, March 25, around noon, he was at Engel's house eating lunch with Isaac, Engel's servant. After lunch they both left and went over to Samuel's house. Isaac then told Seligman that he "had killed the boy, but he did not tell him anything how he had killed him, but that he killed him in Engel's house, . . . [and] that he had killed him on Thursday night . . . , and that Schweitzer, a [Christian] inhabitant of Trent near the canal, was the one who had delivered and brought the said boy [still] alive to the house of the said Engel." Tortured again, Seligman added that Isaac also told him that on Thursday night he "had struck the boy with his fist on the back of his head, whereupon the boy vomited up blood through his mouth, and that they collected this blood into a small pot [*cadinello*]. And that Schweitzer received twenty coins [*renenses*] for bringing the boy to Engel's house." Schweitzer then carried the boy to Samuel's house.

Schweitzer, who was then engaged in a dispute with Samuel and Israel over money, was also implicated in the crime by Vitale, Samuel's servant, who was interrogated both with and without torture on March 29.[36] Vitale confirmed it was Seligman the cook who had discovered the body, but he could not add any more information about the discovery. He did, however, speculate that Schweitzer might have been the one behind Simon's death, dumping the body into the canal under Samuel's house. On April 3, interrogated again, this time under torture, Vitale confirmed his earlier testimony; during the trial the Jews' supporters would maintain that Schweitzer, the Christian man, had played a role in Simon's death.[37]

A third testimony that strengthened de Salis's case against the Jews and influenced his decision to charge them with the killing of Simon was given on March 28 by a German-speaking Christian woman, Margareta Gelbegret. She claimed that some twelve years earlier, when she was living next door to Samuel in the house now inhabited by Tobias, her son had also disappeared but was later found alive in Samuel's house.[38] Margareta, like other Christians interrogated in the initial stages of the trial, had items pawned with Jews.

Although the three testimonies by Giovanni da Feltre, Margareta Gelbegret, and Seligman (Mayer's son) provided much-needed grounding to support the legal charges against the Jews, none of the testimonies from March 26 through April 4 contained the details or rhetoric found in Tiberino's letter. In fact, even Seligman's damning testimony contradicted what Tiberino wrote. Others did too. Schweitzer, the Christian man whom Seligman and Vitale implicated in the murder and who was arrested on March 28 and interrogated on March 31, also doubted that Jews could have killed Simon.[39] Schweitzer recounted his conversation with Andreas,

Simon's father, on Thursday night after Andreas had failed to find his son, telling him, according to the Latin account of his testimony, that Simon must have fallen into the canal. Andreas responded that he had looked for the boy there, but did not find him. As they spoke, two bystanders reported that some people were saying the boy was in the Jews' house, though others speculated that he must have drowned. "Whatever it is," Schweitzer replied, "[now] it is not the time to look for him," and went to bed. The next day, Schweitzer went to participate in the Good Friday celebrations in the Trent churches. After coming back home, Andreas and Schweitzer went again to look for Simon, now both believing the boy to be dead, drowned in the canal. Toward the end of his interrogation, Schweitzer was asked if he "knew or in his soul pondered how the boy had been killed or how he had arrived into Jews' hands." Schweitzer responded that he "greatly doubted" how this would have been possible, because he "knew that the boy had first disappeared on Thursday evening, and these Jews never exit their homes after noon on Thursday." But he offered that one Iohannes, a gravedigger who buried Jews, may have brought the boy into the Jews' house. During the interrogation, Schweitzer also admitted to discord between him and some Jews, especially Engel and his wife.

Schweitzer's testimony raised questions about the validity of the accusations against the Jews. And although he testified relatively early in the trial, on March 31, in the official records sent to Rome his testimony was relegated to the very end of the volume, after the testimonies of all the Jews and reports of their execution.[40] In contrast, the testimonies by Giovanni da Feltre, Margareta Gelbegret, and Seligman, son of Mayer, which made the accusations against Jews plausible, were placed right at the beginning of the trial records.[41] They appeared at the beginning not because they were delivered earlier—indeed Seligman's material includes testimonies from later dates—but because they helped set the stage for the narrative the official records sought to tell to justify the proceedings against the Jews. Still, however damning their testimonies might have been, they contained nothing that could have given Tiberino material for his April 4 story. Even the testimonies of two key figures—Samuel on March 29 and 31 and on April 3 and the April 4 testimony by the old Moses, who in Tiberino's story circumcised Simon—undermined the version Tiberino prepared.

Samuel's description of the finding of Simon's body and the immediate aftermath, including Tobias's notification of the bishop, overlapped with that of the others and did not implicate him or other Jews.[42] Even under torture he asserted that neither he "nor other Jews are killers."[43] Indeed, "none of the Jews was guilty of this, nor did he believe that the said boy had been killed; he drowned"; after all, Simon's mother lived next to the canal. On April 3, subjected to more torture, he again affirmed his own innocence and that of "other Jews, because they are not guilty."[44] And, while undergoing torture, suspended on the ropes, he turned to the podestà, asking, "Lord podestà, where did you learn that Christian blood is valuable and useful?" De Salis responded that he had learned it from "Jews like Samuel." After this exchange the torture intensified, and Samuel screamed to God for help.[45] He was kept on the ropes for "two-thirds of an hour" and then was let down and returned to prison.

In the days preceding Tiberino's April 4 letter to the Senate of Brescia, all the Jews, with the exception of Seligman, son of Mayer, denied culpability, and with small variations their stories were in agreement. Also, on April 4, during his first recorded interrogation, the old Moses affirmed the innocence of all the Jews and presented arguments against blood accusations, explaining rules in Jewish law that made such charges absurd: "It must not be believed that he, Moses, or other Jews did that, because in the ten commandments of Moses given by God it is commanded to Jews that no one may kill or eat blood, and on account of that Jews cut the throat of animals they intend to eat so that a great amount of blood may leave the animals' bodies, and then they salt the meat, so that more blood can be extracted."[46] Moses's argument was similar to that offered earlier by the popes in their medieval bulls protecting Jews from such false accusations. Moses added an example of a false accusation in which a Christian, "enemy of the Jews," brought the body of a Christian boy to a Jew's house. The Jew was arrested and tortured, but he did not confess to anything. The Christian man eventually did, revealing the accusation was completely false.

From the early days of interrogations Tiberino could not have learned the details he included in his April 4 address to the Senate of Brescia. Even if one accepts that not everything said then was included in the records, surely if there had been even one witness or one testimony that had produced the damning details found in Tiberino's account, it would have been included in the records sent to Rome. After all, such evidence would have made the charges against the Jews even stronger. Instead, the early testimonies weakened the case against the Jews. That changed a few days after April 4, when confessions under torture began increasingly to conform to Tiberino's account.

"What Should I Say?"

These are the words Vitale, Samuel's servant, spoke to the interrogators on April 13, 1475.[47] Similarly, on April 15, after having been asked repeatedly if he was telling the truth, Lazarus, a Jewish traveler who found himself in Trent when Simon died—whose testimony is not included in the records sent to Rome, but can be found in the German version at the Yeshiva University Museum in New York City and in the Latin protocols in Vienna—finally pleaded with the interrogators, "Tell me what you want me to say and I will say it."[48] From early on, the interrogators seemed to have had a specific "truth" in mind when questioning the Jews, and wishing to hear it, turning to torture to elicit it. When first interrogated, under only the threat of torture, the Jews offered what would become the first version of events—for days, this version remained quite consistent, containing details about the finding of the body and affirming Jewish innocence. This remained the case even when torture was first implemented.

But this first version was not "the truth" the officials were looking for, and when the Jews did not change it after several days, they were subjected to more torture, sometimes excessive, and more questions. Over time all the Jews broke and confessed to the murder of Simon. For example, when the second Seligman, son of Mayer, answered, "I do not know," to a question about the whereabouts of Brunetta, Samuel, and others when the body was retrieved from the canal under Samuel's house, the podestà, "seeing that he did not want to tell the truth ordered him undressed and lifted" on the ropes.[49] And Vitale's question "What should I say?" came at the end of long interrogation under torture, in which he was even made to listen secretly to Israel's confession, also under torture, in which Israel implicated Vitale.[50]

The "truth" the officials were looking for was sketched in Tiberino's letter. If the early accounts emerging from the first interrogations were relatively consistent—denying Jews' role in Simon's death—the increasing pressure, repeated questioning, and relentless torture led to the first confessions to the murder being made on April 7. These initial confessions were contradictory and confusing, but gradually they gained some coherence, often with language and phrases evoking Tiberino's account. Such language is most pronounced in the testimony by Tobias from April 9, but phrases paralleling those in Tiberino's account are also found in the Latin testimonies of Engel on April 8; Seligman the cook on April 10; and Seligman, son of Mayer, on April 11.[51] It must be remembered that the Latin protocols sent to Rome were dated November 15, 1475—months after Tiberino's story had been widely disseminated in print.

Tobias was first interrogated on April 3, 1475, more than a week after Simon's body was found. The first questions concerned the circumstances of the finding of Simon's body and the description of his injuries. When the body was found, Tobias said, the Jews decided the authorities needed to be notified; they wanted officials to come to the scene because they feared they might be implicated in the crime. As Tobias appears to have noted, "We wanted that one or two [officials] from the castle be here, so they could see the crime committed against us, because some Christian must have killed this boy and then thrown the body in the canal, so that it would be brought by water into the house, and this way they would have a reason to say that we, Jews, kill."[52] Under torture, he confirmed what he had said earlier. On April 7, more explicit questions about Jews killing Christians were asked, and Tobias again denied everything, observing it was Christians who said that Jews killed Christian children. He was then tortured excessively and, "almost dead," had to be sent to his cell to rest.[53]

The next day, April 8, Tobias's recorded testimony began to resemble Tiberino's address.[54] According to its Latin protocols, on Wednesday March 22, Samuel, his son Israel, Moses, Mayer (or Mohar), his son Seligman (Bonaventura), Engel, and Tobias gathered in Samuel's house to plot how to obtain the "blood of some Christian child," whom Tobias was chosen to find. He objected to undertaking this task because he was "poor and had children to take care of."[55] Samuel then ordered Tobias to do what he was asked and promised to take care of his family. The next day, Tobias began to wander the streets until he came to Canal Street (*via fossati*) and passed by Andreas's house, where he saw the boy. He held out his hand for Simon, who took it. Speaking softly to the boy and giving him a coin to encourage him to go, Tobias took him to Samuel's house. Samuel was already waiting at the door. Tobias passed Simon over to Samuel, who closed the door, and Tobias returned home. At home, Tobias could neither eat nor sleep. On Saturday, he went to Samuel's house to attend services in the synagogue, where he saw the body exposed "on a table where they put books, and this table is set in the middle of the synagogue." This time Tobias did not describe the killing; asked why Jews needed Christian blood, he explained that they required it during jubilee years and that this was a jubilee year. As for other reasons, Tobias claimed ignorance, saying he was "an illiterate man," a curious statement given that most scholars present Tobias as a physician. The descriptions of the plot, the kidnapping, and the delivery of Simon, as well as the discussion of the jubilee year as seen in Tobias's recorded testimony, resemble Tiberino's account. But it is in the testimony of the following day, April 9, that the language becomes similar to that of Tiberino's letter. For example, apparently Tobias said that when all were gathered before Passover at Samuel's house, Samuel said that they "had much meat and fish," to which Engel said that only one thing was missing, and everyone understood that he meant Christian blood.[56] Tobias's description of the killing and the April 10 testimony of Seligman the cook also contained verbiage similar to that found in Tiberino's April 4 letter to the Senate Brescia.[57]

In his April 4 letter Tiberino claimed that Jews uttered curses in Hebrew while killing Simon—"*Tolle Iesse mina elle parecheff elle passussem pachmalem*"—which according to Tiberino explained meant: "Let us butcher this boy just like Jesus, the Christian's God, who is nothing."[58] These Hebrew words in a slightly different spelling are also found in the April 11 testimony by Seligman, son of Mayer,[59] even though he said he did not know what these words meant. Still, Tiberino's supposed translation was incorrect. The phrase, except for the word "tolle," comes from Psalm 20: 7–8, which is part of the daily prayers: the words *iesse mina* in Tiberino's letter come from יֵשַׁע יְמִינוֹ (*yesh'a yemino*; deliverance of his right arm), the last words of verse 7, and *Elle* comes from the beginning of verse 8: אלה ברכב ואלה בסוסים (*elle ba-rechev ve-elle ba-susim*; these on chariot, and these on horses). The rest of the psalm was understood as an affirmation of the validity of Jewish worship of God.[60] But the words "passusem pachmalem"—*ba-susim* and *ba-gemalim* (on horses and on camels)—may also refer to Exodus 9:3, which is included in the Passover Haggadah to describe a threat of pestilence that would strike the Egyptians if Pharaoh would refuse to let the Hebrews go.[61] The German translation of the trial protocols includes a Hebrew transcription of the words, a transliteration, and an inaccurate Latin interpretation of them: "Suspensus Jhesus hereticus ista in equis et ista in camelis crucibus."[62] The phrase in the psalm, *yesh'a yemino*, "deliverance of his right arm," was mistranslated because of the onomatopoeic character of the words *Yesh'a* as Jesus (*Yeshu* in the Hebrew tradition) and *yemino* as *ha-min* (heretic) to mean "Jesus the heretic." To be sure, in Christian Europe, these original verses may have been understood by Jews in a polemical way against Christian beliefs, but they certainly did not mean what Tiberino and the Trent officials claimed them to mean.

As the trial of the Jews continued, questions were raised about the legality of the proceedings, and on April 21 the trial was suspended by the order of Duke Sigismund of Tyrol, the city's secular overlord. It was allowed to resume on June 6, thanks to Bishop Hinderbach's lobbying and propaganda efforts, and resulted in the executions between June 21 and June 23 of seven men: Isaac, Engel, Tobias, Vital, Mayer, and both Seligmans (Bonaventuras). The two Seligmans asked to be baptized before execution, saving themselves from death at the stake by being first decapitated. The old Moses was found dead in his cell, on June 18, four days after finally confessing. Still, he was formally sentenced after death, his body dragged to the site of execution and tied to a wheel.[63] The final summaries of the Jews' testimonies recorded before their execution aligned with Tiberino's account, and, chronologically, the events they recounted fit more closely the passion of Christ.⁶⁴ If following the first autopsies after the boy's body was found on Sunday, March 26, it was believed that Simon must have died no earlier than Saturday, by the end of the first phase of the trial, his death was noted to have occurred earlier during the Holy Week, in effort to fit Simon's death into the story of the passion of Christ. By the time the Jews were executed in June, the narrative was firmly set, an updated version of Tiberino's letter was printed in Rome, and iconography representing Simon widely disseminated. (Eventually, Simon's feast would be established on March 24 to mark his death on a date corresponding to Good Friday in 1475.)

With the eight men dead, there were still several Jews, including men, women, and children, in custody. After the news of the executions and the other Jews' imprisonment reached Rome, the pope intervened. On July 23, 1475, he ordered another suspension of the trial and soon sent his envoy Battista de' Giudici, bishop of Ventimiglia, to Trent, giving him broad authority to investigate if the trial had been conducted fairly, and to examine the charges against the Jews and alleged miracles around Simon's body.⁶⁵ Despite his broad authority, de' Giudici was thwarted at every level, and his attempts to end the trial and secure the release of the women and children failed. After a brief hiatus, the trial and the imprisonment of the remaining Jews continued into the first months of 1476, while in Rome a commission of cardinals was deliberating about its validity. Everything hinged on the validity of trial records and evidence marshaled to convict the Jews.

The Narrative in the Trial Records

The legality of the trial was challenged first by Duke Sigismund of Tyrol and then by Pope Sixtus IV. At issue were its jurisdiction, procedures, the excessive use of torture to obtain confessions, and the confiscation of Jews' property before completion of the trial. To defend themselves against the charges, Trent officials had to produce trial records. For that reason, the records of the trial as they came down to us are a consciously structured narrative aimed at addressing these charges. Some eleven full or partial records of the trial of the Jews survived in Latin and German, although there may have been other copies that circulated among the allies of Bishop Hinderbach with his permission.⁶⁶ Some, like the records of Brunetta's trial, have been lost even though their existence is mentioned in other sources.⁶⁷

The earliest surviving protocols of the trial can be dated to November 1475.⁶⁸ They are the official copy of the records in Latin sent from Trent to Rome as evidence in the investigation of the validity of the trial of the Jews. This copy, written on parchment, contains only materials from the first phase of the trial of the major male defendants, excluded are the women and the minor male figures, such as Lazarus. Yet as an official, notarized copy sent to Rome, it is significant because it played a major role in decisions from Rome regarding the validity of the trial and the cult of Simon.

There are differences between the surviving records, even Bishop Hinderbach noted errors on the margins of his personal copy.[69] There exist no "raw" copies of interrogations from the trial taken in the vernacular in real time during the interrogations, and there is "no trace" of the copy of the records prepared by Bishop Battista de' Giudici, who had been sent by the pope to investigate matters or of copies obtained by Jews and their advocates.[70] Neither is there any trace of the "authentic" copy, sealed by both Hinderbach and de' Giudici and sent to Rome in September 1475.

All preserved records of the Trent trial are thus those prepared by Hinderbach's officials; they are mediated by their purpose, time of their creation, and language. As R. Po-Chia Hsia has noted, it was not just the "problem of translation" of speech into text, which is always an issue in historical records, but also of translation "from one language to another," with four languages at play—German, Hebrew, Italian, and Latin—and none shared by all involved.[71] In a region where German and Italian cultures mixed and clashed, some people, including the podestà, spoke only Italian, whereas others knew only German; few shared both. And thus, a translator was needed to bridge the linguistic gaps during the interrogations and in the creation of the records. In the official records in Latin, the already mediated encounters during the interrogations were even further removed from what was said. Moreover, the German protocols are translations from Latin completed after the Trent affair finally ended in 1478, with a papal bull pronouncing the trial lawfully conducted.[72] The Hebrew language was used for snippets from Jewish prayers and rituals and was sometimes only transcribed phonetically in Latin letters, but at least in one instance—the German manuscript now at the Yeshiva University Museum—words were also written out in places in Hebrew characters.[73] With so much lost just in translation, the trial records cannot be taken at face value to learn what was said or asked during the trials; rather, they document how those responsible for preparing and preserving the records wanted the proceedings to be represented and remembered. The protocols are, as David Stern has noted, "extremely tendentious documents" that were "composed in order to defend the actions" of Bishop Hinderbach and other Trent officials.[74]

The apologetic nature of the trial records is most evident in the preface written by the translator of the records into German, identified by scholars as the Dominican Erhard von Pappenheim. Von Pappenheim explicitly addressed the criticism of the trial and emphatically affirmed its validity. The hefty volume of the trial records in German now at the Yeshiva University Museum opens with a German translation of the papal bull by Sixtus IV from June 20, 1478, in which the pope accepted the validity of the trial (but not of the cult).[75] The bull itself is preceded by a comment, written in red ink: "Here in the first place is the papal bull, in which, praise be the diligence and judicial proceedings, our Holy Father the Pope recognizes and declares the duly conducted trial and sentencing against the Jews of Trent, recorded below, on account of the holy, innocent boy named Simon, and that the said trial against the said Jews was conducted in a judicious and upright manner, as one may learn hereafter."[76]

After the translated papal bull, written in black ink, von Pappenheim asserted, again in red ink, "Justice commanded, in such grave matter, that the truth be thoroughly and properly examined through judicial torture, so that such a great evil would not go unpunished, or that anyone innocent might suffer or be suspected on its accounts. Therefore, the podestà in Trent himself ordered the Jews to be seized, which he was obliged to on account of his office, and earnestly examined according to court proceedings."[77] Von Pappenheim also adjusted the order of the protocols, foregrounding Samuel "in view of the fact," as he explained, "that [Samuel] was almost the leader, the instigator and originator of most things, and in my opinion, certain things are said more clearly in his confession."[78] And this also is how Samuel was described in a major legal opinion issued in 1478 by Giovanni Francesco Pavini, a Roman legist who sided with Hinderbach.[79]

From the language to the organization of the records, every decision had a specific effect. The surviving protocols—not just those in the German translation—were not organized chronologically, and their organization varies in the different copies. They all begin with the inquest held in the first two days after Simon's body was found, but then the trial records are organized by person, and only within that chronologically. This order should not be surprising, because it is quite likely that the raw records were also organized this way, with separate quires devoted to each person and created by the clerk present during the interrogations.[80] Yet such organization of files, as the German text shows, also allowed for flexibility in their arrangement. For example, the order of persons in the Latin records sent to Rome followed the chronological order according to the time of the first interrogation. But in the Vienna manuscript, Lazarus, who was interrogated in April 1475, appears only toward the end, after the records of the trial of women from 1476, and is missing from the Vatican copy altogether; by contrast, in the German translation of the records, the interrogations of women end the volume.[81]

As von Pappenheim's introduction suggests, he and likely also other clerks may have understood that order mattered: if the records were to appear chronologically the effect would have been different. The early testimonies by both Jews and Christians frequently raised doubts about the charge that Jews killed Simon. They showed relative consistency in telling how the body was discovered and what Jews were doing between the time of Simon's disappearance and the discovery of his body. The reader would have noticed the increasing application of torture, the desperation of Jews not knowing what the prosecution wanted to hear, and then a gradual shift to admissions of guilt to correspond with Tiberino's account. But when organized according to the person, with a choice of early testimonies—like those of Giovanni da Feltre, Margareta Gelbegret, and Seligman (Mayer's son)—foregrounded to increase the plausibility of Jewish responsibility for Simon's murder in order to justify the trial, the readers saw inconsistency, changing stories, final admissions of guilt, and execution of the accused, one by one. Already from the early pages, they knew how the story would end, with Jews admitting to killing Simon in the cruelest way. By the time they reached the testimony of, for example, Moses, who explained, using similar arguments found in medieval papal bulls of protection, why it was absurd to accuse Jews of such crimes, the readers' minds would have been made up and the Jews' denials and defenses would have rung hollow. Such order shows Jews as liars, changing their story with each interrogation.

Contemporary actors understood that these records were meant to tell a story—one already well known thanks to Tiberino and others; and one that, by the time the surviving official records were sent to Rome on November 15, 1475, was already visually represented in print and paintings, eliciting even a prohibition against such representations from the pope himself. The records thus played an important role in the affair and subsequent history, cementing in place Hinderbach's version of the affair.

At the time, the stakes were quite high, even higher than proving the guilt or innocence of the accused Jews. Were the trial to be deemed invalid, this judgment would potentially undermine the validity of the cult of Simon, which was being promoted with great passion by a bishop who in Trent represented both religious and political authority. The bishop's credibility was thus at stake. In a borderland like Trent, where Italian and German cultures met and clashed, and where political influence of the Holy Roman Empire was confronted by the powers dominating the Italian peninsula, the trial also revealed fissures between local, imperial, and papal authority, as each sought to assert their standing. In the long run, the records would affirm the validity of the cult of Simon, undermining the centuries of protection of Jews; in the twentieth century, their reexamination contributed to the abolition of the cult. And, for contemporaries, the contents of these records did not go uncontested.[82]

Fight over the Records

As soon as the trial began in late March 1475, Jews activated their connections and sought to stop it. In late April, Duke Sigismund of Austria, who, as the duke of Tyrol, had Trent Jews under his protection since 1450, ordered the trial suspended, beginning a period of intense lobbying by both Jews and their supporters, and Hinderbach and his friends, with Hinderbach increasing his efforts to promote the cult and his version of the story.[83] On April 30, Hinderbach wrote to the poet Rafaele Zovenzoni, sending him a copy of Tiberino's address and asking him to write poems glorifying "our new martyr," while regretting that he could not at that time punish the Jews.[84] In this lengthy letter the bishop complained about the Jews' influence over "false Christians" who were helping Jews at the court of the duke. Hinderbach himself hoped to intercede with the duke and present the truth to him "in light clearer than noon light." In May, Hinderbach's ally in Innsbruck, the seat of duke of Tyrol, informed him that "many Jews from Padua, with one Doctor from Treviso" were intervening with the duke, sparing no expenses to vindicate the Jews.[85] In response, Hinderbach sent Zovenzoni a list of new miracles, in hopes that the duke might be persuaded of the truth of the charges and come to understand that those supporting Jews were "corrupted by their diabolic or Jewish love of money."[86] To squash the Jews' "machinations," the bishop included some materials, among them Tiberino's account, proving the martyrdom of the "most innocent little boy," hoping their effect would be to decrease the "false commendation of Jews or false Christians." But Hinderbach's lobbying with the duke of Austria did not end there. As he later wrote to Pope Sixtus IV, to counteract Jewish supporters and "their iniquity and perversity" at the court in Innsbruck, he sent his own envoys with "information about this crime, with all circumstances and similar cases."[87] In June, succumbing to Hinderbach's intense lobbying, the duke allowed the trial to resume, and Samuel was the first to return to the torture chamber on June 6.[88] The others did too, and by June 23 all eight were executed.

News about Trent reached Rome as well. What was happening in Trent had ramifications not just for Jews but also for canon law and the authority of the pope. Accusations against Jews for killing Christians to use their blood were prohibited by popes, and the claims of miracles, if false, could be "injurious" to the Catholic Church. Miracles needed to be carefully examined and vetted. Well documented and verified, they could elevate an individual to sainthood and help the authorization of a shrine. Hinderbach understood that documented miracles had the power to help fulfill his goal to canonize Simon. Thus he took pains not only to document but also notarize them, making each record resemble formal court affidavits, with witness depositions in the presence of notaries.[89]

Miracles linked to Simon, and frequently reported to Rome as the papal commission deliberated, played a supporting role in affirming the validity of the trial.[90] If, on the one hand, the trial needed to be valid to justify the claims of Simon's martyrdom and sainthood, then, on the other, miracles demonstrated that he was indeed a martyr and a saint, and therefore the trial proceedings, in which Jews confessed to killing Simon, must be valid—a circular argument, to be sure, but one that worked in the long term. Hinderbach understood this relationship, and in his June 30 letter to Sixtus IV, he extolled the miracles and reported the "devotion and ardor" of pilgrims.[91] He also defended "the truth of the crime, and the legal and legitimate trial conducted by the [city] captain, the podestà, and other officials and administrators of justice."

The pope was concerned with both aspects of the trial: the validity of the accusations and proceedings against the Jews, and the claims of miracles. On July 23, 1475, exactly a month after the two Seligmans, the last victims of the first wave of the executions, lost their lives, Sixtus IV informed Hinderbach that he was sending an envoy to examine the affair and ordered him to suspend the proceedings.[92] By the time the pope intervened, Tiberino's account of "beato Simone" had been widely disseminated; a version was printed in Rome on June 19 by Bartholomeus Guldinbeck and reprinted on July 24, the day after the pope ordered the trial suspended.[93] On August 3, the pope gave his envoy, Battista de' Giudici, detailed instructions for his mission and, in a separate document, exhorted Hinderbach to cooperate with de' Giudici, a respected Dominican, "a professor of sacred theology, man endowed with learning and integrity," while assuring that he did not doubt Hinderbach's "zeal for justice and Christian religion."[94] The envoy's task, the pope informed Hinderbach, was to dispel detractions about the case that reached him from "many princes" and to understand everything in a "clearer light."

The first task outlined in the papal mandate to the envoy was to obtain "full protocols of the trial, namely, confessions, depositions of witnesses, and others which pertain to the truth."[95] The authentic copies were to be sealed by both Hinderbach and de' Giudici to ensure they had not been tampered with. De' Giudici was also to investigate if Jews did indeed procure the boy, "as it is said," and killed him, "with what ceremonies and torments," what they may have done with blood, and if they did any similar act at another time. The bishop of Ventimiglia was also to find out if "any deception may not have been committed in this accusation" and whether it was true or false that the Jews were guilty. The third task was investigation of the miracles to determine whether they were indeed "true miracles" or whether there was some "delusion or deception" involved, because "we have heard here that such great fame of these miracles" drew great crowds of people and even "images were painted in every place in towns." This was a serious matter, and de' Giudici was to examine these claims diligently, so that the pope would know whether to "approve or condemn" them. And then there was a legal question regarding the Jews' confiscated, or about to be confiscated, property. De' Giudici was to ensure that it all would be inventoried by a notary so that nothing was destroyed. The pope also gave de' Giudici authority to seek the release of the women and children, "so the innocent may not be punished for the guilty" (*cum non sint insontes pro sontibus puniendi*). Finally, while the pope asked the bishop of Ventimiglia to work together with Hinderbach, he, ominously gave permission, as a last resort, for de' Giudici to move the investigation to another city if he was unable to conduct his business in Trent.

Hinderbach welcomed the papal envoy with splendor and honor when he finally arrived in Trent on September 2, 1475, but it was only a performance. A campaign to impugn his reputation had already begun. Just four days after his arrival, de' Giudici wrote to Cardinal Stefano Nardini, archbishop of Milan and a close advisor to Pope Sixtus IV, about the rumors circulating about him in Trent, not just in the court of the bishop of Trent but also on the streets: they accused de' Giudici of coming to Trent to help Jews and being "corrupted" by Jewish money. But it was not just words but also deeds that terrified de' Giudici: one of his servants was killed in Rovereto, a nearby town under Venetian rule.[96]

Although on his arrival, de' Giudici immediately requested copies of the records of the trial, for seventeen days he was not given access to any material, receiving only promises instead.[97] These records, de' Giudici wrote, were necessary to move to the other items of his agenda. But Hinderbach was playing games. He appeared to de' Giudici as "pious and merciful," telling the papal envoy that he frequently told the podestà not to be cruel to the prisoners, because "if the innocent are tortured and die, even though they are Jews, their blood will cry out to God in heaven against you."[98] While Hinderbach used these sweet words, on September 6, just four days

FIG. 2.2 Tobias capturing Simon, *Hystorie von Simon zu Trient* (Trent: Albert Kunne, September 6, 1475), fol. 2v. Bayerische StaatsBibliothek, 2 Inc.s.a. 62#Beibd.

after the arrival of the bishop of Ventimiglia, the first illustrated version of Simon's story was printed in German in Trent by Albrecht Kunne, showing the boy's kidnapping and death, asserting his martyrdom and miracles, and strengthening public opinion against de' Giudici's efforts.[99] (Figs. 2.2–2.5)

Still, despite the printed stories, doubts about Simon's status abounded, increasing the urgency for de' Giudici's thorough investigation. The corpse of the boy was fetid, which contradicted claims that it was miraculously preserved. On September 5, the day before Kunne released the booklet about Simon, de' Giudici had seen the corpse of Simon and nearly vomited from the stench.[100]

Other obstacles were mounting as well. The Trentini, now engaged in a full-fledged conspiracy to promote the cult and fearful that the bishop of Ventimiglia would discover the truth of the fraudulent miracles and the unjust treatment of the Jews, made de' Giudici's task impossible to fulfill.

FIG. 2.3 Simon's martyrdom with Simon held by Moses, *Hystorie von Simon zu Trient* (Trent: Albert Kunne, September 6, 1475), fol. 3v. Bayerische StaatsBibliothek, 2 Inc.s.a. 62#Beibd.

They did not want to give him access to the remaining Jewish prisoners or allow him to interview additional witnesses. The envoy was under constant surveillance by Hinderbach's men, unable to examine witnesses, and, it appears, even to have visitors. The officials were also dragging their feet about de' Giudici's access to the trial records. As de' Giudici would later write, there were "many good words" he had heard from Hinderbach, but "little or nothing" was done to "investigate the truth."[101] Hinderbach later admitted that officials did not want to give de' Giudici access to all the original files, fearing they would give "means of defense into the hands of enemies [*timens gladium defensionis in adversariorum manibus dare*]."[102] To make

FIG. 2.4 Simon as martyr, *Hystorie von Simon zu Trient* (Trent: Albert Kunne, September 6, 1475), fol. 4v. Bayerische Staatsbibliothek, 2 Inc.s.a. 62#Beibd.

matters worse, the living conditions of the envoy's quarters were apparently quite uncomfortable.

Given the problems that de' Giudici faced in Trent, the papal envoy felt he had to move out of the city to fulfill his mandate and conduct his own investigation. The bishop of Trent, the city captain, and the podestà, de' Giudici argued, by preventing him from performing his tasks, disobeyed the pope and acted like "the Pharisees, who simulated devotion they did not have. . . . They feign zeal for the faith while acting scandalously . . . with acts and words resembling those of vipers."[103] On September 23 de' Giudici finally secured copies of the trial records, sealed as requested by the pope, and falling ill, he immediately departed from Trent, ostensibly for Verona. But he stopped in Rovereto, where he would stay to continue his investigation.[104]

In Rovereto, he was able to have visitors. As early as the day after his departure from Trent, de' Giudici informed Hinderbach that Jews' advocates reached him asking for help to free those still imprisoned and requesting "with such importunity" copies of the trial. The issue of the court records became central to his conversation with the Jewish representatives, which took place in the presence of Hinderbach's allies, Giovanni Menchey and Approvino. Perhaps because of the presence of Hinderbach's allies, the papal envoy apparently wanted to steer the conversation away from them, as if to minimize their importance, and wondered, for example, why Jews needed such records. If to protect the living, then de' Giudici was working with Hinderbach and his officials on freeing them; if to defend the dead, there was really not much to be done. But the Jews insisted the records

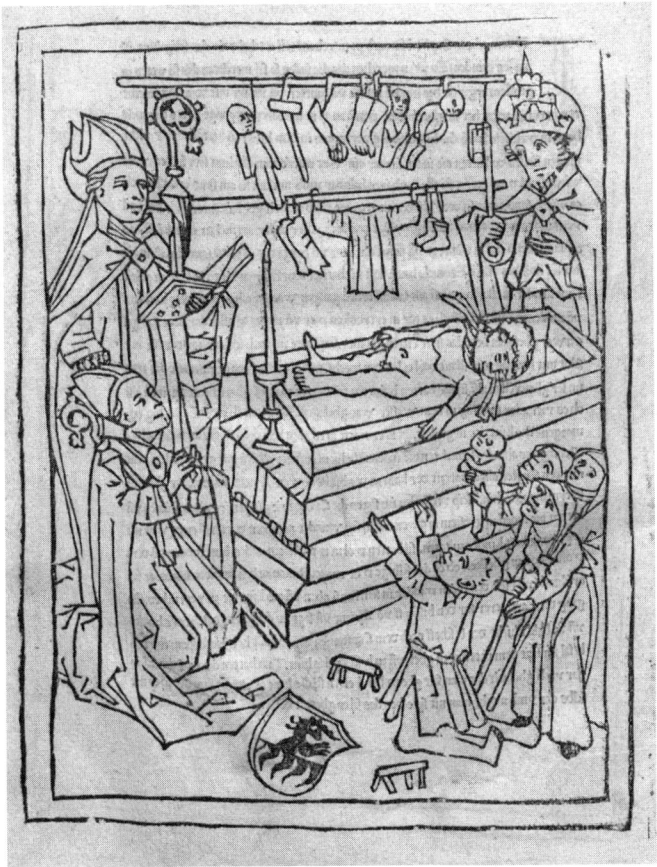

FIG. 2.5 Simon on the altar, *Hystorie von Simon zu Trient* (Trent: Albert Kunne, September 6, 1475), fol. 9v. Bayerische StaatsBibliothek, 2 Inc.s.a. 62#Beibd.

were important "not to defend the dead, who cannot rise again, but the truth." They understood, as did de' Giudici and Hinderbach, if for different reasons, that the ramifications of the trial were far greater than obtaining justice for the Jews in Trent. The Jewish advocates wanted to defend "the living, not just those incarcerated but also those around the world," who would be imperiled if what was in the trial records was to be regarded as true, because "it is said to contain the confessions of all the Jews, that from decade to decade, especially in the year of the Jubilee, they use the blood of Christian boys."[105] With such weight given to the transcripts of the trial and the Jews' apparent "importunity" to get them, de' Giudici felt the need to reassure Hinderbach that he should "sleep peacefully"; the sealed trial records in his possession "shall not be open until Rome."[106] Yet, if these transcripts ever reached Rome, they do not seem to have survived. Neither did another copy that de' Giudici apparently secured, in addition to the sealed one destined for the pope.[107] The earliest surviving records, as we have seen, were sent from Trent, signed by the podestà Giovanni (Ioannes) de Salis and his notary Petrus de Malefaratis on November 15, 1475.[108]

Truth and Authenticity

The question of the authenticity and trustworthiness of the trial records remained pertinent throughout the affair and beyond.[109] The Jews' advocates needed authentic records to defend their innocence; de' Giudici felt that "without them it was impossible to discover the truth" and "affirm the martyrdom of Simon."[110] Soon after arriving in Trent, de' Giudici issued broad calls, threatening penalties and censure to "all who find themselves in possession of writings or trial records, both of the assertions of martyrdom, confessions and condemnations of Jews and those of any miracles."[111] But the bishop of Trent prevented any of those announcements from being posted. Later, the papal envoy reflected that Hinderbach did all he could to control the flow of information, allowing him access only to "witnesses sent by himself," whereas those not sent by the bishop were either unable to come or unable to speak freely. Given de' Giudici's inability to examine those advocating on behalf of the Jews, and thereby to conduct "duly" his investigation, he feared that existing records "grounded in the examination under torture" would not reveal the full truth.[112] But at issue in the fight over records were also questions of "additions and omissions" in the protocols sent to Rome that were not in the original records de' Giudici was allowed to see in Trent.

The distrust over existing records went deeper, even during de' Giudici's sojourn in Trent, where he clashed, as he recounted later, with Hinderbach's supporters seeking to discredit him and with Trent officials over the trustworthiness of notaries engaged in producing the records.[113] Notaries, as Laurie Nussdorfer has shown, were "brokers of public trust"; documents drafted by them "were a superior form of proof in a court of law."[114] Thus, disqualifying a notary was tantamount to disqualifying documents produced by him. The Trentini tried to disqualify Raphael, a notary who worked for de' Giudici, and instead sought to engage, as the papal envoy put it, "some corrupt Tridentine partisan [*aliquis corruptus parcialis Tridentinus*]."[115] For his part, de' Giudici concluded, after examining some miracles and finding them fraudulent, that "all notaries in Trent were falsifiers" and did not "transcribe faithfully and correctly." He suggested hiring another notary, whom he considered trustworthy and who knew German, Italian, and Latin.[116] The undermining of trust in notaries continued even after the papal envoy left Trent. According to Hinderbach's allies in Trent, de' Giudici impugned the integrity of another notary, Giovanni de Fundo, by claiming that documents prepared by him were also false.[117] And in Rome, the issue of notaries was noted in the legal opinion issued and published in 1478 by Giovanni Francesco Pavini, in which he questioned the fact that Bishop de' Giudici used "only one notary," who was "suspected" of committing "grave" offenses.[118] The public fight over notaries cast a cloud over the authenticity of any records coming out of Trent and, according to the Trentini, also those produced by the bishop of Ventimiglia.[119]

The issue of falsification of records came to the fore in the trial that began on May 14, 1476, of the priest Paolo de Novara, a copyist in Trent.[120] Paolo de Novara was a key witness to what may have been omitted or added into the records. Among the documents he transcribed were the sealed trial records given in September 1475 to de' Giudici and a copy of the full records, sent to Emperor Frederick III then in Vienna, which must have been transcribed between the last interrogation recorded on April 12, 1476, and the beginning of Paolo's trial in May.[121]

The trial focused on Paolo de Novara's contacts with Jews and the bishop of Ventimiglia. He was accused of passing information back and forth between the Jewish women imprisoned in Trent and other Jews, especially their relatives who lived elsewhere. One of those relatives was Crassino of Novara, the father of Engel's wife Dulceta (or Süsslein), whom Paolo called "Bona or Bella." Paolo de Novara was accused of conspiring with Crassino and other Jews to poison the bishop of Trent and other officials involved in the trial, to steal Simon's body, or to use "some substance" to make the body "fetid," and, crucially, to go to Rome to testify that trial records were doctored to omit excessive torture of Jews.[122] Paolo reported that Jews believed it was Bishop Hinderbach who had orchestrated, together with Schweitzer, the killing of Simon. He raised questions that also troubled the bishop of Ventimiglia about Jews' guilt, false miracles, including the fact that Simon's corpse was rotting and thus was not miraculously preserved, the falsification of trial records that served the Tridentini to underscore Jews' guilt and thus confirm Simon's martyrdom, and the unlawful confiscation of Jews' property by Hinderbach. During his trial lasting several months and involving torture, Paolo resorted to self-mutilation: he tried to cut out his tongue so he would not be asked to speak and he claimed to be possessed by the devil. And thus he was forced to undergo exorcisms. Following the exorcisms, Paolo dialed back his allegations, denied that records had been tampered with but affirmed that much of the obstruction was engineered by the Jews. Paolo de Novara's trial, with its outlandish claims of Jews' plots against the officials in Trent, served to confirm the narrative promoted by Hinderbach about undue Jewish influence and the corruption of the bishop of Ventimiglia and others, helping Hinderbach discredit the Jews and their supporters. The trial was meant to serve as evidence to exculpate Bishop Hinderbach of wrongdoing and cast doubt on any evidence marshaled against him.[123]

Hinderbach was masterful in promoting his side of the story and undermining others, almost at any cost. A key part of his scheme was controlling information. While he was reluctant to give de' Giudici access to the records and to the incarcerated women, he was more lax about giving his supporters that access. For example, according to Hinderbach's letters from September 1476, the Franciscan preacher Michele de Carcano (Michele of Milan), charged with preaching about "our new blessed martyr Simon," was allowed "to see and examine" the trial records and to talk with the Jewish women, who remained imprisoned despite papal orders to release them; Michele was later to act as an advocate for the cause of Simon in Rome.[124] In October of the same year, Hinderbach also sent copies of the records to Bishop Jacopo Zeno of Padua; in November he mentioned in a letter to Francesco Sansone (or Francesco Nani), the renowned minister general of the Franciscan order, that another preacher, Johannes Petrus, minister of the province of St. Antonio of Padua, "saw and read" the trial records against Jews.[125] Then at the height of the investigation by the papal commission in Rome in 1477, Wilhelm Rottaler, Hinderbach's agent at the Roman Curia, requested copies as well.[126] But in February 1478, as the case in Rome was winding down, when the bishop of Feltre, Hinderbach's strong supporter, also requested copies, Hinderbach demurred, saying they were too voluminous to be copied and sent out.[127]

Hinderbach and his allies did all they could to use the trial records to promote the cult and defend their case, while impugning the integrity of Battista de' Giudici's investigation, the documentation he collected, and any evidence provided by Jews.[128] For example, the protocols of the trial of Brunetta, Samuel's wife, who is prominently displayed in later iconography of Simon's martyrdom (e.g. Fig. 1.2), went missing. Perhaps her trial included something incriminating against the Trentini, because Brunetta is said to have retracted her testimony, and Jews were said to have had the protocols in their hands. Amplifying the suspicion that Hinderbach's advocates may have destroyed the protocols is the fact that they tried to do everything they could to discount any evidence provided by Jews.[129]

Battista de' Giudici's Failed Mission and the Limits of Papal Power

Although the papal envoy secured the (now-lost) sealed records of the first phase of the trial, he was unable to accomplish much else. Frustrated, the bishop of Ventimiglia attached to his letter of September 24, 1475, a copy of his mandate to remind Bishop Hinderbach of the pope's wishes.[130] But if de' Giudici's letter, written in the presence of Hinderbach's close ally Approvino, expressed hope and even confidence that the surviving prisoners would soon be released as the pope had requested, in a second letter sent two days later, the tone was more confrontational. It implied that by not releasing the prisoners Hinderbach was disobeying the wishes of both the pope and the duke of Austria.[131] But Hinderbach remained unmoved: he kept the women and children in prison and continued to promote the cult.

Notified about, and perhaps even alarmed by, the obstruction of the Trent officials, on October 10, 1475, Pope Sixtus IV issued a *breve* to all rulers and officials in Italy prohibiting the veneration of Simon in sermons, paintings, and historical works until Bishop de' Giudici could determine "the truth of the matter."[132] He also ordered the protection of Jews and their property. Two days later, on October 12, the pope sent two additional letters, one addressed to Hinderbach and one to de' Giudici.[133] He exhorted Hinderbach to free the women and children, "whose innocence cannot be doubted." To de' Giudici the pope granted full authority, including the power to use excommunication and other ecclesiastical censures and penalties to compel cooperation from officials in Trent. In late October the papal envoy did use these newly articulated powers, threatening Jacob de Sporo, the captain of the city of Trent, with excommunication if the women and children were not released within three days or if they were subjected to torture. Disregarding the threats, on November 3, the podestà de Salis began the trial of the women, subjecting them to torture between November 4 and 6. On November 8, 1475, in response, de' Giudici excommunicated de Salis.[134]

Despite the excommunication, the women remained in prison, and the torture continued. Not all records of the interrogations seem to have entered the official protocols; a gap exists between November 8 and 17, when Anna, Tobias's wife, was subjected to torture. On November 18, a physician ruled that Brunetta, Bona, and Dulceta were too sick to be subjected to torture; he was especially worried that Dulceta, suffering from dropsy, might die within days. Yet the next day, the podestà, then officially under excommunication by the papal envoy, ordered Anna, Israel's widow, to be sent again to the torture chamber.[135] But Odoricus de Brezio, responsible for sorting out the Jewish loans and debts, intervened and spared her because of Anna's valuable skills: she knew how to read and was the only one able to decipher Jewish loan ledgers. Not until March 1476 was she interrogated and tortured. Dulceta, as the physician had feared, died less than two months later, on January 15, 1476.

The efforts to release the women failed, despite the plenary powers vested in Bishop de' Giudici by the pope, the ensuing excommunication of de Salis, and orders to set them free sent directly from the pope.[136] Hinderbach must have realized there was no mechanism to force him to obey papal orders. The impotence of the papal envoy and his failure to secure the release of the women and children underscored the limits of papal power and influence, something Hinderbach had understood since his time as a student in Vienna, where he embraced conciliarist ideas emerging from the Council of Basel (1431–1445).[137]

In the end, Hinderbach triumphed. His pièce de résistance came in January 1477, when three Jewish women—Bella, who assumed the name Elisabeth; Anna, now Susanna; and Sara, now Clara—converted in a high-profile spectacle, in which Hinderbach participated.[138] The women were first asked to confirm publicly that their conversion was sincere "free, spontaneous, voluntary, and without coercion, violence, fear, terror, or intimidation."[139] Several weeks after the conversion, on Sunday, January 26, 1477, the three women were led to the Church of St. Peter. They knelt before Simon's corpse and touched his coffin with one hand, and, with the other hand, in a gesture of contrition, performed in the presence of the luminaries of the city, including Hinderbach and crowds of faithful who "came to listen to the word of God," an act of penance. They confessed to their own and their husbands' role in killing Simon, "the use of his blood both in food and drink, and also to injuries, derisions, and blasphemies against our Lord

Jewish Christ, and his glorious mother Virgin Mary." Then they asked for the forgiveness of "God, glorious Virgin and his mother Mary, and saint Simon and his parents."[140] A procession around the church, a celebration, and reception followed; finally, there was a ceremony at the bishop's residence, Castle Buonconsiglio, where the women were said to have expressed their gratitude to Hinderbach. He permitted them to visit the church daily and bring votive offerings to "the sacred and incorrupt body of the *beatus* Simon, innocent boy and martyr."[141]

Hinderbach wasted no time in informing his allies in Rome about this important development. By early February the news had reached Rome, eliciting a response on February 10, 1477, from the Franciscan preacher Michele de Carcano of Milan, who rejoiced at the news about miracles through which God "manifested glory" of the new martyr, and in particular at the great miracle of the conversion of the Jewish women who had been, the preacher said, "most obstinate in their perfidy."[142] On February 12, Wilhelm Rottaler, Hinderbach's agent at the Roman Curia, also reported receiving the news and immediately passing it on to members of the papal commission.[143] Hinderbach and his allies hoped to use the women's conversion to thwart Jews' efforts to release them—after conversion they could no longer be united with Jews; and "to confuse other Jews and their supporters," who were attempting to stir opposition and spread "nonsense and fabricated lies" over the validity of the trial.[144] Indeed, Hinderbach's allies did not hide that they saw the women's conversion and the spectacle of contrition as "corroboration of the trial against the perfidious and impious Jews and the protocols [of the trial]."[145]

Conspicuously missing from this spectacle was Brunetta, the only Jewess commemorated in Simonine iconography. Arrested with the men on March 27, 1475, Brunetta was treated differently from the other women from the start. But her interrogation records are missing. A Hebrew letter from 1475 reporting the martyrdom of the men suggests she withstood torture without confessing to anything, but it does not mention her death.[146] Her ability to withstand torture made the Trent officials suspect she might have been bewitched.[147] To counteract the spell, Hinderbach ordered she be washed head to toe with the urine of a virginal boy—a remedy he discovered in Vincent de Beauvais's *Speculum historiale,* one of Hinderbach's favorite books. "Finally, after many attempts," Hinderbach wrote, Brunetta converted on her deathbed, taking the name Catherina.[148] But, as Anna Esposito has noted, there is room to doubt Hinderbach's claim.[149] The only evidence of Brunetta's conversion comes from Hinderbach himself: a marginal note in his copy of *Speculum historiale* and his own epitaph to Brunetta. As someone truly obsessed with record keeping, the notarial affirmation of anything that would help his cause, and informing his supporters about any helpful developments, Hinderbach was unusually silent about Brunetta. Confusion may have been compounded by the fact that there were two women named Brunetta: one was Samuel's wife, and the other was Engel's mother. In October 1477 one Brunetta, Engel's mother, is said to have died in prison and was ordered buried in a local cemetery. In a note about her death she is still called by her name Brunetta, because she was still known as a Jewess, in contrast to the women who converted and assumed new names.[150] The other Brunetta, Samuel's wife, seems to have been still alive in December 1477, months after the three other women converted.[151] Perhaps in this instance, even Hinderbach understood the limits of public fabrication. Although he may have concocted Brunetta's conversion in his private notes, he may not have been willing to claim in public a conversion of someone who had not accepted baptism. Others in Trent must have known her true fate. Or, perhaps, Brunetta died after the pope ruled the trial to be legal, and thus her conversion had no legal standing. Perhaps she was the reason for the Jews' continuous, if futile, efforts to free "Jewish women" even after they had converted. Still, given Hinderbach's propensity to broadcast news about Jews or Simonine miracles, and Brunetta's notoriety in Simon's story, his silence seems telling. Brunetta's presence in Simonine iconography depicting his death is perhaps another clue suggesting that she never converted (Fig. 2.6).

Years later, in a verse epic written sometime around 1481 and published in 1511, some twenty-five years after Hinderbach's death, Ubertino Pusculo, one of the poets writing about Simon at Hinderbach's request, lauded Brunetta's strength as the only one to "conquer the tortures men are afraid of" without confessing. He described in detail her legendary defiance:

> You alone, stripped naked in front of men, resolutely refused to reveal your crimes. Glowing charcoals had already burned your feet, and vile-smelling fumes had driven away the podestà and the rest, when you, fixing your fierce gaze on the man who was scorching your feet with lighted charcoal, called him a butcher! There was no longer any hope of her being conquered by torture, or of any truth being wrung from her lips; she was kept in jail but no longer interrogated, nor having conquered all forms of punishment was any more being inflicted on her.[152]

But "touched by God," she had a change of heart and converted with the knowledge and approval of Hinderbach; she then died, and her funeral was held with great pomp. If this account were true, the silence of Hinderbach and others at the time is particularly striking.

The question of telling false tales and fabricating evidence in Trent was certainly raised by Battista de' Giudici, whom the Trentini sought to dis-

FIG. 2.6 Broadsheet bound with Johannes Matthias Tiberinus, *Passio Beati Simonis pueri Tridentini a p[er]fidis judeis nup[er] occisi*. Rome: Bartholomaeus Guldinbeck, 1475 at the Bayerische StaatsBibliothek, Rar. 337. Brunetta is named "Pruneta."

credit by casting him from the very beginning as a friend of Jews and then forcing him to assert his anti-Jewish bona fides. For de' Giudici the affair in Trent was a threat to "the Christian religion."[153] Although true miracles were, the papal envoy argued, frequently sent by God to confirm faith, "false" miracles, fabricated through human acts, contribute to "its destruction." Indeed, Antichrist, he argued, will bring false miracles to throw into question "the true miracles of the apostles, martyrs, and old saints." But the Church, "founded on the passion of Christ and the blood of the apostles, martyrs, virgins, and confirmed by their miracles, ... has no need for the lies of the Trentini," who defend "their inventions" with force "in total contempt of the apostolic see, and injury to the law."[154] De' Giudici was outraged that the officials in Trent and their friends elsewhere had the audacity to question papal authority over the matter, as if "the investigation of truth belonged to temporal lords and not the apostolic see." The envoy saw an attack on himself as an attack on the pope. The Trent affair was not about "Jewish perfidy," but about the authority of the Holy See. Not only did the officials in Trent hold in contempt the orders of the pope, "the true vicar of Christ," but they also permitted such contempt among the people.[155]

Law and Procedures

The clash between the bishop of Trent and papal envoy de' Giudici revealed their different understandings of papal authority and power. It also highlighted legal disagreements within German and Italian legal praxis regarding grounds for prosecution, legal procedures, use of torture, and the standing of witnesses.[156] Indeed, protests about the legality of the trial led to its initial suspension in April 1475 and to papal involvement in the affair later that summer. The disparities between materials provided by de' Giudici and those provided by Hinderbach and his allies led to the establishment of a commission of cardinals in Rome to investigate the Trent affair and determine if that trial was valid.

Once challenges mounted, Hinderbach, who had for years served as an imperial ambassador to Rome, immediately activated his network of friends to support his cause, and in fact many members of the commission were favorable to him.[157] He also began a letter-writing campaign to support his side of the story and especially to defend the legality of the trial by minimizing the extent of torture used and asserting his power and jurisdiction over the case.[158] For Hinderbach, it was essential that the trial be deemed legal; its legality would confirm Jewish responsibility for Simon's death and thus support claims of the boy's martyrdom and his holy status. De' Giudici's findings had to be destroyed, his integrity undermined.

For Battista de' Giudici several key issues emerged during his investigation: the excessive use of torture to force Jews to confess to the crime, the falsification of trial records, and his inability to examine all the witnesses. In his opinion, "Jews were killed" and their property confiscated "against the law."[159] But beyond the specific questions about the trial, de' Giudici was also concerned with Hinderbach's defiance and disobedience of papal orders. Having arrived with a clear mandate from the pope, de' Giudici claimed to have the authority to investigate matters thoroughly. The Trentini disagreed, arguing, as de' Giudici would recall later, that "the investigation of their *beatus* pertained not to the pope but the emperor," and thus the pope had no authority over the case and "neither should nor could adjudicate" it without offending the emperor.[160] That the Trentini "dared" to make such a claim outraged the bishop of Ventimiglia.[161]

The question of jurisdiction became central to the judgment regarding the legality of the trial. Jurists in Rome, sympathizing with Hinderbach, seem to have concurred that the pope had limited jurisdiction in Trent and that legal matters there belonged to the secular powers, which were rooted in Trent's relationship with the emperor and duke of Austria.[162] Indeed de' Giudici understood this political framework and frequently referred to the duke's authority.[163] Yet, having a much more expansive view of papal power, the bishop of Ventimiglia also invoked the authority of the pope in his requests and actions. Hinderbach's defiance of the pope's orders was, in de' Giudici's view, tantamount to "contempt" of papal authority.[164]

Hinderbach strongly disagreed. Writing to the cardinals in Rome, he claimed that the officials in Trent always acted with "obedience and devotion" to the apostolic see.[165] They did not disobey the pope; rather, the pope's authority simply did not pertain to cases like that in Trent.[166] It was de' Giudici who abused his power and acted "against the will of our most holy lord" by intervening in temporal powers of the bishop of Trent and inappropriately delegating legal tasks, thus throwing into question the validity of the evidence he collected.[167] With the procedures at Trent under scrutiny, Hinderbach assured the cardinals that the trial was based on "much clear evidence" and, in fact, proceeded "according to sacred canons, civil and canonical norms, statutes and customs of the city of Trent."[168] The clash over procedure and records revealed the "relationship between the procedure adopted in Trent," the legal praxis in Italy that was deeply grounded in the Roman law, and legal praxis in the Empire; it also highlighted differences in understanding the jurisdiction over Jews.[169]

According to legal historian Diego Quaglioni, the trial in Trent was in accord with the procedures of an inquisitorial criminal trial.[170] To proceed with a criminal case there needed to be evidence of a crime (*indicia*) and public voice (rumors, *fama publica*) pointing to a culprit, or notoriety.[171] With that in place, the authorities had to begin an investigation, which typically focused on questions framed around the specific allegations and *indicia* of the crime. There was never a presumption of innocence.[172] In Trent, as Quaglioni has argued, that is what happened. When Simon first disappeared, it was first feared he accidentally drowned in one of the canals. But soon rumors began to circulate that Jews may have kidnapped and killed him. Finally after the body was found under the Jews' house, the medical examiners ruled that the boy could not have drowned by accident. With public rumors and the conclusions of the medical examiners in place, the authorities had grounds to open up a criminal trial against the Jews. This is also the argument presented to the commission of cardinals by Hinderbach's supporters.[173]

The flow of the inquisitorial process helps explain why the trial records foreground the early testimonies of Giovanni da Feltre, Margareta Gelbegret, and Seligman (Mayer's son). Their discussion of hearsay that Jews killed Christian children provided legal support to instigate a formal inquisitorial process against the Jews: it was evidence of *fama publica* and notoriety.[174] Later, when de' Giudici was applying more pressure, especially as the trial of women was beginning in November 1476, defensive Bishop Hinderbach would seek to collect historical evidence to substantiate the charges against Jews and judicial action further by sending the Dominican Heinrich of Schlettstett to obtain notarized copies of earlier trials against Jews in the Holy Roman Empire, such as in Ravensburg, Pullendorf, and Endingen, and by citing chronicles, especially, Vincent de Beauvais's *Speculum historiale*.[175] These were then to be sent to Rome to support Hinderbach's side.

But it was the early phase of the trial in 1475 and its representation in the official records that were critical for the subsequent claims of the legality of the procedures. Once the authorities, after examining the body, accepted the idea that Simon did not drown accidentally, but "was kidnapped, subjected to ritual tortures and killed in hatred of Christian faith," the investigators "had no other goal" but to obtain from the accused the "full and concordant confession of their guilt," or what they understood as "the truth."[176] And that "truth" was articulated quite early on by Giovanni Mattia Tiberino.

There were, however, legal issues with these early witnesses. Some had a conflict of interest, having pawned possessions with Trent Jews. Others, like Giovanni da Feltre, the convert imprisoned in Trent for another crime and thus an *infamis persona*, were not legally qualified to serve as witnesses.[177] Even Hinderbach understood that, flagging the issue in his notes on the protocols of the trial.[178] And most important, despite the claims of the officials in Trent and their advocates in Rome, other than Simon's body, the hearsay, and these early testimonies allegedly confirming the authorities' accusations, there were no proofs and no witnesses that Jews had committed a crime. Jews' confessions were therefore legally necessary, and hence, it was argued, it was legal to use torture.[179]

The abuse of torture during the trial was a key point of disagreement. De' Giudici claimed that official records were stripped of descriptions of the excessive application of torture. But Hinderbach pushed back. Torture applied in Trent was "moderate, and lesser than even that used typically against Christians for less serious crimes," therefore the confessions were valid.[180] This line of defense was accepted by the jurists in Rome. Giovanni Francesco Pavini concurred with Hinderbach. With sufficient *indicia* suggesting Jews' culpability, there was a legal basis for the use of torture and, given the inconsistency of confessions, also for its repetition.[181] (Paradoxically, Ubertino Pusculo's description of Brunetta's ability to withstand torture confirms de' Giudici's claims that excessive torture was indeed applied.[182])

The issue of the Jews' confessions under torture and the validity of their condemnation did not disappear from the debates over the legality of the trial. One anonymous jurist close to the bishop of Ventimiglia—most likely, the Italian jurist from Padua, Antonio Capodilista—raised these questions in his legal brief, arguing that Jews were "impiously and unjustly" captured and tortured, since there was no adequate evidence for their arrest, torture, and condemnation.[183] If the Trentini claimed as proof of their case the fact that Jews ratified their own confessions, the author of this opinion challenged that claim by arguing that, although the accused might confirm a confession made under torture, such a person "cannot be condemned" based on such confession if evidence does not support it. The author questioned especially confessions claiming that Jews killed Christian children to obtain their blood. Those "of sane mind and zealous for justice" would not accept as plausible confessions that "Jews killed Christian with different torments to obtain their blood for use in their Passover matzah." The Jews' law, which they observe "with exactitude [*ad unguem*]," prohibits the use of any blood. Surely, Jews "deny that Christ was the son of God and true Messiah," but how was it possible to believe that Jews used Christian blood "for the salvation of their souls"? He went on to savage other "ridiculous" claims that Jews use Christian blood, among them that they needed it to contain the Jewish "smell." It was an absurd idea that "the smell ceases, if it were [even] true that they smelled," when they "put in their Passover matzah or wine a little blood of a Christian boy."[184] Finally, far from truth was the claim that Jews used blood in circumcision; no physician had ever heard of it. The whole affair was fabricated. "What is preached about Simon [is] ... false and full of lies ... intended to cover a crime as is done in parts of Germany," he wrote alluding to blood accusations against Jews in the Holy Roman Empire.[185] The Jews' accusers wanted to promote the veneration of a "fetid and putrid corpse." And that was, he argued quoting Jerome's commentary on the Epistle to Philemon, an abomination: "If someone said a holy is not holy, or asserted an unholy is holy it is abominable before god, and he who believes a man to be holy who is not holy and joins the same man in fellowship of god, he profanes Christ."[186] Crucially, Jerome's proof text for this comment was Proverbs 17:15: "To acquit the guilty and convict the innocent—Both are an abomination to the LORD." The anonymous author thus concluded that the trial of Jews of Trent was unjust and abominable, once again connecting the validity of the trial to the validity of the cult. While the anonymous Italian jurist, apparently Antonio Capodilista, was surprised about beliefs held about Jews, or legal process, these beliefs were quite common north of the Alps from where Hinderbach hailed.

Hinderbach found Capodilista's treatise abominable and indeed mocked it as "anti-Christ."[187] The trial of the Jews, as argued by Hinderbach's ally Giovanni Francesco Pavini in Rome, and jurists closer to home, such as Giovanni de Giglis and Giovanni Antonio de Vaschetis (Guaschetta), was legal and followed conventional practices from beginning to end.[188] Their opinions rested not just on questions specific to the trial in Trent but also on broader questions regarding the place of Jews in Christian society and law; Pavini even attached to his response on the legality of the trial a treatise on the Jews' legal status.[189] As Diego Quaglioni has noted, for medieval Christian jurists, Jews presented a "key" legal problem, bringing to the fore the question of the relationship between "divine law, natural law, and civil law, and even between *ius commune* and *ius proprium*."[190] Whereas de' Giudici and his allies argued that in matters of blood accusations the podestà in Trent had no authority to try the Jews, Giovanni Antonio Guaschetta— who early on in November 1475 had asserted the validity of the first phase of the trial and kept Hinderbach informed about de' Giudici's work— affirmed, in 1477, at the height of the work of the commission in Rome, that the podestà did in fact have such authority based on "the statutes, laws, and customs" of Trent.[191] According to the statutes, Guaschetta argued, the podestà was obligated to conduct "diligent investigation" in cases of murder, robbery, and forgery, and because Jews were counted among legal residents of Trent—they were, he argued, *Tridentinos*—"statutes concerning the Tridentinos apply also to Jews living in Trent." Thus, because the podestà had the authority to try the Tridentinos, he also had jurisdiction over Jews. This followed, Guaschetta argued, ancient Tridentine customs and laws applied to similar crimes in Germany.[192] Moreover, citing Baldo degli Ubaldi's opinion about jurisdiction over Jews with regard to "human actions," Guaschetta stressed that Jews were "not only subject to Roman law, but also . . . to other Tridentine statutes."[193] Giovanni Francesco Pavini concurred.[194]

But Pavini, whose legal opinion focused on two main issues—defending procedures in Trent, *de iure et stilo* (of law and method), and discrediting the actions of the papal envoy—went a bit further. In a direct pushback against de' Giudici's assertion of papal authority and his view that the Trent officials' obstruction was "contempt" of the pope, Pavini's argument to support the city's jurisdiction over Jews and the trial sought to circumscribe papal authority.¹⁹⁵ He first summarized the mandate Pope Sixtus IV gave the bishop of Ventimiglia to argue that not only was de' Giudici's jurisdiction in Trent limited and he, in fact, exceeded it, but that the pope's jurisdiction was also limited in territories under imperial jurisdiction.¹⁹⁶ The pope had jurisdiction over miracles and determination of sainthood, but de' Giudici did not use due diligence to investigate that question properly. As for the arrest of Jews and confiscation of their property, that authority belonged to the officials in Trent. Indeed, Pavini offered a legal parallel: the pope had no jurisdiction over Jews passing through "Saracen" territory; only the "[Saracen] emperor" along with a secular judge had it, and because Jews are not baptized, they are not bound by canon law. Thus "the prince of the land" has jurisdiction over Jews in cases of public crimes. And in Trent, "in criminal cases one appeals to secular judges."¹⁹⁷ Moreover, "the apostolic see did not get involved in similar cases occurring in Paris under the rule of king Philip" nor in cases "in our times in Regensburg and Passau," Pavini wrote referring to a blood accusation in Regensburg in 1476—a direct outcome of the Trent trial—and the 1478 Passau host desecration, which Hinderbach's allies were using to strengthen their case in Rome.¹⁹⁸

Pavini even challenged the Jews' defense that papal bulls issued by Popes Innocent IV and Gregory X, which had been entered into the documentation concerning the Trent affair, protected them against blood accusations.¹⁹⁹ These did not apply, Pavini argued, in this case. Pope Innocent IV reacted against calumnies against Jews that resulted in their persecution without proper procedures, when they were not formally accused, did not confess, and were not convicted. From the text of Innocent's bull it is "clear" it was intended for "calumnious accusations" and not for legally conducted trials.²⁰⁰ In Pavini's treatise, grounded in sources and arguments provided by the bishop of Trent, Tiberino's account also played an important role, because together with the trial records, it provided a basis for Pavini's summary of "facts." Moreover, Pavini even sought to substantiate Tiberino's claims that the blood of the victim flowed in the presence of murderers.²⁰¹ Pavini's work played an important role in the commission's decision in Rome; in fact, Hinderbach's advocate in Rome, Approvino, arranged for it to be printed, paying thirty ducats for three hundred copies.²⁰²

On June 20, 1478, after months of delays, Pope Sixtus IV issued a bull addressing the Trent affair.²⁰³ The succinct document reveals that the pope carefully considered the opinions of both Hinderbach's circle and the bishop of Ventimiglia. Based on the conclusions of the commission, the pope did rule the trial lawful (*processum rite et recte factum*); the podestà acted against some Jews, who "were said to have killed inhumanely a Christian infant," based on public rumors, *fama publica*—a legal term obligating authorities to investigate a crime.²⁰⁴ In a narrow sense, the trial was ruled legal, but the language, especially the phrase that "Jews were said to have killed," suggested that the pope did not accept the Jews' guilt, a necessary element to recognizing Simon's martyrdom and status as *beatus* worthy of veneration. Indeed, invoking Canon 62 of the IV Lateran Council, the pope explicitly exhorted Bishop Hinderbach not to allow devotion that "may result in the harm to God, or contempt of the apostolic see" or may be done "in contravention of the canonical sanctions."²⁰⁵ Pope Sixtus also stood by earlier papal protections of Jews expressed since the medieval period in *Sicut Iudaeis*, the frequently reissued papal constitution on behalf of Jews. Apparently alluding to the various calls for the expulsion of the Jews and retribution against them in Trent and beyond, the pope enjoined Hinderbach—in words echoing *Sicut Iudaeis*—to make sure that "no Christian, on the pretext of the foregoing matter [of Simon] or for any other pretext, barring the judgment of an earthly power, should presume to kill, mutilate, wound, or unjustly extort monies from them [the Jews], or prevent them from observing their rites, permitted by law." Sixtus threatened "those who oppose this decree or rebel against it" with "the weight of ecclesiastical censure and other [pertinent] laws."²⁰⁶ And finally, the pope again ordered that children of the Jews condemned in Trent be reunited with their baptized mothers. The bull was clearly a compromise, a result of intense lobbying efforts by both the defenders of Jews and Hinderbach's agents. But it was only a partial victory for Hinderbach. It remained firmly within the medieval tradition of papal policies concerning Jews and did little to advance Hinderbach's ultimate goal of having Simon recognized a saint.

Jews as Historical Actors

If the medieval cases only provided a glimpse into Jewish actions in the aftermath of anti-Jewish accusations, the Trent affair for the first time documented them in great detail. Jews were hardly passive victims of the affair. Soon after the trial began in late March 1475, Jews from the region activated their networks in Tyrol, as well as in northern Italy, reaching first the court of Duke Sigismund of Austria and then church leaders in Rome, as well as dukes and rulers in other places.²⁰⁷ On May 19, 1475, for example, Gregorius Ems reported to his friend Hinderbach that "many Jews from Padua with a doctor from Treviso" were intervening in Innsbruck on behalf of Trent Jews.²⁰⁸ They were said to spare no "gold or silver" to convince those in power to intercede on behalf of the accused. And they were not without accomplishments. In September 1475, a Jew named Sloman (or Solomon) from Tyrol or Austria received Duke Sigismund's permission and escort to stay in Trent.[209] And when Bishop Battista de' Giudici of Ventimiglia arrived in the region, Jews from northern Italy, among them Jacob of Riva and Jacob of Brescia, reached him to plead for help.[210] In Venice, Jews wanted the authorities to prevent preaching about Simon and against Jews, a request granted by the doge of Venice in November 1475.[211]

Hinderbach and his allies spun the Jewish interventions as corruption. They portrayed any documented contact with Jews as discrediting for the person with whom Jews met or for the documents produced.[212] Indeed, Hinderbach claimed Jews offered money to him, the podestà, and the city captain, pleading to liberate those arrested.[213] This effort failed, because the Trent officials were not easy to bribe. The most eminent victim of this propaganda was the papal envoy de' Giudici—slandered from beginning to end as corrupted by Jewish money, he was called *odiosus,* or odious, and even *pseudo-episcopus,* a pseudo-bishop.[214] De' Giudici had to defend himself by offering his previous preaching against Jews as evidence that he was conscientious in his quest for truth and not easily corruptible.[215]

Although Hinderbach proudly claimed he and his officials did not succumb to Jewish bribes, the issues of corruption and bribery touched him as well, albeit from a different angle. Hinderbach knew very well that interventions were costly and money played a role in the process of making his case; his advocates repeatedly pleaded with him to pay their expenses in Rome. Moreover, implying that Hinderbach was bribing the faithful, Battista de' Giudici accused the bishop of Trent of distributing alms to promote the cult of Simon.[216]

From the thousands of documents left behind as a result of the trial, including the tendentious and hostile to Jews letters sent by Hinderbach's informants, the documents produced by Bishop de' Giudici, the trial records of Paolo de Novara, and the testimonies of women, it is clear that Jews were not without advocates, influence, or the ability to act. The records of Paolo de Novara's trial, a highly problematic source aimed at undermining de' Giudici's claims that trial records sent to Rome had been amended, reveal some mechanisms of communication that Jews seem to have used to get both to those in power and to those in prison in Trent.[217] Paolo de Novara, the priest who served as a scribe in Trent, knew the Jew Crassino also from Novara, the father of Bona, Engel's wife. Paolo apparently served as a go-between, passing messages from the imprisoned Jews, especially the women, to the outside world: their relatives and the papal legate. The task was risky; it involved hiding letters in secret locations in Trent and sometimes even consuming them on the spot to destroy the evidence of contacts. To discredit any evidence of malfeasance by the Trentini, the Paolo's trial records show him acting and speaking against them as a result both of his corruption by Jews and his "possession by the devil."

The actions by Jews in response to the blood accusation in Trent spurred Hinderbach's imagination and fears about them. One striking fear, also revealed in Paolo's trial, was of an purported Jewish plot to poison Hinderbach and other Trent officials, clearly grounded in medieval myths about Jews poisoning wells, which Hinderbach, an avid consumer of books, must have found in history books and chronicles.[218] More real was Hinderbach's frustration with and fear of Jewish influence in sites of power that created obstacles to his cause; he was receiving reports of such advocacy as late as the spring of 1478, just before Pope Sixtus IV issued his June 20 bull ruling the trial legal.[219]

In addition to making personal appeals to release Jewish prisoners and exerting continuous efforts to obtain trial records, to counter the Trent accusations, Jews also furnished in their defense medieval imperial privileges and papal bulls of protection.[220] Although these documents, first issued in the aftermath of blood accusations in Fulda and Valréas in the thirteenth century, did not prevent similar accusations from happening again, they clearly had some effect. In Trent, they raised questions about papal authority over blood accusations, forcing Hinderbach and his allies to articulate a legal framework justifying their jurisdiction over the affair and to defend their anti-Jewish accusations in light of earlier papal condemnations. The dissemination of these previous bulls of protection also meant that some of their language was included in Sixtus IV's June 20 bull.

But direct Jewish voices are largely missing from the mass of documents related to the trial of Jews in Trent, except for one contemporary letter and a *qinah,* a lamentation.[221] There are, admittedly, a few Hebrew letters, which Paolo de Novara carried when he was caught, but they are not related to the trial.[222] The contemporary letter relevant to the trial, probably written soon after the first executions of the Jewish men in June, offers a glimpse into how the affair was perceived by Jews. It contains elements echoing arguments made by Jews' supporters about excessive torture that "one had not ever heard of," about the likelihood that Christians who killed Simon dumped his body in the canal, and about Hinderbach's staging of the trial to confiscate the Jews' property.[223] The letter locates the Jewish victims in the tradition of Jewish martyrdom, calling Samuel and Moses "sons of martyrs."

Also within the Ashkenazi tradition of martyrdom was the *qinah,* a lamentation emphasizing suffering and martyrdom of the Jewish victim. Only one lamentation about Trent is known to have survived, perhaps because the Jewish community in Trent was too small to survive the affair with no survivors who continued to live as Jews to write and recite such lamentations.[224] In this *qinah,* the victims, especially old Moses, are pure offerings, "more acceptable to God than a burnt offering."[225] They are saints on the altar; martyrs who died a martyr's death, remaining faithful Jews.

This lamentation inverts the meaning of what happened in Trent. It was not Simon who was a martyr and a sacrifice on the altar; it was the Jews. It was not the Jews who committed a crime, but "the bloody city of Trent" that "spilled innocent blood for money." Trent harbored "great fear that all nations would witness their shame," because they "tortured an old man on the wheel," a man who "did not participate in the killing." For this Trent deserved curses. Only revenge for "the blood of your servants, the Children of Israel" spilled in Trent could be comfort for what took place there.

Given that the Trent affair left such a deep imprint on Christian society and culture, the minimal imprint it left on Jewish culture is surprising.[226] Among Christians it shaped thinking about Jewish culture and practices and helped them imagine and visualize the unimaginable.[227] But the Jewish responses to the trial were nothing extraordinary—action through intervention, diplomacy, and marshaling of previous privileges of protection, on the one hand, and commemoration through poems and lamentations, on the other. This was a typical Ashkenazi response to anti-Jewish libels.

But if the Trent affair nearly disappeared from Jewish memory, it had a profound impact on Jewish history. As the Jews intervening in the affair correctly sensed, the outcome of the affair would have an effect not only on those directly touched by the accusation in Trent but also on those around the world: deeming the accusation valid would not only affirm a new saint but also provide "proof" of Jewish crimes.

And yet, as Battista de' Giudici astutely noted, the Trent affair was not just about Jews: it was a Christian affair. It was about political authority and influence, a clash between the bishop and the pope. This unusually documented case thus offers a view into politics, sophisticated machinations, diplomacy, and lobbying in late medieval Europe. It highlights the regional understanding of papal powers and their limits. Ruling the trial invalid and fully challenging the cult of Simon would have undermined the bishop's authority and widened the rift between Trent and Rome—between the "Germans" and the Italians; a rift that would become more acute just a few decades later in the aftermath of the Reformation. Conversely, ignoring the trial and the newly emerging cult would have demonstrated the pope's powerlessness. The bull of June 20, 1478, sought to prevent that. The trial in Trent was ultimately a German affair caught between German and Italian cultural and legal frameworks, with markedly different impacts and readings of law and facts within these two cultural milieus.[228]

In his lifetime Hinderbach did not fully achieve what he had sought. To be sure, he and his officials were cleared of wrongdoing, and the trial was deemed legal; but Simon remained a rogue cult, unrecognized by Rome, with papal policies protecting Jews still in place. In the long term, however, Hinderbach's efforts would pay off. He displayed a remarkable historical consciousness and, to use Alexandra Walsham's words from another context, an "impulse to preserve the past for the future."[229] The bishop of Trent was not merely "safeguarding documentation" of this legal case but was also actively "controlling and organizing knowledge" while marginalizing and "silencing . . . competing narratives."[230] It is for this reason that this most-documented case of blood accusation is also one about which we know relatively little beyond what Bishop Hinderbach wanted us to know.

CHAPTER THREE

Echoes of Simon of Trent in European Culture

"THERE IS AT THE EDGE OF ITALY'S territories a lofty city, Trent, touching with its walls the Alps to the north and mingling Germans with Italians." So wrote Ubertino Pusculo in 1481 in a lengthy Latin poem commemorating the death of little Simon.[1] Pusculo was correct: Trent represented a liminal space in more than one sense. This liminality—political, cultural, and chronological—would be felt in the legacy of the 1475 trial of the Jews in Trent, with dramatic consequences for the way anti-Jewish accusations would be handled and remembered for centuries in Italy, as well as in northern and eastern Europe. The Trent trial was not simply, as R. Po-Chia Hsia has argued, "testimony of political and intellectual exchange between southern Germany and Italy during the Renaissance," it was also a place where these cultures clashed.[2] And that clash was represented not only in the immediate responses to the trial but also in the subsequent trajectories of Simon's legacy in literature, law, and art.

Unlike most earlier medieval persecutions and trials of Jews accused of murdering Christian children whose impact was felt only locally, the story of Simon of Trent spread far and wide. The Trent trial left not only an unprecedented amount of archival materials but also an unprecedented literary and artistic legacy. The 1475 trial took place just years after the invention of the printing press, which for the first time allowed for the broad

FIG. 3.1 Simon of Trent in the pirated edition of Hartmann Schedel, *Liber chronicarum cum figuris et imaginis ab initio mundi usque nunc temporis* (Augsburg: Johann Schönsperger, 1497), 285v.

dissemination of texts and imagery. With the strong backing of Bishop Johannes Hinderbach, the flood of publications flowing from the trial in Trent for the first time visually and textually substantiated the medieval tale of "Jewish murders of Christian children," influencing anti-Jewish trials and their visual representation as far as eastern Europe. No fewer than thirty-three individual publications about Simon appeared in print before 1500; there were additional instances where the story was included in works of a broader scope, such as chronicles, including the 1493 *Liber chronicarum* published in Nuremberg by Hartmann Schedel, and its pirated editions (Fig. 3.1). And some of these works were published by the most prominent printers, among them Nicholas Jenson of Venice.[3] The bishop's investment in visual art carved the events of 1475 into the memory and topography of the city of Trent and the region, and the printed works and images helped disseminate the story far beyond the town, with effects lasting even until today.

"To Honor This New Little Martyr"

By far the most influential were Giovanni Mattia Tiberino's early accounts of April 4 and April 17, 1475, printed in the form of short pamphlets in Latin, Italian, and German.[4] Their publication was meant to influence not only the trial but also the political players. The April 17 version was published in Rome on June 19, perhaps coincidentally, only one day before the sentencing of the accused Jews in Trent and two days before their execution, under an explicitly evocative and lengthy title summarizing the story, "Of a child kidnapped and cruelly killed in the hatred of Christian religion, after numerous gravest tortures on the Eve of Passover, and then thrown into the river, in the city of Trent in the Jubilee Year" (*De infantulo in civitate Tridentina per Iudeos rapto atque in vilipendum christianae religionis post multas maximasque trucidationes Anno Iubileo die Parasceue crudelissime necato ac deinde in flumem cadaver dimerso Historia feliciter incipit*). Less coincidentally, this version was then reissued on July 24, the day after Pope Sixtus IV ordered Bishop Hinderbach to suspend the trial of the remaining Jews.[5]

Tiberino's early pamphlets set the tone and narrative framework not only for the trial but also for future representations, both textual and visual, of the story. They were distributed in manuscript form to Hinderbach's supporters and published multiple times in both German and Latin; fragments describing Simon's "martyrdom" would later enter the monumental *Annales ecclesiastici* started by Cesare Baronio and continued by Odorico

Rinaldi, and a full text of Tiberino's original version would become part of the Bollandist impressively extensive *Acta Sanctorum*.[6]

Yet, despite its unequivocal and inflammatory rhetoric, Tiberino's work included a few details that revealed a level of complexity and ambivalence, providing the substance for different legacies of the trial to emerge on the Italian peninsula, beyond the Alps, and especially in the later centuries, in Poland. For Tiberino what happened in Trent was "an unheard-of crime," but not every Jew embraced the plan to murder a Christian child. Even some of "the villains," like Tobias, who was said to have kidnapped the child, appear as somewhat conflicted. When the decision was made to find a child and kill him, Tiberino noted, Tobias and another Jew, Engel, initially opposed the plan "out of anguish" that a murder would take place in their homes. Admittedly, their opposition stemmed from the very limited space in their homes that would make it "difficult to hide such vast crime from their children." Samuel then tried to convince his servant Lazarus to agree to kidnap a child and offered him money. But when Lazarus declined the offer, "collected his belonging and left to live abroad,"[7] Samuel turned to Tobias once more: he was thought to be able to "satisfy" this demand, because he had "dealings with Christians, and nearly all are known to you. You can easily catch one, for no one notices you when walk around the city."[8] But Tobias again "declined, and pointed that out on many counts it was a hazardous assignment." He was then "coerced with curses" and threats of a permanent ban from the synagogue.[9] These threats were then sweetened with a promise of monetary rewards that had earlier been ineffective on Lazarus.

Similar ambiguity is also noticeable in Tiberino's discussion of reasons as to why the Jews of Trent sought a Christian boy. On the one hand, Tiberino claimed that Jews "devoured" the "drained-off blood . . . to keep themselves free from the powerful stench they exude."[10] On the other, they needed to sacrifice the boy because Moses, "the bearded of man," knew "by prophetic inspiration the time and hour of the Messiah who was to come."[11] This passing comment about the imminent coming of the Messiah implied that the murder was tied to a specific event and was thus circumscribed. Indeed, Tiberino's earlier statements that this was "an unheard-of crime, . . a most important event such as no era—from the Lord's passion up to these times—has ever heard of" only strengthened the perception of the unique nature of the Trent story. At least this was the way the story of Simon of Trent was understood by later Italian writers who, with just a few exceptions, focused not on the inherent "Jewish need for Christian blood," but on its singular character: it was a story of one child and one town, its cruel nature notwithstanding.[12] In contrast, writers across the Alps and later also in Poland would absorb from Tiberino the vituperative statements that focused on the cruelty of the Jews and their imagined need for blood, implying the serial nature of their "deadly rituals" and applying them to all Jews.

To be sure, even in Italy, the fiery language found in early Simonine literature, and strongly encouraged by Hinderbach, did not disappear as that literature flourished, albeit in waves, from the late fifteenth all the way to the late eighteenth century. As the patron of most of the early works about Simon, Bishop Hinderbach had clear goals in mind. On April 30, 1475, Hinderbach wrote to poet Rafaele Zovenzoni of Trieste,

> I ask you that in your lyrical poetry you curse this as an utterly impious act, truly perpetrated by the Jews themselves, and that in our words you honor this new little martyr of ours as he deserves, so that this affair may be revealed to all Christians and by being on everyone's lips, may be publicly known and proclaimed—to the praise of almighty God and the heightening of our Christian faith, and to the glorification of this new little martyr and of our city, and a greater appreciation of the blessings, present to us here and now, which God has granted us amongst his other gifts![13]

Hinderbach hoped that both prose and poetry about Simon would help overcome opposition to the trial of the Jews, which he thought had slowed the court proceedings in Trent. Indeed, Hinderbach confided in Zovenzoni:

> From the Jews the penalty they deserve would long since have been exacted, had there not been false Christians thirsting more for those people's gold than for the death or punishment they deserve, and who by certain false suggestions or grand promises have had such influence with the most illustrious archduke of Austria—on whose opinion and authority my own authority inevitably hangs—that now, when the truth has been coaxed and forced out of the Jews, he has brought about a temporary moratorium in this matter, until he has been more clearly informed about the actual fact. And I fear that this same idea is also being bandied about at the court of the most merciful emperor.[14]

The bishop hoped that the "veto or wish of the prince of Austria" to interrupt the trial, which he believed had been inspired by "the false and immoral suggestion of certain misguided people, will soon cease and be revoked and that he himself and everyone else will be informed of the truth of this matter, which is clearer than the midday sun."[15] Hinderbach then invited Zovenzoni to come to Trent and "see and marvel at this holy and venerable little body, which by the grace of God is still preserved whole and unimpaired, and is on view for all those coming here." Indeed people came from all over Italy and from Hinderbach's "native Germany" to see

Simon's body, filling St. Peter's Church and rendering it "far too small to contain them." In fact even the chapel "where the body has been laid was not big enough to house all the tokens left there." Hinderbach assured Zovenzoni that he would also see "God's wonders, which He works in the person of this small boy" and that "this race of Jews, impious and utterly cut off from Christ's grace, is paying the penalty they deserve for so great a crime."

The poet obliged. He composed a poem dedicated to his patron, "the godly Johannes Hinderbach," in which he addressed directly the highest authorities, "bishops, and you, most holy emperor," and "leaders and kings, peoples and fathers who worship Christ," calling on them to "arise," "unsheathe" their "flashing swords; [and] slaughter the nefarious nation of the Jews and drive it out of the whole earth."[16] But in his poem, written in "the standard classical Latin meter for narrative and didactic poetry" modeled on Vergil and Ovid, Zovenzoni seems to be grappling with Jews' clear historical connections to God: "The Virgin was Jewish, that child-bearer of our Christ whom alone the Holy Spirit overshadowed. Jewish, too, was Moses, and so were the holy prophets; and the sacred manna came down from the sky to the Jews alone; for whom, as they marched on, the waters of the sea receded, when Pharaoh was overwhelmed by a disastrous squall. For them almighty God sometimes sent a column of flames, so that it might shine in the darkness, and he also destroyed your enemies, Judea."[17] Yet the Jews repaid all this with ingratitude: they "stoned to death and put to the sword all those who prophesied the truth to [them]," wrote Zovenzoni, repeating the traditional Christian charge of Jewish ungratefulness to God that culminated in their rejection of Jesus as the messiah—a charge repeated annually on Good Friday in the chant *Improperia*. That same unfaithfulness and ingratitude were on display in Trent, where they "treacherously allured a nursing boy," whom they then tortured by cutting his foreskin, piercing him with needles, and using pincers to tear off pieces of his flesh, Zovenzoni wrote, almost reveling in the description of cruelty. The Jews then "stretched the infant out on the cross, and weighted down as he was, each of them pierced him with a needle." Simon's moment of death in Zovenzoni's words evoked the Christ's own moment of death: "He lifted his eyes to heaven, when his blessed spirit blazed forth toward the citadels of the sky."[18] After his death, Zovenzoni wrote, once more alluding to Christ, "the holy boy Simon . . . cure[d] the lame, the deaf, and the blind."[19]

Zovenzoni closed his poem, addressing the Christian rulers once more: "O you who hold kingly scepters, will you allow this race—this race I pray—to exist any longer on the earth? Sixtus our father, forbid—you, Frederic, forbid—those people who thirst for our gore to live with us in our cities any longer! Sigismund, archduke of the Latin Empire, show your mettle now, spread forth flames to incinerate the Hebrew crime, and innocent blood will then proclaim you among the powers above!"[20] He then praised his patron Hinderbach as the "father of peace and justice," fervently justifying his actions. "O my triumph and my stronghold, father Johannes Hinderbach, go forth! No one," Zovenzoni asserted, "orders you *not* to destroy those faithless circumcised bodies, *not* to give their ashes to the whisking winds to scatter." In fact, this is "what God enjoins; this is what your holy power of justice enjoins, and so do your piety, your faith, and your shining virtue, which will surely bestow you on the companies if heaven's denizens."[21]

Zovenzoni was not the only poet whose services for the cause Hinderbach secured. Giovanni Mattia Tiberino, Giovanni Calfurnio (Johannes Calphurnius), and Ubertino Pusculo all praised Hinderbach as a patron of poets and "a muse," the only one "bringing help to wretched poets" and dispensing "bounty from a full horn."[22] And all of them devoted their artistic energies to helping Hinderbach make his case to those in power—composing powerful poems about Simon's death, justifying Hinderbach's actions, and supporting him as he faced pushback from Rome, Venice, and Innsbruck, which according to Tiberino amounted to "a war."[23]

These Renaissance poems, while graphic in their language, were not written for popular consumption. Composed in classical Latin and alluding to classical authors, they were written for an audience of those in power in both the Church and the state. They were the ones before whom Bishop Hinderbach needed to justify the trial, "to defend justice's honor and his own," and who would have to be convinced to expel the Jews from their domains and help Hinderbach secure the canonization of the boy.[24] One of the most powerful poems is Tiberino's "I Am the Boy Simon," published first in 1476, in the midst of a papal challenge to Hinderbach, as a lamentation at the end of *Hystoria completa,* and then, with some modifications, in 1482, in a collection of Simonine epigrams, in which he gave "voice" to Simon, who "still could not speak," for he "had hardly been born."[25]

"I am the boy Simon," begins the poem, in which Simon addresses Christian supporters of the Jews—those "who forever pay court to such ravening dogs."[26] By describing Simon's suffering from the perspective of the boy, Tiberino made the story much more palpable yet intimate, heightening the effect of graphic details. "I was seized," Simon says, and then taken to Samuel's house, where "the impious Jewish race" was gathered in "a terrifying assembly" with "pitiless looks in their eyes, they were not men—rather snakes and fearsome monsters!" They "laid bare my chest in front of the synagogue. Each tore out my flesh with pincers.... They all pricked my chest with needles, thick and fast; they subjected Jesus and me to much abuse. So I collapsed; my head fell down between my soft forearms, and my life, set free, went off to join those above." Simon then turns to Pope Sixtus IV, imploring him to "help us, Sixtus, I pray, anchor of our ship of faith: give support to our bishop! He is a doughty champion; he is the devoted priest whose prayers have found favor with God the Father." Simon calls on the pontiff to "take up your sacred shield and sword and your triple crown; get rid of the obstinate dogs, blessed Holy Father!" The boy prays, "May kings also help up; may you, mighty emperor, help us, together with your peoples and princes! Deliver to their doom the Hebrews who savagely devour the property and precious goods of Christians day and night, who are so glad when Christian blood is shed, who chew warm and gory limbs of men." In his poem, Tiberino skillfully contrasted the fragility and humanity of Simon, "a young lamb" in one of the poems, with the inhuman bestiality of the Jews, who became "monsters" and "ravening dogs."[27] This evocative address to Christian rulers, put in the mouth of the dead boy, was meant to appease Pope Sixtus IV, who was continuing, in 1476 when the poem was written, to subject Hinderbach to a review in Rome and to refuse to recognize the cult of little Simon of Trent.

If in the poem "I Am the Boy Simon," Tiberino only gently made a comparison between Simon and Christ, he was much more explicit in other poems included in the 1482 collection.[28] "Whenever your dread passion comes into my mind, holy Simon, Trent's everlasting light," Tiberino wrote, "Then I recall Christ's most holy passion, and a tear slowly trickles from my eyes."[29] Like Christ, who "shone forth from divine and human seed," Simon too came from dual seed: "Italian and German" (likely a deliberate parallel to symbolize the "divine power" of the pope by the reference to Italy, and the secular or "human" power of the emperor by referring to Germany). Simon's mother, like "the most holy perpetual Virgin, God's mother," was called Mary. "On a cross Christ exchanged life for death; stretched out on a cross this boy collapsed." Like Christ, Simon was cursed and mocked, and like Christ, his body was discovered on the third day. Just as Christ performed so many miracles, so too does Simon. And just as the "the guard of the tomb [of Jesus] was bribed but the Lord shone forth," so too was bribed "Mr. Judge," a pun on the name of the papal envoy Battista de' *Giudici*, whose name corresponds to the Italian word for "judges."[30] Indeed, Jews stopped at nothing: "they secretly denied that Simon must be made a saint, and went to law, earnestly seeking false witnesses in the Roman Curia."[31] For "three winters" Jews sought to "twist the truth."[32] They fought, as the poet Ubertino Pusculo put it, with gold "against justice."[33] And if Christianity triumphed and Judaea was lost (Tiberino uses the classic phrase "capta est Iudaea"), so too, now "the rest of the pack of dogs languishes, defeated in Rome; all the laws have been in my lord's favor."[34] The poems, along with Hinderbach's defiance in promoting the cult through art despite papal prohibitions to do so, confirm what Battista de' Giudici found objectionable—that the Trentini venerated Simon as if he were a "second Messiah."[35]

These Latin works had a lasting impact: they shaped subsequent Latin accounts published in chronicles and collections of the lives of saints into which Simon would be inserted even before Pope Sixtus V formally granted liturgical services (*officium*) to his cult in 1588 and before vernacular narratives were published in German and in Italian. As R. Po-Chia Hsia has noted, these authors were "conscious creators of a clearly articulated political message" seeking to "shape public opinion" through their works in support of Hinderbach's mission.[36] In June 1478, three years after Simon's death and the initial trial of the Jews, Pope Sixtus IV issued a bull partially exonerating Hinderbach of wrongdoing from a legal standpoint.[37] Sixtus IV had intervened, the bull explained, by ordering an investigation after "many people began to complain loudly" about the trial of the Jews. And each phase of the trial was examined "with great care" by "a number of our venerable brothers cardinals of the Roman Catholic Church, and also archbishops, legal experts, and the auditor of trials of our apostolic palace," who "reported to our consistory that the trial itself had rightly and properly been concluded." Yet, if the pope justified the trial "as the gravity of the affair demanded," he did not authorize the cult, a significant decision, given he had earlier authorized other local cults; for example, those of Giovanni Capistrano, Giovanni Bono, and the Franciscan martyrs of Morocco.[38] Indeed, Sixtus IV warned the bishop not to "allow ... anything illicit to be done that might result in injury to God or contempt of the Apostolic See, or which might be perceived as potentially and inexcusably contravening canonical sanctions."[39] By including language from *Sicut Iudaeis*, the pontiff also stood by the centuries-old papal policy of protecting Jews.

This was not exactly the victory Hinderbach had hoped for. And Tiberino would have none of it. His poem penned very soon after Sixtus's 1478 letter and defiantly titled "Salve, Sancte Simone" mutes the pope's concerns altogether while overstating Hinderbach's "victory."[40] "A third winter has slipped by, and a third summer is now passing," Tiberino wrote, "as Johannes pursues his war with the Jews." But justice had "finally flown down through the air from heaven," confirming "the holy acts of Trent's bishop." The papal bull, Tiberino claimed, "confirms that you [Simon] were killed in the image of Christ our God and assents to your inclusion in the companies of saints, and it acknowledges that the Hebrew race, which is second to none in cruelty, is still—as it has been from of old—wicked." The bull said none of that, but there was no question that Hinderbach and his propagandists were very much aware of the power of decisive assertions, however untrue they were. They mastered what in modern parlance would be called the power of spin.

In the end, they were right. The sophisticated, and not inexpensive, public campaign by Hinderbach, with its widely disseminated chapbooks, broadsheets, ballads about Simon, and popularization of the still-unauthorized cult through preaching and art, was quite successful.[41] Pilgrims flocked to the Church of St. Peter in Trent from the beginning, leaving behind donations in many currencies. This money was put to use right away to preserve Simon's body and to promote the cult through art.[42] As early as June 1, 1475, even before the first executions, the accounts show that six marcs were paid for two paintings depicting "the boy with Jews, and his passion," and another two marcs for completed works representing "the boy's passion, S. Vigilius, and many images."[43] On June 8, a lead coffin for the body was ordered and then one made of silver.[44]

Despite the papal reluctance to recognize the cult of Simon, the bishop's efforts to promote it did not abate, and pilgrims continued to visit the new shrine (see Fig. 2.1). Many local churches sought to obtain Simon's relics and in their absence commissioned paintings and altars.[45] In September 1476, Francesco Raimondo, vicar of the province of the Franciscan order, thanked Hinderbach for sending a chalice with "a small quantity of the martyr's blood."[46] The Church of Santa Maria dei Servi in Venice had "two pieces of the dress, which [Simon] wore, and also a small piece of one of his shoes."[47] These requests continued; in 1479, Battista di Campofregoso, a duke of Genoa, also requested relics, and as late as the seventeenth century, the queen of Spain obtained Simon's toe.[48]

The multipronged campaign promoting the cult helped spread the story far and wide, giving it a far greater impact than earlier anti-Jewish trials. Whereas the 1470 trial of the Jews in the town of Endingen, just north of Freiburg, remained a regional affair, plays and ballads about it notwithstanding,[49] the story of Simon's death found its way—thanks to Hinderbach's efforts—to both local and more general printed chronicles, guaranteeing it a permanent place in Christian narratives of world and church history.[50] One of the first world chronicles to include Simon's story during Hinderbach's lifetime were some editions of *Fasciculus temporum* by Werner Rolewinck, such as the 1480 Venice edition and the 1482 Basel edition, though each emphasized a different aspect of the story. In 1483, the story was included, in different wording in *Supplementum chronicarum* by

Jacob Philip Foresti of Bergamo.[51] But it was Hartmann Schedel's splendid *Liber chronicarum*, describing the history of the world from creation to 1493, the year it was published in both Latin and German, in which Simon received a special place. The boy's "martyrdom" was featured in one of the chronicle's longest narratives (based on a text from a Latin edition of Foresti's *Supplementum*) and was adorned by one of the most intricate woodcuts in the whole chronicle (see Fig. 1.2); this woodcut was clearly modeled on the much cruder woodcut from early illustrated chapbooks and broadsides published as early as 1475 (see Figs. 2.4 and 2.6). Schedel's splendid and widely disseminated chronicle, with an estimated print run of some 2,500 copies in both Latin and German, was soon pirated and published in Augsburg in 1496, 1497, and 1500. The Augsburg edition was also adorned with woodcuts, but these were far less impressive than the original 1493 Nuremberg edition (see Fig. 3.1). Still even in the Augsburg edition, the story of the "blessed Simon" covered two facing pages, along with a much cruder mirror copy of the remarkable original, and informed the readers that thanks to the efforts of Bishop Hinderbach, who ordered a shrine to be built, pilgrims "from all over the world" could witness miracles.[52]

Simon's Cult after Hinderbach's Death

That Hinderbach was central to the popularization of the cult is demonstrated by the fact that, with his death in 1486, the number of publications about Simon dropped dramatically—a point noted by the seventeenth-century writer Michelangelo Mariani, who in his 1668 work, written after a reexamination of Simon's body, mentioned "a break and cooling down" in the development of the cult and the cessation of "divine favors" linked to "the wondrous boy" after 1487.[53] Indeed, visiting Trent in 1497, Arnold von Harff of Cologne noted—in contradiction to Hinderbach's supporters earlier—that "miracles caused by the little martyr ceased, and for that reason the pope refused to canonize him."[54] According to Mariani, the hiatus in "divine favors" manifested through Simon's relics that followed Hinderbach's death was caused by the subsequent bishops' preoccupation with wars, a Venetian invasion of the Trentino in 1487, the crisis related to the League of Cambrai in 1508, and wars resulting from activities of "the monster of Lutheran heresy."[55] These crises notwithstanding, Bishop Hinderbach's death in 1486 clearly must have played a key role.

But in the mid-sixteenth century the spell was to end. "After millions of obstacles," Mariani wrote, "an ecumenical general Council" was called in

1545 to take place in Trent "to the immortal glory of the Catholic faith and the perpetual scorn of heresy."[56] The Council was called in response to the Protestant Reformation, and was tasked with reforming the Catholic Church and defining its doctrine. Of the 517 "fathers" who participated in "the great Council," Mariani reported, some expressed great interest in Trent's "most blessed innocent martyr," promoted by Cristoforo Madruzzo, bishop of Trent and Brixen at the time.[57] While in Trent for the Council, the Church leaders no doubt visited the city's churches, walked past sites related to Simon's story, and likely saw the relics of the boy's body.[58] Indeed, on December 28, 1545, the feast of the Holy Innocents, Bishop Madruzzo and other dignitaries attended a mass at the Church of St. Peter and saw Simon's body, specially displayed on that day.[59] A similar mass, explicitly "in honor of B. Simon," took place towards the end of the Council, in 1562.[60]

In 1571, eight years after the conclusion of the Council of Trent, Laurentius Surius (or Lorenz Sauer), a German Carthusian hagiologist and historian, published in Cologne the second volume of his collection of the lives of saints, which was organized by months; this volume covered March and April. In the entry for March 24, Surius included Tiberino's pivotal account of Simon's death sent to the Senate of Brescia on April 4, 1475.[61] Surius claimed that his work was based on the lives of saints by Luigi Lippomano, a multivolume work published between 1556–1560, though they differed in structure.[62] Lippomano was indeed among the 517 "fathers" at the Council of Trent mentioned by Mariani and was no friend of the Jews, participating actively in the first documented host desecration trial of Jews in Poland in 1556, but his opus magnum contains no mention of Simon of Trent.[63] Surius appears to have added the boy on his own initiative, perhaps inspired by one of the editions of the chronicle by Werner Rolevinck, a fellow Carthusian. Surius's version of the lives of saints was the first to include Simon.

That the German Surius, and not the Italian Lippomano, known for his obedience and service to popes, included the story of Simon in the collection of the lives of saints may be a testimony to the legacy of the 1475 trial north of the Alps, on the one hand, and, on the other, to Lippomano's reluctance to embrace Simon, whose cult after all had not yet been officially sanctioned by Rome. Lippomano's collection was republished, but it was the much more user-friendly version by Surius that became a European bestseller, inspiring new adaptations and providing materials for other chroniclers—including Cesare Baronio, as well as Abraham Bzovius and Odorico Rinaldi who continued Baronio's work—thereby securing for Simon a permanent place in the history of Christianity.

A Path to Papal Recognition

Simon's contested path to papal recognition as *beatus* or, as some wished, a saint, reflects the cult's chronological liminality between the medieval and the early modern era. In the early Middle Ages, according to Fidel Gonzalez-Fernandez, a historian and a prominent official at the Congregation for the Causes of the Saints at the Vatican, "the canonization was essentially based on two elements: the *memory* the Christian community preserved of the presence of the saint in its bosom, and miracles, as a sign of [the saint's] presence even after death."[64] The recognition of the saint belonged to a bishop or a local synod, and included a ceremony of inscribing the saint "in the catalogue of saints" or "the translation of [the saint's relics]." The impetus behind the recognition of the saint usually came from the people (*populous Dei*) participating in "a spontaneous movement of Christian piety." But this proliferation of local cults led to "anarchy" that needed to be curbed by Church authorities.[65] By the High Middle Ages, critical voices had inspired greater verification of local claims of sainthood. In 1171, Pope Alexander III prohibited veneration of saints and relics without prior authorization from Rome, and from the thirteenth century on, following the promulgation of Gregory IX *Decretales,* papal canonization became the law, making it clear that miracles claimed to be performed by "candidates" for sainthood had to be sanctioned by papal authority.[66] This task of verification was delegated to three cardinals, a procedure that remained in place until 1588.[67] With the Protestant attacks on the cult of saints in the Catholic Church, the Council of Trent decided both to affirm the validity of the worship of saints and to consider regulating them.[68]

But even though the status of a saint was increasingly regulated, in the late fifteenth century the title *beatus* did not yet have any legal valence—the legal status of "a saint" came with canonization and the records of miracles were collected to achieve that. Standardization of procedures regarding beatification came later, with a formal process made uniform only in the seventeenth century with the beatification of Francesco de Sales in 1662.[69]

In the meantime, new cults continued to emerge, made easier by a medieval loophole that left room for private prayers directed at the dead who were "believed to be good men" or "saints" requesting their intercession before God.[70] And even though the law left little doubt about the illegality of *public* cults unauthorized by Rome, with private prayers allowed, the line between the two was often blurred. It became clear that the Holy See was unable to control the new "private" cults, which gradually grew into public veneration. Despite Rome's explicit threats and condemnations, including warnings to suspend local bishops disobeying the law, local bishops tolerated and often actively promoted these homegrown cults in the hope they would be later formally recognized by Rome.[71] The rise of Simon's cult in Trent illustrates this problem.

The cult of Simon of Trent emerged at a moment when new measures were being sought in order to root out such illegal cults by regulating public worship and defining who in fact could be called a *beatus*. Ludovico Carbone, an Italian scholar active in the second half of the fifteenth century and a contemporary of Pope Sixtus IV, clearly articulated the difference between saints and *beati*, affirming at the same time the sole authority of the pope to authorize public worship. In his book *Summa summarum casuum*, where he discussed the question whether "the Church could err in canonization of the saints,"[72] Carbone argued that any object of public worship had to be affirmed by the pontiff; those venerated in private places by private individuals could at the very most be called *beati*.[73] If for the Catholic scholars the distinction was clear, the terms "saint" and *beatus* were often used interchangeably, causing confusion among the public.

The development of the printing press enabled the rapid dissemination of images and stories of venerated figures such as "Little Simon." It is in this context that Pope Sixtus IV decided to intervene to halt the development of the pilgrimage site devoted to the Trent toddler. Sixtus worried that Bishop Hinderbach's efforts, which in Hinderbach's understanding were in line with medieval customs, would lead to something "that might result in injury to God or contempt of the Apostolic See."[74] In his letter to Hinderbach of October 10, 1475, for the first time Sixtus applied explicitly the legal concepts of authorized public worship of saints to the term *beatus*, by explicitly forbidding to call the boy *beatus*, to preach in public about him and about miracles related to him, and to disseminate images of him. In prohibiting "public proclamation of Simon as a martyr," even though no official liturgy was attached at the time to venerating the child, Pope Sixtus IV interpreted the existing law in a new way, effectively condemning any "public manifestation" of veneration without prior approval of the Holy See.[75] This marked the first step toward what would by the seventeenth century become a formal process of beatification, and turned Simon into a precedent in the Church's legal system.

But the significance of Sixtus's condemnation of the use of the term *beatus* to describe Simon can only be appreciated in relation to other cases of *beati* the pontiff approved. In 1481, Sixtus IV allowed for the public celebration of a mass and hours "freely and with clear and serene conscience" in veneration of "five Franciscan martyrs" killed in Morocco in 1220.[76] A year later, Sixtus canonized Catherine of Sweden, a fourteenth-century Swedish noblewoman whom he called *beata*, suggesting this was a new status before formal canonization.⁷⁷ He authorized the cult of "this *beata* Catherine" so that the faithful could venerate her "in public and in private" without fear of idolatry. And in 1483, Sixtus authorized a public cult of Giovanni Bono, a medieval Italian ascetic, "so he may be venerated as a *beatus*."⁷⁸ In this light, Sixtus IV's explicit prohibition of using the term *beatus* in relation to Simon acquires more weight and signifies a shift from the permission to use that term to refer to private veneration of "servants of God" to a definition of the term to signify a public cult in need of official papal approval. This idea would be formally articulated by Pope Leo X in his *breve* from 1515 stating that "no one may be venerated as *beatus* without authorization of the Apostolic See."⁷⁹ And in 1625, Pope Urban VIII in his decree *Super non cultu* explicitly prohibited the public veneration of those not officially "canonized or beatified" by the Holy See, calling attention to the need for procedures regarding beatification.⁸⁰

In Trent, however, because of Bishop Hinderbach's unwavering efforts, Simon's cult remained active, despite papal opposition. Even a liturgy (*officium*) existed already during Hinderbach's time.⁸¹ Thus, by the time church dignitaries arrived in Trent to celebrate the Council of Trent in 1545, the imagery of Simon, ubiquitous in the churches in the northern Italian territories of Trentino and Lombardy, had created "facts on the ground."

Responding to the crisis caused by the Protestant Reformation, which among other things furiously attacked the cult of saints, the Church Council at Trent took steps toward thorough reforms, including the reform of the procedures and criteria for sainthood, even as it unambiguously affirmed in principle the validity of saint veneration.⁸² The Council called for review of liturgical books and of procedures of elevating saints to altars, whether on grounds of their martyrdom or their saintly lives. It enjoined "new miracles" and "new relics" and made the elevation of saints to the altars dependent, especially in disputed cases, on final approval of the pope—not local bishops.⁸³

In subsequent decades, liturgical books were indeed revised. The breviary, a liturgical compendium containing public and canonical prayers, was revised in 1568 and the missal in 1570.⁸⁴ In 1580, Pope Gregory XIII ordered a commission of scholars and church officials to reform the liturgical calendar *Martyrologium romanum*,⁸⁵ which had existed in many versions that "were not perfect, or without errors."⁸⁶ The commission included two canons at San Peter's in Rome, Silvio Antoniano and Giambattista Bandino; Roberto Bellarmino, a Jesuit lecturer at the Roman College, a future cardinal and a saint canonized in 1930; Cesare Baronio, a scholar and priest, later made a cardinal by Pope Clement VIII; Lodovico Torres, a bishop of Sicily and subsequently a cardinal; and two religious, Michele Ghisleri, a

Theatine, and Bartolomeo Gavanto, a Barnabite.[87] But of all of those men, Cesare Baronio, who was even given a stipend for working on the reform of the calendar, played the most important role; his name became attached to the 1586 edition of *Martyrologium romanum*.[88] At the time of his appointment to the commission, Baronio was working on his monumental *Annales ecclesiastici*, which was to become one of the most comprehensive works of ecclesiastical history. With access to manuscripts in the Vatican library and the knowledge he already had from his research on his history of the Church, Baronio was well positioned for the task.

The work of the commission was not without tensions: the group could not agree on the methods, sources, and changes to be made to the liturgical calendar. Some complained that too many Greek saints were added, others that new saints not previously included in the old *martyrologium* were added from other sources.[89] Still others wanted "martyrs of our times" to be included in the calendar not only so they could be honored but also, as Curzio de Franchi, a canon at San Peter's in Rome involved in the reform of the breviary, wrote, "to show that in all times the Holy Church was illuminated [*illustrata*] by martyrdom."[90] Yet, the addition of such saints and martyrs had to be done with caution, and de Franchi was concerned that the calendar would be rushed to print without proper vetting.

Cesare Baronio shared de Franchi's sentiment to include "the names of the saints celebrated and honored all over the Christian world."[91] In fact, in 1581, Cesare Baronio's own father, Camillo, wrote to his son inquiring about San Cesidio, a local martyr and "protector" of his town, sending along a description of Cesidio's passion. Other local officials wrote too, requesting that their local saints and martyrs be included.[92] Cardinal Ludovico Madruzzo, prince-bishop of Trent from 1567, known for his active promotion of the cult of Simon, may have been one of them, requesting inclusion of Simon of Trent in the new, revised, and authoritative *martyrologium*.

It is unclear what measures Madruzzo or anyone else took to lobby Baronio to include Simon in the *martyrologium*; what is known is that Baronio carefully evaluated all saints and martyrs, adding some and deleting others. Some of his decisions were met by controversy; others were accepted without any opposition.[93] A century and a half later, Prospero Lambertini, the future Pope Benedict XIV, would claim in his opus magnum on beatifications and canonizations that Simon was an exceptional case inserted in *Martyrologium romanum* by the order of Pope Gregory XIII himself.[94] That was certainly not made explicit in the *Martyrologium* itself, but when the revised liturgical calendar, into which Simon was inserted, was first published in 1583, its subtitle assured the faithful that it was "edited by the order of Pope Gregory XIII" and "restored in accordance with the truth of

Church history [*ad . . . ecclesiasticae historiae veritatem restitutum*]."⁹⁵ Underscoring the full papal imprimatur of the newly revised *Martyrologium romanum* on January 14, 1584, Pope Gregory XIII issued a *breve* titled *Emendato iam*, in which he prohibited the use or publication of any other versions, as well as any additions to it. Any local figures venerated in local churches not included in this authorized edition of *Martyrologium romanum* were to be listed separately.⁹⁶ The *breve* was intended to stem potential protests over the saints and martyrs found in earlier editions but omitted from the revised version.

The 1586 edition of *Martyrologium romanum*, published under the new pope, Sixtus V, too, went out of its way to underscore its validity. Placed at the beginning in the 1586 edition was a letter "To the Candid Reader" by Dutch bishop William Damasus Lindanus, written in 1585. It affirmed that the book had been reviewed by Church authorities and was found to contain nothing that would contradict "orthodox faith and doctrine." In fact, the revisions and emendations were made to assure the faithful of the verity of the elogies of the martyrs and saints they worshiped; they were not to worry about "vain," "apocryphal," even "superstitious" tales that may have "contaminated" earlier versions of the *Martyrologium*.⁹⁷

Given such intense scrutiny of the content of the new *Martyrologium romanum*, the inclusion of Simon of Trent was purposeful—a deliberate affirmation of the cult. With Simon included in the *Martyrologium*, arguably Pope Sixtus V had no choice but to grant an *officium*, a liturgy in Simon's name, which he did in 1588. What had once been from Rome's perspective a "rogue" local cult became a cult that was fully, if perhaps reluctantly, embraced by the pontiff and the Roman Curia. The papal bull granting the *officium* was issued the very same year Pope Sixtus V established the Congregation of the Rites, which was to become responsible for regulating the veneration of saints.⁹⁸ The decision to grant the *officium* in the name of Simon was thus both a corollary of the inclusion of Simon in the *Martyrologium romanum* and a deliberate decision that has to be seen as a part of the reform of the liturgical calendar and of broader reforms of the canonization procedures.

The process by which Simon of Trent entered Baronio's *Martyrologium romanum* also illustrates the early modern scholarly methodology of validating evidence. In 1583, Simon appeared under March 24 with a short note: "Tridenti passio sancti Simonis innocentis puelli, a Iudaeis in odium Christi saeuissime trucidati, qui multis postea miraculis co-ruscauit." (In Trent, passion of holy Simon, an innocent boy cruelly killed by Jews in hatred of Christ, who later displayed many miracles.)⁹⁹ The 1584 edition, published in Rome, removed the phrase "in odium Christi." Baronio's 1586 edition of the *Martyrologium* retained the new wording and included an annotation pointing to the sources that supposedly verified Simon's story: Giovanni Mattia Tiberino's account to the Senate of Brescia; Laurentius Surius's lives of saints published in 1570–1571; and Joannes Molanus's edition of *Usuardi martyrologium*, which was published first in 1568 with no references to Simon and then republished in Louvain in 1573 with a brief reference to the boy: "Tridenti, passio beati Simonis pueri" (in Trent, a passion of the blessed boy Simon).[100] At first glance, it thus seemed that there were three distinct, authoritative sources for Simon's story, but a genealogy of Baronio's footnote reveals that there was effectively only one: Tiberino's 1475 account, which was then used by Surius, whose lives of saints was in turn used by Molanus in the 1573 edition of *Martyrologium*, which in turn was used by Baronio. Thus, one could argue that Surius, the Carthusian monk from Cologne, was pivotal in helping sanction the questionable cult of Simon in Trent.

Vernacular Tales and Other Trials North of the Alps

Stories about Jews killing Christian children had, of course, been well known north of the Alps even before the trial in Trent. One Italian jurist, who opposed the Trent trial as "fictitious and full of falsehoods," noted that such stories were told in Germany; Hinderbach himself requested copies of trial records against Jews from the German lands when he was defending the legality of the trial in Trent.[101] Indeed, in 1470, just five years before the events in Trent, similar tales had inspired a trial of Jews in Endingen who were accused of having killed an entire Christian family—the parents and their two young children—passing through the town some eight years earlier. The trial, discussed in detail by R. Po-Chia Hsia, ended with the execution of the Jews.[102] And although the Endingen trial had serious political ramifications for the power structure and jurisdiction within the empire and even produced a ballad and a play—a *Judenspiel*—commemorating the events, and still performed as late as 1616, this case remained, like most earlier instances of anti-Jewish accusations, a regional affair, remembered only in local chronicles (and known to Johannes Hinderbach).[103] In fact, subsequent printed chronicles do not mention this case at all.

In contrast, the impact of Simon's story was much more profound. Laurentius Surius's source, Tiberino's address to the Senate of Brescia of April 4, 1475, was immediately translated into German; by the fall of that year it appeared in illustrated editions, including one issued a few days after

Battista de' Giudici arrived in Trent to investigate the affair.[104] A German song about Simon by Matthaus Kunig, also heavily indebted to Tiberino, was published in Venice soon thereafter, and in 1498, a German translation of Tiberino's poem "Sum puer ille Simon" was published by Johann Zainer in Ulm.[105]

The tale of Simon's death provided inspiration and narrative validation for subsequent accusations against Jews. The case in 1476 in Regensburg, where a trial of seventeen Jews lasted for more than four years but ended with their release, was directly tied to the Trent affair.[106] One of the accused Jews in Trent—Israel, son of Mayer (Mohar) of Brandenburg, who converted to Christianity soon after being arrested and took the name Wolfgang—implicated the Jews of Regensburg in an alleged murder supposed to have taken place some eight years earlier.[107] In March 1476, when the bishop of Regensburg, Heinrich IV of Absberg, stopped in Trent on his way from Rome, Hinderbach quickly informed him about the crime allegedly committed years ago in Regensburg and gave him a copy of Wolfgang's testimony.[108]

But Trent's legacy in Regensburg was not limited to Wolfgang's accusation. The very questions asked of the Jews arrested in Regensburg were shaped by the narrative of Simon's martyrdom. The magistrates wanted to know who purchased the child, how much was paid for the boy, "who held the child," who "tortured him," how the child's blood was collected, whether Jews needed "blood from a Christian child every year and why." They asked, "How were the needles used? How were the pincers used? Why was a handkerchief tied around the child's throat? How was the foreskin on the penis cut off?" All twenty-four questions suggested that indeed, as R. Po-Chia Hsia has observed, "the Regensburg magistrates sought not justice but a duplication of the ritual murder trial in Trent."[109]

The influence of the Trent case was also detectable in the trial of the Jews in Freiburg in 1503.[110] That year on Good Friday, a body of a boy was found in the pastures. The body was immediately identified as Matthew Bader, a son of Philip, a shady character who just a few days later would be arrested for theft. Bader told the authorities he had sold the child to Jews, but they promised that "the child would not be killed; all they needed was a little Christian blood."[111] Soon, Jews were arrested and tortured. In the end, the affair turned into a political showdown between the city officials and Emperor Maximilian I, who had been attempting to consolidate his domains and "subjugate the Swiss Confederation," where Freiburg was located.[112] During the proceedings, the trials in Trent and Endingen were used as proof of the Jews' guilt; and a contemporary poem about the affair in Freiburg also reminded listeners about Trent. In the end, however, the emperor's intervention and his unequivocal condemnation of the trial saved the Jews. The legacy of this official intervention would be felt in subsequent trials of Jews north of the Alps and in Italy, providing a legal basis for imperial condemnations of ritual murder trials in 1540 in Sappenfeld, a trial that also closely resembled what had happened in Trent, and in 1563 in Worms. These imperial condemnations provided additional legal documentary support of Jews that would be used to counter similar accusations in seventeenth- and eighteenth-century Italy and beyond.[113]

North of the Alps, thus, the immediate impact of the story of Simon of Trent and of vernacular songs about him was more trials of Jews. Such trials tapered off only in the late sixteenth century as a result of both the legal transformations of the Holy Roman Empire and of what R. Po-Chia Hsia has called the Christian "disenchantment of Hebrew and Jewish rites," made possible by the study of Jewish languages and religious texts by Christians, which demystified Jewish rituals and beliefs.[114]

But as these trials were disappearing from German lands, they were emerging in Poland, with Simon's legacy quite palpable as a result of the vernacular adaptation of Laurentius Surius's work. In 1579, just a few years after the first printing of Surius's *Lives of Saints,* a Polish Jesuit, Piotr Skarga, published his own vernacular version of *Lives of Saints,* written "to inspire devotion, strengthen faith, . . . and hope."[115] Much like Surius, who had adapted and added to Luigi Lippomano's opus magnum, Skarga carefully chose what to include and to translate faithfully, and what merely to adapt for Polish readers, adding his own commentary and new materials. For Skarga, this was an important task, because reading the *Lives of Saints,* he argued, was "better" and safer than reading the Bible, where the stories were "not simple" and often contained "hidden meaning," impossible to understand without the guidance of the clergy. Since Skarga's book was safe, such additional guidance by priests was not necessary.

It was in his *Lives of Saints* that Skarga introduced to Poland an abridged adaptation of Tiberino's account of Simon of Trent in Polish.[116] But whereas Surius placed Simon on March 24, the day that would become his feast in the *Martyrologium romanum,* Skarga placed Simon's story on "the last day of March," perhaps because some early liturgical calendars and missals located the story on March 30, or perhaps because of the story that followed.[117]

After retelling Simon's story, Skarga turned to a case from closer home. "And the unfaithful Jews," Skarga wrote, "committed openly the same [crime] in our times in the Great Duchy of Lithuania in 1574 after the death of King Sigismund August, when his kingdom was orphaned."[118] That year, a Jew, one Joachim Smerlowicz, who was leasing a brewery and a distillery in the small town of Punia, fifty-six miles from Wilno (now Vilnius in Lithuania), conspired with two of his "godless" Christian servants to abduct a Christian child "to slaughter and drain of blood" in preparation for the "Jewish easter." The victim was to be the seven-year-old daughter "Kalżuchna, or Helżbieta" of a widow, Urszula of Lublin, who lived in Punia. And so, when the widow left her house on the Tuesday preceding Palm Sunday, March 30 of that year, the Jew entered it. But because "the girl knew him, she was not frightened," and like Simon, "she gave him her little hand." But the Jew "like a brutal wolf" grabbed her, covered her mouth with a kerchief, and took her into a barn, slaughtering her "mercilessly," and draining her blood "as if from a goose." He collected the blood, Skarga claimed, to give it to other Jews waiting across the river and did not even bother to hide the girl's body. When the mother discovered the girl's dead body, she immediately suspected the Jew and raised the alarm. Smerlowicz was captured but then released on bail. He did not even lose "one hair," Skarga complained. The mother appealed to higher authorities, even the Sejm (the nobles' Diet), "begging for justice." And although all the lords knew about this "cruel murder," because the girl's body was brought to Wilno for everyone to see the injuries (in 1579 it was still on display in the Church of the Holy Cross), all was in vain; unlike in Trent, Skarga complained, in Lithuania, the "cruel murder" went unpunished.

In Skarga's Polish story, the Christological connection of Simon's story was lost, perhaps because the supposed victim was a girl; instead Jewish cruelty and the Jews' role in Polish society and economy were the focus. After Skarga warned readers that because this crime had been left unpunished, God might extend His punishment "on the people of this land," he ranted about the ills Jews brought on Christian society.[119] Concerned as he was with heresy, one of the main ills for Skarga was that "rabbis falsify the interpretation of the Holy Scriptures," "blaspheme against the name of our Lord Jesus Christ," and "arm heretics with arguments against the Church." But Jews hurt the Polish society also in other ways, he claimed, by practicing usury, corrupting lords with profits from leasing lands and businesses, teaching the lords to treat their serfs cruelly, and ruining the merchant class. If this were not enough, by employing Christian servants, Jews led them away from Christ, and impregnated Christian maids.

Yet, unlike the poets writing in the wake of the Trent trial, Skarga did not advocate expelling the Jews or forcing them to convert. Instead, he was inspired by a practice recently implemented in Rome in a papal bull *Vices eius nos*, issued just two years earlier in 1577 mandating that each Saturday Jews "be forced to listen to sermons."[120] Skarga urged Polish lords to do so as well. In Skarga's *Lives of Saints*, Simon's story became a tool to be used for conversion when all other policies concerning Jews had failed. In Poland, both anti-Jewish accusations and anti-Jewish books would mimic Skarga's tone: Christological language was nearly absent, and stories were told to evoke social reality.

Italian Legacy

In Italy, too, the immediate years following the trial in Trent were marked by a flurry of incendiary literature and copycat accusations. But unlike the early Latin poems and accounts about Simon, which had an apologetic tone justifying Bishop Hinderbach's actions, the vernacular tales, rhymed poems, and songs—even those written during his lifetime—were largely devoid of the focus on Hinderbach. Instead, their goal was to generate excitement about and devotion to Simon by muting some aspects of the story and amplifying others. They sought to stir anti-Jewish sentiments by calling for expulsions of Jews not just from local cities but also from all Christian domains and by undermining the traditional policy toleration of Jews within Christianity.

In May 1475, an Italian translation of Tiberino's letter to the Senate of Brescia appeared in Verona—it was the first dated pamphlet about Simon to be printed.[121] And soon, a seventeen-page rhymed version of Simon's story in Italian, *Li horribili tormenti del beato Simone di Trento* (The Horrible Torments of the Blessed Simon of Trent), was published in Treviso by Gerardus Lisa (Gerardo da Fiandra), the first work about Simon to be originally composed in Italian. And it, too, was heavily influenced by Tiberino.[122] This heavy dependence on Tiberino may not have been accidental. The work circulated widely, and Gerardo da Fiandra, the printer of *Li horribili tormenti*, published at least two editions of Tiberino's text along with other accounts about Simon written by Thomas Pratus.[123]

Although *Li horribili tormenti* follows Tiberino's narrative closely, it amplifies its highly incendiary language and omits ambiguities found in Tiberino's Latin account. While Tiberino's text at times displayed ambivalences, the author of the rhymed Italian story offered a simpler, more violent message: "An atrocious and perfidious Jewish people, full of iniquity and all kinds of defects," committed "a great crime" in Trent "this holy Easter," disparaging "the faith of Mary."[124] The whole affair started when "Moise, the perfidious Jew, an evil dog, convened together with three other Jewish dogs in Trent" to plot to kidnap a Christian boy in order to kill him. They did so, the author wrote, in order to collect his blood with which "this perfidious people joyfully makes their unleavened bread."

Li horribili tormenti is replete with canine and beastly metaphors for Jews who were described as "rabid dogs" tormenting Simon, "a delightful treasure," akin to Christ himself.[125] Emphasizing Jews' enmity, the author called for vengeance and their expulsion: "O, father, good shepherd, expel these dogs . . . with fury." Like Tiberino, he prayed that "the perfidious Jews may no longer be able to live among Christians" and pleaded to "avenge those who died."[126] Clearly not all Christians shared the author's sentiments, for some protected Jews. He called them "blind" and warned, as did Tiberino, that "famine and wars" were punishments for the Jews' blasphemies and curses "against Christians" and "the virgin Mary together with her son."[127] Condemning Christians for "conversing with mortal enemies of Christ and his mother," the author stressed that "there is no people" in the world that "accepts them"; in fact, no one "suffers to be their friend," and only "the devil accompanies them."[128] Although there was only one solution—to "expel these traitors, enemies of God and our mercy" so that "similar errors are no longer committed"—Christians seemed unable to take action and "expel them like dogs," tolerating such "painful deceptions [the Jews] commit against true God." It was "no wonder," the author bemoaned, "that pagans have no respect for our faith."

Although these early works did not succeed in effecting the expulsion of Jews "from Christendom" in the immediate years following the trial in Trent, Jews in northern Italy did become victims of copycat accusations. In April 1479, two Jews, Donato and Belhomo, in Pavia in the duchy of Milan were accused of kidnapping a Christian boy named Turluru "for use in the ceremonies of the Jews."[129] The event took place just four years after the notorious trial in Trent, 150 miles away, the imagery of Jews killing Christian children still fresh in the region.

On April 20, 1479, the ducal podestà of Pavia, Giovanni Calzavacca (or Calzavacha) wrote to Bona of Savoy, who was a regent of the duchy of Milan on behalf of her minor son, Giovanni Galeazzo Sforza, reporting that one of the accused Jews, Donato, a servant to the Jew Belhomo, had been detained by Antonio Malvicino, an official of the cardinal. Donato had since confessed to having sold the boy to Belhomo.[130] Based on the allegations, the podestà ordered the arrest of Belhomo and his companion, Saya di Piacenza. According to Calzavacca, such crimes indeed demanded punishment and "similar errors were not to be tolerated," but he was concerned that the cardinal's officer usurped the jurisdiction that belonged to the ducal podestà. Calzavacca asked the dukes to order the cardinal to release Belhomo's servant to him, so he could proceed appropriately in this case.[131]

Matters moved along quite speedily. The next day, the dukes of Milan sent a letter to the cardinal's officer informing him that Calzavacca was to see the incarcerated Jew and that Belhomo was to be sent to the chief justice in Milan. But by the time Calzavacca was shown the dukes' letter, the Church official had already let "many citizens know the tone of the letter," and a pushback against releasing Belhomo to the authorities in Milan had begun.[132] Representatives of Pavia decided to bypass the podestà and wrote directly to the Sforzas, pleading against sending the Jews, "who, as it is said, have killed a boy in great scorn of all of Christianity," to Milan. "The punishment," they wrote, "should be done in the jurisdiction where the crime was committed, that is in Pavia."[133] The following day, despite protests, the cardinal's officer, Antonio Malvicino, conceded and promised to transfer Donato to the podestà Calzavacca. On April 25, Calzavacca arranged for the prisoners to be transported to Milan.[134]

In Milan, the question of jurisdiction had to be settled first. On April 28, 1479, the duke of Milan and the senators assured Antonio Malvicino and two public officials from Pavia that the duke had no intention of trampling on Pavia's authority and jurisdiction. The duke and senators wanted Pavia's officials to understand that any "atrocious case" that would "offend Christian religion" would belong to the purview of ducal jurisdiction and be heard in Milan, and if the accused were found guilty, they would then be returned to the podestà of Pavia for punishment. But in the case at hand, the investigation found that "this accusation was false and slanderous." As had happened other times, the boy Turluru supposedly crucified by Jews had been found "alive and without any injuries." Since the accusation against Jews in Pavia was unfounded, the arrested Jews were to be released and their possessions restored; they were not to be held liable for judicial expenses. The duke warned that any future attacks and scandalous accusations against Jews would not be tolerated.[135]

On May 19, 1479, Bona of Savoy and her son issued a powerful charter of protection for Jews, who, they emphasized, were "always ready and keen to do what is good and useful to our state."[136] They denounced "new inventions" like those that had taken place "in the last two months" in several locations when a child went missing. Such incidents threatened to cause "a great scandal and disorder to the detriment and danger of the state," because the Jews in these places were subjected to torture and "confessed to have committed that of which they in fact were innocent." In Pavia, "had God through his grace not caused [the boy] to be found, they would have been treated even worse than in Trent."[137]

No "sane" person, the decree stated, "would believe the craziness of which they are accused," because Jews' law prohibited both murder and eating blood.[138] Therefore, if Jews found abominable not only the use but even visual contact with human blood or a corpse, "how much greater an error it would be to kill someone in order to use his blood."[139] To those who claimed that Jews "did it in contempt of Christ," one could respond that "it was not true, not even partly true [*verissimile*]." There were Jews who "became Christians and Doctors of the Church of great reputation and authority," among them Saint Paul, Nicolas of Lyra, and "many others who were very familiar with Jewish rites and customs," and if they had known about "such custom among Jews, certainly they would have shown that." Moreover, "the Church would not only not have granted them so many privileges, but would not have tolerated them" at all, as it had in "all the Christian provinces." Instead it would have "driven them away and persecuted them, and so would other secular and ecclesiastical lords."

And to those who might say that perhaps the murder of children for their blood was "a secret custom," the decree continued, one might similarly respond that there were many baptized Jews "respected in their faith" all over Christendom, whom one could ask and demand to know "if it was true or not."[140] But one should not attempt to find that out from "fickle persons but mature and of good intellect." Still, some might say that there might be "some madmen [*alcuni pazzi*] who through their imagination are set to commit such vile crimes."[141] To them one could respond that "generally, the madmen are poor, and not heads of households"; they are rejected by others. And even if Jews wanted to commit such crimes, others would have objected and not participated in them, either because they would not want to break the laws, "both divine and human," or because of the danger to their persons and property. The "madmen" would not know how to organize these matters and keep them secret. And, then, why would anyone go to so much trouble if there were so many rich Jews "in the lands of the Turks, Moors, Saracens, and other infidels," who had "slaves and servants and could have boys at their will to do with them whatever they wanted without any regard and dangers and without being hindered" as they were in Christian lands. If these arguments were still not sufficient to prove these accusations absurd, one could look at Jewish history in Rome, where Jews settled after the destruction of their temple in Jerusalem by Vespasian. Over these centuries, no one had ever found them to commit such crimes, and "if they had, it would have been impossible not to discover it after some time."[142]

The dukes of Milan ruled that any cases of similar accusations against Jews were to be transferred to Milan. They outlined the parameters of acceptable judicial process, requiring both accusers and witnesses to be of respectable status, with copies of all evidence sent along to ensure it was not gathered through abuse. The decree prohibited subjecting Jews to torture without "participation and express consent" of authorized officials. False accusations against Jews or causing them any harm were expressly prohibited under severe penalties.[143]

But if the decree of the Sforzas might have been effective in the duchy of Milan, elsewhere accusations continued to crop up. In 1480, despite the Venetian doge's condemnation of the accusations, three Jews from Portobuffolè, near Treviso in Veneto, were executed in Venice as a result of similar charges. They were accused of killing a boy, who came to be known as Sebastiano Novello, although no body of the boy was ever found. Giorgio Sommariva, one of the Renaissance poets writing about Simon of Trent, devoted a poem to Sebastiano "to make this great crime well known."[144] And in 1482 in Volpedo, after a child had been killed, a monk and a Jew were implicated, giving rise to a murky story of Giovannino di Volpedo.[145] Finally, in the seventeenth century, there arose a cult of Lorenzino da Marostica, who was said to have been killed in 1485.[146] But these anti-Jewish accusations soon subsided in Italy, coinciding with the "cooling" of the Simonine cult and the decline in the number of publications about Simon after Hinderbach's death. (The accusations would reappear in Italy in the seventeenth and eighteenth centuries, but never with the deadly results seen in the fifteenth century.)

The first work to be published after the hiatus of the first half of the sixteenth century seems to have been Ambrogio Franco's *Martirio del Beato Simone Tridentino* (The Martyrdom of the Blessed Simon of Trent), which appeared in 1586, three years after the induction of Simon into *Martyrologium romanum* and the very year of publication of the calendar's authorized edition by Cesare Baronio.[147] Three years later, in 1589, Antonio Gesti, a parish priest at the Church of St. Peter in Trent where Simon's body was placed, published his *Martirio di S. Simone di Trento* to commemorate the first procession organized to celebrate Pope Sixtus V's bull granting the office and explicitly recognizing Simon's cult the year before[148] (Fig. 3.2). Gesti acknowledged this papal recognition in the presumptuous appellation he gave Simon—*San Simone*, or Saint Simon—even though Sixtus V had not, in fact, canonized Simon. Gesti's book, which was heavily dependent on the narratives developed in 1475 and on Franco's earlier work, was republished, also in Trent, in 1593 and again in 1642; it received a small popularity bump in the eighteenth century, being republished in 1722, 1739, and 1761. Yet, books by Franco and Gesti were little more than imitations of what had already been available in print in the fifteenth century.

One of the first books displaying a noticeable departure from those earlier histories was the anonymous chapbook *Ristretto della vita e martirio di S. Simone fanciullo della città di Trento* (A Short Account of the Life

MARTIRIO
DI S. SIMONE.
DI TRENTO.

Nel quale si tratta de la gran crudeltà
che vsarono gli empi Ebrei
in martirizarlo,

*Et come è stato posto nel Cattalogo de Santi, & la
solenne Processione fatta nella sua prima Festa,
Con molti miracoli fatti da esso Santo.*

IN TRENTO, Per i Fratelli de Gelmini.
Con Licenza de'Superiori.

FIG. 3.2 Antonio Gesti, *Martirio di S. Simone di Trento nel quale si tratta de la gran crudeltà che usarono gli empi ebrei in martirizarlo, et come è stato posto nel cattalogo de santi e la solenne processione fatta nella sua prima festa con molti miracoli fatti da esso santo* (Trento: Per i fratelli de Gelmini, 1589). Bayerische StaatsBibliothek, V.ss. 839.

and Martyrdom of S. Simon the Boy from the City of Trent), said to have been published in Rome in 1594.[149] To be sure, it too was heavily indebted to Tiberino's account, but *Ristretto* was a book for young readers. In the preface, the author encouraged them to embrace Simon as their patron and protector, warning them to be cautious about dangers posed by Jews. To help his young readers better understand the work, the author included a short list of "Hebrew vocabulary, which are in this story."[150] The incomplete list includes the proper name Mordecai and words such as *Judim* (explained as "Jews"), *achala* ("eat"), *bereschit* ("The Book of Genesis"), *scirascirim* ("The Song of Solomon"), *Chabala* ("Vain knowledge of the Jews, who often hide under this name magical arts and necromancy"), *ascittato* ("slaughtered"), *achargato* ("destroyed"), *rabino* ("a teacher who knows a lot"), *cholmalchim* ("all kings of the crown"), *pesulim* ("snitches"), *zacchen* ("old"), *raffe* ("a physician"), *azimelli* ("bread without yeast"), *messia* ("He whom they expect in vain"), and *goim* ("Christians"). The list also includes the term *ghetto,* explained as "a place of the Jews," suggesting that when the book was written, it was still a relatively unknown term but one that was already strictly associated with Jews.[151]

Although *Ristretto* follows Tiberino's narrative, its anonymous author added commentaries and explanations, and invented a dialogue. Despite the general warning against Jews and allusions to other stories of Jewish murders of Christian children in the introduction, these additions and explanations in effect present the Trent case as unique and offer a nuanced interpretation of the story. That message comes across already in the beginning of the story.[152] Just around Easter, the author wrote, which was that year observed "not only by Christians but also by Jews, [whose celebration] little differs from ours," Jews met to discuss how to celebrate the festival. They met in the synagogue, in which "they gathered when it pleased them to perform their ceremonies (especially the Sabbath [*lo sciaba*])," to listen to Rabbi Moses, "whom they considered as a prophet." Moses was ninety years old; he had "a boorish face [*faccia rustica*], black eyes, bristly eyebrows," unkempt hair (*zazzera*), and a beard, "long as that of a Satyr." His "dirty and filthy" clothes stunk. But he addressed those gathered solemnly, because he wanted to reveal a secret: "You should know that as a diligent rabbi, I have always studied the books of our law, [trying to find out] when the Messiah whom we so expect may come; finally I found out thanks to the Kabbalah, examining *Beresci,* all the Prophets, and *Scirascirim* of Solomon, that the Messiah is to come before, I say, a year passes."[153] Indeed, Moses hoped to tell them the month and day of his arrival. He implored them to rejoice and disclosed that they needed to do something special this Passover:

Remember that during the time of the Pharaoh when God wanted to pass over our ghetto [sic], he commanded us to mark doors with blood of a young immaculate lamb. This is how we were saved. And so, too, now that the Messiah will come, it is important that he find our houses sprinkled in blood of an innocent lamb, which (and this shall remain a secret among us) must be a Christian child killed by us, with whose blood we will sprinkle our homes, mix into our unleavened bread, and give to all the Jews, our friends in all parts of the world.[154]

This was to be a sacrifice "in contempt of the Christ of Christians and in honor of the Messiah, whom we are expecting," needed to be made because, Moses continued, "I find that there is no dearer thing we can do for him [the Messiah] than this." All this was based, the anonymous author of the *Ristretto* interjected, on a "false" interpretation of "the Scriptures and the holy Prophets" and on "the fables of their rabbis."

The author then related that Samuel, his son Israel, Angelo (Engel), Mohar (also referred to as Mayer, here *Moccar*), and Tobias the physician all praised the idea. But not all the Jews were in agreement. Two Jews from Germany, Lazzaro (Lazarus) and David, were visiting Trent at the time on their way back home from Rome; one stayed with Tobias and the other with Samuel. Samuel, thinking that the two should be involved in procuring the child, tried to convince them to do so "out of good heart," "zeal for their religion," "the benefit of Judaism," and to be rewarded with money, too.[155] The two German Jews were shocked to see their fellow Jews wanting to become involved in such a dangerous act. So Tobias tried to persuade them as well, saying that no one would recognize them because they were foreigners, and they could leave the city immediately after they had done what was asked of them. They "prudently" pushed back; they "did not want to commit such a crazy thing" and said that all the other Jews, including Moses, were wrong: "God did not command such a thing, on the contrary, [God] says 'Thou shall not kill.' This was a new ceremony against the law, which does not want to spill innocent blood" of a child, "even a Christian." These ceremonies were invented out of thin air, with no basis whatsoever. Moreover, David and Lazzaro added, "Jews were not permitted to eat blood." At that point, they left the town without staying for Passover as they had intended.[156]

This exchange from *Ristretto* between the Trent Jews and the two German visitors contains actual arguments against blood accusations used in earlier trials and official statements defending Jews. They demonstrate the absurdity of such charges by stressing that the alleged crime went against two divine commandments that Jews meticulously observed—the commandment against murder and the prohibition against the consumption of blood. These defenses were well known in Christian Europe. Already in 1247, Pope Innocent IV wrote that, according to "a precept in the Old Testament," Jews were not allowed to consume blood at all and specifically around Passover or to touch the dead, and thus such accusations against Jews had to be condemned.[157] By providing these historically accurate Jewish defenses in the *Ristretto,* the anonymous author offered a version of the Trent story that effectively did not implicate *all* Jews or Judaism more generally. In fact, Judaism emerges rather unscathed from this exchange. Instead, the author allowed that the "crazy" new teachings based on incorrect interpretations of the law led a few misguided Jews to commit this crime, but "not all Jews do this."[158] Such an explanation was unprecedented in the vernacular literature published since the 1475 trial. Despite its anti-Jewish tone *Ristretto* was in fact quite sympathetic to the Jews, acknowledging that some confessions during the trial were extracted under torture when the tortured Jews could no longer bear the pain.[159]

The book ended on a triumphant note for the cult's supporters, recounting the execution of the Jews despite efforts made to save them by Jews in Venice, Florence, and Rome; the establishment of the cult of Simon; and its recognition by Popes Gregory XIII, who "placed him in the *Martyrologium,*" and Sixtus V, who granted him the liturgy and indulgences.[160] But most importantly the book related the conversion of the two German Jews, Lazzaro and David, who, "as it was said, did not want to consent to [commit] such cruelty." They converted, so *Ristretto* recounted, after hearing in Germany "about the miracles of the saint and the honor bestowed on him"; following their example other Jews converted as well. In the end Simon's death was not in vain: the Jews were punished and his cult flourished, stimulating Jewish conversions. To inspire more Jews to accept Christianity, the author included a prayer for their conversion at the end of the book.

Although *Ristretto* offers an unusual complexity in its recounting of the story, it does not even hint at any opposition to the trial. In contrast to the many works published in the years immediately after the trial, which were forced to address some real resistance to the charges against Jews and to the rising cult of Simon, no work published after Sixtus V authorized the cult by granting the office and indulgences in 1588 discussed the initial papal ambivalence toward the trial and the cult nor did they mention the investigation ordered by the pontiff. And if any resistance was intimated at all, it was usually explained away by Jewish bribery—all "in vain," of course. With the cult officially sanctioned, this lack of mention of any opposition may be explained by a desire not to challenge papal authority and to present the story of the cult as unchallenged from the very beginning. Yet, as the cult consolidated, the influence of Tiberino's original narrative written on April 4, 1475, which became a source for subsequent writers, including Laurentius Surius, and Cesare Baronio, might provide another explanation for why there were no mentions of resistance. Written just days after Simon's death, Tiberino's address to the Senate of Brescia could not have, of course, described the strong opposition that would later emerge. And although his subsequent works did do so, they did not enter the chain of memory about the Trent affair.

One of the works that did draw on writings other than Tiberino's popular account was Michelangelo Mariani's *Il glorioso infante S. Simone*, published in 1668 in Trent. Persuaded by Giovanni Benedetto Gentilotti, the parish priest of the Church of St. Peter in Trent,to write about Simon, Mariani initially intended to compose a short work recounting "the legend." But having embarked on research, he felt compelled "to write formally the whole history."[161] Mariani wrote his book to "revive" the memory of Simon's martyrdom, which he called an act of "impiety and cruelty" unprecedented "since the Passion and death of Christ."[162] So unprecedented was it that "the innocent Simon, it can be said, in some way represents a new Christ [*novello Christo*], at least in regards to his passion," because Jews "crucified him and tortured him . . . with the same intention." And for that reason alone, Mariani argued, Simon deserved to be canonized.

Il glorioso infante S. Simone, "a panegyrical history," as Mariani called it, begins with several poems in Latin, evoking works by Renaissance poets such as Zovenzoni and Tiberino. In fact, the opening poem, signed M. M., suggesting Mariani's authorship, begins with the words, "Ille ego sum Simon," which are uncannily similar to Tiberino's "Sum puer ille Symon." In fact, Mariani's poem is a near-plagiarized abridgment of Tiberino's original.[163] Gentilotti also contributed a Latin poem in Simon's honor, as did a few others. Although these brief poetic works in Latin and Italian, sometimes amounting to just a few stanzas, are reminiscent of those by the Renaissance poets at Hinderbach's service, they diverge from them as well, introducing new themes and motifs. One of Gentilotti's poems alludes to the infants massacred by Herod: to those "innocents," Gentilotti assured, Simon was to bring solace.[164] And one Franciscan, Giovanni Giacomo Giovani da Taranto, focused on the apple said to be given to Simon to quiet him down.[165] In his poem "On the Apple with which S. Simon Was Betrayed," Giacomo remembered the apple that "ruined Adam" and contrasted it with the apple with which Simon, "a martyr of Christ," found his glory—this apple was allegedly given to Simon to quiet his cries. For his part, Mariani was even more explicit: if the original apple, a symbol of Adam's sin, was the reason why Christ needed to die, here the apple caused "the innocent Simon's death" to increase "the glory of his martyrdom in the likeness of Christ, whom he symbolizes."[166] The circle is now complete: innocence lost through an apple was regained through Simon's martyrdom. The comparison of Simon to Christ is unequivocal. But that comparison in and of itself was not new; this motif had been, after all, widely embraced already by the Renaissance poets. What seems new here is the notion of the redemptive value of Simon's death akin to that of Christ.

Mariani played with similarities, contrasts, and opposites between Jesus's and Simon's stories. As with Jesus, Mariani argued, God permitted Simon's death to render him "a martyr of innocence."[167] But in contrast to Jesus's crucifixion, Simon's mother—also named Mary—"could not run to this Calvary,"[168] for she was not notified of the execution. Still, when the boy disappeared, she looked for him with her husband just as Mary and Joseph, "the holy parents of Jesus, went to look, with anxiety and grief, for their divine child," when he stayed behind in Jerusalem.[169] But unlike Jesus's parents, Mary and Andreas of Trent did not find Simon debating the sages in the temple, and in sorrow, they had to return home empty-handed.[170] A still more sorrowful discovery was made three days later. Unlike the disciples of Christ, who after three days found him resurrected, the people of Trent found the boy, "all filthy," lying in a canal and "enveloped in the crimson [tunic] of his own blood."[171] Trent became Gethsemane, and Mariani was happy to provide a list of equivalents between Jesus's and Simon's passions.[172]

The crimson tunic plays an important role in Mariani's book, a deliberate choice, given that Simon was dressed in a gray tunic when he died. A crimson tunic had resonance for both Jews and Christians. For Jews "the garment stained in crimson" with blood of Jewish martyrs was to provoke divine vengeance on the enemies of the Jews.[173] In Christianity, a crimson tunic or robe, the *porphyrion*, was closely connected to Jesus's crucifixion. The soldiers "stripped Jesus and put a scarlet robe on him" so they could mock him as "the King of the Jews."[174] But more important for the context of Mariani's discussion of Simon's martyrdom and suffering, when Mariani spoke of "the glorious crimson [tunic], made of blood,"[175] he evoked the Christian understanding of Isaiah 63:1–6, according to which the "garments stained crimson" were meant to be stained with blood, as in Rev. 19:13, where Jesus was to be "clothed in a robe dipped in blood."[176] In both Jewish and Christian societies the crimson robe called to mind blood, redemption, and divine vengeance.

Mariani did not shy away from using other biblical motifs. In the same way that God preserved baby Moses from the Nile, it was God's will to preserve Simon, the "beautiful treasure" in water, despite the Jews' hopes that the current would take the body away. Yet, whereas Moses was preserved for the benefit of Jews, God preserved Simon's body in the water "to liberate the people of Trent" from them.[177]

Mariani also addressed controversial motifs present in earlier tellings of the story. They might have been acceptable in the Middle Ages and at the end of the fifteenth century when the Trent trial took place, but would have been deemed questionable in 1668. One such controversial motif was that of blood flowing from a murder victim in the presence of its murderers. It had first appeared in 1271 in Pfortzheim, where Jews were accused of killing a seven-year-old girl, and it recurred with some frequency, especially north of the Alps.[178] Though not mentioned in Tiberino's first letter to the Senate of Brescia, it was one of the justifications for the trial in Trent and appeared in Ubertino Pusculo's *Symonidos,* written in 1481 and published posthumously in 1511 in Augsburg.[179] For Pusculo, this was one of the miracles testifying to the Jews' guilt, but Mariani, clearly aware of the motif's controversial nature, treaded somewhat more cautiously. He claimed to have discussed the matter with "judges and other men of faith" who nonetheless confirmed the phenomenon from "experience."[180] Still, Mariani was forced to admit that the idea that blood flows from the body of a homicide victim in the presence of the murderer was not accepted everywhere. "It is not practiced in Italy, and even less in Rome," where this type of "proof" not only is not accepted but also is deemed "deceptive and dangerous." Judges in Italy were "very cautious," as were Italian theologians, who feared that such bleeding may be caused by "diabolic arts" and inculpate an innocent.[181] Yet, in Simon's case, Mariani concluded, it was a valid miracle, attested to by reputable physicians who had been called to examine the boy's body and its subsequent incorruptibility. Trent again became a liminal space—trapped between judicial practices and beliefs of Italy and those of northern Europe.

If Mariani was cautious in his discussion of judicial practices, he was not shy about propagating Christian beliefs about Jewish Passover rituals.[182] Every year, he claimed, Jews used Christian blood in the wine and unleavened bread, and they sprinkled it on their tables and in their dwellings "in memory of what ancient Hebrews did when they painted the doorposts of their houses" when they were preparing to leave Egypt, claiming it to be "the blood of [the] covenant that the Lord has made with you." To justify this ritual, Mariani argued, they quoted passages from the "Old Testament," which he was unwilling to cite for fear of giving Jews even more justification.

It was clear that Mariani read the accusations against Jews with the biblical story of Exodus in mind, where blood and the slaughter of sacrificial animals and first-born sons feature prominently, as do redemption and punishment. No other Jewish text contained anything that Mariani could use to sustain his accusations. Indeed, by 1668 there were enough Christian Hebraists, including Catholic censors in Italy, who would have sounded the alarm if any Jewish writings contained information about beliefs or practices supporting tales of ritual murder. Though Mariani did not directly address the fact that Christian scholars of Jewish texts could find no evidence for these purported Jewish practices, he gestured to this point by maintaining that there was in fact no written tradition to kill Christian children, only oral, transmitted "by the elders from father to son."[183]

Simon's story posed another problem for Mariani, similar to the problem Christians faced in interpreting the story of Jesus's death. On the one hand, both deaths were presented as cruel; on the other, they were supposed to be divinely mandated—and in both Jews were said to have played a crucial role. Indeed, Mariani pondered, had Trent listened to the Franciscan Bernardino da Feltre's admonitions and banned the Jews from its territories in early 1475, Simon's death may have been prevented.[184] But then he asked, "Without the cooperation of the wicked ones, how would one acquire such a worthy innocent Martyr for the glory of Trent?" In fact, even the Church, which drew its greatness "from persecutions, could not claim the palms of glory of so many martyrs without the iron of the tyrants, as St. Augustine well observed. . . . For if one cannot score a worthy victory without a fight, how can one fight without enemies?" Thus to be victorious the Church needed enemies and, by extension, Jews.[185] Mariani effectively upturned the meaning of centuries-old Catholic teachings based on Augustine's commentary on Psalm 59:10. According to Augustine,

> The Jews who killed him and refused to believe in him . . . were dispersed all over the world . . . and thus by the evidence of their own Scriptures they bear witness for us that we have not fabricated the prophecies about Christ. . . . It follows that when the Jews do not believe in our Scriptures, their own Scriptures are fulfilled in them, while they read them with blind eyes. . . . It is in order to give this testimony which in spite of themselves, they supply for our benefit by their possession and preservation of those books, that they themselves are dispersed among all nations, wherever, the Christian Church spreads. . . . Hence the prophecy in the Book of Psalms: "Do not slay them, lest at some time they forget our Law; scatter them by your might."[186]

If, for Augustine, Jews were needed as witnesses to the truth of Christianity because of their books, for Mariani, they were necessary as enemies to prove the Church victorious.

To further this idea, Mariani underscored Jewish enmity, and dismissed any Jewish defenses, including those raised earlier by the popes and more recently in the *Ristretto*.[187] That Jews were not allowed to consume blood was indeed a biblical prohibition but, Mariani reasoned, Jews did not follow the Bible; they followed "a certain particular statute called the Talmud, formulated in Babylonia with the goal of derogating the Law of Moses."[188] Moreover, to "legitimize" their "spurious" teachings, they dared to falsify the Bible to obscure any references to Christ. And this alone, Mariani concluded, should inspire Christian rulers to rethink their toleration of the Jews. Thus Mariani's argument was not only a transformation of Augustine's argument for tolerating Jews but in the end also a call for its abrogation.[189]

Mariani's sources were, as he noted, the "most ancient" authors, especially the works by Giovanni Mattia Tiberino and the more recent Ambrogio Franco.[190] Yet Mariani also spent time in the archives of Castle Buonconsiglio, which had been the bishop's palace and the very place where the Jews of Trent were imprisoned and tortured. Mariani claimed to have examined "all pieces of information provided." Among those crucial documents were the court records from the trial, which became the "principal foundation of this history." Though some of the writers mobilized by Bishop Hinderbach seem to have seen the trial records, none before Mariani used them so self-consciously.[191] He quoted directly from the court records to buttress the validity of his own history.[192] Hinderbach's records once more influenced how the story was told.

Mariani's use of archival documentation represents a new epistemological era, where documentary evidence was becoming key in presenting a story as persuasive. For example, the validity of claims of Simon's martyrdom and of the incorruptibility of his body was underpinned by direct references to a report on the reexamination of the body that took place in 1654 and was reaffirmed by another inspection in 1668, witnessed by Mariani himself.[193] Indeed, he asserted clearly, "The body of S. Simon, notwithstanding the signs of torture, with which it was afflicted, can be seen intact and unspoiled. . . . It is only missing a toe from the left foot, which is in Madrid, taken there by the Queen of Spain, when she was visiting these lands."[194]

And yet, the very same documentary evidence Mariani used to sustain the miraculous nature of Simon's body supposed incorruptibility indirectly undermined the claim. As Mariani noted a few pages later, the body had to be re-embalmed and regularly inspected.[195] In May 1654, Mariani reported, Hippolytus Guarinoni, a prominent physician originally from Trent, was charged with re-embalming the body, apparently not for the first time. Following his studies in Padua, Guarinoni settled in the Tyrol, spending many years in Volders near Innsbruck. Clearly very familiar with the story of Simon of Trent, Guarinoni took an interest in a local story of Andreas Oxner, a three-year-old boy said, according to a local legend, to have been killed by Jews in 1462 in Rinn, just a few miles away from his residence in Volders. In 1620, Guarinoni wrote an account of Andreas's death, which, though evidently left unpublished, spurred a local cult akin to that of Simon of Trent. The two boys would become inseparably linked in the eighteenth century, when Pope Benedict XIV recognized the cult of *beatus* Andreas, making him the second case of anti-Jewish accusations formally recognized by the Church. But we are getting ahead of the story.

On Saturday, May 2, 1654, following the celebration of the mass at the altar devoted to Simon, the body of the boy was raised from his coffin and examined in the presence of clerics and other church officials.[196] Guarinoni, with the help of his much younger assistant, took one of the nails "with which the holy martyr was wounded and tortured" and gently, but methodically, touched every "opening" resulting from all the blows, counting them diligently, and making sure no wound had been missed. The two men discovered wounds on the head that, as Mariani claimed, had been previously unnoticed, and some still had blood visible after all these years. They counted 5,812 (!) wounds, of which Guarinoni produced a detailed report.[197] (Guarinoni died a few weeks after producing his report, on May 31.)

In April 1668, another inspection of the body was called for; with clergy and physicians present, two clerics took Simon's body out of the larger casket and placed it, still in the crystal case, on the altar.[198] But, as Mariani, who was present, wrote, the inspection was only visual. Those present decided not to remove the body from its encasement. Somewhat contradicting his earlier claims about the body's uncorrupted state, Mariani admitted that moving it would have been "too dangerous." With a full inspection impossible, it was decided to affirm Guarinoni's report from 1654.

His use of the archive enabled Mariani to develop themes unknown from earlier works, among them efforts by Jews to accuse Bishop Hinderbach of malfeasance before the pope and other men of power. Although earlier works noted Jewish attempts at bribery, Mariani seems to be the first to develop the motif of more serious Jewish "plots" and to address the pope's discomfort with the whole affair.[199] Upon gathering at a council, Mariani reported, Jews from all over Europe decided to seek intervention from the pope against Bishop Hinderbach. They hated the bishop so much that they tried to "poison the waters in the [bishop's] residence," the Castle of Buonconsiglio, where Mariani himself was now staying.[200] But, having been discovered by a priest friendly to the bishop, the plot did not succeed.

Still, Jews "were able to get access to His Holiness" [Sixtus IV], and what they reported to him was full of "sinister information" and "so different from the truth" that the pope felt compelled to order an inquiry, sending his envoy to Trent to investigate the matter further. And because of this, "one can say that the Jews with this apostolic mission obstructed the canonization of this holy and persecuted boy."[201]

Mariani's claims evidently were primarily based on the records of Paolo de Novara's trial.[202] Jews' attempts to stymie all efforts to venerate the boy went so far that they even tried to "pulverize" his body or at least, Mariani wrote, "render it fetid in order to discredit it in the world."[203] By offering gold, they tried to enlist a local priest to "apply poultice on the incorrupt body of the Blessed Boy to render him putrid and turn into powder." Yet the Jews' mission went beyond corrupting Simon's body: the priest was also to poison the waters of Castle of Buonconsiglio and thus the bishop himself, release the imprisoned Jewish women "so they would not convert," retrieve the transcripts of the trial in order to "falsify" them, and, so defaced, send them to Rome. But despite the Jews' stratagems, the plot was discovered, and Simon's cult grew and spread beyond Trent. Pilgrims flocked to the town from Italy, Bavaria, Swabia, Austria, and many other lands.

Mariani's use of archival documents was, however, either incomplete or selective. Receipts of expenditures funding Bishop Hinderbach's own efforts to preserve the body as to prevent fetid smells have been preserved among his papers.[204] Already in April 1475, Hinderbach paid one Venetian ducat sixteen *solidos* and an additional sum of two marcs and 5 *libras* for "the preservation of the boy and for perfumes" [*ad puerum conservandum et pro aromatibus*].[205] The body had to be treated again on May 21, 1475, and on March 28, 1476, when Giovanni Mattia Tiberino was paid one marc for "purification and consolidation of the body of the *beatus* Simon."[206] Some entries about preserving Simon's body were quite explicit. For example, on September 8, 1479, one Johannes of Verona "treated the body of the blessed Simon so it may not putrefy [*ne putrefaceretur*]."[207] Obviously the preservation of Simon's body was not miraculous, confirming the suspicions of Battista de' Giudici, sent by Pope Sixtus IV to investigate the Trent trial and the new cult.[208]

Although early on, Mariani admitted that he had written his book to revive the "memory of Simon," it is not until deep into it that he shed light on the real reason for his writing. On June 29, 1624, the Church of St. Peter suffered a fire, and although Simon's body was "miraculously" unharmed, the rest of the church was seriously damaged.[209] Temporarily, Simon was moved to another church, but jealousy and fights among different churches in Trent over which one should house his body erupted. And although the body, encased in a beautiful silver and crystal case, was returned to St. Peter's Church, the church itself was in need of restoration.[210] In fact, decades later, the restoration of the chapel devoted to the boy was still not completed, "paintings of the Martyr and the miracles of the Saint" left in draft.[211] Mariani's book was thus a seventeenth-century fundraising work, propagating the cult and emphasizing that Simon deserved canonization, for indeed the goal was not "to declare him *beatus*, but saint, not Innocent, but a Martyr of Innocence, killed precisely in hatred of Christ and his Faith."[212] This legal distinction was clear by 1668.

FIG. 3.3 Michelangelo Mariani, *Il glorioso infante S. Simone: historia panegirica* (Trent: Zanetti Stampator Episcopale, 1668). Bayerische StaatsBibliothek, V.ss. 844.

Mariani drew a parallel between Simon's martyrdom and that of the "innocents of Bethlehem," a popular story widely represented in iconography in Italy and with which Simon had long been associated. But, according to Mariani, Simon was more worthy of worship than even the innocents of Bethlehem, who were "simply killed—albeit in hatred of Christ—to save the kingdom for Herod." But Simon "was forced to die precisely because of hatred of the very person of Christ and all Christian faith."[213] The essential point was, Mariani argued, perhaps addressing Simon's detractors, that because Simon was not of the age of reason, the status of Simon's martyrdom stemmed from Christ, Simon's "own prototype."[214] "Iste puer magnus coram Domino [the child is great before the Lord]," so Mariani ended his book, alluding to the liturgy for the nativity of John the Baptist and explaining the meaning of the engraving of Simon inserted before the title page of his book (Fig. 3.3). It depicts Simon, in a triumphant pose, trampling the head of the Jew or rather "the Jewish perfidy," as Mariani explained.[215]

Mariani's book was truly innovative. He sensationalized the account of Simon's life, death, and the aftermath, furnishing new details based on hitherto unused archival documents, and dressing it in elaborate theology. He shone light on the story of the innocents of Bethlehem as a justification for Simon's sainthood. That story would reappear again less than a century later in Pope Benedict XIV's bull *Beatus Andreas,* in which the pope would discuss the question of eligibility for sainthood of child "martyrs."

Iconographic Legacies of the Trent Trial

No other case of ritual murder accusations against Jews inspired as rich a literary production as did the case of Simon of Trent; and none other left an equally impressive—both quantitatively and qualitatively—iconographic legacy, which was tantamount with inventing "an iconographic vocabulary" of ritual murder.[216] These two were, of course, related. Tiberino's detailed description of Simon's death provided fertile ground for artistic imagination, and Bishop Hinderbach, eager to promote the cult from the very beginning, was ready to exploit it.

The surviving ledger of payments suggests numerous commissions of paintings of Simon within the first year, some to be gifted to Hinderbach's supporters.[217] As early as May 1475, Hinderbach commissioned a painting to depict "the boy with the Jews" and the boy's martyrdom. On June 1 he paid six marcs to a painter in Brescia for a painting with two images representing "the boy and Jews, and his passion," and another two marcs for "remaining completed works of the boy's passion and S. Vigilio, and other images."[218] In October, Rafaele Zovenzoni thanked the bishop for sending "the most holy image" of the boy, which moved him to tears.[219] And by the fall of 1475 iconographic depictions of Simon's story began to be disseminated in the earnest, first focusing on the imagery of *Simon victima*, Simon as victim (Figs. 0.2 and 2.1), and *martyrio*, depicting "the passion of Simon as he was being killed by Jews," and then gradually transforming into what would later become the dominant, at least in Italy, imagery of Simon in glory, known as *Simonino in gloria*, or *Simon triumphans*.[220]

On September 6, 1475, a few days after Battista de' Giudici arrived in Trent, local printer Albertus Kunne published a thirteen-leaf chapbook in German commissioned either by the bishop or his chamberlain Hermann Schindeleyp, which recounted the story of "the holy child" Simon "killed by Jews in Trent."[221] The chapbook was the first work ever printed in Trent, and was revolutionary in the history of printing.[222] It was the first to contain woodcuts directly related to the text and the story (Figs. 2.2–2.5) that faithfully illustrate the words on the opposite page; until then woodcuts were typically generic, with the same ones often reused in different contexts.[223] In the 1475 chapbook, the first image shows the scene of several Jews—all named—conspiring to kidnap a Christian child; the second depicts Tobias capturing Simon and bringing him to the synagogue; the next two images are devoted to Simon's martyrdom—in one, Simon is depicted with arms stretched out and held by Moses, the only bearded figure, and Samuel, with Tobias pulling his flesh with pincers, Israel handing nails or needles to Angel, while Vitale looks on. These are followed by an image of a Passover seder (Fig. 3.4), which in turn is followed by a scene depicting the Jews' efforts to hide the boy's body in the river flowing under Samuel's house.

The next two images are devoted to the discovery of the body (Fig. 3.5) and its deposition on the altar, while the remaining three illustrate the execution of the Jews. Jews in this chapbook are not only named but they are also iconographically discernible through their pointed hats, a symbol used in Christian art to mark Jews visually since the twelfth century.[224] (The hats were painted yellow in one copy preserved at the August Herzog library in Wolfenbüttel.[225]) This distinction is most striking in the image of the capture of Simon, in which Simon's headgear is different from that of Tobias, but is similar to those covering the heads of the Christian officials depicted in the discovery of Simon's body (Figs. 2.2 and 3.5). The pointed hat is an important marking device in the three images depicting the execution of the Jews: it is conspicuously present on the heads of the naked figures led to the stake and missing from the very last image in the book,

FIG. 3.4 Passover seder, *Hystorie von Simon zu Trient* (Trent: Albert Kunne, September 6, 1475), 6v. Bayerische StaatsBibliothek, 2 Inc.s.a. 62#Beibd.

depicting the execution of the three Jews who had converted to Christianity (Figs. 3.6 and 3.7).

Kunne's imagery not only tells a sophisticated story of Simon and the aftermath of his death but also evokes Christological imagery familiar from medieval Catholic devotional art; it was meant both to inspire devotion to Simon and to justify actions taken against the Jews. And it was not simply the image of Simon stretched in the form of the cross that alluded to Christ. Scene one, for example, depicts Jews plotting to kidnap a Christian child, illustrating the text that is based on Tiberino's narrative, in which one of the Jews noted that they had everything ready for the festival—the fish and the lamb—but were missing only one thing, the Christian child. The fish and the lamb, seen in the woodcut, were symbols commonly associated with Christ (Fig. 3.8). Scene three, which illustrates Simon's circumcision, closely resembles northern European, especially German, depictions of Christ's

FIG. 3.5 Examination of Simon's body after its discovery, *Hystorie von Simon zu Trient* (Trent: Albert Kunne, September 6, 1475), 8v. Bayerische StaatsBibliothek, 2 Inc.s.a. 62#Beibd.

circumcision, in which the child is held on the knees of a bearded man and another man circumcises the infant, with women either entirely absent or gazing at the ceremony from the sidelines (Fig. 2.3); in the Italian depictions, by contrast, women are often present during the ceremony, with Mary even touching or holding the child.[226] One also wonders if scene six (Fig. 3.4), depicting the Passover seder, would have reminded viewers of the imagery of the Last Supper.[227] With bread and wine on the oblong table, typical of Italian representations of the Last Supper, the bearded Moses sits in the middle and reaches out for bread in front of him. He is flanked by other Jews: the nearest to the viewer is a Jew with a money sack conspicuously visible, reminiscent of the position Judas has in many of the paintings of the Last Supper. Even the women on the side resemble the occasional depiction of Mary Magdalene at the Last Supper.[228]

Echoes of Simon of Trent in European Culture   131

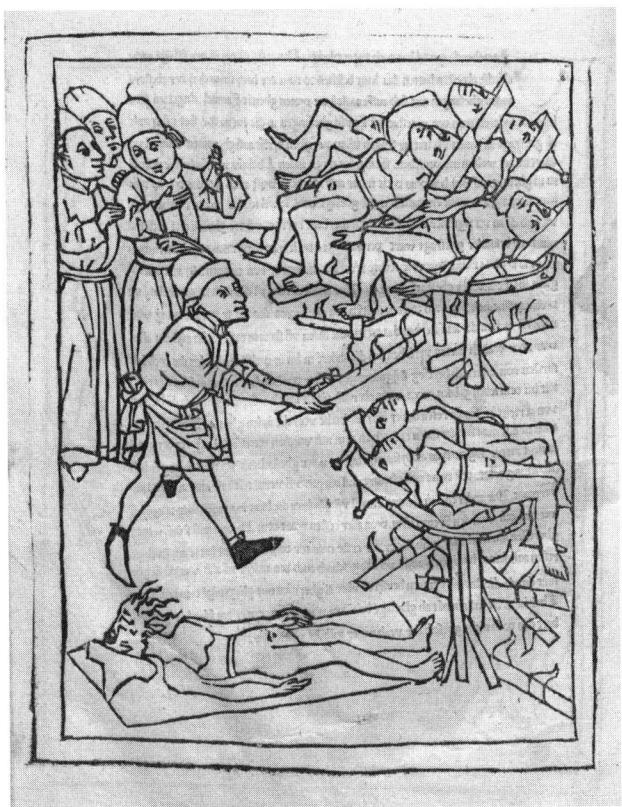

FIG. 3.6 Jews put to the flames, *Hystorie von Simon zu Trient* (Trent: Albert Kunne, September 6, 1475), 11v. Bayerische StaatsBibliothek, 2 Inc.s.a. 62#Beibd.

As David Areford has noted, Kunne's pictorial story of Simon's death and its aftermath is also redemptive. One image (see Fig. 2.5) shows the child's body on the altar with people surrounding it and Hinderbach kneeling next to it, with Saint Peter, the namesake of the church where Simon's body had been placed, "at the boy's head and Vigilio, the city's bishop saint . . . at his feet."[229] The redemptive meaning is also encoded in the last three images portraying the execution of the Jews: the evil deed was punished and several souls were saved through baptism (Figs. 3.6–3.7).

Soon after Kunne published this illustrated version of Simon's story, another illustrated chapbook was published in Augsburg: a German translation of Tiberino's work by Ginther Zainer. It has thirteen woodcuts that also correspond closely to the text and the story, but are different from those found in Kunne's work.[230] In Zainer's work, Jews do not have distinct

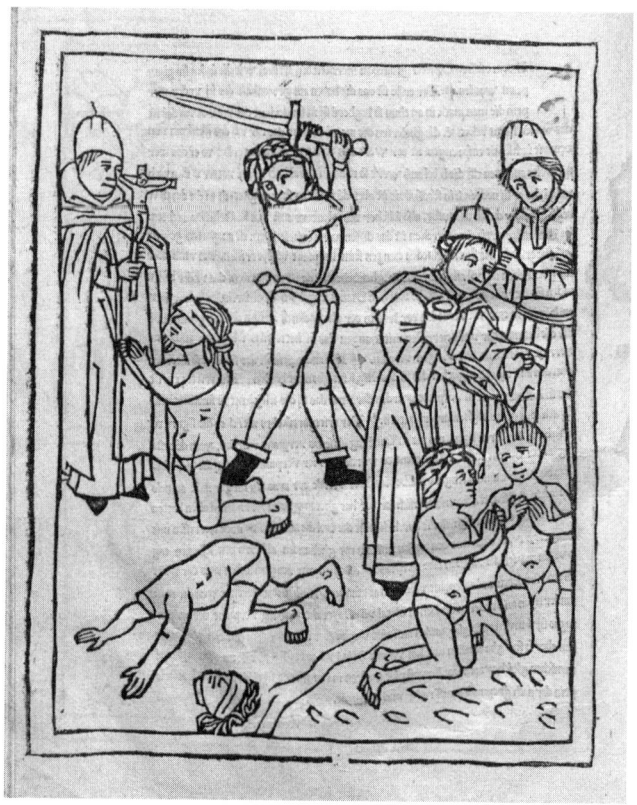

FIG. 3.7 Execution of the baptized Jews, *Hystorie von Simon zu Trient* (Trent: Albert Kunne, September 6, 1475), 12v. Bayerische StaatsBibliothek, 2 Inc.s.a. 62#Beibd.

pointed hats. In fact, some wear no head covering at all, and most are not easily discernible as Jews (Fig. 3.9).[231] The same is true of a 1475 broadsheet depicting Simon's martyrdom (Fig. 2.6), which likely was the model for the depiction of Simon in Schedel's 1493 chronicle (Fig. 1.2). Other pamphlets and broadsheets with woodcuts depicting Simon continued to appear in the region and beyond.[232] These often sharpened the anti-Jewish tone by heightening the contrast between the holiness of the innocent child and the cruelty of Jews through features stereotypically associated with Jews: hats, disfigured ugly faces, and sacks with money. These were then juxtaposed with Simonine imagery that alluded to imagery clearly associated with Christ.[233]

This rapid proliferation of imagery, devotion, and preaching about Simon disturbed Pope Sixtus IV. In his October 10, 1475, letter to "all rulers and officials in Italy," in which he prohibited calling Simon *beatus* and preaching

FIG. 3.8 Jews with Christian symbols of fish and lamb, *Hystorie von Simon zu Trient* (Trent: Albert Kunne, September 6, 1475), 1v. Bayerische StaatsBibliothek, 2 Inc.s.a. 62#Beibd.

in public that "he was a martyr, killed by Jews" by being "crucified," the pope also forbade "to paint images," write historical narratives about Simon's death and the alleged miracles following it, and "to sell" and "display them in public for sale."[234] Such images were not to be held in churches or private homes.[235] All this, the pope warned, "incited Christians against all Jews and their property," endangering their lives.

Not even a month after the pope's letter, on November 5, 1475, the doge of Venice, Pietro Mocenigo, seconded the papal prohibition, decreeing that "no person of any condition may dare or presume in any place to depict or

⁋ Vnd da nun die vesperzeyt vergangen was / Da
gieng der verräter der Thobias auß / vnd gieng allenthalben vmb bey seinem nachbawern / Vnd da er
kam in die gassen die man nennet auf dem Graben /
Da gieng er schnell hinter vnd fürsich / vnd fand ein
gar schön tegenkind sitzent vor der tür seines vatters
das hieß Symon / newnundzwaintzig monade alt
Das was also schön das nyemandt an im erschen
mochte / das an im von natur vergessen wäre vnd
straffberiet sach das kind an / vnd lüget fleyßlich ob
nyemand des kindes acht hette / Da er nyemand sach
da reckte er im dar seinen finger der thobias mit im
lachend als man mit kinden thüt / Das ynnigklich
schön kind daz dan als ein lämlein senftmütig was
vnd leychte auf zebewegend / Nam mit seinem zarten
händlein lindlich den finger vnd stünd auf an dem
finger vnd gyeng mit im gnappend swachlich mit
seinen swachen füssen an dem finger / Da nun der ver-
räterisch blütverkauffer mit dem vil schöne kind vo
seines vatters hauß kam / da nam er mit seiner mu-
bilchen band das vil schön kindlin des kindes vnd

FIG. 3.9 Tobias ordered to kidnap a Christian child. Johannes Tiberinus, *Die Geschicht und Legend von dem seligen Kind und Marterer gennant Symon von den Juden au Trent gemartet und gemortet*. Translated by Ginther Zainer. (Augsburg: Ginther Zainer, 1475).

have depicted, or buy or sell [images] of that little boy called Simon of Trent who was killed, as they say, by the Jews, or to preach about him in either public or private places, or to make any references to his sanctity or miracles, or to write or print anything about these miracle."[236] Mocenigo's decree was recorded in Brescia on November 18, with an explicit statement from Brescia's podestà Luca Navagerio prohibiting the promotion of Simon's imagery "on paper or on walls [*non debbia penzere ne far penzere in carte in muro*]" and selling and displaying the images of Simon as "a martyr" or "blessed" [*ne vendere imagine alguna da martyre ne beato*] in private and public.[237] Yet, despite these papal and secular prohibitions, church officials in the region continued to request Simon's relics, and the imagery of Simon's "martyrdom" was soon found in churches. In fact, one of the earliest mentions of such images comes from Brescia in an April 13, 1476, note in a local chronicle by Elia Capriolo about a miracle in a local Carmelite church, where apparently tears began to flow from "a painting of the blessed Simon of Trent."[238] In some places the frescos were placed on the outside walls and building facades for all to see.[239] Hinderbach did not skimp on funds to commission paintings depicting the story.[240] And some churches embraced the iconography that was rapidly spread by the printing press, using them as models. This is certainly evident in the sequence recently discovered in Albino in the district of Bergamo, painted in the 1480s in the Church of San Bartolomeo.[241] It seems that the painter knew the representations of Simon's story published by both Kunne and Zainer.

As depictions of Simon's story spread, regional differences in imagery across Europe became visible. Although in some places the full narrative of Simon's story was pictorially depicted following Kunne's chapbook, two images—the scene of Simon's martyrdom, his arms spread, his body cut and stabbed by the Jews (*marytrio*), and Simon's naked lifeless body, with wounds exposed for the world to see (*victima*)—became the dominant iconographic representations of Jewish ritual murder north of the Alps, whereas Simon Triumphant became dominant in Italy.[242] The most prominent example of the *martyrio* is found in the 1493 chronicle of the world by Hartmann Schedel, who owned several early broadsheets depicting Simon (Fig. 1.2). The image of Simon *victima* could be found, most famously, at the entry gate to Frankfurt, where it remained until the second half of the eighteenth century, despite numerous Jewish protestations (Fig. 0.2).[243]

Still, if the emotive imagery of Simon's martyrdom emerged, as Laura del Prà has argued, from the evocative Simonine narrative, it was not devoid of devotional significance. Its focus on the violent act of killing, which doubtless was aimed at demonizing Jews as dangerous murderers, alluded to the suffering Christ, increasingly depicted in late medieval Christian art, especially in fifteenth-century northern Europe, as the bloodied and suffering "Man of Sorrows."[244] Simon's outstretched arms resemble the crucified Christ, while Jews collecting his blood evoke the imagery of Christ on the cross bleeding into a chalice. Reminding viewers of the Jews' perceived role in Christ's death, even the devotional Simonine imagery was at times infused with anti-Jewish undertones. One of the most explicit examples may be a late fifteenth-century fresco in St. Martin's church in Cerveno, with a scene of Simon's martyrdom directly under a much larger fresco representing the crucifixion of Christ.[245]

In Italy, the anti-Jewish tone in Simonine iconography gradually softened and later almost disappeared, at least until the eighteenth century. To be sure, as part of Hinderbach's efforts to promote Simon's cause during the first years, the images of Simon tortured by Jews, his arms outstretched, with Jews on both sides holding "a knife and needles," were widely produced and reproduced also in Italy.[246] But after about 1480, the motif of violent martyrdom was largely displaced by the iconography of *Simon triumphans*, Simon Triumphant—depicting Simon in glory, usually standing naked, though occasionally dressed in a red or gray tunic—and, reminiscent of iconography of Jesus Triumphant, holding a white banner with a red cross or another object revealing the tools of his passion (Figs. 0.3, 3.2, and 3.3).[247] Currently, of the images of Simon surviving in northern Italy, only about 20 percent show the martyrdom scene; the vast majority (about 70 percent) are images of Simon Triumphant.[248]

One of the first surviving and datable instances of Simon Triumphant comes from Rovato's Church of Santo Stefano, near Brescia.[249] Dated to August 1478 and thus painted just two months after the bull exonerating Hinderbach, the fresco shows Simon in the triumphant pose symbolizing the living host, an image of a child often evoked to illustrate transubstantiation, his body suspended over an altar.[250] Images of Simon Triumphant reminded viewers of the imagery of the Child Christ, which became increasingly popular, as David Areford has noted, in northern Italy in the decades preceding Simon's death.[251]

If the post–fifteenth-century iconography of Simon in Italy was dominated by single images of Simon in glory, sometimes along with Mary and the Christ Child, Simonine imagery north of the Alps focused on Jews' barbarity, embracing the image of Simon's "martyrdom" or Simon the victim. In rare instances Simon Triumphant images are combined with more explicit anti-Jewish motifs. For example, in the 1511 edition of Ubertino Pusculo's work published in Augsburg, there are two images of Simon Triumphant trampling on a Jew; such images appear rarely in church iconography in northern Italy.[252] In 1668, an engraving of Simon Triumphant trampling

Jews was included in Michelangelo Mariani's work *Il glorioso infante S. Simone* (see Fig 3.3).[253] Simon, dressed in a tunic, stands holding a banner with *arma Simonis*, the tools of his passion, attached to a pole in the shape of a cross; he is looking toward heaven, pointing his finger at angels and cherubs—one of which is offering the boy a crown of laurels—and stomping on Jews lying on the ground.[254]

After the flurry of artistic production in the first decades following the trial, few new works of art were produced in the first half of the sixteenth century. But the enduring artistic traces inside churches and chapels, and on building facades, no doubt contributed to the formal recognition of the cult of Simon and to the granting of the *officium*, a service in his name, in 1588 by Pope Sixtus V. For the locals, the 1588 bull was a formality; as far as they were concerned Simon was recognized as a saint in 1583, when he was first inserted into *Martyrologium romanum*, with Pope Gregory XIII's blessing.[255]

The official papal recognition of Simon's cult led to a renewed interest in his story. Newly printed works, some accompanied by woodcuts and engravings, began to appear, with Ambrogio Franco's 1586 *Martirio del beato Simone Trentino* (The Martyrdom of Blessed Simon of Trent) beginning the trend. These post-1583 works often display images of Simon Triumphant. The 1588 publication of the *officium* featured the same woodcut as the 1589 work *Martirio di S. Simone di Trento* (Martyrdom of St. Simon of Trent) by Antonio Gesti, parish priest of the Church of St. Peter in Trent, and as the 1608 edition of Franco's book, now published under the same title as Gesti's, depicting Simon in glory holding a banner and the tools of his passion, *arma passionis* (Fig. 3.2).[256] The 1655 edition of the liturgy (*officium*) for March 24, Simon's feast day, published in Trent by the episcopal printing house, is also adorned with an image of Simon Triumphant, this one similar to the 1586 edition of Ambrogio Franco's *Martirio*.[257] Single-sheet images, presumably sold to pilgrims, were also printed. Simon appears in his glory in paintings and prints in the company of the saints Vigilio (first bishop of Trent), Massenza, the martyrs of Anaunia, and others. But even that imagery has a precedent in Albert Kunne's 1475 illustrated chapbook.[258]

Tridentine Topography of the Cult

There is little doubt Bishop Hinderbach was seeking to establish the cult of Little Simon from the moment the child's body was found, but it is unclear when a formal pilgrimage route reminiscent of the Way of the Cross was established in the city. Still, soon after Simon's death, Hinderbach ordered some of the sites to be converted into devotional spaces, among them Samuel's house, which was to be turned into a chapel "in honor of the passion of our lord Jesus Christ and all his innocent saints and martyrs."[259] By 1515 pilgrims coming to Trent could visit, as German Has Stockar recounted in his diary, "the church of the holy boy, . . . where his body is venerated as a relic, . . . the childhood home of the holy boy, and the house of the Jews."[260]

But whether organized processions were part of the city's annual cycle is not known; the early sources make no mention of them. If they did occur at some point in the decades before 1588, they must have been forgotten, because in 1589, a year after Pope Sixtus V's *breve* granting the liturgy and indulgences, Gesti's *Martirio di S. Simone di Trento* not only discussed, as the subtitle states, "the great cruelty of the wicked Jews, with which they martyred him," but also promised to tell "how he was included in the catalogue of saints," and about "the solemn procession done during his *first* feast" (emphasis added) and "many miracles performed by this saint."[261] (The part of Gesti's work describing the story of Simon's death and aftermath seems to be heavily based on Ambrogio Franco's 1586 *Martirio del beato Simone Trentino*.)

That Gesti called Simon a "saint" in his title, while in 1586 Franco used the term "blessed" *(beato)*, indicates the unclear status Simon had in the eyes of many. For Gesti, Simon had already been recognized saint by Pope Gregory XIII when the boy was included in the liturgical calendar *Martyrologium romanum*.[262] Franco's use of the term *beato* in 1586, in turn, suggests he may have understood that a formal canonization process was necessary to call Simon a saint.

For Gesti, Sixtus V's granting of the *officium* in 1588 was but a formality to allow observance of the cult throughout the diocese, and the sought-after grant of a plenary indulgence was most worthy of ceremonial commemoration.[263] As a result of the "happy" fact that "the Holy Martyr" was placed in the "catalogue of the saints," the canons of the Trent cathedral "ordered" that the first solemn procession be organized during the first vespers of March 23 (in Italy, unlike in northern Europe, days were counted from sunset to sunset) to thank God for "the great favor and to honor" the little martyr. The faithful who visited Trent on March 24, the new feast day devoted to Simon, went to confession and took communion in the Church of St. Peter, where "there is a consecrated altar dedicated to the Martyr, with his body, which is found intact, and the instruments of his glorious martyrdom," and the worshipers would be now rewarded with a remission of sins.[264]

Gesti described this solemn procession in detail. The Church of St. Peter, where Simon's body was on display, was "adorned with rich and graceful tapestries and different lights, as would require such solemn occasion."[265] A high platform, "adorned with different cloths, and silk and golden textiles," was placed in the middle of the chancel. At noon "the body of the holy martyr" was placed on this decorated platform for all to see. Gesti reported that a great multitude of people came from different parts of the city and abroad both to see "the Sacred Body" and to receive "holy indulgencies in remission of their sins."[266]

Just before the vespers, cathedral canons dressed in festive garments arrived with "all the reverend priests and clerics, not only from the city but also from many places and rural parishes in the diocese, and with the reverend religious."[267] After a public prayer, the procession began, in which the distinguished clergy were joined by members of many pious fraternities carrying "candles, banners, and crosses." Among them were "over two hundred children, dressed in most beautiful vestments of gold and silver, [holding] in hand flags with the image of the saint." Four priests then lifted Simon's body in a coffin made of gold and silver from the platform and placed it on an ornate catafalque to be seen by people watching the procession. The catafalque was adorned with a baldachin made of cloth-of-gold. Then "all the councilors, doctors, and nobles of the city followed devoutly." Finally came women accompanied by children, carrying banners, torches, and candles. All in all, Gesti claimed, more than thirteen thousand participated.[268]

The route of the procession included almost all the churches in Trent: from St. Peter's the participants went to the Church of Holy Trinity, the Cathedral Church of St. Vigilio, and Santa Maria Maggiore, "stopping in each and placing the body in a place prepared in the chancel of these churches."[269] When the procession returned to St. Peter's, the participants chanted the vesper prayer devoted to Simon and "Te Deum laudamus," a hymn in Catholic liturgy sung in thanksgiving to God on special occasions. By 1668, in place of Simon's body, a reliquary with his blood was used in the procession, though later, it seems, the coffin with his remains was carried again.[270]

Although the route of the annual procession continued to include all churches in Trent, other places related to Simon's story were available for pilgrims to visit regardless of the time of year. Among the sites pilgrims and travelers could see was Simon's house, which in 1668, as Michelangelo Mariani reported, was uninhabited, so that "this place would not be profaned by an earthly foot."[271] Above the entry door, Mariani wrote, "One could see the painted image of the triumphant holy martyr, and below a painting of his kidnapping and an inscription in German and in Latin, 'In this house was born the blessed Simon, whose body rests in the Church of St. Peter's, and who in the year of our Lord Jesus Christ 1475 was kidnapped on this street.'"[272] The house, today on via del Simonino, still shows the now-faint painting of Simon triumphant, but the images of Simon's kidnapping and martyrdom have been replaced by a statue of Simon (Fig. 3.10).[273]

Another site in the pilgrims' itinerary was Samuel's house, turned into a chapel by Bishop Hinderbach and restored in the late sixteenth century, perhaps because of the papal recognition of the cult, thanks to the efforts of Cardinal Ludovico Madruzzo. Despite the restorations and the building's transformation into a church, Mariani claimed, there remained original details: the door through which the boy was passed by Tobias into Samuel's hands—a scene widely depicted in Simonine iconography—"the vestibule of the synagogue, the place of the very synagogue, which now serves as a church."[274] Inside, one could also see the cellar where the body had been found and the water in the canal into which the corpse was said to have been thrown. There was also, as Mariani noted, a painting of "the whole history of the Holy Martyr."[275] Samuel's house, now church, was, by Mariani's time, "expressly" included on the route of the annual procession. Having visited Simon's house and the place Tridentine citizens believed to have been the place of his martyrdom, pilgrims could now walk to the place of his apotheosis, the Church of St. Peter's, where they could view the boy's body along with instruments of his passion, or *arma Simonis*; the *ex voti*, which served as proofs of the boy's miraculous interventions; and other relics related to the boy: a chalice with his "uncorrupted" blood, his shoes, and vestments.[276]

And pilgrims did pass through. "Not only the low folks," Michelangelo Mariani wrote, "but also primates, grand personalities" supported the cult and visited Trent. In the fifteenth century, the queen of Denmark, for example, came to worship the little martyr.[277] Queen Maria Anna of Spain stayed, with Ferdinand IV of Hungary, in Trent for several months in the 1640s (the date in Mariani's book is 1649, but Maria Anna died in 1646[278]). In 1651, Eleanora Gonzaga passed through Trent on her way to Vienna where she was to marry Emperor Ferdinand III. Four years later, Christina Alexandra of Sweden visited Trent on her way to Rome, following her abdication from the throne and conversion to Catholicism. Ambassadors, nuncios, and other high officials inevitably stopped in Trent on their way to or from Rome, and they, Mariani claimed, could not but be moved by the "sacred curiosity." What is more, even "heretic princes love to revere the Holy Innocent Simon," seeing him not so much as an object of curiosity but as "a representation of the Passion of Christ."[279]

FIG. 3.10 Fresco on the site of Simon's house, today on via del Simonino, still shows the painting of Simon triumphant. Previous images of Simon's kidnapping and martyrdom have been replaced by a statue of Simon, also in the triumphant pose. Author photo.

Finding Simon of Trent in Poland

Pilgrims helped publicize the cult. Mariani reported hearing about the faithful venerating Simon not only in Italy, France, and Germany but also in Poland and Flanders.[280] He was certainly correct; the cult of Simon was known in Poland, thanks not only to Skarga but also to Polish pilgrims and travelers visiting Rome who stopped in Trent. Some even settled in the region. Painter Marcin Teofilowicz (1570–1639), known in Italy as Martino Teofilo Polacco, was active in Tyrol and Trent. His oeuvre included paintings of Simon of Trent. One, "Madonna with a child, Saint Francis and Little Simon," was in fact placed in the church established in Samuel's house, the former synagogue; another, now in Spormaggiore, is "The Coronation of the Virgin," which prominently depicts local saints, including Simon of Trent in the right bottom corner.[281] Books about Simon made their way to Poland as well. The Camedule Brothers in Bielany near Cracow possessed a copy of Ambrogio Franco's *Martirio di S. Simone di Trento* (1608).[282]

But perhaps most notorious for spreading Simonine iconography in Poland was Stefan Żuchowski, a Polish priest who visited Trent in 1699 on his way to Rome, just one year after he had spearheaded a trial of Jews in the town of Sandomierz, where he was a canon, accusing them of murdering a Christian child.[283] In Trent Żuchowski would have surely seen Simon's body and relics, displayed prominently to the public. A contemporary of his, albeit a Protestant, described the sight: "The dead body of Simon lies for all to see completely naked and rather black in the middle of the altar in St. Peter's Church in Trent, surrounded by bright glass. And no stranger will come to Trent who will not ask to see this hallmark of the city. I myself did this with a friend when I traveled to Italy."[284] Żuchowski would have also seen the numerous works of art on public view: the representation of Simon's kidnapping painted above the entry door to Simon's house on via Simonino and the 1668 series of paintings by Pietro Ricchi in the chapel devoted to Simon in St. Peter's Church. He would have also seen the spaces and paintings in Samuel's house, the former synagogue turned into a chapel.[285] He also bought a book about Simon while in Italy—Giovanni da Padova's *Martirio crudele dato da gli ebrei a S. Simone innocente da Trento*, published in Trent in 1690.[286]

A few years after his return to Sandomierz, Żuchowski again became embroiled in a lengthy trial against Jews of his town, once more accusing them of killing a Christian child. This trial, which lasted from 1710 to 1713, left behind not only grief and pain in the Jewish community but also literary and iconographic traces of the tragic events. Żuchowski published two apologetic books about the trials he had spearheaded. He also sponsored a series of sixteen grand paintings inspired by the liturgical calendar *Martyrologium romanum* for the collegiate church, now a cathedral, in Sandomierz.[287] Twelve of the paintings represent scenes of martyrdom for each month and day. Four others show local instances of "martyrdom," including *Infanticidia*, a vivid painting representing Jews killing a Christian child. And although this painting was indeed intended to illustrate the two cases of ritual murder that Żuchowski championed in Sandomierz, its presence within the *Martyrologium romanum* tied it to the Trent story, both because traditionally martyrological calendars sought to connect local martyrs with the universal liturgical calendar accepted by the church and because Simon had been officially included in the *Martyrologium* since 1583.

Yet if the painting *Infanticidia* in Sandomierz alludes to Simon of Trent only indirectly by association with the *Martyrologium romanum*, far more explicit are seven paintings in the chancel of the Church of St. Paul's in the town.[288] These paintings, despite claims they represent local events, most definitely depict the Trent story. Until their recent restoration, frames on at least three of them contained inscriptions in Latin.[289] One, on the painting showing the kidnapping of the child (Fig. 3.11), read, "Tobias Judaeus puerum rapit et eum synagogam clam inducit" (Tobias the Jew snatches the boy and furtively leads him to the synagogue). There was no Tobias in Sandomierz; of course, Tobias of Trent was a major figure known for his role in kidnapping Simon and was widely represented in iconography.[290] Furthermore, the text found on the frame closely echoed the opening words from the liturgy for Simon of Trent: "Tobias iniquus rapuit beatum Simonem et eum in Synagogam clam deduxit" (Hostile Tobias kidnapped the blessed Simon and brought him furtively to the synagogue).[291] The text in Sandomierz is shorter, but this may be because of the space available on the frame.

Inscriptions on the other frames are more general and mention no specific names. The painting depicting a meal at a table once bore the line "Dicunt judaei perforavimus venas pueri nunc in contemptum Jesu Sanguinem eius bibamus" (Jews say we pierced the boy's veins, now we drink his blood in contempt of Jesus). This line, too, closely resembles a sentence from Simon's *officium* used to celebrate mass in his honor in Trent: "Tenentes puerum saeui carnifices, dicebant ad invicem perforemus venas eius et sanguinem eius bibamus" (Holding the boy the ferocious tormenters were saying to one another we shall pierce his veins and drink his blood).[292] The line in Sandomierz seems to be a conflation of two lines in the Simonine liturgy: "in contemptum Iesu" can be found a few lines after the one referring to the drinking of blood.[293]

FIG. 3.11 "Tobias the Jew snatches the boy and furtively leads him to the synagogue," St. Paul's Church, Sandomierz, Poland, eighteenth century. Photo by Roman Chyła, 1996, before restoration.

The painting depicting the scene of the boy's death displays Simonine iconographic clues—including the white scarf with which Simon was said to have been strangled (Fig. 3.12)—and contained an inscription, "Extensus in modum crucis puer ac *forticibus* [forcipibus] et *acutus* [acubus] toto corpores *sanciatus* [sauciatus] elevatis oculis in coelum sanctum emisit spiritum" (The boy, extended in the form of the cross and hurt all over the body with pincers and nails, having lifted his eyes toward heaven, gave up his holy spirit).[294] Like the two other inscriptions, this too is an almost verbatim rendition of a phrase found in the *officium*.[295] And like the other inscriptions, this one also omits the name Simon.

The differences between the text of the Simonine liturgy and the inscriptions in Sandomierz may be explained by the limited space in the frames, efforts to tie the story of Simon to local events, or perhaps even memory lapses by the painter Carlo de Prevo.[296] But if they were due to the painter's memory, understandably shaky after decades of living in Poland, it would suggest that the painter, about whose life before coming to Poland little is known, may have hailed from Trent or its surroundings or from a town familiar with the Simonine cult, liturgy, and iconography. For even though Stefan Żuchowski visited Trent in 1699 on his way to Rome and may have even brought a copy of the *officium* or some broadsides home, he could not have retained as detailed knowledge of Simonine iconography as is on

FIG. 3.12 A scene of boy's death with Simonine iconographic clues, including the white scarf with which Simon was said to have been strangled. St. Paul's Church, Sandomierz, Poland. This image is derivative of a scene in a broadside dedicated to Aliprando Madruzzo, now at the Wolfegg Castle in the Wolfegger Kabinett (Capriotti, *Lo Scorpione Sul Petto*, 150, fig. 60; another version in Zgliński, "Nagrobki i Kult Ofiar," 311).

display; he may have, however, requested that the Italian painter represent the story in Sandomierz.

The Italian influences are uncanny. The two scenes in the Church of St. Paul in Sandomierz of the meal and of the killing of the boy bear a startling resemblance to two scenes in broadsides published in Trent at the end of the sixteenth or early seventeenth century (one was dedicated to Aliprando Madruzzo, who died in 1606, and another is undated with a different image at the center).[297] The gestures and layout of the paintings are clearly based on these broadsides. Even more striking is the resemblance of the painting depicting Tobias to one of the narrative scenes of a 1597 painting, "San Simonino da Trento" by Pietromartino di Anversa (also known as Pier Martino Fiammingo), a Flemish painter from Antwerp active in the 1590s in Umbria,[298] originally displayed on the third altar on the left of the Church of Santa Maria dei Fossi (or degli Angeli) in Perugia, now at the Galleria Nazionale there.[299] This painting was no doubt created in light of the renewed interest in Simon's story following the formal recognition of his cult. The color scheme and presentation of the Sandomierz representation of Tobias are very similar to this painting. The vestment and position of Tobias, as well as the vestment and position of the child, are nearly identical

FIG. 3.13 "Raptus," a scene from a painting by Pietromartino di Anversa, "San Simonino da Trento" (1597), Galleria Nazionale dell'Umbria, nr. 485.

(Fig. 3.13). Also similar are the buildings, with a bell tower, a gate, and open shops. Indeed, even the painting of ritual murder in the Sandomierz cathedral bears some resemblance to Pietromartino's work.[300] Given the location of Pietromartino's painting in the church in Perugia, the section with Tobias kidnapping Simon would have been at eye level and visible to the faithful. Perhaps Carlo de Prevo spent some time in Perugia and knew the painting well.

There are also differences between the paintings in the Sandomierz church of St. Paul and that by Pietromartino di Anversa. But they too underscore the significance of the story and early Simonine iconography. In Pietromartino's portrayal of Simon is dressed in accordance with historical records in a gray tunic and a white apron, whereas in Sandomierz, Simon is shown wearing a red tunic with a white apron. Red, or crimson, as we have seen, was a symbol of Christ's tunic and was used in both literary imagery and in Simonine iconography to connect the alleged child victims with representations of Christ.[301] Simon appears twice in this outfit in Sandomierz, once with Tobias and another time standing in the corner while Jews sit and celebrate around the table, a scene copied from a Simonine broadside.[302]

In Pietromartino's painting, the representation of Tobias—his hat and black cloak—seems reminiscent of late sixteenth-century representations of Sephardic Jews or, especially in Flanders, the "marranos," crypto-Jews from Spain and Portugal; this may be a surprising choice of imagery given that Tobias was an Ashkenazi Jew, but perhaps less so given that Pietromartino hailed from Flanders. Moreover, like Tobias, the marranos were seen as "mediators" between Jewish and Christian societies.[303] That the Sandomierz paintings would be so closely related to the story of Simon of Trent may be surprising and only partly explained by Stefan Żuchowski's trip to Trent. The Italian artist, Carlo de Prevo, may have been intimately familiar with Simonine iconography, including Pietromartino's painting.

But in Sandomierz, the link to the Simon story was quickly forgotten, and in modern times it has been totally lost. A 1915 book described the paintings as "an illustrated history of the little boy, Jerzy Krasnowski, killed in Sandomierz in 1710."[304] Some two decades later, the Polish writer Jarosław Iwaszkiewicz also saw the paintings as a reflection of the trials in Sandomierz when he referred to the river visible in one of the paintings as the Vistula.[305] And the recent restoration of the paintings in the Church of St. Paul entirely removed any traces of this connection: the texts on the frames that linked the paintings in the Sandomierz to Simon of Trent were painted over. To viewers today the story represented there is entirely local, with no outside connection, no historical and iconographic legacy. To be sure, even in the eighteenth century when these paintings were commissioned and created, their content was chosen in the context of the local trials of Jews. (At least two allude to the local story by displaying a child's body vomited by a dog, and in another a child is inside a barrel, though this motif is already present in Piotr Skarga's version of Simon's story.[306]) The fact that the descriptions of these paintings do not mention Simon's name only underscores the conscious play on both Simon's story and the local trials. But unlike today, when the connection between Sandomierz and Trent is entirely forgotten, in the eighteenth century the connection to events from Trent would have served to justify and frame the accusations of local Jews. That is certainly how Stefan Żuchowski saw it.[307] And although the Sandomierz iconography was heavily rooted in the Italian tradition, the paintings' focus on the cruelty of the Jews and not the apotheosis of the child reflects northern European sensibilities. In Sandomierz, the motif of the child as a victim of a cruel murder triumphed.

Simonine iconography could also be found in other places in Poland, at times connecting Simon's story with local cases. One such painting, now lost, used to hang in Kalwaria Zebrzydowska, near Cracow, in the monastery of the Bernardines, as the observant branch of the Minor Order of the Franciscans is known in Poland.[308] The painting depicts a scene, familiar from Simonine iconography, of Jews donning prayer shawls and torturing a boy who stands in a basin filled with blood, arms stretched in the form of a cross, his feet held by one Jew, while other Jews prick the child's naked body with nails.[309] The painting, though harking back to Simonine imagery, was created to illustrate the 1753 "martyrdom" of a boy in Markowa Wolica near Żytomierz, now in Ukraine, a cause célèbre that would lead to a diplomatic mission of Polish Jews to Rome. Indeed, the work shows thirteen Jews, the number killed as a result of the trial in Żytomierz.

Yet the link between the painting in Kalwaria Zebrzydowska and Simon of Trent seems undeniable not only because of its iconography. Its difficult-to-read inscription (surviving only in a poor-quality photograph) mentions the "martyrdom of boy Simon" and describes the death of a boy in Markowa Wolica; that boy's name, however, was Stefan.[310] The switch of names may have been a mistake, or it may have been a conscious choice to magnify the meaning of the death of a peasant boy in Poland by conflating it with the most famous case of "a child killed by Jews." (Polish scholar Jolanta Żyndul has suggested that the painting in Kalwaria Zebrzydowska may have been donated by Bishop Kajetan Sołtyk who was personally involved in the 1753 trial.[311])

This painting is linked to Simon of Trent in yet another, perhaps more tangential way. Franciscan friars minor were historically key actors in both the spread of anti-Jewish sentiments in Europe and in the case of Simon of Trent. Giovanni Capistrano (1385–1456) preached widely in northern Italy, as well as in Poland and Bohemia, against heresy and the Jews. In Trent, the Franciscan preacher Bernardino da Feltre was a key figure in inciting anti-Jewish violence, and perhaps even in inspiring the trial in Trent; more generally, Franciscan friars were important promoters of the cult.[312] Perhaps coincidentally, Pope Sixtus V, who formally recognized the cult of Simon, was also a member of this order.

In Poland, too, the Franciscan Bernadine monasteries became loci for bodies of children whose deaths were blamed on Jews. In Wilno, in 1592, the Bernardine friars agreed to bury the body of a boy Szymon Kierelis in their church, and in 1623 they placed a plaque commemorating his death; in 1639 in Łęczyca, the child's body was placed in a glass coffin in their church, and a commissioned painting depicted Jews surrounding the body.[313] The placement of the painting in the Bernardine monastery in Kalwaria Zebrzydowska thus seems unsurprising.

Significantly, too, Kalwaria Zebrzydowska was an elaborate complex of chapels devoted to each stage of the passion of Christ, modeled on the Calvary in Jerusalem and known since 1669 as the Polish "Jerusalem." It became the site of an annual reenactment of the passion of Christ. Since the painting of ritual murder in Kalwaria Zebrzydowska depicts the scene of *martyrio* of "the child Simon," harkening to Jesus's crucifixion, its Christological connection was amplified, reminding pilgrims of the role Jews were said to play in both.[314]

The artistic legacy left by the cult of Simon of Trent reveals even sharper geographic differences than its literature. Perhaps because the battle for Simon's beatification and sainthood preoccupied his Italian promoters, in Italy the iconography of Simon Triumphant dominated even in the years immediately following the trial. Over the next century or so, artists played with the semiotic symbols of blessedness or sainthood, assigning Simon rays or aureole depending on how they interpreted his status. In northern Europe, and especially in Poland, where the iconography of Simon entered later, patrons and artists chose to stress the cruelty of the act of murder (Fig. 3.14) and almost always connected it to local recent trials. For them Simon's story provided legitimacy for the local events.

The long-term legacy of the story Simon of Trent was thus stronger and deeper than even Bishop Hinderbach could have imagined; it reflected the cult's geographic, cultural, and chronological liminality. The original story as told by Giovanni Mattia Tiberino and his colleagues hired by Hinderbach in the immediate aftermath of the trial contained a rich palette of motifs to be exploited: Jews' supposed cruelty, hatred of Christianity, need for

FIG. 3.14 Gottfried, Johann Ludwig. *Omstandigh Vervolgh Op Joh. Lodew. Gottfrieds Historische Kronyck* (Leiden, 1698), p. 1408.

Christian blood, and economic exploitation of Christians, as well as calls for the removal of Jews from Christian society. But they also stressed Simon's holiness and hinted at the uniqueness of the case. And as the story spread, its trajectories tracked cultural differences across European lands, with northern and eastern European writers and artists exploiting the motifs of the Jewish need for blood and their cruelty and hatred of Christians. Italians, although not eschewing the descriptions of cruelty, noted the story's uniqueness and celebrated the holiness of the boy. In Italy, Simon was not one of many child victims but the main story. Elsewhere in Europe, especially in Poland, the story served to justify local accusations against Jews.

CHAPTER FOUR

Blood Libels and Cultures of Knowledge in Early Modern Europe

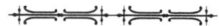

REGIONAL DIFFERENCES WERE EVIDENT not only in the iconography and reception of Simon's cult but also in the content of Christian knowledge about Jews and their ceremonies and, relatedly, the sources of that knowledge. It would be difficult to overestimate the role that early printed works played in shaping these regional epistemological trajectories. Although still steeped in medieval traditions, many early printed chronicles expanded their scope from regional or monastic contexts to tell "a universal history." Readers of those chronicles encountered Jews there even if they did not seek out works devoted to Jewish topics because inserted into their narration of the world or of European or regional histories were "events" and stories about Jews. With these chronicles Jews entered into the broader Christian memory of the past, but the role these Jewish characters played in that past molded the way readers would view Jews or "the Jews." Early printing also shaped more explicit Christian literature about Jews. In Italy and in German lands, Christian Hebraism meant that some Christians could read Jewish books. Although this knowledge was marshaled for polemical purposes, often to discredit Judaism and provide Christians with arguments against Jews, it nonetheless, with few exceptions, provided enough knowledge of Jewish customs to counter or at least mitigate accusations against the Jews.

This was not the case in Poland-Lithuania. There, as elsewhere, the earliest books about Jews shaped subsequent literature for centuries to come. But the first books about Jews were published in Poland decades after the beginning of the Reformation, which had spurred among Catholics fears of heresy and non-Catholic sources of knowledge. This made works published by Christian Hebraists, many of whom were Protestants, suspicious; it also limited what literature about Jews became available in Poland. In the end, in Poland there would be no vernacular or even Latin equivalent to books penned by Christian Hebraists in German lands and on the Italian peninsula or to works written by Jewish converts to Christianity in German lands.[1] What Christians in the Polish-Lithuanian Commonwealth absorbed about Jews from books became limited to explicitly anti-Jewish vernacular works by writers who had never studied Jewish texts. And although unlettered Christians might have learned about Jewish practices through personal interaction, sharing living space, and seeing the daily lives of Jews, for the reading public in Poland "knowledge" absorbed from books was largely shaped by anti-Jewish works steeped in ignorance about Jewish literature, religion, and religious practices. As a result, in Poland-Lithuania, unlike in Italy, the German lands, or even France, there were no voices sufficiently knowledgeable about Hebrew texts to challenge anti-Jewish accusations.

Grammars of Memory

Chronicles shaped historical memory. As Heinrich Schmidt has argued, they wrote events "into a future," making "their presence last." European chronicles, rooted in biblical and Roman models, formed what Judith Pollmann has called "an archive" of "useful knowledge that was considered to be 'true.'" They recorded "what was memorable and therefore important," mentioned or even inscribed crucial documents, and narrated power relations.[2] Chroniclers had the choice to omit stories or include them, leave them for posterity or doom them to oblivion. Chronicle narratives also supplied morality tales through stories of disorder that always ended with a resolution and return to order.

Scattered among thousands of stories, sometimes from the creation of the world to the contemporary moment, are dozens of seemingly random tales about Jews sometimes with accompanying images. Stories about Jews before the Christian era were grounded in the Bible and other ancient sources, including Josephus, but for the postbiblical period, the major sources were local annals, chronicles, and lore.

Glancing at these chronicles' indexes, which frequently did not include all the stories in each volume, provides a taste of what European readers could see that Jews historically "did" and what "was done" to them. The most famous, though not the most popular, chronicle of the world by Hartmann Schedel, published in Nuremberg in 1493, includes eleven postbiblical stories about Jews. The nine indexed under the heading "Jews": "Jews treat irreverently the venerable sacrament in the town of Deckendorff"; "Jews were burned throughout Germany because they poisoned Christian springs"; "Jews were killed and plundered by the inhabitants of Prague"; "Jews were burned by the order of Albert, the Duke of Austria"; "Jews killed a boy named Simon in the city of Trent"; "Jews in these times pierced sacred Eucharist with blood pouring"; "Jews in Nuremberg and other adjacent places were sent to fire"; "a Jew stabbed an image of Christ and blood flowed"; and "a baptized Jew returned to Judaism and was sent to fire." In short, according to Schedel, Jews kill, desecrate images and the Eucharist, poison wells and springs, and convert to Christianity but often revert to Judaism. In return they are expelled, burned, plundered, and killed.[3] The verbs are ominous. These Jewish characters were not the Jews Christians encountered everyday as their neighbors. They were imaginary figures created by Christian writers—dangerous and demonic, enemies who needed to be contained and punished.

To the stories Schedel added images that stand out on the pages and are larger and more detailed than those accompanying stories not about the Jews. For example, the story of a Jew desecrating a crucifix in the early seventh century is only seven lines long, but the image is the largest on the page (Fig. 4.1), nineteen lines in height.[4] Similarly, William of Norwich is mentioned briefly in just one sentence—"Boy William in England was crucified by Jews on Good Friday in the town of Norwich, of whose subsequent wonderful sight one can read," with an allusion to the story in Vincent de Beauvais's *Speculum historiale*—on a page containing stories of prominent Christians: Hildegard of Bingen (seven lines), Gratian (fifteen lines), Peter Lombard (nine lines), and Peter Comestor (eleven lines).[5] But the image depicting Jews crucifying William is the largest of all the images on the page, twenty-three lines high (Fig. 1.1). Three stories—the 1298 persecution of Jews by Albert I, the 1337 Deckendorff host desecration together with the persecutions in 1348 during the Black Death, and the 1492 host desecration in Sternberg—are accompanied by a prominent image of Jews being burned, also the largest on the page (Fig. 4.2);[6] And of course, there is the iconic image of Simon of Trent, which takes up more than a half-page (Fig. 1.2).

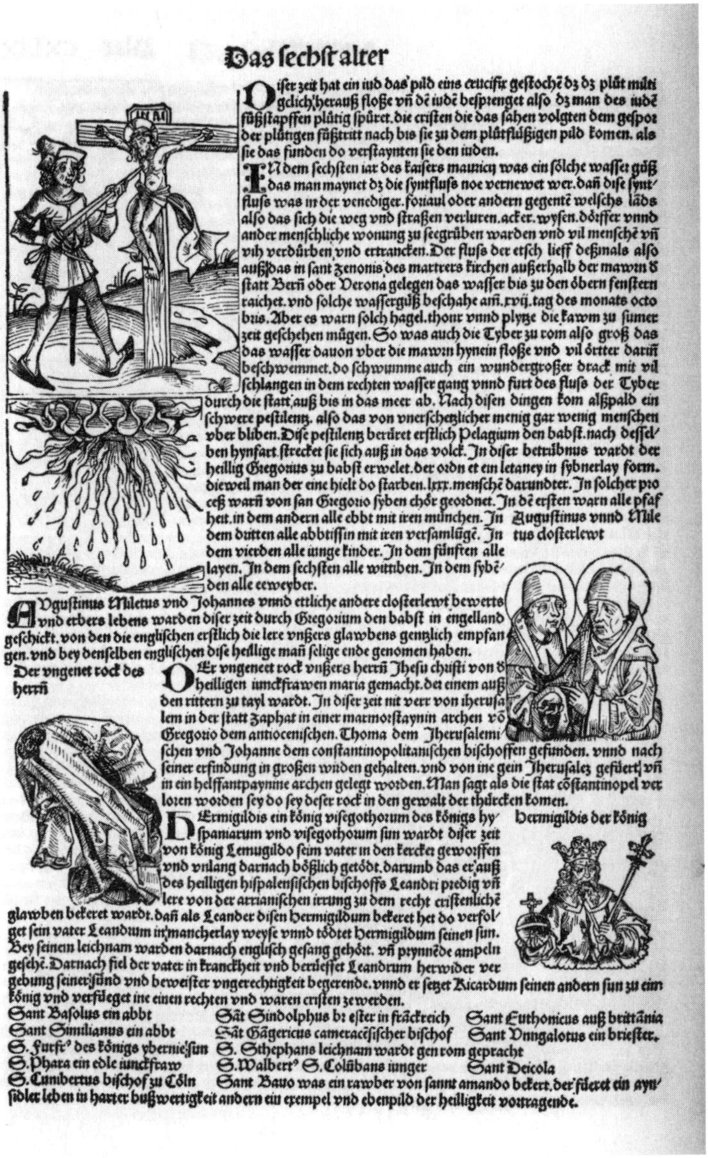

Das sechst alter

Diser zeit hat ein iud das pild eins crucifix gestochẽ dz dz plůt milti glich heraußflosse vñ dẽ iudẽ besprenget also dz man des iudẽ fůßstapffen plůtig spůret. die cristen die das sahen volgten dem gespor der plůtigen fůßtritt nach bis sie zu dem plůtflüßigen pild komen. als sie das funden do verstaynten sie den iuden.

IN dem sechsten iar des kaisers mauricy was ein sölche wasser güß das man maynet dz die syntfluss noe vernewet wer. dañ dise synt-fluss was in der venediger. foriaul oder andern gegentẽ welschs lãds also das sich die weg vnd straßen verluren. acker. wysen. dörffer vnnd ander menschliche wonung zu seegrůben warden vnd vil menschẽ vñ vih verdůrben vnd ertrancken. Der fluss der etsch lieff deßmals also auß das in sant zenonis des marters kirchen außerhalb der mawrn d' statt Berñ oder Verona gelegen das wasser bis zu den öbern fenstern raichet. vnd solche wassergüß beschahe am. xvij. tag des monats octobris. Aber es warn solch hagel. thonr vnnd plytze die kawm zu sumer zeit geschehen mügen. So was auch die Tyber zu rom also groß das das wasser dauon vber die mawrn hynein flosse vnd vil örtter dariñ beschwemmet. do schwumme auch ein wundergroßer drack mit vil schlangen in dem rechten wasser gang vnnd furt des fluss der Tyber durch die statt auß bis in das meer ab. Nach disen dingen kom alßpald ein schwere pestilentz. also das von vnerschetzlicher menig gar wenig menschen vber bliben. Dise pestilentz berüret erstlich Pelagium den babst. nach dessel-ben hynfart strecket sie sich auß in das volck. In diser betrübnus wardt der heillig Gregorius zu babst erwelet. der ordn et ein letaney in sybnerlay form. dieweil man der eine hielt do starben. lxxx. menschẽ darundter. In solcher proceß warñ von san Gregorio syben chör geordnet. In dẽ ersten warn alle pfafheit. in dem andern alle ebbt mit iren münchen. In dem dritten alle abbtissin mit iren versamlũgẽ. In dem vierden alle iunge kinder. In dem fünften alle layen. In dem sechsten alle wittiben. In dem sybẽ-den alle eeweyber.

Augustinus vnnd Miletus closterlewt

AVgustinus Miletus vnd Johannes vnnd ettliche andere closterlewt bewerts vnd erbers lebens warden diser zeit durch Gregorium den babst in engelland geschickt. von den die englischen erstlich die lere vnßers glawbens gentzlich empfangen. vnd bey denselben englischen dise heillige mañ selige ende genomen haben.

Der vngenet rock des herrñ

DEr vngeneet rock vnßers herrñ Jhesu christi von d' heilligen iunckfrawen maria gemacht. der einem auß den rittern zu tayl wardt. In diser zeit mit vert von iherusalem in der statt Zaphat in einer marmorstaynin archen võ Gregorio dem antiocenischen. Thoma dem Jherusalemischen vnd Johanne dem constantinopolitanischen bischoffen gefunden. vnnd nach seiner erfindung in großen wirden gehalten. vnd von ine gein Jherusalẽ gefüert vñ in ein helffantpaynine archen gelegt worden. Man sagt als die stat cõstantinopel verloren worden sey do sey deser rock in den gewalt der thürcken komen.

Hermigildis der könig

HErmigildis ein könig visegothorum des königs hyspaniarum vnd visegothorum sun wardt diser zeit von könig Lemugildo seim vater in den kercker geworffen vnd vnlang darnach bößlich getödt. darumb das er auß des heilligen hispalensischen bischoffs Leandri predig vñ lere von der arrianischen irrung zu dem recht cristenlichẽ glawben bekeret wardt. dañ als Leander disen Hermigildum bekeret het do verfolget sein vater Leandrum in mancherlay weyse vnnd tödtet Hermigildum seinen sun. Bey seinem leichnam warden darnach englisch gesang gehört. vñ prynnẽde ampeln geschẽ. Darnach fiel der vater in kranckheit vnd berüeffet Leandrum herwider vergebung seiner sünd vnd beweister vngerechtigkeit begerende. vnnd er setzet Ricardum seinen andern sun zu ein könig vnd verfüeget ine einen rechten vnd waren cristen ze werden.

Sant Basolus ein abbt | Sãt Sindolphus br ester in frãckreich | Sant Euthonicus auß brittãnia
Sant Similianus ein abbt | Sãt Gãgericus cameracẽsischer bischof | Sant Vnngalotus ein briester.
S. Fursr' des königs ybernie sun | S. Sthephans leichnam wardt gen rom geprachtt
S. Phara ein edle iunckfraw | S. Walbert' S. Colũbans iunger | Sant Deicola
S. Cunibertus bischof zu Cöln | Sant Bauo was ein rawber von sannt amando bekert. der füeret ein aynsidler leben in harter bußwertigkeit andern ein exempel vnd ebenpild der heilligkeit vortragende.

FIG. 4.1 A Jew desecrating a crucifix, Hartmann Schedel, *Weltchronik* (Nuremberg: Anton Koberger, 1493), CXLIX verso

FIG. 4.2 Burning Jews, Hartmann Schedel, *Weltchronik* (Nuremberg: Anton Koberger, 1493), CCI verso.

Schedel was not the first to depict Jews visually—some of the earliest depictions of Jews in print come from works published in the aftermath of the Trent trial. But he was the first to use such prominent and detailed images in a book in which Jews appeared only as a side topic (the pirated, less splendid versions also included crude copies of the original images).[7] But his model of signaling a story through an image would be influential. The publisher of Sebastian Münster's monumental *Cosmographia* would later include several recurring images to alert readers to stories about Jews (Fig. 4.3).

Some of the tales about Jews appear only in Schedel's *Liber chronicarum*, but he did not start the trend.[8] With books becoming available through print, authors increasingly interacted with previous works, creating a veritable chain or, perhaps more accurately, a web of historical memory.[9] Schedel's work was based on material found in earlier printed chronicles, most notably the exceedingly popular Werner Rolevinck's *Fasciculus temporum*, which went through nearly forty editions before the author died in 1502, and Jacob Philip Foresti of Bergamo's *Supplementum chronicarum*, which first appeared in 1483 in Venice and was likewise extremely popular, with more than twenty editions between 1483 and 1581.[10] They in turn had benefited from Vincent de Beauvais's *Speculum historiale*, a medieval chronicle published in 1473 and then 1474. (The 1474 edition was used by Bishop Hinderbach of Trent in the trial in Trent.) Some stories found in Schedel had earlier appeared in the works of Vincent de Beauvais, Rolevinck, and sometimes also Foresti. For example, William of Norwich, Richard of Pontoise, and Werner of Bachrach are also in *Speculum historiale* and in Rolevinck, but the desecration of the crucifix is found in *Speculum historiale*, Foresti, and some editions of Rolevinck.[11]

Not surprisingly, in the works of Schedel's predecessors, postbiblical Jews were also confined to the roles of vicious killers and enemies of Christians, sometimes deceived by a devil; they were, in turn, killed and burned or, if allowed to live, converted. In the 1479 edition of Rolevinck's *Fasciculus temporum*, there is a quick succession of these tales concerning Jews: desecration of the crucifix, a Jewish father burning his son to death for having taken communion with Christian children, William of Norwich, Richard of Pontoise, a conversion of a Jew in Toledo, Werner of Bachrach, the expulsion of Jews from France, and burning of Jews for poisoning wells.[12]

Rolevinck's and Foresti's chronicles were translated into many languages, including Italian, German, French, and even Dutch. But not all editions contained the same material. Some included stories that others did not, varying in wording depending on a language, perhaps to reflect different regional

clxxx **Das ander bůch**

menge der Juden in Franckreich/von dené gieng auß ein geschrey/das sie alle jar ein Christen kind heimlich zůwegen brechten/vnd fürten es vnder das erdreich an ein verborgen ort/vnd marterten es do/vnnd schlůgen es am Karfrytag an ein creütz. Do Künig Philippus das vernam/ließ er die Juden fahen vnd reytigen. Darnach anno Christi tausent ein hundert zwey vnd achtzig/vertrib er alle Juden auß seinem reich/außgenommen die/die sich zům Christen glauben bekerten. Aber darnach do er kriegs halben gelts notürfftig was/ließ er sie widerumb gehn Paryß kommen/vnd Ludouicus nach jhm öffnet jnen das gantz land. Anno Christi tausent dreyhundert vnd sieben/hat man in Franckreich gar tyrannisch gehandlet mitt den Tempelherren/vnd mit jhrem gantzen orden. Vnnd vyl meinen das der künig Philippus(der den obersten des ordes seyend was/darumb das sie reich wäre)hab mehr auß liebe des gůts dañ des Christen glaubens halben/also hertziglichen wider sie gehandlet. Dann mit verwilligung des Bapsts Clementis/hat er alle Tempelherren auff ein zeit lassen fahen/deren nun fast vil waren in Gallia/vnd ließ sie mancherley peinigen/vnd zůletzst mit fewr verbrennen. Man hielt jnen erstlichen für/wölcher der straff wolt entrinnen/der solt sein orden verdammen/ als ein vnnütze sect/ aber es ward keiner gefunden in der grossen zal/der etwas wider seinen orden reden wolt/biß jhm die seel außgieng. Die weil dise welt gestanden ist/hatt Gallia kein ellenderen anblick gesehen/vnd kein standhaffigers exempel. Jacobus der diser Ritterschafft oberster was/ward mit anderen dreyen ein zeit lang behalten/vnd gehn Lugdun zů dem Bapst Clementen geschickt. Vnd als jhn Clemens zů verjehen ermanet/hat er etwas von den orden bekannt. Aber do er widerumb gehn Parys ward gefürt/vnd in die mitte gestelt/begert er das man jn höret. Als das geschahe/hatt er theür geschworen das sein orden solches nit verschuldet habe/das er also gepeiniget solt werden. Vnd ob er schon verjähen hab/wäre das auß des Bapsts nötigung geschehen. Er wußte wol daß das leben seiner mitbrüder were alwegen on besteckig gewesen. Das verlabe er mit lauter stimm/vnd mit vnerschrocknem hertzen gab er sich in todt. Vnd als er mit sampt den anderen dreien obersten seines ordens mit bittem penen ward gemartert/haben sie doch ein sollichs standhafft angesicht erzeigt/gleich als entpfunden sie nit der peinen. Dise sach ward hernach des künigs halb noch argwöniger/das jn der gey mehr darzů weder Christellche liebe hat getriben. Dañ bald nach vertilckung der Tempelherren/wurde alle Juden durch das gantz Gallia beraubt jrer güter/vnd allein mit einem kleid auß dem künigreich getriben. Jedoch wendt künig Philips jre böse thatten für/damit er seinen geitz beschöner. Anno Christi tausent drey hundert zwey vnd zwentzig/wurden vil leprosen oder auffsetzigen in Franckreich gepeiniget. Dann durch der Juden anweysung/schwůren sie zůsammen/das sie wolten vergifften alle brunnen durch das gantz Fräckreich/damit die leüt strben/oder auch auffsetzig wurden/die darauß truncken. Also griffen sie die sach an/vnnd machten Confect von blůt vnd menschen harm/darzů brauchten sie etliche gifftige kreüter/

vnd

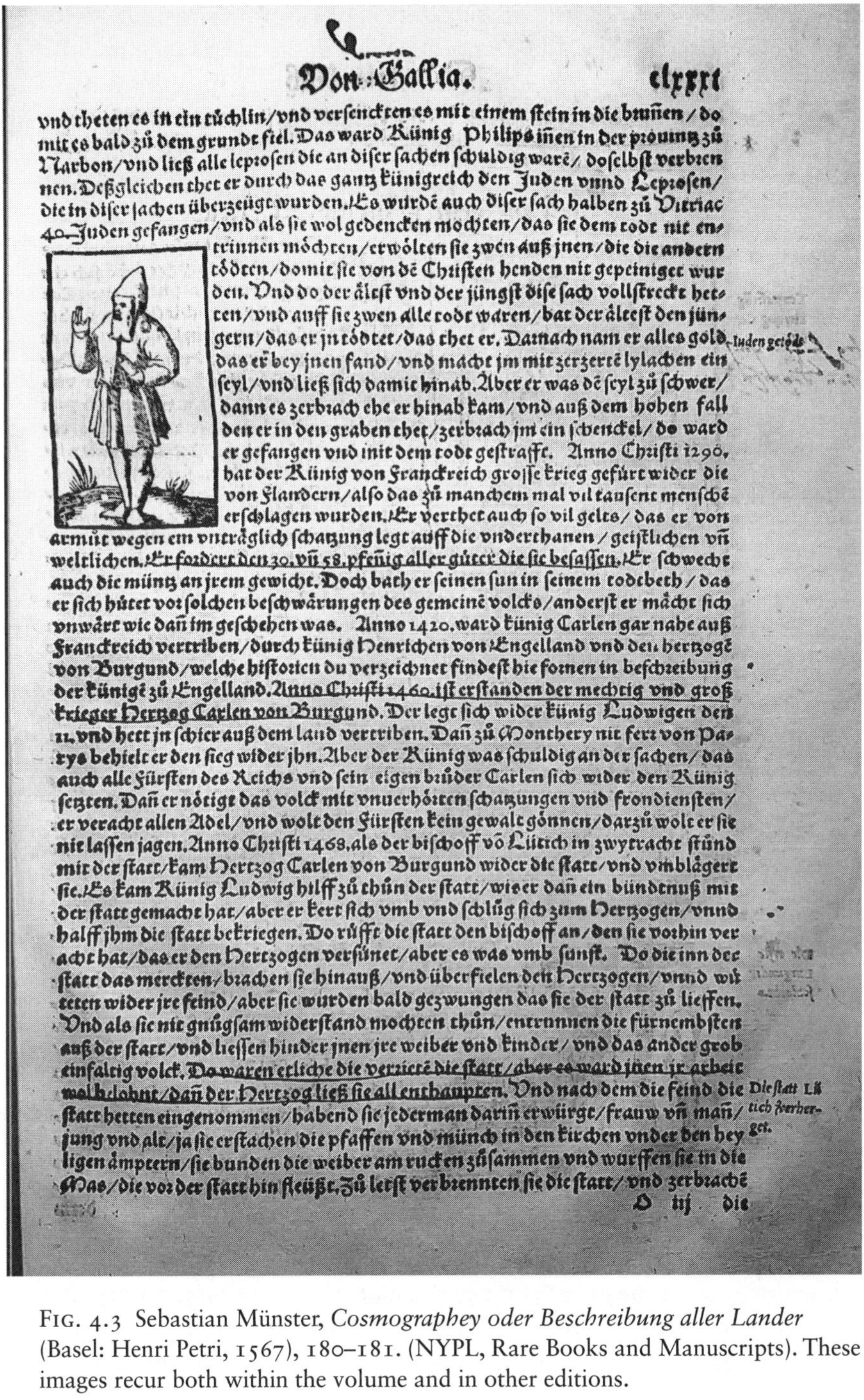
Von Gallia. clxxxi

vnd theten es in ein tüchlin/vnd versenckten es mit einem stein in die brunnen/ do mit es bald zů dem grunde fiel. Das ward Künig Philips innen in der prouintz zů Narbon/vnd ließ alle leprosen die an diser sachen schuldig waren/ doselbst verbrennen. Deßgleichen thet er durch das gantz künigreich den Juden vnnd Leprosen/ die in diser sachen überzeügt wurden. Es wurden auch diser sach halben zů Vitriac 40. Juden gefangen/vnd als sie wol gedencken mochten/das sie dem todt nit entrinnen möchten/erwölten sie zwen auß jnen/die die andern tödten/domit sie von den Christen henden nit gepeiniget wurden. Vnd do der ältest vnd der jüngst dise sach vollstreckt hetten/vnd auff sie zwen alle todt waren/bat der ältest den jüngern/das er jn tödtet/das thet er. Darnach nam er alles gold das er bey jnen fand/vnd macht jm mit zerzerten lylachen ein seyl/vnd ließ sich damit hinab. Aber er was den seyl zů schwer/ dann es zerbrach ehe er hinab kam/vnd auß dem hohen fall den er in den graben thet/zerbrach jm ein schenckel/ do ward er gefangen vnd mit dem todt gestrafft. Anno Christi 1290. hat der Künig von Franckreich grosse krieg gefürt wider die von Flandern/also das zů manchem mal vil tausent menschen erschlagen wurden. Er verthet auch so vil gelts/ das er von armůt wegen ein vnträglich schatzung legt auff die vnderthanen/ geistlichen vnd weltlichen. Er fordert den 30. vnd 58. pfennig aller güter die sie besassen. Er schwecht auch die müntz an jrem gewicht. Doch bath er seinen sun in seinem todbeth/ das er sich hüttet vor solchen beschwärungen des gemeinen volcks/anderst er mächt sich vnwärt wie dann im geschehen was. Anno 1420. ward künig Carlen gar nahe auß Franckreich vertriben/durch künig Henrichen von Engelland vnd den hertzogen von Burgund/welche historien du verzeichnet findest hie fornen in beschreibung der künigen zů Engelland. Anno Christi 1460. ist erstanden der mechtig vnd groß krieger Hertzog Carlen von Burgund. Der legt sich wider künig Ludwigen den 11. vnd hett jn schier auß dem land vertriben. Dann zů Monthery nit fert von Parys behielt er den sieg wider jhn. Aber der Künig was schuldig an der sachen/ das auch alle Fürsten des Reichs vnd sein eigen brůder Carlen sich wider den Künig setzten. Dann er nötiget das volck mit vnuerhörten schatzungen vnd frondiensten/ er veracht allen Adel/vnd wolt den Fürsten kein gewalt gönnen/darzů wolt er sie nit lassen jagen. Anno Christi 1468. als der bischoff von Lütich in zwytracht stůnd mit der statt/kam Hertzog Carlen von Burgund wider die statt/vnd vmblägert sie. Es kam Künig Ludwig hilff zů thůn der statt/wider dann ein bündtnuß mit der statt gemacht hat/aber er kert sich vmb vnd schlůg sich zum Hertzogen/vnnd halff jhm die statt bekriegen. Do růfft die statt den bischoff an/den sie vorhin veracht hat/das er den Hertzogen versünet/aber es was vmb sunst. Do die inn der statt das merckten/ brachen sie hinauß/vnd überfielen den Hertzogen/vnnd wůteten wider jre feind/aber sie wurden bald gezwungen das sie der statt zů lieffen. Vnd als sie nit gnůgsam widerstand mochten thůn/entrunnen die fürnembsten auß der statt/vnd liessen hinder jnen jre weiber vnd kinder/ vnd das ander grob einfaltig volck. Do waren etliche die vertirten die statt/ aber es ward jnen jr arbeit wol belohnt/dann der Hertzog ließ sie all enthaupten. Vnd nach dem die feind die statt hetten eingenommen/habend sie jederman darinn erwürgt/frauw vnd mann/ jung vnd alt/ja sie erstachen die pfaffen vnd münch in den kirchen vnder den heyligen ämptern/sie bunden die weiber am rucken zůsammen vnd wurffen sie in die Maß/die vor der statt hin fleüßt. Zů letst verbrennten sie die statt/ vnd zerbrachen

O iij die

Juden gefolt

Die statt Lütich zerberget.

FIG. 4.3 Sebastian Münster, *Cosmographey oder Beschreibung aller Lander* (Basel: Henri Petri, 1567), 180–181. (NYPL, Rare Books and Manuscripts). These images recur both within the volume and in other editions.

sensibilities. Rolevinck's first official edition of *Fasciculus temporum* describes events up to 1474, the year of its publication. It was then updated in some, though not all, subsequent editions. Johannes Hinderbach had a copy of the 1477 edition and added to it, by hand, the Trent story.[13]

The first to introduce the Simon of Trent story into *Fasciculus temporum* was the Cologne printer Nicolaus Götz in 1478, presumably after the news of the outcome of the investigation in Rome had spread.[14] Simon's story appears as the last event reported just before the colophon, in a short paragraph about "the Blessed Simon" who "was martyred in the city of Trent in year 1475 . . . three days before Easter," when, "as is reported, Jews make their unleavened bread with Christian blood." The infant Simon, the texts says, was captured, crucified, and desanguinated.[15] Götz's edition would begin a trail of transmission in transalpine European editions. With minor spelling adjustments, this version of Simon's story appeared in editions published in Basel (1482; the 1481 edition has no mention of the story), Strasbourg (1487–1492), Lyon (after 1495), and Paris (1512, 1524).[16] But not all editions followed the trail. In Cologne, Heinrich Quentell, the other publisher of the *Fasciculus*, chose not to include the story in the post-1478 editions, and Simon is not found in Quentell's 1479 or 1481 versions. Neither did the story enter the 1480 Utrecht Dutch edition or the Geneva French edition of 1495.[17] To be sure, these editions of *Fasciculus temporum* transmitted other horrifying anti-Jewish stories—Rolevinck's various editions of *Fasciculus* passed on some ten of about forty such tales found in the early modern chronicles.

In 1480, another version of the Trent story was inserted into a Venice edition of the *Fasciculus*. Quite tellingly its wording is significantly different, starting a new trajectory. The Venice editions focused on the death of Simon as a reenactment of the passion of Christ and the subsequent punishment of the Jews, and made no mention of the use of blood for matzah.[18] A similar wording was then used in *Chronicon* by Mattia Palmieri of Pisa, which in turn became part of a popular compilation of chronicles that included Eusebius and other authors.[19]

Yet Schedel's splendid chronicle did not use the language from Rolevinck's *Fasciculus* to describe the Trent affair. Much of his description in the original Latin edition from July 1493 was plagiarized nearly verbatim from Foresti's *Supplementum chronicarum,* but not from the first edition, published in 1483. Rather, Schedel drew from one of the later editions printed in 1485, 1486, 1488, or 1492, which also mention the story of a "similar crime" from the town of Motta, appended in Schedel's chronicle just below the woodcut of Simon; the Motta story is absent in Foresti's first 1483 edition.[20]

In 1491, Foresti's *Supplementum chronicarum* was also published in Italian, and many more editions followed thereafter. Here, too, the Italian text differs in some significant ways from the earlier Latin version. The Latin version, which had served as a basis for Schedel's text, explicitly claims that Jews needed Christian blood at Passover for their unleavened bread.[21] The Italian editions omit this detail. Instead they state that Jews, who were to celebrate "Passover according to their custom, kidnapped this boy and secretly carried him to a suitable house of one of the Jews named Samuel."[22] After describing Simon's torments in detail, the text discusses the podestà Giovanni de Salis and the trial during which he ordered Jews tortured "in such a way that one by one (*per ordine*) Jews described the whole affair." Out of "the zeal of Christian faith" and a sense of "justice" de Salis then sentenced them all to death. The body of the boy was placed in a church and "performed many miracles;" and, to accommodate the pilgrims, the citizens of Trent built him a new church. The Italian version ends with a sentence about Pope Sixtus IV and his envoy, the bishop of Ventimiglia: "Pope Sixtus at the time in order to be sure of the perfidy and evil of these executed Jews and of the great miracles that the body was performing sent Bishop of Ventimiglia and he found that according to the renown spread it was true." This sentence offers an interpretation of the events Hinderbach would have been happy to approve. But it does signal uncertainty. The Latin version, even in the post-1491 editions, is silent about the pope and the bishop of Ventimiglia, instead adding a few more words about Simonine miracles. Schedel, for his part, added still more details, among them a mention of Hinderbach, who apparently had studied at the University of Padua together with Schedel's uncle.[23]

After the Reformation, the chronicles and the "facts" they presented began to reflect the language and concerns of the splintering religious communities. Although many Catholic and Protestant chroniclers continued to repeat what they found in earlier sources, theological concerns also influenced how the stories about Jews were retold. This post-Reformation trend is especially evident from the second half of the sixteenth century, when Catholic and Protestant scholars turned to history for polemical purposes. The contrast is particularly stark between the Protestant Johannes Sleidanus and his Catholic respondents, among them Laurentius Surius, who inserted Simon of Trent into his lives of saints. For Sleidanus, the history of the Reformation was to inspire rulers to support the Reformation. It was a political history embodying a religious argument that "the Reformation represented a logical event that fulfilled God's will."[24] In Sleidanus's vision of history, based on the scheme of four empires from the biblical book of Daniel, the Reformation was "the last stage of the four ages,"[25] and the original documents, copiously used throughout, served him to underscore the "union of the sacred and civil state."²⁶ In that context, Jews were of no concern, except in references to the biblical past.

Sleidanus's work elicited a strong response from Catholic writers. And there, Jews were quite prominent. The Cologne Carthusian Surius responded with his *Commentarius brevis rerum in orbe gestarum*—first published in 1566—focusing solely on the events of the sixteenth century. Each new edition of the book was updated to the year of publication. And while most attention was paid to the reformers who were identified with anti-Christ and the devil, and who also appeared in syntax similar to Jews—often "burned," or committing "crimes"—Jews continued to play an important role in this anti-Protestant polemical history as well. The chronicle includes events such as the 1506 Lisbon massacre, and crucially, given the anti-Protestant context, also reports stories of host desecrations: 1510 in March-Brandenburg, where Jews were tried, tortured, and executed in Berlin (in the process they also confessed to killing a Christian child), and a 1556 trial in the Polish town of Sochaczew, which Surius placed explicitly in the context of the issue of contesting communion under one species.²⁷ Although Surius inserted the story of Simon of Trent in his lives of saints, in this polemical history, he only mentioned blood libel in relation to the confessions from the 1510 trial. This should not be surprising, because in the context of anti-Protestant polemics, blood accusations against Jews had no theological significance. But the stories of host desecration were significant, as were stories of iconoclasm and miracles related to desecration of images. Decades later, Johann Mayr, a priest from the Catholic Bavarian town of Freising, would add to his history of the sixteenth-century stories of the expulsion of Jews from Regensburg in 1519—in its aftermath their synagogue transformed into a church—and a host desecration in Pressburg (today's Bratislava) in 1591.²⁸

But the quintessential work of Catholic historiography was Cesare Baronio's *Annales ecclesiastici,* twelve massive folio volumes published between 1588 and 1607 and covering the first twelve centuries of Christianity. In light of Protestant attacks on the Church as corrupt and disconnected from the ancient church of early Christians—and partly in response to the first Protestant church history, the *Magdeburg Centuries*—the *Annales* offered "a comprehensive and critically scrutinized catalogue of documents demonstrating the identity between the *ecclesia primitiva* and the Roman Church of his own time." Here, as Stefania Tutino argues, "historical questions were plotted against theological debates," with an extensive use of primary documents.²⁹

Because Baronio often eschewed earlier chronicles and lore and grounded his work in official records, the *Annales* provides a more complex representation of Jews' place in Christian history. Postbiblical Jews of antiquity are palpably present in the first volumes of Baronio's opus, and the "margins of his book swarm with references to the Code of Maimonides and other Jewish sources."[30] And even in its history of later periods, the work, which was earnestly concerned with avoiding "lies . . . odious to the God of truth," contains fewer spurious anti-Jewish stories than earlier chronicles, and focuses more on papal letters and conciliar legislation.[31] Church laws concerning Jews were often restrictive, but Baronio also included statements by popes or other prominent churchmen protecting Jews from violence.[32] This is best illustrated in his descriptions of the Second Crusade and the events of the 1140s, discussed in volume twelve, where Baronio presented the debate among Christian leaders over the place of Jews in Christianity and the validity of attacking them as enemies of Christianity.[33] Baronio turned to Otto Frising's *De gestis Friderici* to provide a quote about attacks on Jews by the monk Radulph and his followers. For Baronio, Radulph was a heretic, whose actions Bernard sought to "repress." And then, Baronio turned to Peter the Venerable and his ambivalent view of Jews, who should not be killed but yet should not go "unpunished" for their "excesses." Listed among these excesses were not only usury and exploitation of Christians but also a "detestable crime" described by chronicler Robert of Torigni—the story of William of Norwich. Here Baronio used the same vocabulary of earlier chronicles—Jews are attacked, plundered, and killed; they are enemies and killers—but he mitigated this with a discussion of their defense and efforts to repress violence against them. Still, given Baronio's prominence and his own assertions about the truth, the inclusion stories such as that of William of Norwich gave them additional historical weight.[34]

But since Baronio's *Annales* covered events only until 1198, most anti-Jewish stories of child murders, host desecrations, and others known from earlier chronicles were not included. Those who continued the *Annales*—Abraham Bzovius, Odorico Rinaldi, and Henri Spondanus—seem to have been more dependent on the legacy of the earlier historical works than was Baronio, who focused more on archival documents he had access to in the Vatican library; and they did include those stories.

Abraham Bzovius (Bzowski), a Polish Dominican and early continuator of the *Annales,* tried to follow Baronio's model, including some original sources in the seven additional volumes numbered thirteen and up that brought the *Annales* to the second half of the sixteenth century in volume twenty. In volume thirteen, covering 1198–1299, readers encountered Jews early, on page three.³⁵ There, under 1198.3, Bzovius discussed their expulsion from France, noting an incident some years earlier when Jews "snatched" a Christian infant in accordance with "the impious custom of this perfidious people." The child was led to a subterranean cave and crucified "in derision of Christ [*in Christi ludibrium*]." King Philip Augustus decided to confiscate the Jews' possessions and expel them from his kingdom. The volume contains thirty "events" related to Jews: miraculous conversions; expulsions (from France and England); host desecrations (1213, 1290, and 1299); blasphemies against Mary (1263); and no fewer than seven stories of child murders. In addition to the one in France, Bzovius noted two in England. One is from 1234 [*sic*] in Norwich, where "Jews secretly abducted a Christian boy and fed him for a full year, so that during the upcoming Passover" they could crucify him. But they were discovered a few days before committing the crime and "suffered deserved punishment."³⁶ The second, based on Matthew Paris, is the account of Little Hugh of Lincoln in 1255.³⁷

Although it is perhaps not surprising that Bzovius would have included stories ubiquitous in earlier chronicles, he also utilized other newly available sources and inserted less well-known stories.³⁸ He is one of the few chroniclers to mention the 1236 case from Fulda, which played an important role in setting a legal precedent of imperial protection against anti-Jewish blood accusations, but was unknown beyond obscure medieval monastic sources. Fulda is briefly mentioned in Johannes Trithemius's chronicle of the Hirschau Abbey published in 1559 and 1601 (Bzovius's source)³⁹ and more fully in the compilation of local and monastic German chronicles by Christian Wurtisen published in 1585.⁴⁰ As these medieval monastic chronicles began to be printed, they provided historical "primary source" material for historians like Bzovius and others writing their own annals and introduced hitherto unknown stories about Jews to the broader reading public.

But there were consequences of the dissemination of these medieval stories centuries later. Printed during the early modern period, these medieval chronicles were used in the nineteenth century as historical primary sources for national histories. Monastic chronicles published by Wurtisen and others entered the majestic *Monumenta Germaniae Historica,* a massive collection of primary sources for German lands that was conceived in 1819, right after the end of the Holy Roman Empire, and began to be published in 1826, becoming a go-to collection of primary sources for German historians. These sources, in turn, helped shape and reinforce the image of Jews in the newly emerging national story. The medieval stories of the horrifying and unusual thus became part of the known historical record, which portrayed Jews in a harmful light, committing horrendous deeds for which they were—as the chroniclers asserted—"justly" punished. Modern readers of the national past were now exposed to repeated stories of massacres and burnings of Jews; of Jews committing suicide rather than converting to Christianity; of Jews poisoning wells, killing Christians, and defiling the sacred. As these historical sources created new national memories in modern times, Jews thus represented did not fit as full members of the emerging nations. Instead, they were a historical enemy within, hateful and hated, a people who kill and are killed.

But Baronio's model of combining stories from chronicles with papal edicts and church canons provided a platform for a more complex presentation of Jews. Both Abraham Bzovius and Odorico Rinaldi followed it, though unevenly over the course of the additional volumes. Historical documents were plentiful in the volumes covering the thirteenth century, but subsequent volumes became more reliant on traditional sources—chronicles and the increasingly available anti-Jewish works—and thus more anti-Jewish stories entered them.[41] Still, both Bzovius and Rinaldi included under years 1200 and 1199 *Sicut Iudaeis,* the medieval papal constitution protecting Jews. But only Rinaldi included both the 1236 *Lachrymabilem Iudaeorum in Regno Francie* and the 1247 papal letter against accusing Jews of killing Christians.[42] Overall thirty-one papal documents or canons related to Jews were cited verbatim or mentioned by these two continuators of Baronio's *Annales*. For the first time, seventeenth-century readers were able to see that Jews were also protected by Christian authorities, and not necessarily always because of bribes. That last issue was addressed apologetically by Rinaldi, who wrote that Mathew Paris's assertion that Jews bribed their way out of prison and into the protective arms of the pope had given grounds for "calumnies" of corruption against the pope.[43]

So although many chronicles showed Jews only as usurers, blasphemers, abusers of sacred objects, and killers of Christians acting out of a deep-seated hatred of Christianity, the Catholic *Annales ecclesiastici,* while still not shying away from spurious stories about Jews, mitigated their impact by including papal letters of protection. Of nearly one hundred stories concerning Jews found in the continuations of Baronio's *Annales* by Bzovius and Rinaldi, nearly twenty were of murders (blood libels, ritual crucifixions, or murders of Jewish children for conversion) and eighteen of Eucharistic miracles involving Jews. But there were also the thirty-one papal documents and canons, many of which explicitly condemned violence against Jews. The stories of persecution of Jews were often told as a backdrop to explain papal protection of them. In contrast to earlier chronicles, where multiple stories of persecution of Jews were always justified by stories of their crimes, in the full version of the *Annales* stories of persecution are frequently countered by acts of protection. Even a casual glance at the index provides a more complex grammar for historical memory.

But that complexity was difficult to transmit. In subsequent abridged versions and in other annals inspired by Baronio, Bzovius, and Rinaldi, this complexity was gone. These "facts," to use Mary S. Morgan's concept, did not "travel well."[44] If facts are "settled pieces of knowledge," the new "facts" about papal protections of Jews presented in the *Annales* did not fit the cultural knowledge shaped over the previous century or two by ubiquitous stories about Jewish enmity and crimes, which had made it hard to accept that Jews deserved protection. As a result the historical evidence of papal interventions on behalf of Jews was lost from common knowledge and was often challenged when Jews and their protectors furnished such documents. The evidence of papal protection of Jews, especially regarding blood accusations, ran against the established narrative patterns—although published in the *Annales* but excluded from the more popular abridged editions, it remained in the domain of private elite knowledge.

The "facts" that did travel well and stuck throughout the various editions and epitomes of the annals and other chronicles were the stories that fit the larger narrative and belief system about Jews. Although these stories may have started as local tales or lore, their inclusion in these authoritative chronicles and compilations of primary sources turned them into historical "facts." Tiberino's narrative of Simon's death, for example, became a primary source for the Bollandist *Acta Sanctorum*, testifying to the verity of Simon's martyrdom and sainthood. These invented "facts" about Jews then turned into patterns to be used as evidence in a legal context, in trials and legal treatises. Marquardus de Susannis, for example, in his legal treatise *De Iudaeis et aliis infidelibus* (Of Jews and Other Unfaithful, 1558) turned to chronicles for "facts" to justify expulsions of Jews.[45] He mentioned the poisoning of wells, blasphemies, and several examples of murders of children: William of Norwich, along with the other Norwich story from 1234 mentioned in later chronicles, and Simon of Trent. For de Susannis and others, the chronicles were sources of "reliable knowledge" that provided authoritative historical evidence.

Indeed, whereas Catholic scholars may have included stories of host desecrations in their works to boost the validity of the dogma of transubstantiation, stories of Jewish murders and other "crimes" were so entrenched as "facts" among European Christian writers that even Protestant scholars included them in their works, helping embed them deeper in the body of

European cultural knowledge about Jews. Sebastian Münster, the Catholic-turned-Protestant scholar, boasted that his *Cosmographia* "described the people of the whole world, their studies, sects, customs, habits, laws, religions, rites, kingdoms, principalities, commerce, antiquities, lands, creation of lands ... and other things if the sort which are celebrated by historians and cosmographers and most of all which are in some way able by their excellence and dignity to come to our knowledge."[46] And yet he included more than a dozen anti-Jewish stories.

That Münster was not immune to such stories has surprised some scholars. He was after all one of the most famous and accomplished Hebraists of his era. He studied not only with fellow Christian scholars, such as Konrad Pellikan and Johannes Reuchlin, but also with Jews, notably Elia Levita. He published a Hebrew and Aramaic grammar, a dictionary, and a translation of the Hebrew Bible into Latin and of the Gospel of Matthew into Hebrew. His importance for the development of Christian Hebraism cannot be overstated.[47] And yet, in his *Cosmographia,* an exquisite example of the historical-topographical genre of the time, he did not shy away from medieval tales about Jews, even from introducing new ones into circulation. For example, Münster's *Cosmographia* appears to be one of the earliest European printed works to mention the expulsion of Jews from England[48] and only the second to note the expulsion of the Jews from Spain, which appears to have been first mentioned briefly in the *Chronicon* by Mattia Palmieri of Pisa published in the 1536 edition of Joannes Sichardus's compilation of various chronicles.[49]

To be sure Münster did not mindlessly copy earlier chronicles, and his Protestant sensibilities are certainly palpable in his omission of host desecration stories and of language implying sainthood of Christian children said to have been killed by Jews. But these stories nonetheless served Münster, as they did his predecessors, to justify instances of local anti-Jewish violence and persecution. Thus, for example, in his description of France and its kings, Münster briefly noted that "in 1180 there was a great number of Jews in France," about whom a "rumor" spread that "each year" they kidnapped a Christian child and tormented him on Good Friday. Having learned about it, the king expelled them two years later, in 1182.[50] But Münster makes no mention of a shrine to the boy in Paris. The same is true of his description of Simon of Trent. Although, at first glance, the lengthy passage seems to describe Simon's story dispassionately—even including some nuance by acknowledging that when the Jews' house was first searched the boy was not found there and by incorporating the Jews' explanation that the flowing water must have washed Simon's body into the canal—the text nonetheless gives a detailed description of the tortures Simon was supposedly subjected to and asserts that Jews killed the boy "out of hatred of Christ." Yet Münster said nothing about Simon's veneration among Catholics.[51] Notably, these stories could have served as potentially anti-Catholic propaganda, but they were not deployed in that way in the *Cosmographia*. Indeed, although Münster mentioned the story of Jews "martyring" a boy in Berne, which had been inserted in some editions of Rolevinck's *Fasciculus*, he did not include the story of the venerated Werner of Bachrach, though he could have noted it in his discussion of Alsace. In Münster's *Cosmographia* the stories about Jews are almost always stories of cruelty and disorder, which end with fully justified punishment of the Jews as "authors of all kinds of crimes" either through a judicial process or vigilante violence.[52]

Münster's *Cosmographia* built on both ancient works and the late Renaissance descriptions of the world and peoples. Ptolemy, Strabi, and Pliny provided early models. Christian writers of the late antiquity and the medieval period then reimagined the world within the framework of Christian eschatological chronology, as living in the last of the six ages.[53] Later, Renaissance scholars applied this to their vision of the world, which is certainly evident in Hartman Schedel's *Liber chronicarum*. His work, though presented as a chronology, also provided a description and visual illustration of the world.[54] With the European expansion into the Americas and Africa, European writers began to be interested in descriptions of the world and of customs of peoples inhabiting various lands. The monstrous, tragic, and terrifying became part of the story.

Münster built on this new interest and new body of knowledge. But he also did his own research through traveling and soliciting information from local contacts. It took some eighteen years before the first edition of the *Cosmographia* saw light in 1544. The book took not only time to prepare but also money, which had to be raised to support the costs of print and production of woodcuts. This may explain why Münster, who "believed that the Hebrew language and Jewish scholarship could be put to the service of Christianity, expanding and refining its body of knowledge," included more than a dozen anti-Jewish stories in his majestic opus.[55] The *Cosmographia* was a bit of a "pay-to-play" project. Münster appealed to lords and local leaders to provide content and funding: "Cities of the German nation! Do not regret the gulden or two you might spend on a description of your region. Let everyone lend a helping hand to complete a work in which shall be reflected as in a mirror, the entire land of Germany with all its peoples, its cities and its customs."[56] The cities included in the *Cosmographia* were, unless Münster explicitly noted otherwise, those that paid and provided local information, such as Rufach, whose description and illustrations came from the Protestant theologian and Hebraist Konrad

Pellikan and the humanist Konrad Wolfhart.[57] Rufach's description, which appeared first in the 1550 Latin edition, tells of political violence in 1298 ("or according to others 1296") and its devastation, followed by "calamities" caused by Jews "who in almost all regions conspired to ruin Christians" and who were punished for their crimes. The citizens of Rufach in 1309 burned many of "their Jews, who had a synagogue in the city," and years later they also killed those who had remained.[58] The passage ends with a description of famine and a mention of a painting commemorating it that could still be seen at the time. The stories about Jews in the *Cosmographia* thus may be those contributing patrons wanted included as part of the description of their lands and cities.

Münster constantly updated his *Cosmographia,* and some stories, like the Rufach story, appear in some editions but not others.[59] But the printer also made aesthetic choices, perhaps in consultation with Münster. The German and Italian editions include images of a crucified child near the story of Richard of Pontoise in 1180 and Simon of Trent (Fig. 4.3). The German and, to a lesser extent, the Latin editions have additional images of bearded and marked Jews to signal stories related to Jews, especially those involving violence and persecution. Visually and in text the *Cosmographia* reinforces the image of the dangerous, ugly Jew. By crowdsourcing stories, Münster gave to local people voice and the power to determine how they wanted their towns represented to the reading public. He thus captured the way they saw Jews and their place in their local stories. In contrast to Baronio, Bzovius, and Rinaldi, who complicated the representation of Jews in history, Münster allowed for local memory about them to become "facts." The book's impact was probably significant, given that it went through some thirty-five editions in less than a century, with an estimated fifty thousand German-language copies in circulation and ten thousand in Latin.[60] While Christians may have found in Münster's *Cosmographia* a confirmation of their beliefs about Jews, the sixteenth-century Jewish historian Yosef Ha-Kohen used it as a source for his history of Jewish persecution.[61]

Münster's *Cosmographia* exemplifies a genre in which geographic descriptions also included sites and stories associated with specific locales. Georg Braun's magnificent *Civitates orbis terrarum* similarly pairs images with texts, and here, too, anti-Jewish tales were included. But unlike Münster, Braun seems to have mentioned only stories linked to existing physical sites. Under Brussels, he described the Basilica of S. Gudula and the associated story of host desecration said to have happened there in 1369.[62] In an impressively detailed description of Trent, he added information about the Church of St. Peter's, "of the Germans," in which there was "the body of B. Simon" killed by Jews "years ago."[63]

A survey of these early modern works, especially the chronicles, reveals a certain pattern. German chronicles and annalistic compilations, in Latin or German, provided European readers with the most vituperative stories about Jews, replicating material taken from earlier works. Rolevinck and Schedel provided most such stories in the early period. They, along with Alfonso de Espina's *Fortalitium fidei*, published in at least four editions in the fifteenth century (1471 in Strasburg; 1485 and 1494 in Nuremberg by Anton Koberger, publisher of Schedel's chronicle; and 1487 in Lyon), provided foundational material for subsequent works. These stories came predominantly from northwestern Europe. And although some documentary annals and chronicles included sources explicitly condemning violence against Jews and thus complicating the prevalent narrative about the place of Jews in the Christian world, only the tales of Jewish cruelty and violence against them appeared repeatedly across the genres. These stories were not inconsequential; they had legal value. Already in the Trent trial, Johannes Hinderbach scoured earlier chronicles and books for stories about Jews to justify the legality of the trial and executions. These early modern printed chronicles would later also be used as evidence in other trials of Jews. But the documentary evidence of protecting Jews was gradually lost from both history and memory, because the works that had a broader reach did not include them.

Strikingly, the earliest printed chronicles about Poland included few such anti-Jewish stories and showed little influence of western European chronicles. An exception is the work by Marcin Kromer, a Polish bishop, diplomat, and chronicler, first published in 1555, which mentions attacks on Jews in "Italy, Germany, [and] France" stemming from a popular belief that Jews poisoned wells.[64] Polish chronicles focused on local stories, and by mid- to late sixteenth century, when these chronicles were published, few anti-Jewish Polish stories had spread. Some Polish chronicles mention privileges granted to Jews by King Casimir the Great, explaining them by his relationship with the Jewess Esther, first mentioned by Jan Długosz in his fifteenth-century chronicle, which itself was only known from manuscripts.[65] The chroniclers held that generous privileges were granted to Jews because of Esther's influence on the king.[66] Some Polish chronicles did mention the 1399 legend of host desecration in Poznań, which would become more popular in the late sixteenth and in the seventeenth centuries its dissemination in printed pamphlets.[67] Others, among them chronicles by Maciej Miechowita and Marcin Bielski, discussed an attack on Jews in 1406 (or 1407) in Cracow instigated by a sermon given by a priest named Budek, who claimed that the night before, Jews had killed a Christian child, committed abominable things with his blood, and also attacked a priest carrying the consecrated host.⁶⁸ The story resonated with local Christians, leading to an attack on Jews because, as Bielski claimed, people had grievances against Jews for bribing authorities and escaping justice when they sold stolen objects.

For the most part anti-Jewish stories found in earlier European chronicles did not begin to filter into Poland until the late sixteenth century, when they would enter vernacular explicitly anti-Jewish works. Marcin Bielski's chronicle of the world, published in 1564 and inspired by Münster's *Cosmographia*, is most notable for largely omitting them. For example, although Bielski mentioned the expulsion of Jews from Spain,⁶⁹ he did not include the story of Jews "martyring" a boy in Berne found in Rolevinck and Münster⁷⁰ nor the discussion of anti-Jewish persecution that Münster had inserted in the descriptions of Strasburg and Speyer.⁷¹ Trent is described in ten words without mentioning Simon: "Trent, city and castle, partly [belonging to] the Duke of Austria, partly to the Bishop of Trent."⁷² With the exception of a handful of Polish examples, events related to postbiblical Jews, so ubiquitous in other European chronicles, are virtually nonexistent in Bielski's description of the world.⁷³

But Bielski did devote a chapter exclusively to Jews.⁷⁴ The chronicler focused on the Talmud and what he considered its absurd teachings, as well as some Jewish customs, often described erroneously and with derision. After discussing the Jewish holidays, dietary laws, betrothal practices, mourning rites, and ethical teachings that he implied condoned questionable practices, adultery, and even murder, he briefly turned to the accusations that Jews used Christian blood: "As for the [claims] that they drink Christian blood, which they drain from innocent children, as our [writers] claim, I could not verify for sure from baptized Jews; nor regarding their procurement from the Eucharistic wafer [*boże ciało*], since it is difficult to tell which one is consecrated, which is not."⁷⁵ And although Bielski raised doubts about child murders, the use of blood, and host desecrations, he asserted that Jews did indeed "secretly buy children, though not for to murder [them] or for their blood, but to sell them expensively to Turks." His claim was based on what he apparently had heard from an Armenian. Bielski transformed an accusation found in other books into a new story, which given Poland's proximity to the Ottoman Empire, seemed plausible. Still his chronicle quite consciously was purged of spurious stories blaming Jews for the deaths of children.

The same cannot be said of a Bohemian chronicle by Václav Hájek of Libočan, *Bohemian Chronicle*, published first in Czech in 1541 in Prague and then in German in 1596.⁷⁶ Though, as Zdenek David argues, Hájek was quite familiar with western European chronicles, his chronicle had a distinct local flavor. It contained a staggering forty-six stories about Jews, among them eleven known from other western chronicles, including William of Norwich and Simon of Trent, and new stories pertaining to Bohemia that had appeared nowhere before.[77] Here too Jews kill Christians, rob or even burn their churches, poison wells, desecrate hosts, and defraud Christians. As punishment, they are in turn attacked, hanged, burned, or expelled. For example, one of the earliest stories about Jews in Hájek's chronicle, said to have taken place in 1053, conflates well poisoning and blood accusation.[78] It recounts that during a plague when many Christians were dying in smaller towns where Jews lived, no Jew died. At the same time a Jew was caught for attempting to kill a Christian child to use his blood. He confessed to wanting to kill the child for his blood, which was then to be distributed among his family and used for magic. Having learned about these crimes, the duke punished the Jews by burning, whereupon the dying stopped. In Hájek's work, as in the earlier western European chronicles, Christian violence against Jews is always justified by Jews' alleged crimes. Hájek's chronicle fits in the European genre. With these stories he established a pattern of Jewish behavior, using the same action verbs and adjectives, and giving the readers a limited menu of what they could imagine Jews did and what could be done to them.

Regional Epistemologies

Early modern Christian readers seeking information about Jews did not need to resort to leafing through pages of weighty tomes.[79] Polemical works about Jews had been published since the earliest days of printing, and by the early sixteenth century publishing patterns emerged, reflecting regional interests and shaping epistemological trajectories. An important early influence was Alfonso de Espina's *Fortalitium fidei*, written on the Iberian peninsula before 1461 and published several times north of the Alps. In this work Espina outlined theological questions and provided a long list of anti-Jewish tales about "existential past and present."[80] The theological questions, largely based on earlier polemical works available in Iberia, served as a model for later polemical works, and his anti-Jewish stories became yet another source of "historical" knowledge for those who sought proof of "Jewish cruelties."[81] But whereas de Espina combined two distinct areas of anti-Jewish literature in one volume—theological polemic and spurious anti-Jewish works—later works tended to split these genres according to distinct regional interests. In the German lands and on the Italian peninsula, such literature tended to focus on the polemic against Jews and Judaism, even if the means and topical focus differed. In Poland, in contrast, the theological aspect of anti-Jewish literature was minor, with the predominant emphasis on "Jewish cruelties."

German lands developed their own regional focus. Traditional anti-Jewish polemic that emphasized theological issues such as the Trinity, the incarnation of Jesus, circumcision, baptism, and other issues did, of course, exist there. A late fifteenth-century work, *Pharetra fidei*, published in Cologne in the 1490s and republished in Landschut in 1514, offered a polemical dialogue on theological questions between a Jew and a Christian, declaring that "we cannot defeat these vile and rejected Jews except with their own weapons."[82] But in the early modern period there emerged a new genre, marking what R. Po-Chia Hsia regarded as "a shift from theology to folkways, from doctrine to cultural practices," with books focused on Jewish practices and observances.[83] With more than seventy such works published in German or written by Germans, and only a handful authored or published outside the German lands, such "polemical ethnographies" became a predominantly German phenomenon.[84]

The trial at Trent may have been, as Hsia has argued, an important trigger of interest in Jewish rituals in the German cultural sphere, especially among those who were part of the proceedings, such as Friar Erhard von Pappenheim.[85] Von Pappenheim, who had translated a copy of the trial records into German, also wrote a commentary on a Hebrew manuscript of the Haggadah that demonstrates the extent to which the trial tainted his reading of Jewish practices.[86] Strikingly, this post-Trent interest in Jewish customs did not take root in the Italian cultural sphere, despite the Trent affair leaving a mark. The "ethnographic" focus remained a German development shaped largely by early sixteenth-century vernacular works by Jewish converts to Christianity and then sustained by Protestant scholars who studied, as Elisheva Carlebach has observed, "Jewish ritual for the purpose of elucidating the original [Christian] practices that had now become objects of serious contention between Christian denominations."[87]

The broader Jewish and Christian cultural and political context in German lands may further explain why the "ethnographic" polemic was a German development. For the Ashkenazi Jews of the German lands, the *minhag*, or custom, was "the core" of their culture, and *minhag* literature as a genre developed among them from the late eleventh century on.[88] By the fifteenth century, the genre was widespread, to the point that custom often served as a basis for some legal decisions. The genre even spread to individuals and individual communities, which recorded their own customs. This literature, as Carlebach has convincingly shown, became a model for the "ethnographic" polemic. In fact, Antonius Margaritha, a Jewish convert and author of one of the most influential polemical works on Jewish observances, first published in 1530, was a product of this cultural milieu. As a cantor's brother, he knew the importance of "cantorial instructions" when he translated Hebrew prayers for his readers. Although many important rabbis wrote works focusing on Jewish practices, one did not have to be a scholar deeply immersed in rabbinic literature to read or even write such books. *Minhag* books became a hallmark of secondary elites. It is thus perhaps not surprising that the first such polemical works were penned by Jewish converts who did not display a high level of sophistication in the understanding of the halakhah and rabbinic literature. Victor von Carben and Johannes Pfefferkorn pioneered the genre in the German vernacular with the help of Cologne Dominicans, publishing the earliest such books in the first decade of the sixteenth century. Von Carben's work, disorganized and laden with errors, did not make as big an impact as the pamphlets penned by Pfefferkorn, who had begun his anti-Jewish crusade in 1507 with the pamphlet *Der Juden Spiegel* (The Jews' Mirror), in which he challenged some Jewish beliefs and practices and promoted anti-Jewish policies that would subsequently make it into works by Martin Luther and others.[89]

Pfefferkorn's first work on Jewish customs, the 1508 *Ich heyss eyn Buchlijn,* came with five woodcuts, of which four were full-page images representing scenes of Jewish ceremonies related to the High Holidays. In all of them, Jews are blindfolded as they perform ritual acts such as *taschlikh* (a symbolic casting off of sins), *kapparot* (a ritual of atonement), and *malkot* (a ritual flagellation). These woodcuts were some of the earliest—except for the publications emerging after Trent and the chronicles—visual representations of postbiblical Jews disseminated in Europe. Their goal was unmistakably to highlight the strangeness of Jewish observances.[90] In 1509, Pfefferkorn published another booklet, in both German and Latin, in which he promised to offer "a complete explanation of how the blind Jews celebrate their Passover."[91] To be sure, he (or his Dominican handlers) offered a Christological interpretation of Passover, asserted Jews did not understand that the true Passover sacrifice was Christ, and used the text to polemicize against Jews, especially to show that they harbored heretical beliefs. Still, Pfefferkorn did not provide any ammunition for those claiming Jews killed Christian children during Passover for their blood or as a ritual sacrifice. In fact, in the first chapter, he discussed almost matter of factly the preparations for Passover, including making Passover "bread," the matzah, which he noted was made from special flour—considered sacred—mixed with water in such a way as to avoid fermentation. Pfefferkorn's book on Passover represented a continuation of his effort to undermine the legal status of Jews in the Holy Roman Empire, but it did not cross the line of providing support for anti-Jewish libels.[92]

Pfefferkorn's attacks on Jewish books and ceremonies led to a pushback from Christian scholars. Dragged into this controversy was Johannes Reuchlin, who defended the value of Jewish books and demonstrated Pfefferkorn's ignorance of Jewish texts.[93] In 1512, also as a statement against Pfefferkorn's attacks on the Passover liturgy, the Franciscan friar Thomas Murner published the Haggadah in a Latin translation; it was the first printed illustrated Haggadah.[94] The frontispiece shows three Jews reclining around a table, with matzah at the center covered by a cloth, and four cups of wine in front of each figure—visually symbolizing the four cups of wine drunk during the Passover seder (Fig. 4.4). The remaining images also depict Jews sitting around the table with cups of wine. In contrast to the illustrations in Pfefferkorn's book, Murner's Jews are not blindfolded, nor do they have any derogatory features, only the badges visible on the frontispiece.

Yet Murner's haggadah was still polemical, and not only against Pfefferkorn. The introduction noted that contemporary Jewish celebrations of Passover were not part of biblical observances, but rather an invention during their exile, "observed outside of Jerusalem, against the precepts of Moses." In fact, the Jews "dare[d] to invent new rituals of Passover," which Murner considered heretical. Murner's translation of the Haggadah was also framed within the tradition of Christian polemical interest in Hebrew learning through references to two medieval examples, Paul of Burgos and Nicholas of Lyra. Still, in the context of Pfefferkorn's crusade against Jewish books, Murner, as Lawrence A. Hoffman has suggested, "hoped to demonstrate that the Haggadah contained nothing worth destroying."[95]

As the commentary on the Haggadah by Friar Erhard von Pappenheim makes clear, a discussion of Passover rituals was often an opportunity to indulge in interpretations supporting blood accusations against Jews. Yet neither Murner nor Pfefferkorn went in that direction. In fact, in *The Jews' Mirror*, Pfefferkorn addressed the issue directly: "It is a common saying that the Jews have to have Christian blood and also have the monthly flow," he wrote. "We really put them in the wrong by making such a claim."[96] He saw such accusations as obstacles to Jewish conversion, and although he did not preclude the possibility that some Jews may have killed Christians, he pleaded,

> Therefore I ask all faithful Christians to disregard such unfounded talk in order not to give the Jews a reason to be stubborn. It is quite possible that some Jews persecute us and sometimes kill children of Christians because they envy and hate Christ and us. However, they do not do this for the blood but in order to dishonor and harm the parents. For there are bad people in all estates, and although there is once in a while a bad person like that, this does not mean that everyone is of that nature. Therefore, avoid making such accusations so that the Jews will not believe we need them as evidence for our Christian faith, which is clearly without flaws proved by the Holy Scriptures and by miracles.

FIG. 4.4 Thomas Murner, *Hukat ha-pesah: ritus et celebratio phase iudeorum* (Frankfurt: Beatus Murner, 1512). NYPL Spencer Coll. Ger 1512.

Pfefferkorn's arguments made their way into Luther's 1523 pamphlet *Jesus Was Born a Jew*, in which he expressed hopes for Jewish conversion and pleaded with Christians to treat Jews kindly and not claim that they needed Christian blood "so that they don't stink."[97] By 1543, in his book *On Jews and Their Lies*, Luther reembraced the tales of Jews' need of Christian blood and even mentioned Trent.[98]

Although the earliest works of this "ethnographic" genre of polemical literature emerged before the Reformation, the genre "reached its mature form" after the publication of a more sophisticated work on the subject in 1530 by another convert to Christianity from a prodigious Jewish family, Antonius Margaritha.[99] The genre flourished also in the context of Protestant anti-Catholic polemic and interests, as Protestants began to study "Jewish ritual for the purpose of elucidating the original practices" of early Christians, thereby highlighting the corruption of the Catholic Church.[100]

Margaritha's *Der gantz Jüdisch Glaub* (The Entire Jewish Faith) provides a fuller description of Jewish customs and a translation of Jewish prayers into German.[101] Margaritha, recalling earlier Christian polemicists, including Thomas Murner, wanted "to expose Judaism as an unbiblical religion."[102] He was also concerned with what he thought was an unfairly high status of the Jews and sought to undermine it by proposing policy measures that would curb their perceived power and influence. Published just before the 1530 Imperial Diet in Augsburg, Margaritha's booklet addressed Christian authorities. He hoped that given his status as a son of a rabbi, the book would have an impact.[103]

In *Der gantz Jüdisch Glaub* Margaritha argued that Jews harbor a deep-seated hatred of Christians and thus posed a danger to Christian society. According to Elisheva Carlebach, the work framed Jewish rituals as "elements of a deliberately concealed anti-Christian complex," exposing "the most trivial Jewish everyday behaviors as 'secrets' to be probed for clandestine evil intent."[104] It disturbed the emperor, who summoned to Augsburg the Jewish leader Josel of Rosheim for a debate with Margaritha. The incident ended with Margaritha's imprisonment and expulsion from the imperial city.[105]

Margaritha's book was hostile to Jews and often inaccurate, but it became an instant bestseller. In the first year of its publication, it was reprinted four times, and then again in 1531, 1544, and 1561. It got another burst of popularity at the end of the seventeenth century, with editions in 1698, 1705, and 1713. Not only did Margaritha's book shape the genre of polemical "ethnographies," including later works by Christian scholars, but it also influenced Luther, who used snippets of it in his own writings against the Jews. For example, Margaritha's claim that, when seeing Christians, Jews mispronounced the greeting "Seyt Gott will komm" as "Sched will komm"—here comes the devil—found its way into Luther's 1543 book "On Jews and Their Lies," and then into other polemical anti-Jewish works.[106]

But for all of Margaritha's hostility, the book offered nothing to support blood accusations. In fact, in a subtle way, it refuted it. In his description of Passover matzah, Margaritha emphatically stated there was nothing in it—"only flour and water"; not even salt or fat was added.[107] Although not all converts unequivocally denied the accusations against Jews, that many did was significant and was noted by some high-profile writers and authorities. Protestant reformer Andreas Osiander in his essay *Whether It Was True or Believable that the Jews Strangle Children of Christians and Use Their Blood* (written in the aftermath of a trial of Jews in Pösing—now Pezinok, Slovakia—in the kingdom of Hungary in 1529) raised this point explicitly.[108] He argued, echoing the *bulla aurea* from Emperor Frederick II in the aftermath of the violence in Fulda, that baptized Jews who became Christians would have no reason to conceal from Christians what their enemies—the Jews—did. In fact, Ossiander added, Pfefferkorn "and the friars of Cologne" would have been all too happy to reveal "child murders," had they known about them. Similarly, Paul Ricius, a learned man who also became a Christian, knew nothing about child murders.[109] This remained an important point; in 1759, Cardinal Ganganelli would note it in his report on blood accusations. But, as Elisheva Carlebach has pointed out, even when some converts, such as Ernst Ferdinand Hess in 1598, did "report practices in which Jews reportedly used Christian blood for ritual or magical purposes," the allegations were dismissed as counterproductive falsehoods and an obstacle to the goal of converting Jews to Christianity—a point already raised by Pfefferkorn and repeatedly evoked for centuries.[110] One of the most explicit expressions of this view came from Johann Christoph Wagenseil at the beginning of the eighteenth century. "It is certain," Wagenseil wrote, "that these lies and the untruths accompanying them arouse in them nothing but a hate against Christians, and make them at the same time have a horror of [Christian] religion.... Among those lies (as Luther calls them) the biggest and bitterest which Jews are forced to suffer at the hands of Christians is that they are publicly accused of needing Christian blood.... [B]ecause of those damned lies the Jews have been plagued, tormented, and many thousands of them cruelly executed."[111]

The result in German lands was a polyphony of voices about blood accusations. On the one hand, some continued to repeat such stories in chronicles and in reports of new trials. On the other, some, emphatically or just implicitly, denied, for different reasons, the charge that Jews killed Christian children.

The genre of custumals of Jews exploded in the seventeenth and eighteenth centuries and became increasingly embraced by Christian writers. One of the most successful such books was Johannes Buxtorf's *Synagoga judaica*, published just a few years after the convert Ernst Ferdinand Hess published his inflammatory book.[112] *Synagoga judaica,* addressed explicitly to the Christian reader, promised to "consider" with utmost diligence the "great ingratitude, disobedience, and stubbornness" of the Jews through a detailed description of Jewish ceremonies. Buxtorf, a reformed theologian and a professor of Hebrew at the University of Basel, ostensibly wanted to answer the question whether Jews indeed observed "zealously" the laws of Moses. But, in fact, his real purpose was to expose the "unbelief" of the Jews and show to Christians that Jews of his time no longer obeyed biblical laws but instead followed "fables" and other traditions. He wanted to arm Christians with tools against Jewish "unbelief" and help them avoid the "wrath of God." Like most others, Buxtorf took issue with the Talmud, underscoring that Jews privileged it over the Scriptures. Buxtorf based his description on a wide array of Jewish sources, ranging from the Talmud and the sixteenth-century compilation of Jewish law—the *Shulḥan 'Arukh*—to prayer books and Yiddish sources, such as sermons, guidebooks, and *minhag* books. And yet, despite the undeniable anti-Jewish premise and tone, the descriptions of the ceremonies and practices, mostly based on written sources, were not inaccurate; their goal, to be sure, was polemical but not spurious.

Synagoga judaica was, as Stephen Burnett has argued, "a theological examination of Judaism" through an "ethnographic description" of beliefs and ceremonies.[113] Scattered among Buxtorf's descriptions of Jewish practices are bits of information implicitly refuting blood accusations. For example, Buxtorf provided minute details related to the preparation for and observance of Passover. Discussing the days preceding the festival, he explained the observance and meaning of *Shabbat ha-gadol* (the Sabbath before Passover), the removal of leaven from the household, and the careful preparation of the Passover matzah: "usually round, full of little holes pierced with a metal tool . . . made only with clear water." Without salt or fat, the matzah, Buxtorf added, is quite "unpleasant" to eat.[114] A lengthy chapter about the Passover seder gives a step-by-step description, in which Buxtorf noted a few anti-Christian elements of some rituals; for example, he claimed that during the ritual of spilling wine, Jews cursed Christians. Describing in detail the ritual, which so obsessed the Trent interrogators, Buxtorf explained that Jews spilled drops of wine during the recitation of the ten plagues, which were to befall not onto Jews and their houses but "their enemies, evidently Christians."[115] The evening ended with a fourth cup of wine and a blessing based on scriptural passages, Psalms 79:6 and 69: 25: "Pour out Thy wrath upon the nations that know Thee not, and upon the kingdoms that call not upon Thy name," and "Pour out Thine indignation upon them, and let the fierceness of Thine anger overtake them." The blessing was in fact a curse "against all peoples who are not Jews,"

Buxtorf wrote.[116] Though Buxtorf never referred to anti-Jewish accusations, it was clear from his detailed description that no blood, Christian or otherwise, was part of the Passover celebration. In fact, as he showed later when describing dietary practices, no blood was *ever* part of the Jewish diet. In a section on food, he noted the fastidious avoidance of eating meat and milk together, and the removal of blood from meat.[117] So evidently based on Jewish sources, Buxtorf's exceedingly popular book became an important cultural artifact that subtly debunked blood accusations against Jews by providing a detailed description of Jewish ceremonies.

Some of the works on Jewish ceremonies came with images, a trend begun by Pfefferkorn. Margaritha's *Der gantz Jüdisch Glaub* sported illustrations based on Pfefferkorn's, though smaller and a mirror image of them, suggesting that the artist had Pfefferkorn's book in front of him. Later books included elaborate scenes of many ceremonies, including Passover and the preparation for it. In the long term, the works demystified Jewish practices. They still presented them as superstitious and absurd. But now these practices were revealed; they could no longer be secret. The 1705 book by Friedrich Albrecht Christiani, *Der Jüden Glaube und Aberglaube* (On Jewish Faith and Superstition), opened with a demeaning image of Jews with a dog and sow, and included many inflammatory passages and illustrations of some "superstitious" customs, including *kapparot* and *malkot*.[118] But other plates provided detailed and faithful representations of objects and rituals. Sometimes, as in case of Bernard Picart's elaborate *Cèremonies et coutumes religieuses de tous les peuples du monde,* the images are exquisite and do not focus just on the absurd.[119]

Picart's work differed from "ethnographic" books on Jewish ceremonies produced in the German lands, because his description of Jews was not intended to stand alone: it was one part of a seven-volume massive work on the ceremonies and customs of different religious groups around the world. The book emerged from the early modern genre of travel literature and "ethnographic" descriptions that followed the colonial expansion of Europe, rather than from anti-Jewish polemical instincts, an impetus for the German genre.[120] For Picart, Jews were important in the context of the history of religion, and in that sense his work resembled Joannes Boemus's on the customs of "all people" first published in 1520 in Latin and translated into many languages, including Italian and French, or that of Claude Fleury, whose work on Jewish ceremonies and rites focused on the biblical period.[121] Picart's work fit the new epistemological shift to a focus on witnessing and observation, rather than on textual studies or reports by converts. Even though his descriptions had polemical aspects, his work was not a direct anti-Jewish polemic.[122]

Picart included several copperplates with ritual objects and scenes to illustrate his elaborate descriptions of Jewish ceremonies. Though not all Picart's Jewish figures are portrayed in a flattering way—some sport a prominent "Jewish nose"—nonetheless the images are not inflammatory, though not devoid of polemic. Like Pfefferkorn and Margaritha, Picart added in the first 1723 edition of his work illustrations of rituals of Rosh Hashanah, Yom Kippur and the rest of the High Holidays, but omitted the "bizarre" practices that others emphasized (*tashlikh, kapparot,* and *malkot*). An illustration of *malkot,* the Yom Kippur flagellation practiced among Ashkenazi Jews, was added to the 1741 Paris edition, which copied meticulously Picart's original plates; but that image was appropriated from August Calmet's *Dictionnaire historique,* published also in Paris in 1722.[123]

Artists made it symbolically known that Christians were now privy to internal Jewish practices. Many illustrations depict Christians gazing or even participating in the ceremonies: for example, in Pfefferkorn's and Margaritha's books it is a Christian synagogue attendant, the only figure not blindfolded; in Bernard Picart's copperplates, centrally located women wear crosses; in Johann Alexander Boener's depictions of Jews in Fürth, Christians witness Jewish ceremonies outdoor, as they also do in Paul Christian Kirchner's *Jüdisches Ceremoniel* and Johann Bodenchatz's *Kirchliche Verfassung.*[124] The presence of Christians in these illustrations made visible a significant point: it signaled to the readers that Jewish ceremonies, now exposed and witnessed by Christians, were no longer "secret" and concealed. And if in these polemical ethnographies Jews might still be portrayed as blind to the truth of Christianity, as observing "bizarre" and exotic rituals, and even as blaspheming against Christ; and even if they might harbor hostility, indeed hatred, toward Christians—in their actions, Jews just curse: they do not kill. In this light, Jews no longer seemed dangerous. Jews and their rites may have been ridiculed, but those practices were "far different from the murderous rites fantasized in host desecration and ritual murder discourses."[125] With these books, European Christian readers now had tools to learn more about Jews that in a way that countered knowledge passed on through anti-Jewish tales in chronicles, where Jews appeared as secretive, dangerous killers to be murdered and plundered.

Indeed these works did not shy away from the topic of anti-Jewish accusations; blood accusations appeared in them again and again. Pfefferkorn was the first to address it explicitly. Margaritha chose a stealthier way, discussing the rituals of Passover and Passover matzah. But later writers addressed it as well. For example, Friedrich Abrecht Christiani in *Der Jüden Glaube und Aberglaube* passionately defended Jews against blood accusations, offering "my body and my life" as "a pledge that no Jew should be as bold to have the courage to kidnap and kill a Christian child."[126] Jews, he argued, were "too timid by nature to exercise such a cruel act, especially since they know that they have been subjected to exile among the Christians and under the Christian authorities." He acknowledged the stories from "two-three hundred years ago," such as at Trent and elsewhere, but laid the blame on "priests and monks" whose inventions led to persecution and massacres of Jews by the mob. Neither did Bernard Picart skirt the issue, although he was not as unequivocal about it. Despite elaborately describing the Jews' avoidance of blood, both by biblical commandment and in preparation of meat, in a chapter about "crimes laid to the charge of the Jews" he allowed for ambiguity.[127]

In contrast to German lands, in Italy there existed only a handful of books devoted to Jewish ceremonies intended for Christian readers. The earliest was *Historia dei riti ebraici* (History of Jewish Rites) by the Jewish scholar Leone Modena, written ostensibly as a response to Buxtorf's popular *Synagoga judaica* and published first in Paris in 1637; it was later republished and translated into other languages a number of times. The French version was included in Picart's *Ceremonies*. At the end of the seventeenth century, Giulio Morosini, a convert to Christianity, published a polemical work in which a large part was devoted to Jewish ceremonies, and in 1737, another convert, Paolo Medici, published his response to Modena's *Riti*. But in contrast to the Ashkenazi Jews, no indigenous *minhag* literature seems to have developed among Italian Jews. The *minhag* books published on the Italian peninsula were Ashkenazi Yiddish, sometimes Yiddish-Italian works, or occasionally Italian translations of Yiddish works, such as the *Sefer minhagim* published in Venice by Giovanni de Gara in 1589 and republished numerous times thereafter, or even Benjamin Slonik's guidebook for women, *Seder mizvot nashim* (A Book of Women's Commandments), first published in Yiddish in 1577 in Cracow, then translated into Italian by Jacob Halpron, and published in 1616 in Venice. The Italian edition of Slonik's guidebook evoked a strong negative response by a Bolognese preacher, Girolamo Allè, who feared that the availability of such books in Italian, combined with the proximity of Jews and Christians, would lead to a "pernicious" Jewish influence on Christians.[128] With few works discussing Jewish rites and ceremonies, anti-Jewish polemic on the Italian peninsula was dominated by theological questions shaped early on by Pietro Galatino's work, *De arcanis catholicae veritatis* (Mysteries of the Catholic Truth), which itself had been influenced by medieval polemical works.[129]

If polemical interests by German-speaking Christians, coupled with the Ashkenazi tradition of *minhag* literature, offer a convincing account of why the "ethnographic" polemical genre was such a German phenomenon, the relative lack of interest in Jewish ceremonies in the Italian context can also be explained by the fact that Italian Christians did not face the same challenges to Christian ritual that Catholics in German lands faced from Protestant attacks during the Reformation. The political situation played a role as well. Because of the frequent expulsions of Jews from German cities and principalities, which may have played a role in creating the *minhag* literature to preserve local customs in periods of instability, some Christians, including Johannes Reuchlin, feared that Jews, "the bearers of this ancient testimony," would soon disappear from Europe and thus "doubled their effort" to study the Hebrew language and literature.[130] In Italy, the political situation was different. Jews were not expelled; indeed from 1555 their presence was assured, albeit in the increasingly segregated districts that became known as "ghettos."

On the Italian peninsula, the early polemical literature was driven by Christian Hebraists, mostly Christian Kabbalists, not out of fear of the disappearance of Jews or polemical impulses but because of their interest in Jewish texts as sources of knowledge about Christianity.[131] In fact, Pietro Galatino, in his letter to Reuchlin, wrote that his book dealt with "mysteries of the Catholic truth contained in the Talmudic books."[132] This Christian theological interest in Hebrew books was, from the mid-sixteenth century, reinforced by an overt papal policy to censor books and convert Jews. Censorship required competent readers of Hebrew, and although many Jewish converts to Christianity served that role, there were also Christians who studied Hebrew.[133] The conversion policy, which mandated regular preaching, in turn effectively created a market for polemical conversionary books, which tended to focus, like medieval polemical works, on validating the "incontestable" truth of Christian dogmas through Jewish texts and demonstrating Jewish "blindness." For centuries, the Italian anti-Jewish polemic remained by and large theological.

Pietro Galatino's *De arcanis catholicae veritatis,* written in defense of Johannes Reuchlin and published in 1518, was of pivotal importance in shaping subsequent Italian polemical literature.[134] Twelve chapters not only introduce the readers to basic information about Jewish tradition—such as the concepts of the "written" and "oral" Torah—but also demonstrate "mysteries of Catholic truth" received from "Hebrew books and old scriptures." For Galatino, as for other Christian Hebraists, Hebrew books were instruments for confirmation of the Christian faith according to *hebraica veritas*—the Hebrew truth.

Although Galatino was accused of plagiarizing Raymondo Martini's *Pugio fidei,* an important thirteenth-century polemical work, it was

Galatino's work that had a demonstrable impact on polemical anti-Jewish works on the Italian peninsula and beyond, because until the seventeenth century, *Pugio fidei* remained relatively obscure.[135] And based on the number of surviving manuscripts, according to Ora Limor, *Pugio fidei* had "a limited success" also in the medieval period.[136] Likely because of that, the book was not brought to print until 1643, when it was first published in Paris. It was followed by three more seventeenth-century editions and one in the eighteenth century.[137] By contrast, some other medieval polemical works against Jews—for example, Isadore of Seville's work—were printed already in the fifteenth century.[138]

Plagiarized or not, Galatino's work became quite popular and reached numerous readers across Europe even before the works Galatino had drawn on became available in print. First published in 1518 in Ortona by the Jewish printer Gershom Soncino, *De arcanis* was then reprinted posthumously in Basel in 1550 and 1561, and in Frankfurt in 1602, 1603, 1612, with a final edition in 1672. It was Galatino's *De arcanis*, not *Pugio fidei*, with which scholars engaged explicitly. For example, Modena refuted *De Arcanis* in his Hebrew work *Magen va-herev*, and Christian writers, even opponents of the Kabbalah, referred to *De arcanis* in their works.[139]

Each chapter in Galatino's book addressed separate theological questions, most of which had already been articulated in the Middle Ages: the Trinity, the incarnation of "the Son of God and Divinity of the Messiah," the first coming of the Messiah, "the redemption of the humankind because the Messiah has come," the mother of the Messiah, the "mysteries" of the Messiah, "the eternal rejection of the Jews and the calling and salvation of the gentiles," "the new divine law" to be established by the Messiah, the cessation of "old law" with the establishment of the new, and the second coming of the Messiah.[140] But even though *De arcanis* is a polemical work, seeking Jewish conversions, the book left readers with a sense of appreciation for postbiblical Jewish texts because Galatino used rabbinic sources to demonstrate Christian truth. Indeed, Galatino concluded, the Christian truth could be found in Jews' own postbiblical books, even if they were blind to their meaning.

Galatino's *De arcanis* used the figures of Reuchlin and his accuser, the Dominican Johannes Hoogstraten, to demonstrate two ostensibly contradictory points: the Talmud contained falsities, lies, and blasphemies, but it also contained truths.[141] Galatino argued that Christians should know and study the Talmud, showing that Pope Clement V himself supported a Latin translation.[142] It is perhaps not surprising that two years after Galatino's *De arcanis*, Christian printer Daniel Bomberg began to publish the first full edition of the Talmud with Pope Leo X's endorsement.[143]

The topics and examples contained in *De arcanis* were later used by other polemicists, who at times reorganized their order and flow. Fabiano Fioghi's *Dialogo fra il cathecumino et il padre catechizante* (A Dialogue between a Neophyte and a Father Catechizer), published first in 1582 and then republished twice in the seventeenth century, did just that.[144] The book's dependence on Galatino was undeniable. Like Galatino, Fioghi sought to refute Jewish arguments and convert Jews, showing that mysteries of Christian truth are contained in Jewish works. As a result, while claiming that Jews were blind to the truth of Christianity contained in their own books, Fioghi, himself a convert, validated Jewish sources—both the Hebrew Scriptures and rabbinic works. Nowhere in this work did he allude to anti-Jewish accusations, even when the opportunity arose, for instance, when discussing Passover or the Eucharist.[145]

This was true also for other works published in Italian. In his 1618 treatise against Jews focused on the "Passion and Death of the Messiah," Pietro Pichi, a Dominican preacher nominated by Pope Paul V to the official position of a preacher to Jews, referred to "the authority of ancient rabbis," the Talmud included, to prove Christian doctrines. For Pichi and other Italian polemicists, Jewish sources were in fact useful and were not to be ridiculed in their entirety. Jews simply could not see the truths their books contained; hence Pichi pleaded with them to "read your own masters, who in your Talmud explained the truth about the Messiah … who because of the sins of the world had to be martyred and killed."[146] The preacher expressed his desperation at Jews' failure to convert and their continued persistence "in their perfidy;" his concern: they would never be saved.[147] Jews, Pichi wrote, were "like men, who are near death, about whom one thinks as dead rather than alive; who are counted among the dead because there is no longer hope for life." Despite his pessimism and reminders about the state in which Jews found themselves—"the poorest of all nations," with no kingdom of their own, "servants and slaves to all nations on earth"—Pichi repeatedly called Jews "brothers."[148] To be sure Jews were punished for their role in the death of Christ—"the gravest sin"—but he nonetheless claimed that Jews did not kill Jesus. They were participants but not direct killers: Jesus "was not exactly killed by Jews, but by gentiles … not by Priests but by other strangers," but Jews "were present there, and assisting: they accused him and sent him to death."[149] Even though Pichi asserted that Jews hated Christ and that the terrible things that had happened to Jews were a punishment for their role in the crucifixion, he never accused Jews of crimes against contemporary Christians. His argument, vituperative adjectives notwithstanding, was theological, his polemic textual.

Most Italian polemical works argued that it was contemporary Judaism, "its most unhappy state," as one writer put it, along with its "vanities," and, in the words of another, "profane and harmful law of the Talmud" that were to be challenged, but not Jews themselves.[150] In another work, Pietro Pichi wanted to ridicule the idea of transmigration of the souls, the *gilgul,* which he thought was "contrary to the Divine Scriptures"; he was also troubled by the Jewish interpretation of the biblical Edom to mean Christianity and of Esau as Christians, thus transposing all the biblical curses against Edom and Esau "against us."[151] According to Pichi, Jews "believe in all kinds of tales and blasphemies;" they speak "great evil" against Christianity, and curse Christians.[152] And yet, frustrated as he was that Jews were "hard as a rock," Pichi nonetheless prayed to find "arguments to convince and convert" them and asked God to "open their heart and recognize the truth."[153]

In Pichi's work and others, the issue was what Jews believed or failed to believe, not what they did. It was about thoughts not deeds. To be sure the Jews had hateful fantasies, Pichi claimed, but they were not about the now, but about the future. These fantasies expressed hope, as did "David Kimhi in the explanation of the prophesy of Obadiah that when Rome will be destroyed with all Christians, redemption of the Jews will arrive." But Jews, "as all rabbis interpret, will not be liberated, nor will they ever leave this captivity, unless Christian religion is destroyed first."[154] Indeed, decades later, Francesco Carboni, another seventeenth-century writer writing about "the unhappy state of Judaism," noted the "wickedness of their thoughts [*malvagità de loro pensieri*]," and mentioned only a few obscure examples of attempts by Jews to act out their "enmity" toward Christians, mostly tales from Spain.[155] Instead, he claimed, Jews continued to "crucify the Christian name" but only "in thought, not being able to do it in deed."[156]

But for all his fierce language, Carboni did not embrace the narrative of Jewish "crimes," though he did address the issue of consumption of blood in the context of dietary prohibitions.[157] Whereas most Christian anti-Jewish polemic that discussed dietary issues sought to justify the consumption of pork by Christians, Carboni focused on the biblical prohibition on consuming blood, realizing that the laws of kashrut grounded in this prohibition raised a serious theological issue. If blood was prohibited by the scriptures, then Christians needed to defend the idea of the consumption of Christ's blood in the Eucharist. According to Carboni, this biblical prohibition was no longer valid, because Christ himself "affirms that blood is the drink of the man, mysteriously appearing in Christian sacrifices." Paradoxically, then, it was Christians, accepting the precept of transubstantiation, who needed to abolish the prohibition against drinking blood. Implicitly, Jews' "stubbornness" in observing biblical precepts due to their "blindness" to the coming of the Messiah made the accusations of killing Christians to obtain blood and of desecrating the Eucharist for the purpose of making it bleed absurd. By being "obstinate" in observing these "no longer valid" laws—abolished "with the coming of the Messiah"—Jews refrained from consuming blood; their law was quite strict about it. In fact, to use blood, they would have had to accept the premise that "the Old Law" was indeed abolished! By this logic, Jews could not both be obstinately observant of the law and use human blood. Their steadfast refusal to eat pork implicitly strengthened their defense against blood accusations. For Christians like Carboni, the argument about the abolition of Jewish dietary laws was not only about justifying Christian consumption of pork, an arguably trivial issue, but also about validating transubstantiation, a dogma central to Catholicism.

For all its virulent language, Carboni's work was deeply theological, and even he conceded that despite the "blasphemies" and "vanities" of the Talmud, it contained truths the rabbis concealed. The Talmud covered, Carboni wrote, following Jeronimo de Santa Fe, "three types of matter."[158] One concerned civil and criminal matters, similar to "imperial laws among us Christians"; the second dealt with issues of matrimonial law, forbidden and permitted foods, festivals, and prayers "in the same way that we have the Decrees of the Holy Doctors of the Church"; the third concerned "stories and discourses about law," creation, "works of the Holy Fathers, miracles . . . the coming of the Messiah," and related topics. These were called *Haggadoth* "that is narrative, in plural." But, he continued, these narratives were not presented separately; they were diffused among the many books of the Talmud, enabling the rabbis to hide these stories. In short, the Talmud might include "abominations," but it also contained valid knowledge.

Theology thus dominated anti-Jewish polemic on the Italian peninsula. It drew heavily from Hebrew sources; many pages were filled with quotes in Hebrew characters in support of Christian doctrines. The intoxicating power of Jewish sources used to demonstrate the verity of Christianity became an important aspect of Italian conversionary polemic. This was a battle of ideas providing simultaneous apologetic arguments in support of Christianity and a polemic against Judaism. Conversion remained an important aspect of Christian, especially Catholic, policies concerning Jews, especially in Italy. That goal was manifest in the establishment of *domus catechumenorum*, a home for neophytes, and the prooemium of the 1555 bull *Cum nimis absurdum*, which established the ghetto in Rome and reaffirmed earlier Church policies that sought to "use legal pressures" to convert Jews.[159] The conversionary policy was crowned by the 1584 bull *Sancta mater ecclesia,* which reaffirmed the thirteenth-century *Vineam sorec,* and forced Jews to attend weekly Catholic sermons.[160]

In Italy, conversionary policies of the Church, coupled with the fact that the original interest in Hebrew was stimulated not by anti-Jewish polemical and conversionary goals, but rather by Christian theological interests, meant that Jewish sources, even if censored and occasionally even ridiculed, were studied and considered valid. In fact, some conversionary polemic emerged from the act of censorship itself. In 1608, *Dottrina facile et breve per ridurre l'hebreo al conoscimento del vero Messia & Salvator del mondo* (Easy and Short Doctrine to Bring the Jews to the Knowledge of the True Messiah & Savior of the World) was published in Venice. Its author, Thomaso Bell'Haver Crucifero, was a member of the Holy Office responsible for the supervision of Hebrew books. His job as a censor of Hebrew books before they were printed ignited "a desire" to write his own book.[161] Bell'Haver "has read many things in the Holy Language, and seen the errors of the Jews, and their perverse interpretations," which he also "discussed" with rabbis. In his book, he wanted to "rebut" all these arguments, "false interpretations of the rabbis," and demonstrate "the Catholic and Christian truth." Bell'Haver wrote out of concern for "Jewish souls" and from the hope that, if Jews only opened their eyes, they would see there was "no other Messiah than that crucified on Calvary." The book, a mix of Italian, Latin, and Hebrew, was to be used by preachers and others conversing with Jews to facilitate their conversion. Certainly, the book is indebted to Galatino, but the fact that there were Catholic censors of Hebrew books who read those works and consulted with rabbis was one more reason why on the Italian peninsula accusations against Jews seemed less entrenched in polemical works.

These cultural and policy goals—conversion and censorship—shaped the content of polemical literature. Italian polemical literature was generally not anti-Jewish, but rather anti-*Judaic,* focusing on refuting the tenets of Judaism. Although in early modern Italy there existed a whole body of Simonine literature, only on very rare occasions did Italian polemical writers even mention the anti-Jewish stories found so frequently in European chronicles. When they did, the discussions were brief. By and large Italian writers focused on the battle of ideas, not the demonization of real Jews.

Yet there were exceptions, such as the Jesuit Giovanni Piero Pinamonti's 1694 conversionary work *La sinagoga disingannata* (*The Synagogue Disenchanted*), which was not based on Hebrew sources. Pinamonti focused on theological issues, seeking to affirm for the world "a truth and only Faith." He also addressed laws and real-life situations, such as economic issues that might prevent Jews from converting, as well as the "sinful" ways of Christians.¹⁶² He claimed that Jews were "not treated better in any place in the world as among Christians, where, with few exceptions, everyone allows them to live in peace."¹⁶³ Among Christians, Jews were treated justly but, he continued, "if they were our judges," similar justice could not be expected from Jews. Indeed, no one could deny, Pinamonti claimed, that Jews harbored hatred toward Christians, as one could see "in stories of many innocent children tormented and crucified by Jews in many countries, or as one saw during the last wars in Hungary, in which, as it is written in many places, they publicly fasted, and prayed to God that the Turks win and Christian be defeated."

In chapter 16 of *La sinagoga disingannata*, Pinamonti addressed a larger question: whether Christian law was just and, in turn, whether Jews were justly or unjustly persecuted by Christians. Citing Bzovius, Spondanus, and Rinaldi, he listed examples of "Jewish crimes"—poisoning wells, killing William of Norwich, and the Poznań host desecration—and he concluded that Jews were never persecuted unjustly but always, deservedly, for their "crimes" (*scelerezze*).¹⁶⁴ To buttress his argument, he noted that when Jews were in fact persecuted unjustly, Christian leaders intervened. This was the case during the Second Crusade in 1146, when Bernard of Clairvaux intervened, and on other occasions when the popes stepped in to protect Jews as well. Being just, therefore, "Christian law is the true law of God."¹⁶⁵ In Pinamonti's argument, the existence of both anti-Jewish trials and of Christian defenses of Jews was evidence of the validity of the accusations.

Pinamonti returned to accusations that Jews killed Christian children in a chapter proving that Jews' "misfortune" was punishment for "the crucifixion of Christ," which, he claimed, was praised by rabbis in the Talmud. "If they could repeat it," he wrote about the crucifixion, "they would do it again, as they had done many times with the innocent children, lashing them, crowning them with thorns, and crucifying them with extreme cruelty because of hatred of Jesus Christ."¹⁶⁶ Yet despite this vitriolic language and his embrace of the ritual murder stories, he avoided making the claim that Jews needed Christian blood. As with Christian polemicists in the German lands, his knowledge of Jewish practices prevented him from making such claims. In a chapter concerning changes Christians made to divine commandments related to dietary laws and circumcision, Pinamonti did not focus, as others typically did, on the question of the consumption of pork but, like Carboni, on the consumption of blood.¹⁶⁷ He discussed in detail the commandment "you must not eat flesh with its life-blood in it" (Gen. 9:4) and described Jewish kosher slaughtering practices. He found them superstitious, but when examined carefully, they clearly contradicted any idea of the Jewish need for Christian blood.

For the Jesuit Pinamonti, the existence of stories of Jews killing Christian children in authoritative Catholic chronicles could not be discounted: but if true, they were stories of "ritual crucifixion" done in reenactment of Christ's passion and in "hatred" of him, not cannibalistic rites to obtain the children's blood. The conversionary instinct was so strong in the Italian context that even though Pinamonti stressed what he saw as errors and blasphemies of the Jews, and gave examples of Jewish "crimes," he still believed that if Jews were adequately educated they would see the light and convert.[168]

On the Italian peninsula few writers turned to the demonization of Jews qua Jews. Simon's story was known, but it was presented as a singular case. It was only in the second half of the eighteenth century that works akin to those found north of the Alps and in eastern Europe began to appear. Strikingly, one of them, a book by Giovanni Pietro Vitti published in 1761, was based on printed sources related to sources from Poland.[169]

In contrast to his predecessors, Vitti was not interested in conversion or in explaining "so many prophecies"—other authors had tried that. His "only and principal intention" was to "expose to light" the stories of "children and other child martyrs killed in hatred of our faith by Jews" and to demonstrate "the hatred and malevolence the Jews have against us Christians."[170] Grounded in accessible historical works (by Adriano Fino, Alfonso de Espina, Laurentius Surius, the Bollandists, Bonelli, and others), Vitti's book was filled with vitriolic stories of Jews as killers. Thirteen long stories of children said to have been killed by Jews covered nearly 140 pages. Vitti made a list totaling nearly sixty brief examples, inclusive of the thirteen discussed in detail, each with reference to sources.[171]

Vitti's book inverted the trope of Jewish "blindness" in evoking "the blindness of Christians" that enabled them to have close relations with Jews. By digging up stories of Jews killing Christian children from chronicles, the lives of saints, and other books, Vitti aimed to poison personal relationships Jews and Christians might have had; he repeatedly urged Christians to be "more cautious and guard themselves from having intimacy, friendship, and confidence with such pernicious and dangerous enemies."[172] To heighten the rhetorical impact, he set up a contrast between his tropes of Christian love and of Jewish enmity, repetitively stressing Jewish "hatred" and Christian "fondness and favor." He deviously warned readers not to think that he wanted to "impress in the heart of Christians hatred and malevolence against the wretched Jews, as if we wanted Jews expelled from every part of the Christian world, but even completely destroyed."[173] "No," Vitti protested, "this was certainly not my intention; on the contrary, following the authority of the Holy Fathers and of the Church I admit that they have to be loved with love and common affection." In fact, even though Jews were "through their ancestors killers of Christ," they were not "excluded" from "the overall redemption of the Savior," and therefore "neither should we judge them unfit for our love."

Vitti's work is unusual in its scope and focus, but it does underscore the role that print played in disseminating and rooting these spurious stories in Christian memory. He scoured printed European works to provide his long list of anti-Jewish stories, ignoring nearly all works that denied those accusations and disparaging some as written by Protestants. But the impact of Vitti's work increased because it came at a specific moment: only six years after Pope Benedict XIV recognized the cult of Andreas von Rinn and, significantly, after a new wave of books about Simon of Trent, many of which mentioned other stories, appeared under the pontificate of Benedict XIV.

Pinamonti's and Vitti's books notwithstanding, what most Italian and German works shared was that they were based on Hebrew sources, and many, though certainly not all, the writers had some knowledge of Hebrew. Even when some of these polemical works were not directly based on Hebrew texts, they were often derivative of earlier works that had accepted the premise of the value of Jewish sources. This stands in stark contrast with anti-Jewish literature produced in Poland. If the polemical literature of the German and Italian spheres sought to "deny the tenets of Judaism" or—in the German context—"to expose the evil of Jewish rites," and in both "to convert the Jews," in Poland, except for a handful of theologically focused polemical works, most literature about Jews engaged little, if at all, with theological questions—ignoring almost completely polemical works based on Jewish texts, like those in Italy, or the "ethnographic" works produced in Germany.[174]

In early modern Poland-Lithuania, Christians increasingly encountered Jews in everyday life, sharing with them daily, even intimate, experiences. But readers were also able to find them in a variety of books—homiletic devotional works, the lives of saints, and, occasionally, chronicles. Christian works focused explicitly on Jews were relatively few in Poland, although they were published with some regularity from the second half of the sixteenth century.[175] The earliest works had a predominantly theological focus, as did the very first book against Jews printed in Poland and in Polish: the "Epistle of Rabbi Samuel Maroccanus." Published in 1536 in Cracow and reprinted two years later, with more editions in subsequent centuries, the "Epistle" came to Poland relatively late—almost two decades after the religious earthquake had shaken Christians in the western parts of Europe. Notably for Polish books, the 1536 and 1538 editions contained a rare image of Jews.[176]

Known to have survived in more than 300 manuscripts across Europe, including Italy, England, Germany, France, Spain, Poland, and even Denmark, the "Epistle" became a European bestseller also in print.[177] The first printed edition was published in 1475, and some thirteen incunabula editions followed before 1500, with dozens more in the sixteenth, seventeenth, and eighteenth centuries. The Polish version had twenty-seven chapters, three more than the earliest medieval versions. Like other European versions, its aim, using biblical sources, was to prove that Jesus was the Messiah and that the Jewish exile was the result of their rejection of this "truth."[178]

Still, Polish polemical works that focused on theological matters were almost never strictly anti-Judaic; many served as anti-Protestant polemic under an anti-Judaic guise.[179] That is why these works rarely, if ever, engaged with postbiblical Jewish literature, even when they criticized Jews for following the Talmud and, paradoxically given Poland's Catholic context, for not reading the Bible, which was prohibited to Catholics without clerical mediation. In these works, the Jewish interlocutor, always idealized and removed from social reality, served as a polemical trope, a foil for an intra-Christian polemic. In the end, he usually accepted theological arguments marshaled by the main character and converted to the denomination of the book's author.

The landscape began to shift slowly in the second half of the sixteenth century. In 1569, Jan Górski published *Index errorum*, a list of "errors" of the Talmud, copied verbatim—inclusive of spelling mistakes—from *Bibliotheca sancta* by Sixtus Senensis, published in Venice just three years earlier.[180] The list was a short summary of alleged blasphemies against Christ and God in the Talmud, "calumnies" against the law of Moses, and Jewish prayers against Christians. To Sixtus Senensis's Latin list, Górski added a Polish, much more vile "translation" and a short afterword. (For example, where Sixtus called Jews "impious," Górski used the adjective "stinking."[181]) Although Górski's book was of limited success—it was not republished on its own—the book had a lasting impact in Poland. Subsequent writers either copied the passages verbatim or paraphrased them in their own, much more aggressively anti-Jewish works.[182] But it was Przecław Mojecki's *Żydowskie okrucieństwa, mordy, y zabobony* (Jewish Cruelties, Murders, and Superstitions) of 1598 that set a new tone for Polish works concerning Jews.[183] It aimed to vilify Jews in order to discourage Jewish–Christian contacts and offered a vitriolic regurgitation of stories of "Jewish crimes and cruelties" found in European chronicles and other works.[184] Polemical works focusing on theological arguments did not entirely disappear from the Polish scene, but the new explicitly anti-Jewish genre that emerged with Mojecki was neither polemical nor *sensu stricto* anti-Judaic. Instead, it was anti-Jewish, targeting Christians who engaged in close business or personal relations with Jews, its goal to poison Jewish–Christian interactions.

Mojecki's work proved a turning point in more than one way. It created a veritable echo chamber of anti-Jewish ideas articulated in the Polish vernacular, which were then copied and replicated as if in an infinite mirror. The apparent impetus for the book was the death of a child in 1597 in Szydłów, a small town some seventy miles northeast of Cracow, for which Mojecki believed Jews were responsible but not punished thanks to "sacks of Judas."[185] The book offered several dozen "examples of Jewish murders and cruelties from trustworthy historians" to explain "domestic" cases, to influence those who doubted that Jews committed such crimes, and to warn them that God might send a disaster onto the kingdom of Poland in retribution for a weak justice system.[186] Jews, Mojecki contended evoking the Good Friday *Improperia,* had always been an "ungrateful" people; they rejected God by worshiping the golden calf, killing prophets, and succumbing to idolatry.[187] They had been repeatedly warned by the prophets and punished by God, but still continued in their deeds. And following the destruction of the Temple they were dispersed across the earth. Those who settled in Europe were "illegitimate" children, born from Hebrew women given to "German" mercenaries in the Roman army. Educated by women, they spread superstitions that had nothing to do with Moses's teachings. Jews of his day, Mojecki argued, were thus no heirs to ancient Israelites—a point that set the stage for stories about "Jewish cruelties" and implicitly undermined Jewish defenses grounded in biblical prohibitions on murder and the consumption of blood.

Drawing on "authoritative histories" such as *Fortalitium fidei* by Alfonso de Espina; the Bohemian chronicle by Václav Hájek of Libočan; *Supplementum* by Jacob Foresti; Cesare Baronio's *Annales;* and many other sources, Mojecki presented thirty-four examples of "Jewish murders" and several more of host desecration and other "superstitions." They were meant to demonstrate that across Christendom Jews were punished for their crimes, and when they were not, God punished those who failed to provide "justice." For example, in a story said to have taken place in Weißenohe in 1303, Jews killed a child, but bribed their way out of retribution with "gold, with whose power also today they create Judases in Poland."[188] But God afflicted with a sickness the official who refused to punish Jews. While suffering, this official promised to "punish Jews and not to tolerate them in his estates anymore," whereupon he became healthy again and fulfilled his promise by burning at the stake the guilty Jews and expelling the rest. The "martyred" child was buried in a church and produced miracles. In this story, disorder turned into order. In marshaling dozens of examples from Poland and abroad, Mojecki sought to emphasize differences in the treatment of Jews in different regions. The litany of cases from abroad, which ended with brutal punishments of Jews, was followed by a list of examples from Poland, where, according to Mojecki, Jews escaped justice by being largely not just unpunished but not even prosecuted. Mojecki wished Poland to be more like Italy, where "justice was more acute and people more scrupulous and interested in evidence."[189]

Important for Mojecki's argument connecting Poland-Lithuania with European lore was Piotr Skarga's authoritative *Lives of Saints,* which in 1579 introduced to the country the story of Simon of Trent along with a "domestic" story from Punia in Lithuania. Skarga's text about Simon was based on Laurentius Surius's version published in 1571, some seventeen years before papal recognition of the cult; it mentioned the punishment of the Jews only briefly and, of course, made no mention of Simon's inclusion in the *Martyrologium,* which would come a few years later. But by 1598 the cult of Simon was officially recognized, and Mojecki embellished Simon's story with deceptive details. After describing the unspeakable "cruelty" of the Jews to Simon, who was tormented in a way "not resembling the passion of the Lord" in the least, Mojecki stated that "following papal order" and based on known circumstances, Giovanni de Salis was "easily" able to charge Jews, who "after confessing [to the crime] were punished with fire, and all others expelled from the town."[190] God glorified "the martyrdom of the child" with great miracles, so when "the pope inducted him to the fellowship of holy martyrs," the town's citizens built a beautiful church in which his "shriveled and brutally martyred body" could still be seen. In an important twist, in Mojecki's version, it was now not only the kings, emperors, and other Christian officials who punished Jews, but the popes did so as well.

If Skarga's work triggered new attention to stories of Jews killing Christian children, Mojecki's work was to spur not just new copycat works but also more trials and convictions of Jews in Poland-Lithuania. In the full swing of the Reformation, Jews had been tried, prosecuted, and executed for desecrating the Eucharistic wafer, but accusations of murder rarely triggered prosecution, and even when they did, the Jews were generally exonerated.[191] Still, as Hanna Węgrzynek has noted, little material from the sixteenth century survives in the archives; much information about these anti-Jewish accusations comes from later anti-Jewish works, like that by

Mojecki.[192] The first documentable trial seems to have taken place in 1547 when two Jews were charged in Rawa, now a town in central Poland, resulting in a special commission established by a royal decree issued on June 23, 1547.[193] But because the full records have not been preserved, the purported outcome is only known from an anti-Jewish work by Szymon Hubicki, a lector of the bishop of Cracow, published in 1602, more than five decades later.[194] Just how unreliable Hubicki's claims are is exemplified by his claim that, according to a court decree from "feria 5 post cond. Paschae" in 1547 (April 21), Jews were executed at the stake and expelled from the city. Yet the royal commission was established only in June, so the April 21 decree that Hubicki took as evidence of punishment may have been issued by city officials which was then appealed by Jews, resulting in the establishment of the commission. But Hubicki made no mention of any of this, and thus after reading his work one is left with the impression that Jews were in fact convicted and punished.

The nature of the sources makes it difficult to distinguish between accusations in a legal sense, resulting in a court trial, and stories accusing Jews of killing children that circulated in the region either orally or that were later immortalized in print.[195] Still, for the period between 1547, the year of the trial in Rawa, and 1579, when Skarga introduced Simon's story into Poland, some ten stories claiming Jews killed Christian children in Poland-Lithuania are known from either archival references or later polemical works. Of those, it seems, four resulted in a legal action, either a trial or an act of legal protection of Jews, as, for example, in 1575 (or 1576), when King Stefan Batory prohibited unsubstantiated accusations against Jews. After Skarga's introduction of Simon's story in 1579, and even more after the Simon cult was officially recognized in 1588, more such stories began to spread—Hanna Węgrzynek has listed approximately fifteen between 1579 and 1598, known mostly from later polemical works. But even then, Jews were largely accused but not prosecuted; when they were charged with a crime in courts, they were again largely exonerated, though not without facing a torturous ordeal. Such was the case of Jews in Gostynin and Sawina (or Sawin) in 1595.[196] Throughout the sixteenth century, it appears, despite the circulation of some anti-Jewish stories, Jews continued to be able to muster effective defenses, suggesting that the tales of "Jewish cruelties" had not yet become deeply rooted in Polish culture. And this is what Mojecki wanted to change.

Mojecki attacked close Jewish–Christian contacts and the legal framework within which Jews settled and lived in the country. With gifts, he claimed, Jews "have stolen themselves into the hearts of so many venerable people," who then, despite "shameful cruelties," bend the law and statutes and, "in contempt of Christ, love them and partake together in feasts and social events with them, [partner with them] in tolls, taxes, stuff, and fortunes, and turn themselves into an affront, and their subjects, a people saved with Christ's blood, into slaves and ridicule of the Jews."[197] Addressing Jews' protectors, Mojecki tried to dismantle the validity of the Jews' defenses: the statute of Prince Bolesław the Pious of Great Poland issued in 1264 addressing anti-Jewish accusations, the 1334 privilege granted to Jews by King Casimir the Great, and papal bulls prohibiting charging Jews with killing Christians to obtain their blood.[198] The 1264 privilege was invalid, Mojecki claimed, because it was issued only for Great Poland, the domain of Bolesław the Pious, and its confirmation by King Casimir the Great, "our Polish Ahasuerus," was the result of the king's affair with a Jewish woman named Esther. As for papal protections that Jews invoke, claiming that "they should not be accused of needing Christian blood," these documents "mention no name of the pope, nor a place" where they were issued, in contrast to other papal bulls that warn against contacts between Jews and Christians. In fact, in 1568, Pope Pius V expelled Jews from his state, except for Rome and Ancona. In light of this evidence, "it is not likely that Jews would have received any encouragement and protection regarding these crimes from the Bishops of Rome." And even if some pope might have indeed issued such a bull, Mojecki continued, "I cannot see how this could save Jews," because charters granted in good intentions but based "on bad and erroneous information" could not be valid. So if Jews obtained a letter arguing that their law prohibited them from consuming blood, this was a poor excuse. "We know that well" that accusations against Jews were not grounded in "the reason that they commit these murders because of their own law." Rather, Jews commit "these cruelties" because of "their superstitions and hatred of Christians." Jewish law, therefore, cannot be used as a defense. Even so, Mojecki played the devil's advocate: if one were to accept the argument that Jews did not kill Christians because their law prohibited the consumption of blood, history and even the Bible showed that Jews "sin against their precepts." He drew the reader's attention to Psalm 106 (105 in the text), which lists Israelites' acts of disobedience to God, including "sacrificing their own sons and daughters" and "shedding innocent blood of their own sons and daughters" before Canaanite idols. So if they did not "spare their own, would they spare Christians, whom they consider enemies?" But even more generally, Mojecki reasoned, the arguments that Jews' defenders presented could not be accepted, because doing so would mean that Jews could not be accused of anything—"thefts, adultery, usury, sorcery, cheating, and other misdeeds"—for all of these are against Jewish law.

The Polish writer thus took a diametrically opposite approach from the Italian polemicists who insisted that Jews stubbornly adhered to Jewish law and that they needed to abandon it to be able to see the truth of Christianity. By shifting attention from theology and conversion to social issues aimed at poisoning apparently friendly Jewish–Christian relations, Mojecki concluded that Jews in fact did not adhere to their law. In his mind, as captives to "German" soldiers in Titus's army, Jews residing in Europe had never adhered to their law: instead they adhered to superstitions that they learned from their mothers. Christians thus should guard themselves from contacts with Jews, who were dangerous, shunned justice, led Christians astray, taking not just "blood and fortune" but also "our souls."[199] Jews were, Mojecki emphasized, "our main enemies;" following Johannes Eckius, he wrote they were "a wanton people," "full of wickedness," "dishonest, unfaithful, perjurious, thievish, malevolent, purulent, hateful, ... inhuman, vengeful, bloodthirsty, treacherous, homicidal, murderous, blaspheming, spellbinding, filthy, reeky, dissolute, indifferent, slanderous, usurious, ungrateful, overjoyed by all their misdeeds against Christians."[200] He ended by challenging the contention that Jews were needed and useful, wanting instead to demonstrate that their presence in the kingdom was harmful. He hoped his readers could imagine a Poland without Jews.

If one accepts later writers' claims as true, Jews immediately recognized Mojecki's book as dangerous and bought out the print run to destroy it, but no record of this action survives. The documents related to the Council of Four Lands, a Jewish self-governing body, responsible for many fiscal matters, say nothing about this matter, even though there exists other evidence of the costs of interventions in response to anti-Jewish accusations.[201] Today, it seems no more than two incomplete copies of Mojecki's book have survived.

In light of the book's apparent destruction, Mojecki's contemporary Szymon Hubicki wrote his own work, in which he included abridged version of stories found in Mojecki's. Hubicki's book was published on Christmas Eve in 1602 under a similar, though more exact, title: *Żydowskie okrucieństwa nad Naświętszym Sakramentem y dziatkami chrześciańskimi* (Jewish Cruelties against the Most Holy Sacrament and Christian Children). In his work, fatefully, Hubicki included a 1598 decree by the Crown Tribunal in Lublin sentencing Jews to death, issued in the aftermath of a trial of Jews accused of killing a Christian child in village of Świniarów—a trial that took place just a few months after Mojecki's book was published.[202]

The Świniarów case, which ended in Jews' death, apparently inspired Hubicki; he hoped it would become a turning point in Jewish–Christian relations. He dedicated his book to Adam Stadnicki, Marshal of the

Crown Tribunal at the time. In his dedicatory chapter, Hubicki outlined what he and other Christians, including Mojecki, saw as Jews' unfaithfulness and ungratefulness. God had generously provided for them, but Jews "quickly forgot his law and commandments, and began to offend him with unfaithful stubbornness and even idolatry."[203] Hubicki underscored Jews' "open hostility and venom" against "God and our savior," as well as the blasphemies of the Talmud—all typical Christian arguments against Jews. But this section only served to prepare the reader for "examples, both old and new, foreign and ours" of "sacrilege" and "murder of innocent children, whose blood they unspeakably desire." The case from Świniarów was not the only one on his mind; fresher perhaps was a recent host desecration trial that ended with the expulsion of Jews from Bochnia in 1601, because Hubicki began his catalog of "Jewish cruelties" with a host desecration story from 1290 Paris.[204] "Murders of Christian children" was the subject of chapter 7, preceded by a chapter on "Jewish enmity" against Christians. By the time readers arrived at that point, they were well primed.

Peppered throughout Hubicki's book are attacks on Christians who were close to Jews. Indeed, if the stories from abroad showed how Jews were punished everywhere, the same could not be said about the Polish crown, where, Hubicki wrote, "Almost every year, [Jews] spill our blood," but they get away with it thanks to gifts, which make officials "look the other way [*przez spary patrzą*]." Bribery aside, "in clear and obvious matters, they do not believe in these Jewish murders."[205] And yet, "Poland, Lithuania, Ruthenia, and Podolia were filled with similar examples—if one only wanted to collect them." Alas, "it is more likely today that Jews live not only near each other in a neighborhood," but they share the same house with Christian men and women. Hubicki hoped that the Świniarów case, which was tried openly "*in theatro* of the whole Kingdom," would have an impact; still he feared that "bags of pepper, and the sound of gold" turned people deaf, "knowing, they don't know, and don't want to admit these cruel murders into their hearts."

Simon of Trent, according to Hubicki, deserved "the first place in the unhappy register of murdered children."[206] His martyrdom was glorified by God through miracles, and "he was included among the Saints by the head of the Catholic Church," his "shriveled and brutally martyred body displayed for the pious people" to see. Jews were tried and, "according to papal order, after they confessed to everything, executed by fire, with the rest expelled." This historically inaccurate account of the papal role in the execution of Jews in Trent helped undermine any future claims of papal protection in defense of Jews—a hallmark in Polish books.

In a manner more succinct than Mojecki, Hubicki dismissed Jewish defenses against blood accusations grounded in Jewish law, such as its prohibition on using blood. Instead, he focused on historical, and especially biblical, examples of sorcery and, it seems, for the first time in Polish Christian works, Jewish customs and ceremonies. Moses killing an Egyptian became proof that it was "an axiom of their faith" that killing an idolater was not only not a sin but also that "when they offer blood of unfaithful idolaters they offer God the most appreciated offering."[207] Jews cursed Christians every day and believed that "a man can take another man's sin onto himself," such as during the ritual of *kapparot* when they transposed the sin onto Christians.[208] Although Mojecki was clearly Hubicki's main source—with some passages, including the list of sources, taken verbatim—in this section Hubicki also referred to the 1531 edition of Antonio Margaritha's work on Jewish ceremonies, perhaps suggesting he knew German.[209]

Hubicki ended his work with a broader reflection on the status of Jews in Poland and policies and laws.[210] "What should one do with them," he asked. "Expel them?" This, he quickly conceded, would not be possible. So through another story meant to show the haughtiness of Jews, he advocated both marking them and applying laws that would curb their prosperity and wealth. Marking was necessary, Hubicki stated, to "distinguish slaves from lords." Hubicki's verbs worked to deny Jews the right to respect: they cheated, swindled, bribed, engaged in usury; they did *not* work, plow or sow, or engage in crafts. They "snatched bread from the mouths of the children of the Crown." Hubicki ended his book with an address to Polish "politicians": supporters of Jews reluctant to expel them, "into whose hearts" Jews stole themselves with their gifts, who "disdain their own brothers and Christian blood, and socialize with this wicked nation and entrust their secrets to them." He provided once more the long list of anti-Jewish adjectives from Johannes Eckius, introduced to Polish readers by Mojecki, which would henceforth become rooted in Polish literary lore.[211]

Although Hubicki's work was certainly derivative of Mojecki's, his book introduced certain innovations. For Hubicki, chronicles were only one kind of evidence of Jewish "cruelties"; court records were another. Where Mojecki only mentioned the existence of court records, Hubicki provided more detailed information about them, adding concrete dates and references, and even printing excerpts of the 1598 Świniarów case.[212] European chronicles provided Polish writers with a new prism through which to look at Jews who were becoming increasingly embedded in the social and economic fabric of the Polish-Lithuanian Commonwealth. Stories found in them became evidence in trials against Jews, and the trials, in turn, became evidence for the stories. A feedback loop was now closed.

Hubicki's book had a long-lasting impact, with pan-European ramifications felt until the twentieth century. Sometime between 1671 and 1675, when Volume II of the *Acta Sanctorum* was published by the Antwerp Bollandists, a Polish Jesuit, Ludovicus Hoffman, provided the Bollandists with a Latin synopsis of Hubicki's list of blood accusations.[213] Hoffman's summary was then included in the monumental *Acta Sanctorum* in an appendix titled "De pluribus Innocentibus per Judaeos excruciatis" (Of Many Innocents Tormented by Jews) that followed the story of "Albert the Martyr," the boy whose death led to the trial that inspired Hubicki's book.[214] But if Mojecki, Hubicki, and other subsequent writers, like Sebastian Śleszkowski, used examples of acquittals from Poland as a *cri de coeur* to sound the alarm that Jews went unpunished in their kingdom, *Acta Sanctorum* omitted entirely all references to the acquittals or lack of prosecution. What was left was a list of supposed historical instances of Jews killing "innocent" Christians. The *Acta Sanctorum,* arguably the most comprehensive collection of lives of saints, became an authoritative reference book, and the Bollandists' inclusion of anti-Jewish stories provided evidence used to justify trials and accusations against Jews. Vitti used it in his 1761 book, as did the Nazi Julius Streicher in one of the most notorious issues of *Der Stürmer,* published on May 1, 1934, and devoted to "ritual murder," in which he published a three-page "annalistic" list of "Jewish ritual murders from the times of Christ to 1932."[215]

Mojecki and Hubicki started a Polish trail of transmission; their content and even wording would enter most of the anti-Jewish works all the way through the eighteenth century.[216] The stories they included inspired others, even those whose interests did not lie in anti-Jewish literature. In 1613, Szymon Syrenius, a physician from Cracow, added a three-page appendix to his massive herbarium about "the ruthless cruelties of unfaithful Jews" collected from "serious and authoritative writers."[217] Syrenius parroted Mojecki's and Hubicki's dismissal of Jewish defenses based on Jewish law and papal protections and updated the list of "Jewish cruelties," with examples extending to 1612 (the printing of the massive book of more than 1,500 folios was finished in March 1613). He ended with a warning to Christians that God would punish them for not punishing Jews.

The most sustained attack on Jews and their protectors came several years later from two writers, Sebastian Miczyński, a professor in the Cracow Academy, and Sebastian Śleszkowski, a personal physician to Szymon Rudnicki, bishop of Warmia.[218] Miczyński, writing in 1618, addressed the "Sons of the Crown" on the occasion of the convocation of the Sejm, the Polish parliament, imploring them to protect the kingdom. In his book, with the motto "the son of the slave shall not share in the inheritance with a son of a free woman," he argued that the Jews usurped a social position reserved to "the sons of the Crown."[219] After demonstrating Jewish "crimes" and attacking Christians for enabling them by having close relations (*spółkowanie*) with Jews and accepting bribes from them, he focused on policies and laws, both existing and proposed, regarding Jews. He conceded that the Church, through the bull *Etsi Judaeos,* tolerated Jews amidst Christians, but with limitations.[220] Of course, Jews were not to be treated "with extraordinary severity" but, Miczyński added a caveat, they were only to be treated well "when they are obedient, that it when they do not blaspheme against God Lord Christ and the saints, when they do not dare to hold Christian faith in contempt, when they do not harm Christians." But in Poland "everything is different." In fact, everything was "upside down."[221] Miczyński then offered the most detailed thus far discussion of economic issues at stake between Jews and Christians in Poland.

In its call against Christian friendships with Jews, Miczyński's work is not unique. What is significant is its lengthy and detailed polemic against legal protections. Miczyński, expanding the discussion in Mojecki and Hubicki, acknowledged laws that Jews used to protect themselves from Christian attacks and cited them in detail only to undermine them. For example, after quoting seven paragraphs from the 1264 privilege of Bolesław the Pious, the seventh (in the privilege, the thirty-first) focusing on blood libels, Miczyński brazenly stated, "What do I say about these above mentioned Jewish privileges? It is not right that Jews should enjoy them and defend themselves [with them]: because they [these privileges] cannot have any authority and power."[222] Not only could these privileges, here Miczyński agreed with Mojecki, not be valid because Bolesław the Pious granted his charter for Great Poland alone and Casimir the Great's confirmation was tainted by his Jewish lover's influence, but they were also an insult to Christianity, for they caused much harm to Christians. Miczyński implied that Jewish privileges violated one of the premises set out in canon law for tolerating Jews among Christians: that they do no harm to Christians. And since harm the Jews did commit, Miczyński reiterated listing children "recently killed," laws protecting Jews from persecution were thus inherently unjust and unfair.

The same applied to the Jews' use of papal protections against blood accusations. Already in the Bible, Miczyński retorted, there were examples of Jews spilling blood, even of their own children, who were "sacrificed to the devil . . . [and] offered to the Canaanite idols."[223] If Jews did not spare their own children, why would they spare "us Christians"? It was not possible, he continued, that those who were always inspired by the Holy Spirit would issue such protections to Jews. Papal, royal, and imperial privileges were only valid if based on truth, but examples demonstrated that Jews "committed many murders of Christian children," "almost every year," with many "revealed," but many still unknown. Miczyński's work was to date the most sustained attempt to upend Jewish legal defenses. It reinforced and deepened the attack on Jewish privileges and exacerbated distrust in the validity, even the existence, of papal bulls prohibiting anti-Jewish blood libels.

Three years later, in a lengthy, somewhat repetitive, and error-riddled book promising to "reveal treason, malicious ceremonies, secret counsels and practices harmful to the Commonwealth," Sebastian Śleszkowski would wield an even heavier hammer to the Jewish defensive strategy.[224] Like previous authors of anti-Jewish works, Śleszkowski addressed Christian readers, seeking to "warn them" about the "dangers" of close Jewish–Christian interactions. Accusations that Jews killed Christian children were only one in a long list of domestic "dangers" but one that allowed Śleszkowski to attack Jews' presence in the Polish-Lithuanian Commonwealth using precedents from other "Christian countries" that had expelled or killed Jews.[225] Śleszkowski did not hide his frustration with Christians "who not only do not want to believe the truth, clear as sun at noontime but even defend" Jews against charges for "such crimes."[226] He called such Christians "Jew-Christians" (Żydo-Chrześcianie).

To illustrate his point, Śleszkowski included a letter from "an honorable person"—an apparent eyewitness to the 1598 trial in Świniarów—to Cardinal Andrzej Batory, bishop of Warmia. The author described some of the proceedings of the trial, noting that "at the beginning" Jews were "defended with their law, the privileges, and, finally with the bulls of the Most Holy Pontiff."[227] This report of Jews submitting a copy of a papal bull in their defense sent Śleszkowski into a rage: "Shameless Jews, defending their well-known homicide, which they had committed, presented before the Tribunal a fraudulent papal bull, doing great harm to the Holy Father."[228] No pope would ever issue such a bull, Śleszkowski contended, just as a pope would not testify on behalf of a "thief that he did not steal, or a bandit that he did not assault." By presenting such a bull, Jews "hideously slander the pope," and should be punished in the same way as those who present "fraudulent privileges, letters, and bulls to deceive a person and to harm the Commonwealth." As for the presented bull itself, it should be confiscated "and burned along with those who have hitherto held it."

Śleszkowski's proof that the papal bull was fraudulent was a book by Stefano Quaranta, *Summa bullarii*, first published in Venice in 1608 and republished numerous times thereafter (Śleszkowski referred to the 1609 edition).[229] *Summa bullarii*, Śleszkowski claimed, contained "all bulls," but "we could not see this bull" in it.[230] If there were one, it would have surely been included. This "unworthy bull, issued not by a pope but by some Jew-Christian," was nothing but "imposture, sham, and treason, unworthy to say anything else." This relentless attack on one of the most important Jewish defenses not only made Jews more vulnerable but also gradually helped harden in Poland the belief that Jews killed Christian children to obtain their blood.

But Śleszkowski's reasoning was wrong; Stefano Quaranta did not include "all the bulls." Indeed, Quaranta's opus tried to deal with the "immense ocean of bulls" by offering a "short summary" of the laws.[231] Because many laws were promulgated after some volumes of the canon law had been completed, Quaranta wanted to update them, chiefly from the 1586 *Bullarium* published in Rome. He organized some of his material "according to the titles of Decretalium." An authoritative compilation of canon law, *Decretalium* was published in 1234 by Raymondo de Peñaforte—thirteen years before Pope Innocent IV updated *Sicut Iudaeis* to include the paragraph prohibiting blood accusations against Jews—a key reason why the bull with the language concerning blood accusations did not formally enter the canon. The 1247 bull would not be mentioned in "authoritative sources" until 1646, twenty-five years after Śleszkowski's book, when Odorico Rinaldi included excerpts in his continuation of Cesare Baronio's *Annales ecclesiastici*. By that time, the skepticism among Polish writers that the bull even existed, promoted by Mojecki, Hubicki, Miczyński, and Śleszkowski, had become deeply rooted.

Still, this process of convincing Christians about the "truth" of the blood accusations and the "dangers" of Jewish–Christian interactions was evidently tedious and difficult.[232] Repeatedly the authors of the anti-Jewish books expressed frustration with Christians who, oblivious to or unwilling to embrace the accusations, happily continued to engage in daily encounters with their Jewish neighbors. Śleszkowski himself confided he had not known anything about these dangers either. In fact, in his youth he ate and drank in Jewish establishments in Kazimierz. "I thank God," he interjected, "I did not die."[233] But this changed when he began to read books during his studies abroad; his eyes were opened, he confessed, and now he knew better. In one of the most revealing passages, Śleszkowski explicitly explained how books colored his way of seeing Jews. Over years of studies and travel, he read "many authors and collected many writings about this veritable dissoluteness and hitherto unheard-of many Jewish crimes."[234] The new information made him realize that the "complaints and cries," which to "his regret" he had not noticed, matched the unexpected "Jewish crimes" described in "the writings of these authors."

So important were books in Śleszkowski's transformation that he included in his book a list of the authors he drew from. The list is impressive, full of chronicles, descriptions of the world, and polemical works, among them works by Sebastian Münster, Johannes Pistorius, Giovanni Botero, Piotr Skarga, and Sixtus Senensis. But a close reading of Śleszkowski's book reveals a heavy dependence on one particular work: *Tractatus de imposturis et ceremoniis judaeorum nostri temporis* (A Treatise on the Impostures and Ceremonies of Jews of Our Times, henceforth *De Imposturis*) by Marcus Lombardus, referred to by Śleszkowski as Conradus Huserus Tigurensis, the name of the translator of the original German work into Latin.[235] Not only did Śleszkowski refer to Jews as "Talmudists," as did Lombardus, but whole sections were directly taken from *De imposturis* and rendered into Polish, for example the sections on "Jewish festivals and ceremonies" and on Jewish education.[236] The biggest giveaways are the many factual and spelling errors in Śleszkowski's book that can be traced to *De imposturis*. For instance, among the foreign examples of "Jewish murders of innocent Christian children," Śleszkowski included "Wilhelm Hugo," supposedly killed by Jews in England in 1358, and one Simon killed in "Trevir" (Treviso?) in 1475, a clear but erroneous reference to Simon of Trent.[237] Śleszkowski truly appears to have worked from his collection of notes, because in a later reference to Simon's story he used Piotr Skarga's version and located it in Trent.

De imposturis's influence is also palpable in Śleszkowski's policy suggestions. Where Miczyński complained that Jews dominated all trades and crafts but smithing, Śleszkowski only focused on money lending and proposed to force Jews to engage in crafts and farming; he also urged to burn their books, and force them to read the Bible alone; to destroy their synagogues, and force a dress code.[238] *De imposturis* also mentions these measures, which were derivative of proposals recommended by Johannes Pfefferkorn and Martin Luther. As a Catholic in service to a bishop, Śleszkowski might not have wanted to cite Luther as his source, even if he in fact had access to Luther's work. But *De imposturis* made him aware of the measures in Luther without even reading his work.[239]

Few Polish writers before these anti-Jewish works began to propagate blood accusations had addressed the issue, even indirectly. Marcin Czechowic, the anti-Trinitarian polemicist and leader, briefly mentioned it in his 1581 polemical work, written ostensibly in response to a Jew named Jacob, who noted that since "Christians say and hold great belief that Jews need Christian blood and your holy bread," Jews who might have considered converting to Christianity would use it as an excuse not to, and "thus Christian faith would have to be weakened."[240] Marcin meekly responded,

"I don't understand it, I am not aware of it, I don't know about it, and I don't want, nor can, nor am able to talk about it.... As to the blood, whether it is needed by all Jews, for some purification, or the Papist wafer I do not accept it nor do I believe it. This is an error and fabrication." Yet he conceded that sorcerers sometimes used human blood, so perhaps some Jew might have sought it too.

In no Polish published works did there arise an implicit or explicit defense of Jews and a rejection of such accusations, though specific trials elicited defenders and written opinions against such charges. With no detailed, even if still polemical, ethnographies in the Polish vernacular that provided tools for understanding Jewish ceremonies and rebutting the blood accusations, by the time explicitly anti-Jewish works began to be published in Poland, they formed a largely harmonious voice, reinforcing the validity of anti-Jewish libels. There was no polyphony, as in German lands, that moderated anti-Jewish charges, gave Christian readers an alternative view of Jews and their rites, and provided materials and arguments rebutting tales of Jewish crimes so perniciously present in chronicles and other descriptions of the world. Neither was there in Poland, in contrast to Italy and German lands, much interest in Jewish writings as a potential source for Christian truths to which Jews, Christians argued, were oblivious or "blind." In fact, for Sebastian Miczyński, Kabbalah was all about "sorcery and witchcraft" and not a source of Christian truth as it was for Galatino and other Italian writers.[241] These assertions about "sorcery and witchcraft" led to a dangerous syllogism: because sorcerers often used blood, and Jews engaged in sorcery, Jews therefore needed blood.[242] Meanwhile authoritative sources like Skarga provided new, hitherto unknown tales, crucially that of Simon of Trent, whose papal recognition as a legitimate cult in 1588 further served as a confirmation of Jewish "crimes."

Jews still had legal defenses and supporters willing to help and protect them; indeed, arguments in defense of Jews were known in Poland and were even acknowledged in these anti-Jewish works only to be strenuously discounted as invalid. The Polish writers' frustration at the frequent acquittals of Jews or dismissals of accusations shows that these promoters of anti-Jewish stories had an uphill battle. But they also had tools: books by respected authors widely available across Europe. The cultural knowledge among those able to read was thus increasingly drenched with stories that Jews killed Christian children for the purpose of getting their blood—with no alternatives to read. As a result, there developed in the Polish-Lithuanian Commonwealth a unique pattern: the circulation of stories of Jewish "cruelties" not counteracted by reliable knowledge of Jewish works and customs, as was the case in the German lands. Nor were such stories, with the meek exception of Czechowic's *Odpis*, counterweighted by the concern to convert Jews, as in Italy, where, interest in conversion meant that polemical works tended to emphasize Jewish stubbornness in observance of Jewish law, thereby implicitly nullifying the claim that Jews consumed Christian blood, forbidden in Jewish law. In Poland, there was no clear goal to convert Jews until the eighteenth century, and works dealing with theological questions tended to use Jews as tropes in an intra-Christian polemic; anti-Jewish works were in turn intended to demonize Jews and discourage apparently cordial Jewish–Christian contacts. As Miczyński wrote in exasperation, "I hear: it is best to sell to a Jew, buy from a Jew, Jew does things best, best serves, best helps in need."[243] And Śleszkowski asked explicitly, "Why do Jews appear to some people better than they are described here?"[244] Crucially, these Polish authors worked tirelessly to discount the validity of papal defenses of Jews—not in contempt of the popes but from the disbelief that they would have issued such documents.

Polish works, it bears repeating, were heavily indebted to, and often plagiarized from, existing European works. Books by Alfonso de Espina, Václav Hájek of Libočan, Jacob Foresti of Bergamo, Cesare Baronio, Laurentius Surius, Marcus Lombardus (Condrad Huser), and later, Abraham Bzovius and Johannes Spondanus played important roles in shaping cultural knowledge about Jews among the educated and the literate. And because interest in Jews among these literate circles came late to Poland-Lithuania in comparison to other European countries, by the time it did arrive in the late sixteenth century, Hebraism and enthusiasm for studying Jewish texts and genuinely engaging with them had waned in much of Catholic Europe. Thus Polish writers missed the period of passionate Hebraism among German and Italian Catholic intellectuals of the late fifteenth and early sixteenth centuries.

Each region developed a distinct approach to writing about Jews that was tangibly shaped by the availability of books. In the German world, traditional theological polemic notwithstanding, early sixteenth-century books on Jewish ceremonies spurred an epistemological trajectory that created a specifically German style of anti-Jewish polemic that revealed and demystified Jewish rites and ceremonies in books published not only by converted Jewish informants but also by Christian Hebraists familiar with Jewish rabbinic sources. On the Italian peninsula, Renaissance scholars' fascination with the Jewish Kabbalah and Hebrew sources shaped anti-Jewish literature and also helped demystify, if differently than in the German lands, rabbinic works and Jewish law, promoting among Italian Christian scholars an appreciation for the usefulness of Jewish sources not only in anti-Jewish polemic but also for the discovery of Christian truths. Such

Christian exposure to Jewish texts, in German lands and in Italy, meant that Christians were able to attest, explicitly or implicitly, that no Jewish teachings supported blood accusations. This is where the Polish cultural sphere stands out: with little or no indigenous Polish interest in Jewish writings and few, if any, capable Polish Christian Hebraists, no genuine anti-Jewish polemic developed in the region. Instead, the early books and subsequent works developed a genre of aggressively anti-Jewish works that drew from historical books and archives to prove the "cruelties" of the Jews and discourage Jewish–Christian contact. With the Jewish population in the Polish-Lithuanian Commonwealth the largest in Europe, everyday Jewish–Christian contacts were frequent. Jews and Christians shared spaces, and even illiterate Christians could witness Jewish rites and ceremonies in daily interactions with Jews. But literate Christians were also exposed to different stories in the books that presented patterns of Jewish behavior akin to that of enemies of Christians, who harm and kill Christians and desecrate their sacred objects. This created a dissonance between everyday experiences and, as Śleszkowski put it, "what is described" in the books. And so, contrary to the perception that it was the uneducated "rabble" who incited trials and anti-Jewish persecution, it seems that in Poland-Lithuania books created and transmitted a body of knowledge that implanted this inimical image and anti-Jewish accusations in Polish literary culture. Those who had access to books and could read were imbued with ideas of the Jews' enmity and danger. And they also frequently had a say in the trials against Jews.

CHAPTER FIVE

Ashkenazi and Sephardic Jews Respond to Blood Libels

THERE WAS notably little interest among Jews in responding to anti-Jewish accusations in print, but the surviving Jewish literary responses to blood accusations seem to underscore the known, though debated, cultural differences between Sephardic, Italian, and Ashkenazi Jews, each grounded in their own epistemic realities. The responses also reveal that blood accusations affected both Sephardic and Ashkenazi Jews in the early modern period, albeit in different ways. Sephardic Jews were not victims of real-life blood accusations—Ashkenazi Jews were—but the persistence of these beliefs in Christian culture had a direct impact on the Sephardic Jews' ability to establish themselves in their new European homes, and they engaged more explicitly in challenging anti-Jewish accusations. Their works, written not only in Hebrew but also in languages accessible to non-Jews, such as Latin, Italian, English, Portuguese, and Spanish, engaged with non-Jewish authors and offered polemical arguments rebutting the slanderous charges.[1] Some of those rebuttals had been known to and even used by Christian authorities before these Jewish works were published, but some offered new defenses that were later used to protect Jews from similar libels and were even deployed by Christians writing in defense of Jews.

Among Ashkenazi Jews, who were the main victims of the accusations, literary responses were rare.[2] In contrast to the Sephardic Jews who offered polemical refutations of the accusations written in the languages read and spoken by non-Jews, the Ashkenazi Jews preferred to turn to songs and tales in Yiddish, such as the book *Sefer geulat Israel* (*Seyfer geules Isroel, The Book of Jewish Redemption*), recounting among others a story of blood libel in Poznań and published in the waning years of the seventeenth century.[3] To quote Max Weinreich, the songs and tales became a means to "inform the world about different events," since at the time "people did not write telegrams" about the news, such as fires, expulsions, or libels, but "a song to be sung to a melody."[4]

These historical Yiddish songs commemorate the "martyrdom" of the accused Jews and emphasize their fidelity to God and the Jewish community, despite experiencing horrifying suffering and persecution. These rhymed songs and tales built on Ashkenazi medieval martyrological imagery. They also fulfilled communal needs, providing reassurance and affirmation of faith and loyalty to the community, when faith, loyalty, and life itself were challenged. But these songs, insular as they might seem, were also deeply embedded in local Christian cultures and traditions.

Christian Accounts of Jewish "Crimes" in Jewish Writings

In contrast to premodern Christian writers, who produced chronicles, histories, and anthologies of the lives of saints, kings, and other prominent historical figures, Jews were not keen on writing chronicles and histories, and few works by Jewish writers qualify as such.[5] Premodern Jews remembered historical events through commemorative annual liturgy, not through the many genres of historical writings common among Christians.[6] The few existing Jewish chronicles can be divided into histories of the rabbis and their works, the *shalshelet ha-kabbalah* (chain of tradition), or chronicles of calamities that befell Jews.[7] Samuel Usque's *Consolation for the Tribulation of Israel*, published in 1553 in the vernacular of Portuguese Jews and conversos, was explicitly written as a reflection on persecutions endured by Jews throughout history; and Joseph Ha-Kohen's *Emek ha-bakha* (The Vale of Tears), a sixteenth-century chronicle disseminated in manuscript form until the nineteenth century, was intended to commemorate the suffering of Jews since the destruction of the Second Temple, perhaps as part of the observance of Tisha be-Av, a day of mourning in Judaism.[8]

A hallmark of Sephardic and Italian Jewish historical and polemical works was their use of non-Jewish works, even those explicitly anti-Jewish, as sources for their histories of Jewish suffering. One of the earliest Sephardic works of this type, Samuel Usque's *Consolation,* known to and used by other Jewish writers, including Joseph Ha-Kohen and Isaac Cardoso, the seventeenth-century Jewish physician and polemicist,[9] relied heavily on the fifteenth-century work by Alfonso de Espina, *Fortalitium fidei* (*The Fortress of Faith*), an exceedingly popular polemical work aimed at providing preachers with arguments against heretics, Jews, and Saracens—"the enemies of Christian religion"—and other anti-Jewish writers with examples of "the crimes of Jews."[10] Jewish writers, among them Usque and Cardoso, appropriated de Espina's scurrilous work not as evidence of "Jewish cruelties," of course, but as a source documenting the persecution of Jews by Christians. Cardoso explained that Christian anti-Jewish works represented "the fiction of history," for "they impute cruelty to the Jews in order to conceal their own. Let [these] histories be read," he implored, "and one will see the tyrannies and cruelties they inflicted upon [the Jews] throughout centuries."[11]

In reappropriating stories from anti-Jewish works, Jewish writers offered their own interpretations of events.[12] This is evident in one of the shortest stories included in Usque's *Consolations,* an account of an event said to have taken place in France, in which eighty-four Jews were sent to the stake. Usque wrote, "Because the Christians in France hated the Jewish usurers, the poor Israelite people living in Paris were charged with having killed a Christian in order to celebrate the Passover with his blood."[13] Hearing the news about the alleged murder, the king, who was away from Paris "on a hunt," immediately turned back and "angrily condemned to the stake eighty-four Jews, who were allegedly accomplices in the crime." This story, found in *Fortalitium fidei,* had been included in Vincent de Beauvais's popular *Speculum historiae,* a bestseller among early printed books in Europe.[14] For Usque providence played a role in Jewish persecutions (and revenge for them): the execution of "the oppressed lambs," who although "innocent" were "charged with what was prohibited by their Holy Law and contrary to its precepts," was fulfillment of the prophecy, "You shall be fuel for the fire" (Ezekiel 21:37). Prophecy notwithstanding, the reason behind the existence of anti-Jewish libels was, Usque argued, Jews' money-lending activities, or usury, because the supposed basis for the accusations—the alleged need for Christian blood—was absurd due to precepts of "the Holy Law," a clear reference to the prohibition against consumption of blood in Jewish law.

Usque cited Jewish law explicitly in defense of Jews in another story; in this Spanish tale, Jews accused of needing blood were actually saved by the king.[15] "See, brothers," wrote Usque through his Jewish character Ycabo, "how my iniquities blind the world when the time for my punishment comes.... For though the very people who accuse me know that there is no such cruel precept in my Law, they claim that I want to offer sacrifices of human limbs."[16] Ycabo, mirroring the argument made by Pope Innocent IV in response to the 1247 accusation in Valréas, exclaims that if "in order for us to slaughter even a hen, we must do it mercifully according to the precept..., [h]ow much more unnatural would it be to kill human beings to hold divine services with their blood, which is an abominable and forbidden thing." Usque ended the tale here, attributing the reason for these persecutions to divine providence: "Since my sins may roll on until Moses's prophecies are somehow fulfilled, 'The Lord will send a discomfiture against you because of evil of your thoughts' [Deuteronomy 28.20]."

Elements of Usque's work, including the stories from de Espina's *Fortalitium fidei*, were integrated into Joseph Ha-Kohen's *Emek ha-bakha*, sometimes with the same errors Usque had introduced.[17] Though the repetition of Usque's errors suggests that Ha-Kohen did not use de Espina's magnum opus as a direct source, it is abundantly clear that in other instances Ha-Kohen did turn to non-Jewish works for Jewish history. This is evident in his earlier but much larger published work, *Sefer divrei ha-yamim*, from which came many of the stories included in *Emek ha-bakha*. Most prominently, Ha-Kohen used Sebastian Münster's popular *Cosmographia*, first printed in German in 1544, translated into five languages, and published nearly forty times between 1544 and 1628.[18] Ha-Kohen appropriated almost all the events pertaining to Jews found in *Cosmographia*, from stories of imperial protection of the Jews, as in Bern following a blood accusation in 1287,[19] to the most ridiculous tales, such as one in 1270 about a Jew who fell into a privy on the Sabbath and was refused help by other Jews. In response to this incident, according to Ha-Kohen, the pope—in Münster's *Cosmographia* it was the bishop of Magdeburg—ordered that all Jews had to observe, under penalty of death, all the precepts of the Sabbath also on Sunday.[20]

If in Christian eyes these histories denoted "Jewish crimes," for Jewish writers they chronicled Jewish suffering. Jewish authors, of course, did not use the stories uncritically; they edited and reworked them, omitting the most controversial material. For instance, in reporting violence erupting in 1348, Ha-Kohen first quoted Usque ("the Portugese") and then paraphrased Münster ("Sebastianus"):

> Many Jews gathered in their houses and locked the door behind them, and set themselves on fire, when they saw that destruction is upon them [*ki-kalta aleihem ha-ra'ah*; play on Esther 7:7]. And the fire burned their houses and their families. And in the city of Mainz, a large church bell melted because of the blaze. And they saw what happened: in the imperial cities they tore the

Jews' houses to the ground, and with the stones from them and from the tombstones they built walls and towers. And they expelled many at the time.[21]

In paraphrasing Münster, Ha-Kohen chose to omit the section about Jews poisoning wells and Münster's rather explicit statement that "many Jews of both sexes were baptized, less out of love of God but more out of fear of punishment."[22] Ha-Kohen's selectivity shifted the emphasis onto Jewish suffering and avoided tainting the memory of the persecuted Jews.

Far more sophisticated and detailed were Ha-Kohen's versions of more recent events, some of which he or his family may have experienced or had access to better information about. The expulsion of Jews from Spain in 1492; the violence in Lisbon in 1506; the adventures of Shlomo Molkho, a messianic figure active in the sixteenth century; and the story of Simon of Trent were all marked by insightful analysis. Though Münster did discuss the Trent case, devoting to him a lengthy paragraph,[23] Ha-Kohen seemed to have eschewed Münster's account and presented his own longer, more detailed interpretation of what may have happened in 1475. According to the Jewish chronicler, "an evil man" (*ish ha-beli'al;* 1 Samuel 25:25) murdered a boy named Simon in Trent; unseen, he put the body in a cistern near the house of a Jew, Samuel, whereupon Christians "accused the Jews, as it is their custom," of killing the boy.[24] At first they did not find the child, but when the child's body was found—Ha-Kohen did not make clear that it was the Jews who found the body in Samuel's house and reported the finding to the bishop—"all the Jews were to be seized. Their lives were then embittered. They were tortured with the cord, so that they confessed to what they had not plotted. One very old man named Moshe, and he alone, did not admit to this great lie."[25] The remaining Jews were sentenced to a painful death, "pinched with [hot] pincers, and burned" at the stake; "their pure souls rose up to heaven."

If Ha-Kohen's recounting of the Trent events and Jewish suffering seems formulaic, his description of the political complexity of the case is not. He demonstrated an uncommon knowledge of details and an acute awareness of the dynamic driving the long trial and its aftermath. Jews sought help, Ha-Kohen reported, from two Christians from Padua "learned in religion and law," but the men were ultimately chased away from Trent. In the meantime, "it was said that the child was holy" and performed miracles, and people began to flock to Trent "not empty handed," insightfully added the chronicler to draw attention to the material benefits of veneration sites. Motivated by the popularity of Simon's shrine, the bishop beseeched the pope to "make the boy a saint, for he is holy [*kadesh et ha-yeled ki kadosh*]." But the pope demurred and sent a cardinal, "a legate," as Ha-Kohen called him, to investigate the affair thoroughly. He saw that "the whole affair was delusions and nonsense [*ta'atu'im ve-hevel*]," for "he discovered [the boy's body] had been embalmed in spices and perfumes, as is done to the dead. And then he chided them [the bishop of Trent and his entourage], saying publicly that it was all a lie. This infuriated the people, and the legate had to flee." Despite the bishop's relentless efforts—"in fact, over and over, almost daily," Ha-Kohen asserted—"the pope did not canonize the boy."

Joseph Ha-Kohen seems to have had a sophisticated understanding of the status of Simon, being aware of the difference between Simon's appellation as *beatus* and as a saint: "They called him Beato Simone, but saint he is not called to this very day." Ha-Kohen's *terminus ad quem* was 1575, the year he is said to have made the last changes to his chronicle. By then, Simon's story had entered at least one comprehensive collection of the lives of saints (Laurentius Surius's *De Probatis Sanctorum Historiis* published in 1571), but, as Ha-Kohen astutely noted, the cult had not yet been officially recognized by the pope. Simon of Trent would earn a short description in the newly updated liturgical calendar *Martyrologium romanum* in 1583, eight years after Ha-Kohen's death, and his cult would be officially recognized in 1588 with a liturgy and indulgences, which added to confusion about the boy's status. Still, for Ha-Kohen, the lack of papal recognition at the time seems to have been vindication for the unjust trial and persecution of Jews, and proof of the falsity of the accusation. So too were other examples he cited such as an accusation in Novi (now Novi Ligure), near Alessandria in 1513, where the city's mayor explicitly defended Jews and assured them he did not believe such accusations.[26]

Some aspects of Ha-Kohen's account of Simon's story were certainly known in Italy from the works celebrating Simon's martyrdom and defending the actions of the bishop. In Ubertino Pusculo's *Symonidos*, for example, Jews were said to have "hired doctors of law" from Padua. And though, according to Pusculo, their intervention was in vain, the Jews did manage to gain the support of some lords and kings. This, in turn, emboldened them to seek help from the pope himself, who sent his envoy to Trent.[27] In Pusculo's words, the envoy was "a paid employee, completely at the Hebrews' expense"; he "challenged the little boy's miracles" and "laughed at them." But some details, like the mention of embalming spices and perfumes, suggest that Ha-Kohen may also have had access to unpublished sources about Simon, such as Battista de' Giudici's account, *Apologia iudaeorum* and *Invectiva contra Platinam*, or other sources not publically known; or perhaps Ha-Kohen recorded oral counterstories circulating during his life.[28]

In Jewish polemical literature, Simon of Trent would appear one more time—in the last section devoted to refuting calumnies against the Jews that "they kill Christian children in order to use their blood in their rituals" of Isaac Cardoso's opus *Las excelencias de los hebreos,* published in Amsterdam in 1679.[29] Cardoso offered arguments demonstrating the absurdity of the accusation and recounted several stories he found in Christian anti-Jewish works, including de Espina's *Fortalitium fidei,* Laurentius Surius's *De probatis sanctorum historiis,* and Jacob Philip Foresti's extremely popular *Supplementum chronicarum.*[30] One of these stories is about Simon of Trent.

The story of Simon of Trent was for Cardoso a "baleful tragedy fabricated against Jews."[31] After briefly recounting the narrative from Trent based on the accounts by Surius and Foresti, Cardoso, who at the time lived in Verona, 62 miles from Trent, noted almost in passing that "they dedicated a shrine to the child, where one can still see [the boy's] black and disfigured corpse."[32] This side comment was a direct polemical jab at the Christian story of Simon, which emphasized the incorruptibility of Simon's body as evidence of his saintly nature. Just in 1668, eleven years before Cardoso's book was published, this point was explicitly emphasized in Michelangelo Mariani's *Il infante glorioso S. Simone,* written to "revive the memory of the memory of his martyrdom" because this "glorious innocent . . . deserved to be canonized by the Church."[33] Indeed, the task was to declare Simon a saint, not just *beatus;* to make him not just "innocent" but "a martyr killed in hatred of Christ."[34] Mariani devoted a significant section of his book to the state of Simon's body, given that it was written after the body was reexamined by medical experts who confirmed its "incorruptibility."[35]

Still, with Cardoso's work an exception, after Simon's cult was officially recognized, his story could no longer be invoked as proof of papal disbelief in blood accusations. In fact, papal recognition of the cult had the opposite effect: it made it easier for anti-Jewish accusers to legitimize their claims and more difficult for church officials to dismiss the charges altogether.

Few works of this sort—historical or polemical—were published by Ashkenazi writers north of the Alps. The best-known work describing historical events is David Gans's *Tsemaḥ David* (*Sprout of David*), published in Hebrew in 1592. Its section devoted to Jewish history resembles a list of rabbis and their works, peppered with short descriptions of other events from Jewish history, but it has little to say about blood libels.

With the exception of the *Yudisher teryok* (*A Jewish Theriac*) by Solomon Zevi Hirsch of Aufhausen—an apologetic response, or "an antidote," to an anti-Jewish work by a German Jewish convert, Samuel Friedrich Brenz—Ashkenazi works, mostly songs and tales, were markedly different from the elaborate accounts produced by Sephardic writers, who developed what Yosef Hayim Yerushalmi called a Sephardic tradition of Jewish apologia that was deeply embedded in Christian works about Jews.[36] This cultural difference was on display in the remarkable Sephardic work *Shevet Yehudah (The Scepter of Judah)* by Solomon ibn Verga, which provided one of the most extensive discussions of blood libels in early modern Jewish literature, and its Yiddish translation.[37] The Yiddish *Shevet Yehudah* was subjected to what Michael Stanislawski called "Ashkenization," highlighting in the process the differences between Sephardic and Ashkenazi Jews.[38]

Polemical Responses, Sephardic Style

In contrast to Samuel Usque's often circumscribed, brief explanations for the accusations against Jews, Solomon ibn Verga's *Shevet Yehudah*, a book of "the widest popularity" in the early modern period, discussed the subject more extensively and more assertively.[39] Of seventy-six tales in sixty-four chapters, eight concerned ritual murder.[40] The first and longest is the seventh, which recounts a fictional encounter between King Alfonso of Spain and Thomas, a wise and learned man.

Ibn Verga's King Alfonso faced a dilemma and needed advice. A certain bishop, the king said, preached to large audiences that "Jews could not celebrate the festival called in the Hebrew language Passover without blood from a Christian."[41] Although the king was skeptical about the bishop's accusations, he was worried that so many people believed them and did not know how to handle the situation; if he defended the Jews, the king feared, he would lose the respect of his subjects, who, in turn, would see him as "a stranger or a Jew for not taking revenge on Jews."[42] He hoped that Thomas, a Christian known for his knowledge of Jewish religion, customs, and tradition, would advise him on how to "respond to these fools" and clarify whether there was any foundation in Jewish books to support such claims. If Thomas showed that the bishop's claims could be substantiated, the king said, he was ready to expel Jews from his kingdom. If not, he would do everything he could to protect them.[43] In response Thomas offered sophisticated arguments grounded in logic and reason, as well as his knowledge of Jewish tradition and customs, to demonstrate the baselessness of the bishop's claims. His refutation was so compelling that at one point the king appeared a bit incensed when he realized Thomas might have thought that the king himself embraced the bishop's accusations.[44]

First of all, Thomas said, God did not want to harm Jews, because God did not want to harm anything he created, not a fly, let alone Jews who "had received the law."[45] As for the accusation that Jews needed blood to celebrate Passover—that was "far from reason." People, after all, were naturally disposed to abhorring things they were not used to eating. One should only ask a Christian to eat a dog or a cat, and he will run away like a Jew runs away from pork! The Jew flees from pork because he is not accustomed to it due to God's commandments. Thus, if Jews do not consume pork, which is more agreeable to human "temperament and nature," they would certainly not consume human blood. In fact, if Jews "do not eat blood of any animal, or, according to rabbis (*talmudiim*), not even fish, how much more would they abhor human blood, which is not consumed by any people!"[46] Jews carefully drained blood of the slaughtered animals to fulfill the biblical commandment of not consuming any blood. As for human blood, Thomas gave an example of what happened when a Jew bit bread and his gums bled—he was not allowed to consume it unless he cleaned the bread.[47]

But the conversation and the king's questions soon expanded beyond the blood accusation. The king was also disturbed by the distinction Jews made between themselves and non-Jews and the claims that apparently the Talmud allowed them to harm gentiles. To rebut them, Thomas first had to explain the difference between the Hebrew terms *nokhri, nozri,* and *goy*—a stranger, a Christian, and a gentile—then he asserted that the Talmud considered robbing and harming a gentile worse than harming a fellow Jew.[48]

As the tale progressed, the discussion, whose purpose was to debunk reasons for the anti-Jewish accusations, shifted from Jewish customs and beliefs to the Jews' economic and social status.[49] As Jews gained status and visibility, Thomas argued, envy and hatred against them increased. When the Jews arrived in the kingdom, they arrived as "poor slaves," and for many years they lived humbly and did not wear ostentatious clothes. And then no one accused them of drinking blood! But now Jews were rich and Christians poor. And as Jews became more prominent, and wealthy, openly wearing luxurious clothing of silk, these accusations emerged, as did calls for their expulsion.

But the principal reason for the hatred of Jews, Thomas argued, was that they became rich through usury. They now possessed hereditary properties, houses, and fields of the Christians. Thomas's advice was to prohibit Jews from practicing usury and to issue restrictions that would remove them from positions of power and curb their display of luxurious clothing and lifestyles—a policy recommendation that corresponded to already known Christian Jewry laws, including those summarized in de Espina's *Fortali-*

tium fidei.⁵⁰ Thus, while condemning the blood libel, Thomas's advice helped the king solve his uncomfortable dilemma.

While Thomas and the king were talking, some Christians came before the king saying that a dead Christian was found in a house of a Jew, who must have killed him to extract blood.⁵¹ Exasperated, the king asked Thomas to respond to "these fools." Thus Thomas repeated what he had just explained to the king, saying that the king now understood that what bothered Christians about Jews was their usury and possession of Christian properties and lands. The king promised that what was taken from Christians through usury was to be returned to his subjects.⁵² And while the men praised the ruler for his justice and wisdom, the king forced them to admit that the Jew did not kill the Christian man. Conceding, the men said that they felt exploited; they "worked the land," but had nothing left from it. Their goal was to have the Jews expelled, and so they concocted this plot. The king pressed on, "According to what you said, the Jew did not kill the Christian, but you killed him." The men protested, saying that when they found the man, he was already dead, and they planned to take the body to the cemetery, but then decided to dump him in the house of the Jew. The king was happy he saw through the falsity of the accusation against Jews, and he let the men free, and ordered that the incident be recorded in the chronicles. Thus in Tale Seven, ibn Verga laid bare the anatomy of blood accusations against Jews, and debunked them, while providing explanations of Jewish rituals and highlighting the real and rational reasons for the hatred of Jews—money and envy. Blood libels, went the story's take-home point, were often concocted to engineer the expulsion of Jews.

A similar message is reiterated in the next tale, in which representatives of the Jewish community came to plead for the king's support and protection following an accusation of blood libel and a slew of attacks on Jews around Passover.⁵³ Though the king admitted that "the Jews have no guilt in this [crime]," he saw them as guilty of "other kinds of sins" that were the true reasons why people rose against Jews every day. Once more ibn Verga's king connected the Jews' increased social status to the rise of animosity against them. "You arrived," the king said, "to our kingdom poor and hungry, and Christians received you with love, but you paid back with evil for the good." Once more, usury was the source of many evils. If Jews were slaves and exiles (*avadim ve-golim*), why, the king wanted to know, "do you wear garments of the princes?" In response, the Jews offered only vague apologetic and gendered explanations. Though like most of ibn Verga's tales, the story ends well and the Jews are saved, there is no doubt that in ibn Verga's mind Jews shared some of the blame for their misfortunes. To be sure, they were innocent of the crime of which Christians, wishing to expel Jews, accused them, but their life in luxury at the expense of Christians was a source of their tribulations.⁵⁴

Ibn Verga's anatomy of blood accusations was so powerful it was embraced and appropriated by other Jewish apologists. A century later, in 1656, after more than ten editions of *Shevet Yehudah* had appeared in Hebrew, Yiddish, and even Latin, Menasseh ben Israel, the prominent Sephardic rabbi and community leader, published his *Vindiciae judaeorum*; it was an apologetic work written in response to the 1655 publication *A Short Demurrer to the Jewes Long Discontinued Remitter into England* by William Prynne—a vocal opponent of the readmission of Jews to England on the grounds that Jews "had been formerly great Clippers and Forgers of Mony, and had crucified three or four Children in England at least."⁵⁵

In his rebuttal of Prynne, Menasseh followed ibn Verga's Thomas almost to the letter.⁵⁶ Christian "calumniators" sometimes themselves "cruelly butchered" their victims or after finding a corpse they "cast [it] as if it had been murdered by the *Iewes,* into their houses or yards," only to "accuse innocent *Iewes* as the committers of this most execrable fact." All this was false, Menasseh wrote, for "it is utterly forbid the *Iewes* to eat any manner of bloud whatsoever, *Levit.* Chapter 7. 26 and *Deuter.* 12 where it is expressly said וכל דם [*ve-khol dam*], *And ye shall eat no manner of bloud,* and in obedience to this command the *Iewes* eat not the bloud of any animal." Menasseh then discussed what Jews did when they found a drop of blood in an egg and the case of blood from the gums left on bread. Like ibn Verga's Thomas, Menasseh exclaimed, "Since then it is thus, how can it enter into any man's heart to believe that [Jews] should eat humane bloud, which is yet more detestable, there being scarce any nation now remaining upon earth so barbarous, as to commit such wickednesse?"

Menasseh also retold, almost verbatim, ibn Verga's Tale Eight of the king ("King of Portugal" in *Vindiciae judaeorum*) who could not sleep:

> He went up into the balcony in the palace from whence he could discover the whole city, and from thence (the moon shining clear) he espied two men carrying a dead corps, which they cast into the *Iew's* yard. He presently dispatches a couple of servants, and commands them, yet with a seeming carelessnesse, they should trace and follow those men, and take notice of their house; which they accordingly did. The next day there is a hurly burly and a tumult in the city, accusing the *Iewes* of murder. Thereupon the King apprehended these rogues and they confesse the truth; and considering that this businesse was guided by a particular divine providence, calls some of the wise men of the *Iewes,* and asks them how they translate the 4. Verse of the 121 Psalm, and they answered, *Behold, he that keepeth Israel will neither slumber,*

nor sleep. The King replied, if he will not slumber, then much lesse will he sleep, you do not say well, for the true translation is, *Behold, the Lord doth not slumber, neither will he suffer him that keepeth Israel to sleep.* God who hath yet a care over you, hath taken away my sleep, that I might be an eye witnesse of that wickednesse which is this day laid to your charge.[57]

To underscore further the ludicrous nature of the blood accusation, Menasseh, citing among others Tertullian, the early Christian writer not particularly friendly to Jews, noted that "the very same accusation and horrid wickednesse of killing children and eating their bloud, was of old by the ancient heathens charg'd upon the Christians."[58] But the example of ancient accusations against Christians focused on the "blood accusation." In response to Prynne, Menasseh ben Israel also had to address the accusation of "Christian homicide" in "hatred and detestation of Jesus of Nazareth."[59] Blood libel, associated with consumption of blood, could be easily discredited by demonstrating its absurdity and obvious violation of biblical laws; the accusation of killing Christians in "hatred of Jesus" required a different strategy. Of course, murder was in violation of the biblical prohibition, "Thou shalt not kill." But the Christian chronicles told of many examples of such murders. Menasseh's strategy was to discredit the sources of these stories, a task of particular importance because Prynne's book emphasized the quality of the historical sources he consulted to support his attacks against Jews.

On the title page of *A Short Demurrer,* Prynne promised to offer "an Exact Chronological Relation of Their First Admission into, Their Ill Deportment, Misdemeanors, Condition, Sufferings, Oppressions, Slaughters, Plunders, by Popular Insurrections, and Regal Exactions in; and Their Total, Final Banishment by Judgment and Edict of Parliament, out of England, Never to Return Again: Collected out of the Best Historians." One of these "best historians" was Matthew Paris, known for including in his chronicle several stories of Jews murdering Christian children in England, which for Prynne were "the principal causes of [the Jews'] banishment" from England. Prynne paraphrased the medieval chronicler almost verbatim, copying even his mistakes; for example, placing the story of Jews crucifying a boy in Norwich in 1240, perhaps an erroneous reference to William of Norwich. "In the year of our Lord 1240," Prynne begins his story, "the Jews circumcised a Christian child at Norwich, and being circumcised, they called him *Jurninus,* but reserved him to be crucified in contumely of Jesus Christ crucified."[60] To counter Prynne's attack, Menasseh ben Israel, playing shrewdly on English anti-Catholic sentiments and the black legend, immediately discounted the account as "popish" and challenged its logic:

He was first circumcised, and this perfectly constitutes him a *Iew*. Now for a *Iew* to embrace a Christian in his armes and foster him in his bosome, is a testimony of great love and affection. But if it was intended that shortly after this child should be crucified, to what end was he first circumcised? If it shall be said it was out of hatred to the Christians, it appears rather to the contrary, that it proceeded from detestation of the *Iewes,* or of them who had newly become proselytes, to embrace the *Iewes* religion. Surely this supposed pranck (stories to be done in popish times) looks more like a piece of the reall scene of the Popish *Spaniards* piety, who first baptiz'd the poor *Indians,* and afterwards out of cruel pity to their souls, inhumanely butchered them; then of strict-law-observing *Iewes,* who dare not make a sport of one of the seales of their covenant.[61]

Then, paraphrasing the Dutch theologian and polemicist Johannes Hoornbeek, Menasseh reinforced the notion that such accusations were based "either upon uncertain report of the vulgar, or else upon the secret accusation of the Monks belonging to the inquisition, not to mention the avarice of the informers, wickedly hanquering after the *Iewes* wealth, and so with ease forging any wickednesse."[62] The history books so praised by Prynne, among them Thomas of Canterbury, could be given "no more credit than his other fictions and lies where with he hath stuffed his book."[63] The chronicles were "popish," their authors "too much addicted and given unto fables and figments."[64] (The chronicles may have been "popish," but Menasseh's own arguments against blood libels had been articulated explicitly in two separate letters by Pope Innocent IV in 1247.[65])

As if to fortify his polemic with an anti-Catholic tone, Menasseh recounted several recent cases of accusations against Jews, all from Catholic domains—for example, Ragusa, Lisbon, and Madrid—and almost all involving torture.[66] Menasseh's emphasis on torture to discredit the anti-Jewish accusations was likely purposeful: although on the continent torture was accepted as a legitimate judicial procedure, in England it was not.[67] Evoking anti-Catholic sentiments would have strengthened his appeal in England, where King Charles I was executed just a few years earlier. So too was the use of Hoornbeek a good strategy, because the Protestant polemicist was no particular friend of the Jews. His extensive book sought to convert Jews, even if along the way it conveyed serious doubts about the frequent accusations against them.[68] Through a careful choice of his sources and sophisticatedly tailored arguments against anti-Jewish accusations, Menasseh was able to demonstrate that such charges against Jews had no grounds—they were based on fables, popish fables at that—and thus Jews deserved to be formally readmitted to England.

Legal Strategies and Tools

Whereas Menasseh ben Israel's refutation of Prynne's accusations was forceful and clearly effective in ultimately securing permission for Jews to live in England, another seventeenth-century Jewish polemicist, Isaac Cardoso, chose to add to his polemical response legal documents that could be used in defending Jews accused of ritual murder or blood libels. And used they were—published and republished in the seventeenth and eighteenth centuries, these documents became legal tools for Jews as blood accusations continued to plague them in the early modern era.

The last chapter of Cardoso's wide-ranging polemical and apologetic work *Las excellencias de los hebreos*, "The Tenth Calumny against Jews that They Kill Christian Children to Use Their Blood in Their Rituals," was a powerful retort to blood accusations. It condemned Christian historical accounts of supposed Jewish murders of Christian children as "fictions of history," bemoaning the fact that enemies of Jews did not accept any evidence debunking the accusations.[69] Even "*breves* of the Pontiffs, decrees of the emperors, and orders of the princes" condemning such accusations were not enough to discourage the blood accusations, because many considered those documents false, Cardoso claimed.[70] Indeed, though some Christians knew well that these accusations were fabricated and found them "abominable," the commoners did not believe these learned men and were unwilling to "obey Princes when hatred dominates reason and the fury closes the door to acquittals."

Frustrated by this disbelief, Cardoso listed key documents by Church and secular authorities condemning blood accusations, along with those he found in the archives in Padua and Verona, where he lived.[71] The documents included the 1236 papal decree defending Jews more generally, the 1247 decree by Pope Innocent IV explicitly condemning the blood accusations, and the decree by Emperor Frederick III issued in the aftermath of the 1470 accusation in Endingen that was reissued in 1544 by Charles V and reconfirmed in 1566 by Maximilian II. Cardoso also published the Spanish translation of documents from local archives in Verona and Padua: the 1479 decree by Bona and Giovanni Galeazzo Sforza of Milan, mistakenly dated 1470; the 1475 condemnation of similar accusations by Venice's Pietro Mocenigo issued in the aftermath of the Simon of Trent trial; and a 1603 decree from Verona issued during the trial of Giuseppe Abramino, accused by a certain Bernardino Bretorio of abducting his son, which cited all the previous documents in defense of the Jews.

Although Cardoso may have come across the list of these documents in the 1603 Verona decree, they were first mentioned by the French Catholic polemicist Richard Simon, who wrote a treatise in defense of Jews following the trial of Raphaël Lévy of Boulay, accused of killing a Christian child in 1669 in Metz.[72] Simon also challenged the historical examples brought by the accusers to bolster their charges against Jews and demonstrated that there was "a great number of stories in favor of Jews." Crucially, he cited in defense of Jews exactly the documents Cardoso singled out in his book.[73]

Richard Simon and Isaac Cardoso began a chain of transmission that would shape Jewish legal strategies for at least a century, if not longer. In 1681, two years after the publication of Cardoso's *Las excellencias de los hebreos,* an Italian Jew, Isaac Viva Cantarini, republished these documents in Latin in his *Vindex sanguinis,* a booklet written as a rejoinder to a work by Jacobus Geusius about human sacrifice.[74] In 1705, in the aftermath of a trial of Jews in Viterbo, Rome's Rabbi Tranquillo Vita Corcos reprinted those documents in his materials defending the accused Jews before the papal courts.[75] These documents then made their way in the second half of the eighteenth century into the now famous but at the time secret report written in response to the pleas of the Jews from Poland by the Consultor of the Holy Office, Lorenzo Ganganelli, who would become Pope Clement XIV. This chain thus connected France, Italy, and Poland (one could also add England, because *Vindex sanguinis* also reveals influences of Menasseh ben Israel's *Vindiciae judaeorum*) in the transmission of Jews' political and legal strategies.

Torture and Martyrdom

Isaac Cardoso's outrage over accusations against Jews may have been inspired by the 1669 trial of Raphaël Levy of Boulay in Metz. Levy, as Cardoso noted, was tortured. He did not confess to the crime he was accused of, nor did he implicate anyone in the community; he is said to have prayed *Shem'a Israel,* "Hear O Israel," during his torments.[76] The slanderous accusations against Jews gave Cardoso an opportunity to reflect on questions of justice and judicial procedure. Lamenting the injustice done to Jews and stressing that "the Divine and Holy Law" did not condemn on the basis of "signs and conjectures," but rather on the basis of "true and faithful testimonies," Cardoso also invoked Ulpian, the third-century Roman jurist whom Cardoso called "one of the Princes of Jurisprudence," who expressed reservations about torture.[77] Though "torment and corporeal suffering," according to Ulpian, "were employed to extract truth," torture was nonetheless "weak and dangerous, and inimical for the truth." Cardoso paraphrased Ulpian's cautionary statement, noting that some people were able to endure torture so much that it was impossible to extract any certain information from them. Similarly, some had so little ability to endure the pain that they preferred to die, and they "not only confess[ed] to incriminate themselves but also accuse[ed] others of [crimes] they had never committed." In his 1681 *Vindex sanguinis,* Isaac Viva, citing Johannes Hoornbeek, echoed Cardoso's words: "Some Jews, confined to prison, confessed to this crime, either because of the fear of suffering torments, or, in fear, hoping for the grace of a quick death sentence."[78] These comments by Cardoso and Viva illustrate the unambiguous condemnations of the efficacy of torture found in many Sephardic works. Menasseh ben Israel also discussed torture, if briefly, in *Vindiciae judaeorum,* and it is quite explicit in Solomon ibn Verga's *Shevet Yehudah.*

Between the fourteenth and sixteenth centuries, torture increasingly became integral to European jurisprudence, as it entered official codes of law, including the Carolina of Charles V, which became law in 1531.[79] However, the use of torture did not go unchallenged. European debates over torture date back to the Roman period, when it was used to extract evidence from slaves. The premise behind torture was to obtain confession, the "crown of proof," because, as Roman law had it, "pain was the primary channel of truth."[80] In addition to Ulpian, Augustine in *City of God* warned about the use of torture, especially in dealing with witnesses. Augustine saw torture as the punishment of innocent people "for a crime that is still doubtful" just to "discover whether [the accused] is guilty." The crime was doubtful because "it is not ascertained that he did not commit it." Thus, Augustine argued, "the ignorance of the judge frequently involves an innocent person in suffering."[81] Indeed, sometimes "an innocent person is tortured to discover his innocence" or, worse, is "put to death without discovering it." Torture could not secure certainty because people often lied. In his commentary on Augustine's *City of God,* Juan Luis Vives, a sixteenth-century Spaniard whose parents are said to have fallen victim to the Inquisition and who was a contemporary of Solomon ibn Verga, noted that "neither the man who can endure reveals truth, nor the man who cannot."[82] In fact, Vives argued, quoting Publilius Syrus, "Pain compels even the innocent to lie." (Montaigne later embraced Vives's views.[83])

Stories in Solomon ibn Verga's *Shevet Yehudah* embody the legal reservations expressed by Ulpian, Augustine, and Vives. At times, it seems that ibn Verga knew these works, because the ideas and sometimes even the wording echoed earlier writers.[84] Ibn Verga provided convincing and sophisticated illustrations of the worthlessness of judicial torture and confessions extracted through it. In Tale Eight, after discussing the ills Jews supposedly cause in society through their usury and wealth, the king received a letter from the judges investigating an accusation of ritual murder against a Jewish man; his viceroy wanted to order the Jew to "hard" torture to make him confess.[85] But the Jewish envoys immediately protested, saying that during torture the man would surely say that "he killed him and ate his blood." The king then recalled an incident in the early days of his reign, when two golden spoons were stolen while there were two Jews "coming and going" in his palace, and "all people in his court said that Jews stole them as it is their custom." The two Jews were tortured and indeed confessed to the theft, whereupon the king ordered them hanged. But three days later the spoons were found in the possession of one of the king's own servants. As the story about the theft was being told, the king's advisor recalled that in earlier days torture was never used to condemn people. The next day, a boy came to court with information about the murder: his master had lost his inheritance to the Jew in whose house the body of the Christian was found, and he had offered the boy a reward if he killed the Jew, but the boy did not want to do it, so the master devised a plan to accuse the Jew of ritual murder. The Jew was saved, but the moral of the tale was clear: Jews were accused of ritual murder because of their usury, and torture never produced reliable testimonies.

The dynamic of Tale Eight reveals a king caught between popular hatred and his disbelief of accusations. In fact, as Jeremy Cohen has noted, "In almost every instance the king knows the accusations to be groundless and, frequently, with the help of a beneficent prelate or counselor, he too seeks to dismiss them. Yet conspirators characteristically persist, accusing the king of favoring the Jews over the Christian faithful."[86] In Tale Seventeen, too, this dynamic is played out to reveal not only the groundlessness of anti-Jewish accusations but also the unreliability of torture. Though the king "in the Kingdom of France" saw through the lies of accusers claiming that a Jew killed a Christian before Passover, they brought false witnesses who said they saw the Christian enter but not exit the Jew's house, and they managed to gain the support of the king's advisors. They also began to spread rumors that the king favored "those who despised Christian faith" over the Christian faithful, forcing the monarch to order the accused Jew to be tortured.[87] The Jew subsequently confessed and implicated fifty other Jews. The pleading Jews tried to remind the king that torture was not reliable and that, according to old statutes, only confessions regarding the accused himself could be accepted, but not if they implicated others.

At the court was a Moorish ambassador, and the king asked him if similar accusations against Jews took place in his kingdom.[88] The ambassador was aghast that Christians believed such absurd accusations against Jews, because they were "contrary to reason." In fact, no nation on earth, not even one inclined to do abhorrent things, did what the Jews were accused of in Christian kingdoms. The ambassador then proceeded to offer a scathing critique of the use of torture: "In our kingdom, confession under torture is a mere conjecture," needing to be supported by other evidence and unable to serve as a basis for conviction (*din ve-mishpat*). One advisor interjected, saying Jews did not hold such hatred against Muslims as they did against Christians on account of Jesus: "They take a Christian, name him Jesus, eat his blood in order to take revenge on him." The ambassador then pointed out the difference in beliefs between Christians and Muslims, which explained why such accusations emerged among one but not the other—it was Christians who believed Jews had subjected Jesus to many sufferings and killed him. This story, he continued, is shown in images in many churches, reinforcing these beliefs. Muslims, by contrast, did not believe that Jews killed and tortured Jesus, but that he ascended to heaven alive.

The debate continued, angering the Christians. Feeling humiliated by the Moorish ambassador and pressured by the common people, the king ordered the Jews punished.[89] They were to be put in barrels with nails protruding inside and, in a manner known from Roman antiquity, rolled down a hill.[90] Just as the king was about to push the barrels, he was felled by an invisible force. Sensing divine intervention, he freed the Jews. This was a just move, because it was later revealed that, as in other tales in the book, a Christian had planted the body in the Jew's home and accused him falsely. The Christian slanderer was then punished.

But perhaps the most explicit example of the argument against the use of torture is Tale Twenty-Nine.[91] "During the reign of the just and old king Alfonso," people came before judges claiming they had seen on the eve of Passover "a Christian man enter a house of a Jewish man, and after that they heard him scream, 'Christians help me!'" The investigators sent to examine the Jew's house found nothing there. "Last year," they said, "in this matter, they also accused [Jews] but it turned out to be a lie." Seeing the judges' reluctance to prosecute Jews, the people rebelled and approached the king, who summoned the accused Jew. The Jew denied that a Christian had entered his house. The king then challenged the accusers: "If you heard [the Christian man] scream, 'Help me!' ... why didn't you break the door in the Jew's house, and save the abused man from his abuse?" They did nothing, because they feared the judges would punish them for breaking the door, the accusers responded. Hearing this, the king called them liars; skeptical that the Jew had attacked the Christian man, he pointed out the Jew's old age.

The following day the accusers brought more witnesses, among them the disappeared man's wife Beatrice and his friends, who claimed that the man had gone to the Jew to retrieve his pledge.[92] In light of these new allegations, the king ordered the Jew to be examined under torture. The accused Jew confessed to having killed the Christian man and was sentenced to death by fire. But as the verdict was being announced, a bishop arrived, who asked if the case concerned the husband of a certain Beatrice Guzman, one of the bishop's serfs. It turned out that the bishop had seen the man the day before in a village nearby; he was very much alive. As the king realized the Jew had confessed to a crime he had not committed, the bishop warned against trusting any testimony or confession extracted under torture. The Jew then explained that while being subjected to horrible tortures he had lost his mind, and to avoid more suffering, he "chose death," confessing to the murder. As the king expressed his gratitude to the bishop for saving him from spilling "innocent blood," the bishop reiterated that one should not place any "confidence and certainty in what a man would say under blows and torments."

As these tales show, in ibn Verga's *Shevet Yehudah,* in the end everything ends well, and justice is done. The stories presented logical arguments against blood libels, with some practical advice on how to approach royal officials and the king himself. *Shevet Yehudah* quickly became popular and highly influential, reaching broader Jewish and Christian audiences as it appeared in multiple Hebrew editions and in translations in Latin, Spanish, and Yiddish. It was used by other sixteenth-century Jewish writers, including Samuel Usque in his *Consolations for the Tribulations of Israel* (1553, Ferrara) and Josef Ha-Kohen in *Emek ha-bakha,* and his history of the kingdom of France and the Ottoman Empire. In the seventeenth century, Menasseh ben Israel used these stories in *Vindiciae judaeorum* to refute the scurrilous work by William Prynne opposing the readmission of Jews to England on the grounds that they killed Christian children.[93]

These Sephardic works can be contrasted with the Yiddish works addressing blood libels.[94] The Yiddish editions of *Shevet Yehudah,* beginning with the first one, published in Cracow in 1591, changed some motifs to conform to Ashkenazi sensibilities. The translator, as Michael Stanislawski has put it, "slyly but substantially transformed a classic of Spanish-Jewish historiography and the Sephardic weltanschauung into a radically different sort of work."[95] The Yiddish versions, for example, amplify the role of God, which is only occasionally implied in the Hebrew original (for example, in Tales Sixteen and Seventeen).

They also display a discomfort with details about blood accusations. The short introduction before Tale Seven in Yiddish, absent from the Hebrew, mentions the claim that Jews used Christian blood for Passover, and notes a bishop as the source of the accusation.[96] Other tales are less explicit about blood and tend to talk about "gentiles" dropping bodies in Jews' houses, as in Tales Eight or Eleven (Twelve in the Hebrew original) in the 1724 Fürth edition.[97] In Tale Eight of the Hebrew original, as Stanislawski has noted, the accusers expect that under torture the Jew "will confess and we will learn the truth, for the Jew will say that he killed [the Christian] and ate his blood." The reference to confessing to eating blood is notably removed from the Yiddish version.[98]

If in *Shevet Yehudah* all ends well, though in the Yiddish version with God's explicit help, the outcomes in Yiddish songs and tales are nearly the exact opposite. To be sure, the Yiddish songs and tales too offer practical advice on approaching Christian authorities, pleading with and bribing them, but they almost always end, despite the Jews' intercessions, with the martyr's death of the accused Jews. The surviving songs and tales celebrate martyrdom, heroic death, and affirmation of Jewish beliefs in the face of persecution and torments from the gentiles. In contrast to the Jewish protagonists in the Sephardic *Shevet Yehudah*, the heroes and martyrs of the Yiddish tales almost never confess under torture, never convert, and certainly never implicate anyone else in false crimes. And the rare exceptions serve to underscore the dominant message.

Yiddish songs and tales about anti-Jewish accusations—both ritual murder and host desecrations—share a similar structure. When an accusation is made against Jews, they are arrested and sent to be tortured, where they are pressured to confess and, almost always, to convert. Yet despite these pressures and pain, they do not break under torture, remaining steadfast in their faith and loyal to their community.

This is the message of the song devoted to "three martyrs from Vilne [Wilno]."[99] When R. Yehezkel, one of the three heroes of the song, is asked to incriminate the community leaders, he steadfastly refuses, defiantly saying to the executioner, "Until now you have been my lord, but today I will be free from you, I want to go to my higher lord. He will help me endure the *kiddush ha-shem*." Yehezkel is executed along with his companions, dying a martyr's death in the presence of multitudes.

But if ibn Verga's Jews who confess to crimes they did not commit provide polemical arguments against torture and blood accusations, the premise behind the Yiddish tales was not as explicitly polemical. Here, torture serves to create the image of the holy martyr, a *kadosh*, whose steadfastness is glorified and presented as a model to be followed by all.[100] Although Jews in these tales try to muster political support to prevent the deaths of the accused and plead with God for mercy by prayers and fasting, the accusations are *gzeyres*, decrees from heaven; they are not human inventions requiring logical arguments in defense of Jews as they are presented in the Sephardic works. In these Yiddish historical songs and tales, as in much of the medieval Hebrew martyrological poetry, most connections with the highest authorities usually fail; instead, prayer and atonement, faithfulness to God and to the community are praised while the martyrs die painful deaths.[101] Jewish martyrs become "sacrifices prepared on a sacrificial altar" "for our many sins;" an *'akedah* reminiscent of the binding of biblical Isaac, and sometimes *kapparot,* or *kapoyres,* redemptive sacrifices on whose account the sins of the community (*kol isroel*) would be forgiven.[102] This rhetoric seems to be an inversion, perhaps even a displacement, of the Christian ethos of martyrdom and of Christ's redemptive sacrifice for the sins of humanity.

This message is retained even in songs that are not about anti-Jewish libels. One song tells the story of the martyrdom of R. Shlomo Zanvil of Krzeszów. The crime of which Shlomo Zanvil was accused is unclear. Though the texts calls the affair *'alilat sheker* (a libel), the punishment he received—hanging, with his right hand cut off—suggests he must have been accused of some sort of theft, though definitely not sacrilege, because then the punishment would have likely been burning at the stake.[103] The cultural weight of the song is amplified by the fact that it was to be sung to the tune of *El Male Raḥamim,* a chant performed during funerals and in some Ashkenazi communities also during Yom Kippur.[104] The drama of Shlomo Zanvil's death is set over the last days of the High Holidays, the climax taking place on *Hoshana Rabbah,* a day Jews considered the last day to seek forgiveness for sins of the previous year.

On *Hoshana Rabbah,* Shlomo was tortured, and the priests pressured him to convert. But predictably for such songs, Shlomo managed to withstand both, willing "to go like a sacrifice to the [ritual] slaughter."[105] Like the medieval Jewish martyrs, he affirmed he "was born a Jew and will remain a Jew," and is said to have died with *Shem'a Israel* on his lips. Though Shlomo stood accused of a crime other than an anti-Jewish libel, he attained martyr status by being pressured to convert. It was on the merit of the death and suffering of such "holy and pure" martyrs, the Yiddish songs asserted, that "the sins of Israel" would be forgiven.[106]

The story of Adil Kikinesh of Drohobycz, a rare example of an accused Jew (incidentally a woman) to confess, illustrates the point that pain and suffering were endured for the sake of the community.[107] According to the story, recorded by ethnographers in the nineteenth century and told for generations, Adil Kikinesh, whose beauty, wisdom, voice, and "clear pronunciation" were said to have besotted "princes and priests" alike, was accused in 1718 of convincing her Christian maid to kill a Christian boy to obtain blood for Passover matzah.[108] The accusation was concocted out of envy by some priests seeking to destroy "the beautiful Adil." Imprisoned, she realized that the whole Jewish community was now in danger. To save it, she took the full blame and was sentenced to death. Although Adil's Christian maid eventually revealed the secret plot against Jews, the court did not reverse the sentence; instead, Adil was offered life if she converted to Christianity. Like all other Ashkenazi martyrs, Adil remained steadfast in her faith and decided to die. With her execution scheduled in the public square in Lwów, a major city in Poland, Adil requested pins to attach her skirt to the skin of her legs so her body would not be exposed to onlookers as she was dragged through the streets. She was said to have died on the seventh of Elul, 5478 (September 2, 1718).[109] On her tombstone, Adil was remembered as "the holy and pure woman" who "sanctified the great name, and gave her soul for all Israel."[110] In contrast to ibn Verga's *Shevet Yehudah*, where the false confession of accused Jews serves to prove the unreliability of torture, Adil Kikinesh's false confession serves to save the Jewish community and turns her into a martyr.[111] In effect, through her death Adil Kikinesh, like the male martyrs from earlier songs, became the community's redemptive sacrifice.

The early modern Yiddish historical songs are deeply rooted in the Ashkenazi ethos of martyrdom, *kiddush ha-shem*, which dates back to the Crusades and the 1171 Blois, and from which also emerges the notion of Jewish martyrs as redemptive sacrifices.[112] Their deaths, as Susan Einbinder has shown, served "as expiation for communal sins."[113] There are rare exceptions to this pattern of martyrdom. One is the story of the accusation in Poznań in 1696 (still unverifiable in the archives), published in *Sefer geulat Israel* (*Seyfer geules Isroel*; Prague, ca. 1696) and in *Sefer ma'aseh ha-shem* (*Seyfer mayse ha-shem*).[114] According to this story, in 1696 Itzḥak bar Ḥayim Meshorer went to a fair and was killed by a Christian (*ain orel,* from Hebrew, *'aral,* uncircumcised), but the Christian was not held accountable for the Jew's death, because his friends helped him escape to a monastery or a church (*unter galuḥes*).[115] The Jews demanded the murderer be handed over, but he was not. Then on Isru Hag, following the festival of Shavuot, the naked, mutilated body of a Christian student was found in the fields—his feet and hands chopped off, his heart and tongue cut out, and his face slashed. A Christian man immediately began to spread rumors that three Jews killed the young man, and soon people began saying the student was killed to avenge the death of Itzḥak bar Ḥayim Meshorer. As the Christians became riled up for an attack on Jews in the city, the Jewish community leaders sought help from the authorities, who ordered the gates to the city locked. But the lords, facing a dilemma similar to those of the kings in ibn Verga's stories, feared the multitude of the mob and were less eager to protect the Jews. The frightened Jews thus went to the priests to seek protection from attack.

In the meantime, a Christian woman came to Poznań, trying to sell bloodied clothes that, it turned out, had belonged to the dead Christian student. The woman claimed she had found the clothes, and people immediately began to say that Jews must have killed the student and hid his clothes, which the woman then discovered. To further incite the public, "enemies" of the Jews also sought to bring the father of the slain student to see his son's mutilated body. But when the father arrived in Poznań, he recognized that Jews had not committed the crime and asked for the body of his son to be buried. Immediately, some Christians, outraged, claimed the Jews must have bribed the father.

With this turn of events, the Jews took matters into their own hands. When the woman caught selling bloodied clothes turned out to be from Rogoźno (*ragoshny*), about 25 miles north of Poznań, Jews activated their networks, sending information about her to the Jews in her town.[116] They immediately located the house where the woman lived with her son and daughter, and once inside, they saw a bloodied shirt. Asked where the shirt came from, the woman's daughter answered that her brother brought it home and asked her to wash it. Jews then began to search for the brother, finding him in a tavern. They surrounded him so he could not escape and notified the local official. Sympathetic to the Jews' pleas, he arrested the "murderer" and took him to "a room" (*a shtibl*), where he subjected him to torment (*tut im abisl payn*). Pleading with the official not to beat him, the young man confessed to the murder.

Hearing about the man's confession, the Jews immediately sent a messenger to Poznań to inform the authorities about the new developments in the case, who then ordered the man to be sent to Poznań for further investigation. But when the man arrived, the Jews' enemies (*reshoim*) urged him to blame the murder on the Jews, to say that Jews had given him money to kill the student. He did so under torture, but then kept changing his testimony. Jewish religious leaders, meanwhile, ordered a fast and prayers. The community held a day of atonement (*yom kipurim*) to plead with God for deliverance from this libel. Jews from many communities, old and young, men and women, participated in the prayers.

Meanwhile the *reshoim* tried to bribe the executioner to torture the Christian man lightly so he would not confess to the murder, but would continue to implicate the Jews and consequently be let off. This plot came to naught; it was discovered by a Jew who immediately reported it to the authorities, whereupon the accused man was sent to receive "proper" torture. After the third round of torture, the man finally confessed to the murder. His previous testimonies were lies, he said, for he had been asked by the Jews' enemies to implicate Jews in the murder. But now, knowing he would surely die, he did not want to lose his soul and decided to take back his accusation. Although he exculpated the Jews, he did implicate his own mother in witchcraft. Subjected to the last round of torture, he remained steadfast, continuing to exculpate the Jews. The murderer was sentenced to death by quartering, as "he did himself" to the student, and the Jews were saved—by their own ingenuity in finding the murderer, by prayers, and by the effectiveness of torture, which in the end led to the confession of truth.

As the Poznań story demonstrates, the Yiddish tales have a strikingly different take from the Sephardic works on the use of torture. Whereas ibn Verga, along with other Sephardic writers, explicitly questioned the validity of torture already in the first half of the sixteenth century, the much later Ashkenazi works accepted torture as a valid, if terrifying, part of judicial proceedings. Not only did Jews in the Yiddish stories not break under torture but also, as in the Poznań story, the actual murderer's confession under "proper" torture was touted as truth and credited with saving the Jews. The plot to ease the torture of the Christian murderer suggests that under light torture he would lie, but under heavy torture he would tell the truth, further implying that torture was accepted as a reliable means of investigation. In the Yiddish tales, the innocent never confess to anything they did not do, but the guilty eventually do—the exact opposite of the famous dictum *etiam innocentes cogit mentiri dolor,* "pain compels even the innocent to lie."[117]

On the surface, the Yiddish songs seem insular, and on some level they were, because their purpose was to speak to other Jews to glorify the martyrs. But, like the works of their medieval Hebrew predecessors, they are also evidence of Jews' acculturation and their deep embeddedness in early modern Christian Europe.[118] The authors display a detailed knowledge of the law and legal procedures, reflecting the legal thinking and practices of the time. They seem to have accepted the legitimacy of torture, which in the seventeenth century in Poland and the German lands was not only an accepted procedure of the judicial process but also one performed, at least in Germany, by increasingly professionalized executioners who, as Joel Harrington has shown, were seen as important servants of the state performing necessary tasks.[119] Thus, if the early decades of the Spanish Inquisition gave torture a bad name in Sephardic circles and in regions that embraced the Spanish black legend, in the Ashkenazi world, torture was part of the law—the imperial or royal law—that Jews also used for their own protection. And that is what is on display in these Yiddish tales.

But there is more. Sephardic Jews have frequently been seen as interlocutors with Christian cultures and contrasted with Ashkenazi Jews' supposed insularity, but the Yiddish tales, despite their inward orientation, closely reflect the surrounding Christian values and culture. European Christians saw pain as "the primary channel of truth" and valued its salvific meaning. For Christians, suffering was a means of drawing "closer to God," an ethos based in the figure of Christ who chose "suffering and death for the redemption of humanity."[120] The trope of martyrdom is also present in German witch trials in which the accused women compared themselves to true Christian martyrs. For example, one Anna Murschel, tried in 1599–1601 in Lutheran Württemberg for witchcraft, claimed, as Laura Kounine has shown, that she was able to endure "such suffering pain and martyrdom" during torture thanks to "help and assistance of God's mercy." She "could confess nothing," because she knew her "innocent in [herself] and before God the Almighty."[121] In another case from 1603, one woman accused of witchcraft wished "to God that she was [a witch], so that she would like to abandon martyrdom . . . [and] die for that."[122]

Indeed, the imagery found in both medieval Jewish poems and early modern Yiddish songs is boldly Christological, perhaps aimed at contesting Christian motifs of sacrifice, piety, and redemption. In some, the bodies of the medieval martyrs are not destructible by fire,[123] a motif that appeared in early Christian literature and would be later shared by the Eucharistic wafer.[124] Perhaps the most explicit example of the reappropriation of these Christological motifs in Jewish poetry is Solomon Simḥah's poem "Shaḥar avi todah" (At Dawn I Shall Bring an Offering), commemorating the death of thirteen Jews of Troyes in 1288.[125] Solomon Simḥah, placing the words in the mouth of the Jewish martyr Samson, evokes motifs closely associated with Christ:

> Behold me here
> God, to worship you—may my sacrifice be acceptable!
> Among these saints, who surpasses me?
> From my own blood pouring down I shall make a libation of wine
> On the fiery altar wine and tears will go up.

Later in the poem, the martyr tells how "for the sake of his Holy Name [he was] burned, beaten, and tortured" and became "the double-portion of bread/His hands, his feet, his head—for behold it is the Sabbath." These passages adapt the motifs closely associated with Jesus's own sacrifice, even echoing Eucharistic themes, for a Jewish use: the blood of the Jewish martyr becomes the libation of wine; his body becomes the bread. The "double-portion of bread" was not the Eucharistic bread, of course, but rather the manna. In this medieval Jewish poem it was set to contrast with or perhaps contest the Christian interpretation that manna was a prefiguration of the Eucharist, as expressed by Jesus in the Gospel of John: "I am the bread of life . . . I am the bread that came down from heaven. . . . Your ancestors ate the manna in the wilderness, and they died. This is the bread that came down from heaven so that one may eat of it and not die. I am the living bread that came down from heaven. Whoever eats of this bread will live forever, and the bread that I will give for the life of the world is my flesh" (John 6: 35, 41, 45–51). The rhetorical question "Among these saints, who surpasses me?" manifestly gestures toward Jesus who "surpasses" all the saints in heaven. The references to being "burned, beaten, and tortured" and to the martyr's hands and feet also seem to echo the beaten and tortured Jesus as he spoke to his followers after his resurrection: "Look at my hands and my feet, see that it is I myself" (Luke 24: 39–40). Jesus's suffering and his injured body, hands, feet, and head bloodied by the crown of thorns were increasingly prominently portrayed in Christian art.[126]

The prominence of the imagery of suffering in Christian society, the role of pain and suffering in the stories of Christian martyrdom, and instances of Jewish suffering and martyrdom prompted late medieval Ashkenazi rabbis to debate the question of martyrdom and pain, with some even arguing that a person committing an act of martyrdom did not suffer pain.[127] Yet, in the popular early modern Yiddish songs and tales, the role pain plays in the description of martyrdom is stark—it reifies the martyr's sacrifice.

As Brad Gregory has noted discussing early modern Christian martyrdom, "the impact of martyrdom helped solidify group identities."[128] The Yiddish tales sought to reassure Jews about their faith by featuring Jewish martyrs who never convert, despite persistent efforts on the part of Christians. The Jews' faithfulness to their God had (or was at least portrayed as having) a powerful impact on the onlookers. If in the Christian context, to return to Brad Gregory, "from the perspective of civil and ecclesiastical authorities, the condemned ought to have begged for forgiveness and reconciliation," in the case of Jewish executions the offer to convert should have been attractive, because it offered either an easier death, which was the option more frequently encountered in real trials, or life, an option given in the stories.[129] The Jews' conversion would have provided Christians with a story of victory, but the Jews' martyrdom reaffirmed Judaism instead.

In the song about "the three martyrs from Vilne," one of the martyrs, R. Moshe, was told that not only would his life be saved but also he would be "made rich" and "equal to the greatest lords" if he converted.[130] He did not succumb to the priests' "stupid speech," choosing painful martyrdom instead. In another story the Jewish writer conveyed the impact all martyrs hoped to have on the onlookers, witnessing "the sight of men and women going to their deaths willingly," even, as many early modern Jewish and Christian sources put it, "with a joy like to a wedding" and "bearing extreme pain with extraordinary patience."[131] The non-Jews, witnessing the painful execution of R. Abraham, "trembled tearfully," hearing the holy man's pious and moving speech.[132]

Ashkenazi Jews, of course, did not have a monopoly on martyrdom. By the late Middle Ages and certainly by the 1391 persecutions in Spain, aspects of the medieval Ashkenazi ethos of martyrdom began to appear among Sephardic Jews.[133] For example, as Miriam Bodian has shown, the Spanish rabbinic scholar and community leader Hasdai Crescas described the death of his son in 1391 as "a burnt offering." But despite Crescas's comparison, in contrast to Ashkenazi Jews among whom "the image of the martyr as a 'burnt offering' ... became a key element in the idealized self-image of Ashkenazi Jewry for generations to come," such an image "never became a part of the idealized self-image prevalent among Spanish Jews."[134] In the early modern era, Spanish and Portuguese conversos celebrated, if rather cautiously, those willing to die defiantly and publicly "in the Law of Moses." Menasseh ben Israel noted them in *Hope of Israel;* Isaac Cardoso discussed them in *Las excelencias de los hebreos.*[135] But for Sephardic Jews, adjusting to openly Jewish life, as Bodian has persuasively shown, the defiant tropes of martyrdom were "unhelpful and indeed a liability."[136] And for Ashkenazi Jews, who faced real-life accusations, the Yiddish tales of martyrdom, grounded in deep and potent tradition, provided models for how and why to survive torture and how to avoid implicating other Jews.

If as scholars have shown the real-life acts of martyrdom occurred among both Sephardic and Ashkenazi Jews, the Ashkenazi and Sephardic literary responses to blood libels are marked by sharper cultural differences, grounded in longer cultural traditions and practical needs, both of which informed the choice of genre and contents. Ashkenazi works tended to focus on martyrdom, atonement, and offerings; they sought to sustain hope, make sense of the suffering Jews periodically experienced as a result of anti-Jewish libels, and to prevent their conversion, a choice always offered during criminal trials in Poland and the German lands. The Yiddish songs became *musar* literature that called for piety and repentance in the Jewish community to prevent the *gzeyres* God sent upon Jews in the form of accusations "for our many sins."[137] If the anti-Jewish accusations were in fact *gzeyres* from God, for which some Jews were chosen to become sacrifices, then blaming the gentiles and polemicizing against these accusations would undermine the meaning assigned to these deaths. Gentile accusations played a crucial role in making effective the Ashkenazi narratives of punishment, repentance, and redemption. As the Yiddish songs relished in the descriptions of suffering and torture, they mirrored the paradoxical need for Jewish "crimes" in Christian narratives that served to underscore Christian "truths."[138] But the Yiddish songs also imparted values and provided concrete models on how and why to withstand torture in the face of similar accusations. For the rest of the community, they also offered guidance on how to respond practically to such libels by organizing financial and political support, or, as in the story about an accusation in 1696 in Poznań, how to take matters into their own hands and find the true perpetrators of the crimes.

The Sephardic works, in contrast, preserved the polemical character of the responses, reflecting a long Iberian tradition of Jewish–Christian polemic that was much stronger than among Ashkenazi Jews, while muting actual acts of martyrdom known to have been committed by conversos. But the Sephardic writers also responded to practical needs. Although not subjected to accusations themselves, they were forced to prove the baselessness of such accusations as they sought to reestablish their lives in Italy, England, or the Netherlands. Their literary responses, thus, reach out to Christian readers as well.

CHAPTER SIX

"Who Should One Believe, the Rabbis or the Doctors of the Church?"

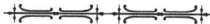

IN NO PLACE after Trent, it seems, was there a more evident link between tales about Jews murdering Christian children disseminated through books and criminal trials against them than in the Polish-Lithuanian Commonwealth, which witnessed a rise in anti-Jewish accusations and trials at the same time they were subsiding in western and southern Europe. The trials in the Polish-Lithuanian Commonwealth created a feedback loop: books provided evidence of Jews' culpability and led to their prosecution, while the trials that ended in their conviction provided new material for subsequent books that were in turn used as evidence in later trials. They all helped root the belief in Jewish murders of Christian children more deeply in the Christian consciousness in the Polish-Lithuanian Commonwealth.

Not every accusation led to a trial, and not every trial ended with the persecution and deaths of Jews. But those cases in which Jews were not tried or punished by and large remained hidden in the archives and away from public view, invoked only occasionally by Jews' opponents as proofs of corruption and a "failure of justice." In contrast, the trials that spilled Jewish blood entered both public memory and a transmission trail in books, pamphlets, and commemorative art and plaques in churches. This feedback loop between literature and courtroom in the Polish-Lithuanian Commonwealth stood in stark contrast with events in western Europe, where, as R. Po-Chia Hsia has shown, by the second half of the sixteenth century, the number of such accusations and trials decreased.[1] Indeed, when a trial against a Jew, Raphaël Levy, got underway in 1669 in Lorraine, a backlash that ensued reverberated across many regions and provided new materials to push back against similar accusations.[2]

In Poland-Lithuania, two moments seem pivotal: the publication in Polish of Simon's story in 1579 by Piotr Skarga, "the incomparable preacher" as Sebastian Śleszkowski dubbed the noted Jesuit, and the 1598 book by Przecław Mojecki, which presented "Jewish cruelties" in a small succinct package, offering Polish readers a new lens through which to look at Jews. Mojecki's book challenged officials' frequent reluctance to prosecute accusations against Jews and laid the groundwork to undermine the validity of Jewish defense arguments by sowing skepticism about papal and imperial protections that continued to be felt until the modern era.[3] These anti-Jewish books not only spawned similar books but, by raising doubts about the legal position of Jews, disseminating venomous stories, and selectively publishing decrees condemning Jews to death, they also began to influence the outcomes of trials against Jews. They provided legitimacy for later accusations and prosecutions, and a new framework within which to view the deaths of children—so much so that, by the second half of the eighteenth century such accusations in the Polish-Lithuanian Commonwealth not only continued but they became more acceptable.

The Trial of 1598 and Its Aftermath

In March 1598, just a few weeks after Mojecki finished his book *Jewish Cruelties, Murders, and Superstitions,* a four-year-old boy named Wojciech (Albert in Latin) disappeared near the village of Świniarów (today about twenty miles east of Siedlce in eastern Poland).[4] A few days after Easter, which that year fell quite early, on March 22, Albert's father apparently went to work in a field, and the boy followed him, but stayed behind on the road leading to the village of Woźniki some two miles away and became lost.[5] Although Passover was not until April 20, Jews were implicated in the boy's disappearance and were tried in the nearby town of Mielnik. The accused Jews were then transferred to the Crown Tribunal in Lublin, and after a trial lasting more than two weeks they were publicly executed on a Sabbath in July 1598.[6]

Since no court records survive, only narrative summaries of the affair in Polish by anti-Jewish writers—Szymon Hubicki, from 1602, and Sebastian Śleszkowski, from 1621—the timeline of the affair is difficult to establish. Hubicki published only excerpts of the records, focusing on the consumption of blood. Śleszkowski republished these excerpts, framing them as a decree from the Crown Tribunal and adding a Latin preface to buttress their authenticity. Śleszkowski also described the final part of the trial in July apparently on the basis of then-existing court records, and added to his own reconstruction of events a contemporary letter of an eyewitness at the trial. The apparent fragmentary court decree from Śleszkowski's work was then included in later anti-Jewish works, including those by Stefan Żuchowski and Jakub Radliński.[7] Thus began the transmission of court documents demonstrating Jewish guilt popularized in Polish anti-Jewish works.

According to Hubicki's version, on March 25 or 26, Jews kidnapped Albert, whom they found sleeping on the side of the road. They were said to have taken him to a tavern they ran in Woźniki, and killed him at night, disposing of his body in nearby swamps with help from a female Christian servant named Nastaska, identified by Śleszkowski as a cook in one of the Jews' homes.[8] A few days later, Nastaska reportedly became drunk and mentioned something to a Christian man during a fair in nearby Łosice. In the meantime, a boy looking for "ducks' or lapwings' eggs in the swamp" came across Albert's body and notified the authorities. Jews were soon accused and summoned to the castle in Mielnik. After a dispute over jurisdiction, the case was transferred to Lublin, the seat of a recently established Crown Tribunal.[9] Hubicki's summary is followed by what appear to be confessions in Polish of three Jews—Jachim, Aron (known also as Gromek), and Isaac—excerpted from court records in a manner to justify the death sentence. Full interrogations were apparently recorded in *Acta Advocatialia* of Lublin, but they have been lost, and none of the anti-Jewish writers felt the need to publish them, likely because, as Śleszkowski's Latin preamble and trial summary suggest, the Jews vehemently denied committing the crime.[10] In contrast, the fragmentary confessions that entered public memory thanks to Hubicki (and then others) focused on the Jews' culpability and admission to using blood. The fragments became, as Śleszkowski wrote, "a proof" that Jews killed Christian children. They also created a new paper trail of evidence to serve in the future. A fuller account of the records would have weakened that message.

According to the published fragment of the confession of Jachim, one of the three Jews on trial, he came across a pot of blood hidden under the Jewish children's bed on Thursday "before Jewish Easter."[11] Jachim was a poor man, and "since it is a Jewish custom to send the poor Jews to the rich for sustenance," he was sent to celebrate Passover with Marek, a Jew of Woźniki, who apparently told him to look around for food if he got hungry. On Thursday, the hungry Jachim began to root around in the storeroom, where he found bread and, under the children's bed, a "new red pot" with what he thought was honey. But when he touched it with his finger, he found that it was a red substance. Puzzled he asked Marek's wife about it, and the Jewess answered that it was "blood of a Christian child, but don't tell anyone,"[12] whereupon the pot disappeared. Jachim added that when the Jews were arrested and sent to Lublin, Marek begged everyone to "keep our hearts with God and say nothing, confess nothing, even if they tortured us." But Jachim implicated Nastaska, the Christian woman, who in his version found Albert's body in a barrel in the cellar of the Jewish tavern where she went, before "the Jewish easter," to retrieve beer, considered *hametz* and therefore not permissible for Passover.[13] Nastaska's role changed from testimony to testimony. According to Aron, she took care of the boy for weeks while he was hidden in the cellar, keeping him company when he missed his family. She was also said to have helped dispose of the body. In the fragment of her own testimony, Nastaska relayed her conversation with Marek's wife, who she said told her, "If we did not have Christian blood for the festival [*wielik deń*], we could not have a festival, that is Easter."[14] The suspects were waterboarded, including with vodka, then shaved, stretched on the rack, and their skin burned—apparently an effective strategy that made them confess to the killing. The effects of physical torture were compounded by the fact that the Jewish prisoners were starving, because they refused to eat food provided by the court, but were prohibited from getting kosher food delivered by Jews for fear of "sorcery or poison." Aron agreed to convert in hopes of being spared, but when he learned he would still have to die but as a Christian, he balked. Though the fragment of the ostensible sentencing decree mentions torture just briefly, underscoring that the confessions were "voluntary" and "spontaneously" made in the presence of the leaders of the Lublin Jewish community, the gory details were published in Śleszkowski's book.[15]

The narrative lines of these confessions, fragmentary as they are, do not hold together. The timelines are contradictory, especially given that Passover that year was on April 20–27, almost a month after the disappearance of the boy. The supposedly secret demonic activity by Jews was all but secret, as Jews are said to have talked openly and brazenly about the killing and the blood with each other and with Christians. Though Jews were supposed to be using blood to fulfill their own rites, the story's elements are framed within a distinctly Christian understanding of religious practices. For example, the Jewess was said to have added the blood to the unleavened Passover bread, as if to fabricate the Eucharistic wafer, which was believed to contain Christ's blood; the blood was also added to wine, believed to have a special "power." The letter from an eyewitness to the trial in Lublin, published by Śleszkowski, reported that one of the interrogated Jews had claimed that only rabbis drank the blood. According to this letter, the Jewish prisoners lashed out at the Jewish leaders in Lublin, saying, "All the tortures we suffer now is all because of you. You order us, the young in villages and towns to find small Christian children, but you drink their blood on Easter." This is a salient projection of the functions of a Catholic priest onto the elders of the Jewish community, especially the rabbis. In Catholicism, only priests were allowed to partake in Eucharistic wine, and only they could effect transubstantiation—to turn a wafer into a body and blood of Christ and the wine into his blood.

Though distorted, these fragments of the 1598 affair nonetheless reveal glimpses of plausible Jewish responses to the charges and their legal defense strategy. Already in Mielnik, where the first court proceedings took place, sometime in April 1598, after the decomposing body of Albert was discovered in the swamps, Jews demanded to have the case transferred to a royal jurisdiction. Once that request was granted, Jews presented privileges and charters to the Crown Tribunal in Lublin that protected them from such accusations, along with papal bulls stating "they did not need Christian blood."[16] Presenting such royal or papal decrees was a common defense by Jews, and in Lublin too, this strategy at first seemed effective: Jews gained defenders among the noblemen serving as deputies at the Tribunal.[17] But when some of the Jews confessed to the killing, the Marshal of the Crown Tribunal, Adam Stadnicki, who considered Jews "heathens" and "dogs," tried to shame their supporters for accepting the Jews' legal defenses and their money and defending them.[18] The Jews' confessions and Stadnicki's attitude seem to have played a pivotal role in the trial, which resulted in the first convictions and executions of accused Jews in the Polish-Lithuanian Commonwealth and became a legal precedent soon used by other accusers and anti-Jewish writers.

The letter published by Śleszkowski also referred to Jewish responses to the trial and its verdict. When the accused Jews were convicted and sentenced to be executed in front of the Lublin synagogue, Jews lobbied both local officials and religious figures and engaged in prayer and fasting in hopes of changing the outcome. They did not succeed, but these apparent responses are in line with how Jews were known to react in similar cases, and from Yiddish songs and tales.

The 1598 affair—the first high-profile case against Jews for murdering a Christian child that resulted in a conviction and a public execution in

Poland—was a turning point, acknowledged as such by both contemporaries and later readers. A century or so later, Stefan Żuchowski, the instigator of two trials of Jews in Sandomierz and the author of two anti-Jewish accounts of those trials, noted the novelty of the 1598 trial. "It seems to be the first" such judgment of the Crown Tribunal against the Jews, Żuchowski wrote, presenting the 1598 fragmentary decree as evidence in his own case against Jews and reprinting it in one of his books.[19]

The 1598 affair may be significant for another reason: it may have also been the first time that traditional Jewish legal defenses failed in Poland. For example, when Jews were accused of killing a Christian in 1576 in Gostynin, King Stefan Batory intervened, reiterating long-standing prohibitions against similar accusations.[20] The king reminded officials of the requirements to provide four Christian and three Jewish witnesses for an accusation to be valid, and to transfer such cases to royal jurisdiction. When in April 1577, Nachum Abramovich, a Jew from the small town of Wojnia (or Wohyń, as identified by Hanna Węgrzynek[21]) in the Podlasie region was accused by burghers, or townsmen (*meshchane*), of killing a Christian child, the royal decree from the year before proved useful.[22] Nachum was arrested and led to the local prison by the townspeople, but the local Jews brought to the attention of the court a privilege granted them by King Stefan Batory.[23] The court rejected the case on procedural grounds, basing its decision in part on testimony by two Christian women, Marina and Kakhna, who claimed that "the *meshchane* were forcing [them] to testify against Jews" and denied that "the Jew Nachum did anything like" that.

The 1577 case shows that the officials' insistence on following proper laws and procedures mattered. And following proper procedures included the acceptance of privileges and charters issued to protect Jews from such accusations. Though it is unclear whether Mojecki's book played a direct role in the outcome of the 1598 trial, the timing is suggestive: just months after his book sought to undermine the validity of Jewish legal defenses, the strategy of presenting royal charters and papal bulls failed. His book introduced to Polish readers doubts about the validity of documents presented by Jews, and other books continued to raise them.

But another development proved important. In 1576 and 1577, the king was still a supreme judge, the *judex supremus*. A year later, in 1578, a Crown Tribunal was created to replace the king in that role.[24] The Tribunal became a court of the highest instance in the Crown of Poland, and since 1581 also in Lithuania, both led by nobles elected at local dietines. The convening of the Crown Tribunal was an important annual event, attracting huge crowds beyond those whose cases were considered.[25] High-profile political figures, parties to judicial proceedings, and spectators all were part of a veritable theater of power and influence.[26] With the establishment of the Tribunal, appeals to the authority of the king became more difficult and less effective. Jews, and others who stood before the tribunals, now had to persuade all noble deputies to the Tribunal.[27]

The creation of the Crown Tribunal was part of a set of broad political reforms within the Polish-Lithuanian Commonwealth. In 1580, a new tax system led to the creation of the Council of Four Lands, a Jewish self-governing body responsible for the collection of taxes and other fiscal matters.[28] This new body also facilitated Jews' responses to blood accusations and made collecting funds to defend those accused more effective. As the fragmentary records of the 1598 case demonstrate, Jewish leaders were often present during anti-Jewish trials, actively lobbying on behalf of the accused.

A convergence of countrywide political transformations, local conflicts, and culture seems to have played an important role in making the 1598 case so pivotal.[29] As Hanna Węgrzynek has shown, the last decade of the sixteenth century was marked by a spike in accusations, which went mostly unprosecuted—until 1598.[30] Three years before, in 1595, Jews were tried in relation to another accusation in Gostynin. That same year, in Sawin, a town near Chełm, and a day's distance from Lublin, Jews were similarly charged with killing a Christian child, but Jewish leaders, now organized through the Council of Four Lands, were able to "quiet down" the libel.[31] And in 1597, a year before Mojecki's book came out, Jews were accused of killing a child in Szydłów, but apparently the case was dismissed. For Mojecki it was a travesty of justice that inspired him to write his book on "Jewish cruelties," which came out a few months before Albert's body would be found.[32]

In the three years before the death of Albert, the region had been a site of three libels in which Jews were freed. And so when in 1598 Mojecki's new book arrived ranting against Jews' influence and corruption and offering the first argument invalidating Jewish legal defenses, it did not ring hollow. With the Council of Four Lands now in place, Jews were indeed more organized and more visible, just as the proceedings at the Crown Tribunal were more visible than those previously headed by the king.

And so when Albert's body was found in Świniarów, stories and rumors, amplified by Mojecki's book, were already circulating about Jews, waiting to be exploited when the need arose. Albert's death provided such opportunity. The two villages of Świniarów and Woźniki were owned by Istvan Pete, a nobleman of Hungarian origin, who seems to have arrived in the Polish-Lithuanian Commonwealth with the Hungarian-born king of Poland, Stefan Batory. Pete leased his estate to a nobleman named Skowieski and a tavern to Jews, among them Marek, who became one of the accused Jews. An apparent conflict arose between the two lessees: Skowieski is said to have borrowed a significant amount of money from Marek, the Jewish tavern keeper, and was upset about the Jews' good relations with their landlord. According to Śleszkowski's account, Jews claimed that Pete had asked Marek to notify him if Skowieski harmed the local peasants. When Albert's body was found, Skowieski wasted no time in arresting the Jews and their Christian servant, having found an excuse to punish the informants.

The public execution of Jews in Lublin for killing Albert in 1598 reverberated across Poland-Lithuania. It was described in letters, such as the one written by an eyewitness to the trial and published by Śleszkowski. The Jesuits in Lublin, who were collecting funds to build and decorate a new church, wrote about it in their annual report (*litterae annuae*) to Rome, which report was then printed and dispatched across the world to other Jesuits, providing one more piece of historical "evidence."[33] In it, the Jesuits mentioned that although Jews had been punished for their "most deplorable crime," some Christians wanted to ensure that the deed not be buried in the archives of memory and sponsored the dissemination of the case in "printed books" to expose the "crime" to the world [*orbi universo detegendum*]." In 1604, Albert's body was transferred into the newly built Jesuit church, thereby potentially turning it into relics and increasing the boy's profile.[34] But there is no evidence that the Lublin Jesuits had sought to do so right away. The *litterae annuae* for 1598 mention nothing about the boy's body, though they note other donations for the church, including a silver crucifix.[35] Despite this initial silence, Albert's body seems to have been laid at first in the Jesuits' private chapel.

In their *littera annua* for 1604, the Jesuits in Lublin reported to Rome about the celebration of the feast of Holy Innocents, a festival associated with child martyrs, in their new church. They described a chapel adorned to honor the Holy Innocents, "in particular a four-year old who had been slit by Jews a few years earlier" and whose body was deposited there by Cardinal Bernard Maciejowski, the new bishop of Cracow and a supporter of the Jesuits in Lublin.[36] Maciejowski, apparently in an effort to create a Polish "Simon," petitioned Rome for the recognition of Albert's cult, sending "published books and images" as evidence.[37] But no records of this material seem to exist in Rome; the assertions come only from polemical works and from an account in the Bollandist *Acta Sanctorum*, which was comprised of some of the information found in the Jesuits' annual reports and in Hubicki's book, with the added mention of miracles, a detail absent from the internal Jesuit reports.[38] In a letter from 1616 preserved in the Bollandist Archives, Polish Jesuit Fryderyk Szembek offered a list of Polish saints and compared Albert to "S. Simon" of Trent.³⁹ Although the display of the body by the Jesuits in their church in Lublin was not unusual—several other children's bodies had been displayed in Poland-Lithuania, among them that of Szymon Kyrilis in the Bernardine monastery in Wilno and another, unnamed child in a Norbertine monastery in Witów, near Piotrków Trybunalski—their effort to have him recognized as *beatus* or a saint was.⁴⁰ And although Rome never recognized the cult, Albert's story did enter the monumental *Acta Sanctorum* along with an appendix of other "cases" taken from Hubicki's 1602 book. The 1598 death of Albert of Świniarów transformed, in more than one way, the legal and cultural landscape of blood accusations in the Polish-Lithuanian Commonwealth and thrust Polish cases into the European market of knowledge.

A Tale of Two Trials in Lublin, 1636

With the 1598 trial providing a precedent, the number of trials and convictions of Jews in the Polish-Lithuanian Commonwealth increased.⁴¹ But not all trials of Jews accused of murdering Christians ended with their execution. In 1636 in Lublin, two trials took place in quick succession: one resulted in the Jews' release and the other in their conviction and execution.⁴² The first case would have been likely doomed to oblivion had it not been obliquely mentioned in the sentencing decree of the second. Together they entered the paper trail that stretched across Europe.

In 1636, after a body of a Christian boy named Mathias was found in the river, two Jews, Bieniasz and Lachman, stood accused of killing him around Passover. They were both extensively interrogated under torture, but unwaveringly denied killing the boy, asserting both their own innocence and the innocence of all other Jews. "I am not guilty, and Jews are innocent; Jews do not need blood," said Bieniasz in his testimony.⁴³ He repeatedly stated that neither he nor other Jews ever killed Christian children. Lachman, too, when asked why Jews used Christian blood, said, "These are fabrications against us; Jews do not use blood."⁴⁴

The investigators were clearly fishing for incriminating information in their inquiries about Jewish ceremonies. When Lachman was asked what the word for blood was in Hebrew, he answered "dam," and then another question followed immediately: What did Jews drink in the synagogue from a special cup?⁴⁵ Lachman answered, "Wine, which [even] children drink so that they would go to school." The interrogation continued: "Asked why they smeared eyes after the Sabbath, he answered we extinguish the candles in wine or in beer, and out of piety smear eyes [with the wine] after the

Sabbath." But Lachman added, "I am not fluent in knowledge." The questions were about a *havdalah* ceremony marking the end of the Sabbath, during which some Jews indeed followed the ritual of dipping their fingers in the wine used to extinguish the candles and wiping the wine on their eyes. But the question was not innocent. One oft-cited reason for why Jews needed Christian blood was that they smeared it on their eyes. This line of interrogation was evidently trying to establish the validity of this claim. After other questions, the interrogators returned to the issue of the use of blood. Lachman repeatedly asserted, "We do not use any blood; we do not even eat a bloody piece of beef. No Jew needs Christian blood."[46] He said again under torture, "Jews do not need blood. I cannot say that about Christians if they killed this child, I do not want to take them on my conscience (*na duszę*), but Jews did not kill this child, nor did they drown him." Indeed, the next day, when he was asked about it again, he said, "I know for sure [*wiem dowodnie*] that Jews do not use or need Christian blood."

Other questions, too, were formulated to provide a comparison of Jewish ritual practices with the alleged reasons for Jews' need of Christian blood often found in anti-Jewish literature. Such comparison was to validate the accusation. With little to no reliable sources about Jewish ceremonies available to Christians in Poland, the interrogations served as an opportunity for "ethnographic" research. *Afikomen,* a portion of matzah used during the Passover seder, fascinated Christians and raised their suspicions. In almost every trial, Jews were asked about it. Bieniasz was asked when Jews "were given *effikomen* [*sic*]." He responded that during Passover (literally, "easter") they ate matzah without salt and emphasized that "in this matzah there is flour and water."[47] Lachman was asked if the *afikomen* was distributed in the synagogue, a question again revealing the Christian framework since communion is distributed in church. He answered, "It is not given in the synagogue; every Jew bakes matzah at home, without salt."[48] The next day when he was asked about the water used for baking matzah, he answered that each Jew drew it from the pond or a well for his own use.[49] Lachman was also asked, "What blood do Jews use for circumcision," another question that emerged from lists of uses of blood published in anti-Jewish works. He replied that Jews used no blood in circumcision.

A Jewish widow named Fegella (Feigele) and two Christians were also interrogated. Feigele, Bieniasz's sister who ran a tavern and sold soup and vodka, was asked repeatedly about the use of Christian blood. She too denied any use or need for it: "Jews are not allowed to use blood, and they find even a bloody piece of beef repugnant."[50] As a woman, Feigele was also asked if she engaged in witchcraft. This too she denied repeatedly. The testimony of the two Christians is revealing. Joseph, a Christian who served

Jews on their holidays, lighting candles and doing small jobs, implicated Jews in the crime, interpreting a commotion following the rumors of the child's death as a plot to cover it up.[51] Bieniasz and his wife were apparently up at night, and Bieniasz spoke to other Jews. "How did he know that Jews killed Christian children," the officials asked Joseph. "I heard," he answered, "when people were saying that Jews killed children." But Joseph might have had his own reason to argue that Jews killed the boy. The other Christian brought before the interrogators, Joannes Korpiska, who worked with four other Christians in a Jewish slaughterhouse, said Joseph was the one seen near the river around the time the child disappeared.[52] Joannes described what Jews did in the slaughterhouse, including which meat they sold to Christians. But when asked which Jew killed Mathias, he said he did not know.

The Jews consistently denied the charges and the claims that Jews had any need for any blood, let alone Christian blood. Christian witnesses were more ambivalent, but except for Joseph's suggestive testimony, there was no proof that Jews had committed the crime. The full records of the trial did not survive; neither did the verdict, if one existed. But it appears that the Jews were allowed to take an oath, as required by law, and be released; perhaps for that reason no formal decree survived.[53] Bieniasz seems to have died soon after, perhaps of wounds suffered during torture, and was considered a martyr by the Jewish community.[54]

The Jews' denials may have appeared persuasive to the interrogators because they had taken special steps to prepare the prisoners for questioning and elicit the truth, among them exorcisms to prevent any "evil schemes."[55] Blessed salt, a common item used in exorcisms against demonic influence, was put in Bieniasz's mouth; on his neck were placed relics and a piece of the Eucharist, while Psalm 52 was chanted, beginning with the verse, "Why do you boast of your evil, brave fellow? God's faithfulness never ceases."[56] When Lachman was interrogated, in addition to the use of salt and relics, he was also sprinkled with holy water.[57] These steps notwithstanding, Jews persisted in denying the charges. Christian witnesses, it appears, were not subjected to similar rituals.

A few weeks later, in August 1636, another trial in which some Jews were implicated took place in Lublin.[58] Although this was not a case of murder—indeed the alleged victim testified in the trial—one of the Jews was executed, his head displayed outside the city, his body burned to ashes. In this case a Carmelite monk, Paul, was said to have badgered a Jewish surgeon, Marek, for months, asking him to remove his testicle. He confided that some two years before he had used a knife to cut off one of his testicles, lying to his superiors that he had injured himself on an iron spit. Marek tried to

"Who Should One Believe, the Rabbis or the Doctors of the Church?" 247

refer him to Christian surgeons, but likely because Paul wanted to keep his request secret, he insisted that Marek perform the surgery. Finally, Marek convinced him to go to a Lutheran surgeon, Smith, who after receiving payment agreed to do what the monk had asked. Apparently to protect his craft and not have Marek present, Smith sent Marek away to fetch a silk thread.[59] By the time Marek returned the procedure was over, and Smith placed the testicle, resembling "a pigeon's egg," on the table for Marek to dispose of in the fire pit. According to Marek's testimony not much blood was released: "only three drops fell onto his pants." A carriage was called to take Paul away. Still wanting to keep everything a secret, Paul insisted that Marek tell the driver that a dog's bite caused his injury. It is unclear how the monk returned to his monastery and what led to the arrest of Marek, Smith, and two other Jewish helpers. But charges against them were likely brought by Paul's superiors.

These charges came when the memory of the previous case was still fresh. In fact, Marek was asked if "he had been present when Jews kidnapped a Christian child recently."[60] He emphatically responded, "I was not, and it is a calumny; Jews do not need any blood." Nevertheless the court officials linked the two trials during sentencing, and this time they sentenced the Jew to death. The sentencing decree noted—in contradiction to Marek's testimony—that Marek, while "singing a song known only to him, murmuring with his fouled mouth," was collecting "copiously flowing blood into two small bronze bowls."[61] This decree, full of inflammatory language calling Marek and the Lutheran surgeon "cruel accomplices, rapacious wolves" and their "cruelty not human," was soon published in Cracow as a pamphlet. Perhaps the tribunal officials regretted not sentencing Bieniasz and Lachman earlier, or perhaps the story of Jewish and Lutheran surgeons "desanguinating" a monk resonated with them. The case also came not long after Sebastian Śleszkowski had published a screed against "Jewish doctors," warning Christians who use "Jewish, Tatar, and other infidel doctors" of the danger not just to their souls but also to their bodies.[62] Or perhaps the trial was allowed to proceed simply because the powerful Carmelite superiors were able to influence the court to punish Marek, even though the monk Paul was still alive. This unusual case entered the paper and memory trail, was included in subsequent anti-Jewish publications, and was used in court as evidence against Jews. In 1698, Stefan Żuchowski published it, along with the 1598 decree and another from 1639, in his book in support of his own case against the Jews of Sandomierz.[63]

The 1636 trials and their outcomes reverberated beyond Poland. On September 19, 1636, Jerzy Słupecki, a nobleman present in Lublin during the proceedings, wrote a pained letter to Hugo Grotius, the Dutch philosopher and legal scholar with whom he had studied as a youth.⁶⁴ The two trials raised doubts for Słupecki, who until then had considered such accusations against Jews "rather fabricated than derived from truth" and who was aware "from daily experience" that Jews "greatly abhor all blood." Słupecki saw "no sufficient reason to believe that Christian blood was useful to them." He therefore asked his "most noble and distinguished" former teacher "whether in your region too a charge of this sort has been laid against Jews, and then, whether any of those accused of the crime had ever been convicted by proof of direct evidence, and finally, whether there is anything of this matter in the books of the Talmud." Słupecki hoped that Grotius "owing to [his] exceeding erudition" would be able to "explain what I ought to think in the future on this issue." Grotius responded with what one scholar called "a shameful equivocality."⁶⁵ He praised Słupecki for "good-heartedness" by not "believing easily the accusations of those who burn against others with religious hatred."⁶⁶ Early Christians, he noted, along with "those of our age who had seceded from the pope, and before then the Waldensians" were also accused of all types of crimes, and so too "Jews, ever since they became exiles from their land and served hostile masters, undoubtedly have been vulnerable to insults." But then Grotius equivocated. Jews were not "always innocent," he wrote, "since they hold that it is lawful and pious to curse Christians, as appears in the Talmud and other books." Jews could not refrain "from deeds where they were satisfied with their strength." And "as for murdering children and collecting their blood," he referred Słupecki to "authorities" of late medieval and early modern historiography and polemical literature—Stumphius, Michael Neander, *Fortalitium fidei*—for stories about "Munich, Zurich, Bern, Wissenscho in Turigia, Uberlingen . . . Deissenhofen by Lake Constance." And if some of these might be doubtful, "with more certainty than these, Sabellicus affirms the same in Enneads 10, book 7 about the Jews of Trent; and about Tyrnavia in Hungary, Bonfinius, book 4, chapter 5 of 10."⁶⁷ Moreover, Grotius added, blood had a place in magic and superstition, including the belief that "children's blood is a remedy for leprosy." And if this belief "has brought many kings an evil reputation,"⁶⁸ Jews often practiced medicine and "could have the readier recourse the more they hate Christians," especially "if they were not deterred by the fear of punishment."⁶⁹ Grotius, sensing that his letter did not resolve Słupecki's doubts, acknowledged that all this "is manifestly either an ancient charge or myth; which is the case, in our opinion, it is not easy to say."

Although Grotius's letter did not allay Słupecki's doubts, it did reveal the power of books circulating in Europe. Even an erudite scholar like Grotius, a champion against torture, could not discount historical books that presented example after example of "what the Jews... did."[70] And even though he conceded that "among the Dutch, Jews have not been suspected of such atrocities," he suggested this was so "either because, treated more mildly, they become milder too, or they are recent immigrants who live carefully." But turning to stories found in historical chronicles, Grotius added, "Certainly, it was not for frivolous reasons that they were expelled long ago from the entire Netherlands, no less than from France, to say nothing of Spain, where I do not deny they were treated unfairly." If Hugo Grotius, who had access to more sophisticated, if still quite polemical, literature about Jews, was influenced by the stories circulated widely in early modern chronicles and annals, it is hardly surprising that Polish court officials and writers, who were not as well read and educated as many western European intellectuals, would accept these stories as proof of Jewish guilt. Słupecki's questions, however, signal that doubts nonetheless lingered and that not everyone wholeheartedly accepted the charges. Grotius' equivocating response, but not Słupecki's questioning letter, was published in 1687 in a posthumous collection of the philosopher's letters, ensuring its wider circulation.[71]

Many trials ending with Jews' deaths sooner or later became known more broadly through print, but trials in which Jews were not convicted and executed largely remained in the archives. In 1659, in another case also in Lublin, whose fragmentary records have survived, several Jews were accused of murdering a Christian child, interrogated, and tortured, but appear to have been released.[72] They denied killing the child and called the accusation "a calumny [*potwarz*]." Under torture they reiterated that "no Jew is guilty" and that Jews "did not need Christian blood." Two Christians, a male and a female, were also interrogated; both "denied that Jews needed blood."

Four years later, in July 1663, Maryna Janowa Litwinianka from Wohyń was accused of killing her son Demian and was tried in Brześć (Brest).[73] She had found her son dead, apparently drowned in the marsh. While still in the marsh cleaning the body, she was spotted by two neighbors, one of whom was Demian's godfather. Suspicious that she might have strangled the boy, the two men examined the body for signs of violence. They found none. Maryna then took the body to her house and went into town to notify officials about her son's death so she could receive permission to bury him. But when she came back home, the body was not where she had left it, and another neighbor, Jerzy Łomski, attacked her, accusing her of killing her son, and then had her arrested. When the boy's body was presented in court, it now showed signs of violence: seven wounds, "two on the belly and five on the back." Maryna protested the accusation, but was repeatedly tortured.

Łomski and others tried to convince her to blame Jews for killing Demian. The "generals and jurors" present during the torture watched, "as it is required by law, how the master first pulled her mercilessly, without any leniency, because," the court clerk noted, "he was watched by the townsmen, who made sure that he should not show her any mercy. And he tortured her tyrannically three times, and then he burnt her, asking if this was Jewish doing; and she said: 'I would rather tell on my father than on Jews.'" The townsmen speculated that, given the amount of torture Maryna was subjected to, "the Jews must have given her some drink [to ease the pain]." But one of the jurors protested that there was no window in the prison and that they were "accusing Jews unjustly [*niewinnie żydów tym pomawiaią*]." The "common people" came to the court,[74] where they too "said that we did not accuse Jews and instigate against them, and we do not want to instigate against them, because we have no proof, and we have not heard anything from anyone." In the end, the Jews were not tried. Maryna continued to refuse to confess to killing her son or to implicate the Jews. Ultimately, she succumbed to her wounds and died. In this trial, it was the common people, and some jurors sympathetic to Maryna's cause, who protested against accusing Jews of the child's death. The court report, strikingly sympathetic to Maryna, reveals the mechanisms of such libels: it shows both the spread of knowledge about stories of "Jews killing Christian children," which could be readily abused, and the limits of such knowledge, when local populations and local officials refused to play along. But this case remained unknown until it was published in 1901 in a collection of documents issued by the Vilna historical committee, while the 1659 case from Lublin seems to have remained unknown until now.

A French Interlude—The Trial of Raphaël Levy and of the Jews of Metz

That there were trials of Jews accused of murdering Christians that ended in sentences favorable to them was noted in 1670 by French scholar and theologian Richard Simon, who intervened in the defense of Jews in Metz, accused of killing a three-year-old boy named Didier the previous year. Didier's disappearance and apparent death in a forest bordering France and the duchy of Lorraine in September 1669 led to a lengthy legal battle mired in questions about borders, jurisdiction, and authority.[75]

Raphaël Levy, a Jew from Boulay, which was in the duchy of Lorraine, traveled on September 25, the eve of Rosh Hashanah, to Metz, which had

"*Who Should One Believe, the Rabbis or the Doctors of the Church?*" 251

been under French rule since the sixteenth century, to purchase wine, oil, and fish. That same day little Didier, dressed in a red bonnet, apparently disappeared after his mother, who was from Glatigny, a village under French rule, lost track of him in the forest.[76] A week later, on October 2, rumors began to spread that Jews had kidnapped the boy; the next day, the parents, subjects of the French king, denounced the disappearance to the authorities in Metz, claiming that Raphaël Levy of Boulay was responsible. Levy was summoned to Metz, and upon short questioning was released; he voluntarily returned on October 9 to prove his innocence and was released again. But on October 12 he was ordered to return, arrested, and detained. A long trial ensued, ending with Levy's public execution on January 17, 1670.

The trial of Levy laid bare the local political context that played a key role in the dynamics of anti-Jewish trials, often exacerbating the plight of the Jews. This was the case in Trent as well as in other places. Statements issued on Levy's behalf described him as a "voluntary prisoner," because, as a subject of the duke of Lorraine, he complied voluntarily with an order by French authorities to go to Metz.[77] While in Metz under French jurisdiction, Levy was characterized as "a foreign Jew" and as a result had no effective advocates.[78] Apparently feeling abandoned, by the end of the affair he blamed Metz Jews for his troubles. "You are the reason why I am in the state you see me," Raphaël is said to have told a Jewish leader from Metz who visited him in prison before his execution.[79] But according to a Yiddish account of the trial, Jews did try to save him. On Sunday, October 26, 1669, a Jewish envoy from Metz was sent to Frankfurt to seek help.[80] He returned the following Friday, carrying "the Emperor's ordinances, saying that Jews were not capable of such a crime" and that similar accusations had already been found to be "false."[81] The emperor apparently prohibited anyone to appear in court without his knowledge. The Jewish account claims that the imperial decree was translated into French and entered into evidence, but no such letter has been preserved in the Levy file in Metz.[82] Despite this apparent intervention and Raphaël Levy's persistent denials even under torture, he was sentenced to death by burning on January 16, 1670, and executed the next day.[83]

During Levy's trial several other Jews from Metz were implicated. But, unlike Raphaël Levy, they were subjects of King Louis XIV, which made for much clearer lines of intervention. Formerly a free imperial city, Metz in the middle of the sixteenth century came under the rule of France, a country from which Jews had been expelled since 1394. The acquisition of Metz, along with sections of Alsace and Lorraine, by France meant a significant and precarious change of status for the Jews living in these territories. They needed to secure their position. And they did in 1567 when King

Henri III confirmed their right of residence, placing them thus under direct royal protection.[84] But medieval expulsions were not forgotten, and some—exploiting France's medieval policies—advocated for the expulsion of Jews from these newly French territories, making the Jews' position in Metz quite unstable. Not surprisingly, the Levy affair presented another opportunity for a push to expel Jews. It was when these new efforts reached Paris that the news about the affair reached the king as well. The Metz Jews might have hoped that King Louis XIV would be sympathetic to their pleas. Not only were they under his protection but the king himself had visited their synagogue in 1657 and confirmed their earlier privileges of residence and commerce.[85]

If, given their precarious situation, the Jews of Metz seem not to have intervened on Levy's behalf in Paris—he was, after all, a "foreign Jew," not a subject of Louis XIV—they did seek help once the case metastasized to include their own members. Indeed, despite being under royal protection, in comparison with Jews elsewhere, the political position of the Jews of Metz was significantly weaker. Unlike in the Holy Roman Empire, Poland-Lithuania, or the Italian peninsula, where Jewish communities were both larger and more established, Jews in France had not been able to develop reliable channels of influence and access to the royal court. They were only allowed to live in France in the recently acquired territories of Alsace and Lorraine, and could not reside anywhere else in the country, including in the capital Paris. Sephardic Jews who did live in France, especially in port cities such as Bordeaux, did so clandestinely as Christians.[86] As a result, there were no Jewish communities or networks to lean on at times of crisis.[87]

The urgent crisis in Metz following the Levy affair intensified after publication of a 1670 anonymous pamphlet, *Abregé du procés fait aux Juifs de Mets* (A Summary of the Trial against Jews of Metz), that offered a detailed summary of the case along with several official decrees issued during the trial, and, at the end, a 1615 decree by Louis XIII affirming the expulsion decree of Jews from France.[88] *Abregé* has been attributed to the historian and political writer Abraham-Nicolas Amelot de La Houssaie, who apparently wanted to use the Raphaël Levy case to pressure political players in Paris to influence Louis XIV to expel Jews living in France. In *Abregé*, Amelot tried to locate the Metz trial in what he saw as a long history of Jewish "crimes," going as far back as the Bible. His key evidence came from books of history. Baronius, Amelot wrote, "report[ed] a numerous examples of repeated crimes" and "extraordinary cruelties exercised by Jews on Christian children."[89] The "Nuremberg chronicle," he continued, included three stories of children killed by Jews, "one in England, another in Italy in Frioli [sic], and the third in the city of Trent."[90] Indeed, the story of Simon

"Who Should One Believe, the Rabbis or the Doctors of the Church?" 253

was so well known that one could see it painted on the wall in Frankfurt. But these were not just simple crimes: "these are species of deicide, for in derision of the Passion of the Son of God, the Jews put to death these innocent victims after having exercised upon them all the cruelty and all the fury, which animated them before on the Calvary." Before turning to the Levy case, ostensibly his principal subject, Amelot briefly but explicitly signaled that this case was not unique. Indeed, "whole volumes would be needed to describe all the impieties, all the sacrileges, and all the abominations which the Jews commit every day in hatred and in contempt of the Christian religion." Thus primed, the reader was told Amelot's version of what happened in Metz, which noted conspiracies and ruses, as well as secret messages in Yiddish passed between the accused and the Jews.[91] Even the Jews' explanation that Didier might have been devoured by beasts in the forest—an otherwise plausible explanation of the child's death—was called a "Jewish stratagem" to exculpate them—a stratagem with biblical roots in the story of Joseph and his brothers, who sold him into slavery but lied to Jacob that he had been devoured by beasts.[92] Like Polish anti-Jewish writers, Amelot included texts of court decrees condemning Raphaël and his "co-conspirators." And like the Polish writers, Amelot also showed some of the economic underpinnings of the persecution of Jews, allowing him to pivot to advocate for their expulsion from France.[93] In printing the 1615 decree of Louis XIII he reminded readers that Jews had been previously expelled from the kingdom for "crimes" similar to those for which Raphaël Levy was executed. The historical memory shaped by printed chronicles of what Jews "did" and what was "done" to them resurfaced again.

Amelot's book did not go unanswered. A Piedmontese Jew, Jona Salvador, approached the still young, but rising in prominence, French scholar and theologian Richard Simon for help.[94] Simon, proficient in Hebrew and other Semitic languages, agreed to challenge the premise of Amelot's book and to defend the Jews in a short work titled *FACTUM servant de réponse au livre intitulé Abrégé du procès fait aux Juifs de Metz* (Factum Serving as a Response to a Book Titled "Abbreviated Trial against Jews in Metz"), in which he did not pull any punches. In the first paragraph he declared that the anonymous author of *Abrégé du process* acted in "bad will against the Jewish nation" by publishing his work "to render this nation odious," despite orders of the royal council, issued with the king's knowledge of the affair, that "expressly forbids" any action against the Jews of Metz.[95] But even the "proofs" the author brought in support of "the judgment rendered against Raphaël Levy" and "to prevent justice of the King through his calumnies [*médisances*]" were "so feeble" that it should not be necessary to refute them.[96] To offer these proofs, one would have to be "either malicious or ignorant," Simon wrote, as he addressed Amelot's first claim that some precepts from the Bible supported the plausibility of Jews' crimes. The "second proof" offered by the *Abregé* author came from histories, especially Baronio's ecclesiastical history, which Amelot claimed "reported numerous examples of crimes of kidnapping followed by extraordinary cruelties perpetrated on Christian children by Jews."[97] Simon then challenged Amelot's disingenuous invocation of Baronio.[98] The author of the *Abrégé* must have meant not Baronio himself but "Baronio's continuators, who in truth provide several examples of these alleged cruelties." Simon also attacked Amelot's cherry-picked examples: the author should have admitted that these books were also "filled with a great number of stories in favor of Jews." Indeed, Baronio's *Annales,* and to a lesser extent those of his continuators, contained stories of Jewish "crimes" predominantly cited in relation to the documents of protection of Jews he published.

Simon was deliberate in his use of language; although he acknowledged the presence of these anti-Jewish stories in the *Annales* by Baronio and his continuators, he called them "alleged cruelties." Simon also drew attention to the fact that these accusations emerged in a specific moment in history. Indeed, Baronio could not have provided such a "great number of examples of these imaginary cruelties," because "he finished his annals in the twelfth century," and Jews began to be accused only around the time when "Christians were preoccupied with the conquering of the Holy Land." Before the Crusades, then, Jews were "rather charged with impiety against the images than against the men, because that was the argument of the time." By contextualizing the rise of accusations against Jews, not only did Simon challenge Amelot's long view of "Jewish crimes" but he also demonstrated that most anti-Jewish stories were related to internal Christian developments. Simon thus effectively shifted the blame from Jews onto Christians.

Simon then turned to the age of the Crusades and discussed the monk Radulph, who found a place in Baronio's annals ("after Otton de Frising," as Simon noted).[99] Radulph, "a man of good appearance and more zeal than wisdom," incited the people of France and Germany to "crusade against Jews," teaching "publicly that they all should be put to death as enemies of Christian religion." As a result in many cities "innocent blood of the Jews was spilled by these seditious people"—to which Bernard of Clairvaux, whom Simon called "Saint Bernard," responded in letters to the archbishop of Mainz in which he called Radulph "a homicide and a father of lies." Other preachers too threw "great invectives against the Jewish nation, exaggerating the sin of their fathers who killed Jesus Christ" and attributing this "crime to the children." All this, Simon continued, resulted in "the monks [who] not only preached, but filled their books with these tragic stories that were soon after spread throughout the cities. They made such an impression on the people that the popes and princes needed all their authority to stop the course of the cruelties that were being waged against these unfortunates." In this remarkable section, Simon explained not only the root of violence against Jews, explicitly presenting them as innocent victims of "seditious" Christians, but also upended the epistemology of relying on chronicles for stories. He traced the roots of the stories about Jews found in chronicles to the same impulses that incited anti-Jewish violence, and key to them was the story of Jesus's crucifixion and its contemporary uses.

Simon went on to give examples of papal protection of Jews, again stressing it was the Christians who were the perpetrators of "unjust" violence. He began with three bulls, all printed in Rinaldi: one by Pope Gregory IX, issued in 1235 and "addressed to all Christians," another from 1236, *Lacrimabilem Judaeorum Franciae,* which "can be read in Rinaldi," and the third, from 1247 by Innocent IV, defending Jews against blood libels.[100] Pope Gregory IX defended Jews, Simon stressed, and "pronounced an anathema against those who continued to persecute them." In his bull to France, the pope "deplored the pitiable state of Jews" there, "afflicted unjustly by Christians, who instead [of] devoting themselves to the holy war by the means of piety and justice, invented all sorts of malice," perpetrating cruelties without remembering that "the Christians are indebted to the Jews for the foundations of their religion." Simon assured readers that "these are the words of the pope" who himself "reproached these false zealots" for abusing religion as a pretext "to plunder with more liberty the goods of these poor innocents."

The 1247 papal bull by Innocent IV "sent to bishops and archbishops of Germany and France" prohibiting accusations that Jews consumed the heart of a child on Passover allowed Simon to raise doubts about blood libels.[101] But Simon also cast doubt on host desecration accusations, discussing the 1338 letter from Pope Benedict XII to Duke Albert of Austria, which exposed frauds perpetrated by priests "in hatred of the Jewish nation." More examples followed. They were enough, Simon argued, to show how unjust were these accusations against Jews. He stressed that they all came from "the books of Christians," especially Rinaldi, who "composed his *History* in Rome, at the Vatican Library, mostly from the writing of the popes in favor of Jews." To be sure, Simon conceded, the same author included many stories "to their disadvantage," but given the objections from popes and emperors, any person would be able to see the spuriousness of these stories. Examples from secular leaders followed, including the decrees against these calumnies from "Giovanni Galeazzo Sforza, duke of Milan, Pietro Mocenigo, the doge of Venice, and the Emperors Frederic III, Charles V, and Maximilian III, who conformed in their [opinions] with the pontiffs." Also in court records one could find sentencing decrees favorable to Jews, such as the case in Verona in 1603, where "a Jew named Joseph was accused of committing a similar kidnapping to the one imputed to Raphaël Levy." Joseph's accuser, like the author of the *Abrégé*, also drew attention to examples from history books, but "the judges were very well educated in the Hebrew laws and customs that after examining the affair they recognized Joseph's innocence and [the accuser's] calumny."[102] In Simon's view there was correct and false knowledge. Each could influence the outcome of the trials against Jews—in Metz with the support of the author of the *Abrégé*, false knowledge was being used against Jews, whereas the judges of Verona had the correct wisdom and knowledge to recognize the Jews' innocence. Simon then pleaded with royal officials and the king himself to follow the example of previous rulers and popes, and extolled the value for Christians of knowing Hebrew. The French scholar, recognizing that the Jews of Metz had been charged with a calumny, then examined the specific circumstances of the Metz trial and argued that there were no convincing legal proofs to condemn them.

Richard Simon's response was not widely circulated; it was printed in a small number of copies intended only for royal officials in Paris.[103] But despite the limited circulation, the booklet appears to have had an impact beyond influencing the royal court in Paris. To be sure, the king intervened favorably on behalf of Jews, in part because he saw the Metz Parlement as defying his authority. Still more importantly, Simon succeeded in outlining a legal strategy and arguments that would be used subsequently in defense of Jews.

Sandomierz, 1698 and 1710

In January 1712, the legal strategy outlined by Richard Simon made its way to Poland as evidence in defense of several Jews subjected to a lengthy trial following the death of a boy, Jerzy Krasnowski, in Sandomierz in August 1710. These ideas did not reach Poland directly from Richard Simon's text but rather through a 1699 bilingual Latin-German book *Maximi fructus monitum,* published in Fürth in the aftermath of an affair in Sulzbach, where a Christian woman accused Jews of killing her husband and son.[104] The Fürth publication, whose Latin section was used in in the trial of Sandomierz Jews, mentioned some of the documents noted by Richard

"Who Should One Believe, the Rabbis or the Doctors of the Church?" 257

Simon and articulated similar defense arguments against blood accusations. More explicitly these arguments were invoked in a report by the theological faculty of Leipzig in 1714, after the trial in Sandomierz concluded.

The 1710 trial, which lasted more than three years, was spearheaded by a local priest, Stefan Żuchowski. This was the second such trial he instigated against Jews in Sandomierz; the first one was in 1698. The two Sandomierz trials underscore both the role individuals played in blood libels and the effectiveness of the propaganda introduced by Mojecki's 1598 book that undermined in Poland-Lithuania the trust in official documents issued by popes and kings in defense of Jews. Żuchowski played a key role in both trials, investing time, energy, and money not only in the legal proceedings against Jews but also in publishing books and court records and sponsoring works of art to commemorate the "cruelty of the Jews."[105] An avid reader, Żuchowski applied the arguments found in historical books to challenge in court the Jews' traditional defenses.

Żuchowski was quite litigious, and the two cases against Jews were not his only fights in courts—he challenged both Jews and Christians on fiscal and religious matters.[106] He was famously embroiled in a lengthy case with Sandomierz Jesuits.[107] But it was the two trials against Jews that largely defined his legacy, thanks to his books and his patronage of works of art that still survive.

During the Easter season in 1698, Margaretha, a three-year-old girl, died in Sandomierz, a royal city; her body was found weeks later in an ossuary of the Collegiate Church of Mary Virgin (now a cathedral).[108] On April 9, 1698, her mother, Catherina Mroczkowiczowa, appeared before the magistrate "in regard to the cruel murder of Margaretha, her daughter." On that same day, Catherina Mroczkowiczowa, her husband, and their domestic servant also testified that the girl "had died on white Sunday in the afternoon and we saw her die. There were no signs of cuts or injuries on the body, nor were they cause of the child's death."[109] Other witnesses added, "We know and watched the child suffer from a serious illness, and we know about the illness. We did not see any signs of injury on her body and face when the child was sick."[110] But no one said who had placed the body in the church ossuary. Because of that improper disposition of the body, Mroczkowiczowa was to be punished by standing for three market days shackled by her neck to a column in front of the city hall.[111] This punishment was meant to discourage clandestine burials. Though the surviving court records do not state this, Żuchowski's book suggests that Catherina had been denied burial of her daughter by the local priests and cemetery attendants because she could not pay for it.[112] As a priest, Żuchowski fervently denied that claim as a calumny, and to support his accusation that Jews were the culprits, turned to Sebastian Śleszkowski's virulently anti-Jewish book arguing that Jews were prohibited from burying their victims properly, which is why Margaretha was not properly laid to rest.[113]

The emphasis on Margaretha's lack of injuries and her long illness in the April 9 decree, sentencing Mroczkowiczowa to public shaming, suggests that the body found in the ossuary must have appeared mutilated. And indeed, on April 12, almost a month after the girl's death, priests of the Collegiate Church of the Virgin Mary came before the castle court with her body, alleging a violent death.[114] Mroczkowiczowa speculated that perhaps rats or cats had gnawed on her daughter's corpse. That day, the case, in which the charges had been downgraded on April 9 from potential murder to "clandestine burial," became with the change of venue to a castle court and new claims of violence once more a murder case—but this time Jews became more explicit targets.

After the clergy presented Margaretha's body in the castle court, Catherina Mroczkowiczowa was summoned again.[115] This time her testimony changed. She claimed she had brought her daughter still alive to Berek Alexander, a prominent Sandomierz Jew, on the Thursday before Easter, and retrieved her covered in wounds. The girl "now very weak" died three days later. Catherina then hid her for several days before dumping the body in the ossuary.

The change of judicial venue and character of the case were not accidental. The magistrate court had refused to treat it as anything more serious than a clandestine burial and explicitly "refused to promote the case" as murder "by Jews."[116] But those who sought to have the court target Jews found an ally in Andrzej Dunin Karwicki, the deputy *starost* (a royal official at the castle court), who together with the priests from the church escalated the case to accuse both the mother and the Jew Berek of murdering Margaretha. Even miracles of blood were reported, Żuchowski claimed, sustaining the accusers in their resolve to target Jews.[117] With time, the accusers also received support from local nobles and the bishop of Cracow.[118]

Once the case turned into one targeting Jews "for sacrilegious spilling of Christian blood,"[119] questions of jurisdiction became salient. Because Sandomierz Jews were royal subjects not bound by local jurisdiction, the case would have to be moved to a royal jurisdiction. Jews sought to use this change in venue to their advantage, while Żuchowski advocated that Jews should be subject to the same laws as Sandomierz Christians, in hopes of simplifying the process and making it less costly.[120] In the end the trial was transferred on Berek Alexander's behalf to the Crown Tribunal in Lublin. And after much uproar surrounding the case—with Jews seeking help and intervention at the highest levels and Żuchowski, together with Sandomierz

"*Who Should One Believe, the Rabbis or the Doctors of the Church?*" 259

deputies armed with the bishop's blessing and a mandate from a local royal official, relentlessly pursuing a conviction of the accused—both Catherina Mroczkowiczowa and Berek Alexander were convicted and executed on July 21, 1698.

With the exception of a few fragments preserved in Sandomierz, court records of the trial have not survived.[121] What did survive is Stefan Żuchowski's rhymed narrative, published together with the final decree sentencing Mroczkowiczowa and Berek Alexander to death and his short prose explanation of the case.[122] Despite its anti-Jewish slant, Żuchowski's account captures the legal and political complexity of the trial, which was not a slam-dunk against Jews. Jews had defenders and were able to access powerful individuals, including King August II; the charges against them were not universally accepted.[123] In Lublin, they produced in defense of Berek twenty witnesses, including "students," a group generally known for their attacks on Jews. Berek never confessed to the crime, even under the most extreme torture, whereas Mroczkowiczowa kept changing her story, creating significant legal problems in a judicial system relying on confessions.[124] Żuchowski's narrative perhaps exaggerates the drama and difficulties he faced in order to score narrative points for achieving his ultimate goal of convicting Mroczkowiczowa and Berek. He even presented the trial as a divine test.[125] Still, one cannot easily dismiss the difficulties Żuchowski and his allies encountered. Despite the bishop's blessing, not even all the clergy lined up in support of Żuchowski's efforts, and at one point Berek was dismissed from Lublin only to be rearrested.[126] Berek's steadfast denials and arguments challenging the very premise of the charge that Jews killed Christian children made it difficult for the court to convict him, forcing the accusers to resort to religious rhetoric that cast the judges as defenders of God and divine order. "Heaven asks," Żuchowski wrote, "not for revenge but faith, so the [judges] may present an offering of sacred justice, so that our benevolent Christ may not lose his case with Israel for the second time."[127] The judges should "not fail their conscience" and should "promote God's glory."[128] Indeed, they should not be concerned with costs and money, because "it is not about thousands, or gains, but about blood and God's mandates trumped in it"[129]; they should avoid God's wrath for not bringing justice by acting as "defenders of faith and justice."[130] Żuchowski and his allies wanted to remind the Sandomierz deputies not to forget the city's glory and its heroic defense against Tatars and to proceed with similar courage in this case.[131]

As Żuchowski's fears deepened that the prisoners might be let go, one Reverend Kaluski, the preacher to the Tribunal, addressed the deputies, urging them to do "no favors to the Jew" and not to be tempted by "sacks of money" Jews want to pay for "innocent blood." The language evoked the image of Judas and Christ, heightening the court drama.[132] And while some deputies bought into the preacher's message, others pushed back. The testimony of the witnesses, Berek's steadfast denials, and the arguments marshaled in his defense—that Jews did not need to kill Christian children, that such accusations were "a lie" and "a fable," and that the Bible prohibited Jews from consuming any blood—were hard to overcome.[133] The accusers sought to undermine the defense by stating that Jews did not adhere to the Bible but rather to the Talmud.[134] To explain Berek's steadfastness, Żuchowski expounded the idea of Jewish martyrdom: Jews felt it was better to die and suffer tortures than to confess to this crime.[135] This was of course true. Jews did indeed glorify martyrdom in such cases, but in Żuchowski's hand this refusal to confess was evidence of Jews' obstruction of justice, not, as Jewish law and lore suggested, of their innocence. Still, the costs of the trial and its direction made some of the actors, especially the clergy, want to give up.

The turning point, at least in Żuchowski's narrative, came when he and his supporters brought before the court historical examples from chronicles. Such stories about Jews killing Christian children were not new, they argued. There were numerous difficult-to-deny "examples of our blood spilled" found in "foreign and our chronicles."[136] Tyrnau, Prague, Paris, Vienna, Trent, Ancona, and Saona were listed among examples that had trickled down from foreign chronicles into Polish anti-Jewish books. Of Polish examples, Żuchowski reminded the deputies of the case from 1598, tried at the Lublin Crown Tribunal no less, and others whose decrees he printed at the end of his book. Żuchowski explicitly presented chronicles and legal precedents as evidence of Berek's guilt. Though, formally, as Waldemar Kowalski has argued, "literature and precedent had no evidential weight," their use seems to have influenced the trial.[137] Soon Mroczkowiczowa and Berek were sent to torture, and witnesses testifying in Berek's defense were impugned and ignored. "God ruled the hearts in this sacred case," Żuchowski wrote, and the trial turned Żuchowski's way.[138] In his book, he gleefully recounted the excessive torture Berek was subjected to and the exorcisms applied to him. At that point Jews once more sought to reach the king and their other defenders.[139] But the deputy with the king's letter arrived too late, and Żuchowski and his supporters prevailed.[140] For Żuchowski it was not just a personal victory but also a triumph of divine justice, a divine test the judges were able to pass.[141]

Żuchowski knew that doubts lingered about the trial—even the king expressed outrage. And so the priest ended his book with a rhyme in which he not only claimed a leading role in the trial but also challenged those who disbelieved his story: "I led the trial, and described the truth/for which I may not be liked/If you don't believe me and don't have faith/you read [this] through Jewish glasses/[and] the blind should not (they say) judge colors."[142]

That Żuchowski was a key player in the trial is evidenced not only by his own narrative but also by the court decree sentencing Mroczkowiczowa and Berek to death.[143] But the involvement of clergy in criminal trials was questionable from the perspective of canon law, and a special dispensation and a reason for that intervention were required. Żuchowski did receive such permission from the bishop of Cracow, who justified it by reference to injuries to "orthodox faith, crime of *laesae* of divine honor," and, by the fact that the body was deposited in a church ossuary without authorization in "the violation of sacred space."[144] Żuchowski accepted the dispensation with enthusiasm and a sense of vindication, but the issue of the clergy's role in criminal trials would not go away, returning the next time Żuchowski became embroiled in another trial against Jews in 1710.

One year after Berek and Mroczkowiczowa were executed, Żuchowski traveled to Rome. On his way, he stopped in Trent where he saw both Simon's relics and the rich iconographic legacy of the Trent trial. That is where he might have acquired for his library Giovanni da Padova's *Martirio crudele dato da gli ebrei a S. Simone innocente da Trento,* published in Trent in 1690.[145] He may have also brought broadsides that disseminated imagery of Simon's story (Fig. 6.1). The visit in Trent certainly left a deep impression on Żuchowski, and he immediately connected the stories of Sandomierz and Trent.[146] On his return, inspired by what he saw in Trent and read in chronicles and other books, Żuchowski wanted to sponsor a series of paintings commemorating Simon and other children he believed had been victims of Jews.[147] The planned series of paintings was never executed, but a smaller series commemorating Simon's story, heavily influenced by existing iconography including the broadsides, was placed in the Church of St. Paul in Sandomierz. And after the second trial in 1710–1713, a larger painting, titled *Infanticidia,* was commissioned for the Collegiate Church.[148]

The second trial of Sandomierz Jews is unusually well documented. But like the trial in Trent, the preserved records come predominantly from its instigator, Stefan Żuchowski, in the form of his apologetic narrative and the documents he chose to preserve. As such, they provide insight into Żuchowski's thinking and intentions, but hide under many layers other aspects of the trial.[149]

At dawn on August 18, 1710, the body of a boy, Jerzy Krasnowski, was found on the porch of Rabbi Jakub Herc's house, located next to the synagogue. Jakub Herc, born around 1660 in Moravia, came to Poland in the

FIG. 6.1 S. Simonino da Trento, a broadside by Giovanni Parone (1643–1730) at Biblioteca Communale di Trento, TI 1 f 294, http://www.stabat.it/?q=scheda/283.

"Who Should One Believe, the Rabbis or the Doctors of the Church?" 263

1690s to assume the post of rabbi in Pacanów, a small town just over fifty miles southwest of Sandomierz. There, Herc married and started a family, first had a daughter and, then in 1697, a son Abraham.[150] With his family, Herc moved to Sandomierz to assume his post as rabbi in 1700, just two years after the 1698 trial, which had not yet faded from local memory. In 1710, soon after the body was found on that fateful August morning, the rabbi, his thirteen-year-old son Abraham, and his seventeen-year-old son-in-law Jakub Schario fled the town. They were apprehended the same day in the village of Gorzyczany, a few miles away, and brought back to town.

Perhaps encouraged by his success in 1698, Żuchowski immediately became involved in the affair. He visited the body, sent it to the magistrate, and "ordered the painter (Karol de Prevo from Lubnic who was working on grand paintings in our Collegiate Church) to paint a true image of the body, with all the scars, which later was a clear record of Jewish cruelty."[151] The body was examined, and the rabbi's residence. Multiple wounds were found on the body, as were, apparently, drops of blood in the rabbi's house. For Żuchowski, the 1698 case became both a precedent to be used as evidence of Jewish guilt and a guide to follow. When the town officials seemed reluctant to try the Jews, Żuchowski was successful in having the case transferred to the Crown Tribunal in Lublin. He again secured support from the bishop of Cracow for his involvement in the criminal trial and made sure the boy's body was quickly dispatched to Lublin.[152]

In Lublin, things did not go smoothly for Żuchowski at the beginning. There, as in Sandomierz, Żuchowski and the Sandomierz officials with whom he teamed up initially encountered resistance to their cause, though admittedly, they also garnered local supporters. The Sandomierz priest presented the boy's body to the court and claimed, as he did in 1698, a miracle of blood; he then transferred the body to a local church.[153] Soon, nine Sandomierz Jews were ordered arrested and sent to Lublin.

At first the Jews were interrogated without torture. Then, on September 1, Żuchowski along with other clergy and Sandomierz citizens filed formal charges against them, in a choreographed ceremony designed to have the most impact.[154] The arrested Jews were brought before the court and forced to face not only Żuchowski but also "a painting of three children killed in Sandomierz," a way to remind the court through visual means that the case before them was not the first "Jewish cruelty" committed in that town. The charges were framed in inflammatory language presenting Jews as "viperous" people, "insatiably" desiring Christian blood, just as did their ancestors crying "his blood upon us and our children," and in line with previous cases Żuchowski considered indubitable evidence of guilt—the 1598 case, his own triumph of 1698, and others.[155] He demanded the expulsion of Jews from Sandomierz, confiscation of their property, invalidation of debts owed to them, repossession of the synagogue, which he justified with the precedents of confiscation of Lutheran and Calvinist churches, and its conversion into a chapel "commemorating the detestable crimes" with paintings "of the killed children."[156] Ultimately, he advocated for the total expulsion of Jews from "the Polish Kingdom and the Grand Duchy of Lithuania."[157] Some of these measures resembled those that had been implemented in Trent.

Yet the Jews had their defenders—Christians who for three hours read the testimonies taken in Sandomierz and presented familiar defense arguments on behalf of Jews, chief among them that Jews could not consume any blood.[158] The next day, after the Jews' defenders spoke, Żuchowski demanded time for himself. He "threw" examples "both foreign and domestic of Jewish murders of children," including eight, so he claimed, recognized as "holy martyrs" by the Church, like "Simon of Trent, whose uncorrupted body I have myself seen."[159] He reminded the Crown Tribunal of the five cases it had tried in the past, whose decrees Żuchowski had included in his first book. Just from these decrees one could see, Żuchowski argued, "the unmistaken truth that Jews need Christian blood and for that reason they commit these cruel crimes." And invoking Augustine's meditation on the cross, Żuchowski urged the deputies to use their authority and out of their religious zeal to "rein in the unheard-of audacity of repeated crimes by the hardened Jewish spite." Żuchowski's historical approach once again proved fruitful. On September 3, 1710, the nine Jews imprisoned in Lublin were sent to be interrogated under torture. There were four main areas of questioning.[160] The first spoke to Żuchowski's claims: "What do you Jews, and you [personally], use Christian blood for, why, on which holidays you do it, what is evicomen [afikomen], do you draw lots, which one of you should obtain [the blood], do you use it in matzah or wine?" The remaining three questions were specific to the Sandomierz accusation.

To Żuchowski's dismay, one of the Jews' defenders, a deputy from Mazovia, demanded to be present at the interrogations. Moreover, the Lublin officials initially refused to follow the tribunal's order to subject Jews to torture.[161] Complicating matters further was the fact that when the interrogations began, the executioner, charged with applying torture, died suddenly on the first day, his death witnessed by the deputy from Mazovia. Two of the imprisoned Jews, the rabbi's son-in-law and one named Szmer, died that day as well, stirring fears of plague. Others were saved "half-alive." All this disrupted the proceedings, with interrogations resuming only on September 23.[162] Except for the rabbi's son Abraham, whose testimony was ambivalent and potentially inculpating, all remaining Jews denied the charges and offered largely consistent testimonies.

While the Sandomierz Jews remained in prison, Polish Jewish leaders were reaching out to supporters and succeeded in opening another area of inquiry led by the palatine, a royal regional governor.[163] At times, individual Jews found supporters in lords with whom they did business; for example, Lord Tymiński asked for the release of Liczman, one of the imprisoned Jews.[164] With the Jews insisting on their innocence, the case against them was not as clear-cut as the accusers would have wished, so they began to focus on Abraham's inculpating testimony and, later on, his expressed desire to convert to Catholicism. Meanwhile, as in 1698, Żuchowski, along with some clergy in Lublin, began a public relations campaign to gain support for their cause among the deputies to the tribunal and across the country. His extensive political contacts were also likely consequential for advancing his agenda of not only executing the imprisoned Jews but also expelling all the Jews from Sandomierz.[165] With Bishop Kazimierz Łubieński of Cracow fully on his side, Żuchowski sought support from the papal nuncio (as did the Jews), though the nuncio himself did not report much in this regard to the secretary of state in Rome.[166] In 1711, the synod of the Cracow diocese bestowed on Żuchowski the title "Commissary for Jewish Affairs," a new office created just for him.[167] In April 1712, the meddlesome priest finally succeeded in securing a decree from King August II ordering the Jews' expulsion.[168] The decree, however, was never executed.

In light of the fear of plague in Lublin, the proceedings were suspended in the fall of 1710, and the case was transferred back to Sandomierz, where it languished for years, because royal officials were unwilling to take it on—a conflict over jurisdiction now stalling the case.[169] Imprisonment, torture, and the travel resulted in the deaths of some of the imprisoned Jews; only three remained alive to the end of the affair in November 1713 when they, too, were executed. Although Jews' defenders fought for their freedom until the end, Żuchowski's relentless pursuit of victory, his inventive tactics that amplified earlier anti-Jewish stories and trials through the use of paintings and printed books in court, his impugning of witnesses who testified in defense of the Jews, and his undermining defense arguments while exploiting damaging testimonies of Jewish converts, among them the rabbi's son Abraham, resulted in his admittedly uneasy win.[170]

Satisfying as the outcome of the trial might have been to Żuchowski, who was indeed quite proud of his actions, he clearly knew well, as he had back in 1698, that doubts about Jews' guilt remained—after all, they had never confessed to the crime. He also must have sensed that his political stature was hurt as a result of his actions. After the trial ended, he decided to publish an apologetic work justifying his efforts and offering, as Waldemar Kowalski has argued, a manual for prosecuting Jews for killing Christian children.[171] Żuchowski stated in his book that he was not "so cruel as to desire Jewish blood, but I cannot be as godless as to sell out human blood ... as a priest of character I must vindicate" the crime; and he offered forty reasons why the Jews were guilty, including similar cases he knew from books, the state of the body, alleged perjury, and, importantly, previous accusations.[172]

The publishers of Żuchowski's book would have concurred with Kowalski's assessment. They hoped, as they noted as the end of the book, that Żuchowski's opus would be useful to those who might need it in future trials. They promised that readers would find "effective information how to proceed in similar cases," along with a detailed account of the trial, including "documents of clear and reliable truth."[173] Indeed, the book was not intended to be a popular read—Żuchowski, for example, assumed readers' knowledge of Latin, a skill limited to some clergy and educated officials. And though the book offers indeed a detailed account of the trial, it does not necessarily present "clear and reliable truth." Rather, it is Żuchowski's apologetic version of the events, justifying his actions and the final verdict. Although he and his supporters felt a sense of pride and triumph, the legacy of the trial became a difficult-to-remove stain on the history of Jewish-Christian relations in Poland.

Żuchowski's victory rested on his earlier success in 1698 and on his use of previously published books and court trials. His tactics in the trial were innovative and, when presented later in a book format, in the long run proved dangerous for Jews. He methodically built up his argument, first presenting the selective teachings of "Church fathers" about Jews, along with canon law before turning briefly to historical "evidence" of a wide variety of Jewish crimes based on authoritative sources.[174] Then he discussed specific Polish examples and legal restrictions in various locales on Jews' residence and economic activities, before finally turning to the Sandomierz case and his "evidence" against Jews, including a more detailed list of "foreign" and "domestic" examples of "such Jewish murders."[175] Żuchowski thereby established the long history of Christian views in literature and law about Jews across Christendom. Strikingly, whereas elsewhere accusations centered on *odium*—Jews' alleged enmity or hatred of Christ and Christians—in Poland the centerpieces of accusations were blood and "Jews' cruelty."

Żuchowski painstakingly outlined this argumentative framework.[176] While Miczyński and Śleszkowski had already raised doubts about the existence of papal protections of Jews against such anti-Jewish accusations

"*Who Should One Believe, the Rabbis or the Doctors of the Church?*" 267

and about Jews' innocence, demonstrated in their persistent denials even under the most egregious torture, Żuchowski perfected these methods. He articulated the epistemological foundations of blood libels, simultaneously both undermining the very plausibility of Jewish defenses and underscoring the logic of accusations against them.

In Sandomierz, as in previous trials, Jews entered into evidence a copy of papal condemnations of blood accusations. They filed a Polish translation of the May 12, 1540, bull by Pope Paul III addressed to the bishops and archbishops of Poland and Hungary.[177] Issued in the aftermath of the 1536 blood libel in Tyrnau (Trnava), the bull reiterated previous papal condemnations of the blood accusations, specifically referring to Pope Martin IV's 1420 bull, and implored clergy and secular rulers to prevent such unjust persecution. The translation of the bull presented in Sandomierz was based on copies registered earlier in Polish court records, revealing the paper trail of the transmission and preservation of privileges and significant legal documents. According to its preamble, the copy brought in defense of Jews in Sandomierz was taken from the records of the castle court in Chełm, just over forty miles away from Lublin and nearly 100 miles from Sandomierz, where it was registered in January 1701 by Isaac Fortis, a physician of Italian origin and a powerful representative of the Council of Four Lands known as Isaac *hazak rofe'* (strong doctor, a play on the name Fortis).[178] That copy was based on an extract from the city of Brest, where it had been registered in the castle court records sixty years earlier, in March 1641 by an official from the Brest Jewish community, Zelman Szmuyłowicz. The Brest record, in turn, was based on an "authentic" parchment copy issued in Rome, which was supposedly inscribed in the castle court records in Cracow, then the seat of royal power, on September 7, 1540.[179] The Sandomierz Jews also obtained two copies of imperial protections issued by Charles V in Worms in 1544 and submitted certified copies of the privilege issued in September 1710 by an imperial official in Vienna, where it evidently had been confirmed by Emperor Joseph I in 1707; the German copy was translated into Polish and registered in Sandomierz in November that year.[180] Along with these papal and imperial letters, Jews' defenders also submitted a volume of the Talmud, apparently printed in Venice and expurgated, and the 1699 Fürth publication *Maximi fructus monitum,* which provided compelling arguments against blood accusations.

Maximi fructus discussed in detail biblical prohibitions on the use of blood and underscored the fact that Jews zealously observed the law, invoking the example of Eleazar in the second book of Maccabees, who died a martyr's death rather than consume pork.[181] The anonymous work then discussed not only the medieval papal bulls but also the fact that the 1572 bull of Pius V expelling Jews from the Papal States, so frequently used in Catholic anti-Jewish literature, did not mention ritual murder or blood accusations, even though it mentioned other Jewish "crimes."[182] Crucially, the author noted that charges that Jews killed Christians were a European phenomenon. Jews lived in "in many regions of Asia and Africa, mixed with Christians, but we never hear of such crimes from mouths outside of Europe. . . . Lamentably only in Europe did this lie arise" most strongly in Germany, Italy, and Poland.

Żuchowski rejected *Maximi fructus* by ridiculing it as "similar to this project once published in Germany [that argued] that *mulier non est homo* [a woman is not a man]."[183] And any defense from the Talmud was also dismissed—after all, Żuchowski emphasized, that work was condemned and burned. To discredit an official papal bull and imperial defenses of Jews was potentially treacherous, especially for a clergyman. But the long paper trail of the bull presented in Sandomierz, in and of itself meant to assure the courts of the authenticity of the documents, left an opening for Żuchowski to attack it. He dismissed the imperial document on the grounds that it was copied in Vienna, arguing that Jews were expelled from Vienna in 1670 "for killing a Christian child" (a historically inaccurate assertion) by Emperor Leopold I, making it implausible that Emperor Joseph I, his son, would have confirmed such a privilege.[184] More troubling for Żuchowski was the 1540 bull by Pope Paul III. But here too the long preamble outlining the bull's legal trail in Poland provided fodder for Żuchowski's attack. The bull the Jews presented, he wrote, was taken from a Polish version inscribed by Fortis in official records, with a claim that the original was registered in Cracow in Latin. But no trace of it could be found in Cracow's records; thus, he added with irony, "I don't know perhaps it was issued in Ruthenian or Polish from Rome." Using Śleszkowski's argument, Żuchowski noted that the bull was not mentioned in what he called *Bullaria Quratanti,* an abridgment of canon law by Stefano Quaranta, *Summa bullarii,* nor in the *Epitome canonum* by Cardinal Laurentio Brancato de Lauraea, first published in 1649 and republished numerous times.[185] But more implausibly, Żuchowski continued, by the time Paul III became pope, "four children martyred by Jews were included among the Holy Martyrs of the Church."[186] He only named two: "Richard of Paris in 1188" and "most importantly, Simon of Trent in 1475, killed under Sixtus IV, and in the memory of Paul III himself." According to Żuchowski, issuing such a bull would have been tantamount to "revoking canonization of the holy children." Although Żuchowski's argument was ahistorical—Simon's cult was not recognized until 1588, decades after Paul III's pontificate, and none of the children had ever been "canonized"—he captured the epistemological dilemma Christians faced in the aftermath of blood accusations. "If Jews do not martyr children," he wrote, "then those accepted as such by the Church cannot be called Martyrs, because neither Lord God can perform miracles to confirm a fallacy, nor can the Popes in any way, basing their [opinion] on these miracles, include among the Saints those who are not holy, and among the Martyrs those who were not martyred." Indeed, at the crux of accepting the belief in blood accusation and rejecting the possibility of papal defenses of the Jews was the fact that by 1588 the popes did indeed recognize at least one such child, Simon of Trent; and, moreover, authoritative Catholic sources, among them the *Annales ecclesiastici* begun by Baronio and the Bollandist *Acta Sanctorum,* included as true stories of other "child martyrs." He challenged readers to think about the absurdity that popes, bishops, and papal nuncios would have protected criminal deeds. Elsewhere, in the same spirit, Żuchowski asked, "Who should one believe, the rabbis or the Doctors [of the Church]?" before answering, "I believe the masters of truth, the Holy Doctors."[187] Żuchowski's attack on documents issued in defense of Jews did not just raise doubts about their validity—as did those of earlier writers—it raised doubts about their very existence, by framing the questions as: "Whose side are you on?" and "who do you believe? The Holy Fathers, the authoritative Christian sources, or the Jews?" This line of attack provided powerful new tools for Jews' accusers.

Żuchowski went on to upend the claims of authenticity of the 1540 bull issued in defense of Jews by arguing that soon afterward—in 1555, 1572, 1592, and 1623—the popes dealt with Jews harshly.[188] He also challenged Jews to furnish an authentic parchment copy of the bull complete with papal seals. Privately, Żuchowski had earlier reached out to Rome to find a copy of the bull. His contact there was unable to find it, likely because he did not have access to the secret archive of the apostolic secretary, where a record of Paul III's letter was in the collection "Minutae brevium."[189] For Jews, given this line of attack, securing an explicit statement from the pope confirming or reissuing the 1540 bull became increasingly urgent.

The fallout from the Sandomierz trials was not clear right away. Żuchowski's book, published posthumously, was certainly known and used in the decades that followed.[190] But one thing is certain: Żuchowski's actions and the materials that emerged in the trial raised questions about anti-Jewish blood accusations and prompted King August II to order in 1714 the theology faculty of the University of Leipzig to prepare a report responding to the question whether "the Jewish people, according to the laws of their religion, or the superstitious beliefs introduced to them" needed Christian blood and whether to get it they killed Christian children.[191]

The report, prepared by Gottfried Ollearius and issued in May 1714, provided one of the most comprehensive denial of anti-Jewish accusations based on a plethora of legal documents and works by Catholics, Protestants, and Jews. It began by historicizing the accusation, pointing out it had been unknown for the first thirteen centuries after Christ.[192] Why, Ollearius asked, would the Jews have refrained from committing this crime all that time and begun doing so only at that moment? How would the Christians of the past not know about it? The report linked the increase in hatred against the Jews to the Crusade era, especially the preaching of the monk Radulph. But the violence Radulph was preaching against Jews was condemned, the report continued, by Bernard of Clairvaux in his letters to the archbishop of Mainz. Still, sermons against Jews continued, and "monkish" fables of Jews using Christian blood were invented, which made their way into books.[193] After describing the 1235 bull by Gregory IX protecting Jews against Christian attacks,[194] the report turned to documents related to the accusation that Jews killed Christian children: the 1247 bull by Innocent IV written to the bishops and archbishops of Germany; the decrees by Emperor Frederick III, Bona and Giovanni Galeazzo Sforza of Milan; the doge of Venice Pietro Mocenigo—all found in the writings of Richard Simon, Isaac Cardoso, and Isaac Viva, and all referenced in the report itself.[195] No one had ever proved this accusation definitely; quite the opposite, the Leipzig report said, explaining that even Johannes Pfefferkorn, who allowed that perhaps there were some Jews who killed Christian children "out of anger, hatred or revenge," denied that Jews needed Christian blood. Johann Christoph Wagenseil, too, the report continued, testified in his "Refutation" that he never met a single Jewish convert—and he dealt with quite a few and asked them all—who confirmed that Jews used Christian blood. The report even cited *Shevet Yehudah* in which Thomas, a learned Christian man, refuted blood accusations in a discussion with King Alfonso of Spain.[196] Perhaps surprisingly, after the discussion of *Shevet Yehudah*, the report turned to Johann Andreas Eisenmenger's *Endecktes Judenthum*. Eisenmenger's notorious anti-Jewish book, which appeared just a few years earlier, was at best ambivalent on the issue of blood accusations. Drawing on chronicles and other historical accounts, Eisenmenger, as R. Po-Chia Hsia has shown, "affirmed the historical veracity of blood libel."[197] He listed a number of cases, from the fifth to the seventeenth century, among them Simon of Trent, the 1598 case from Poland, and the 1669 trial of Raphaël Levy in Metz.[198] Yet the Leipzig report cited Eisenmenger not for these examples, but rather to support the report's refutation. Eisenmenger, the report stated, offered "a few more" reasons why Jews did not use blood.[199] And indeed, in *Endecktes Judenthum* on the pages immediately following the list of "the historical examples," Eisenmenger discussed *Shevet Yehudah* and Abravanel's commentary on Ezekiel—the exact sources used in the Leipzig report to defend Jews, demonstrating that the Leipzig report was directly engaging with Eisenmenger's spurious book.[200] True, the church *Annales* contained many examples of Jews killing Christians, the report stated in reference to *Annales ecclesiastici* begun by Baronio and continued by others, as did *Fortalitium fidei* and Gilbert Genebrand's *Chronography,* but "the circumstances of most of these histories are so much against each other," outlined "with such differences by different authors" that they almost invalidate themselves, as Wagenseil himself noted in his discussion of Simon of Trent.[201] The Leipzig scholars then dismissed the accusations as stuff of the times of "ignorance and easy believability," perpetuating the myth that blood accusations could be blamed on the ignorant and poorly educated, rather than, as historical sources actually suggest, the literate elites of early modern Europe. Like Pfefferkorn, the theologians did not exclude the possibility of some Jews killing Christians, but they vehemently denied the idea that Jews needed Christian blood—a key charge in Polish cases. Listing nine purported uses of blood, among them those included in the Sandomierz trial—that Jews needed Christian blood to cure their smell or as a cure for bleeding following circumcision or as love potions—the authors of the Leipzig report demolished them one by one as incoherent and absurd.[202] At the end the report examined Jewish religious practices and cited Jacques Basnage's critique of histories claiming Jews killed Christian children—they were all steeped in cruelty and injustice, without thorough process and investigation.[203] In fact, the accusations were often a pretext for unjust violence, the report said citing anti-Jewish riots from Prague in 1305 related in Bzovius. But even if, it concluded, some Jews committed crimes, the whole people should not be persecuted.

The report remained private, without traceable echoes in Poland or beyond, at least until 1751 when it was published by Christian Friedrich Börner as part of the selected works of the Leipzig theology faculty.[204] The papal nuncio at the royal court did not mention it, even as he kept, throughout 1714, the secretary of state in Rome apprised about the conflict between Żuchowski and the Sandomierz Jesuits.[205] Still, anti-Jewish accusations eased in the Polish-Lithuanian Commonwealth for more than two decades after the second Sandomierz trial. Perhaps the backlash against Żuchowski was stronger than expected, and some in the Polish-Lithuanian Commonwealth saw the trials as a miscarriage of justice. Or perhaps the dire political and military situation during the Great Northern War, the civil war that ended with so-called Silent Sejm of 1717, and the contested royal election of 1733 with the subsequent war may have contributed to the hiatus.

Poznań, 1736–1740

This break in anti-Jewish accusations ended in 1736, when Jews in Poznań were accused of murdering a Christian child, with the ensuing trial lasting for several years. On the evening of April 13, 1736, a two-year-old boy, Maciej Kazimierz, disappeared. His father Wojciech (Albertus in the Latin records) Jabłonowicz tried to find him, to no avail. On April 27, the boy's mutilated body was found in a field in Górczyn, a village a few miles away from Poznań.[206] Although no Jews were mentioned in the initial court filings, the language and description of the wounds left the door open for accusations against them. After a lengthy description of the mutilation, the autopsy noted that the intestines were "healthy" and "the excrement" still inside the child's body. And although the child had disappeared two weeks prior "he had milk inside and no blood."[207] The surgeons concluded the boy was "murdered and martyred."[208] In June a Christian woman, Helena Sowińska, and her ten-year-old daughter Rosa were arrested. Although they denied the charges, they apparently implicated another woman, Agnieszka Kubarka, who worked as a caretaker at a Jewish cemetery. By September, major figures of the Jewish community in Poznań were arrested "not only on the presumption and suspicion" but also because of "probable signs of infanticide"; more specifically, they were blamed for "martyring" the boy.[209]

Perhaps aware of the fatal outcomes of such trials in Crown Tribunals, most recently in Sandomierz, the Jews of Poznań sought to invoke a 1633 law—passed after the 1630 trial of a Jew in Przemyśl accused of desecrating a consecrated communion wafer—that reaffirmed the legal parameters of the magistrate and palatine jurisdiction, both in general and, more specifically, in criminal cases involving Jews, confirming exclusive palatine jurisdiction over such cases.[210] (In Sandomierz, the palatine sided with the Jews. Perhaps had this law been invoked and the case not transferred to Lublin, the fate of the Sandomierz Jews would have been different.) In response to the accusation, Poznań Jews also mobilized networks of support, reaching Dresden, where King August III resided with his court and other dignitaries, among them the papal nuncio and the bishop of Poznań. The Jews even reached Church authorities in Rome through the Jewish community there.

Żuchowski's explicit rejection of papal and imperial defenses and the permission he as a member of the clergy was granted by Church authorities to be involved in the trial must have alarmed Jews. Perhaps this is one of the reasons why during the Poznań affair and in the following decades Polish Jews made increasingly visible overtures to Rome for help. To be sure Polish Jews had appealed to Rome before: in 1654 Naftali of Gniezno, aided by the Roman Jewish community, pleaded with Church authorities in Rome,

"Who Should One Believe, the Rabbis or the Doctors of the Church?" 273

and in 1664, Jews succeeded in obtaining a letter from the general of the Dominicans addressed to Dominicans in Poland urging them to stem "calumnies" against Jews.[211] In 1684, it seems Polish Jews were close to receiving a broader condemnation. In November of that year, the Holy Office of the Inquisition sent a notice to the papal nuncio in Poland "for his attention and no one else's'" asking him to urge the bishops of Poland "to publish a ban" warning the faithful "not to listen" to such rumors and trials and not to "impute such excesses" to Jews.[212] The Holy Office explained that blood accusations against Jews were false, citing the biblical prohibition against consuming any blood (Lev. 3:17 and 17:10), as well as chapter three of a section from Moses Maimonides's *Mishneh Torah* on prohibited foods, *ma'akhalot assurot*.[213] Such a ban was never issued in Poland, and over the decades there is little evidence in the correspondence between the papal nuncios in Poland and the secretary of state in Rome about any blood accusations against Jews until their detailed exchange during the Poznań affair.[214]

That exchange began in November 1736, when the papal nuncio included short notices about the case in reports of events in Poland. Amidst news about episcopal and cathedral positions, the nuncio reported several criminal cases, including the executions of a mother accused of infanticide in Poznań and of a nobleman for fratricide in Piotrków. Regarding the Jews of Poznań, he wrote about a decree from the castle court stopping the trial for eight days following the death of the "deputy rabbi of Jews here, in prison accused of murdering an infant"; the deputy rabbi's body was to be returned to Jews in Poznań, but the other Jews, the decree ordered, were to remain in prison.[215] A few days later, the ciphered dispatch noted that the trial had not yet been resumed.[216] It was not until December 14 that the nuncio informed Rome about the resumption of the trial, noting briefly that two officials were sent "to examine other Jews who are in prison and to confront the accusation that have been brought against them."[217] But no significant report about the trial found its way into the nuncio's dispatches until January 21, 1737.[218] That day, the papal nuncio apprised Rome that he had been "notified about the case, which causes agitation among the Jews of Poznan and is pending in the castle court in that city." "From the first days," he wrote, that the Jews in Poznań were accused of the crime, "envoys of that community came here to appeal to His Majesty the King." They also appealed to the nuncio himself "so that I may speak in their favor not only to the Lord Deputy Chancellor of the Crown, but also Monsignor Bishop of Poznań, who is here at the time." The nuncio approached the issue with caution, "so that the affair may be examined with necessary maturity and so that the true perpetrators of this shameful murder may be found." To be sure, the nuncio did not want Jews to be harmed, but he did not exclude the possibility that the crime "may have been committed by one or a few Jews." But still, he argued, even though the accused Jews may be members of that Jewish community, the whole community "should not be punished for the crime of the few." More certain proof of the crime needed to be obtained. Though tepid in his response to Rome, the nuncio insisted on a fair process. He intervened with the bishop of Poznań, who was visiting Dresden at the time, and the deputy chancellor of the court, both of whom requested copies of the trial documents. The nuncio also insisted that Jews have more time to prepare their defense.

This detailed letter was written in response to a dispatch from Rome, dated December 29, 1736, in which the secretary of state informed the papal representative in Dresden that the Roman Jewish community had appealed to the "Holy Father" on behalf of Jews in Poznań, who had been accused of "an alleged killing of a Christian boy."[219] The secretary instructed the nuncio to offer assistance to the Jews, if they were indeed innocently accused, but if it turned out they did in fact commit the murder, they should "merit the most severe punishment." Thus, "given this uncertainty," the pope left the decision whether to act in favor of the Jews "to the wisdom" of the nuncio.

As the trial in Poznań dragged on, the nuncio blamed the lengthy deliberations on the Jews' procedural maneuvers.[220] Numerous motions and countermotions were filed, and the king was frequently asked to weigh in.[221] Testimonies were contradictory. The women who implicated the Jews did not provide consistent testimonies, and Jews, for their part, denied the charges throughout the proceedings. With no clear end in sight the king decided to appoint a commission to examine the matter. It was made up of both lay and ecclesiastical notables, but as the nuncio's auditor reported to Rome from Warsaw in February 1737, the Jews preferred the case to be judged by the king, and "so the case returned here," to the king's court.[222]

The trial had an impact not only on the individual Jews who were accused but also on the Jewish community as a whole. It was financially draining, and some Jews—"not only the poor, but also those who have something to live on"—converted to Christianity.[223] For nearly four years, the accused Jews were kept under arrest, despite concerted efforts to get them released. In April 1737, representatives of the Jewish community appealed to court officials to release the imprisoned Jews for Passover, under the financial surety from the whole community of Poznań. The request was denied and the Jews remained locked up—most of the time in the city hall, though at least for part of the trial in the synagogue.[224] Although two Jews died during interrogations under torture in the early stages of the trial, as

"Who Should One Believe, the Rabbis or the Doctors of the Church?" 275

did Rosa, Helena Sowińska's daughter, all the other Jews were eventually released in 1740 after taking an oath affirming their innocence.[225]

After 1737, the nuncio largely stopped reporting on the trial, though the subject of the Jews did not disappear entirely from the dispatches. In late 1738 and early 1739, issues of an economic nature and relating to the proximity between Jews and Christians in Poland began to emerge. It seems that the Poznań affair shone a bright light on the close relationships of Jews and Christians in Poland, a topic certainly noted in the court records.[226] But the nuncio's interest in the affair may have also encouraged Church officials to raise broader questions about the status of Jews in the Polish-Lithuanian Commonwealth. Even the Holy Office of the Inquisition in Rome, troubled by the blatant violations of canon law, became involved after the bishop of Włocławek submitted a complaint against a Cistercian abbot in the town of Peplin in Pomerania, regarding the permission the abbot granted Jews to settle in a borough near Gdańsk (Danzig).[227] Among the discomfitures related to Polish Jews noted by the Holy Office were claims, based in part on a lengthy secret letter by Italian physician Carlo Garani in Lwów, that Jews controlled the keys to some churches, charged 20 percent interest on loans, falsified coins, traded in holy objects stolen from churches, and borrowed money with synagogues as security. "Even Dominicans and Jesuits lent to Jews great amounts."[228] The Holy Office and the secretary of state demanded more information. In April 1739, the nuncio passed a response from the Cistercian abbot of Peplin to the Holy Office addressing grievances raised by the bishop of Włocławek.[229] The nuncio added his own opinion, stating that because it was impossible "to expel the Jews from many places [in this country] . . . without a significant detriment to revenue," it would be "unjust" to require that the abbot follow the orders of the bishop, who did not have any jurisdiction over the monastery and its properties—"especially since the tolerance of Jews is a necessary evil against which the Republic cries but does not have a way to stop it." The Holy Office, however, did not fully accept the nuncio's explanations and in July forwarded to him a list of instructions to be implemented in Poland to stem "the scandal" caused by the Jews there.[230] Although it acknowledged that Jews were "a necessary evil" impossible to "expel," the Congregation of the Holy Office disagreed that it was "impossible, or very difficult" to implement remedies and observe the "laws and Apostolic constitutions concerning them issued by the Church and by the zeal of the Highest Pontiffs." It encouraged the nuncio to "excite the zeal of the Majesty the King and the pastoral care of the bishops to cooperate with all power from their side to the laudable ends beneficial to the Christian Republic." The Holy Office wanted the secular and ecclesiastical authorities to implement existing laws and cease financial relations with Jews, especially investing with them.

But there was another reason for these increased anxieties about Jews in Poland. In 1738, Charles of Parma married Maria Amalia of Saxony, the daughter of Poland's King August III. In the aftermath of the War of Polish Succession, Charles of Parma became the king of Naples and Sicily. The Church authorities in Rome became concerned that Charles would invite Jews to live in the kingdom of Naples, and they wanted the nuncio to Poland to inform Rome about the situation of Jews in Poland and intervene with August III in hopes of influencing his daughter and preventing the settlement of Jews in the kingdom of Naples.[231]

Even as their status in Poland came under closer scrutiny, Jews continued to lobby Church officials in Rome to obtain a formal papal statement condemning accusations against them like the one in Poznań. It seems they were encouraged to seek such a statement when the accused Jews were released in 1740 at the conclusion of the trial. In the summer of 1743, the papal nuncio Serbelloni sent a memorandum on behalf of the Jews of Poznań and all Poland, reporting a plea delivered by Solomon Zalman and Moses Kalisz.[232] The memorandum summarized the previous protections of the popes and secular leaders and provided an account of the Poznań trial, emphasizing the official recognition of "the truth" and the Jews' innocence. It also drew attention to the steep costs of the trial for the Jews, leading to debts now difficult to repay. The Polish Jews asked for two things. The first was "a new bull declaring the unsustainability of the calumny" and naming the Polish Jews explicitly as beneficiaries. The long attacks on papal protections of Jews were bearing fruit, and the Jews' detractors had rejected previous papal protections claiming that Polish Jews were never mentioned in them (though they were in the less well-known 1540 bull). The second request related to the debts incurred because of the lengthy trial. The Jews asked for a letter of recommendation to a bishop or another authority who would be able to influence Jews' creditors, "almost all of whom were clergy," to have pity on them and give them a little leeway in repaying their debts.

In July, Secretary of State Cardinal Silvio Valenti Gonzaga requested more information from the nuncio before he was willing to take up the matter with Pope Benedict XIV.[233] On August 12, the nuncio sent his response, reattaching the memorandum and recommending that the secretary of state reject the Jews' request. The fact that Jews were indeed deemed innocent in the Poznań case suggested that the Polish tribunals proceeded "according to the rigor of the law," implying that a papal bull was not needed. But it was likely the second request that doomed the Jews' efforts to obtain letters of protection from Rome both in 1743 and for decades to come. It reminded Church officials of the unacceptable, from its perspective, relationship between Jews and Christians in Poland, especially of the business relations between Jews and the clergy and the debts Jews had contracted with Church institutions, an issue that was about to reach a point of crisis also in regard to the Jewish community in Rome.[234] In his letter, the nuncio reminded the secretary of state of the discussions on the same topic in the Holy Office just a few years earlier and highlighted once more specific details about the Jews' status in Poland that clearly violated Church laws and that outraged the nuncio from the moment he arrived at his post.[235]

On August 31, Cardinal Valenti responded with a most fateful letter.[236] He agreed with nuncio Serbelloni "to reject" the Jews' requests and thanked him for a clear explanation why. Valenti promised to stay vigilant "in case Jews ever tried a new appeal."

Four years after this exchange between Serbelloni and Valenti, in April 1747, Polish Jews would be accused of murder again, this time after the severely mutilated body of a man was found lying in the mud behind an inn in the town of Zasław (now Iziaslav in Ukraine).[237] Eight Jews were sentenced to what the court termed "the most serious and cruel punishment," which included live impaling, flaying, quartering alive, and on one instance the removal of a heart.[238] The text of the sensational, and highly unusual, verdict was composed as if with the intention to be printed and disseminated widely. Indeed, five copies were immediately made, one explicitly indented for the printer, "who is to print it word for word."[239] The verdict was then published at least twice in cheap pamphlets.[240] Duke Paweł Sanguszko, the grand marshal of Lithuania and owner of the town of Zasław, expressed his gratitude that the verdict was printed "for the perpetual memory of the nefarious crime."[241] Sanguszko's letter was itself also printed as a small, quarto leaflet, "for information, lest there be any doubt about the Zasław Decree against Jews accused of killing a Christian, published this year."

Yet despite this wide dissemination across the Polish-Lithuanian Commonwealth, no mention of the trial was made in the correspondence between Rome and the papal nuncio to Poland, though there can be no doubt that the Jews sought support and protection as they did during the affair in Poznań.[242] The only trace of Jewish voices in the historical records is found in a penitential prayer to commemorate "the souls of the martyrs of Zasław" who gave up their lives faithful to God.[243]

The Zasław affair is significant in several ways. It appears to be the first trial in a private town to be fully supported and promoted by its owner. It also appears to be one in which Jews were unable to get any protection. In retrospect, it was the beginning of a new wave of accusations that was to last for two decades, affecting the eastern territories of the Polish-Lithuanian Commonwealth. This new wave was marked by brutality and questionable legal practices. It was now increasingly difficult to claim, as did nuncio Serbelloni in the aftermath of the Poznań affair, that Polish courts followed the "rigors of the law." With this escalation in anti-Jewish accusations, the Polish-Lithuanian Commonwealth seemed to be moving in the opposite direction from western European regimes, which were increasingly turning away from torture, the death penalty, and similar types of persecution.

CHAPTER SEVEN

"Jews Are Deemed Innocent in the Tribunals of Italy"

THE POLISH Jews' hope for intervention from Rome was not a random wish. "Jews are deemed innocent in the tribunals of Italy," wrote Lorenzo Ganganelli of the Holy Office in 1759, contrasting the outcomes of trials of Jews accused of killing Christian children in Poland and Italy.[1] Although "deemed innocent" in courts, the Jews in Italy were not immune to accusations of killing Christian children. And this should not be surprising, given the prominence of the cult of Simon of Trent on the peninsula popularized by works of literature and art.[2] The 1475 trial in Trent led to an initial wave of accusations. Yet, after that initial wave, the Jews in Italy, though still occasionally subject to libels, would not be convicted in any of the trials in either secular domains, or in the Papal States. These acquittals and sometimes even the outright dismissals of charges were a result of careful, often protracted reviews of the cases by the relevant secular or ecclesiastical authorities. These outcomes reflected the power of existing laws and precedent, the ethos of good governance (*buon governo*) grounded in "good justice" (*buon giustizia*), and the cultural awareness of Jewish customs.[3] Significantly, the outcomes of two trials of Jews—in Verona in 1603 and Viterbo in 1705–1706—helped shape the responses and expectations of both Jews and Catholic officials to subsequent accusations. Their legal arguments were grounded in published works and precedents, and the outcomes became precedents themselves, their impact felt beyond the Italian Peninsula.

Viterbo, 1705–1706

The year 1705 brought back to life the image of Jews as enemies of Christians. In April 1705, leaders of the Jewish community in Venice appealed to the Senate of the Serenissima to intervene on their behalf. At issue was "a large painting" displayed for two days "on Rivoalto [Rialto Bridge] near the Church of St. Jacob, in which Jews were depicted as killing a boy, with other images and inscriptions aimed at stirring the people against the Jews."[4] The Jewish supplicants reminded the Senate that similar allegations of Jews killing Christian children had already been condemned by the very Senate and Doge Pietro Mocenigo in April 1475. The Jews included a copy of the decree for the Senate's consideration. In the 1475 document, issued in the middle of the Trent trial, the Venetian authorities sternly prohibited the spread of similar stories and allegations under "most severe punishment," emphasizing that "in our lands and regions Jews shall live securely and free from any injuries."[5] And lest in the future "preachers and others ... stir the population toward insults of this kind," the doge ordered that this decree be registered in the Senate Chancellery "for future memory." In 1705 the centuries-old decree proved exceedingly relevant and still effective. The painting displayed on the Rialto Bridge was ordered to be immediately removed and destroyed.

Although the authorities in Venice took a decisive step to remove the incendiary painting from the Rialto Bridge and prevent disturbances affecting Jews in their city, news about the painting spread across the peninsula, inspiring, it seems, a real criminal accusation of murder against Jews. In June 1705, in Viterbo, a town in the Papal States, Jews visiting the town for the fair of Madonna della Cerqua (or Quercia) were accused of attempting to kill a Christian boy, spurring a lengthy trial that ended in November 1706 with their acquittal.[6] Since 1593, Jews had no right to reside in the city—the result of the bull by Pope Clement VIII, *Caeca et obdurata Hebraeorum perfidia* ("The blind and obdurate perfidy of the Jews"), which expelled Jews from the territories of the Papal States, except for Rome, Ancona, and Avignon, although Jews would be allowed to live in cities later acquired by the Papal States.[7] In the late seventeenth century, however, Jews occasionally received temporary permits of residence in Viterbo during the fairs held there.[8] And so, in 1705, some Roman Jews were in Viterbo for the duration of the fair, which that year ran from May 27 to June 19.[9]

Six days before the end of the fair, on Saturday, June 13, a twelve-year-old boy, Girolamo Antonio Gallerani, the son of a local shoemaker, accused the Jews temporarily residing in Viterbo of trying to kill him to obtain his blood. Girolamo claimed that five Jews came out of their quarters and asked if he wanted a job for which they would pay him.[10] The Jews then, according to Girolamo, "made him go with them," and after reaching the end of Campo Grande, where the fair was held, they led him "to a hidden place where they could not be seen by anyone." Once there, they threw him down on the ground and "placed a halter (*il capestro*) to his throat in order to strangle him." Girolamo then said that the Jews pulled his hat over his eyes and "put their hands into his mouth" so he would not scream. Evoking the imagery of the martyrdom of Simon of Trent, he claimed they had a knife and a basin "to collect his blood for use in sorcery." But according to the boy, after he appealed to the Madonna and S. Antonio, whose festival was that very day, miraculously, the halter broke. And "although he was half-dead, he fled from their hands."

Almost immediately after Girolamo made this accusation, the news spread, and the matter was turned over to a lay court (*curia laicale*). And "though half-dead," Girolamo was examined by "physicians and surgeons," who found that on his neck he had three lines"; the boy seemed frightened and was short of breath. The boy then recounted what had happened to the prosecutor Antonio Volpini.

Some sixty-four Jews were immediately apprehended. The very next day, June 14, they were all lined up for Girolamo to pick out the perpetrators. Girolamo "recognized one of those who attacked him, touching him with his hands. It was Gioiello di Core, who was immediately arrested."[11] Another Jewish lad, Josef Samen, was also implicated, and eleven others were detained for further questioning; the remaining Jews were released. Jews immediately activated all their connections in Rome, Viterbo, and the rest of the peninsula. Ten Jewish leaders wrote to both the Holy Office of the Inquisition in Rome and the Roman Jewish community, seeking their intervention in face of the accusation of the attempted murder of a Christian boy "to collect his blood."[12] In their supplication, they emphasized the danger facing the incarcerated Jews specifically because of those charges.[13]

In Viterbo, the case was still in the hands of the *curia laicale*. And although the accused Jews remained in detention for months, the accuser Girolamo was also interrogated numerous times, providing contradictory testimonies. The Jews wanted the case transferred to the episcopal court (*curia episcopale*) in Viterbo and then to the Holy Office in Rome. They did not fully trust the lay court and seemed to have an ally in the episcopal court in the person of Paolo Bonanzi, a prosecutor. After much legal wrangling, the case was eventually turned over to the episcopal court.

By August, thanks to Jews' persistent efforts, the Holy Office in Rome was forced to consider the case.[14] In their appeal to the Holy Office, Jews insisted that neither the lay court nor the episcopal court found any convincing "proofs of such crime." Indeed, the results of both investigations, they wrote, "demonstrate clearly the falsity of the said calumny." Despite this, the governor of the city still continued to detain eleven Jews. The Jewish community in Rome was financially strained, having to provide not only for the incarcerated Jews but also for their families, now destitute "here in Rome," as well as the representatives in Viterbo for the duration of the suit.[15] These financial strains, although very worrisome for the Jews, were, of course, not of particular concern to the Holy Office, although the question of fiscal solvency and debts of the Jewish community in Rome would become an issue a few decades later. Emphasized thus in the Jews' appeal were matters pertaining to religion: "invention of the said miracle" and the claim that Jews needed blood "for sorcery and superstition."[16] Jews pleaded that the case be moved to the "Holy Tribunal" and the incarcerated Jews to the prisons of the inquisition. When given a choice, Jews often showed a preference for the Holy Office, which they hoped would bring justice and truth.[17]

The charge that Jews killed Christian children had already been "recognized as calumnious" earlier that year, the Jews noted in their plea, when the Senate in Venice intervened on the Jews' behalf to have "a painting depicting many Jews in an act of killing a Christian child" taken down.[18] "It is difficult to believe that in the said city the calumny and imposture implied in the painting would have been legally condemned [*si sia intentata*]," but supported in Viterbo by "a judicial action." Despite the Jews' appeals, on August 24 the Holy Office decided that the case did not fall under its jurisdiction, marking the case as *causam non spectare ad S. Officium*. The decision, certified on September 4, 1705, was announced to the Jews on September 22. On September 25, the case was transferred back to Viterbo.[19]

Not giving up hope, the very next day, Rabbi Tranquillo Vita Corcos and the leaders of the Jewish community in Rome appealed to Placido Eustachio Ghezzi, an official at the office of *Sacra Consulta*, asking that the Sacra Consulta take up the case.[20] The Sacra Consulta, founded in 1559 as part of the reform of the state, was a council responsible for appraising "the legitimacy of trials by peripheral courts" and for adjudicating conflicts over jurisdiction in the Papal States. It effectively functioned as a court of highest instance for appeals in criminal and civil cases.[21]

Rabbi Corcos appealed to the Christian "kindness" and "fraternal love, which [means] more than filial [affection]," thanks to which Jews had been "tolerated and embraced" by so many secular and ecclesiastical Christian princes.[22] The rabbi juxtaposed "this love" by Christian rulers to "cruel and terrible prejudice [that] emerges from the bosom of the ignorant commoners," who "accuse [Jews] of crimes so far from the truth, in order to make them despised both by the public and the very charitable princes." Yet, even when Jews were "falsely" accused of these crimes, especially "infanticides, based on the false belief that Jews wanted to use their blood for sorcery and superstitions, [which are] utterly contrary to the Law of Moses," the Jews' innocence had always been recognized by popes and secular princes alike. Corcos referred to Gregory IX, who "following the example of his predecessors, Calixtus, Eugenius, Alexander, Celestine, Innocent, and Honorius" extended his defense of Jews "in cases of similar impostures" in a brief *Lacrimabilem Judaeorum Franciae* from September 5, 1236.[23] In his *breve*—issued soon after Emperor Frederick II had granted Jews his own charter of protection in the aftermath of one of the most notorious cases of anti-Jewish violence that took place in December 1235 in Fulda—Pope Gregory IX called for justice in the treatment of Jews and condemned their oppression and the calumnies against them. Yet, the pope did not explicitly deal with the accusations of infanticide; the first to do so was Innocent IV, who in 1247 wrote first to archbishops and bishops in France and Germany, and then to "all faithful Christians, most explicitly urging clergy, princes, nobles, laity, and citizens to abstain from charging innocent Jews with similar diabolic fraud, impostures, enormous crimes, such as infanticides of Christians."[24] Pope Innocent's letters are some of the most powerful condemnations of the anti-Jewish accusations. In them, the pope admonished Christians not "to accuse [Jews] of using human blood in their religious rites, since in the Old Testament it is their precept not to use blood of any kind, let alone human blood."[25]

These thirteenth-century condemnations had already been cited during the Trent affair, and although they were never inducted to canon law, they were repeatedly used by Jews to emphasize the long history of papal protection against accusations of infanticide. The archive of the Jewish community in Rome contained other documents related to intercessions in the aftermath of similar accusations, and Corcos was happy to make use of some of them in his methodically composed entreaties to Sacra Consulta. In the second half of the seventeenth century, a Polish Jew, Jacob ben Naftali of Gniezno, traveled to Rome seeking intercession against clergy and students of seminaries and colleges who attacked Jews and spread "calumnies among the most ignorant people"—charging that Jews needed "to mix Christian blood" in their unleavened bread and that they "also need, for the same reason, bits of the Eucharistic bread."[26] These "repugnant" accusations,

Jacob ben Naftali stressed, contradicted the divine law, which prohibited consumption of any blood. As for the unleavened bread, there was nothing extraordinary in it; it just could not contain any leaven, and according to Exodus, must not be fermented. Indeed, the Polish Jew argued, the unleavened bread had been established thousands of years before "the birth of Christ," and thus it would have been impossible to use "the said blood." This claim was "invented after the coming of Christ." Such claims, Corcos noted, had already been condemned by Church and secular authorities, among them Emperor Charles V, and more recently in "a letter written to the same effect in 1664 by Father General of the Dominican Friars," copy of which was kept in the archive of the Jewish community in Rome.[27] Corcos then directly quoted both Jacob ben Naftali's letter and the intervention from the general of the Dominicans in one of his treatises he sent to the Sacra Consulta in the defense of Jews.[28]

To compose his sophisticated addresses to Ghezzi, Corcos had clearly drawn not only on archival sources but also on earlier printed works. He cited decrees already known from earlier publications: the 1475 condemnation of similar accusations in Venice, the 1479 decree by Bona and Giovanni Galeazzo Sforza of Milan, the 1603 decree from Verona, and the 1544 letter by Charles the V, which was subsequently confirmed in 1566 by both Frederick III and Maximilian II.[29] All of them were first listed in Richard Simon's work in response to the 1669 trial in Metz, then published in Isaac Cardoso's apologetic *Las excelencias de los hebreos* in 1679, and then again in 1681 in a short pamphlet against blood accusations by Isaac Viva Cantarini, *Vindex sanguinis*. A telltale that Corcos used Isaac Cardoso's *Las excellencias de los hebreos* is the typographical error copied from Cardoso that dated the 1479 decree by Bona and Giovanni Galeazzo Sforza to 1470. But notably absent from Corcos's appeal was the case of Simon of Trent, even though it was discussed by Cardoso.[30] Corcos would likely not have wanted to draw attention to a story of Jewish murder of a Christian child that was sanctioned by the Church.

Like many other defenders of the Jews, Corcos focused on biblical injunctions against murder and consumption of blood.[31] All the biblical proofs "demonstrate clearly not only that God prohibits Jews the consumption of human blood . . . but also that the primary cause [for this] is the rigorous prohibition to eat blood of beasts and animals," which was to prevent the spilling of human blood. This was, Corcos pointed out, also noted by Thomas Aquinas in a section of his *Summa theologica,* which dealt with sacrifices in the temple.[32] Although Aquinas discussed the exclusion of both fat and blood from priestly use and consumption, Corcos's focus was on blood only. Blood was, Corcos paraphrased Aquinas, to be "poured at the foot of the altar in honor of God" for several reasons: first "to prevent idolatry, because idolaters used to drink the blood of the victims"; second, "to form human life living. For they were forbidden the use of the blood that they might abhor the shedding of human blood"; and third, Corcos added, following Aquinas, "on account of the reverence due to God: because blood is most necessary for life, for which reason life is said to be in the blood."[33]

Rabbis too prohibited the consumption of any blood, Corcos wrote; the topic was addressed most explicitly by "Rabbi Moses Maimonides of Egypt," who wrote in his *Mishneh Torah* on the section of prohibited foods, "Human blood is especially prohibited by the rabbis when it is separated from the body . . . but [in case] blood that happens to flow from the gums, if the patient swallows it, he does not commit an error, but biting bread or indeed other food, and leaving the blood on it, he first has to cleanse the blood and then continue to eat, treating the blood as if it were separated."[34]

Evoking arguments similar to those raised during the mission of Jacob ben Naftali of Gniezno to Rome, Corcos argued that the belief in the use of blood for the Passover bread was unsustainable. How could one support the belief that "the bread, which had to be prepared with such caution and consideration, and for which scrupulous purification from any kind of pollutions was especially necessary, would require an ingredient, which in and of itself is considered polluted and filthy, and which cannot be used without committing a mortal sin"?[35] Why would anyone require human blood in the unleavened bread, if the bread was not eaten "in commemoration of the massacre by His Divine Majesty of the enemies of the Hebrew people, but rather of Divine Providence, which knew to persuade those who obstinately kept [the people] subjected" to let them go in liberty, without "leaving that much time for the dough to become fermented"? If this "imagined superstition" were true, would not so many converts from Judaism to Christianity, "who were excellent scholars, like Nicolas of Lyra, Paul of Burgos, and others well-informed about the Jewish rituals, have shown it in their writings?"

In Corcos's mind, the Viterbo accusation was undeniably connected to the earlier incident in Venice. And even though the Senate of Venice condemned the insinuations that Jews killed Christian children, "a similar calumny was fabricated no more than two months later" in Viterbo.[36] Corcos implied that the motifs invoked in the Viterbo accusation—not only of blood but also of a basin and a knife—were related to the recent public iconographic depiction in Venice of Jews killing a child. Yet although in Venice, the attempt to promote this calumny was ultimately in vain, some believed that it could bear fruit in Viterbo, and "unfortunately, they succeeded at least in causing anxiety and evident dangers to all Jews, who find themselves here ... and who, because of this, were detained in prisons, without any trace of crime." If Venice was a trial run, then Viterbo took matters further.[37] Pleading with Ghezzi and the Sacra Consulta for justice to protect Jews from accusations of "crimes of which they are absolutely innocent," Corcos urged them to "imitate examples of so many popes, and decrees and judgments by secular princes, especially those of the Republic and the Senate in Venice," all of which followed the tenor of the "apostolic declarations."

In 1706, a much-expanded version of the treatise that included specific source references and an extensive discussion of rabbinic sources was published along with the *Sommario,* which contained the texts of several of the documents mentioned in the treatise, including the 1664 letter to Poland, a fragment of the decree by Charles V, and the latest condemnation issued in Venice in April 1705.[38] This version of Rabbi Corcos's treatise directly addressed the Jews' failed attempt to have the trial moved to the Holy Office in Rome. But here this failure became a tool of the defense. "To render this supposed crime credible," Corcos wrote, the prosecutor in Viterbo claimed that Jews acted "in scorn and contempt of the Christian religion."[39] Yet, the Congregation of the Holy Office "has already meticulously examined the trial, and noted *Nihil extare, quod spectet ad Sacram Congregationem Sancti Officii* [there is nothing here that pertains to the Sacred Congregation of the Holy Office]." Thus, "it cannot be doubted" that "no act appears to have been committed in scorn of the religion, because if this Supreme and Zealous Tribunal merely suspected a similar crime, it would not have neglected to punish those accused severely."[40] The fact that the Holy Office dismissed the case meant that the prosecution's argument was deeply flawed.

To accuse Jews of enmity was utterly unfounded. Not only did Jewish law prohibit murder, a topic that Corcos had already discussed at length in the first version of his defense, but it also prohibited Jews from deceiving non-Jews; indeed, Jewish law mandated honesty in dealing with gentiles.[41] Citing Johannes Buxtorf's *Synagoga judaica,* Corcos asserted that on all Sabbaths and other Jewish holidays, Jews prayed to God "for peace, quiet, and the felicity of the Prince, in whose domains they lived, and for all his subjects."[42] Yes, perhaps some "crazy Jew" might commit murder or a similar crime, but Corcos protested against condemning the whole nation for the actions of one. In fact, in all nations there were those who "disobeyed and did not observe laws of the princes" or "the divine laws." There were to be sure even sorcerers and the wicked among Jews, such as Dathan and

Abiram, biblical figures who conspired against Moses. There were also many "inobservant Israelites." But still, Corcos shrewdly pleaded, just as it would not be appropriate to deem "Christians in general as impious, because Luther and Calvin were impious," so too it was not reasonable "to call the whole Israel a villain or a sinner."[43]

Corcos's supplications were published by the official papal printing house, the Stamperia della Reverenda Camera Apostolica, which had prerogatives to publish officially approved Church documents from papal bulls, encyclicals, and *brevi* to apostolic privileges, edicts, and indulgencies, all of which were intended to be disseminated widely or at least "through our entire Church state and all of Italy."[44] The official printing house also published approved books, among them the Vulgate version of the Bible, "works of the Doctors of the Church, and other books, which contain and explain the doctrine and traditions of the Catholic faith."[45] It was thus no small matter that Corcos's supplications and other documents in defense of Jews in Viterbo were printed by the Vatican's printing house, after receiving the appropriate approval of Church authorities.[46] The expanded version of Corcos's defense sported the imprimaturs of Giovanni Pastrizio (Ivan Paštric, 1636–1708), a polymath and theologian at the Congregation of Propaganda Fide in Rome, known for his expertise in the Hebrew language and rabbinic literature; Dominicus de Zaulis, a jurist and censor; and a Dominican friar Joannes Baptista Carus.[47] The approbation by the highly respected Giovanni Pastrizio validated Corcos's arguments that were grounded in Jewish sources. Decades later, when in 1758 Polish Jews once more appealed to Rome, any arguments based on Jewish sources would have to be sent to Paris, because Catholic scholars in Rome seem to have increasingly moved away from Hebrew research and learning.[48]

The publication of Corcos's works with such distinguished approbations demonstrated that Jews had friends in high places. Whereas Corcos based his defense of Jews on earlier Christian condemnations of anti-Jewish accusations and on the precepts of Jewish law, a Christian lawyer, Andreas Alberettus (Alberetti), writing at the beginning of 1706, focused on the trial at hand and its broader legal implications. Building on Corcos's argument that elsewhere in Europe and in Italy similar "calumnies" had been condemned and deemed untrue, Alberetti stressed legal consequences for those who filed false accusations. And, so too in the Viterbo case, "after more than six months of examination," nothing had been proven. In fact, the accusation had been deemed "false and malicious," with medical examiners finding no injuries consistent with the allegations of attempted murder and "endangerment of his life."[49]

There were, Alberetti argued in defense of Jews, numerous inconsistencies and confusing statements in the various testimonies offered by the boy accuser Girolamo. Why did he not take the road that was shorter and more frequented by the public, but instead one that was longer and empty? Even more, it was unclear which road he did take.[50] For example, he repeatedly changed the location of where the Jews supposedly called out to him and apprehended him.[51] He "modified and varied" the description of the rope supposedly used by Jews. One time he said it was new; in another testimony he said that it was old and weak. But the major contradiction, consequential for the Church authority, came in the story about the breaking of the rope. First, Girolamo said that it broke because of the force Jews used when they threw him to the ground. But then he said that "it was not because of violence and pulling, but because he placed his own hands on his neck and called out to Mary the Virgin," who miraculously freed him from the grip of the Jews. The claim of false miracles was potentially heretical and detrimental to the faith. The list of contradictions went on and on. Girolamo often said different things in different courts, so that his testimony varied between the secular court and the ecclesiastical court.[52] The discrepancies and false statements made in this trial demonstrated clearly that one was dealing with "a calumny."[53] These falsities together with the lack of evidence that the crime had even occurred "superabundantly" demonstrated that the two Jews from Rome, Gioiello di Core and Josef Samen, still imprisoned after nine months of legal proceedings should be deemed innocent and freed immediately.[54]

If that were not enough, Alberetti argued, judicial procedures were not adhered to properly. Some of the witnesses were legally problematic. The only witness who allegedly saw Gioiello in action was the accuser himself, Girolamo, whose testimonies could not be trusted. Two other witnesses who were called to testify against Gioiello were criminals, charged with theft and incarcerated with him.[55] They too were hardly trustworthy. In fact, one of them, Zamparinus, who had tricked Gioiello into making false statements, had already been tried at the Sacra Consulta for insulting the governor of Ischia.[56] Moreover, there were omissions in the testimonies and final court account. No mention was made, for example, of the fact that Girolamo drank wine with his relatives. All this, Alberetti claimed, undermined the legitimacy of the judicial process.[57]

To reinforce these patent problems with the judicial process and the questionable nature of the accusation itself, excerpts of testimonies from court documents and "extrajudicial" evidence were published in March 1706, also by the Stamperia della Reverenda Camera Apostolica.[58] The printed commentary on the margins of the quotes from the court records served to underscore discrepancies between different testimonies. The publication offered additional details, one suggesting the boy's drunkenness on the day of the alleged attack, and reports of more in-depth investigations, which included site visits and testimonies of other witnesses. Those site visits demonstrated what could be heard or seen from the places near the spots of the claimed attacks, providing yet another method to undermine the boy's version of the story. The boy's story simply did not hold: there were too many contradictions, big and small, about the location of the attack, the number of Jews involved, and the condition and color of the rope and other tools supposedly used by Jews. The long verbatim excerpts from existing court records of Girolamo's contradicting testimonies provided compelling evidence for the defense.

But perhaps the most powerful material was the testimony of the parents and the medical examiners. Girolamo had apparently told the investigators that his father had interrogated him about the incident "in order to know if it truly happened to me."[59] The father "did not believe it." He said to the boy "that it was not true and that he wanted me to tell the truth" and threatened that he would beat him if he had told lies. And so, "fearing my father, I told him that it was not true," Girolamo said. But then when his father left the house, the lad called his mother and confided that his response to the father was motivated by fear. Girolamo's father, for his part, first told the officials that he had initially not believed that Jews had attacked his son.[60] But he then seems to have backpedaled, saying he realized the boy might have denied the Jews' role out of fear of being beaten. "I am the only one," the father said, "who beats him," as he had done numerous times for "his pranks."

There may have been a reason for the father to change his story. When the physician Marcucci arrived on Sunday, the day after the alleged attack, he was told that Girolamo's neck hurt, but not why it hurt.[61] The father took the doctor aside, telling him that the boy was well and that what Girolamo had said on Saturday against the Jews was not true. Marcucci then urged the father to go "in [good] conscience" to the authorities and report that the allegations were untrue. But after the doctor left and the mother came back from mass, the family, fearing that Girolamo would be prosecuted for "the calumny," decided not to "retract the accusation." And this was the reason, the Jews' defense argued, why "between the three of them, the boy, the father, and the mother" could not keep their story straight.

In December 1705, two medical authorities, Giovanni Trulli, a public health official (*protomedico*) and the dean at the university "La Sapienza" in Rome, and Luca Tomassini, a medical official for the magistrate, were asked to opine about the causes of Girolamo's injuries.[62] Though it was too late to examine the evidence in situ, they reviewed the testimonies and descriptions of symptoms and injuries reported by Girolamo and recorded by the investigators. Trulli and Tomassini concluded that the symptoms described were not consistent with the alleged cause of the injuries: an attempted strangulation. Given that symptoms of strangulation, they wrote, were different from those described, "without any doubt" the reported symptoms and injuries were either feigned, or merely caused by epilepsy, or, truly, caused by drunkenness, or by having eaten sallow, wet, and difficult to digest foods, or perhaps by having taken a long walk during a hot summer day. . . . All can be identified both in theory and practice." The physicians' opinion was delivered to Ghezzi, the official at the Sacra Consulta in January 1706.

The argument presented by Jews and their defenders must have been persuasive. Two months after the defense opinion was rendered, it was decided that the case be transferred from Viterbo to the Sacra Consulta in Rome, and the two incarcerated Jews, Gioiello di Core and Josef Samen, were moved to a new prison in the city.[63] They reached Rome on April 13.[64]

Still the case was not yet over. In September 1706, the final four-page summary of the issues undermining the accusation against the Jews was published in Italian by the official pontifical printing house.[65] It focused on the repercussions of affirming these accusations against Jews based on such problematic evidence, which failed "any principle of proof."[66] "Owing it to justice," the judge "is obligated to find the truth." The Statute of Rome mandated that judges investigate crimes with a presumption of innocence of the accused; it was the accuser who needed to sustain the accusation.[67] The case against the Jews in Viterbo was contrary to this principle, and the procedures so flawed that it was hoped that this would be remedied in Rome. With the Sacra Consulta weighing in, the trial's outcome, positive for the Jews, it was assumed, would not be easily "dismissed." But as the matters stood, with this "false stain" that they slaughtered Christian children, "the unhappy Jews" were unable to function in society "without [being] universally hated," "without danger of being killed, and without being able to do business at the fairs"—all this despite being "tolerated and defended by the Holy Apostolic See."[68] An accusation "so vicious" must not be legitimated by the trial. The whole case should be dismissed and Jews let free.

Intervention in this lengthy affair was expensive and challenging for the already financially strained Jewish community in Rome.[69] Numerous letters were sent to different officials and persons of influence in efforts to release the Jews or gain access to the incarcerated. More than 1,200 scudi were collected to cover some of the expenses from Jewish communities in

Florence, Mantua, Ancona, Venice, Livorno, Ferrara, Reggio, Lugo, Cento, Verona, Fiorenzola and Piacenza, Modena, Pesaro, Casale, Siena, and Senigalia (known at the time as Sinigaglia, or Sinigalia).[70] The efforts by Jews and their supporters proved effective, though the results were not immediate. In November 1706, after seventeen months, the case was finally resolved by the Sacra Consulta. On November 5, the governor of Rome was ordered to release the incarcerated Jews, and the next day Gioiello di Core and Josef Samen were free again.

Creating a Defense Blueprint

One of the byproducts of the protracted trial of Viterbo in 1705–1706 was the consolidation of arguments in defense of Jews. Preparing their defense of Gioiello di Core and Josef Samen, Jewish leaders in Rome obtained copies of previous decrees condemning similar anti-Jewish accusations and presented them as legal precedents. It was not only that both secular and ecclesiastical leaders granted Jews general patents of protection against such accusations but also that in actual cases against Jews the authorities had found them innocent.

The most recent of those decrees was issued in April 1705 in Venice following the incident with the offensive painting on the Rialto. That decree, not surprisingly, directly referred to a Venetian precedent, the 1475 ruling by Doge Peter Mocenigo condemning accusations against Jews. But of the accusations of murder that resulted in an investigation and an exculpating decree, one of the most recent took place in Verona in 1602–1603 when a Jew, Giuseppe Abramino, was accused by a certain Bernardino Bretorio of abducting his son, and "either trying to take a Christian soul from the bosom of Mother Church and lead him to the Jewish perfidy and damnation," or "killing him in mocking of the death of our Savior, and of taking the innocent blood."[71] Giuseppe Abramino "denied committing such a wicked crime," and his lawyer demonstrated "with various passages from the Holy Bible" that Jews held "the shedding of blood in horror." Indeed, the defense argued, "many princes considered the rumor of use of blood to be vain and false," which they publicly conceded in many privileges, as did Giovanni Galeazzo Sforza, the duke of Milan on March 29, 1479, and Pietro Mocenigo, the doge of Venice on April 22, 1475, and "finally, Frederick III, Charles V, and Maximilian II on May 8, 1566," who drew on and affirmed earlier papal injunctions "to believe" such accusations. Based on this defense, the authorities in Verona decreed, "all suspicion of committing such a crime is annulled and thereby the illustrious podestà along with the most excellent Senate liberate the above mentioned Giuseppe." The documents that served as the foundation for the defense of Jews and the exculpating decree in Verona were then inscribed in Verona's official records and came to be more broadly known thanks to Richard Simon, Isaac Cardoso, and Isaac Viva.

Of the three documents mentioned in Verona, the 1479 decree by Bona of Savoy, the regent of Milan on behalf of Bona's minor son, Giovanni Galeazzo Sforza, was perhaps one of the most powerful denunciation of anti-Jewish accusations issued by Christian authorities. It called the accusations "craziness" and stressed that Jewish law prohibited consumption of blood.[72] Indeed, there were many baptized Jews "respected in their faith" all over Christendom, who would have revealed this "secret" crime if it were true. The decree dismantled the accusation with logic, pointing to the centuries of a Jewish presence in Rome to prove that these accusations were absurd. For hundreds of years, no one had ever found Jews to commit such crimes, and "if they had, it would have been impossible not to discover it after some time."[73]

If the edict of Milan so forcefully and persuasively debunked the charge that Jews killed Christian children that it came to be used in the subsequent defense of Jews in similar accusations, the decree reissued by three successive emperors—Frederick III, Charles V in 1544, and Maximilian II in 1566—further undermined the validity of these anti-Jewish charges by building on, as well as lending an executive support to, earlier papal condemnations.[74] The emperors' decrees clearly articulated a mutual relationship between imperial and papal power. On the one hand, earlier papal condemnations lent legitimacy to the imperial condemnations. On the other, the cases in which Jews were "most gravely bothered, taken captive, tortured, condemned to death, robbed of their possessions, evidently despite the fact that the Most Holy Fathers, Our Pontiffs, declared and prohibited to believe [these accusations]" were to be judged solely by the emperor, "as the supreme lord and judge of the Jews." Even though these imperial decrees were in fact assertions of imperial power over Jews, the fact that they drew a lineage to and highlighted their dependence on earlier papal pronouncements made the decrees crucially important for the defense of Jews living on the Italian peninsula, subject to papal authority, as they were in Papal States.

If the 1603 decree from Verona provided references to existing documents, in his defense of the Jews accused in Viterbo, Tranquillo Vita Corcos then brought them to life and supplemented them with additional sources and explanations, thus creating a comprehensive blueprint for the future defense of Jews. The Jewish community of Rome evidently recognized the relevance of Corcos's elaborate treatises beyond Viterbo, saving many unbound copies for future use.[75] And used they were just a few years later, in 1711 in Ancona, in 1721 in Senigalia, and then eventually in the 1750s in defense of Jews of Poland, with Cardinal Lorenzo Ganganelli referring precisely to the same documents and sometimes even using similar wording to that found in Corcos's works in his report on blood accusations issued for the Holy Office of the Inquisition and Pope Clement XIII.

Ancona, 1711

Ancona was one of the few cities within the Papal States where Jews were allowed to reside, albeit in a ghetto. In 1711, during Holy Week, a three-year-old Christian boy disappeared, so wrote the Jews of Ancona in their supplication to Pope Clement XI.[76] Since that year Easter and Passover coincided, "some Christians" began to "slander" Jews, denouncing them to the episcopal vicar, and claiming that the child had been seen in the ghetto where he was taken "by Jews [who wanted] to make use of his blood."[77] As the rumors spread, people in town began to "whisper" about "setting the ghetto on fire." To make matters worse, even "the judge himself" embraced this rumor and ordered "a rigorous search of all Jewish homes," which would have been destroyed "had the child astonishingly not been found the next morning in the house of a Christian tanner, far away from the ghetto." The boy had apparently fallen into one of the tanning vats and drowned. If that were not enough, the following day, on Good Friday, April 3, which was also the eve of Passover, a woman was heard wailing that she could not find her six-year-old son. She began to incite the city against "the ghetto." But a short time later the boy was found outside of the city gates. The Jews asserted that it was no accident that this rumor was spread; rather, it was a concerted effort inspired by hate. In similar situations in the past, the pope's "predecessors Calixtus, Eugenius, Alexander, Celestine, Innocent, and Honorius" excommunicated "such slanderers," the Jews of Ancona wrote, citing almost verbatim one of the supplications by Tranquillo Vita Corcos.[78] They also mentioned the decrees of Bona and Giovanni Galeazzo Sforza, of the three Holy Roman Emperors—Charles V, Frederick III, and Maximilian II—the 1475 decree from Venice, the 1603 verdict from Verona, and most recently, the results of the incident in Venice and the trial in Viterbo in 1705–1706. Copies of the treatises by Tranquillo Vita Corcos and transcripts of some of the mentioned documents were attached.[79]

The Holy Office took the Jews' complaints seriously, and on May 17, less than two weeks after first considering the supplication, it requested from the officials in Ancona more information about the incidents in which Jews were accused of kidnapping Christian boys.[80] The bishop's deputy (*vicario episcopale*) of Ancona, who was apparently about to leave the city, quickly composed the requested report and forwarded it to the Holy Office in Rome.[81] According to the vicar's report, on March 24—not April 2 during Holy Week as the Jews' supplication suggested—Gasparro Baldassare Nicolò, a three-year-old boy and the son of Antonio Pallotta and Maddalena Angelini, disappeared, having been reportedly last seen on a street not far from the ghetto. Or, so it was reported by Don Donato Conditi, a parish priest at the Church of St. Giaccomo in Ancona, and by Giuseppe Angelini, the boy's uncle, who came to the vicario soon after the child disappeared. Many people searched through "all the streets and alleys of the city, sounding the bell, and shouting, as it is always done in similar cases," but the boy could not be found. Thus, "what was left was to search diligently the ghetto." The vicario then requested help from the *bargello,* the chief constable of the episcopal court, and ordered him to notify the Jewish leaders to provide help in the search efforts. But the next morning the secretary (*cancelliere*) of the criminal court reported that a body of a child was found in a small well. The secretary had already seen the body and testified that it "was found intact, without any wounds or signs of abuse." How the boy fell and drowned, he could not say, but one girl of about the same age as the boy was said to have pushed him with a stick during play. Nonetheless, the vicario did not try to deny that before the boy's body was found some Christians had gone into the ghetto at night to look for him.

As for the second boy—Antonio Valentino, the son of a tanner Giuseppe Bonafortuna, who, according to one account was six years old and twelve according to another—his story was more complicated.[82] The incident took place on Thursday during Holy Week just as the gates of the ghetto "were being closed"; its timing was perhaps why the Jews conflated the two incidents in their supplication. That morning Antonio Valentino went with his boss Giovanni Catani (or Catanei), a local shoemaker, into the ghetto to the house of Rabbi Giuseppe Cipolletta to deliver a pair of shoes for the rabbi's daughter. But the shoes were too big, and so Antonio was sent back with a pair that was a little smaller. They did not fit either, so the boy had to go back a third time. When he entered the house there were two men, one of whom was the rabbi's son and the other his servant, as well as a Jewish widow named Canizza. (Later testimonies would indicate that even more people were in the house.) The Jews asked him if he had seen a piece of paper, in which a few coins were wrapped. When the boy denied seeing it, they took him to a room "where the chickens were" and locked the doors.[83] One put his hand on the boy's mouth "so he would not scream, the other took off his shirt." They then apparently offered him something to eat and drink "so he would stay quiet." When the boy did not return to the workshop, the master, Giovanni Catani, came to look for him, whereupon Antonio was set free and went back to work. The boy said nothing, the vicario wrote, about what had happened in the ghetto until he got home for lunch. There he told his mother, who in turn told his father. Hearing this the father went to the Office of the Inquisition and, it was claimed, tried to lodge a complaint against the Jews.

But in the court records sent to Rome, Giovanni Catani's version of the events was different. He said that when he went back to the rabbi's house, the Jewish women and men present there asked him to make the boy confess if he had taken that piece of paper with money.[84] But the boy cried and, so Catani suggested that they undress him to see if he had that paper. But "the rabbi did not allow that, saying it was not required." Back at the shoemaking workshop, the boy told the workers that "Jews locked him in a room ... place a hand on his mouth so he would not scream." Catani then, along with the boy's father, informed the Office of the Inquisition.

In the meantime, an anonymous letter arrived at the Holy Office in Rome informing it about "a barbarous act committed in the city of Ancona by the perfidious Jews."[85] "Because of [the] zeal of Christian piety," the anonymous author decided to write directly to the Holy Office because nothing was being done about this "barbarous act" in either the secular or ecclesiastical tribunal. This might have been, he speculated, because of the Jews' persuasiveness or their money.

The letter recounted the events of that Maundy Thursday, telling the story of Antonio's dramatic visit to the rabbi's house, where the "twelve-years-old" was trapped in a room, his mouth and eyes covered as he was disrobed, tied with the help of the Jewish widow Canizza, and thrown to the ground so he would be quiet.[86] Canizza offered him money and something to eat and drink so he would stay quiet. But the boy, the anonymous informer wrote, "was continuously shrieking" until his boss, Giovanni Catani, arrived, whereupon Antonio was quickly dressed and sent away. The letter pleaded that the Holy Office "find the perpetrators because of the sinister end the said Jews had in mind for the poor and innocent boy ... to fulfill their barbarous law, which during the days close to their Passover" makes them "attack and kill a Christian." The Holy Office needed to intervene because the Jews had succeeded in getting away with such crimes "through the power of money and oppression of Christians." The Holy Office in Rome did not ignore the letter. After debating the matter, it decided, on June 1, 1711, to forward a copy to the inquisitor in Ancona and to request more information "about the second case."[87]

Soon after the request from Rome arrived, the inquisitor began his investigation, which was to last until June 22. On that day, he sent his response, along with an "authentic copy of the court records" related to "the supposed attack on Holy Thursday by Jews against Antonio Ventura [sic] Bonafortuna, a Christian boy represented in the anonymous letter."[88] The inquisitor explained why initially the Holy Office in Ancona had not dealt with this matter; that was simply because "no denunciation was brought before this Holy Office, and the rumor running around the city was about a supposed theft," not about "a menacing" act done by Jews to the Christian boy.

On June 11, Antonio Valentino, the boy at the center of the controversy, was called in for questioning.[89] He recounted the events of Holy Thursday, during which he visited the rabbi's house three times, because the shoes did not fit "his daughters."[90] It was during that third visit that the Jews detained him. When asked who was in the house, he said that the first two times he was only in the front rooms of the house, and there was only the rabbi's wife (named Isotta) and his two daughters, for whom the shoes were intended; but when he arrived for the third time, there was also the rabbi's son Moise Aron and another Jew—the servant of the widow Canizza. It was those two who undressed him and continued to threaten him, asking if he had taken the piece of paper with money, until his master Giovanni arrived. Antonio then told both his master and his father about what had happened in the rabbi's house, and the master told him to report the incident to the Holy Office. He went there after lunch and first told a priest and then the vicario.

The same day, the boy's father, Giuseppe Bonafortuna, was also called to the Holy Office.[91] According to Giuseppe, his only son, the twelve-year-old Antonio, came home at lunch crying. Antonio told his father about the incident in the ghetto that morning: his visits to the rabbi's house and the Jews' attempt to undress him in search of the lost piece of paper with money. After the father heard the story, he went to the rabbi's house himself. The Jews told him that the boy had stolen the money; and after "quarreling" with the father they told him they would file a complaint against his son. That was when he decided to denounce the Jews to the Holy Office. The vicario was not there, but one of the people present, Father Morganti Filipino, seeing it as a case of theft, told him that the vicario would not have "taken up such matters." Filipino added the father must have "known well" that his son once "was in the store in [Filipino's] house" and stole money, and he "was found red-handed stealing it." Having heard that, Giuseppe Bonafortuna left the Holy Office. "Why didn't he return to the Holy Office?" the official wanted to know. It was because he did not want to be bothered with this case anymore.

Next was Giovanni Catani, the shoemaker, Antonio's master.[92] According to Catani, after Antonio went to the ghetto for the third time, he was missing for about an hour, and at that point a Jew, whose name he could not recall, came to his workshop and asked him to come to the house of the rabbi to talk. Once there, the rabbi told him about the missing paper with money, claiming that Antonio must have taken it. Catani then suggested that they undress the boy to see if he was hiding the money. But the rabbi said it was not necessary, because after he had brought the shoes the second time, he left the house—implying that he might have disposed of the stolen money; they just wanted to make the boy confess where the money was. Hearing this, the shoemaker said that the boy was trustworthy; he had worked in the shop for a long time and had not stolen anything. They then left without waiting for the Jew's response. Asked if he had heard about any other abuses of the boy by Jews, he answered he had not.

The next day, on June 12, Antonio's mother was examined.[93] She said that on Holy Thursday, her son came home around lunch "half-dead, and trembling." He told her about what had happened, whereupon she and her husband, together with their son Antonio, went to the ghetto. She did not enter the rabbi's house "because of the prohibition against Christian women entering Jewish homes." While the Jews blamed Antonio for stealing the money, the boy lay the blame on the rabbi's daughters. And so, the Jews threatened to file a formal complaint against Antonio. But the widow Canizza interrupted, saying that "she had already done that." To which the mother responded, presumably from outside the house, "We will also go and file [a complaint]." Following this exchange, Antonio's mother left with her husband and son and went to the Holy Office to denounce the Jews. When asked if there was anything else the Jews had done to her son, she added nothing to what had already been said by others.

Over the next few days, Antonio's coworkers were interrogated about the affair.[94] Their testimonies were vague, adding nothing new to the case. Still, they all agreed that Antonio was a "good boy." But a priest Antonius questioned on June 15 said that after the parents had arrived to report the incident in the ghetto he told them that their son had stolen something from his house. Hearing these words, "they both left, without filing another complaint."[95]

The investigation ended on June 20, and on June 22 the findings were dispatched to Rome, although one more testimony, that of Bartholomeo Lucatelli, a tanner who knew Giuseppe Bonafortuna, was added on June 28.[96] He had been absent from the city during the investigation. Bartholomeo said that Giuseppe had told him about what had happened to his son in the ghetto, mentioning that Jews had tried to crucify and kill his son. He added that he had also heard that Antonio's mother went to denounce Jews to the Holy Office. After the holidays, Bartholomeo went to the ghetto and talked to the Jewish moneylenders (*banchieri*). He told them not to worry about this quarrel at the Holy Office because it was "not a matter of faith and religion but of theft," whereupon the Jewish moneylender said, "Giovanni Catani spread the rumor so that 'the rabbi would be quiet and not talk about the gold that had been stolen.'"

When the investigation prompted by the Jewish supplication and the anonymous denunciation finally concluded, it was evident that in neither case in Ancona were the Jews guilty of any crime. Accusations that the Jews harmed the two Christian boys were caused by malicious rumors that easily spread throughout the town. If in the aftermath of the events in Viterbo it may not have been clear why Jews would have sought to have their case transferred to the Holy Office, the incident in Ancona offers some possible answers. Jews appear to have had confidence in the Holy Office: it was not easily seduced by rumors and acted only when in possession of evidence that was substantive enough to begin proceedings. When the anonymous letter reached Rome, expressing frustration that local authorities had not acted to punish the Jews and demanding justice for "the barbarous act," its demands dovetailed with those of the Jews, who also sought Rome's intervention. But a thorough investigation revealed that the whole incident was prompted by disgruntled individuals seeking revenge at the hands of the Holy Office. And the Holy Office refused to play along, clearing the Jews of all "calumnies" against them.

The Holy Office again had the Jews' back in 1721 in nearby Senigalia, where, as *The Historical Register* reported in England, "the common people had begun to insult the Jews, and would in all probability, have proceeded farther, had not that Tribunal interpos'd their Authority."[97] On July 14, 1721, the Holy Office in Senigalia issued a decisive decree "forbidding everybody to rail at, abuse, or insult the Jews in any manner whatsoever, upon pain of imprisonment and other arbitrary punishment, as the superiors should think fit, even upon the deposition of one single witness." The officials—the vicar general, the vicar of the Holy Office of the Inquisition, and the notary—exhorted, as the *Historical Register* reported, "everybody to pay obedience to this order, that they may not incur the penalties aforesaid."

Jews were indeed "deemed innocent in the tribunals of Italy," as Lorenzo Ganganelli would write decades later, and were exculpated by lay and ecclesiastical authorities. But it was not because the story of Jews killing Christian children was unknown or culturally unacceptable in Italy. The relative ubiquity of the imagery and of the publications reminding Catholics of the story of Simon of Trent and the very fact that such accusations even took place suggest the opposite. Italian scholar Tommaso Caliò has argued that the judicial persecution of Jews on the Italian peninsula was stifled because it interfered with long-term conversionary policies of the Church.[98] Although the medieval argument that the persecution of Jews prevented their conversion was known, with some Christians warning against such spurious accusations and their impact on Jews' conversions, this ideology alone would not have been sufficient to prevent the persecution of Jews, and their acquittals. After all, harassment of Jews in order to convert them had been an accepted method in the Papal States since at least the mid-sixteenth century. It was rather the ethos and framework of the legal system, with its insistence on *buon governo* (good governance) and *buon giustizia* (good justice), with proper judicial process as a sign of both, that should be particularly credited with saving many Jewish lives on the Italian peninsula. This stress on "good justice" allowed for a gradual move away from confession as the crown of evidence and prompted not only legal scholars but also local inquisitors and other officials to consider other types of evidence before ruling on guilt or innocence. Canon law prohibiting the clergy from pronouncing death sentences and participating in criminal cases that would end in capital punishment may have been a moderating factor on the peninsula, much more so than north of the Alps.[99] In the Papal States, "God's good order," as Irene Fosi has recently argued, was the goal to emulate, and Rome was to be the model for other rulers.[100] True, the ideal often clashed with reality, but the fact that it existed at all and was, at least in theory, embraced by Church authorities and other rulers on the peninsula meant that the courts there were more deliberate and attentive to legal precedent than in Poland-Lithuania, where the ideal of justice was to be swift and where, in contrast to the Italian peninsula, the ethos of a weak state and governance dominated to the point that "anarchy" was understood to be a guarantor of Polish stability.[101] In Poland, thus, in contrast to Italy, the combination of a lack of knowledge about Jewish customs and the weak judicial system meant that trials against Jews were often deathly. In Italy, the legal framework protected the Jews, even though within canon law itself that legal framework would tie the Church official's hands to issue explicit public condemnations of blood libels.

CHAPTER EIGHT

The "Enlightenment" Pope Benedict XIV and the Blood Accusation

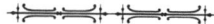

Despite Italian courts' acquittals of Jews from blood accusations, Rome's refusal to address Polish Jews' request for a condemnation of such accusations in 1743 after the blood libel in Zasław was a sign of a shift in policies toward Jewry under the new pope, Benedict XIV, elected in August 1740, the year the trial of Jews in Poznań ended. His pontificate coincided with a particularly bloody wave of accusations in Poland, during which Polish Jews were desperately seeking an official statement from Rome in their defense, but in vain. Not only did Benedict XIV decline to defend Jews but he also became the first pope since Sixtus V to authorize an office and mass in honor of a purported child victim of Jews. Although admittedly he never validated the blood accusations, the pope explicitly discussed the veneration of such child victims, thereby lending a hand to accusers of Jews who saw in his statements a general substantiation of anti-Jewish accusations.

Modern scholars have lauded Pope Benedict XIV as a man of the Enlightenment who condemned slavery and installed a woman as a professor of sciences at the University of Bologna; he has been praised as a jurist and a theologian who took a scientific and critical approach to evidence even as he deliberated about miracles.¹ But Benedict's legacy as an "enlightened" pope has been tarnished by his actions—and inactions—toward Jews: his views on their social and legal status, their conversions to Christianity, and especially anti-Jewish accusations, which he expressed both in his magnum opus and in his 1755 bull *Beatus Andreas*.² For all his engagement with contemporary sciences and arts, Prospero Lambertini, the future Benedict XIV, was also a product of the legal and cultural heritage on which Church teachings were based. That powerful legacy was palpable in his treatment of Jews.

Prospero Lambertini on the Martyrdom of Children

In 1734, the first volume of Prospero Lambertini's massive opus on the beatification of "servants of God" and canonization of the *beati* was published in Bologna. At more than five hundred pages, this volume was only the first of four additional thick tomes, the last appearing in 1738.³ The whole four-volume work, fully titled *De servorum Dei beatificatione et beatorum canonizatione,* became one of the most influential—and still used—books on the subject, its importance no doubt amplified after its author Prospero Lambertini became Pope Benedict XIV. The work was heavily influenced by Lambertini's two decades of experience with the Congregation of the Rites, where he served as *Promotor Fidei,* popularly known as the "Devil's advocate," responsible for vetting cases slated for beatification and canonization. He left the post in 1728 to become the archbishop of Bologna.

The approval of cults for public veneration was a serious matter; a lot was at stake, for "true sanctity and true miracles," Lambertini noted, could only be found in "our Roman Catholic Church,"⁴ and false miracles threatened the edifice of faith. The gravity of the matter required strict procedures. Lambertini thus devoted a significant portion of his work to those procedures, the evaluation of sources, and the officials responsible for them—notaries, archivists, and, of course, the Promotor Fidei. The multivolume book addressed, it seems, all potential questions and issues that could arise about the candidates for beatification or canonization; even details about expenses related to the process. It was bursting with historical precedents from antiquity to the most recent years, some coming from Lambertini's own experience as the Promotor Fidei, who was responsible, as he wrote, for "raising objections" to the cases brought before the Congregation of the Rites. *De servorum Dei*'s goal was to assure that the evidence was solid and no false cults were authorized.⁵

Lambertini divided candidates for beatification or canonization into two categories: confessors and martyrs. Confessors were those whose heroic deeds in the name of faith and God earned them devotion, but "who died in peace," not as a result of persecution and hatred.[6] Martyrs were those "who died in defense of the true faith," though some argued that also "those who suffered most atrocious torments for the faith, even if they survived and died in peace," deserved to be regarded as martyrs.[7] Martyrdom raised many questions about both the martyr and the persecutor, such as consent and age of the martyr, circumstances of martyrdom, and the identity and intention of the persecutor.[8] Child martyrs presented a particular problem.

According to canon law, as articulated by Lambertini, "all those who suffer martyrdom for Christ, and after death were distinguished by signs and miracles; all those who, after praiseworthy performance of heroic virtue died a precious death in the presence of the Lord, and after death flourished in glory of miracles are subject to canonization."[9] But could children who had not reached the age of reason be canonized? No, Lambertini answered. Before reaching the age of reason, children could not be "distinguished by heroic virtues." Accepting children as saints would have meant that "the pope would have to canonize all children who were baptized and died soon after baptism. This is absurd."[10] But what about children baptized not by water but by blood—"that is those killed in hatred of Christ and his faith," such as the "innocent children killed by Herod in place of Christ." Lambertini admitted that their eligibility for sainthood was subject to debate, because these children not only died before reaching the age of reason, a condition for canonization regarding martyrs, but also they were not baptized as Christians. Still, some scholars agreed that children "killed in hatred of Christian faith" were "true martyrs," because the intention of the persecutor played a role as well, even though the children themselves could not have expressed their willingness to die for Christ. Hatred was in fact a necessary condition of martyrdom.[11] And this was an interpretation often invoked by medieval writers, such as Thomas Monmouth, in regard to children said to have been killed by Jews.

Lambertini too noted that the Holy Innocents were not the only children "killed in hatred of Christ and his faith." Other examples could be found in *Martyrologium romanum,* among them Urbano, Prilidiano, and Epolonio venerated on January 24, the feast of San Babila. None of these examples related to Jews.[12] But then there was "Simon, a boy from Trent, who had just completed twenty-nine months of life when he was killed in 1472 [sic] by Jews in hatred of Lord Christ."[13] Lambertini observed that "the body of the killed infant" had been examined by the physician Giovanni Mattia Tiberino, who then wrote "the story of his martyrdom," which was then "published by Surius under March 24." After Simon's death, Lambertini continued, miracles followed, and soon a public cult emerged. But Lambertini did not shy away from doubts. He noted that Pope Sixtus IV had warned officials and prohibited Simon's veneration until "the truth of the deeds" could be ascertained by an apostolic commissary. Lambertini then reprinted Pope Sixtus IV's letter from October 10, 1475, which prohibited, under the penalty of excommunication, the veneration of Simon as *beatus* and martyr until the martyrdom and miracles could be verified. But once the nature of Simon's martyrdom and miracles was verified, the cult was approved "by apostolic authority"—at the request of Pope Gregory XIII, Simon was inserted into the *Martyrologium romanum* and finally granted the office and mass, as well as indulgences by Pope Sixtus V. Lambertini's main sources for Simon's story were Surius and the Bollandists, though he did occasionally mention others. The Bollandists, Lambertini cared to add, had also mentioned other children "killed by Jews in hatred of Christ" and venerated—Ioannetto of Cologne, Richard of Paris, and "in England, boy William"—but the Jesuit scholars did not see the "original" documentation about them to suggest that a proper process of beatification had been followed. Still, some scholars had argued that these cases provided sufficient evidence that "children killed in hatred of the faith," with or without "baptism of water," could be canonized. Lambertini disagreed.[14] In his objection, he again turned to Simon of Trent. Simon could not be used as a precedent for canonization of children; his cult was recognized more through "equipollent beatification" than "canonization," that is through beatification without a formal process. In fact, Simon's veneration was authorized by the pontiffs, but only "in one particular church." Since there was no "formal" or even "equipollent" papal recognition that Simon "should be venerated as a martyr of the universal Church," Simon was never canonized.

That was a crucial distinction Lambertini made between saints and *beati*, and between canonization and beatification more generally. "In the canonization of the saints," he argued, "Christian religion grows, because when saints multiply, so does the cult of saints," making their lives and virtues known to the public, increasing devotion, and inspiring acts of Christian virtue.[15] But children, although they could be considered "true martyrs," could not be considered saints, in part because canonized saints provided inspiration for others to follow and imitate and one could not imitate the death of children.[16] Even Simon of Trent, whose *acta* requesting formal canonization did exist in "the secret archive of Castel Sant'Angelo," about which even the Bollandists did not know, could not be considered for canonization.[17] Indeed, Simon's case could not even be referred to "as formal beatification and even less as solemn canonization, but [only] as equipollent beatification."[18]

Although the recognition of saints through canonization was final and infallible, beatification was not, and of the two types of beatifications, equipollent beatification was weaker, even revocable.[19] In formal beatification one had to prove "virtues or martyrdom, as well as signs and miracles," before the pontiff permitted "the servant of God [to] be called beatus and be venerated in a particular place." In contrast, equipollent beatification is based on "the renown [*fama*] of the virtues, or martyrdom, or of the signs or miracles." And in this process one also had to ascertain either that the cult had been active from "immemorial times," "with the knowledge and tolerance of the Apostolic See or the bishop," or that it was introduced or continued "with the permission of preceding pontiffs, or the Congregation of the Sacred Rites." In such a case the pontiff confirmed the bishop's decree and approved the cult. With equipollent beatification, then, Lambertini continued, "it is certainly probable" that the "judgment of the pope is not infallible, nor that it affects the Faith." There is some fear that "the pontiff might have erred in this or that case" and that he might later reject a cult he had approved. That is because in equipollent beatification there was not the same process of approval of virtues or martyrdom or miracles. The "judgment, in one word," is based on the *fama* and "antiquity," rather than being considered "judiciously." Because equipollent beatification is not definitive, it cannot be prescriptive, but only permissive. Yet, even though the judgment in formal beatifications is "certainly more weighty," still such beatification is nonetheless still only permissive, because at most it permits veneration in "a particular region or to a single pious family." In contrast, when it comes to canonization, papal judgment is infallible and irrevocable. The cult of Simon of Trent was, then, approved by the least rigorous method—equipollent beatification. While Lambertini did not challenge the cult—indeed, he affirmed it—this point would bear fruit when the cult was repealed in the twentieth century.

For Catholic jurists like Lambertini, Simon of Trent constituted both an uneasy legal problem and an important precedent. Although Simon was not, as Lambertini repeatedly stressed, recognized formally as a canonized saint—his veneration only approved for a specific church—he was inserted in the *Martyrologium romanum*, a universal liturgical calendar, leading some to interpret the insertion as equipollent canonization. When Lambertini returned to this issue in his discussion of the liturgical calendar, he conceded that Simon was a special case inserted there at the request of Pope Gregory XIII.[20]

As with the discussion of papal infallibility in the context of beatifications, the issue of children "killed in hatred of faith"—not all of whom were said to have been killed by Jews—gave Lambertini an opportunity to emphasize papal authority in authorizing such cults—a major theme in his *De servorum Dei,* and very much in line with the argument about centralizing papal power and the Church that was being increasingly articulated in the eighteenth century.[21] Lambertini emphasized the role of the papacy in his discussion of Simon of Trent, while stressing that in all such cases of child martyrs, the pope had to make a judgment whether to authorize the veneration of "children killed in hatred of faith."[22]

Strikingly, Lambertini used the examples of "children killed by Jews in hatred of Christ and the faith" not to focus on Jews but to highlight specific problems related to the Church's approval of veneration of "the servants of God" through beatification or canonization. Werner of Oberwesel, for example, who is said to have died in 1287, was noted for the fact that the formal *acta* focused not on his martyrdom—though "without doubt," Lambertini wrote, "he suffered the bitterest death, since his martyrdom lasted three days"—but on miracles.[23] Still, that examples of the supposed child victims of Jews, known from chronicles and *Acta Sanctorum,* were cited as precedents in his general discussion of canonization procedures signaled an acceptance of charges that Jews in fact killed Christian children "in hatred of Christ."

When Lambertini became Pope Benedict XIV, his earlier recognition of these stories, as Nicola Cusumano has argued, elevated them even higher.[24] For the first time since 1588, when Pope Sixtus V granted office and mass to Simon of Trent, a pope—by citing these stories as precedents in canon law—validated the accusations that Jews killed Christian children "in hatred of Christ and the faith." True, the examples did not affirm blood accusations and stressed only equipollent beatifications, the weakest in the scale of proof and potentially revocable. Still, as precedents in church law, these examples now reinforced through a papal voice what previously was only a matter of chronicles and histories, however authoritative they may have been.

Debates over Child Murders and Blood Accusations in Lambertini's Lifetime

Important as they were as precedents in canon law, Lambertini's discussion and examples of child martyrs might have also been colored by lively pan-European debates about child murders and blood accusations against Jews during his lifetime. In 1694, the year Prospero Lambertini graduated from

Rome's Collegium Clementinum with degrees in theology and canon law, a Jewish boy named Simon Abeles died in Prague. Simon was buried the next day, in accordance with Jewish custom, in the Jewish cemetery.[25] His death would have been unremarkable, except that apparently he had earlier expressed a keen interest to convert to Catholicism. Simon Abeles's sudden death led to suspicion that his father Lazar killed his own son to prevent his "apostasy," though Lazar denied the charge, claiming Simon died of illness. Five days after the boy's burial, his body was exhumed and examined by the medical faculty of the university in Prague, who concluded that Simon did not die of illness but of a violent blow to his head. Without doubt he had been violently murdered.[26] By the fall of 1694, Simon's father was dead from an apparent suicide in prison, and another Jew, Löbl (Levi) Kurtzhandel, implicated in the affair was publicly executed, and, according to Jesuit accounts, many Jews apparently accepted Christianity. According to two accounts, one by Johannes Eder and the Jesuit report sent to Rome on October 20, 1694, three days after his execution, Löbl had converted moments before his death.[27] In contrast, in a Jewish commemorative song in Yiddish, he is presented as a martyr who "did not want to break from God" and died "happy as if he had been saved."[28]

Simon Abeles's death and the subsequent trial became a *cause célèbre*, captivating Catholics, Protestants, and Jews across Europe. Illustrated broadsheets, books, pamphlets, plays, and even musical dramas telling the story of an "innocent" Jewish boy wishing to convert to Christianity, but cruelly murdered by his father, were disseminated in several languages and continued to attract attention even decades later.[29] One such narrative was structured around court records, lending it credibility; another offered a story of Simon's "martyrdom," connecting it to the story of his namesake, Simon of Trent.[30] In these many formats, the story became a propagandistic tool not only for Jewish conversions but also in the Catholic–Protestant polemic. For example, the Christian scholar and Hebraist Johann Christoph Wagenseil responded to the Abeles affair in 1699 and used it to polemicize against Catholics.[31]

Jews, too, responded with their own counternarrative, quite typically packaged as a Yiddish song that was also disseminated through print. The song, "sung to the tune of Rabi Rabi Shimon," praised Lazar Abeles and Löbl Kurtzhandel as martyrs and holy men not only because they died as Jews but also because "his father resolved to bring the youth to death" for his "heresy."[32] The Yiddish song, although no doubt drawing from medieval tropes of Jewish parents sacrificing their children to prevent apostasy, seemed to be aimed at directly countering the ostensible epidemic of conversions of Jews in Prague and the aggressive conversionary efforts by

Prague Jesuits.³³ Simon Abeles was a "bad youngster," his wayward ways were deemed calamitous for the Jewish community, and his death was thus justified.

As the literature about Simon Abeles circulated across Europe, in 1699, an accusation that Jews killed a Christian girl erupted in Sulzbach; in response, the printed booklet *Fructus maximi monitum* was produced, defending Jews against blood accusations, and later used in the 1710–1713 trial in Sandomierz.³⁴ In 1700, Johann Andreas Eisenmenger published his *Endecktes Judentums*, in which he expressed ambivalence about these anti-Jewish accusations, but nonetheless included several sources that proved useful in refuting the Jews' need for blood.³⁵ Both *Fructus maximi monitum* and *Endecktes Judentums* were known to the Hebraist Johann Christoph Wagenseil, who used arguments from both in his most extensive defense of Jews against these accusations, *Benachrichtigungen wegen einiger die Judenschafft angehenden wichtigen Sachen* (Notifications of Important Things in the History of the Jews), published in 1705. (Since Wagenseil praised the count of Sulzbach for defending Jews against these accusations, which led to the publication of *Fructus maximi monitum*, it is not implausible that Wagenseil himself was the anonymous author of the 1699 booklet.³⁶)

Wagenseil's lengthy refutation of blood accusations against Jews in the *Benachrichtigungen* is found in part two of this work, titled "Reflections on the Untruth that Jews Need to Have Christian Blood."³⁷ It is sandwiched between a section devoted to the Jews' conversion and one devoted to questions of usury. In his refutation, Wagenseil relied on his own knowledge of Jewish customs and Jewish texts based on his reading of Jewish sources and conversations with Jews and Jewish converts. As did *Fructus maximi monitum*, Wagenseil also provided references to papal and imperial decrees in defense of Jews, reprinting in full the 1475 decree by Doge Pietro Mocenigo of Venice, from which he singled out a sentence that raised doubts about the verity of the charge that Jews killed Christian children.³⁸

Wagenseil's discussion of Mocenigo's decree was in the longest section in part two—a section devoted to Simon of Trent.³⁹ Wagenseil had visited Trent and seen Simon's body. The visit made him question the accuracy of the representation of Simon on the Brückenturm in Frankfurt, whose likeness was reproduced at the beginning of Wagenseil's book. But more importantly, Wagenseil raised doubts about and refuted the arguably most important version of Simon's story by Giovanni Mattia Tiberino, which had served as the main source for many authoritative chronicles and shaped the narratives of the trial in Trent. Wagenseil's refutation emphasized the many contradictions in the story and its subsequent retellings in chronicles, martyrologia, and travel books. He also noted the fact that the Jews' confessions were extracted under torture.[40] Indeed, these contradictions, Wagenseil suggested, prevented Simon's canonization, despite the fervent efforts of the Church officials in Trent.[41] Yet Wagenseil's polemic against blood accusations and Simon's story was not based on humanitarian grounds; rather, his refutation was part of his conversionary efforts. For Wagenseil, blood accusations were one of the main obstacles to Jewish conversions, an argument in line with objections to blood libels expressed in earlier German polemical works.

In France, too, the Protestant historian Jacques Basnage devoted sections of his monumental *History of the Jews* to refuting anti-Jewish accusations.[42] Drawing from Isaac Cardoso's *Las exelencias de los hebreos,* Basnage shared arguments advanced by Jews—in "all the facts"—against "this calumny," explaining the mechanisms of the accusation: bodies are deposited in Jewish homes "to have a pretext to accuse Jews," and the deaths of children drowned in ditches or lost in forests and mauled "by the beasts" are then ascribed to Jews.[43] Basnage asserted that Jews certainly did not consume blood, and even the accusations of ritual crucifixions were absurd. "Indeed, what is the point of the Jews crucifying a Christian as their fathers did Jesus Christ? Do they believe to be insulting us? But an insult that so obviously shocks humanity, and which is accompanied by so many perils, must seldom rise in the human spirit."[44] Among these perils was a strict enforcement of severe laws against murders of children. According to Basnage, "these crucifixions of young Christians have often been very much pretexts used to animate populace and kings against them."[45]

As Basnage attacked the logic of the charges, he enumerated reasons that made these accusations suspect, despite being repeated so often:

> First of all, we only find them in recent centuries: The Jews are not accused of having done anything of the kind in the first days, when the multiplication and prosperity of the Church, which established itself on the ruin of the Synagogue, rendered their jealousy and hatred more piquant. Why did they think of crucifying Christians in the last centuries, where they could not hope for impunity; and did they not do it under the government of the pagan emperors, where this crime would not have appeared so enormous, and where it would not have been punished so severely? It is only, for example, since the middle of the thirteenth century, that we see children slaughtered.[46]

Second, Basnage argued, there was a clear pattern in the anti-Jewish accusations: "these accusations are always followed by an act of cruelty and injustice on the part of Christians." It was "these popular emotions" that stirred doubts in Basnage.[47] Third, miracles always accompanied the death of the child. The crimes of which Jews were accused brought them no benefit—but they did benefit Christians.[48]

Although Lambertini might not have read books published in German or French, this heated discussion about Jews did reach the Italian peninsula. In 1705, when he was thirty years old and had just been appointed to the position of a consistorial advocate in the Roman Curia, three linked events took place: Paolo Medici, the prolific Jewish convert and a professor of Hebrew in Florence, published his Italian translation of Johannes Eder's story of Simon Abeles; in Venice, a large painting of Simon of Trent was displayed on the Rialto; and in Viterbo, the trial of the Jews accused of trying to kill a Christian boy began, ultimately leading to the involvement of both the Holy Office of the Inquisition and then the office of Sacra Consulta in Rome.[49] As an official in the Roman Curia, Lambertini must have at the very least heard about the Viterbo case. And, in 1736, two years after Lambertini had published the first volume of his opus magnum on beatifications and canonizations, Paolo Medici published *Riti e costumi degli ebrei confutati* (Jewish Ceremonies and Customs Refuted), a hostile refutation of Leone Modena's apologetic work about Jewish ceremonies written for a Christian audience, which had first appeared in 1637 and then was frequently republished. Medici's book became a veritable bestseller, going through some ten editions in Lambertini's lifetime and nearly twenty overall. The goal of the work was not only to refute the customs of the Jews but also to pursue traditional theological arguments demonstrating the proofs of Jesus's messiahship in order to encourage Jews' voluntary, or even forced, conversions. The hostility of Medici toward Jews is palpable throughout his work, particularly when he projected his own feelings onto his descriptions of Jews' hostility toward Christians and Christianity. Simon Abeles came in as a handy example of that hostility.[50]

Medici largely avoided the topic of blood accusations, except for a paragraph in his lengthy chapter XXXIII—titled "Of the punishment that the Synagogue presently suffers because it did not want to accept the Messiah. Of the obstinacy, blindness, and hatred that it professes toward the Christians and especially toward the neophytes"—that would leave a mark on subsequent discussions of the topics. In this chapter, in which Medici enumerated false messiahs and discussed what he saw as Jews' blindness and obstinacy, the convert returned to the topic of Jews' "hatred" toward Christians and Jewish converts to Christianity, like himself. It was in this context that he touched upon the anti-Jewish accusations. "The hatred," he wrote, "Jews profess toward Christians cannot be represented adequately with words. We will infer it from their evil deeds and the frequent killings of Christian children, abuses of the crucifix and other images in the Kingdom of Spain and Portugal from which they were driven out by a royal edict."[51] Medici was not the first convert to accept the stories presented in Christian chronicles as true. Indeed another Italian Jewish convert, Giulio Morosini, had devoted a long section of his massive book on Jewish customs to such accusations, including Simon of Trent, solely because they appeared in so many chronicles.[52] But whereas Morosini's book remained relatively obscure, with only one edition in 1683, Paolo Medici's popular work and this paragraph in particular were cited by many others seeking to prove blood accusations against Jews, all the way to the modern era.[53]

Medici's work was also read by Benedetto Bonelli, an erudite Franciscan historian from Trent, who decided to write a defense of the cult of Simon of Trent to counter attacks by Basnage and Wagenseil.[54] Although Basnage's attacks could have been dismissed by pointing to their glaring errors, Wagenseil's attack on Simon of Trent struck a particularly raw nerve.[55] Given Wagenseil's reputation as a renowned scholar, Bonelli spent years, if not decades, conducting research in the archives and tracing the earliest mentions of Simon in printed works and in works of art.[56] The result was a monumental work, bursting with footnotes to numerous sources, that methodically defended the cult and refuted Wagenseil's arguments, one by one. That Bonelli embraced the dominant narrative of Simon's death is not surprising. He used Bishop Hinderbach's archive and the printed records, including the earliest ones, most of which had been financed by the bishop.

Over the long centuries, some of the most powerful Jewish defenses against these libels were past imperial and papal decrees. They were so powerful because Jews' accusers could not easily dismiss them, even though they tried. In Poland, Mojecki, Żuchowski, and other writers took pains to undermine their validity. And Bonelli's instinct might have been similar, but during his research he uncovered some archival evidence that troubled him. In a letter written in August 1740 to Abbot Girolamo Trattarotti, he confided that he had found in the Trent archives "two manuscript copies, produced at the time of martyrdom of the Blessed Simon," of the papal bulls, "in which they excommunicate those Christians who falsely accuse to Jews of having kidnapped and killed Christian children. . . . They made me think."[57] A few weeks later, Trattarotti, who was a learned Church leader from the nearby town of Rovereto and who would later become famous by addressing the question of witchcraft, gave Bonelli a plausible explanation for the policy of excommunication. "Regarding [the bulls], issued against those who falsely accused Jews of having killed Christian children," Trattarotii wrote, "it's possible that they are most authentic [*verissime*]."[58] Given the number of such incidents, it was possible that sometimes Jews were accused "falsely." This is what the bull would have sought to correct, threatening the punishment only of those accusing Jews "falsely." In his book, published in 1747, Bonelli pushed the argument further, focusing on several key phrases in Innocent IV's bull. The bull stated that some Christians "unjustly deprived" Jews of their property" by "falsely charging them with dividing up among themselves on the Passover the heart of a murdered boy," "maliciously" throwing dead bodies near Jews, and because of these "imaginary crimes" they raged against Jews, even though "Jews are not accused of these crimes, nor do they confess to these crimes, nor are they convicted of them."[59] This was a bull, Bonelli argued, about the proper "administration" of justice; it was against condemning the innocent, who were not "accused, did not confess, and were not convicted." This was not a blanket protection of Jews, as other pronouncements by the same pope concerning them demonstrated. The pontiffs, thus, Bonelli stressed, "rigorously prohibit" the condemnation of people solely on the basis of "vain suspicions and popular rumors," without an appropriate "judicial procedure." The imperial decrees were not blanket defenses, either, Bonelli claimed, making a conscious effort to historicize them. They were issued in specific times and places and were not intended to apply to every accusation.[60]

Bonelli, perceiving himself as a serious scholar following new "scientific" methods, did not accept all the claims presented by others as true. In fact, he disagreed with many other writers, by decisively arguing that Simon was not a saint, but only *beatus,* who had been beatified equipollently.[61] Bonelli marshaled historical evidence that Simon had not been regarded as a saint—neither in the earliest printed sources nor in the Simonine iconography.[62] Indeed, he cited *De servorum Dei* by then-pope Benedict XIV to show that Simon was never formally canonized and therefore, contrary to Wagenseil's assertions, "canonizations are not performed in the Catholic church as lightly as the sectarians would want us to believe."[63] Bonelli thus transformed Wagenseil's attack on Simon into an affirmation of Church practices regarding venerated figures. If Bonelli turned to Lambertini's *De servorum Dei* in his work, Lambertini would, in turn, use Bonelli's *Dissertazione* in another formal statement he would make, as a pope, about children said to have been killed by Jews. In the early 1750s, Pope Benedict XIV would have to respond to repeated requests to beatify and then canonize a two-and-a-half-year-old boy named Andreas Oxner, venerated in a small village near Innsbruck as a victim of five unnamed Jews.

Beatus Andreas

The story of Andreas Oxner of Rinn, who supposedly died in 1462, remained undocumented and perhaps even unknown until 1621, when a play narrating his "martyrdom" written by Hippolytus Guarinoni, a physician originally from Trent but educated by Jesuits in Prague, and working near Innsbruck in Tirol, was performed in a Jesuit College in Hall, just under a three-hour walk from Judenstein where Andreas was said to have been killed, with the emperor's brother Leopold and Prince Radziwiłł of Poland in attendance. A manuscript copy of the play contains a map of the area, visually connecting local sites with the story of Andreas.[64] In 1642, a seventy-three-verse vernacular poem by Guarinoni was published. Andreas's story eventually made it to the Bollandists, who received a manuscript from the Jesuit Ernest Bidermann (d. 1688) with Andreas's story, thereby opening the way for the boy to be included in *Acta Sanctorum*. Yet, modern scholars have argued that Guarinoni, inspired by the story of Simon of Trent, invented the story about Andreas and all its historical details.[65]

But it was in the eighteenth century that the propagation of the cult gained momentum. In 1724, Ignatius Zach published "a detailed description of the martyrdom of the holy and innocent child Andreas of Rinn" amounting to more than 250 pages and 50 chapters, with 26 copperplate engravings, among them a map of the area based on the drawing in the manuscript of Guarinoni's poem.[66] Still, it was perhaps the brief mention of "Blessed Andreas a boy killed by Jews in hatred of the faith" in Lambertini's opus magnum that spurred more decisive local efforts to have the cult authorized.[67] Around 1740, the church in Rinn was adorned with four new ceiling frescos by the painter Josef Ignaz Mildorfer depicting the story of Andreas: the sale of Andreas to Jews, his killing, the miracle of blood appearing on Andreas's mother's hands, and the apotheosis—Andreas in glory.[68] Four years later, a procession took place on the occasion of moving what were believed to be Andreas's bones to a high altar in the church in Judenstein; a year later, in 1745, Hadrian Kembter published the *Acta* "concerning the truth of the martyrdom" of the boy Andreas.[69] The work was carefully structured to comply with the requirements for beatification and canonization articulated in *De servorum Dei* by Lambertini, then Pope Benedict XIV.

Although Lambertini mentioned Andreas of Rinn only in passing in his *De servorum Dei*,[70] as pope he was forced to address his veneration more formally when proponents of the cult of Andreas in Tyrol began to seek its formal recognition in Rome. After their request reached Rome, the pope rejected it, in September 1751, on the grounds that a proper process needed to be followed before a concession of office and mass could be granted.[71] The Tyrolean postulators were unhappy by this response, but they were not unprepared. After all, Kembter's *Acta* had been published a few years earlier. The pope accepted the materials, and on December 15, 1752, he conceded the mass and office for Andreas[72] (Fig. 8.1). The plenary indul-

FIG. 8.1 Andreas of Rinn, an early twentieth-century devotional card. The inscription in the middle reads "The holy Andreas of Rinn in Judenstein."

gence came just over a year later, on January 14, 1754. Anyone who visited the church in Judenstein, where the supposed relics of Andreas were deposited, participated in confession, and took communion would thus benefit from the removal of temporal punishment for those forgiven sins that would otherwise have to be faced in purgatory.

Still not "content," the abbot of Wilten, near Judenstein, insisted that the boy be formally canonized. It was in response to these indefatigable efforts that Benedict XIV issued a letter, *Beatus Andreas,* in which he considered formally the question of "children cruelly killed by Jews in hatred of Christian faith."[73] *Beatus Andreas* was addressed to Benedetto Veterani, then the Promotor Fidei in the Congregation of Rites. In twenty-nine paragraphs

Benedict reiterated much of what he had already articulated in his *De servorum Dei* about the distinction between those who deserved to be beatified and those who deserved to be canonized, and the particularities of children who, like Andreas, had not reached the age of making a conscious decision about martyrdom.

The case of Andreas, Benedict argued, should follow the precedent of Simon of Trent, who was also beatified equipollently and subsequently received a mass, office, and indulgences from Pope Sixtus V, but who was never canonized. Still, there was one distinction between the two cases. Because of Pope Urban VIII's stricter rules for approval of cults and who might be admitted to the *Martyrologium romanum*, Andreas would not be inducted into this liturgical calendar.

The tone of *Beatus Andreas* revealed the pope's impatience and frustration with the petitioners. Benedict would have preferred if they had accepted in humility what he had granted them in accordance with other precedents. The pope understood that the proponents of the cult of Andreas sought to make his case a precedent in canon law and he needed to resist that. But the unique precedent of the Holy Innocents of Bethlehem complicated his stern stance. The Holy Innocents were the only children formally recognized as saints by the Church; other children, Benedict argued, did not merit similar honors, for reasons he had laid out in his *De servorum Dei*. Although the pope did not decisively foreclose the potential for canonization in the future, his demands for a rigorous process, and his concerns about the merit of the case of Andreas and of similar cases, effectively stopped the canonization efforts. Yet, by repeating numerous times the phrase that Andreas—like Simon and other children known from the chronicles—was "cruelly killed by Jews in hatred of Christian faith," *Beatus Andreas* validated the charge and thus the historicity of similar stories passed on in European chronicles. Benedict's *Beatus Andreas* thus became a new "authoritative" source for the proponents of anti-Jewish accusations.[74] To be sure, the pope never affirmed the blood accusation—according to Benedict the murders were *in odio*—but that distinction would be lost on future accusers.

Back in the Polish-Lithuanian Commonwealth

While Benedict XIV was considering the cult of Andreas of Rinn, Jews in the Polish-Lithuanian Commonwealth began to face new deadly accusations. And given that reports of those trials reached Rome around the same time, they possibly had an impact on Benedict's response to the requests from Tyrol. Perhaps the frequently used phrase affirming the "killing in hatred" (not only in *Beatus Andreas* but also in *De servorum Dei*) and the pope's statement that other cases might prompt requests similar to those coming from Austria also were influenced by the news about Polish Jews. What is certain is that both Jews and the Polish-Lithuanian Commonwealth were at that time on Benedict XIV's mind.

While writings about Jews formed only a small percentage of the total oeuvre of Benedict, Jews were not as marginal to his concerns as they appear. When he became pope, he faced a grave financial crisis in Rome. Soon the Jewish community in Rome became insolvent, and the highest Church authorities had to intervene, with a settlement reached only in 1755, the year Benedict XIV issued *Beatus Andreas*.[75] The presence of Jews epitomized the limitations of papal power and authority—as long as they existed within the body of Christendom, the Church could never fully triumph. Nowhere was this better illustrated than in the Polish-Lithuanian Commonwealth, where Jews held a prominent and relatively privileged position. Their position stood in sharp contrast with the tiny Jewish community in Rome, subjected to harsh rules and regulations reminding them of their "place," such as being forced to listen to sermons and being restricted in their mobility and economic activity.[76] Facing what he perceived as both a fiscal and religious crisis, Pope Benedict XIV began to enact increasingly repressive, segregationist, and ultimately also conversionary policies against Jews, first in the Papal States and later in other countries as well.[77]

The approaching jubilee year of 1750 also likely encouraged reflections on sin, disorder, and overall reform.[78] In the late 1740s, and in 1750 itself, several issues regarding Jews in Poland reached Rome. Two Polish Jewish converts to Catholicism were seeking aid and support, alleging persecution "from Jews in Poland in hatred of Christian faith." The papal nuncio to Poland was approached by several bishops from the eastern territories of the Polish-Lithuanian Commonwealth with concerns about Jews, which came on the heels of other complaints about Jewish "abuses" and disregard for Catholic holidays during fairs and markets.[79] Also reopened were complaints about the status of Polish Jews that had emerged during the Poznań affair and were at the time considered by the Holy Office.

Although over the centuries popes and nuncios tended to be resigned to the status of the Jews in Poland they found in violation canon law, repeatedly noting that little could be done about it, Benedict XIV took a more assertive stance, just as he did with the Roman Jewish community. During the jubilee year, the faithful were supposed to "enter . . . properly disposed, fortified by this most salubrious sacrament [of penance]," undertake a pilgrimage to Rome, obtain "the necessities both for bodily nourishment and spiritual refreshment with the aid of upright priests," and return home "informed by the example of holy conduct that flourishes in Rome, firm in the faith, fervent in virtue, and confirmed in their obedience to the Holy See."[80] The preparations for the jubilee and its celebrations were thus focused on improvement, correction of sin, and repentance. In this context, the "disorder" reported from Poland could not go ignored. After extending the jubilee to other places beyond Rome, including Poland, on June 14, 1751, Benedict XIV issued the encyclical, *A quo primum,* which was released to the nuncio on July 17, 1751, for distribution among Polish bishops.[81] The encyclical praised the "Polish nation" for its historical fidelity to the Catholic Church and for its past victories over the enemies of faith, including heretics. It urged the bishops to confront the current threat—the Jews who "multiplied" in towns and villages, dominating the trade there, living intermixed with Christians, and even displacing Christians to the detriment of parishes, which by losing the faithful also lost their revenues. Even worse, Jews had authority over Christians, compelling them to engage in excessive labor and submit to their power. Jews borrowed money from Christians, including the clergy, with synagogues as security, thereby gaining "as many defenders of their synagogues and themselves as they have creditors."[82] The pope praised synodal legislation regulating Jewish–Christian relations already in place in Poland and urged efforts to enforce it alongside earlier papal pronouncements. There was no need for any new regulations.

But the encyclical did offer something arguably quite new. After enumerating the "abuses" of Jews in Poland in violation of canon law, the pope abruptly switched gears. "The famous monk Radulph, led by excessive zeal," Benedict wrote, traveled across German lands and France preaching against Jews "as the enemies of our holy religion," inciting Christians to "destroy them by slaughter."[83] And many, indeed, were killed. "What would he do, if he lived today," asked the pope rhetorically, and saw what was happening in Poland? This "excessive" zeal, Benedict conceded, was opposed by St. Bernard of Clairvaux who wrote to the clergy and people of eastern France, warning them that Jews were not "to be persecuted, they are not to be slaughtered, they are not even to be driven out." The pope cited lengthy passages from Bernard's letters articulating the doctrine of protecting Jews against persecution and violence: they serve a role in the Christological understanding of the world and the Church triumphs "more fully over the Jews in convicting or converting them than if once and for all she destroyed them with the edge of the sword." The abbot of Cluny also wrote to King Louis of France against Radulph, Benedict XIV continued, urging him "not to allow the destruction of the Jews. But at the same time he encouraged him to punish their excesses and to strip them of the property they had taken from Christians or had acquired by usury." The pope then reviewed papal pronouncements about Jews and their place within Christendom, as well as relations between Jews and Christians. Christians should not serve Jews, but rather Jews should serve Christians, Benedict wrote citing Innocent III's *Sicut Iudaeis:* "Let not the sons of the free woman be servants of the sons of the handmaid; but as servants rejected by their lord for whose death they evilly conspired, let them realize that the result of this deed is to make them servants of those whom Christ's death made free." Nor should they be promoted to public office and have authority over Christians. Indeed, Benedict added, referring to Odorico Rinaldi's continuation of Baronio's *Annales ecclesiastici,* Pope Innocent IV approved the expulsion of Jews from France, "since the Jews gave very little heed to the regulations made by the Apostolic See." The lessons from the past were clear. Though Jews should not be attacked, if they disobey Christian law they should be punished by either being stripped of their property, as the abbot of Cluny suggested, or even expelled. This was the first, albeit veiled, papal encouragement to expel Jews from Poland.

To be sure, Benedict dutifully affirmed the papal policy of protecting Jews against violence, but the "dog whistle" of supporting expulsion along with the ostensibly trivial sentence about Radulph—"What would he do, if he lived today?"—was heard, and the results were soon felt by Jews. As the encyclical circulated in both Latin and Polish, with the Polish version much harsher than the original, some clergy soon felt emboldened to act against Jews and free to "enforce" canon law.[84] In November 1753, the nuncio reported that a bishop contacted him on behalf of Jews who reported being persecuted and abused. Though the Jews tactfully noted that such treatment went against what the pope had intended in his encyclical, it was clear that their mistreatment was inspired by it.

But there may have been another side effect of the encyclical. Given that in light of recent trials of Jews, even those resulting in grisly executions— as in Zasław in 1747—Jews, for no want of trying, had not succeeded in obtaining a condemnation of libels against them from Rome, the encyclical's harsh tone may have served to embolden inciters of anti-Jewish accusations.[85] Moreover, although *A quo primum* mentioned a bull by Pope Innocent IV and cited Rinaldi's continuation of *Annales ecclesiastici* as sources, it said nothing about the letter issued by the same pope in 1247 to the bishops of France condemning blood accusations, a document cited explicitly in Rinaldi's opus.[86] This silence, too, must have been heard. And in 1753, a new accusation erupted, this time with the personal and proud involvement of a bishop.

On Good Friday, April 20, 1753, a three-and-a-half-year-old Christian boy, Stefan Studziński, a son of a minor nobleman named Adam, disappeared near the village of Markowa Wolica, seventy-five miles west of Kiev. On Easter Sunday, Stefan's "worried" father went to pray in front of an image of Mary Virgin, prostrating in a cross-like position in front of it. The next day the boy's naked and mutilated body was found in the brambles near the village, his clothes scattered on the nearby bushes.[87] Since Easter coincided that year with Passover, Jews were soon blamed for the boy's death—the accusers claimed that, when the body was being carried into the village and its church, it bled when it passed by a Jewish inn. At the time, the coadjutor bishop of the Kiev diocese, Kajetan Sołtyk, happened to be within six miles of the village and immediately became involved, seeing it as "a cause pertaining to faith and God's honor." Bishop Sołtyk made every effort to get the secular authorities to arrest Jews, but he appeared to face resistance. So he took matters into his own hands and decided to make the arrests himself.[88] All in all, the bishop arrested more than thirty Jewish men and women, "the most respected and the wealthiest," from eight nearby towns and villages, including the innkeepers in Markowa Wolica, and soon began extrajudicial interrogations. In his defense Sołtyk later noted that he had planned to transfer the case and the testimonies he obtained to a secular court. He also claimed that when local Christians were aroused, attacking Jews and wanting "to destroy them entirely," he sought to protect Jews as "valuable" witnesses.[89]

While interrogations under Sołtyk's supervision were taking place, the bishop ordered Stefan's body to be examined and then deposited in a church, where "after two weeks it is *incorruptum,* and does not stink; in fact, a fragrance of something can be smelled."[90] In his letter printed after the trial together with the court sentencing decree, Bishop Sołtyk reported that he had planned to move "the holy body of the innocent martyr" to the cathedral "in all solemnity" and even ordered a tombstone *ad perpetuam rei memoriam* to assure that the case be remembered for posterity.

The prisoners were eventually transferred to a secular court in Żytomierz, a royal town, the capital of the Kiev Voievodship (palatinate) and the seat of the bishopric of Kiev, forty miles west of the village of Markowa Wolica. In Żytomierz, Jews were subjected to interrogations both without and with torture. Some seem to have confessed to committing the crime—though trial records have not survived and the details recorded in the sentencing decree from May 1753 and disseminated in print soon after are confusing and incoherent, because they only address, and misinterpret, certain aspects of the Jewish tradition to make the accusation believable to Christians. For example, apparently Jews found the boy on Good Friday while looking for lost horses in the forest near Markowa Wolica. They then stayed with the boy in the woods until late Friday night, when one of the Jews finally returned to the inn in Markowa Wolica with the horses—all in clear violation of the Sabbath. When they brought the boy to the inn, they fed him bread soaked in vodka and then matzah, also served with vodka and honey. Since Passover had begun three days earlier, the use of bread made no sense, because bread was not allowed in Jewish households for the duration of the holiday. Moreover, according to the published narrative, the Jews waited until the Sabbath was over before cruelly killing the boy in the inn, as if to avoid violating the Sabbath. The decree noted, casually, that the boy's parents lived right next to the inn, and yet, unbelievably, they heard or saw nothing. But logic had never been a strong point in anti-Jewish trials: the belief in Jews' guilt was stronger than any evidence to the contrary.

No matter how contradictory, incoherent, or incomprehensive the recorded testimonies, thirteen of the thirty-one arrested Jews were sentenced to tormenting deaths, designed not to fulfill the law but to create a spectacle. Six Jews were to be led from the main market square to the execution site, their hands wrapped in hemp, dipped in tar, and then lit. At the execution site they were to be flayed and then quartered, with their heads and body parts then displayed in public. Five other Jews were to be executed at another site by quartering. One of these Jews, since he converted to Christianity with his wife and children, was to be spared the brutality of the execution and beheaded to ensure a quick death. Two remaining Jews were sentenced in absentia to live quartering, but they remained fugitives.[91]

The actual executions differed from what was specified in the sentencing decree.[92] On the day that the first six Jews were scheduled to be executed, Ela, who ran the inn in Markowa Wolica, converted with his wife, hoping for an easier death, whereupon Bishop Sołtyk vouched for him and saved his life. Three Jews in the second group to be executed, among them "the richest in these lands," David Chodorkowski, decided to accept baptism, perhaps hoping that the bishop would save their lives as he did with Ela. But they were executed by simple beheading the following day; their bodies, instead of being quartered and displayed in public, were put in coffins and carried with great pomp to the cathedral in Żytomierz before being solemnly buried. One of the Jews, sentenced earlier to beheading, also converted together with his wife, and he too was spared by the bishop. The day of executions, baptisms of the accused, and burials ended with a ceremony of conversion of another thirteen Jewish men and women, administered by Sołtyk himself.

Before long, printed versions of the decree were disseminated, art commemorating the boy's death was commissioned, and copies of paintings, resembling the iconography of Simon of Trent, were reproduced as broadsides.[93] Coming so soon after Zasław and Dunajgród, the Żytomierz trial, notable for the active involvement of a bishop, sent shock waves among Jews in the Polish-Lithuanian Commonwealth; the trial would remain a point of reference for years also among non-Jews.[94]

Alarmed by the accusation and the trial proceedings in Żytomierz, Jewish leaders in the Polish-Lithuanian Commonwealth mobilized to act. Their approach was multipronged. Soon after the executions, leaders of the increasingly influential community of Brody sent a letter to the Ashkenazi Jewish community in Amsterdam, asking for help and describing "the calumny made against the [Jewish] Nation, accused of using Christian blood for Easter, which was followed by so much violence and harshness."[95] Their strategy seems to have been to approach "all the *kehillot* [communities], begging for their help and requesting by all possible means letters of protection that will demonstrate that this is a false accusation, that in past times on various occasions Jews were blamed [for such crimes], and that every time they were proven innocent."[96] The Amsterdam Ashkenazi Jewish community in turn approached their Sephardic coreligionists in that city, who then wrote letters to the Jewish communities on the Italian peninsula, including one dated July 16, 1753, to the Sephardic Jewish community in Ferrara, requesting that it "obtain as soon as possible an authentic copy of a certain sentence rendered in Senigalia dated 14 July 1721, in which the innocence [of the Jews] was proclaimed following a similar calumny, and that it be sent without delay to Rome, so that the Pope may suppress and annul this sentence."[97] The strategy was intended to marshal evidence demonstrating that other courts, notably those in Papal States, such as in Senigalia, invalidated similar accusations and, with this evidence, to appeal to the pope for help in this particular instance. The letter also referred to a previous papal condemnation of such "false accusations," requesting "an authentic copy so that we may use it and show it to those who may be of service to us in this case."

Just twelve days after the Jews of Amsterdam dispatched their letter to Ferrara, the secretary of the state in Rome on July 28, 1753, wrote to the papal nuncio in Poland, who was then residing in Dresden, notifying him that he received a *memoriale* from the Jews in Rome on behalf of the Polish Jews addressed to "Our Holiness Pope Benedict XIV."[98] The letter from the Jews in Rome focused on the charge that Jews were using Christian blood

The "Enlightenment" Pope Benedict XIV and the Blood Accusation 321

for Passover matzah, a "calumny," they wrote, long condemned by the popes.[99] They reminded the pontiff that Jews were prohibited from consuming blood and implored him to intervene. The Jews noted that just a few years earlier, in Poznań, the nuncio intervened in a similar accusation and justice was ultimately done—not without suffering and torments—as Jews were found innocent. The secretary requested from the nuncio more information about the affair. That the secretary of the state in Rome sent this request a mere twelve days after the letter was dispatched from Amsterdam to Ferrara suggests that Polish Jews may have first reached Rome through other channels. Given travel time and the realities of Roman bureaucracy, it would have been impossible for the letter from Amsterdam to reach Ferrara, then for the Jews of Ferrara to reach the Jewish community in Rome, then for the Roman Jews to prepare the *memoriale,* and then for the *memoriale* to reach the curia and elicit a response from the secretary of state—all in twelve days.

On August 15, the nuncio from Dresden forwarded a copy of the *memoriale* with his letter to the papal auditor, who was performing the nuncio's duties in Warsaw. He requested more information about the affair, so he would know whether to intervene on the Jews' behalf.[100] On August 22, the auditor responded, summarizing what seems to have happened: Jews were accused of killing a Christian child, and though the initial accusation was handled by the bishop of Kiev, in the end the whole trial was transferred to a secular court, where the accused confessed under torture and were condemned to death.[101] The auditor also clarified that "in this case, the question whether Jews need Christian blood for their superstition [was not addressed] but rather the question whether or not the mentioned crime was committed." This clarification was for the Church officials of crucial importance. If the accusation had indeed been based on the claim that Jews required Christian blood, then intervention from Rome would have been warranted. But the shift away from this "superstitious" accusation to a murder made the crime more plausible, requiring, according to Church officials, further investigation.[102]

A week later, on August 29, the nuncio sent his report to Rome, deeming the judicial process proper.[103] With this information in hand, the secretary of state concluded that since "according to the legal and judicial proof, [the Jews] were found guilty of this abominable infanticide of a Christian boy," the Church authorities should now work with secular authorities "to punish crimes committed in spite of Christ and hate of those who believe in Him."[104] This formal redefinition of the accusations Jews were facing in Poland on the part of the highest Church authorities—from blood libels to "crimes committed in spite of Christ and hate of those who believe in

Him"—echoed the wording frequently used even in Lambertini's works: it made clear that Jews would not obtain a papal condemnation of accusations against them. Indeed, just a few months earlier, on December 15, 1752, Pope Benedict XIV, the addressee of the *memoriale* on behalf of Polish Jews, had granted a plenary indulgence sanctioning a cult of Andreas of Rinn, described as a victim of Jews, killed "out of hatred toward the Christian Faith."[105]

But the issue would not go away. On January 26, 1754, Samuel Szmulko Naftolowicz and Israel Iser Juzefowicz appeared before an apostolic notary, Joseph Augustynowicz, in the royal city of Lwów and filed a formal complaint against Bishop Kajetan Sołtyk for his treatment of the Jews in Żytomierz, for financial misconduct (accepting money from Jews and executing them later), and for the conversion of two young Jews.[106] To demonstrate the preposterousness of the accusations launched by the bishop against the Jews, they included a decree from the court of Krzemieniec from April 1753, exonerating Jews accused there of killing a Christian girl, who, it turned out, was fatally wounded by her own father, who then tried to frame the Jews. Whereas the case from Krzemieniec remained hidden in the archives, the decree from Żytomierz, where Jews were executed, was republished numerous times, widening the published paper trail against Jews.

There is no evidence that this formal complaint against Sołtyk was forwarded to Rome in 1754. But the documents submitted by Jews became evidence in 1756 when, after another trial, a delegation of Jews made its way to Rome to seek intervention. And this time church officials in Rome decided to act.

CHAPTER NINE

Cardinal Ganganelli's Secret Report

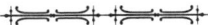

In 1756, only three years after the trial in Żytomierz and a year after Pope Benedict XIV issued his bull, *Beatus Andreas,* another accusation erupted, also with the open support of a bishop, this time in Jampol in the Łuck diocese. In response, Polish Jews again sent an emissary, Eliyakim ben Asher Zelig of Jampol, also known as Jacob Selek or Zelik, on a mission to Rome.[1] With help from Italian Jews, especially the Roman Jewish community and its rabbi Shabbatai Fiani, in early 1758 Zelig succeeded in receiving the attention of the highest Church officials, although not an audience with the pope himself.[2] This time, perhaps thanks to some Italian Jews' high-profile connections, the matter was sent to the Holy Office of the Inquisition for further examination.[3] The Holy Office considered not only the trial in Jampol but also reviewed the 1753 Żytomierz case that had been earlier rejected from consideration by the apostolic nuncio in Poland and the secretary of state.

The charge before the Holy Office was to investigate whether "oppressions, harassments, incarcerations, aggravations, and torments to which the poor [Jews] are frequently subjected" were in fact "based on the claim that their famed unleavened bread is adulterated with human blood and especially that of Christians."[4] This was an advantageous phrasing—for the Jews; had the argument presented to the Holy Office been centered on killing Christians "in hatred of Christianity," with Benedict XIV, the author of *Beatus Andreas,* still alive, the supplication may not have even been considered at all.[5]

Almost two years after the Jews' supplication reached Rome, the Holy Office of the Inquisition voted on December 24, 1759, to approve an extensive report written by the newly minted cardinal Lorenzo Ganganelli, condemning the frequent accusations that Jews killed Christian children to obtain their blood for Passover matzah. In early February 1760, that report, which had been approved a month earlier by Pope Clement XIII, who succeeded Benedict XIV after his death in May 1758, was communicated to the newly appointed papal nuncio to Poland, Antonio Eugenio Visconti.[6] Though lauded by scholars as a vigorous condemnation of anti-Jewish accusations, the report, which appears to have remained unknown until the nineteenth century, is more complex than that, with its intricate genealogy and content and with its author, Cardinal Lorenzo Ganganelli, trying to navigate a dangerous terrain. On the one hand, from the thirteenth century, the popes had indeed condemned blood accusations against Jews—at least until 1540. On the other hand, some popes before, including Pope Gregory XIII in 1583, Pope Sixtus V in 1588, and Pope Benedict XIV, Ganganelli's contemporary, sanctioned popular shrines celebrating the alleged child victims of the Jews in Trent and near Innsbruck. The Ganganelli report shows that beyond anything else his prime task was to consider matters of faith, and to affirm papal authority. The structure of the report and its supporting sources point to Ganganelli's dependence on arguments articulated by Tranquillo Vita Corcos, the Roman rabbi defending Jews in the aftermath of the Viterbo affair in 1705–1706.[7]

The Importance of Procedure and Precedent

An internal report dated March 21, 1758, which has been preserved in the archive of the Congregation for the Defense of Faith, as the Holy Office is now known, provides a glimpse of the issues at play when Zelig's supplication first reached Church authorities in Rome.[8] Although this internal report included elements that would be found in the final version approved on Christmas Eve, 1759, it focused on different questions: "The first if such examination belongs to the Holy Office and if the Holy Roman See should be interested in offering any measures in response to this mentioned aggravation. If so [*quatenus affirmative*], then secondly, should [the Congregation] consider proposing any remedy aimed at correcting the divisive [*divisato*] lawlessness."

Ganganelli methodically laid out the reasons why the Congregation should indeed take action in response to the supplication, while acknowledging there were sound arguments for them to refuse to do so. The first objection was there was no Inquisition in Poland. Thus, the question became whether the Holy Office could even act. Second, when in June 1705 Jews were accused of attempting to kill a Christian boy in Viterbo, "the Jewish community of the ghetto in Rome presented a supplication to the Holy Office, which sought to convince it to take steps in such a case. But having examined the aforementioned supplication, on August 24, [the Holy Office] noted—*Causam non spectare ad S. Officium* [the case does not belong to the Holy Office]."[9] Therefore, Ganganelli continued, if a similar case had already been rejected by the Holy Office, then the Holy Office should treat the current supplication of the Polish Jews the same way. Such a decisive rejection, Ganganelli wrote, would end the hope of the Polish Jews and would save him "from having to write on this matter." Although it would have been easier simply to reject the supplication, Ganganelli thought it did in fact belong to the purview of the Holy Office. Empathy might have also played a role in an anonymous Church official's decision to forward the petition to the Holy Office: "The aforementioned humble supplication to His Holiness Our Father Benedict XIV contains the following annotation to the Congregation of the Holy Office: 'Having said that, I would have no courage any more to proclaim: *Non spectare ad S. Officium*.'"

But in Church bureaucracy, with its complex set of rules of canon law and legal precedents, empathy would not have been a sufficient reason to respond to the supplication by Polish Jews if there was no legal justification to do so. Thus, to handle the Viterbo precedent, which, though not considered by the Holy Office, was resolved by the Sacra Consulta, Ganganelli drew a sharp contrast between that case and the wave of accusations in Poland. If the issue in Poland had indeed been that of a simple homicide, as it seemed to have been in Viterbo, he argued not quite correctly, then the Holy Office should reject the case, as it did in the case of murder in Markowa Wolica in 1753 in Żytomierz precisely because the nuncio's report did not suggest anything but a murder. But a case of "homicide for superstitious ends, seeking to offer a sacrifice in honor of God, and presenting as the offering to Him the blood of a sacrificed Christian, considered by [Jews] the enemies of their Law of Moses ... would certainly be a case to discuss and adjudicate in the Holy Office,"[10] because that was clearly a religious matter. Ganganelli then contrasted the Viterbo case of 1705 with another case in the Papal States, in Ancona in 1711, where rumor had it that "a Christian boy was bled and killed by them for superstitious purposes related to their unleavened bread."[11] When in that case Jews turned to Pope Clement XI for help, the pope forwarded the supplication to the Holy Office, which in fact took it up.

Having proven that on the basis of precedent the case did belong to the Holy Office, Ganganelli then needed to address the objection regarding jurisdiction of the Holy Office over Poland, "where there is no established Inquisition." To do so, he turned to a statement Pope Paul III had made when establishing the Inquisition itself: "the supreme inquisitors have jurisdiction over all patriarchs, archbishops, bishops, and any lay princes, as well as any other people."[12] And, in 1554, Pope Julius III affirmed the "unlimited jurisdiction of the *Suprema* in any place, and especially in cases dealing with Jews." Ganganelli's choice of sources signaled without any doubt an attempt to assert Rome's jurisdiction over a wide variety of matters and to claim universal authority—a centralizing vision that had been embraced by the recently deceased Pope Benedict XIV.

It now remained to decide what sort of measures the Holy Office should propose. What followed was a historical survey of responses by various church and secular authorities to blood accusations against Jews: Bernard of Clairvaux and his response to "Monk Radulph," the 1247 papal bull by Innocent IV, and a list of decisions by secular authorities on the Italian peninsula, including those in 1479 in Milan, in 1475 and 1705 in Venice, and in 1603 in Verona. The cardinal also added imperial condemnations, especially the 1566 imperial decree that specifically referred to papal injunctions against such accusations. And he extensively quoted the 1664 letter sent by the general of the Dominican Friars to Poland prohibiting Polish friars from preaching about "the various calumnies and malicious imputations" that Jews use Christian blood in their Passover bread. The cardinal then went on to discuss a number of books by Catholic, Jewish, and even Protestant writers who debunked the accusations over centuries. This section found its way into the final report voted by the Congregation on Christmas Eve in 1759 and subsequently passed on to Pope Clement XIII for approval. It would not be an exaggeration to say that this section was derivative, almost verbatim, of the treatises by Rabbi Tranquillo Vita Corcos published during the Viterbo affair in 1705–1706. Ganganelli used exactly the same documents Corcos quoted and published, all of which were in the possession of the Holy Office. (Corcos, for his part, had used some of the arguments presented in earlier published treatises by Richard Simon, Isaac Cardoso, and Isaac Viva.)

In the closing statements of his March 1758 report, Ganganelli listed two reasons why the Holy See should respond to the Jews' supplication: on account of *carità* or brotherly love, "the zeal as not to permit Christians an opportunity to oppress the unfortunate unjustly," and "finally, on account of religion, as not to render [the Catholic religion] odious to the infidels because of false suppositions, and thus to discourage them from embracing it."[13] Yet, Ganganelli was surely aware that Pope Benedict XIV, then in his last months of life, would likely be reluctant to take up the issue. Just three years earlier, in February 1755, Benedict had issued the lengthy bull, *Beatus Andreas,* affirming the cult of Andreas of Rinn who was, in Benedict's words, "slaughtered by Jews most cruelly before the completion of the third year of [his] life in the year 1462 out of hatred toward the Christian Faith."[14]

Another of the pope's statements that was difficult to ignore was his 1751 encyclical *A quo primum,* addressed to the bishops and archbishops of Poland in which the pontiff lambasted what he considered conditions that were too favorable for Jews. He singled out Jews' involvement in business relations with the clergy and their protection by Polish lords among many other violations of the canon law. Aware of Benedict's attitudes toward Jews and his past policies, Ganganelli pleaded, even if "His Holiness did not believe in having to renew the paternal words [*insinuazioni*] to the prelates and magnates of Poland, like those Pope Innocent IV had given to the prelates of Germany and France," at least he asked the pontiff "to agree graciously to charge the Apostolic Nuncio not to permit any burden [*aggravio*] and oppression of the Jews in this Kingdom based on the unsustainable supposition that Christian blood is mixed into their Passover bread."[15] Concluding his report, Ganganelli referred directly to *A quo primum,* conceding that indeed the social and economic position of the Jews in Poland was in violation of many church statutes and thus a "burden much injurious to the Christian religion." And for that reason, "Jews in Poland are not worth to expect such compassion, which they may have received, had they not forgotten that they are in position of servitude," but "because the Holy See does not behave according to the precepts of vengeance [*vendetta*], but rather according to the sentiments of piety, I would believe that [His Holiness] could take some of the above mentioned measures."

On the same day Ganganelli submitted his preliminary report, March 21, 1758, the Congregation voted unanimously to agree with his recommendations. In addition to requesting more information from the nuncio in Poland, the members of the Holy Office added this clause: "It is true that Jews in Poland, who are considerably powerful and who oppress the poor Catholics in some areas, do not deserve great compassion from the Apostolic See. Nonetheless, it is not justifiable for Catholics to persecute Jews unjustly for this reason, and thereby render our holy religion odious."[16] Niccolò Serra, the papal nuncio in Poland, was now charged with obtaining more information.

Evidence from Poland

It took nuncio Niccolò Serra several months to respond. In late October 1758, he finally forwarded to Rome two letters: one from the bishop of Kiev, Kajetan Sołtyk, who was involved in the Markowa Wolica affair that had led to the gruesome executions of Jews in Żytomierz, and one from the bishop of Łuck, Antoni Erazm Wołłowicz, who was an actor in the Jampol affair. Serra added a note saying that such accusations against Jews had occurred in the past and had not merited intervention. Still, Jews continued to seek intercession "with great importunity."[17]

The letters from the two Polish bishops were defiant and focused on defending their roles in the accusations. Wołłowicz, the bishop of Łuck, opened his letter by stating that "the perfidious Jews" had left in Poland enough evidence about their "cruelty for the sake of Christian blood"—it could be found in printed books and many court decrees issued in cases of infanticide "from the year 1400 until this time."[18] And so when an accusation against them sprang up in Jampol in the Łuck diocese, after a Christian servant to Jews was found dead, the bishop "requested" justice from Michał Kazimierz Radziwiłł, the Hetman of Lithuania and the palatine of Wilno, as well as the owner of the town. Somewhat apologetically, perhaps sensing Rome's concern with the legality of the process, the bishop claimed that he had only followed the customary legal channels, taking the body to the castle and requesting that "the basis of criminal allegation" be investigated (*requisivi ut realitatem objecti criminii indagare*). If the Jews turned out to be the killers, then serious punishment should be applied. Yet, the bishop remained silent on the fact that in this case Prince Radziwiłł had ordered an investigation on his own and found the Jews innocent. Despite Prince Radziwiłł's conclusion, the bishop, encouraged by local clergy, reopened the accusation and escalated the case to Warsaw, the capital city of Poland-Lithuania. Fifteen Jews were arrested and tortured, some of whom died.[19] While not revealing the details of the Jampol case, the bishop mentioned the case tried in Żytomierz, "a mere 50 miles" from the seat of his bishopric, and pointed to the printed materials related to that trial as evidence of Jews' guilt.

Much longer was the letter from Kajetan Ignacy Sołtyk, the bishop of Kiev.[20] Sołtyk had played a role in the arrest of thirty-one Jews following the death of a three-and-a-half-year-old boy, Stefan Studziński in Markowa Wolica. The letter forwarded by the nuncio was both a summary of the "killing by Jews of an infant Stefan Studziński in the diocese of Kiev" and an apologetic, if defiant, treatise on the bishop's role in the affair in 1753, which was already known in Rome. Sołtyk claimed that the body had been found with many wounds, a clear sign that the three-year-old boy had not died of natural causes but "violently." Right away, it was broadly believed that Jews were guilty, this suspicion "powerfully" bolstered by the fact that some Jews fled the town. Parents, relatives, and friends of the boy soon came to Sołtyk "exposing the injury done to the Christian name and blood, blaming the impudence of Jews, and imploring" him to help. And so, aware of other examples of "Jewish malice" and fearing that more Jews would flee, be protected by the magnates or others "corrupted with their money," the bishop decided to intervene, sending the matter "for investigation of the truth of the crime." The arrested Jews were interrogated both "freely" and under torture. All was done according to law, Sołtyk insisted, because he was well aware that "this was a blood case," which did not belong to his jurisdiction but squarely to the secular court, "namely the Castle Court of the Palatine." Indeed, the highly competent secular court convicted Jews justly, after "oral and corporal interrogations," with no influence "whatsoever" of the bishop or his office.[21]

If Bishop Sołtyk had to deny that he or his office had exerted any influence on the secular court, he also had to address the "calumnies" that he had cunningly accepted money from Jews as a bribe to free them. It was true, he admitted, that he had received from Jews some thousand zloty in Hungarian coins, but the money was from the Jews who were leasing breweries in a town that belonged to the "episcopal table," and five hundred was immediately paid back, according to a promissory note (*chirographum*).[22] It was therefore false, defiantly stated the bishop known for his gambling and resulting indebtedness, to imply that this money was in any way related to the trials and that it was a bribe to help release the arrested Jews.[23] The money, in fact, was partly related to the lease, partly a donation customarily offered to the bishop by Jewish inhabitants of episcopal domains, and partly an ordinary fee paid for the privilege to restore an old synagogue or build a new one. Such privileges, the bishop clarified, were granted "not for free," but were meant as a "monetary penalty."[24] The money was then used for "pious uses" determined by the bishop himself. In this case, the money was to serve "the good of the diocese" and fund the building of a new seminary.

That there was a legitimate explanation for accepting money from Jews was not the only reason why the charge of bribery was preposterous, Bishop Sołtyk argued. "Would he, indeed, who has no power to mete out corporal, let alone, capital punishment be able to redeem life?" In turning to a legal argument over jurisdiction and the distinction between secular and ecclesiastical powers, Kajetan Sołtyk emphasized that it would have been futile to bribe a bishop in this case, because he had no power over such matters.

Such power belonged to a secular court that was not at all "dependent on the bishop." Would it not have been wiser, the bishop pondered, "if the said money given to a bishop" to help release the Jews had been given to "secular judges to whom belongs the sole and arbitrary power to punish or absolve them of the crime?" Moreover, there could not be any doubt that "Jews living among us know very well" that according to Church law clergy were not allowed to be involved in "blood cases." Thus, they would have been imprudent to "solicit imaginary protection from him who can never condemn criminals to death."

Sołtyk also took the opportunity to address another "absurd imputation"—that he ordered the kidnapping of Jewish children in order to convert them. A charge of the use of such violent methods could apply to the "barbarity" and "inhumanity" of Tatars and Turks, but not "to Christians, let alone their pastors."[25] All the rumors that circulated about the bishop were thus outlandish. They were spread, he argued, by his enemies, particularly Joseph Augustynowicz, an apostolic notary, who disseminated "injurious" and defamatory information. There was a grain of truth in what Sołtyk was saying. In January 1754, following the 1753 trial in Żytomierz, Augustynowicz indeed received Jewish delegates from Podolia in his office in Warsaw to take their deposition against Bishop Sołtyk and his role in propagating "the calumny" of Jewish infanticides.[26] And perhaps Augustynowicz was responsible for forwarding some of the information to Rome.

Bishop Sołtyk clearly felt beleaguered, his reputation damaged. He was known for gambling, but now those "rumors" had clearly made their way to Rome. Seeking to repair his standing, he used the letter not only to support the accusations against Jews and justify his role in the trial but also to address any allegations that he might have personally profited from Jewish money. Yet, no matter the "pious uses" Sołtyk claimed to have had in mind, by defending his acceptance of money from Jews, he inadvertently admitted to engaging in business relations with Jews in a flagrant violation of Benedict XIV's 1751 encyclical *A quo primum*.

The letters from the two bishops were not the only evidence provided to the Holy Office. If the bishops emphasized court evidence as proofs of Jewish crimes, Jews themselves delivered a decree from another trial that took place in April 1753 in Krzemieniec, where a girl was found seriously wounded and nearly dead and the Jews were again suspected of the crime. But after further investigation it turned out that it was the girl's own father who had cut the child with a knife and dumped what he must have thought was her dead body in a sack, near the house of a Jew, Merch Leyzorowicz. The next day, the father changed his mind and decided to take the body and drop it next to a hospital run by the Franciscan friars. He then left town. But the child survived and blamed her father for the crime, removing suspicion from the Jews.[27]

With these documents in hand, on September 24, 1759, the officials of the Congregation of the Holy Office of the Inquisition met to discuss the matter.[28] Two months later they would take a vote on the final report.

Frankist Accusations of the Need for Blood in the Talmud

While Ganganelli and the Holy Office were preparing the materials to deliberate on the blood accusations in Poland, a new development took place in the spring of 1759. A heretical Jewish group, later known as Frankists after its leader Jacob Frank—with roots in the seventeenth-century Sabbatian messianic movement—charged that the Talmud, an ancient compendium of Jewish law and stories that had in fact been condemned to flames by the Catholic Church, affirmed the need for Christian blood.[29] Thus, they claimed that Jews who, in contrast to the Frankist sect, accepted the authority of the Talmud did indeed require Christian blood for their rituals.

The group openly emerged in Poland in 1755, when Jacob Frank arrived in the Polish territories, and in February 1756, Polish rabbis began to push back, enlisting the help of Polish Church authorities, who began to investigate the rabbis' allegations of Jewish heresy.[30] But this approach soon backfired. As the sectarians professed their belief in Christian dogmas, such as the Trinity, and embraced Christian religious symbols, they endeared themselves to Church authorities, who were now hopeful, if still somewhat apprehensive, about the group members' prospects as potential converts. Gaudenty Pikulski, a Bernardine theologian who composed a lengthy report about the affair, noted that it was easier to discuss Christianity with a Kabbalist or a Sabbatian than a "Talmudist," because the former "can more easily understand the Mystery of the Holy Trinity."[31]

Seizing the window of opportunity, the Frankists challenged the rabbinic Jews to a debate before the Christian authorities. Presenting themselves as opponents of the Talmud, they became known as "anti-Talmudists" or "counter-Talmudists." This was a shrewd move on their part, one that temporarily shifted the balance of power in their favor. As Paweł Maciejko has noted, the Frankists cast their case in "the broader framework of the Catholic polemics against the Talmud."[32]

Hearings before Church authorities started in 1756, culminating in two major debates in 1757 and in 1759. The first debate in Kamieniec in 1757 was to decide whether the accused "counter-Talmudists" followed the law of Moses or, as the Jews claimed, they did not. The debate ended in favor of the sectarians.[33] Bishop Mikołaj Dembowski issued a decree favorable to them, in which he took the opportunity to outline the parameters of Church authority over both Jews and heretics, quoting earlier decrees by Popes Gregory XIII and Clement VIII, as well as the more recent by Pope Benedict XIV.[34] Although the "counter-Talmudists" did not raise the question of blood in the Talmud at this time, the bishop did not shy away from discussing Jews' hostility to Christians and alluding to Jews' killing of Christian children. Referring to printed chronicles, he mentioned William of Norwich, the expulsion of Jews from Spain, and from France, which he dated, incorrectly, to 1180; he turned to the work of Marquardus de Susannis and its examples of Jewish "hostilities" such as "kidnapping and crucifying children" and spreading "pestilence" around Europe.[35]

Because the rejection of the Talmud became one of the centerpieces of Frankist identity, Bishop Dembowski was emboldened to examine Church teachings about this work and took the opportunity to condemn it. Given the Talmud's "impious, erroneous, scandalous speculations and blasphemies, offensive to pious ears" how could this work not be bad?[36] It had already been condemned to the fire by many popes, among them Gregory IX in Paris in 1242, Julius III in 1553 in Italy, and then again in Italy by Pius V in 1566.[37] In line with the popes, Dembowski condemned the Talmud in his diocese. Because the sectarians presented themselves as Jews following the "Old Testament" and not the Talmud, the bishop became particularly predisposed to them and ready to vilify rabbinic Jews, who now became the guilty party.[38]

Nuncio Serra was informed about the first debate the same year in which it occurred by a Jewish emissary, Barukh Mi-Erez Yavan, who appealed to the nuncio for help.[39] But the event itself and even Dembowski's decree do not appear to have been reported to Rome until July 1758, by then the affair had progressed further.[40]

Seven months later, in February 1759, the most dramatic and dangerous charge by the Frankists was voiced. In formal, printed—and one assumes widely distributed—supplications to the king and the primate of Poland, Archbishop Władysław Łubieński, the sectarians publicly expressed their desire to convert to Catholicism.[41] But they set certain conditions for this major step—before converting they wanted again to debate with "the Talmudists" and, through that debate, to prove not only their sincerity to convert but also "to open the eyes" of the "Talmudists [who were] hardened by their errors, and chuffing with unheard-of and terrible blasphemies against God Himself."[42] The sectarians presented themselves as "the Israelite nation returning by God's grace to their Messiah."[43] In April, nuncio Serra informed Rome about this new movement among Jews, whom he called "the Karaite Jews," and forwarded a copy of the supplication printed in Latin.[44] The Church officials in Rome must have been very pleased: not only did the sectarians profess their belief in Jesus Christ and express their desire to convert but they also declared obedience "to the Messiah's Vicar on Earth, the Roman Pontiff, and his legitimate successors."[45] Rome was anxiously awaiting the results of the second debate, hoping that "this affair will end to the glory of God" to be "remembered in the History of the Church" and to serve as a "consolation to Christianity."[46]

In May, the sectarian Jews, now increasingly known as "anti-Talmudists," again approached the king and the primate for assistance, pleading, among other things for support in the face of their enemies, the rabbinic Jews, and asking for a safe territory to settle.[47] A few days later, they prepared a detailed manifesto outlining the points of the debates, which was then inscribed in the records of the Lwów Consistory on May 25, 1759, printed in Latin, and distributed.[48]

Seven points were listed for the debate, six of which dealt with the question of the Messiah. But the seventh charged bluntly, "The Talmud teaches the need for Christian blood, and he who believes in the Talmud is required to use it."[49] The debate, initially scheduled for July, was postponed to September, and Jews seem to have been forced to participate under the hefty monetary penalty of some one thousand zloty.[50] Even if the local Church authorities might have been thrilled about this debate and the potential conversions, the papal nuncio Niccolò Serra was a little apprehensive. He did not like the fact that Jews were reportedly compelled to participate and expressed doubts about the catechumens, because to his taste their leader Jacob Frank was "held in excessive veneration." To Serra, it all had markings of an emerging sect. Thus, he warned, one needed to "proceed with all possible caution."[51]

Other Church officials also seemed uneasy about the seven points of the proposed debate, particularly the seventh one affirming the verity of blood accusation.[52] With the points of the debate printed in the manifesto, the Jews, Serra reported, were able to prepare well for the debate, at least the first three points to which they responded proficiently. But three other points were controversial because answers to them might have potentially been deemed offensive to the Catholic Church. And so, the Jews demurred. In regard to point five, for example, which addressed the cross as the sign of the Holy Trinity and the "seal" of the messiah, they refused to respond on the grounds that "it was not proper for us to speak against the Catholic religion."[53] The seventh point was particularly charged, for it alleged that the Talmud mandated the use of Christian blood. Since the sectarians' manifesto was printed, it was now out in the open—in print—that a Jewish group seemingly validated the notorious anti-Jewish accusations. Indeed, the nuncio wrote, should it be verified that "the need of Christian blood was a religious principle," then this would lend credence to "the cases of killings of Christians of which Jews have been so many times accused in the courts of this Kingdom."[54]

The rabbis' defense, preserved apparently "in accordance with the original response submitted by them" in Gaudenty Pikulski's work, challenged the "anti-Talmudists'" proficiency in Hebrew, their selective choice of passages that were often taken out of context, and their manipulation and mistranslation of texts. The defense also highlighted non-Jewish authorities who had denied that Jews ever committed the imputed crimes, among them the "Catholic" Hugo Grotius.[55] They argued that in other countries, "Germany, the Empire, Italy, and Turkey" no credence was given to this "tall tale."[56] Similar arguments would be repeated years later in one of the last trials of the Jews in Poland.

Nuncio Serra continued to send dispatches on the question of whether the need for blood was indeed mandated by the Talmud. Though the question remained unresolved, it did touch on the very issue that was simultaneously under consideration in the Holy Office. Still, Rome expressed little interest, its attention focused on the Frankist conversions and their aftermath. Secretary of State Cardinal Torrigiani addressed the question of blood directly only in November, nearly two months after the Holy Office had already discussed the supplementary documents delivered in connection to Jacob Eliyakim Zelig's supplication and nearly two months after Serra had sent his reports.[57] On November 17, 1759, Torrigiani wrote that "even though here it interests us little to know if the texts taken from the Hebrew books and the Talmud are true or false, or approximate" because so many errors were contained in the Jewish books, still, it would be useful to have the matter examined by Catholic experts in the Hebrew language.[58] On December 5, Serra confirmed that it was indeed difficult to "verify the existence of such teaching in Talmudic books" because of the "profound uncertainty of meaning of the texts brought up in the last session held in Lwów." Nothing could, in fact, be concluded, given the lack of scholars fluent "in the dead language," that is, in Hebrew and Aramaic.[59] The confusion reported by the nuncio was likely grounded in the rabbis' defense that consistently focused on the misuse and misunderstanding of the texts the anti-Talmudists had singled out during the debate.[60]

In his December 12 dispatch, Nuncio Serra attached, among documents related to the new converts, evidence they provided "to verify the teaching of the Talmud concerning the use of Christian blood."[61] From then on, the topic of the use of Christian blood dropped out of the correspondence. Instead, subsequent dispatches from Serra about Jews and the new converts focused on concerns about the converts' sincerity, whose goal in conversion seems to have been to obtain "in this Kingdom land to inhabit." From January 1760 on, the topic of the arrest of the then-baptized Jacob Frank on suspicion of heresy was added.[62] It took about two to three weeks for dispatches from Warsaw to reach Rome. Thus, by the time Serra's December 12 dispatch reached Rome, the Ganganelli report had already been presented to and voted on by the Congregation of the Holy Office. It was now waiting to be presented to Pope Clement XIII.

Ganganelli's Final Report

Even though Nuncio Serra's last dispatch touching on the Frankist blood accusations did not reach Rome in time for Cardinal Ganganelli to consider it in his report, by the time the Cardinal finished it, the sensationalistic allegations by the Frankists about the use of blood would have certainly been known in Rome. Yet, in his report, Ganganelli mentioned nothing about the charges made in the disputation in Lwów. The silence is deafening, but perhaps the cardinal, unable to verify the accuracy of the allegations and the Jewish responses, may have preferred not to consider the issue raised at the Lwów disputation. Or perhaps based on the strong evidence from Jewish sources supplied in 1706 by Tranquillo Vita Corcos in his treatises in defense of Jews and sanctioned by the premier Vatican Hebraist and theologian Giovanni Pastrizio, Ganganelli was confident that Jewish texts did not support the use of Christian blood. But Ganganelli simply may not have wanted to complicate matters further by engaging in a debate about statements made by the highly controversial group of converts about the Talmud, a work that, after all, had been banned by the pontiffs. And so, by focusing on the two specific trials that brought Jacob Eliyakim Zelig to Rome, and basing his report on the historical evidence—not Jewish texts—and on the documents requested by the Holy Office from the nuncio following the initial vote in March 1758, Ganganelli avoided becoming involved in the increasingly notorious issue of Frank and his followers, an issue with which the Holy Office would have to deal separately.

By the time Ganganelli finished his report, Clement XIII was pope, who, though respectful of his predecessor Benedict XIV, did not carry the same baggage of writings about Jews. In a tactful but explicit way Ganganelli condemned the Polish bishops for their uncritical acceptance of anti-Jewish accusations. "May God guard me," the newly appointed cardinal wrote, "from simply suspecting that the two Polish bishops, and the apostolic nuncio wished to conceal the truth in a contrived way, or that they sent here fraudulent information. Still, it could be that they themselves were not deceivers but rather deceived."[63]

In addressing directly the two reports by Bishop Wołłowicz of Łuck and Bishop Sołtyk of Kiev (by then the bishop of Cracow), Ganganelli once again took the opportunity to lambast the bishops and affirm papal authority. He cut to the chase, dismissing Sołtyk's report outright as "an apology for his conduct" and a defense of "his greed" for gold.[64] As for the bishop of Łuck, he "has shown himself too prone to believe what cannot be true"[65]—not only because he apparently did not have his historical facts straight but also, more importantly "if the Supreme Pontiffs Gregory IX and Innocent IV judged such accusations to be baseless (as I have already shown), and if the Jews were declared innocent in the tribunals of Italy, I cannot see how they can be considered guilty of such a crime in Poland alone." As if not to leave any doubt, the cardinal stressed, "I would desire that Mgr. the Bishop of Łuck, in order to undeceive himself [*per suo disinganno*], should read the decretal of Innocent IV, cited by me, which can be found in the works of Rinaldi, who continued the work of Baronio. There he would be able to see the same accusations with which he now persecutes the Jews, and would find a complete defense by the esteemed pontiff."[66] Citing Rinaldi was a risky move, because even though he mentioned Innocent's decree, he also included examples of children "most cruelly killed" by Jews. In fact, Lorenzo Virgulti, an eighteenth-century Dominican preacher in Rome, directly referred to Rinaldi's work to justify his preaching against Jews and his discussion of Jewish "hatred of Christians and the Christian religion," poisoning of wells, and infanticides.[67] Some later chronicles, including abridged versions based on Baronio and Rinaldi, included even more stories about Jewish infanticides while omitting any mention of the popes' intervention in defense of the Jews.[68]

Even if Ganganelli may have felt freer, with the death of Pope Benedict XIV, to condemn more explicitly the accusations that Jews killed Christians to obtain their blood for Passover matzah, defending the Jews was not the only goal of his exposition. In fact, his final report was not just a condemnation of the accusations but also a strong affirmation of papal authority in the Church hierarchy, a major issue at the time that was not limited to dealings between Rome and the Polish clergy; it had clearly been on Ganganelli's mind when he wrote his preliminary presentation in 1758. Last but not least, Ganganelli's dissertation also repeatedly affirmed the Church's ultimate hope that Jews would convert to Catholicism, a topic central to Italian anti-Judaic polemic and certainly one actively discussed among Church officials in Poland and in Rome because of the Frankists, and one that was of particular interest to the recently departed Benedict XIV.[69]

In this final report Ganganelli expanded on the arguments both in support of the accusations and against them that he had outlined in March 1758. The purpose of presenting both sides was, the cardinal wrote, "to estimate the probability and credibility of the information ... that has come from Poland concerning the matter under discussion."[70] There were many arguments in support of the accusations—precisely those that the Polish bishops brought to their own defense: "this crime is imputed to the Jews by so many nations, in nearly every period and place (even where they are subjected to strict control)." Moreover, "if it is imputed to them by so many writers with evident proofs, it is possible for everyone to see on what basis of truth the reports [*informazioni*] from Poland on this subject must rest."[71] Ganganelli methodically addressed—one by one—the arguments that supported the accusations. He demonstrated "the unsubstantial character of the authorities cited with regard to the object at issue," championing at the same time the proper hierarchy of the Catholic Church, with the pontiff at its head.

The cardinal reached back in time to the twelfth century, when violence against Jews during the Second Crusade in 1145 was promoted by one "Monk Radulph in Mainz, to repress the audacity of Jews against Christians."[72] Monk Radulph, Ganganelli wrote, "considered it his special duty to preach to the Christian people and excite in them a just resentment against Jews, eager for Christian blood. In fact, the Christians in Mainz, emboldened by the zeal of this monk, were stirred and made a great massacre of the Jews." The chronicler Odorico Rinaldi, Ganganelli continued, also told of "the just resentment of the Princes of Germany and of the King of France in the thirteenth century against the same Jews, who were consequently subjected to corporal and pecuniary punishments." The reason for this was "the same as that for which they have been justly punished in Poland, that is: 'That in the same solemnity [unleavened bread] they make communion with the heart of a slain child ... and have laid their charge the corpse of a dead man.'" But Monk Radulph was condemned by Archbishop Henry of Mainz, who, in turn, informed "the glorious St. Bernard [of Clairvaux]" about Radulph's actions. In his letter responding to the archbishop of Mainz, St. Bernard strongly denounced Radulph and undermined his legitimacy:

> That man of whom you speak in your letter [Brother Radulph] is sent neither by man, nor as man, nor for man, nor yet by God. For if he boasts of being a Monk or a Hermit, and from this takes upon himself the liberty or office of

preaching, he may and ought to know that a Monk has not the office of one who teaches, but of one who laments; for indeed to him a city should be a prison and solitude Paradise. Yet this man on the contrary holds solitude to be a prison and a city Paradise. . . . Truly three things in him are highly blameworthy: "the usurpation of preaching" (with which he stirred up the people to massacre the Jews): "contempt of the Bishops" (who regretted the slaughter of these unhappy people); and "license of approving murder" (by promoting and approving of the extermination of the unfortunates).[73]

Though the letter cited here had been discussed by Richard Simon in the aftermath of the Metz affair in 1670 and was reproduced in Tranquillo Vita Corcos's 1706 treatise in defense of the Jews, Ganganelli used it for slightly different purposes.[74] By citing St. Bernard's letter and interjecting his own comments, Ganganelli sought to put a dent in the argument that if a churchman, such as "monk Radulph," supported and promoted violence against Jews, then this very fact justified such violence and suggested that the Church supported it as well. Wanting to differentiate levels of status within the church hierarchy and make that part of his argument against anti-Jewish violence, Ganganelli thus juxtaposed the questionable monk against some of the highest church figures: a saint and an archbishop.

Pushing the argument further, Ganganelli addressed support for the accusations from some high-profile lay authorities, such as "the King of France and the Princes of Germany." Against them, he presented "a judge whom none can consider suspect"—Innocent IV, "the Supreme Pontiff," who in 1247 issued a strong condemnation of similar anti-Jewish accusations.[75] For Ganganelli there was no question whose authority was the highest. Indeed, no one, the cardinal claimed, could accuse him of relying "on very weak and unsubstantial proofs."[76] And thus because Innocent IV and other popes thereafter condemned accusations against Jews and offered protection to them, their condemnation superseded any secular authority.[77] And when Ganganelli did quote secular rulers, it was only in cases when they "affirmed that in the past the Supreme Pontiffs have forbidden men to believe the accusation of the alleged impious abuse of Christian blood."[78]

True, there were many trials against Jews in many places, as the Polish bishops had pointed out but, Ganganelli stressed, Jews were in fact acquitted in Christian courts and justice was served. In Verona, for example, the "pure love of truth" guided the court. Indeed, there "it was a question of condemning Christian coreligionists and doing justice to Jews."[79] Against these natural "blood-ties," justice was achieved and Jews were acquitted, precisely because the Verona podestà "considered that 'it was forbidden by the Supreme Pontiff to believe in the accusation of the alleged impious abuse of Christian blood.'"

Just as there were many trials resulting in condemnations and acquittals, so too, many books could be found both supporting and refuting the accusations. Ganganelli noted that, although supporters of the accusations pointed to certain Jewish converts who confirmed the charge, one had to consider their character with caution. Here the cardinal may have been alluding to Frankists, but he said nothing about them. Instead, he singled out Giulio Morosini, a seventeenth-century convert, "first a rabbi among his own people, and afterwards a writer among us," and Paolo Sebastiano Medici, "another neophyte, personally known by me," who "put forth various accusations against the Jews." Yet, claims by the two were effectively refuted in print by Jews in Rome.[80] Moreover, the cardinal warned, perhaps alluding again to the Frankists, one had to deal with converts cautiously because "there is wont to occur a certain transport against their own nation, by reason of which they not seldom go beyond the limits of truth."[81]

Still, not all converts were untrustworthy, and those who were more reputable than others had, in fact, refuted claims that Jews needed Christian blood. One such convert was Paul of Burgos, "formerly a Jewish doctor, and afterwards a Catholic and raised to the Bishopric of Burgos," Ganganelli wrote following Corcos's treatise.[82] Paul of Burgos saw anti-Jewish accusations as one of the chief reasons preventing Jews from accepting Christianity, "for they think that we invent lies against them, which presents no small obstacle in our making them believe us." Ganganelli also mentioned Nicolas of Lyra, "of my Order," and Ludwig von Sonnenfels of the University of Vienna among trustworthy "neophytes." (He mistakenly included in this category also Leone Modena, perhaps because of Modena's publications in Italian.) These three examples once again affirmed the authority of the Church: Paul of Burgos was a bishop; Nicolas of Lyra, a Franciscan friar; and Ludwig von Sonnenfels, a professor of a university whose Catholic orthodoxy could not be questioned.

Having ascertained that all reputable authorities denied accusations that Jews killed Christian children, Ganganelli was left with two cases that seemed to undermine his argument—those of Simon of Trent and of Andreas of Rinn, both of which seem to have had an impact on the rise of anti-Jewish accusations in Poland and both of which were sanctioned by popes. Ganganelli was thus forced to admit "as true the fact of the Blessed Simon, a boy three years old, killed by the Jews in Trent in the year 1475 in hatred of the faith of Jesus Christ" and "the truth of another fact, which happened in the year 1462 in the village of Rinn, in the diocese of Brixen, in the person of the Blessed Andreas, a boy barbarously murdered by the Jews in hatred of the faith in Jesus Christ." The two cases, however, were not automatically accepted, the cardinal argued. They were "proven by authentic proofs after much diligent search and considerable lapse of time."[83] (This could not be said about the trials in Poland.) The cardinal continued, "It should then be concluded that, among so many infanticides in hatred of our Holy Faith imputed by writers to the Jews, only two can be said to be true."[84] Still, even after "admitting the truth of the two facts in Brixen and in Trent" one could not contend that they applied to the whole "Jewish nation." These were but "two isolated events." Indeed, the cardinal dismissed other cases of alleged child victims of the Jews included by the Bollandists in their *Acta Sanctorum*. All these cases, Ganganelli stated, citing the bull *Beatus Andreas*, were not "beatified by the Holy See . . . and much less can they be canonized, no suit having been formed, or sent to Rome to the Roman Pontiff in order that he might approve it."[85]

The cases of Simon of Trent and Andreas of Rinn allowed Ganganelli to establish the channels of transmission of papal authority that linked the two cases. Both boys bore the title *beatus* or blessed, and their cults were officially sanctioned by the pontiffs, if not immediately. In Simon's case, Pope Sixtus IV had serious objections to the Trent trial and the emerging cult. He, in fact, "forbade the devotion that was paid to the aforesaid Blessed Simon." It took more than a hundred years before Pope Sixtus V "conceded the Office and Proper Mass in honor of the Blessed Simon, adding to these a Plenary Indulgence to any person who, having confessed and communicated, visited on his feast [March 24] the church in which his relics are to be found."[86] Sixtus IV's *breve*, Ganganelli noted, was cited "in the immortal work *On the Canonization of Saints* by Benedict XIV of glorious memory," whereas Sixtus V's work was mentioned in Bonelli's *Apologetic Dissertation*. Benedict XIV in turn in December 1752 granted the diocese of Brixen the "Office and the Mass" for Andreas of Rinn, in January 1753 the plenary indulgence similar to that conceded to Simon of Trent, and finally and crucially, in February 1755, he issued the bull *Beatus Andreas*. (*Beatus Andreas* remains one of the most powerful affirmations of anti-Jewish accusations ever issued by a prominent Church leader, one that would have strong reverberations for the subsequent defense of Jews.[87])

Given the stature of Benedict XIV as a pope and canon lawyer, and the fact that he had addressed the issue of child victims so recently, Ganganelli could not have ignored either Simon or Andreas. But the way Ganganelli handled these papal endorsements of cults of alleged child victims allowed him to condemn anti-Jewish accusations coming out of Poland without undermining papal authority, indeed affirming it. Earlier papal condemnations of accusations that Jews killed Christian children to obtain their blood were not at all contradicted by Sixtus V and Benedict XIV—the cases they sanctioned were murders "in hatred of the faith," not "blood accusations." This distinction allowed Ganganelli to remain consistent in his argument. The popes did indeed clear Jews of the latter accusation, but as the cases of Simon and Andreas showed, the popes allowed the possibility of the former. Yet Ganganelli's claim was not quite forthright. True, Benedict XIV referred to both cases as killings "in hatred of Christian faith," but blood was an important motif in the story of Simon of Trent, if less so in the case of Andreas of Rinn.

The last papal condemnation of blood accusations against Jews was issued in 1540 by Pope Paul III and then soon forgotten.[88] After that, given Rome's refusal to renew it or to issue a new one, Jews had to resort to invoking either centuries-old papal decrees in their defense or statements by lesser church figures. Although Ganganelli noted that other church officials also intervened on Jews' behalf, as if to underscore the broad scope of the defense of Jews, he neglected to mention the real reason why Jews had to turn to them. On behalf of Jews in Poland, Ganganelli wrote—again drawing on the material provided decades earlier by Tranquillo Vita Corcos—there also intervened "the most reverend father Giovanni Battista de' Marini, General of the Order of Preaching Fathers [Dominicans]," who "moved by pity by the Jews of Poland ... wrote on February 9, 1664, a very urgent letter to Father Alan Choroduski, the provincial of Poland, in which he instructed his friars in that Kingdom to preach from the pulpit and persuade the people to abandon the baleful belief" they held against Jews. Violence against Jews was not justified, de' Marini wrote. Christians should instead display "piety and gentleness ... to them also, when they are oppressed by injury." Ill treatment of Jews was offensive to God, the general asserted. "Let the Jews find out in this matter that we desire not their destruction but their salvation."[89] That last sentence reflected broader Church ideas about Jews and gave Ganganelli one more occasion to affirm them. "Such also were the sentiments," the cardinal wrote, "of St. Bernard against Brother Radulph, and the oracles of Gregory IX and Innocent IV against the Princes of Germany and France."

If the medieval principle of *favor fidei* justified situations that according to existing laws appeared illegal but advanced the faith, here the situation was exactly the opposite. Such "illicit hatreds, false accusations, abuses, contumelies" were "an offense to our God" and caused much "injury to divine honor," because they prevented Jews from converting to Catholicism.[90] This was why Ganganelli hoped that "the Holy See would take some measure on behalf of Jews in Poland, as did St. Bernard, Gregory IX and Innocent IV for the Jews of Germany and France, 'so that the name of Christ may not be blasphemed' by Jews, and their conversion may not become more difficult."[91] Ganganelli here was harkening back to the medieval Church tradition of condemning anti-Jewish violence on the grounds that it discouraged the Jews from converting. By returning to that medieval tradition, he implicitly moved away from the policy of oppressing Jews "so that Jews may convert" that had dominated the Church since the pontificate of Pope Paul IV.[92] As methodical and powerful as Ganganelli's report was in condemning the specific accusations coming from Poland, in the end it largely affirmed medieval policies of the pontiffs regarding anti-Jewish accusations and, by doing so, also reinforced the centuries-old hope that Jews would convert to Christianity.

But Ganganelli stopped short of making specific recommendations of how to address the Polish trials. He simply examined the background of the accusations and the Church's responses to them in the hope that "Jesus Christ will suggest to his Vicar such means as shall be honorable to the Christian name and conducive to the conversion of those unhappy ones." The Holy Office approved the report on December 24, 1759, and then passed it on to Pope Clement XIII on January 10, 1760. It decided that the papal nuncio in Poland was to be briefed about the outcome of Ganganelli's investigation, but that no formal condemnation was to be issued by the pope. This must not have been what Jacob Eliyakim Zelig and the Polish Jews who sent him to Rome had hoped for, certainly not in the context of the Jacob Frank affair that resulted in conversions to Catholicism of hundreds of his followers. Polish Jews had hoped that the pontiff would either condemn accusations against them outright in a new declaration or at least reissue the centuries-old papal bulls to the same effect.

Jews were not even notified about the full report. In fact, the Ganganelli report was not meant as an official response of the Holy See. Written in Italian, it was an internal document for the Congregation of the Holy Office of the Inquisition. When the popes or other members of Catholic hierarchy wanted to publicize matters broadly, they issued documents in Latin (if destined outside of the Italian peninsula) and had them printed by the official printing house. A printed copy of such document would then be dispatched to a nuncio so it could be, in turn, printed and disseminated locally.[93] Documents intended to be read in the Italian peninsula were generally written in Italian, but were still published by the official pontifical printing house.[94] The Ganganelli report was never committed to print. The secrecy surrounding this report underscores the importance of the permission to publish in the Vatican's official printing house the writings by Tranquillo Vita Corcos during the Viterbo affair of 1705–1706.[95] But in the case of the Ganganelli report, the Church officials clearly did not want to make it known. Jews likely never received a copy at the time.[96]

Still, Jews were not ignored completely, though they may not have been fully aware of the outcome of the mission to Rome. According to the decree from the Holy Office signed by Assessor Benedetto Veterani, the papal nuncio in Warsaw was ordered to "take care according to his wisdom and zeal that in other similar cases no harm shall be brought upon the Hebrew nation."[97] If necessary, he should also work with secular and ecclesiastical judges. But Jacob Eliyakim Zelig was not to be informed in detail about the report. Indeed, "all this was to be minimally communicated to Jews."[98] The Congregation agreed that only letters from the Holy Office "addressed to the [current] Apostolic Nuncio were to be given to [the Jews'] delegate who is staying in the City."

On that very same date when the report was presented to Pope Clement XIII, January 10, 1760, a draft of the letter from the Holy Office to be given "open" to Jacob Eliyakim Zelig and intended for the nuncio in Warsaw was prepared. The nuncio was "expressly ordered" by the pontiff to help Zelig, who had come to Rome to "implore [the] Holy See most humbly" for protection from these "intolerable hardships." He was to offer any assistance to Zelig so he "may not suffer any oppression and harassment" by those who might be upset on account of his appeal to Rome.[99] The letter had then to make its way through the Vatican bureaucracy. It was finally signed by the young cardinal Andrea Corsini on February 9, 1760, to be sent to Warsaw with the Jewish emissary.[100]

Meanwhile, the newly appointed papal nuncio to Poland, Bishop Antonio Eugenio Visconti, was readying for his trip to assume his post, which was set to begin on February 22, 1760.[101] Just before his departure, Cardinal Lorenzo Ganganelli paid him a visit to wish him "happy travels."[102] Visconti was not present, so a note was left for him that Ganganelli wanted to "hand over some documents concerning the decided case of Jews in that Kingdom." Among the documents was perhaps a manuscript copy of Ganganelli's report, though it is not clear if the nuncio did in fact receive a copy.

As Visconti was leaving Rome for Poland, Jacob Eliyakim Zelig was still in the Eternal City. On May 23, 1760, Zelig received a letter from none other than Cardinal Ganganelli who warmly recommended Zelig to the nuncio. "After having been held in Rome for a long time to conduct to the end a most important business," Ganganelli wrote, "the Polish Jew Jacob Zelig, returning to his country will have the honor of presenting to you this letter of mine to beseech through me Your Illustrious Lordship [to offer] forceful aid [*valevole padrocinio*] in situations when he may need to reach out to you."[103] Ganganelli reiterated that the favorable report of the Holy

Office had been accepted by "His Holiness" himself and emphasized that this should give more weight to the cardinal's recommendation and should create a "new willingness" on the part of the nuncio to "accommodate my efforts on behalf of the person and the needs of the said Zelig."

Jacob Eliyakim Zelig left Rome not having achieved his ultimate goal. Certainly, his mission to Rome bore fruit, but it did not result in what the Jews had for decades been trying to achieve: "an official papal pronouncement on the blood libel."[104] On this the Holy See had stalled since at least the 1740s, when Jews began asking for such a document in the aftermath of the Poznań trial in 1736–1739, and possibly ever since the seventeenth century when, in the absence of papal condemnations, Jews resorted to obtaining letters from other church officials, like that from the general of the Dominicans issued in 1664.[105]

On his return to Poland, Zelig met with Nuncio Visconti, no doubt hoping for a forceful response in accord with Ganganelli's letter. But with Ganganelli's treatise kept private and the decision by the Holy Office not to issue official pronouncements, the nuncio had little room for a public declaration. What Visconti could do was work behind the scenes when the need arose. And in the absence of a forceful refutation of the anti-Jewish charges, such occasions did arise very soon, testing the power of behind-the-scenes interventions in the absence of public statements.

CHAPTER TEN

Calculated Pragmatism and the Waning of Accusations

THE LETTERS of recommendation that Jacob Eliyakim Zelig received in Rome in 1760 and the behind-the-scenes efforts by Cardinal Lorenzo Ganganelli and others were not exactly what the Jews hoped to achieve, at such great expense, in Rome. Still these measures surely had an effect, albeit at times rather delayed and not strong enough to prevent future accusations, which sometimes were openly supported by the Polish Catholic clergy. Not all the trials were deadly, but those with violent consequences continued into the late years of the Polish state, forcing Jews to employ ruses to achieve what officially they could not—a public condemnation of the charges. The trials did eventually wane at the time of civil war and the first partitions of Poland, but their end was more a result of political circumstances and legal reforms in the collapsing country than of the efficacy of Church interventions.

Soon after Zelig returned from Rome, the effectiveness of his expensive mission was tested again. In January 1761, Jews in the small village of Józefów sued a Christian man, Franciszek Rozmarynowski, for falsely accusing them of buying an infant from a vagabond Christian woman, Catharina Jakóbowa Woyciechowska.[1] In this case Jews were found innocent not because of anyone's intervention, but simply because the child was found alive and well in another village; apparently the mother had left it behind after she became drunk. The court fined Rozmarynowski for making the false accusation against Jews and ordered him to make donations of tallow to local churches and to repay the court expenses that the Jews had incurred as a result of the libel. But Jews were not satisfied with the court decree. By suing the Christian man they wanted him criminally charged for false accusations and punished in accordance with the law, which in some instances mandated death for false accusations.[2] Given the gravity of the accusation against Jews and its potential consequences, the sentence Rozmarynowski received was too mild. The Jews decided to appeal the verdict, but the outcome of their appeal remains unknown.

But it was the trial of Wojsławice in the diocese of Chełm that stirred up the country again.[3] On March 27, 1761, five days after Easter, the body of an infant boy named Nicolas was found with multiple wounds. Right away Jews were suspected of murdering him. Many were arrested, and five were formally charged and imprisoned, among them the local rabbi and prominent community officials. They were kept in isolation, except for visits from clergy, especially the Jesuits, who sought their conversion. Because one of the arrested was said to know how to read Polish, he was given Catholic books and "read [them] daily." Still these efforts bore no fruit until the prisoners were subjected to torture, during which they confessed to this and many other crimes and "softened," with two of the imprisoned men promising to convert. But when they heard that despite their willingness to convert, they would be still be sentenced to death by quartering, they wavered until the Jesuits warned them of eternal damnation and encouraged them to be steadfast in their earlier decision. They were to receive baptism at the site of execution, a ploy to make their conversion and baptism a public event witnessed by "some thousands of people." Still, according to a pamphlet published in Polish narrating the affair, two Jews remained "obstinate" in Judaism, staunchly refusing to convert, while the rabbi hanged himself in prison.

In June, the four prisoners were taken to the place of execution. When they arrived, the two potential converts, accompanied by the Jesuits, received some "good news": after accepting baptism, they would be decapitated instead of quartered alive. After the converts' baptism and execution by sword, the clergy turned to the two "obstinate" Jews. Having witnessed the swift death of the first two, one also accepted baptism. The other, "elderly" and "obstinate," seemed "unmoved." But priests continued to try to convert him, even if their efforts seemed to "have hit a deaf rock." The elderly Jew let himself be taken by the executioner, screaming, "Take me." When he was stretched on the board in preparation for quartering, and everybody fell to their knees and began to pray, one priest called out, "God of Abraham, God of Isaac, God of Jacob, have mercy on me, and in your goodness, give me light!" Hearing these words, "the guilty man looked at the sky, and asked to be lifted" from the board, whereupon he accepted baptism. Then he, too, was decapitated. After this public ceremony, the four bodies, placed in coffins, were taken to a small church where they lay until morning. On the bishop's orders, they were then taken in a solemn procession to the cathedral church, where funeral services were held. Finally their bodies were transported to the Jesuit church, where funeral rites were performed, and they were buried in the presence of the bishop. In the meantime, "the abominable body of the rabbi," who had committed suicide in prison, was dragged through the city and then burned at the stake, "his ashes cast into the wind," while the Jewish community of Wojsławice was ordered to pay fines, including reparations to the parents of the dead child.

The Wojsławice affair embodied exactly what Ganganelli condemned: it terrorized and persecuted Jews in order to convert them. But Polish Jewish leaders blamed the Wojsławice affair on the publication, *Złość żydowska* (Jewish Malice), by the Bernardine theologian Gaudenty Pikulski, which recounted the Frankist affair and ambivalently though sympathetically described the "Counter-Talmudists" while vilifying rabbinic Jews.[4] After the book was published, Jewish leaders mobilized once more, writing a damning letter to the nuncio about the impact of the book.[5] They argued that it presented Jews as "ungodly beasts" who were "worse than tigers." They defended their religion and their lives as decent hardworking human beings who supported their brethren in need. The book, they stressed, was contemptuous of the Jewish faith and harmful not only because of its words but also because it was printed and disseminated. Pikulski's opus was a product of vanity, a money-making endeavor, defying the vow against "pride, vain glory, envy, greed, . . . aspersion, and gossip" that its author as a monk must have taken.

Pikulski's work was indeed a massive—more than 800 pages long—compendium of information about Jewish religious texts and customs, and as Paweł Maciejko has noted, it was "the most comprehensive Christian account of early Frankism."[6] To be sure the book was definitely hostile to Jews, but it was not always inaccurate. In fact, it was written at a much more sophisticated level than any other work touching on Jewish ritual and custom published in Poland until that time, much more than the small anonymous book, *Błędy Talmutowe* (The Errors of the Talmud), issued not long before Pikulski's work.[7] *Błędy Talmutowe* was either an earlier version of Pikulski's work or at the very least served as a source for significant portions of it. But though some passages were quoted verbatim and others paraphrased in it, Pikulski's 1760 work elaborated on Jewish texts and gave Jews a voice, even if it was to be discounted and ridiculed.[8]

Where Gaudenty Pikulski did not differ from his predecessors was in his fixation on host desecrations and blood accusations, for which he offered detailed descriptions and which he placed squarely on the Jewish religious calendar.[9] Pikulski used Hebrew verses and cited Hebrew sources to the point that he was deemed expert in Hebrew, which compelled him to deny it in his introduction to the reader, as if knowledge of Hebrew were something shameful. No doubt some of the information Pikulski included had been fed to him by the "Counter-Talmudists," but some was the fruit of his own research in printed books by Christian authors. Pikulski's book was more dangerous than others precisely because it appeared to be and, to some extent, was indeed so well informed.

The impact of printing was felt elsewhere as well. A pamphlet, *Processus judiciarius*, containing court decrees of the Wojsławice affair was also printed and disseminated in 1761.[10] Although mostly in Latin, it contained a detailed description in Polish of the wounds on the child's body along with a "short description" summarizing the trial and the execution of the Jews. Copies, with the Polish sections translated into Latin, were forwarded to Rome to the Secretary of State and the Holy Office of the Inquisition. The Wojsławice documents would later be included, along with Kajetan Sołtyk's letter written in the aftermath of the Żytomierz trial and several court decrees related to recent trials of Jews accused of murdering Christian children, in a booklet with the same title as Pikulski's massive work, *Złość żydowska*. Republished in 1774, the second expanded edition of this booklet coincided with one of the last trials of the Jews, in Grabie.[11]

The Wojsławice affair was, as many scholars have noted, linked to the Frankists, living in that town under the protection of the noblewoman Katarzyna Kossakowska of the Potocki family.[12] That much could be inferred from the lengthy report printed in Latin that alluded to "*pseudodogmata* called the Talmud (*Talmuty*)." More explicitly this connection with Frankism was noted in a summary of the interrogation of Szloma Pliskowski, one of the implicated Jews, who alleged that Moszko, the Jew who read Catholic books in prison, would often invite "Counter-Talmudists" to debate with them in the presence of Jesuits, thus revealing a longer relationship with the Catholic clergy.[13] Jewish leaders of the Council of Four Lands also mentioned the "Counter-Talmudists" in their supplication to papal nuncio Antonio Visconti sent within days of the trial, in which they again protested the accusations and reiterated that Jews did not need "Catholic blood" as the "Counter-Talmudists" falsely claimed "in the town named

Wojsławice, [owned by] Lord Potocki, the castellan of Słońsk, in whose estate a child of one of his men disappeared."[14] It is perhaps precisely because of the link with the Frankists that the trial received so much attention from both Jews and Church officials.

Nuncio Visconti responded immediately to the Jews' supplication. On April 5, 1761, a week or so after the accusations were first hurled at the Jews of Wojsławice, the nuncio wrote to Feliks Wincenty Potocki, owner of the town, drafting the text of his letter in Italian on the very letter the Jewish leaders had sent him.[15] Visconti's letter was then translated into French and sent to Potocki.[16] "I find myself obliged," Visconti wrote, "by my position and by the charge received from Rome on this matter to inform Your Excellency that after a recent examination by the Holy See [of] all the foundations on which is based the opinion that Jews need human blood to make their unleavened bread, and that because of that they are guilty of killing Christian children, it has been established that there are no proofs sufficiently clear and certain that would be enough to validate" such accusations, and declare them guilty of such crimes. "Therefore," the nuncio continued, "I beg Your Excellency" not to base his judgment on these opinions, "but rather on legal proofs that would establish for sure the crime imputed to them."

Four days later, on April 9, 1761, Visconti apprised Cardinal Corsini, the prefect of the Holy Office in Rome, on the situation in Poland.[17] He began by pedantically recapping that the decree of the Holy Office from January 10, 1760, "regarding the appeal made by Jews of Poland to the Holy See regarding the harm they receive from Christians as perpetrators of homicide based on the belief that they mix human blood, particularly Christian, in their unleavened bread" had been communicated to him before his departure from Rome. After that, when he moved to Warsaw, the Jewish emissary Jacob Eliyakim Zelig presented him a letter from Corsini himself, dated February 9, 1760, specifically requesting that Visconti offer assistance to Zelig. The nuncio obeyed the directives, furnishing Zelig with several letters of recommendation "to the Grand Treasurer of Poland [Karol Józef Sedlnicki at the time], and other prominent persons." But when it came to the "principal point" of the common belief that Jews used Christian blood in their matzah, the nuncio could do no more than only attempt to persuade both secular and ecclesiastical judges not to "permit any harm to the Jewish Nation by condemning them without valid foundations." In fact, recently, the nuncio wrote, one of the prominent noblemen in Poland, Feliks Wincenty Potocki, the castellan of Słońsk, "imprisoned seven Jews" [sic] because of a disappearance of a child in his village. The nobleman threatened "to make them die if he did not obtain from me a proof [*attestato*] that the Holy See had deemed false the common belief in their crime." But because the Ganganelli report was to remain private, the nuncio felt he "could not grant such a proof" and so he decided to write a letter to Potocki himself. The nuncio included the final text in Italian with his dispatch to Corsini. "I do not know what effect my letter will have," the nuncio confessed, "since I have not yet received a response." But he expected that "each year, around the time when Jews celebrate Passover I will find myself in similar circumstances," having to "save the lives and property of these [Jews] always accused of this crime." Visconti then asked Corsini to present his response to the Congregation of the Holy Office for approval and give him further guidance whether he should stick to this form of intervention or instead present "something more forceful." He concluded the letter with an update on Jacob Frank, imprisoned at the time, and his followers.

Nuncio Visconti also wrote to Bishop Walenty Wężyk of Chełm, in whose diocese the village of Wojsławice was located. Although the original letter seems lost, on April 30 that year, Visconti wrote a second, rather apologetic yet assertive letter defending his efforts to protect Jews.[18] He did not send the first letter to cast doubt on the judgment of the courts, even less did he demand the Jews should be released if they were found guilty. "On the contrary," the nuncio desired that "they be severely punished according to the laws" if they indeed had committed such an act. "All I desired was that one proceed against them according to legal proofs, and solid foundations, and not according to the opinion that may be false and [based] on the accusations that may have been calumnies against Jews from another region."

In the meantime, the nuncio's report of April 9 to the Holy Office reached its destination, and on May 6, 1761, the Congregation of the Holy Office discussed the dispatch. Ten days later, they sent their response, in which they commended the nuncio profusely for his efforts to save Jews from harm done to them by "Christians of this Kingdom," who most tenaciously held "the opinion that [Jews] collected human blood for their unleavened bread."[19] Visconti was also commended for the "spirit" of his "decrees." Addressing the second point of the nuncio's letter—the arrest and trial of Jacob Frank in "a secular court"—the Holy Office noted that if the case were to come to Rome, the matter would be given the necessary consideration. In the meantime, the Congregation stressed, Frank should not be released from prison; in fact, he should be kept in "strict custody," so that "no one should have contact with him; not even any letters should be passed between him and the neophytes."

By the end of June, the Wojsławice trial was over, the Jews executed. On July 7, Nuncio Visconti wrote another letter to Bishop Wężyk, once more reiterating that his initial intervention was not to "protect the Jews if they were found guilty based on legal proofs."[20] Indeed, he had desired that they should be "severely punished according to the law if they committed such a crime." And it is "with the same sentiments" that the nuncio was writing again, this time understanding that the Jews had already been executed. Now, however, Visconti demanded the bishop "kindly" provide "all the grounds" used "to arrive to this execution," so that according to "his duties," the nuncio could "instruct the Holy See on this point." After all, the Holy See had given him "precise instructions" to do what he could to prevent harm done to the Jews on the basis of the belief that they "needed human blood to make their unleavened bread." Not only did Visconti demand details of what led to the execution but he also wanted the bishop to provide information that innocent people were not "confused with the guilty." Because the Congregation of the Holy Inquisition in Rome found no proof sufficient to support the prejudice against Jews, "it is up to you as bishop," Visconti wrote, "to use all means in your diocese so that these poor Jews are not persecuted." And if they were indeed found guilty, it was important to know whether there was enough legal evidence to support such a verdict or if, under torture, they admitted to a crime they had not committed. "Sir," Visconti added, "we need to prevent such injustice as much as we can." The nuncio closed on an angry note—"I will be sorry to be obliged to write to Rome that I could not succeed on account of people who could help me but did not want to"—and expressed his hope that the bishop would offer his assistance so he could fulfill "the orders of the Holy See." That same day, Visconti also wrote to Janusz Aleksander Sanguszko, the court marshal of Lithuania, beseeching him to use his authority to prevent judgments based on anything other than "legal proofs."[21] But the letter to Sanguszko may have been related not to the Wojsławice affair but to a new accusation that had just been made in June in the town of Bazalia (Bazylia in the text) in the diocese of Łuck: there, several Jews were accused of murdering a young Christian woman (*virginem*) and incarcerated, resulting in another Jewish intervention with the nuncio and a supplication to intercede with the bishop of Łuck.[22]

The anti-Jewish accusations and the Frank affair, along with matters of the status of converts that interested the Holy Office, did take up a lot of the nuncio's energy.[23] But they were not the only issues the nuncio had to work on. Many dispatches from that period report on the conflict between Russia and Prussia during the Seven Years' War and other matters concerning international politics, as well as on matters relating to the "immunity of church land" from taxation and to other religious groups, such as "the heretics" or Protestants, whose power seemed to be increasing, and

Eastern Orthodox Christians.[24] In fact, two weeks after writing his angry letter to Bishop Wężyk, Visconti wrote again, this time about "the Greeks."[25] "After so many letters regarding Jews," the bishop now needed "exact and very secret information about the conduct of Monsignor Philip Felician Wolodkowicz, the bishop of Wladimir." Still, despite so many other issues, those related to Jews did not go away.

On August 25, 1762, Nuncio Visconti wrote once more directly to Cardinal Corsini, sending him a lengthy, detailed letter describing his futile attempts to save the Jews. Although the nuncio had obeyed the orders of the Holy Office to do what he could to save Jewish lives and property, his efforts did not always bring the desired results.[26] First, his letters "were not always sufficient to save the miserable Jews from death." Second, there were still "in this Kingdom so many clergy and laymen" who accepted the validity of the accusation that Jews killed Christian children and that Jewish law "obligated them to do it."[27] Third, there were indeed "many documents here in Poland that seem to excuse them from this great crime." Finally, the Jews, knowing well of the nuncio's efforts on their behalf to spare them from "the most haughty persecution," had again petitioned him to "obtain an authentic certificate" from his office that could be officially submitted in a secular court (*grod*) or other public office to stronger effect. Visconti then went on to elaborate on each point.

Wojsławice was the example *par excellence* of the inefficacy of the nuncio's earnest behind-the-scenes efforts. After he wrote to Count Potocki and the bishop of Chełm, both responded in a spirit affirming, as Potocki put it, "that in such an affair one would have proceeded with judicial and legal proofs."[28] Bishop Wężyk even referred to past cases tried before the Crown Tribunal as evidence. In fact, the nuncio wrote, "They sent me, though long after the fact, printed text of the trial, which I have the honor to forward to Your Eminence."[29] Like the papal envoy during the Trent trial in 1475, the nuncio was not satisfied with the version of trial records offered; he "would have wanted to have in hand transcripts of the interrogations of the Jews to see on what basis they were convicted." But despite "all the diligence" to obtain them, he never got those transcripts. In fact, he was told that "such interrogations are not preserved in Poland, but they are burned as soon as a trial is finished." This, of course, was not true. The nuncio seems to have been duped. The decree from Wojsławice explicitly stated that the texts of the confessions and interrogations were sealed and given to the prosecution.[30] Many courts in Poland did retain at least summaries of the interrogations. But they would not have met the legal standards adhered to in the Italian courts. Moreover, courts in the Polish-Lithuanian Commonwealth did not have established procedures for archiving the documents, especially in criminal cases. This, too, was in stark contrast with the judicial practices on the Italian peninsula. Concerned with *buon governo,* courts on the peninsula preserved their records for future reference to assure "equity and good procedure." After all, good procedures depended on good records.[31] Visconti's comment reveals his expectations of what documentation should have been preserved in a criminal trial and underscores the differences in legal cultures between Poland and Italy.

As for the second point in his letter of August 25, 1762—that clergy and laypersons accepted anti-Jewish accusations—Visconti's explanation shows not just the pernicious nature of the Frankist claims but also the impact of Benedict XIV's 1755 bull *Beatus Andreas.* Not only were the bishops of Chełm and Łuck asserting that Jews were guilty of "this crime," the nuncio wrote, but also other persons of "first rank" wanted to persuade him that "truly the Jewish nation is guilty of this offense," because Jews were many times convicted in Poland of such murders.[32] Visconti pushed back: "Immediately, I said that in the Talmud there is no law that obliges them to seek Christian blood." But "they responded that there were some fourteen [versions] of the Talmud in the Kingdom," and "moreover, even if no Talmud made mention of it, it would be necessary to know how this was commented upon by the rabbis." "They cite," the nuncio reported, "the seventh article of the converted anti-Talmudists, which I attach here." Finally, "they say that even if one could not prove the use of Christian blood in the unleavened bread, still it could be certain that the Jews killed Christian children either because of hatred, or another motive. That was believed by most worthy authors, and it was once more noted by the Bull of Benedict XIV from February 22, 1755, about the canonization of children killed in hatred of Christ." That the nuncio's interlocutors had referred to *Beatus Andreas* demonstrates that the bull was known in Poland and understood to apply broadly, not just to Andreas of Rinn. That fact did not escape the nuncio either. "This, I did not ignore," he declared.

As for point number three regarding documents favorable to Jews, Visconti reported that Jews had brought him "a decree from Sigismund August, the King of Poland, from 1557, in which he ordered that [Jews] accused of murdering children or stealing the most holy Eucharist" were to be judged by the king alone in order to prevent "injustice committed by private judges who condemned [Jews] based on the opinion that [Jews'] laws forced them to obtain blood of Christians and the most holy Eucharist, even though it is opposed by the statutes and decrees of Pope Innocent that say that one should proceed with caution in accusing the Jewish nation of this grave crime." Moreover, "to validate this prohibition" Jews also "cited a bull granted by Paul III to the Jewish nation on May 12, 1540."

In addition to these efforts, Nuncio Visconti seems to have truly wanted to understand the level of support for the accusations against Jews in Poland, including "the sentiment of the most learned and enlightened persons in this State."[33] He thus approached Piotr Hiacynt Śliwicki, father superior of the brothers of the Congregation of the Mission. Śliwicki pleased the nuncio by passing on "the opinion of Lord L'advocat, the librarian and professor of Hebrew language at the Sorbonne," a copy of which the nuncio decided to include "again" in his dispatch to the prefect.[34]

The opinion of Jean-Baptiste de Ladvocat had been solicited to examine the claims made by the "counter-Talmudists" about the requirement for Christian blood they alleged was found in the Talmud.[35] The extensive report from the Sorbonne arrived in Poland in March 1760, a few months after Ganganelli finished his own text; it fully refuted the allegations, denying any trace of such teachings in Jewish texts. Ladvocat explained, "It was true that in the centuries of ignorance, and until today, one has frequently mounted such horrible accusations against Jews, both rabbinic and Karaite, without distinction."[36] In fact Christians who knew the Hebrew language and the Talmud could not find anything of which "the Karaites," he wrote referring thus to the Frankist "contra-Talmudists," accused the Jews. "No evident proof of the bloody maxim is there." In fact, "the Karaite Jews proved nothing regarding this allegation." Ladvocat's lengthy report was perhaps the most detailed and unequivocal rebuttal and condemnation of the "barbaric" accusations against Jews, its tone and content far stronger than that of the Ganganelli report. But that may have been because Ladvocat was answering a simple academic question; he was not charged with advising on policy and dealing with delicate political realities and past papal decrees, as Ganganelli had to.

Visconti's last point about Jewish supplications for a formal public pronouncement on their behalf touched on a delicate matter. Because the pontiff and the Holy Office had refused to issue a statement or a new bull, or even renew an old one condemning accusations against Jews, the nuncio's hands were tied, his intervention limited to behind-the-scenes operations. As a result, his efforts were, as the nuncio himself pointed out, rather ineffective: Jews continued to be accused and continued to appeal to him seeking to obtain a firmer declaration "that there were no laws among [Jews] that forced them to use blood of Christian children for the unleavened bread." But because Jews understood that the nuncio was not willing to "go beyond the limits" of what he was commanded to do from Rome, they turned to the Royal Court and its main ministers to obtain something more official. Given the situation, Visconti once more asked whether the Roman Curia would provide a firmer public statement.

On September 20, 1762, the Holy Office discussed the nuncio's lengthy letter and decided to uphold the decisions previously made by the Congregation on January 10, 1760, and on May 16, 1761, mandating the nuncio to intervene on behalf of Jews, but only—as he had done so far—behind the scenes by reaching out to local lay and ecclesiastical officials. The Holy Office voted on the measure two days later.[37] Three days after the vote, Cardinal Corsini drafted a response on behalf of the Holy Office.[38] He noted that the nuncio's long letter was read both by Pope Clement XIII and the Congregation of the Holy Office. It was clear from the attached documents that the belief that Jews committed these crimes was "so deeply rooted in that Kingdom, it was not easy to eradicate." This was not only because of the false conviction that Jews used Christian blood but also because of the notion they did so on account of "eternal hatred that the Jewish perfidy holds for the Christian name." The fact that the nuncio was unable to obtain copies of the interrogations of Jews "gives reason to fear" that Jews were often unjustly "oppressed." But Visconti was right to acknowledge that "the Holy See did not want to, nor could, define anything; therefore, His Holiness, along [with] the Holy Congregation, has strongly recommended that in anticipation of future news [about anti-Jewish libels] you should remain firm and unfailing in rejecting appeals for the noted decree." Indeed, Visconti should apply "the same method" he had done thus far in making sure that "no penalty is imposed on these miserable [Jews], let alone capital punishment, unless there are clear, convincing proofs of the crime that exclude any possible doubt."

The letter from Corsini is probably the most explicit articulation of Rome's unwillingness to intervene openly in anti-Jewish accusations. Thus, if the fact that Ganganelli report was never translated into Latin and published with an imprimatur of the Holy See might have been only circumstantial evidence of this reluctance, Corsini left no doubt that this issue had to be threaded on gently. In a country like the Polish-Lithuanian Commonwealth where accusations had the effect of rallying popular support for the Church, especially in religiously mixed areas with large numbers of Jews, the political costs of defending the Jews openly would have been too high. Moreover, how could the papacy condemn such accusations against Jews so soon after Benedict XIV allowed for the possibility that Jews had indeed killed Christian children "in hatred of Christ and his followers"? Benedict's legacy had an enduring effect. And so, by choosing to limit their intervention to behind the scenes, Church authorities believed they were acting both for "the good of the Church" and against the disturbing accusations that Jews killed Christian children for blood. This balance was unsatisfying and ineffective but very much in the spirit of Ganganelli's report, condemning the accusations but simultaneously affirming Church hierarchy and structure.

Making the Condemnations Public

It is possible that after receiving Corsini's response, Nuncio Visconti informed the Jews that there would be no official statement from the Church. But it is clear even from Visconti's letter to the Holy Office that Jews must have already felt frustrated by the futility of his restrained interventions. They understood that, to be effective, a condemnation of accusations against them had to be public, which is why they turned not only to the royal court and its ministers but eventually also to print.

Although the Jews seem to have reached out to the royal court already in 1761, apparently passing on to Count Heinrich von Brühl a copy of the letter Jacob Eliyakim Zelig had received from Cardinal Corsini in 1760, they must have doubled their efforts in late 1762 and 1763. In March 1763, Count von Brühl wrote to the nuncio asking for information about the Holy See's position on the accusation—evidence that he was unaware of the existence of the Ganganelli report.[39] Von Brühl acknowledged knowing about the Jews' "recourse to the Holy See to seek protection against persecution they suffer over the supposed crime in relation to Christian blood." Jews also turned for protection to the king, but before acting on their behalf he asked to know "the intentions of His Holiness in this matter." Von Brühl had established relationships with some prominent members of the Jewish community. For example, Barukh Mi-Erez Yavan had "carried out a number of secret missions on behalf of von Brühl and the king."[40] Von Brühl, therefore, might have been behind some of the Jewish efforts to obtain from the papal representative in Warsaw a more explicit condemnation of accusations against them.

Visconti's response to von Brühl followed instructions he had received from Rome almost to the letter. It was largely a word-for-word copy of what he had written to Potocki and others in 1761 following the Wojsławice affair.[41] The nuncio confirmed that Jews had turned for protection to the Apostolic See and that he himself "had received orders relating to this matter from His Holiness" and had done what he could to obey them. As to "the intention of the Holy Father," the nuncio added, he was happy to say the pontiff "desired everyone to know that the Holy See had examined all evidence, on which is based the belief that Jews needed human blood for their unleavened matzah," the reason they were "considered killers of children." The investigation revealed there were "no clear and sufficient proofs" to sustain this accusation and consider Jews guilty. And, as he had done in other places, the nuncio urged that criminal convictions be based on legally sound evidence alone.

Although Visconti was unequivocal in saying the matter had been examined in Rome and that no evidence had been found to support such accusations, the letter was, like all the previous letters, a personal response, not a broad official statement that Jews had hoped to obtain when they sent Zelig to Rome. If Jews may have been encouraged when Zelig returned with letters of recommendation, it soon became clear that aside from personal interventions no public condemnation of the trials was forthcoming. So they took matters into their own hands and tried to make Visconti's statements "official."

Visconti's letter to von Brühl reached Jewish hands, undoubtedly because of von Brühl's connections with the Jews; but given that, Visconti appeared sympathetic to the Jews' cause, perhaps even with the nuncio's approval. This letter, along with the letters Zelig had received in Rome, were translated from French and Italian into formal Latin and then into vernacular Polish. That done, they were registered along with other royal documents supporting the Jews' innocence against such charges in the official royal registry, which helped bolster their authenticity. Jews then requested official extracts of the now lawfully certified documents and had them published in 1763 as *Documenta judaeos in Polonia concernentia: Ad acta Metrices Regni suscepta et ex iis fideliter iterum descripta et extradita* (Documents concerning the Jews in Poland: Inscribed in the Acts of the Royal Registry and from Them Faithfully Copied and Extracted).[42] These convoluted actions of translating, inscribing in royal records, obtaining official transcripts, and publishing them made for an expensive endeavor. The funds of 2,400 zloty were laid out by the leader—the *parnas*—of the Council of Four Lands, Meir of Dubno, with the expectation that they would be repaid. But they were not. A year later, in 1764, the Council of Four Lands ceased to exist, at least formally, for the purposes of collecting taxes and funds, and Meir had to appeal for reimbursement as late as 1765.[43]

Soon after *Documenta* was published, on June 25, 1763, Friar Stanislaus Kleczkowski of Lwów wrote to "Reverend Father Benedicto a Cavalesio" in Italy about the events in Poland, in particular about the recent publication of "Documents concerning the Jews in Poland."[44] Kleczkowski reported that Jews "so often convicted of infanticides" were seeking to conceal their crimes and to oppose the authority of the Holy See. They thus published this little book, in which they inserted the letter of Cardinal Corsini to Nuncio Visconti, and the nuncio's letter to Count von Brühl, "dated March 21, 1763." Both letters, Kleczkowski wrote, stated that Pope Clement

XIII expressed that Jews should not be troubled on account of infanticides, "because after a diligent examination done in Rome it was revealed that they never used Christian blood." Moreover, "Jews boast that they have obtained some *breve* protecting them. "This," the friar added, "is not accepted (as I know) in any diocese." He also bemoaned that Jews, "the most hostile nation," were supported by the avarice of the magnates, who for their part dared neither to deal with what the Jews did nor to enforce the 1751 bull *A quo primum* issued by Pope Benedict XIV. Because the Jews were spreading "tales," deceiving even Rome about their faith, Kleczewski decided to write to "friends closer to Rome" to find out the truth of the matter. Once the answer was "communicated" to him, Kleczewski would in turn pass it on to others in Poland.

Kleczkowski's choice of "Reverend Father Benedicto a Cavalesio" was not accidental. Benedicto a Cavalesio was none other than Benedetto Bonelli, the author of *Dissertazione apologetica sul martirio del beato Simone da Trento nell'anno 1475 dagli ebrei ucciso* (An Apologetic Dissertation on the Martyrdom of the Blessed Simon of Trent Killed by Jews in the Year 1475); published anonymously in 1747, it sought to demonstrate the truth of Jewish murders of Christian children, and was used by Pope Benedict XIV when he addressed the question of child martyrs. Bonelli promptly forwarded this letter to the Holy Office in Rome, and on August 16 that year, the officers of the Holy Office discussed the matter, voting the next day to send a copy of Kleczewski's letter and of the *Documenta* to Nuncio Visconti and requesting more information about this matter. By August 20, the dispatch was on its way to Warsaw.[45] The Holy Office was not pleased with this turn of events, not least because they learned about them not from the nuncio himself but through remote connections.

The fact that Rome was informed about the publication of the documents in such a roundabout way may suggest the nuncio did not find that publication to be objectionable and felt no need to inform the Holy See about it. Perhaps in his own frustration, so well expressed in his long letter to Corsini at the Holy Office, he colluded with von Brühl to provide Jews with something they might find more useful in their efforts to stop the accusations.

In the meantime, in Poland, in July and August, another trial took place in Kalisz, about seventy-four miles from Poznań. Given the timing in the summer, it appeared not to be linked to the need for blood for Passover matzah, though blood was still central to the accusation. Several Jews, including women, from a number of surrounding towns were charged with brutally killing a Christian girl, Regina, "in order to procure Christian-Catholic blood" because of "superstition and impious hatred of the Christian people."[46] Having drained the girl's blood, the court document said, to satisfy "their blood-thirsty appetite [*cruentum appetitum*]," they dumped the body in a deserted field and carried the blood to other towns with Jewish communities. Finally, it was said, they gave it to a rabbi from the town of Krotoszyn, who had promised to pay for it the hefty sum of thirty Hungarian ducats. Soon after a shepherd found Regina's body, rumors started circulating implicating the Jews. They were promptly arrested and interrogated, including under torture, and most were sentenced to death.

The Kalisz trial laid bare the limits of the effectiveness of the booklet published by Jews at great expense a few months before. A copy of the court decree from Kalisz was sent to Rome, perhaps together with the booklet printed by Jews that the Holy Office had requested on August 20, since both are now held in the Vatican Secret Archive.[47] Little more is known about the repercussions of Jews' attempts to broadcast the Holy See's conclusions by printing documents—on their own—exculpating them from blood accusations. This may not be because "the pamphlet virtually closed 'the frenzy of blood accusations' in Poland,"[48] but because far more pressing matters took center stage. On October 5, 1763, King August III died. After almost a year of turmoil, civil war, and intrigue, Stanisław August Poniatowski, a former lover of Catherine the Great, was elected king of Poland under military pressure from Russia. During this tumultuous period, the nuncio's dispatches from Warsaw were dominated by the politics of the royal election.[49] At the time Nuncio Visconti's prime task was to do everything in his power to rally support behind a Catholic candidate and a strong supporter of the Church, and to protect the interests of the Church.[50]

The Decrease in Accusations in Times of Turmoil and Reform

Once matters settled a bit following the election of Poniatowski in 1764, new reports about infanticides reappeared in dispatches sent to the nuncio and Rome. On May 6, 1766, Walenty Wężyk, now the bishop of Przemyśl, wrote to Nuncio Visconti informing him about another "cruel martyrdom" of a boy near the town of Tyczyn in his diocese.[51] Wężyk attached two color illustrations of the child's decomposing body, along with court documents relating to the trial (Fig. 10.1).

Directly below one of the images was a brief list of injuries and a description of the incident: "The Martyrdom of the child named Nicolas, son of the laborious Ignacy Paszka, Budzywoj peasant, three years and three

FIG. 10.1 Illustrations accompanying forensic description of a decomposing body found near Tyczyn in 1766, forwarded to the Vatican by the papal nuncio Visconti. ASV Acta Nunziatura Varsavia 94, 100v–101r.

months and six days old, kidnapped on March 15 of the current 1766 year, found stabbed on April 7 of the same year." A more detailed list of injuries, attached on a separate sheet, ended with a statement implicating Jews: "No sooner than Jews had come to see this body during the official review, did the blood (in all improbability) begin to flow from the right ear, so beautiful and red as if he was alive and simply injured." The trope of blood flowing from the body in the presence of the alleged murderers was, of course not new, having appeared since the thirteenth century, but it had most recently resurfaced in Poland as evidence against Jews in the trials in Zasław in 1747 and Żytomierz in 1753—both widely known because the court summaries of these trials were published as small pamphlets.[52] The mention of the miraculous flow of blood from the corpse in official court records of postmortems and the bishop's letter again underscored what Visconti had reported earlier to Rome—old stereotypes and beliefs were still deeply rooted in Poland. Indeed, the belief that blood flowing from a corpse was evidence pointing to the murderer had been long rejected in Italy. In 1668, in his strongly anti-Jewish book about Simon of Trent, Michelangelo Mariani explicitly noted that this type of evidence was not used in Italy, "much less in Rome."[53] Evidently, the nuncio's efforts following Cardinal Ganganelli's report and even the Jews' somewhat sly publication of the documents exculpating them from the accusation of killing Christian children in 1763 had a limited impact.

Poland meanwhile was going through major transformations; the newly elected king introduced a number of reforms, ranging from relatively minor changes—opening a school for knights in Warsaw to train young noblemen in statecraft—to major ones, such as tax reform; restrictions on the use of the *liberum veto,* the disastrous practice whereby one member of the parliament could veto any legislation; and reluctantly, under pressure from Russia, the removal of legal disabilities from non-Catholic Christians: the Protestants and Eastern Orthodox. On October 11, 1766, Cardinal Ludovico Maria Torrigiani, the secretary of state in Rome, wrote in a panic, ordering Visconti to try to convince Poles that "the plan now promoted by the Dissidents [Protestants] is incongruous with the peace of the Kingdom."[54] The Catholics had to oppose this reform. It was already not a small thing that the dissidents, Torrigiani complained, were now "tolerated in so many parts of the Kingdom." If "this present toleration," the cardinal warned, were to be "sanctioned and even advanced more, one would take a great step toward first obtaining equality with the Catholics, and eventually also their exclusion." The nuncio was ordered to "exhort the bishops and other zealous persons in this Kingdom to champion the cause of God and his Church."

Subsequent letters sounded even more alarmed about how little effort was being made by the bishops in support of "the Religion and the Holy See."[55] The nuncio's job was to "ignite in any possible way their zeal." No compromise was to be accepted, even the possibility of permitting the "dissidents" to practice their religion privately, because it was difficult to know "what baleful consequences could arise from this step."

But most importantly, the Church was concerned with legal reforms proposed by the Sejm, the bicameral parliament of the Polish-Lithuanian Commonwealth; some of those reforms, it was feared, would curtail the Church's "jurisdiction and ecclesiastical immunity," possibly undermining the authority of the bishops in the Senate.[56] It was of grave importance that the Church not be burdened with more taxes than the laity. Torrigiani reminded the now outgoing nuncio Visconti that ecclesiastical immunity was of crucial importance because the Church had its "own rules dependent on canonical dispositions." Thus, Visconti was to do everything possible to influence the bishops to prevail.

The reforms also had an impact on the Jewish community. The restructuring of the taxation system in 1764 meant the official end, at least from the perspective of the Polish state, of the Council of Four Lands, the celebrated supracommunity governing Jews in Poland and responsible for collecting taxes and managing community affairs. When it came to the repayment of communal debts, the abolition of the Council created serious problems. Not only did Meir of Dubno have a claim against the Council for expenses incurred in relation to the publication of the *Documenta* in 1763 but also Jacob Eliyakim Zelig and his creditor in Italy, Neta of Mantua, had not yet been reimbursed for the expenses incurred during Zelig's stay in Italy in 1758–1760—a massive sum of 3,046 red złoty, or golden coins.[57] The whopping debt was to have been repaid by levying a special tax, because the Council did not have such an enormous amount of funds at their disposal. But the question of the repayment of Zelig's bills languished with other communal debts and was then included among matters to be resolved by the Commission on Jewish Debts of the Royal Treasury in 1767. Despite the fiscal reforms, the removal of the responsibility for tax collection from the Council, and the resulting debt crisis, letters written after 1764 from "the elders and the entire Jewish community" to high officials suggest that some form of Jewish self-government and representation continued. The legal reforms of the Polish-Lithuanian Commonwealth, with their complex ramifications for both the Jewish community and the Church, were also to play a major role in ending the trials against Jews in premodern Poland.[58]

The political chaos in Poland, including the Bar Confederation of 1768 that opposed reforms beneficial to non-Catholics, followed by the first partition of Poland by Russia, Prussia, and Austria in 1772, seems to have brought about a short hiatus in anti-Jewish accusations. That lasted until 1774, when another shocking trial took place in the village of Grabie, belonging to a Benedictine monastery, thirty-eight miles north of Warsaw.[59] On Wednesday, March 30, four days before Easter, a three-year-old girl named Marianna went missing. According to a Christian account sent to Rome, she was apparently last seen near a brewery run by a Jew, Jakub Nodkowicz. When Hieronym Kamieński, the abbot of the Benedictine monastery, arrived in the village the following day, he found it in an uproar and ordered a thorough investigation. Jews soon became suspects. And rumors began to circulate about Jews from nearby towns who were traveling through the village, and about a cry of a child heard among Jews as well as "other great suspicious signs."[60] Abbot Kamieński ordered that Jews connected to the brewery be brought before him. Three adults—Jakub Nodkowicz, his wife, and Jakub Józefowicz, a Jewish brewer from the nearby village of Sadków—and two children, Jacob Nodkowicz's twelve-year-old daughter and his fourteen-year-old Jewish servant, were arrested. (Jewish reports recounted lower ages—eleven years for the girl and twelve for the boy. These discrepancies were likely purposeful: their ages in the Christian document would allow them to be seen as "adults" responsible for their words, whereas the ages noted in the Jewish supplication would make them "children."[61])

The two children were interrogated separately.[62] Nodkowicz's daughter said her parents would have prohibited her from saying "in front of the abbot and a servant of Rev. Thomas Jankowski, as well as others" that her father found the child and "brought her to the brewery. He then gave her to a Jew, the brewer from Sadków [Jakub Józefowicz]." Józefowicz, she continued, in turn took the infant and passed her on to a Jew from another town. After her testimony the brewer's daughter pled with the abbot not to tell her parents what she had just said. The boy told the interrogators a "similar" story and also pleaded with them not to inform his employer about his testimony.

The following day, the abbot sent a letter to a royal official in a nearby town and to a canon in the Cathedral of Płock with Easter wishes and a report about "the unhappy case."[63] More interrogations followed. Jakub Nodkowicz, the brewer from Grabie, denied even being in the village the day the child went missing and insisted he had not committed this crime. But with the testimony of his daughter and of an administrator of the monastery's lands who claimed to have seen him in the village, he eventually relented, saying he would confess. Two days after Easter, and a full week after Marianna went missing, on April 5, her body, covered with "more or less 50 wounds," was found near a ditch (*circa fossas*).[64]

The Jewish children once more confirmed their previous accusation of the adults, and the abbot ordered four more Jews from the area imprisoned in chains, among them an adult son of Jakub Nodkowicz. They were, like the prisoners in Wojsławice, held in isolation. Each was interrogated in the "presence of many."[65] The son, who had moved to another village, was asked if he had visited his father for Passover, which started on March 26 and ended on Sunday, April 3, coinciding with Easter, and if he had seen his father take the child from the ditch and pass her on to the Jew from Sadków, as his sister had testified. The son did not say much. Jakub Józefowicz, the Jew from Sadków, however, did confess: "Yes, I took the child, but I passed her on to a Jew from the village Kocerany, and what was done with her, I do not know." Another prisoner, a brewer from nearby Jeziorko, implicated still other Jews, and when asked "if many Jews knew about it, he responded, 'they all know.'" The abbot then ordered the arrest of additional Jews whom he thought might have been involved. In the end twelve were arrested and held in prison for months. The matter was transferred to Warsaw, where on April 10, the child's body was examined by doctors who found "no wounds caused by nails before or after death."[66]

The next day, the Jews appealed to the king.[67] They recounted the events briefly and offered defenses against blood libels—Jews do not consume any blood, human or animal, because it was prohibited by the Law of Moses. Experts, Catholic and Protestant alike, had "cleared Jews of the calumny that they needed Christian blood." Nowhere were Jews accused of such matters—not in "Germany, France, Spain, Italy, not even in Rome, Holland, and Turkey.... Only in Poland they experience such calumny." There were numerous reasons for that, but the most important one was the way interrogations were done: with an executor using "fire, breaking bones, and applying other tortures." True, the Jews conceded, no nation in the world is utterly pure, without evil among them. But the Jewish religion does not, they stressed, support such superstitions. They appealed to the king's wisdom and mercy for justice and the opportunity to prove their innocence.

Just two weeks later, on April 24, Colonel Lucas de Toux de Salvert, a learned Frenchman residing in Poland, sent to the king, at the Jews' request, a treatise in their defense.[68] Citing western scholars such as Johann Christian Bodeschatz, Jean Leusden's 1663 book *Philologus Hebraeo-Mixtus*, and converts like Caspar Joseph Fridenheim, who published in 1769 a conversionary work, *Mikve Israel-Die Hoffnung Israel* (Hope of Israel), he argued that there was no evidence Jews "use[d] Christian blood to celebrate their ceremonies."

On April 28, 1774, Jewish leaders appealed to the papal nuncio in Warsaw, Giuseppe Garampi. In a long and elaborate letter they complained about "the sad case" in Grabie. Surely, news about it "had already reached Your Excellency's ears," they wrote.[69] The Jews stressed that much of the case was based on confessions extracted under torture and fear, including those of two children, a girl of eleven years and a boy of twelve. The boy was "tied in ropes and beaten with sticks and rods." The girl was also persuaded to confess "with coaxing and terror." Other Jews were tied, suspended, and tortured for many hours "so they may confess." But confessions so extorted, the Jews complained, "hardly have a shadow of truth." If this mode of extorting confessions "by beating, incarceration, suspension, and coaxing, and other ways" seemed just and sufficient to "prudent men and magistrates, whom GOD appointed to administer justice and who must examine such crime," then there was little justice for Jews accused "without any probability." "We are sure," the letter continued, "that prudent and learned men in other regions would be astonished to hear that only in Poland so many Jews perish with violent deaths because of this criminal charge that has no basis," but was grounded "in wrong confessions an executioner extorts through inhuman torments." The "learned" nuncio would certainly know that when "a hand of the executor extorts confession, it does not find out the truth according to true judicial prudence." In real life, this trial demonstrated yet again that, unlike in the Jewish songs and tales, under torture Jews confessed to crimes imputed to them. In their letters to the king and the nuncio, thus, the Jewish leaders ignored the message found in Yiddish literary works valuing torture as a means for martyrdom. Or, perhaps, the argument of their supplication was a sign of changing times.

This appeal to jurisprudence that questioned the value of torture represented not just a shift from Yiddish songs and tales but also a new defense strategy on the part of Jews. For centuries, their supplications and appeals had focused on Jewish law and its prohibitions against consuming blood. Certainly their appeal to Nuncio Garampi also stressed that Jewish law prohibited Jews from consuming blood and even provided him with a short summary of the requirements for making meat kosher, from which blood had to be "diligently" removed and the meat "washed and sprinkled in salt."[70] These were not hidden precepts—all this could be found in "Jewish history, our Talmud, commentaries to the Holy Scriptures written by rabbis, in [our] teachings and ceremonies." Jews "never, certainly not during Passover" had the need for Christian blood. The Jewish leaders "trusted" that the "learned" nuncio agreed. In 1774, however, Jews, clearly highly attuned to the debates about legal reforms and the use of torture in judicial proceedings, not only in Poland but also throughout Europe, used this new approach for their own ends.

Playing into the notion of Poland as a backward country, which nuncio Garampi certainly shared, the Jewish leaders noted that even learned Catholic men elsewhere in Europe had in fact "declared that although Jews in Poland are accused of this crime, they, nevertheless, never commit it."[71] Indeed, from "ancient times" learned Christian men who knew Hebrew examined Jewish books, and "none of them ever" found that Jews killed Christian children. "Only in Poland," where educated men and clerics were "ignorant of the Holy Tongue," did they embrace printed books filled with "calumnies" against Jews. This was only possible with "men who can neither read nor understand our books." Since the destruction by the Romans of "the Holy City of Jerusalem, because of our sins," the letter continued, "God angry at us" left Jews "without Kingdom, without a priest, without the Temple, without sacrifices" and scattered them across the world. But when Jews made their home "in Rome, in France, in Spain, in Italy, in Holland, in Germany, and other kingdoms, indeed even in the Turkish Empire, no nation among whom we lived has held us suspects of such crimes."[72] This happened "only in Poland." And yet, all Jews, everywhere, "with the exception of the Karaites," shared the same religion.

To further bolster their argument, the authors of the letter noted past privileges and letters of protection granted to Jews denouncing such accusations. Among them was a 1671 privilege from Sigismund III, letters from the pontiffs, and most recently from Rome in 1760, one written by "Cardinal Corsini in the name of the Pontiff Clement XIII to nuncio Visconti" and the two letters from Corsini to Visconti and from Visconti to Count von Brühl that were published in 1763. But the authors of the petition to nuncio Garampi said not a word about Ganganelli's report, an indication they knew nothing of its contents. Once more, the Jews "beseeched" the nuncio to publish a formal decree declaring Jews' innocence. They were "sure" that after examining the basis for the accusations, especially the confessions of two children, the nuncio would be able to bring "the truth to light" and accelerate justice to free the "the people" from this "wrong prejudice."[73] All this said, the Jews were not trying to avoid justice: "this we never flee." They asked for "nothing more" but assurance that the case be tried in a competent forum, not by the abbot, and that the confessions extorted under torture not be approved.

It is unclear if Garampi did anything in response. The nuncio had a full plate of other concerns. The trial took place during a tumultuous period: during the pivotal Sejm of 1773–1775 ratifying the partition of Poland, when the nuncio had to be particularly vigilant in protecting the interests of the Church, and in the aftermath of the papal order suppressing the Jesuit order, which was so negatively received that, combined with the crisis of the partitions, it threatened the already weak position of the pope.⁷⁴ On August 23, the Jews sent Garampi another letter, pleading "with tears" for help in the Grabie case, where twelve Jews "of both sexes" remained incarcerated.⁷⁵ With or without Garampi's intercession, at the end of the year, the Grabie case reached the country's highest court, and became part of a broader debate about torture and the death penalty.

At the end of the year, a pamphlet *Replika na powództwo instygatora sądowego i jego donosicielów* (A Response to the Complaint by the Court Prosecutor and His Informants) was published in Warsaw in the Jews' defense.⁷⁶ Though responding to the case in Grabie, the pamphlet was also a legal treatise on court procedure, evidence, and proof. Like the Jews' letter to Nuncio Garampi, it challenged the premodern reliance on confession, especially under torture, and focused on undisputable hard "judicial proofs."

The Jews' defender challenged the very foundations of the accusation—the belief that Jews killed Christian children—and focused on the evidence or lack thereof. The question, the defender argued, was not a historical question whether Jews ever committed such crimes, but "whether or not this infanticide was committed by those imprisoned."⁷⁷ To answer that question it was necessary to examine the circumstances related to "persons [involved], time, and place." When examined, the conclusions would "serve to exculpate the prisoners from the accusation of infanticide." Thus the alleged past cases were not to be used as evidence in court. This argument was a striking departure from almost three centuries of reliance on "facts" described in books and chronicles as court evidence.

First, the accusers claimed that Jakub Nodkowicz of Grabie and Jakub Józefowicz of Sadków collaborated in kidnapping the child. Nodkowicz was said to have kidnapped Marianna and given her to Józefowicz, who was passing through the village. But the "prisoners ask the accusers if anyone saw the kidnapping of the child by the first [of the accused] . . . or the capturing of her by the other." If so, why did not anyone do anything or notify anyone? Why did not anyone rescue the child? If no one saw anything, then "how can they accuse the prisoners? There is no proof." In fact, there were witnesses to Józefowicz's presence in the town—he passed through Grabie in the morning together with carpenters working in his brewery on his way to the nearby village of Cichrowo. But he did not stop at the Grabie brewery and thus did not see Nodkowicz. And so "if he did not meet with the brewer in Grabie, how can one say that one picked up the kidnapped child from the other?" This is not, the author asserted with a snark, "possible in nature."⁷⁸ Thus, if the two main accusers "were far from committing the crime," those who were imprisoned later were even farther. They were imprisoned randomly; some had not lived in Grabie for several years, and others had never lived there. Jews in nearby villages were arrested, some "picked up on their way to Warsaw" without "any evidence." They were indicted of the crime because they "kept silent" without confessing to anything.

Detailed examination of the alleged timeline of the crime also supported the innocence of the accused Jews. If the prosecution argued that Jews killed Christian children because they needed "children's blood for their matzah," then it was important to point out that the day Marianna disappeared, March 30, was the Wednesday before Easter, but Passover had begun four days before on March 26. The child "disappeared after the Jewish festival [had begun]," the author argued. The timing thus proved that "the child could not have been kidnapped because of the alleged Jewish need for children's blood, because Jews prepare matzah, or the unleavened bread, before the holidays; they prepare if for the holidays, not during or after the holidays."[79] Of course, in reality, Passover, a weeklong holiday, did not end until April 3, but it was the rituals of the first night, the seder, that were of greatest importance. Or, rather, at the heart of the accusation was the *afikomen*, the three pieces of matzah used by Jews during Passover seder, on which Christians fixated during blood libels.[80] Indeed, Gaudenty Pikulski had just recently asserted that blood was used in the "matzah called *afikomen*, which Jews consume during Passover. And this matzah hangs in their homes and in synagogues for the whole year."[81] This was, he falsely claimed, just in case "they could not obtain Christian blood the next year, they could then soak this matzah in water and smear the blood on a Christian door." Jews did indeed store a piece of matzah, the unleavened bread made with just flour and water, for the whole year in synagogues but this was to expand the boundaries of households through an *eruv* that would allow Jews to carry items otherwise prohibited outside the house on the Sabbath and Jewish holidays.[82]

The very sources of the accusations also needed to be challenged. The prosecution in Grabie apparently used the decades-old "testimony of Serafinowicz," the converted Jew who provided ammunition to Stefan Żuchowski, the canon of the Sandomierz cathedral, during his prosecution of Jews for murdering a Christian child in 1710–1713. But Serafinowicz's "simple" writings, clearly still in circulation, could not be treated as "legitimate and authentic evidence."[83] Furthermore, the court needed to examine critically the character of the very man who incited violence and turmoil against Jews following the disappearance of the girl—Andrzej Tryndoch, a serf from Grabie who was apparently a murderer. How could one believe a man who "once committed murder" of a Jew, whom he hanged in a forest, and then "boasted about it among the people"? "One cannot believe him at all," especially since the examination of circumstances related to "persons, time, and place" did not provide hard evidence that the crime had been committed by the accused Jews.[84]

The Jews' defender then turned to disproving the very foundation of the accusation: that Jews needed Christian blood. He offered an overview of all passages in the Hebrew Bible that dealt with blood and murder, quoting directly those most explicitly prohibiting the consumption of blood. Repeating almost verbatim passages from the long letter Jews sent to Garampi, the author wrote that Jews lived in many states, "German, French, Spanish, Italian, and even in Rome itself, in Holland, and Turkey for so many years," where they were not accused of "this crime." Why should they be accused of it in Poland, if they, as Jews, "are governed by the same law, same teachings, and same scriptures."[85]

But more importantly, there existed "authentic documents exculpating the Jews [*niewiernych*] of this hideous charge" issued by both secular and ecclesiastical authorities. Most recently, following the mission of "Jakub Jelek" to Rome in 1758, with Pope Benedict XIV still alive, the Apostolic See examined the matter, "as always, with great diligence."[86] Indeed, the author added, "It was important to note that it is a custom of Roman authorities and tribunals to examine closely and exactly each matter." There should therefore be no doubt that the conclusion reached in Rome, which exculpated Jews from the accusations, was based on solid evidence. Quoting extensively from the now publicly known letter from Cardinal Corsini to nuncio Visconti, the author ramped up its significance: "this opinion of the Holy Father and the Apostolic See," he wrote, "has the power of a firm verdict," and as such it was communicated by the nuncio to the royal court officials.[87] This bold statement was, of course, not quite true. Even if the text of Corsini's letter was authentic, it was not issued "as a firm verdict." But it no longer mattered; Church authorities were unlikely to dispute this point now. Still, the assertion suggests either that when the Jews were providing evidence to their defenders and offered the collection of documents published in 1763, they insisted that these statements represented the official position of the Church that had been clearly communicated in Poland, or simply that by 1774 the politics of the letters and their behind-the-scenes nature, as well as the frustration at the lack of forceful official condemnation of anti-Jewish accusations from Rome, were no longer significant. After all, these letters were officially registered in the royal registry and had appeared in print. They became official evidence. The 1763 ruse of publishing what had not been intended for publication finally bore fruit in 1774. Based on the position of the Holy See expressed in the 1763 publication, and a long list of royal decrees and Polish legal statutes, Jews were not to be accused of such crimes.

But the prosecution objected. They argued, as did Bishop Kajetan Sołtyk in his response to the nuncio in 1758 and as had Stefan Żuchowski at the beginning of the century, that there existed many decrees issued by courts that condemned Jews of such crimes. The defender stood firm. Even if one were to allow that "Jews killed some child, since murders happen," and were tried and convicted of the crime as murderers, "as was the case in Sandomierz," still, these past decrees could not be used as evidence "today."[88] One could not conclude, the author argued, that "if Jews killed a child [somewhere], that they did it based on their [religious] teachings, and thus must kill now too." The evidence of crime in the past should not be used as evidence for the specific crime tried today. This was an epistemic departure from previous reasoning used in trials against Jews, at least since Trent if not before.

Seeing their case crumble under the defense's effective challenge, the prosecution suggested the court should "unearth the truth through torture, as is allowed by law."[89] This was a miscalculated move at a time when the question of torture was itself a subject of judicial reform. And the defense would have none of it. Torture was "a lamentable mode of first discovery," but in "our enlightened era it is coming to an end." Using torture was "dangerous," because it served more "to impair than to expose the truth." Torture was all about endurance. If someone "can endure, he will not tell the truth, but if he cannot, he will confess untruth; even though he may be innocent, he will come up with a crime." This was not a new argument; Hugo Grotius made it in the seventeenth century, and even in Poland, the sixteenth-century court clerk and author of popular judicial manuals, Bartłomiej Groicki, urged court officials not to rush to torture but rather to examine the case so that "there would be just and adequate evidence [*dostateczne znaki*]" against the suspect, because "[it is] not always that the guilty person is [the one] who is accused and charged."[90] Confessions under torture, Groicki warned, should not necessarily be accepted unconditionally: "And so one must not believe [confessions under] torture immediately, but neither should it be that [the confessions under torture] be disbelieved on the account that they are an uncertain, erroneous and dangerous matter. Because it happens numerous times that one is so resilient [*cierpliwy*] and tough that he can suffer the torture and will not tell the truth even if he were tortured most heavily. And others are not as resilient and, fearing torture, confess against themselves and others, and they repeat many times what had never happened."[91] But while Groicki still allowed for a cautious use of torture and in Poland, more broadly, torture had been liberally applied;

in the Grabie case its use was presented by the defense as tantamount to the prosecution's admission that it lacked evidence strong enough to convict.[92] The death penalty was a serious matter, and it should only be meted out when strong evidence was in place. The Jews' defender appealed to the court: "Make judgment and do justice, and do not shed innocent blood in this place."

In early 1775, Jews again appealed to nuncio Garampi for help. Whether he intervened is unclear, but in April 1775, "in order to accelerate justice" for those imprisoned for more than a year, the case was transferred to a commission under the chairmanship of Bishop Andrzej Stanisław Młodziejowski of Poznań, the same bishop who in 1774 was charged with executing the papal decree to suppress the Jesuit order and confiscate Jesuit property in Poland.[93] The members of the commission took an oath to judge "according to God, conscience, justice, written documents, and objections, and depositions of witnesses" and not to accept any "rewards and promises" in order to "suppress justice." The commission was asked to examine both the incarcerated and the evidence provided by the medical examiners, who had performed a postmortem on Marianna's body when the case was transferred to Warsaw. If it were to find this evidence insufficient, the commission could then question the two Jewish children, Dina (or Binia) and Berko, both of whom were now Christians named Barbara and Michael. The commission's charge was to condemn to death those found guilty and release from prison those found innocent.

The commission found that in regard to the accusation that Jews killed Christians to obtain their blood, both the Holy See and royal authorities had spoken and found no substance to support this accusation.[94] And yet, despite this, the accusers illegally arrested, prosecuted, abused, and tormented Jews after the body of a Christian had been discovered. The commission questioned the whole trial and its procedures, which were checkered with violence and intimidation and grounded in testimonies of children who "innocently accused" their parents because of "fear and pain." Moreover, the medical examiner in Warsaw found no wounds on the body of the child to indicate foul play. As a result, on June 12, 1775, the commission, fulfilling its charge, ordered the release of the imprisoned Jews. A month later, on July 12, the newly established *Warsaw Gazette* (Gazeta Warszawska) reported the conclusion of the trial on its front page.[95]

In the 1774–1775 trial of the Jews for the infanticide in Grabie two judicial worlds clashed—the old, where confession was "the crown of evidence," and the "enlightened," where material evidence was demanded and where confession, especially that under torture, became unacceptable.[96] Under the old system, the trial was not limited to the specific crime of which a suspect was accused, but also included, and made the suspect liable for, other crimes to which he or she may have confessed during interrogations.[97] Books and chronicles recounting past tales and stories were informally seen as having evidentiary power. In the old judicial world, Polish courts, whose practice and procedures were strongly rooted in medieval Saxon law, the sixteenth-century *Carolina,* and Polish legal manuals based on them, considered several kinds of proof: testimony of the accuser, confession of the accused, witness testimonies, and an oath.[98] Legal manuals used through the eighteenth century, among them those by Bartłomiej Groicki, provided specific guidelines as to who could be considered a witness fit to "give the testimony of truth in court under oath."[99] Age was one factor. In most cases witnesses could not be younger than fourteen, but in "ignominious" cases in which the death penalty was considered they could not be younger than twenty. People older than seventy were also disqualified from serving as witnesses. (The Grabie trial appeared not quite legal even under the old law, but that kind of arbitrariness of courts was indeed one aspect of judicial practice the reformers wanted to eliminate.) In Polish courts, torture was applied in criminal court proceedings extensively. And although certain rules existed to which most courts seemed to adhere, there was also the unsystematic use of torture during the early modern period that paralleled the centrifugal and fragmented nature of the court system in the Polish state. In some cases torture was even applied to those who were considered witnesses, although the line between a witness and a suspect was often a thin one.

Bartłomiej Groicki advocated the careful investigation of criminal cases, stressing the need to consider all kinds of circumstances, such as the reputation of both the accused and his accusers, the location of the crime and the presence or absence of the accused there, times of the crime and the ages of those involved, as well as the reasons for the accusation "whether out of enmity, envy, past threats, or . . . profit."[100] He counseled court officials to seek expert advice if there was any doubt about the confession and urged them not to rush to execution even if the accused had actually confessed.

Following the imperial *Carolina,* Groicki had set up specific procedures to be used during criminal trials: (1) The accused should be examined in front of the court without torture "so that he should confess and tell the truth voluntarily without torture."[101] During that time the accused should be warned about the "severity [*srogość*] of torture, to which he will be subjected if he does not confess voluntarily to that of which he is accused." (2) The accused should be allowed to prove he was not involved in the crime by demonstrating "that he either was not in the place where something like that happened or that he was doing something else at that time."[102] The court was not allowed to prohibit the accused from bringing witnesses to testify on his or her behalf (Groicki used only the masculine form, but women were often suspects as well.) (3) If after such presentation the court was not convinced of the suspect's innocence, it had the right to send the accused to be interrogated under torture in the presence of the judge, two jurors, and the court clerk. But even under torture the suspect should still be allowed to claim his innocence. Should he or she confess to the crime, the clerk "is to write his words, without omitting or adding the smallest [single] word."[103] (4) The confession under torture had to be confirmed "voluntarily" after torture, and the court had the right to ask follow-up questions about the circumstances of the crime and accomplices. Should there be discrepancies between the confession under torture and this stage of interrogation, the suspect could be sent to torture again.[104] As Joanna Pilaszek has noted, the courts distrusted voluntary confessions—"If the accused admitted so easily to all the deeds of which he was accused, he will recall more when led to torture."[105]

Groicki's sixteenth-century manuals were republished as late as 1760.[106] But by the second half of the eighteenth century, some courts became reluctant to execute offenders and struggled to justify noncapital punishment, since according to the legal manuals available to them, capital punishment was required not only for heresy or *lese majeste* but also for thefts, raids and robberies, sexual crimes (in Groicki's manual that included bestiality and male homosexuality, but not lesbian sex, even though it did appear in the *Carolina* itself), bigamy and adultery, pimping, abortion, infanticide, and poisoning, as well as many other offenses. Indeed, until the latter half of the eighteenth century the death penalty was quite commonly applied in Polish criminal courts. Moreover, in the old system, an accused was not, as in modern law, presumed innocent until proven guilty, but quite the opposite.[107] Legal reformers of the Enlightenment era began to call not only for a shift away from this paradigm but also for the accused's right of defense.[108] The essay by the defender of the Jews in the Grabie case demonstrated the new legal thinking and made the case part of broader debates over criminal law in Poland.

The reforms in Poland were influenced by similar developments in Europe. Although formal calls for legal reforms came only during the second half of the eighteenth century, on the Italian peninsula, for example, some of the principles of those reforms were already practiced by the courts, which were urged to use "moderation and circumspection," use torture more judiciously, and make punishment, even for murder, much lighter.[109] Works by European legal scholars who called for legal reforms began to infiltrate legal thinking in Poland in the 1770s. Cesare Beccaria's 1764 essay *On Crimes and Punishments,* published as a response to the Jean Calas affair in France in 1762, was translated into Polish and published in 1772, spurring earnest legal debates. (Jean Calas, a French merchant from Toulouse, was accused of killing his son, who apparently had committed suicide. Calas was tortured and, despite maintaining his innocence, executed. The affair shook European Enlightenment thinkers, many of whom began calling for judicial reforms.) The reformers, in Poland, like in the rest of Europe, argued for the abolition of torture, the end of the death penalty, except in cases of treason and premeditated murder, and for proportionality of punishment to the crimes. And so, the Grabie case came at the very moment when judicial reforms were hotly debated and in the very venue in which they were being considered, with the use of torture and death penalty at the center of both.[110]

The death penalty was a particularly pressing issue in Poland at the time. Russia and Prussia demanded an end to capital punishment in cases of apostasy from Catholicism, with it being replaced, if necessary, with exile—something the Holy See and nuncio Garampi strongly opposed.[111] But, even more importantly, since many noblemen who opposed King Stanisław Poniatowski and took part in his kidnapping in 1771 could have faced the death penalty for treason, many lords became its most vigorous opponents. Although the ban on torture and the partial abolishment of the death penalty (for example, in cases that were considered "witchcraft") did not come until two years later, the trial of the Jews and its ultimate outcome thus became both subject to and a product of these debates and the legal reforms that followed.

Although the Grabie case was not the last accusation of Jews in Poland in the premodern period, those that came after were considered more cautiously. In 1779, for example, in Izbica Kujawska it was the accusers who were convicted. In Olkusz in 1787, a Jewish tailor accused of killing a Christian girl was convicted but not simply on the basis of his confession, but also of material evidence found on him—a knife—that allegedly tied him to the crime. Still, the Jews whom he implicated were freed, and the king, visiting nearby Cracow, condemned the accusation as "medieval superstition" and scolded one of the instigators, Stanisław Wodzicki, for believing "in such medieval tales that Jews needed Christian blood for Passover [*święta wielkanocne*]." The king said, "Despite the fact that all nations mention such trials, and severe punishments were meted out at those accused of this crime, enlightened education of our times has convinced us about the innocence of these victims of prejudice and superstition."[112] Although Wodzicki did not agree with the monarch, and years later reaffirmed his belief in the Jewish need for Christian blood and the resulting murders, he complied with the king's request to end the trial. By the time the Olkusz case took place in 1787, a gap had developed between popular beliefs embraced locally by local instigators and positions embraced by intellectual elites, exposed to Enlightenment ideas, who rejected both the old tales and the old criminal procedures.

And although trials of the Jews largely ended in premodern Poland, they did not end because of the Ganganelli report or papal intervention, as some scholars continue to maintain.[113] They ended, in their lethal effects, partly because of legal and cultural transformations in the state and partly because the state eventually ceased to exist in 1795. In the modern period other parts of Europe saw a resurgence of the accusation in a new guise.[114] After the Damascus affair in 1840, and even more during the wave of modern accusations beginning in the 1880s, Jewish intellectuals and community leaders, along with some Christian supporters—forced again to demonstrate the fallacy of blood libels—turned to the archives to show, like their premodern predecessors, that Christian authorities had already declared Jews innocent, publishing known papal bulls and breves on the subject.[115] It was then that the text of the Ganganelli report was discovered, first in the archives of the Jewish community in Mantua and then in Rome. It is unclear how the report found its way into Jewish archives, because it had not been shared with anyone except the highest Church officials in Rome. Perhaps Jews got a copy after Napoleon seized documents in the Vatican archives, especially those housed in the Holy Office. That "papers certainly disappeared in times of the revolution" was in fact the explanation the Holy Office offered in 1900 to explain why Jews had possession of "certain documents in their defense" they had recently published. The official was referring to the Ganganelli report.[116]

Whatever the history of its acquisition, the report by Cardinal Ganganelli soon received a new lease on life. In 1862 its existence was discussed in the Italian Jewish journal *L'Educatore Israelita* by Marco Mortara, the rabbi of Mantua; in the 1880s, in the aftermath of a number of trials of Jews, including in Tiszaeszlar, the report was published several times in the original Italian and in translations.[117] The report came to be championed as the most extensive condemnation of anti-Jewish accusations and became relevant again during the Beilis affair that started in Kiev in July 1911 and lasted for more than two years, ending with a four-week trial in September and October 1913. When the Beilis trial began, the Jewish community in western Europe mobilized to intervene in Kiev, and Baron Nathaniel Mayer Rothschild, a British banker and politician, requested that the Holy See authenticate the published versions of the report so it could be submitted as defense evidence in Kiev. This move was a response to the fact that one of the supporting witnesses in the trial, Justinius Elisejevitch Pranaitis, a Roman Catholic theologian, testified in support of the accusation and cast doubt on the existence of papal condemnations.

The Ganganelli report's reputation and importance were thus built not at the time of its creation but by later generations. It had a relatively limited impact when first written, with Church officials conscious of the power of public symbolic gestures but still reluctant to make overt statements condemning blood libels against Jews. To be sure, Rome was explicit about instructing nuncios to help Jews avoid persecution and unjust trials, but it was pragmatically reluctant to make a public stand. The papal responses, along with Ganganelli's report, exemplify the tension between such a pragmatic approach rooted in the Church's desires to protect its own corporate interests and the demand to act based on what might be considered moral principles to condemn what is unjust and reprehensible, as the tortures of the Jews were to many Church officials in Italy. Yet the trials and tribulations of Jews in premodern Poland demonstrate that sometimes a symbolic but public statement can be worth more than even most elaborate behind-the-scenes interventions.

EPILOGUE

The Trail Continues

THE DEADLY BLOOD libels might have waned, but they did not disappear. Accusations and trials continued in the nineteenth and twentieth centuries, and in 1946 the persistent myth triggered a pogrom that left more than forty Jewish survivors of World War II dead in Kielce, Poland. In this long story, the significance of the early modern period in the history of blood accusations against Jews has been unappreciated. Although medieval in origin, the blood libel and ritual murder accusations became truly rooted in the European Christian imagination in the early modern period, when stories that had hitherto been hidden in medieval monastic chronicles or limited to local lore were included in widely disseminated printed chronicles, cosmographies, and polemical works. As they entered the "authoritative" accounts of world history, the tales of Jews killing Christians became "facts." To be sure, there were very few such stories among the thousands of "events" of "world history," but few as they were, they created patterns and perceptions that became difficult to root out and that gave their readers the verbs, nouns, and adjectives to describe Jews. And soon, in an interplay between law and culture, these stories came to be used in anti-Jewish trials as evidence against Jews and as validation of new accusations; the new trials, in turn, became material for subsequent books, creating a vicious feedback loop that was to last until the end of the eighteenth century when it began to be challenged.

The trial at Trent was a turning point. Not only did Bishop Hinderbach deploy a sophisticated multimedia propaganda campaign in the aftermath of the death of the toddler Simon in March 1475, exploiting the new print technology to disseminate the story far and wide, but he also turned to earlier stories and freshly printed books to justify his persecution of Jews and the veneration of Simon as *beatus*. Aware of the printed books' utility, Hinderbach made a concerted effort to assure the inclusion of Simon's story in chronicles that were to be printed. And he succeeded. Simon entered chronicles published across Europe, and though his cult may not have been immediately recognized as legal by the pope, the story became a nearly permanent fixture of Christian historical accounts, including authoritative lives of saints, capturing Christian imagination, even—as the manifesto by the shooter of the Poway synagogue, near San Diego in 2019 demonstrates—until our own times.

The Trent trial also had legal consequences. In his explicit prohibition of calling Simon *beatus,* Pope Sixtus IV assured Simon a place in the history of canon law. This was one of the first times a pope had used the term *beatus* in a concrete legal sense. Until then, bishops had had the authority to recognize local cults, but with Simon the landscape of church law concerning sainthood and beatification began to shift. And his case would remain a controversial legal precedent for centuries to come. The formal recognition of his cult in 1588 and, even more importantly, the insertion at the order of Pope Gregory XIII of his name in the newly revised liturgical calendar *Martyrologium Romanum* in 1583 validated, for many, the charge that Jews killed Christian children. This fateful decision ended the centuries-long era of papal condemnations of such accusations against Jews, and from then on, Jews became more vulnerable to those charges. The weight of papal authority affirming Simon's cult and Rome's subsequent silence in the defense of Jews helped anchor the libel more deeply in the European imagination. As one writer pointed out, "Who Should One Believe, the Rabbis or the Doctors of the Church?"[1]

Indeed, Pope Paul III's bull in defense of Jews issued in 1540 to the bishops and archbishops of Hungary, Bohemia, and Poland turned out to be the last papal defense of Jews against accusations of killing Christian children; subsequently it became nearly forgotten in Rome. But this was not the last papal statement on the topic. Sixtus V's 1588 bull granting Trent an office and indulgences for Simon and the 1755 bull *Beatus Andreas* by Pope Benedict XIV concerning the cult of Andreas Oxner of Rinn—the only two other official papal statements on child victims—both affirmed not only cults of purported child victims of Jews but, through explicit language, also validated the claims that Jews committed such crimes. True, these papal recognitions of the two cults were careful to distinguish between blood accusations and accusations of killing Christians "out of hatred," but as crucial as these distinctions were in the legal context, they disappeared when it came to the expansive Christian imagination and memory. The papal refusal after 1583, and certainly after 1755, to reissue public condemnations of accusations that Jews killed Christians for blood, the dominant charge in eastern Europe, spoke louder than the previous protections. And while Rome was ostensibly concerned with ensuring that justice was done and the secretary of state often urged nuncios in Poland to provide assistance to Jews, no official had the courage to intervene publicly. Yet, such a public intervention against blood accusations could have been issued even in light of the recognized cults of Simon and Andreas, because blood was precisely the focus of papal letters defending Jews until 1540, and it was also the motif in the trials in eastern Europe. This deafening silence came to be read as a tacit affirmation of charges against Jews, and the papal recognition of Simon and Andreas as boys "cruelly killed by Jews in hatred of Christ" allowed Jews' accusers to discount the existence of even the medieval papal protections.

For decades, scholars have been baffled why, despite explicit repeated papal condemnations of blood libels in the Middle Ages, no pope after 1540 issued a public statement against them until—so they thought—1759, when in the midst of a wave of such accusations in Poland, Cardinal Lorenzo Ganganelli, the future Pope Clement XIV, prepared an extensive report refuting their validity. This failure to condemn blood libels was sometimes attributed to the Counter-Reformation and to what some thought was a decline in the number of such accusations, at least in western Europe. In contrast, the Ganganelli report in its refutation of blood libels was attributed to the spirit of the Enlightenment. This explanation fit neatly into a familiar story that condemned "Catholic obscurantism" of the Counter-Reformation era and glorified the new spirit of the Enlightenment.

But the story, it turns out, was more complicated. The Counter-Reformation does not directly explain the discontinuance of papal defenses of Jews; but the recognition of Simon and his placement in the *Martyrologium romanum* does. The Enlightenment narrative also needs to be revised. Ganganelli's report, although it reads as a text infused with Enlightenment ideas, presented arguments developed many decades earlier by Jews and their Christian defenders. Moreover, the report remained a secret document unknown beyond the small circle of Vatican officials until the nineteenth century when a new wave of charges hit Jews across Europe and in the Middle East. And then too, the paper trail created in the early modern period became a tool both for the accusers and the defenders of Jews. In Velizh, Russia, for example, early modern Polish printed works against Jews were translated into Russian to support the charge that Jews in that town were responsible for killing a Christian boy in 1823, helping develop a Russian-language historical paper trail of past accusations.[2]

In the late nineteenth century, when new accusations and trials against Jews were taking place, Jewish and non-Jewish scholars, accusers and defenders alike, began to dig in the archives and in old books to find inculpatory or exculpatory evidence.[3] The result was a fascinating replication of the epistemological communities of the premodern era. The Jews' defenders cited and republished the same documents that Jews had used in the early modern period: medieval papal bulls explicitly condemning the blood accusations; the 1475 condemnation by Venice's Pietro Mocenigo; the 1479 decree by Bona and Giovanni Galeazzo Sforza of Milan; the 1603 decree from Verona; the decree by Emperor Frederick III issued in the aftermath of the 1470 accusation in Endingen, reissued in 1544 by Charles the V and reconfirmed in 1566 by Maximilian II; the 1714 report of the theology faculty from Leipzig; and, after 1881, also the Ganganelli report.

The antisemitic accusers did the same: scouring premodern chronicles and the lives of saints, they offered their own "evidence." For example, the French cult of St. Vernier, which had lost its anti-Jewish content, regained it during that time.[4] But the most notorious use of early modern sources was the Nazi publication *Der Stürmer,* which in May 1934 published a special issue almost entirely devoted to "ritual murder." In it were nearly twenty pages of stories and images of Jews killing Christians, among them the Simon of Trent woodcut from Schedel's 1493 chronicle (the work had just been republished in facsimile in Leipzig in 1933); reproductions of images from Rader's *Bavaria Sancta;* photographs of sites, such as the church in Oberwesel with a depiction of Werner being killed by Jews; and a painting from the church in Judenstein, with a scene from the story about Andreas of Rinn (Fig. 11.1). Added to these iconographic reproductions was a three-page "annalistic" list of "Jewish ritual murders from the times of Christ until 1932," with 131 brief examples, the majority from the early modern period. Julius Streicher, the publisher of *Der Stürmer,* wanting to make the stories appear credible to his readers, provided a source citation for each of them: *Acta Sanctorum,* Baronio's *Annales ecclesiastici,* Matthew Paris, Trithemius's *Chronicon,* the Colmar Annals, *Bavaria sancta,* Alfonso de Espina's *Fortalitium fidei*—in short, the early modern sources of historical knowledge.

The Nazi publication elicited a swift response. On May 11, the *Times* of London carried an article about the *Der Stürmer* issue, and for the next several days, it published letters of protest from prominent figures, including the chief rabbi of England, the archbishop of Canterbury, and the president of the Folklore Society, alarmed by this "revival" of "the worst ex-

Fig. 11.1 From *Der Stürmer*, May 1, 1934, a depiction of the story of Simon of Trent that reuses imagery from Hartmann Schedel's 1493 *Weltchronik*, helping turn the image into the quintessential depiction of ritual murder in both antisemitic and scholarly publications.

cesses of medieval fanaticism."[5] In addition, the mayor of Lincoln and the chancellor of the Lincoln Cathedral both "took pains publicly to disavow the legend of 'Little St. Hugh.'"[6]

The next year, the Jewish historian, Cecil Roth, decided to republish the Ganganelli report in the original Italian and in the English translation.[7] Roth preceded the report by a long preface in which he discussed both the history of anti-Jewish accusations, starting with William of Norwich, and the medieval papal defenses of Jews. He ended the preface with the last known communication on the subject from the Vatican during the Beilis affair of 1911–1913, in which a Jewish man, Menahem Mendel Beilis, was accused of killing a thirteen-year-old Ukrainian boy Andrei Yushchinsky in Kiev.[8] The affair mobilized Jews around the world. On October 7, 1913, Lord Nathaniel Rothschild contacted the Vatican not asking to intervene in the affair, but instead to "authenticate" two documents he thought useful in defending Beilis—"a letter of His Holiness Pope Innocent IV and the report of Cardinal Ganganelli," printed copies of which Rothschild attached in his request to the secretary of state, Cardinal Rafael Merry del Val. In his letter to Cardinal del Val, Rothschild reminded him that many popes "have on various occasions extended their merciful protection to my persecuted coreligionists, [among them] Pope Innocent IV."

In addition to the Ganganelli report, which Lord Rothschild claimed "was drawn up at the instance of His Holiness Pope Benedict XIV in 1758 and acted upon by his venerable successor, Pope Clement XIII," he mentioned the 1664 letter issued by Giovanni Battista de Marinis, the general of the Dominican Order. On October 18, 1913, the secretary of state sent his response, in which he wrote, "I am in a position to certify that the typewritten copy of Ganganelli's Report . . . is substantially authentic. . . . As to the extract of Innocent IV's letter, there can be no doubt of the accuracy of [Rinaldi's] quotation, which is confirmed by the fact of Ganganelli citing it in his Report." Cardinal del Val used an early modern authoritative source—Odorico Rinaldi's continuation of Cesare Baronio's *Annales ecclesiastici*—to confirm the validity of a medieval bull, with Ganganelli's use further buttressing its authenticity. Though not an explicit letter defending the Jews, Cardinal del Val's short response was more than what Polish Jews ever obtained. It affirmed, albeit in an indirect way, the medieval papal condemnations of blood, which were, of course, known but not accepted by all. In the end Beilis was acquitted. He died in Saratoga Springs in July 1934 and was buried in Queens, New York.

But Cecil Roth understood that "evidence" exculpating Jews needed to be made public. So he felt compelled to publish not only the text but also a photograph of the Vatican's letter to Lord Rothschild along with the envelope in which the letter arrived to affirm unequivocally the document's authenticity. At some level both Lord Rothschild and Cecil Roth acted in quite a traditional manner: in response to anti-Jewish libels, they, like Jews before them, cited Christian arguments against blood libel, approached Christian authorities for protection, and wanted to demonstrate widely that Christian authorities had explicitly condemned such accusations and exculpated Jews. Like Polish Jews in 1763, Roth made a private letter public, along with, thanks to new reprographic technology, a photograph of the document itself.

The exchange between Cardinal del Val and Lord Rothschild points not only to engaged Jewish diplomacy at the time of crisis but also to the disheartening fact that the long early modern trail paper continues to be relevant in the modern era as the myth of Jews killing Christian children persists in the European and, now also, Middle Eastern imagination, although—thankfully—no longer in the courts.

The long memory trail, the equivocating responses by Church officials, and the papal recognition of both Simon of Trent and Andreas of Rinn in the early modern period have made it difficult to eradicate this bloody Christian tale. And this is why former shrines such as that of Little Hugh of Lincoln, Simon of Trent, and Andreas of Rinn, despite their abolition in the second half of the twentieth century, persist unofficially, attracting antisemitic groups and individuals. This is also why antisemitic websites and chat groups are filled to the brim with articles on "Jewish Murder Plan against White Christians" that are, as one white supremacist online user announced, "backed up by records going back many centuries."

This long story of the persistence of anti-Jewish blood libels despite arguments to the contrary is dispiriting. Viewed in a *longue durée* and cast expansively across time and place, this story reveals what is now understood as "confirmation bias" or "cognitive bias," when readers embrace sources they agree with and find reliable, while rejecting information that contradicts their views, even if that information is in fact accurate. And with so many sources repeatedly telling the same deleterious stories about Jews, it is no wonder that belief in them has persisted. These stories, scattered across printed chronicles, not only introduced the image of "murderous" and dangerous Jews and reinforced the belief in blood accusations but also, as Richard Simon noted in 1670, reflected the same impulses that incited anti-Jewish violence—a statement still true today. Ostensibly incidental knowledge—like the tales and lore recorded as "facts" in the chronicles and cosmographies—has created patterns and perceptions difficult to root out. It matters what people read.

Premodern books focused on story content that is similar to today's "breaking news": "the sensational, exceptional, negative, recent, and incidental," while ignoring "the ordinary, usual, positive, historical, and systematic."[9] And, like today's news, true or fake, this knowledge disseminated through print created a historical record, a footprint that has shaped the way the public thinks about society and events. What the history of the blood libel also tells us is that political leadership matters, as do words and official statements. They might not always be effective nor prevent violence and hatred, but they provide a tangible trail of voices for those who want to turn into action and need moral support. For all the work behind the scenes to help Jews, the lack of an explicit public condemnation came to be read as a tacit approval. Silences are heard too.

Notes

Archival and Printed Primary Sources

Acknowledgments

Index

NOTES

See www.thebloodlibeltrail.org for additional images, interactive maps, and a full bibliography.

Introduction

1. Simon Rocker, "Facebook Refuses to Act over 'Blood Libel,'" *Jewish Chronicle*, February 20, 2014, https://www.thejc.com/news/uk-news/facebook-refuses-to-act-over-blood-libel-1.52591.
2. "May 2015—British Movement News & Views," http://bmsunwheel.blogspot.com/2015/05/may-2015-british-movement-news-views.html. I thank Nicholas Paul for bringing this to my attention.
3. Gavin I. Langmuir, *Toward a Definition of Antisemitism* (Berkeley: University of California Press, 1990), ch. 10, especially 237–238. See also David Carpenter, "Crucifixion and Conversion: King Henry III and the Jews in 1255," in *Laws, Lawyers, and Texts,* ed. Susanne Jenks, Jonathan Rose, and Christopher Whittick (Leiden: Brill, 2012), 129–148. For the text of the Anglo-Norman ballad, see Roger Darhood, "The Anglo-Norman 'Hugo de Lincolnia': A Critical Edition and Translation from the Unique Text in Paris, Bibliothèque Nationale De France Ms Fr. 902," *Chaucer Review* 49, no. 1 (2014).
4. "Christians and Jews: Towards Better Understanding," *Wiener Library Bulletin* 13, nos. 3–4 (1959): 60.
5. In 2009, a new plaque was placed near the shrine, commemorating the eighteen Jews who died as a result of this accusation.
6. Nicholas Sagovsky, "What Makes a Saint? A Lincoln Case Study in the Communion of the Local and the Universal Church," *International Journal for the*

Study of the Christian Church 17, no. 30 (2017): 173–183. On the attraction of such sites, see Magda Teter, "Blood Libel, a Lie, and Its Legacies," in *Whose Middle Ages?: Teachable Moments for an Ill-Used Past,* ed. Andrew Albin, Mary Carpenter Erler, Thomas O'Donnell, Nicholas Paul and Nina Rowe (New York: Fordham University Press, 2019), 44–57.

7. "Chi Siamo: Il *Comitato san Simonino,*" https://sansimoninotrento.wordpress.com/chi-siamo/.
8. Talia Lavin, "The San Diego Shooter's Manifesto Is a Modern Form of an Old Lie about Jews," *Washington Post,* April 29, 2019.
9. *La difesa della razza,* March 5, 1942.
10. Walter Quattrociocchi, Antonio Scala, and Cass R. Sunstein, "Echo Chambers on Facebook (June 13, 2016)," https://ssrn.com/abstract=2795110; Christine Emba, "Confirmed: Echo Chambers Exist on Social Media. So What Do We Do about Them?" *Washington Post,* July 14, 2016. Quote from Quattrociocchi et al., "Echo Chambers," 1–2.
11. Although some scholars conflate the two types of accusations, the distinction between "ritual cannibalism" and "ritual crucifixion" was made by Langmuir, *Toward a Definition of Antisemitism.*
12. On the decline in western Europe, see R. Po-chia Hsia, *The Myth of Ritual Murder: Jews and Magic in Reformation Germany* (New Haven: Yale University Press, 1988). On Poland, see Hanna Węgrzynek, *"Czarna Legenda" Żydów: Procesy o Rzekome Mordy Rytualne w Dawnej Polsce* (Warsaw: Bellona, 1995); Zenon Guldon and Jacek Wijaczka, *Procesy o Mordy Rytualne w Polsce w XVI–XVIII Wieku* (Kielce: DCF, 1995); Daniel Tollet, *Accuser pour convertir: du bon usage de l'accusation de crime rituel dans la Pologne catholique à l'époque moderne* (Paris: Presses universitaires de France, 2000); Meir Bałaban, "Hugo Grotius and the Blood Libel Trials in Lublin, 1636," in *Social and Cultural Boundaries in Pre-Modern Poland,* ed. Adam Teller, Magda Teter, and Antony Polonsky (Oxford: Littman, 2010). Jolanta Żyndul, *Kłamstwo Krwi: legenda mordu rytualnego na ziemiach polskich w XIX i XX wieku* (Warsaw: Wydawnictwo Cyklady, 2011).
13. Shlomo Simonsohn, *The Apostolic See and the Jews: Documents, 492–1404* (Toronto: Pontifical Institute of Mediaeval Studies, 1988), 191–192, no. 182. The English translation is available in Solomon Grayzel, *The Church and the Jews in the XIIIth Century: A Study of Their Relations during the Years 1198–1254* (Philadelphia: Dropsie College, 1933), 262–263, no. 113.
14. R. Po-chia Hsia, *Trent 1475: Stories of a Ritual Murder Trial* (New Haven: Yale University Press, 1992), 3.
15. *Martyrologium romanvm ad nouam kalendarij rationem, & Ecclesiasticae historiae veritatem reftitutum Gregorii XIII Pont. Max. iussu editum* (Rome: ex typographia Dominici Basae, 1583), 66–67, Nono Kal. April. Luna.
16. See Chapter 1 and John M. McCulloh, "Jewish Ritual Murder: William of Norwich, Thomas of Monmouth, and the Early Dissemination of the Myth," *Speculum* 72, no. 3 (1997): 698–740; Thomas of Monmouth and Miri Rubin, *The Life and Passion of William of Norwich,* trans. Miri Rubin (London: Penguin Books, 2014).

17. Langmuir, *Toward a Definition of Antisemitism;* Carpenter, "Crucifixion and Conversion"; Darhood, "The Anglo-Norman 'Hugo De Lincolnia.'"
18. *Benedicti XIV Papae Bullarium* vol. III.2: 215–225. On *Beatus Andreas,* see Nicola Cusumano, *Ebrei e accusa di omicidio rituale nel settecento: il carteggio tra Girolamo Tartarotti e Benedetto Bonelli, 1740–1748* (Milan: UNICOPLI, 2012); Nicola Cusumano, "I papi e le accuse di omicidio rituale: Benedetto XIV e la bolla 'Beatus Andreas,'" *Dimensioni e problemi della ricerca storica* 1 (2002): 7–35. On the cult of Andreas of Rinn, see Bernhard Fresacher, *Anderl von Rinn: Ritualmordkult und Neuorientierung in Judenstein 1945–1995* (Innsbruck: Tyrolia-Verlag, 1998); Georg R. Schroubek, "The Question of Historicity of Andrew of Rinn," in *Ritual Murder: Legend in European History* (Cracow: Association for Cultural Initiatives, 2003), 159–180. On Benedict XIV as the Enlightenment pope, see Rebecca Marie Messbarger, Christopher M. S. Johns, and Philip Gavitt, eds., *Benedict XIV and the Enlightenment: Art, Science, and Spirituality* (Toronto: University of Toronto Press, 2016); Gabriella Berti Logan, "Women and the Practice and Teaching of Medicine in Bologna in the Eighteenth and Early Nineteenth Centuries," *Bulletin of the History of Medicine* 77, no. 3 (2003): 506–535; and the almost adulatory work by Renée Haynes, *Philosopher King: The Humanist Pope Benedict XIV* (London: Weidenfeld and Nicolson, 1970).
19. It was published in a German translation in 1888 by A. Berliner as *Gutachen Ganganelli's—Clemens XIV—Angelengenheit der Blutbeschuldigung der Juden* (Berlin: Ph. Deutch, 1888); then in the original by Loeb, "Un memoire de Laurent Ganganelli sur la calomnie du meurtre ritual," *Revue des études juives* (1889), 179–211; and then with additional materials, by Moritz Stern, *Die Päpstlichen Bullen über die Blutbeschuldigung* (Munich: August Schupp, 1900).
20. Alessandro Maria Gottardi, "Notificazione circa il culto al piccolo Simone da Trento," *Rivista diocesana tridentina* XCI, October (1965): 595–596. I am grateful to Marco Iacovella of the Scuola Normale Superiore in Pisa for helping me obtain a copy of this text.
21. "Can. 1284. Locorum Ordinarii reliquiam, quam certo non esse authenticam norint, a fidelium cultu prudenter amoveant," in Pope Pius X, *Codex Iuris Canonici,* vol. IX, part II, Acta Apostolicae Sedis Commentarium Officiale (Rome: Typis Polyglotis Vaticanis, 1917), 249.
22. Vatican II, "Declaration on the Relation of the Church to Non-Christian Religions *Nostra Aetate.*"
23. Magda Teter, "Painting Inspires Dialogue between Jews and Catholics in Poland," *The Forward,* March 7, 2014, and "The Sandomierz Paintings of Ritual Murder as *Lieux De Mémoire,*" in *Ritual Murder in Russia, Eastern Europe, and Beyond: New Histories of an Old Accusation,* ed. Eugene M. Avrutin, Jonathan Dekel-Chen, and Robert Weinberg (Bloomington: Indiana University Press, 2017), 253–277.

1. From Medieval Tales to the Challenge in Trent

1. Hartmann Schedel and Stephan Füssel, *Chronicle of the World: The Complete and Annotated Nuremberg Chronicle of 1493* (Köln: Taschen, 2001), 7; Hartmann Schedel, *Liber chronicarum* (Nuremberg: Anton Koberger, 1493). The German version is known as *Weltchronik*.
2. Schedel and Füssel, *Chronicle of the World,* 9.
3. Schedel and Füssel, *Chronicle of the World,* 9, 15, 21–24.
4. Aside from the representations of biblical figures, the very first examples of visual representations of Jews in print seem to be illustrated pamphlets telling the story of Simon of Trent in 1475. On some of the earliest visual representations of Jews in printed books, see also, David S. Areford, *The Viewer and the Printed Image in Late Medieval Europe* (Farnham, UK: Ashgate, 2010).
5. Schedel, *Liber chronicarum,* CXLIX verso, CCI verso, CCXX verso, CCXXX verso, CCLIIII verso, CCLVIII verso.
6. Some obscure early modern printed chronicles included a story from 1053 Prague.
7. See, for example, Paul Oskar Kristeller, "The Alleged Ritual Murder of Simon of Trent (1475) and Its Literary Repercussions," *Proceedings of the American Academy for Jewish Research* 59 (1993); Stephen D. Bowd and J. Donald Cullington, *"On Everyone's Lips": Humanists, Jews, and the Tale of Simon of Trent* (Tempe, AZ: Brepols, 2012); Laura Da! Prà, "L'immagine di Simonino nell'arte Trentina dal XV al XVIII secolo," in *Il Principe Vescovo Johannes Hinderbach (1465–1486),* ed. Iginio Rogger and Marco Bellabarba (Bologna: Edizioni Dehoniane, 1992); Anna Esposito, "Il culto del 'beato' Simonino e la sua prima diffusione in Italia," in *Il Principe Vescovo;* Nicola Cusumano, "L'accusa di omicidio rituale: undici lettere di Girolamo Tartarotti a Benedetto Bonelli (1740–46)," *Dimensioni e Problemi della Ricerca Storica,* 2 (2002): 153–194; Gianni Gentilini, *Pasqua 1475: Antigiudaismo e lotta alle eresie: il caso di Simonino* (Milano: Medusa, 2007); Valentina Perini, *Il Simonino: Geografia di un culto* (Trento: Società di studi trentini di scienze storiche, 2012); Laura Dal Prà, "Ancora su Hinderbach e la sua creazione iconografica, con la scoperta del ciclo Simoniniano di S. Maria della Misericordia di Trento," in Perini, *Il Simonino;* Diego Quaglioni, "Uno stereotipo antigiudaico per immagini," in Perini, *Il Simonino;* R. Po-chia Hsia, *Trent 1475: Stories of a Ritual Murder Trial* (New Haven: Yale University Press, 1992); Gianni Gentilini, *Pasqua 1475: antigiudaismo e lotta alle eresie: il caso di Simonino* (Milano: Medusa, 2007); Joseph Jacobs, "St. William of Norwich," *The Jewish Quarterly Review,* no. 4 (1897): 748–755; John M. McCulloh, "Jewish Ritual Murder: William of Norwich, Thomas of Monmouth, and the Early Dissemination of the Myth," *Speculum* 72, no. 3 (1997): 698–740; Gillian Bennett, "Towards a Revaluation of the Legend of 'Saint' William of Norwich and Its Place in the Blood Libel Legend," *Folklore,* no. 2 (2005): 119; Gillian Bennett, "William of Norwich and the Expulsion of the Jews," *Folklore,* no. 3 (2005): 311–314; Denise L. Despres, "Adolescence and Sanctity: The Life and Passion of Saint William of Norwich," *Journal of Religion* 90, no. 1 (2010): 33–62; Miri Rubin, "Making a Martyr: William of

Norwich and the Jews," *History Today* 60, no. 6 (2010): 48–54; Heather Blurton, "The Language of the Liturgy in the Life and Miracles of William of Norwich," *Speculum* 90, no. 4 (2015): 1053–1075; Uri Z. Shachar, "Inspecting the Pious Body: Christological Morphology and the Ritual-Crucifixion Allegation," *Journal of Medieval History* 41, no. 1 (2015): 21–40; Thomas of Monmouth and Miri Rubin, *The Life and Passion of William of Norwich,* trans. Miri Rubin (London: Penguin Books, 2014).

8. Most recently on Richard of Pontoise and King Philip Augustus of France, see Kenneth R. Stow, *Jewish Dogs: An Image and Its Interpreters: Continuity in the Catholic-Jewish Encounter* (Stanford: Stanford University Press, 2006), ch. 3; E. M. Rose, *The Murder of William of Norwich: The Origins of the Blood Libel in Medieval Europe* (Oxford: Oxford University Press, 2015).

9. On Werner of Oberwesel, see later notes and Henri de Grèzes, *Saint Vernier (Verny, Werner, Garnier), martyr, patron des vignerons en Auvergne, en Bourgogne et en Franche-Comtè, sa vie, son martyre et son culte* (Clermont-Ferrand: L. Brustel, 1889); André Vauchez, "Antisémitisme et canonisation populaire: Saint Werner ou Vernier (+1287), enfant martyr et patron des vignerons," *Comptes renus des séances de l'Académie des Inscriptions et Belles-Lettres* 126, no. 1 (1982): 65–79.

10. Gavin I. Langmuir, *Toward a Definition of Antisemitism* (Berkeley: University of California Press, 1990), 209–236. Rubin, "Making a Martyr"; Monmouth and Rubin, *Life and Passion,* "Introduction." Most recently, see, with caution, Rose, *Murder of William of Norwich.*

11. McCulloh, "Jewish Ritual Murder"; Monmouth and Rubin, *Life and Passion.*

12. The most detailed analysis to date of the history of Thomas Monmouth's *Life and Passion of William of Norwich* is McCulloh, "Jewish Ritual Murder," quote on 704.

13. McCulloh, "Jewish Ritual Murder." Langmuir uses that phrase in the index; in the text it appears in various combinations: "crucifixion accusation," "crucifixion libel," and others. See also Robert C. Stacey, "From Ritual Crucifixion to Host Desecration: Jews and the Body of Christ," *Jewish History* 12, no. 1 (1998). Shachar, "Inspecting the Pious Body."

14. Monmouth and Rubin, *Life and Passion,* 26.

15. Jeffrey J. Cohen, "The Flow of Blood in Medieval Norwich," *Speculum* 79, no. 1 (2004): 26–65.

16. See also Sara Lipton, *Dark Mirror: The Medieval Origins of Anti-Jewish Iconography* (New York: Metropolitan Books, 2014), for a discussion of the development of anti-Jewish iconography in this context.

17. Monmouth and Rubin, *Life and Passion,* for example, 31.

18. Monmouth and Rubin, *Life and Passion,* 10. On Marian devotion in England, see Kati Ihnat, *Mother of Mercy, Bane of the Jews: Devotion to the Virgin Mary in Anglo-Norman England* (Princeton, NJ: Princeton University Press, 2016).

19. On rose as a symbol of Mary, see for example, Rachel Fulton, "The Virgin in the Garden, or Why Flowers Make Better Prayers," *Spiritus: A Journal of Christian Spirituality,* no. 1 (2004); Adrienne Nock Ambrose, "The Virgin of the Rosary and Florid Sculpture in Late Medieval Germany," *ARTS* 11, no. 1

(1999); Anne Winston-Allen, *Stories of the Rose: The Making of the Rosary in the Middle Ages* (University Park: Pennsylvania State University Press, 1997), 89. On the blood of Christ represented as roses, see Caroline Walker Bynum, *Wonderful Blood: Theology and Practice in Late Medieval Northern Germany and Beyond* (Philadelphia: University of Pennsylvania Press, 2007), 3.
20. Ambrose, "Virgin of the Rosary," 12.
21. Fulton, "Virgin in the Garden," 9.
22. Monmouth and Rubin, *Life and Passion*, 44–45.
23. Victoria Larson, "A Rose Blooms in the Winter: The Tradition of the Hortus Conclusus and Its Significance as a Devotional Emblem," *Dialog: A Journal of Theology* 52, no. 4 (2013): 303–312.
24. Monmouth and Rubin, *Life and Passion*, 13–17.
25. The vision is found in Monmouth and Rubin, *Life and Passion*, 49–51.
26. Monmouth and Rubin, *Life and Passion*, 19, 25, 26. On similar torture and suffering during the civil war, see Rose, *Murder of William of Norwich*, 18.
27. Monmouth and Rubin, *Life and Passion*, 18.
28. Monmouth and Rubin, *Life and Passion*, 24, 25, 28.
29. Langmuir, *Toward a Definition of Antisemitism*, 221.
30. Monmouth and Rubin, *Life and Passion*, 13; Rose, *Murder of William of Norwich*, ch. 1.
31. Monmouth and Rubin, *Life and Passion*, 43–44.
32. Monmouth and Rubin, *Life and Passion*, 56–57.
33. Paul A. Hayward, "The Idea of Innocent Martyrdom in Late Tenth and Eleventh Century English Hagiology," *Studies in Church History* 30 (1993): 81–92. On child saints more broadly, see William F. MacLehose, *"A Tender Age": Cultural Anxieties over the Child in the Twelfth and Thirteenth Centuries*, E-Gutenberg (New York: Columbia University Press, 2007). MacLehose focuses on England and incorrectly states that Simon of Trent was canonized (ch. 3). On child victims of violent murder as martyrs, see also, with caution, Patricia Healy Wasyliw, *Martyrdom, Murder, and Magic: Child Saints and Their Cults in Medieval Europe* (New York: Peter Lang, 2008), ch. 5.
34. Hayward, "Idea of Innocent Martyrdom," 83.
35. Monmouth and Rubin, *Life and Passion*, 57.
36. Despres, "Adolescence and Sanctity," 47–48.
37. Monmouth and Rubin, *Life and Passion*, 57–58, 63. Also see Despres, "Adolescence and Sanctity," 52–56.
38. Matthew 2:16–18.
39. On the Holy Innocents evoked to support the argument for child saints said to have been killed by Jews, see Chapter 3 and, for Benedict XIV, see Chapter 8. On the cult of the Holy Innocents, see Wasyliw, *Martyrdom, Murder, and Magic*, ch. 2. Jews developed a counternarrative with their own "holy innocents": the infants of the Hebrews killed to heal the Pharaoh's leprosy; Ephraim Shoham-Steiner, "Pharaoh's Bloodbath: Medieval Jewish Thoughts about Leprosy, Disease, and Blood Therapy," in *Jewish Blood: Reality and Metaphor in History, Religion and Culture*, ed. Mitchell B. Hart (London: Routledge, 2009), 99–115. David Malkiel, "Infanticide in Passover Iconography," *Journal of Warburg and Courtland Institutes* 56 (1993).

40. Wasyliw, *Martyrdom, Murder, and Magic,* 34.
41. Monmouth and Rubin, *Life and Passion,* 58.
42. Langmuir, *Toward a Definition of Antisemitism,* 234–235.
43. McCulloh, "Jewish Ritual Murder"; Monmouth and Rubin, *The Life and Passion,* lii–lxiii.
44. Blurton, "Language of the Liturgy," 1053. Anthony Paul Bale, *The Jew in the Medieval Book: English Antisemitisms, 1350–1500* (Cambridge: Cambridge University Press, 2006).
45. Blurton, "Language of the Liturgy," 1054.
46. Blurton, "Language of the Liturgy," 1064–1066, 1068–1069, 1075.
47. Blurton, "Language of the Liturgy," 1071. Theresa Tinkle, "Exegesis Reconsidered: The Fleury "Slaughter of Innocents" and the Myth of Ritual Murder," *Journal of English and Germanic Philology* 102, no. 2 (2003): 212–213.
48. See also Ihnat, *Mother of Mercy.*
49. Wasyliw, *Martyrdom, Murder, and Magic,* 114.
50. For an overview of the development of procedures, see Robert J. Sarno, "Canonization of Saints (History and Procedure)," in *New Catholic Encyclopedia: Supplement* (2010); E. W. Kemp, "Pope Alexander III and the Canonization of Saints: The Alexander Prize Essay," *Transactions of the Royal Historical Society* (1945); Peter Brown, *The Cult of the Saints: Its Rise and Function in Latin Christianity* (Chicago: University of Chicago Press, 1981); Richard Gribble, "Saints in the Christian Tradition: Unraveling the Canonization Process," *Studies in Christian-Jewish Relations* 6, no. 1 (2011); André Vauchez, *Sainthood in the Later Middle Ages* (Cambridge: Cambridge University Press, 2005). For the period following Pope Alexander III's bull of 1180, see Ronald C. Finucane, *Contested Canonizations: The Last Medieval Saints, 1482–1523* (Washington, DC: Catholic University of America Press, 2011), ch. 1. See also Lipton, *Dark Mirror,* 65–66.
51. Vauchez, *Sainthood,* 27.
52. Kemp, "Pope Alexander III and the Canonization of Saints," 13.
53. Jacques Paul Migne, *Patrologia Latina* 84, col. 212 (in a database).
54. Kemp, "Pope Alexander III and the Canonization of Saints," 13–14.
55. Monmouth and Rubin, *Life and Passion,* 31.
56. Monmouth and Rubin, *Life and Passion,* 34–35.
57. Sarno, "Canonization of Saints," 194–195.
58. Monmouth and Rubin, *Life and Passion,* 41.
59. Jean Bolland et al., *Acta Sanctorum Martii* (Antverpiae: apud Iacobum Meursium, 1668), vol. 3: 588–591, esp., introduction on 588.
60. John of Tynemouth and John Capgrave, *Explicit (Noua Lege[n]da Anglie)* (London: Wynkyn de Worde, 1516), CCCIX verso–CCX verso. For a detailed discussion of the dissemination of Thomas's work, see McCulloh, "Jewish Ritual Murder," 710, which discusses the John of Tynemouth version. The Bollandists acknowledged that the 1516 edition was their source in the discussion of Hugh of Lincoln under July 6.
61. Langmuir, *Toward a Definition of Antisemitism,* ch. 10, esp. 237–238. See also David Carpenter, "Crucifixion and Conversion: King Henry III and the Jews in 1255," in *Laws, Lawyers, and Texts,* ed. Susanne Jenks, Jonathan Rose, and

Christopher Whittick (Leiden: Brill, 2012), 129–148. For the text of the Anglo-Norman ballad, see Roger Darhood, "The Anglo-Norman "Hugo De Lincolnia": A Critical Edition and Translation from the Unique Text in Paris, Bibliothèque Nationale De France Ms Fr. 902," *Chaucer Review* 49, no. 1 (2014).

62. Tynemouth and Capgrave, *Explicit (Noua Lege[n]da Anglie)*.
63. Langmuir, *Toward a Definition of Antisemitism*, 240–241. See also a table listing the accusations in Joe Hillaby, "The Ritual-Child-Murder Accusation: Its Dissemination and Harold of Gloucester," *Jewish Historical Studies* 34 (1994): 86.
64. On Robert of Bury, see Bale, *Jew in the Medieval Book*, ch. 4.
65. Hillaby, "The Ritual-Child-Murder Accusation," 74. For a chronological listing, see, for example, Bale, *Jew in the Medieval Book*, 16.
66. On Hugh of Lincoln, see Langmuir, *Toward a Definition of Antisemitism*, ch. 10.
67. Anthony Bale stresses the role of Benedictine networks in the dissemination and support for the cults, Bale, *Jew in the Medieval Book*, 16–17.
68. Wasyliw, *Martyrdom, Murder, and Magic*, 176, n. 113.
69. McCulloh, "Jewish Ritual Murder," 724.
70. Susan L. Einbinder, *Beautiful Death: Jewish Poetry and Martyrdom in Medieval France* (Princeton, N.J.: Princeton University Press, 2002); on Blois, see ch. 2.
71. For a discussion of both, see Stow, *Jewish Dogs*, chs. 3 and 4. For a discussion of the Hebrew sources, see Einbinder, *Beautiful Death*, ch. 2. Robert Chazan, "The Blois Incident of 1171: A Study in Jewish Intercommunal Organization," *Proceedings of the American Academy for Jewish Research* 36 (1968).
72. Rigord, *Gesta Philippi Augusti*, in *Œuvres de Rigord et de Guillaume le Breton, Historiens de Philippe-Auguste: Chroniques de Rigord et de Guillaume le Breton*, ed. Henri F. Delaborde (Paris: Librairie Renouard,1882), 15. For the Bollandist version, see Bolland et al., *Acta Sanctorum Martii*, vol. III, 592. On this, see Kenneth R. Stow, *Jewish Dogs*, 84. I thank Sara Lipton for pointing out the differences between the Bollandist version and that edited by Delaborde. For an extensive study of Jews under the Capetians, see William Chester Jordan, *The French Monarchy and the Jews: From Philip Augustus to the Last Capetians* (Philadelphia: University of Pennsylvania Press, 1989).
73. Stow, *Jewish Dogs*.
74. Stow, *Jewish Dogs*, 76.
75. Bolland et al., *Acta Sanctorum Martii*, III: 591–594, March 25.
76. A succinct summary of the case can be found in Anna Sapir Abulafia, *Christian-Jewish Relations, 1000–1300: Jews in the Service of Medieval Christendom*, ed. Julia Smith (Harlow, UK: Pearson, 2011), 182–184.
77. The sources are published in Adolf Neubauer and Moritz Stern, *Hebräische Berichte über die Judenverfolgungen Während der Kreuzzüge* (Berlin: Simion, 1892), 31–35, 66–69. An English translation of some of the sources is in Susan L. Einbinder, "The Jewish Martyrs of Blois, 1171," in *Medieval Hagiography: An Anthology*, ed. Thomas Head (New York: Routledge, 2001), 537–560. Robert Chazan, *Church, State, and Jew in the Middle Ages* (New York: Behrman House, 1980), 114–117, 301–304; Stow, *Jewish Dogs*, appendix II.

78. Einbinder, *Beautiful Death*, 47. See the "Orleans Letter" in Neubauer and Stern, *Hebräische Berichte*. The English translation is in Chazan, *Church, State, and Jew*, 301–304.
79. Einbinder, *Beautiful Death*, 48.
80. Robert seems to have conflated a number of cases with the one in Blois; Robert de Torigni, *The Chronicles of Robert de Monte* (London: Llanerch Publishers, 1856), 114–115.
81. Einbinder, *Beautiful Death*, 18, 45–46, 57, 59–61.
82. Neubauer and Stern, *Hebräische Berichte*, 68.
83. Einbinder, *Beautiful Death*, 61–62.
84. Einbinder, "Jewish Martyrs of Blois, 1171," 548.
85. On Jewish literary responses, see Chapter 5. See also the "Orleans Letter" for the tropes of sacrifice and atonement; Neubauer and Stern, *Hebräische Berichte*.
86. Neubauer and Stern, *Hebräische Berichte*, 31–34. Cf., English translation in Chazan, *Church, State, and Jew*, 301–304.
87. Israel Yuval, "God Will See the Blood: Sin, Punishment, and Atonement in Jewish-Christian Discourse," in *Jewish Blood: Reality and Metaphor in History, Religion and Culture*, ed. Mitchell B. Hart (London: Routledge, 2009), 98.
88. Neubauer and Stern, *Hebräische Berichte*, 35. English translation in Stow, *Jewish Dogs*, 202.
89. Neubauer and Stern, *Hebräische Berichte*, 32. English translation in Chazan, *Church, State, and Jew*, 302.
90. On the history of the ordeal see Robert Bartlett, *Trial by Fire and Water: The Medieval Judicial Ordeal* (Oxford: Clarendon Press, 1986). On the problems with ordeal by cold water, see 74.
91. Neubauer and Stern, *Hebräische Berichte*, 33. In the account by Ephraim of Bonn, the Christian servant of the lord is subjected to this ordeal; Neubauer and Stern, *Hebräische Berichte*, 67.
92. Stow, *Jewish Dogs*, 102–103.
93. Bartlett, *Trial by Fire and Water*, 53–54.
94. BT Sanhedrin 56a: "Our rabbis taught: The Noahides were commanded regarding seven commandments: (1) Justice, (2) Blasphemy, (3) Idol Worship, (4) Sexual Immorality (5) Murder, (6) Robbery (7) Eating the limb of a living animal." BT Sanhedrin 56b expanded on this teaching, arguing that just as Israelites were commanded to establish courts of justice in all towns, so too were the Noahides [*benei Noah*] required to do so.
95. Neubauer and Stern, *Hebräische Berichte*, 67.
96. Einbinder, *Beautiful Death*, 48.
97. Neubauer and Stern, *Hebräische Berichte*, 34–35. NB: the phrase *basurah tovah* is often used as a name for Gospels. Kenneth Stow discussed these letters in detail in Stow, *Jewish Dogs*, chap. 4.
98. Neubauer and Stern, *Hebräische Berichte*, 34–35. An English version is in Chazan, *Church, State, and Jew in the Middle Ages*, 115–116. The Hebrew word is *kadesh*; Chazan uses the word "beatified" in his translation, but there was no beatification at that time. Stow, *Jewish Dogs*, 201–202.

99. Chazan, "The Blois Incident of 1171." Kenneth Stow challenges the assumption that these letters followed the Blois affair, arguing for a later dating, Stow, *Jewish Dogs*, ch. 4.
100. Stow, *Jewish Dogs*, 110. Historically, medieval French monarchs could not boast of guaranteeing safety to Jews: they were responsible for repeated expulsions; efforts to curtail Jewish economic activity; and the confiscation, censorship, and burning of Hebrew books are what mark French monarchs' official pronouncements concerning Jews, at least since 1182.
101. Neubauer and Stern, *Hebräische Berichte*, VII; for the narratives, see 31–35.
102. Neubauer and Stern, *Hebräische Berichte*, 58–75; for the Blois narrative, see 66–69.
103. According to Thomas of Monmouth, the royal sheriff of Norwich seems to have done the same in 1144, but beyond Thomas's narrative there is no reliable evidence of the responses of Christian authorities to the libels before Fulda and Valréas.
104. "Privilegium et sententia in favorem iudaeorum," in *Monumenta Germaniae Historica*, ed. Ludwig Weiland, Jakob Schwalm, and Margarete Kuhn (Hannover: Hahn, 1896), 2: 274–276, no. 204. "Annales Merbacenses," in *Monumenta Germaniae Historica* (MGH) 17: 178; "Annales Erphordienses," MGH 16:31. Matthias Eißler, "Annales Erphordenses Fratrum Praedicatorum," in *Encyclopedia of the Medieval Chronicle*, ed. Graeme Dunphy. http://dx.doi.org/10.1163/2213-2139_emc_EMCSIM_00129. Gavin Langmuir discusses the two stories in his *Toward a Definition of Antisemitism*, ch. 11: "Ritual Cannibalism."
105. "Privilegium et sententia in favorem iudaeorum," MGH 2: 274–276.
106. "Annales Erphordienses," MGH 16:31.
107. "Annales Erphordienses," MGH 16:31.
108. Langmuir, *Toward a Definition of Antisemitism*, 271–276.
109. "Annales Merbacenses," MGH 17: 178. A different version of this chronicle, with verbatim wording but also some gaps, was first published in the section, "Fragmentum Historicum Auctoris Incerti" of vol. 2 of Christian Wurtisen, *Germaniae historicorum illustrium, quorum pleriq[ue] ab Henrico IIII Imperatore usque ad annum Christi, M. CCCC, ex ijs quidem septem nunquam antea editi, gentis eius res gestas memoriae consecrarunt* (Frankfurt a.M: Apud haeredes Andreae Wecheli, 1585). The section on Fulda is on p. 51, lines 14–24 of vol. 2.
110. "Annales Merbacenses," MGH 17: 178.
111. Or, perhaps, he referred only to the first phase of its inquiry.
112. "Privilegium et sententia in favorem iudaeorum," MGH 2: 274–276.
113. "Privilegium et sententia in favorem iudaeorum," MGH 2: 274–276.
114. See also Shlomo Simonsohn, *The Apostolic See and the Jews: History* (Toronto: Pontifical Institute of Mediaeval Studies, 1991), 49–50.
115. Simonsohn, *The Apostolic See and the Jews: Documents*, 492–1404, 192: no. 183; 194: no. 185; Solomon Grayzel, *The Church and the Jews in the XIIIth Century: A Study of Their Relations during the Years 1198–1254* (Philadelphia: Dropsie College, 1933), 268–271, 274–275, nos. 116 and 118. Grayzel

and Simonsohn have two different dates for the *Sicut Iudaeis*. Grayzel dates it to July, but Simonsohn to June. Others give additional dates. see Grayzel, *The Church and the Jews*, 274, n. 1.
116. Grayzel, *Church and the Jews*, 274–275, no. 118.
117. For a summary of what is known about Valréas and primary sources associated with it, see Auguste Molinier, *Enquête sur un meurtre imputé aux Juifs de Valréas* (Paris: H. Champion, 1883).
118. Molinier, *Enquête*, 13.
119. Molinier, *Enquête*, 8–9. The names mentioned were common among Provençal and Catalonian Jews.
120. Molinier, *Enquête*, 9.
121. Molinier, *Enquête*, 9–10.
122. Molinier, *Enquête*, 10.
123. Molinier, *Enquête*, 10–11.
124. Grayzel, *Church and the Jews*, 262–267: nos. 113–114.
125. Grayzel, *Church and the Jews*, 262–263, no. 113.
126. Simonsohn, *Apostolic See and the Jews*, 190–191, no. 181. English, Grayzel, *Church and the Jews*, 264–265, no. 114.
127. May 9, 1244, to the King of France; Simonsohn, *Apostolic See and the Jews*, 250–251, no. 104.
128. Grayzel, *Church and the Jews*, 264–265, no. 114.
129. Simonsohn, *Apostolic See and the Jews*, 192: no. 183; 194: no. 185.
130. Grayzel, *Church and the Jews*, 274–275, no. 118.
131. Simonsohn, *Apostolic See and the Jews*, 194, no. 185. Grayzel, *Church and the Jews*, 268–269, no. 115.
132. Num. 9: 6–13; some Israelites were concerned about not being able to celebrate Passover because of uncleanliness resulting from touching the dead, but God allows them to celebrate it. *Kohanim*, of the priestly line, are forbidden to touch dead bodies altogether, except for the closest relations, Lev. 21:1–4. For a discussion of rabbinic laws on the subject, see Maimonides, *Mishneh Torah*, "Hilkhot tumat met," in vol. 10 "Sefer tahara."
133. Simonsohn, *Apostolic See and the Jews*, 197, no. 188.
134. Molinier, *Enquête*, 9–11.
135. Molinier, *Enquête*, 9.
136. Molinier, *Enquête*, 10 and 11.
137. For primary sources on the Talmud trial, see Robert Chazan, Jean Hoff, and John Friedman, *The Trial of the Talmud: Paris, 1240* (Toronto: Pontifical Institute of Mediaeval Studies, 2012).
138. Exodus 29, Leviticus 4 and 16. See more in Michael Swartz, "The Topography of Blood in Mishnah *Yoma*," in *Jewish Blood: Reality and Metaphor in History, Religion and Culture*, ed. Mitchell B. Hart (London: Routledge, 2009), 70–82.
139. Mishnah *Yoma* 4:3, see Swartz, "The Topography of Blood."
140. Mishnah *Yoma* 4:3 and 5:5 quoted in Swartz, "The Topography of Blood," 76.
141. Shoham-Steiner, "Pharaoh's Bloodbath." David Biale discusses the medieval period more broadly, beyond the specific context predating 1247. David

Biale, *Blood and Belief: The Circulation of a Symbol between Jews and Christians* (Berkeley: University of California Press, 2007), chap. 3.
142. Shoham-Steiner, "Pharaoh's Bloodbath," 108–109.
143. Shoham-Steiner, "Pharaoh's Bloodbath"; Malkiel, "Infanticide in Passover Iconography."
144. Bynum, *Wonderful Blood*.
145. "Annales Merbacenses," MGH 17: 178.
146. In Valréas, there is evidence of attempts to make a shrine, but these attempts do not seem to have been successful, Grayzel, *Church and the Jews*, 262–265: nos. 113–114.
147. The best and most concise discussion of the cult is Vauchez, "Antisémitisme et canonisation populaire." Kenneth Stow has recently discussed Werner in another context, Stow, *Jewish Dogs*, 60–64. There is also the apologetic and quite dated work by Henri de Grèzes, but it does contain some primary sources, Grèzes, *Saint Vernier*. See also Gerd Mentgen, "Die Ritualmordaffäre um den "Guten Werner" von Oberwesel und ihre Folgen," *Jahrbuch für westdeutsche Landesgeschichte* 21 (1995): 159–198.
148. Vauchez, "Antisémitisme et canonisation populaire," 66, n. 3.
149. Chronicon Colmariense, 1288 "De compositione Judaeorum," MGH 17: 255. Vauchez, "Antisémitisme et canonisation populaire," 66–67. The chronicle was first published in 1585 in vol. 2 of Wurtisen, *Germaniae Historicorum Illustrium;* the specific passage is in 2:50.
150. Chronicon Colmariense, 1288 "De compositione Judaeorum," MGH 17: 255.
151. Vauchez, "Antisémitisme et canonisation populaire," 66–67.
152. Vauchez, "Antisémitisme et canonisation populaire," 67–70. For the examples of claims about bribes, see also "Annales Colmarienses Maiores, Anno 1287/1288," MGH 17:215, and "Chronicon Colmariensis," MGH 17:255.
153. The request is now in BAV, Pal.lat 858. Vauchez, "Antisémitisme et canonisation populaire," 70–71. The mention of Werner in the indulgences granted to the chapel of S. Cunibert were later interpreted as a sanction for his veneration; see, for example, Grèzes, *Saint Vernier*.
154. Vauchez, "Antisémitisme et canonisation populaire." Grèzes's apologetic work about the cult of "S. Vernier" devoted much attention to its controversial nature; Grèzes, *Saint Vernier*. For the text of the 1422 bull by Pope Martin V prohibiting blood libels, see Moritz Stern, *Die Päpstlichen Bullen über die Blutbeschuldigung* (Munich: August Schupp, 1900), 25–29.
155. Grèzes, *Saint Vernier*, ch. XVIII; Vauchez, "Antisémitisme et canonisation populaire," 75; Godefroid Henschen and Daniel Van Papenbroeck, *Acta Sanctorum Aprilis collecta, digesta, illustrata tomus II. quo medii XI dies continentur* (Antwerp: apud Michaelem Cnobarum, 1675), 734–735.
156. Vauchez, "Antisémitisme et canonisation populaire," 77. For an example of a modern rediscovery of the cult's history and a new anti-Jewish framing influenced by modern antisemitism and the rise of new accusations against Jews in the late nineteenth century, see Grèzes, *Saint Vernier*.
157. Bynum, *Wonderful Blood*, 12.

158. On the dispersion of the relics, see Henschen and Van Papenbroeck, *Acta Sanctorum Aprilis, Tomus II*, 735–740, and on Belgium and Italy specifically, see 739–740.
159. Jacques de Voragine, *Hystorie plurimorum sanctorum noviter e laboriose ex diversis libris in unum collecte* (Lavanii: Johannis de Westfalia, 1485), 54v–55v.
160. Laurentius Surius, *De probatis sanctorum historiis. . . . complectens sanctos mensium martii et aprilis* (Coloniae Agrippinae: Calenius & Quentel, 1578), 775–776. Werner's story was added in 1581 to an appendix to the earlier edition, which did not include the story in its volume for March–April published in 1571; Laurentius Surius, *Tomus VII de probatis sanctorum historiis: in quem ordine mensium obseruato relatae sunt cum omnes illae historiae, quae ad secundam sex tomorum editionem accesserunt* (Coloniae Agrippinae: apud Geruinum Calenium et haeredes Quentelios, 1581), 319–320.
161. Henschen and Van Papenbroeck, *Acta Sanctorum Aprilis, Tomus II*, 697.
162. Henschen and Van Papenbroeck, *Acta Sanctorum Aprilis, Tomus II*, e.g., 714, and 718.
163. Henschen and Van Papenbroeck, *Acta Sanctorum Aprilis, Tomus II*, 697–740.
164. Grèzes, *Saint Vernier*, 98; the text of the office is on 151–157; Vauchez, "Antisémitisme et canonisation populaire," 77.
165. Grèzes, *Saint Vernier*, XLVIII. On Benedict XIV and his view of beatification and canonization of purported child martyrs, see Chapter 8.
166. Stow, *Jewish Dogs*, 60–64.
167. Vauchez, "Antisémitisme et canonisation populaire," 78.
168. Daniela Rando, *Dai margini la memoria: Johannes Hinderbach (1418–1486)* (Bologna: Il Mulino, 2003), 473.

2. The Death of Little Simon and the Trial of Jews in Trent

1. Archivio di Stato di Trento, Archivio Principesco Vescovile, Sezione latina 69, document 17. Henceforth, AST, APV, s.l. 69.
2. See for example, Gemma Volli, *I "processi tridentini" e il culto del Beato Simone da Trento* (Florence: La Nuova Italia, 1963), 64; Lamberto Donati, *L' inizio della stampa a Trento ed il Beato Simone* (Trento: Centro culturale "Fratelli Bronzetti" e Centro di studi turistici della città di Trento, 1968); Anna Esposito and Diego Quaglioni, *Processi contro gli ebrei di Trento (1475–1478)*, vol. 1 (Padova: CEDAM, 1990) and *Processi contro gli ebrei di Trento: I processi alle donne (1475–1476)*, vol. 2 (Padova: CEDAM, 2008); R. Po-chia Hsia, *Trent 1475: Stories of a Ritual Murder Trial* (New Haven: Yale University Press, 1992); Iginio Rogger and Marco Bellabarba, *Il Principe Vescovo Johannes Hinderbach (1465–1486)* (Bologna: Edizioni Dehoniane, 1992); Paul Oskar Kristeller, "The Alleged Ritual Murder of Simon of Trent (1475) and Its Literary Repercussions," *PAAJR* 59 (1993); Wolfgang Treue, *Der Trienter Judenprozess: Voraussetzungen, Abläufe, Auswirkungen (1475–1588)* (Hannover: Hahn, 1996); Gianni Gentilini, *Pasqua 1475: Antigiudaismo e*

lotta alle eresie: Il caso di Simonino (Milano: Medusa, 2007); Valentina Perini, *Il Simonino: geografia di un culto* (Trento: Società di studi trentini di scienze storiche, 2012).

3. Jennifer Bishop, "The Clerk's Tale: Civic Writing in Sixteenth-Century London," *Past & Present* 230, suppl. 11 (2016): 112.
4. Diego Quaglioni has written extensively on the legal context and questions of evidence in the Trent trial; see for example, Diego Quaglioni, "Giustizia criminale e cultura giuridica: i giuristi Trentini e i processi contro gli ebrei," in *Il Principe Vescovo Johannes Hinderbach (1465–1486)*, ed. Iginio Rogger and Marco Bellabarba (Bologna: Edizioni Dehoniane, 1992).
5. On Hinderbach, his life, educational and political background, and interests, see Rogger and Bellabarba, *Il Principe Vescovo*; Daniela Rando, *Dai margini la memoria: Johannes Hinderbach (1418–1486)* (Bologna: Il Mulino, 2003).
6. On the political context of Trent, see Josef Riedman, "Rapporti del principato vescovile di Trento con il conte del Tirolo: le cosiddette *Compattate* del 1468," in *Il Principe Vescovo*.
7. On Hinderbach's election as bishop, see Rando, *Dai margini la memoria*, 219–228.
8. The reconstruction of the first days is based on trial records in Esposito and Quaglioni, *Processi*, vol. I.
9. Esposito and Quaglioni, *Processi*, I:111.
10. On the German ethnic presence in Trent, see Serena Luzzi, *Stranieri in citta: presenza tedesca e societa urbana a Trento (Secoli XV–XVIII)* (Bologna: Il mulino, 2003).
11. AST, APV, s.l. 69, document 5A, fol. 9.
12. Johannes Matthias Tiberinus, *Passio Beati Simonis Pueri Tridentini a p[er]fidis Judeis nup[er] occisi* (Rome: Bartholomaeus Guldinbeck, 1475). There is a disagreement among scholars whether *Brixen* means Brixen, a town midway between Trent and Innsbruck, or Brescia, Tiberino's hometown, see Treue, *Der Trienter Judenprozess*, 287. Tiberinus's text of April 4, a version addressed to Rafaele Zovenzoni, was published in the English translation by Stephen D. Bowd and J. Donald Cullington, *"On Everyone's Lips": Humanists, Jews, and the Tale of Simon of Trent* (Tempe, AZ: Brepols, 2012). Zovenzoni and Simonine poetry are discussed further in Chapter 3. On Tiberino, and his work, see Gaia Bolpagni, "Giovanni Mattia Tiberino e la *Passio Beati Simonis Pueri Tridentini*: Edizione e Commento" (PhD. diss., Università Cattolica del Sacro Cuore, 2011).
13. The Latin text with the English translation is in Bowd and Cullington, *"On Everyone's Lips,"* 40–57. Though I have consulted all the other editions, I will use this easily available version.
14. Bowd and Cullington, *"On Everyone's Lips,"* 40–57, quote from 40–41.
15. Bowd and Cullington, *"On Everyone's Lips,"* 42–43.
16. Bowd and Cullington, *"On Everyone's Lips,"* 42–45.
17. Bowd and Cullington, *"On Everyone's Lips,"* 44–45.
18. Bowd and Cullington, *"On Everyone's Lips,"* 46–47.
19. Bowd and Cullington, *"On Everyone's Lips,"* 50–53. Cf. Bowd and Cullington, *"On Everyone's Lips,"* 52–53. Hsia seems to have been using another version,

an earlier draft of the April 17 text, dated April 15: "That is, just as Jesus God of the Christians, who is nothing, we butcher this one, and thus confound our enemies in eternity." For a discussion about Ashkenazi curses, see Hsia, *Trent 1475*, 55.

20. Bowd and Cullington, "*On Everyone's Lips*," 54–57. On Jewish views of Jesus, see Israel Jacob Yuval, *Shene goyim be-vitnekh: yehudim ve-notsrim dimuyim hadadiyim* (Tel-Aviv: `Alma `Am `oved, 2000), ch. 3, and in English, Yuval, *Two Nations in Your Womb: Perceptions of Jews and Christians in Late Antiquity and the Middle Ages* (Berkeley: University of California Press, 2006), ch. 3. On Jesus in the Talmud, see Peter Schäfer, *Jesus in the Talmud* (Princeton, NJ: Princeton University Press, 2007).
21. Bowd and Cullington, "*On Everyone's Lips*," 56–57.
22. Bowd and Cullington, "*On Everyone's Lips*," 42–43.
23. Bowd and Cullington, "*On Everyone's Lips*," 25.
24. For example, AST, APV, s.l. 69, document 10, from April 30, 1475, in which Hinderbach praises Tiberino and sends a copy of his letter to another poet.
25. Esposito and Quaglioni, *Processi*, I: 109–110.
26. Esposito and Quaglioni, *Processi*, I: 119.
27. Esposito and Quaglioni, *Processi*, I: 113.
28. Esposito and Quaglioni, *Processi*, I: 114.
29. Esposito and Quaglioni, *Processi*, I: 124–125.
30. Esposito and Quaglioni, *Processi*, I: 125.
31. Diego Quaglioni, "Il procedimento inquisitorio contro gli ebrei di Trento," in Esposito and Quaglioni, *Processi*, I: 35–36. Also, Diego Quaglioni, "La parola 'data' e la parola 'presa': le donne nel processo," in *Processi*, II: 15–16.
32. Esposito and Quaglioni, *Processi*, I: 134, 135.
33. Esposito and Quaglioni, *Processi*, I: 134–137.
34. This is in the testimonies of Samuel's son Israel; Vital, Samuel's servant; and Samuel himself, all on March 29: Engel (or Angelo) on March 30, Tobias on April 3; and the old Moses on April 4.
35. Esposito and Quaglioni, *Processi* I, 153–155.
36. Esposito and Quaglioni, *Processi*, I: 205–206.
37. Esposito and Quaglioni, *Processi*, I: 207.
38. Esposito and Quaglioni, *Processi*, I: 127–129.
39. Esposito and Quaglioni, *Processi*, I: 394–401.
40. Archivio Segreto Vaticano (ASV), Archivi Arcis Arm. I–XVIII No. 6495, 113r–116r. Henceforth ASV, A.A.
41. ASV, A.A. Arm. I–XVIII No. 6495, 6v–7r, 7v–8v, 9v–17r, respectively.
42. Esposito and Quaglioni, *Processi*, I: 233–235.
43. Esposito and Quaglioni, *Processi*, I: 236.
44. Esposito and Quaglioni, *Processi*, I: 238.
45. The records in Latin have "Deus adiutor et veritas adiuvet me!" in Esposito and Quaglioni, *Processi*, I: 238. In the German translation, the text says, "Gott der helffer und die warhait helffer mir!" in YUM 1988.001 "Trial of the Jews of Trent, 1478," 29.
46. Esposito and Quaglioni, *Processi*, I: 351.

47. Esposito and Quaglioni, *Processi*, I: 212. YUM 1988, 135: "Was sol ich sagen."
48. For Latin, see Österreichische Nationalbibliothek (ÖNB), Vienna, Cod. 5360, 317v: "Dicatis mihi quid vultis quod dicam et ego dicam." The date in the Vienna MS is Saturday, April 15, 1475. In the German MS the date is Saturday, April 13, clearly a mistake. YUM 1988, 319, quote on 320: "Sagt mir was sol ich sagen, sol wil ich es sagen"; also see Hsia, *Trent 1475*, 49, 152, n. 55.
49. Esposito and Quaglioni, *Processi*, I: 154.
50. Esposito and Quaglioni, *Processi*, I: 211.
51. Bowd and Cullington, "*On Everyone's Lips*," 52. Compare to Esposito and Quaglioni, *Processi*, I: 286.
52. Esposito and Quaglioni, *Processi*, I: 308.
53. Esposito and Quaglioni, *Processi*, I: 313–314.
54. Testimony given on April 8 is in Esposito and Quaglioni, *Processi*, I: 314–319.
55. "Tobias dixit quod pauperum erat et quod habebat pueros ad pascendum" in Esposito and Quaglioni, *Processi*, I: 315. Compare to Tiberino's recounting of Tobias's words: "Patres, libenter provinciam hanc, verum ut nostis pauper ego sum, et ad commode vivendum ars mea non sufficit. Sunt et plures mihi filioli...." in Bowd and Cullington, "*On Everyone's Lips*," 46.
56. Tiberino: "'An isto Pareseceve et carnes et pisces abunde nobis sunt. Unum tantum nobis deest.' Respondit Samuel: Et quid te deficit? Tunc, coniectis oculis adinvicem, taciti omnes intellexerunt quod de immolando Christiano infant loqueretur...," Bowd and Cullington, "*On Everyone's Lips*," 44. Tobias's testimony on April 9, according to the official records: "Samuel dixit quod ipsi Iudei habebant multas carnes et pisces paratos pro festis futuris; et tunc Angelus dixit quod verum erat, sed quod unum solum deficiebat ... intelligendo de sanguine pueri Christiani, prout ipse Tobias credit. Et Samuel respondit: 'Quid est illud quod deficit nobis? Et Angelus, se circumsipitiendo respondit: 'Non est tempus dicendi.'" Esposito and Quaglioni, *Processi*, I: 319.
57. Bowd and Cullington, "*On Everyone's Lips*," 48. Compare to Esposito and Quaglioni, *Processi*, I: 320.
58. Bowd and Cullington, "*On Everyone's Lips*," 50–53.
59. Esposito and Quaglioni, *Processi*, I: 157. On Tiberino, see Bowd and Cullington, "*On Everyone's Lips*," 50. YUM 1988, 99, offers the slightly disordered Hebrew text:

תולה ישע מנה אלה בסוסים ואלה בגמלים ברכב

The Latin protocols in the Austrian National Library in Vienna, Cod. 5360, also include testimonies of other figures, including Wolfgang, formerly Israel. In his testimony on November 18, 1475, he also mentioned this verse in a mangled way; Vienna Cod. 5360, 234v.
60. Psalm 20: 7–8: "Now I know that the LORD will give victory to His anointed, will answer him from His heavenly sanctuary with the mighty victories of His right arm. They [call] on chariots, they [call] on horses, but we call on the name of the LORD our God." Rashi understood it to mean that salvation comes through trust in God and that "some of the nations trust in their iron chariot and some trust their horses," but for Jews "salvation" will based on prayer.

61. See, for example, a Haggadah that was contemporary to Trent: David Stern, Christoph Markschies, and Sarit Shalev-Eyni, *The Monk's Haggadah: A Fifteenth-Century Illuminated Codex from the Monastery of Tegernsee, with a Prologue by the Friar Erhard Von Pappenheim* (University Park: Pennsylvania State University Press, 2015), fol. 17r.
62. YUM 1988, 99.
63. Esposito and Quaglioni, *Processi*, I: 366–374.
64. See, for instance, the summary of Seligman's description of the killing on June 11 and Israel's on June 21 (Esposito and Quaglioni, *Processi*, I: 159, 201) and compare to Tiberino's description, especially the wording about circumcision. Bowd and Cullington, "*On Everyone's Lips*," 48–50.
65. AST APV s.l. 69, docs., 20, 25, 29. Also, on Battista de' Giudici, see Diego Quaglioni, *Apologia judaeorum invectiva contra Platinam: propaganda antiebraica e polemiche di curia durante il pontificato di Sisto IV (1471–1484)* (Rome, 1987).
66. R. Po-chia Hsia has summarized them all in English, and Diego Quaglioni and Anna Esposito have outlined methodological problems related to the surviving documents. Esposito and Quaglioni, *Processi*, I: 97–103; Hsia, *Trent 1475*, 137–140.
67. AST APV s.l. 69 docs. 94, 158.
68. ASV, A.A. Arm I–XVIII 6495: "Processus et sententia contra quosdam Hebraeos qui in Civitate Tridentina immanter occiderunt puerum duorum annorum Christianum nomine Simonem, die veneris sancti die 24 Martii 1475." In Esposito and Quaglioni, *Processi*, I.
69. AST APV s.l. 69, 1b. The annotations are discussed in "Note al testo" in Esposito and Quaglioni, *Processi*, I: 439, 441, 444.
70. Esposito and Quaglioni, *Processi*, I: 97. On copies that may have been in the hands of Jews, see AST APV s.l. 69, docs. 94 and 116.
71. Hsia, *Trent 1475*, xxii–xxiv.
72. Hsia, *Trent 1475*, "Introduction." And in more detail, see Esposito and Quaglioni, *Processi*, II: 59–60.
73. YUM 1988.001 "Trial of the Jews of Trent, 1478," 38, 46, 99, 154, 183, 207, 361, 363, 415, 416, 422. In the women's records, the Hebrew words are rendered in red ink in transliteration.
74. David Stern, "The Hebraist Background to Erhard's Prologue," in Stern et al., *The Monk's Haggadah*, 85.
75. YUM 1988, 1–3. On the bull see the later discussion.
76. YUM 1988, 1, transcribed in Hsia, *Trent 1475*, 142, n. 5, and translated on xix. For evidence that Erhard von Pappenheim was the translator of the records, see Stern et al., *The Monk's Haggadah*.
77. YUM 1988, 4. The quote comes from Hsia, *Trent 1475*, xxi, and is transcribed on 142, n. 7.
78. The quote comes from Hsia, *Trent 1475*, xxi.
79. Johannes Franciscus de Pavinis, *Inquisitio et condemnatoria sententia contra Judaeos Tridentinos* (Rome: apud Sanctum Marcum, 1478), 5v (unnumbered).
80. Hinderbach himself mentioned different quires of the originals. See de' Giudici and Quaglioni, *Apologia Judaeorum*, 144–146.

81. Testimony of Lazarus: Vienna Cod. 5360, 316–345v; YUM 1988, 317–349.
82. See discussion below and de' Giudici and Quaglioni, *Apologia Judaeorum*.
83. Historians give two dates for the suspension of the trial: April 21, and 29. Menestrina and Eckert give April 29; R. Po-Chia Hsia and Wolfgang Treue, April 21. The difference may stem from dating of a document and its arrival in Trent. W. P. Eckert, "Il Beato Simonino negli atti del processo di Trento contro gli ebrei," *Studi trentini di scienze storiche* XLIV (1965): 208; Hsia, *Trent 1475*, 50; Giuseppe Menestrina, "Gli ebrei a Trento," *Tridentum* (1903): 348; Treue, *Der Trienter Judenprozess*, 83. On Sigismund's 1450 privilege, see Menestrina, "Gli ebrei a Trento," *Tridentum*, VI–VII: 306–307, n. 303, has the text of the document.
84. ASV APV s.l. 69, doc. 10, 1r-v.
85. ASV APV s.l. 69, doc. 14.
86. ASV APV s.l. 69, doc. 10, 3r-v (May 21, 1475).
87. P. Ghinzoni, "Simone di Trento: nuovi documenti," *Archivio Veneto* 19, no. 37 (1889): 136–138.
88. Esposito and Quaglioni, *Processi*, I: 240.
89. AST APV s.l. 69, doc. 5A, and also doc. 73
90. ASP APV s.l. 69, docs 94, and 123.
91. Ghinzoni, "San Simone di Trento," 137.
92. AST APV s.l. 69, 25 and 29, and printed in Shlomo Simonsohn, *The Apostolic See and the Jews: Documents, 1464–1521* (Toronto: Pontifical Institute of Mediaeval Studies, 1990), no. 982.
93. Johannes Mathias Tiberinus, *De infantulo in ciuitate Tridentina p[er] Iudeos rapto atq[ue] i[n] vilipendium [Christianae] religionis post multas maximasq[ue] trucibationes [isic] ... crudelissme necato ac deinde in flume[n] cadauer edimerso hystoria feliciter incipit* (Rome: Bartholomaeus Guldinbeck, June 19, 1475); Johannes Mathias Tiberinus, *De infantulo in ciuitate Tridentina p[er] Iudeos rapto atq[ue] i[n] vilipendium [christianae] religionis post multas maximasq[ue] trucibationes [isic] anno iubileo die parasceue crudelissme necato ac deinde in flume[n] cadauer edimerso hystoria feliciter incipit* (Rome: Bartholomaeus Guldinbeck, July 24, 1475).
94. Simonsohn, *The Apostolic See and the Jews, 1464–1521*, no. 985.
95. AST APV s.l. 69, doc. 20, published in Simonsohn, *The Apostolic See and the Jews, 1464–1521*, doc. 984.
96. Ghinzoni, "San Simone di Trento," 141.
97. AST APV s.l. 69, doc. 191, 3r, published in de' Giudici and Quaglioni, *Apologia Judaeorum*.
98. Ghinzoni, "San Simone di Trento," 141.
99. *Hystorie von Simon zu Trient* (Trent: Albert Kunne, 1475).
100. For de' Giudici's reaction to seeing the corpse, which he described in his September 6, 1475, letter to Cardinal Nardello, see Ghinzoni, "San Simone di Trento," 141. Translation of the passage from the September 6 letter is in Hsia, *Trent 1475*, 72. On the relationship between printed editions of Simon's story and the legal proceedings, see Quaglioni, "Il Procedimento Inquisitorio," 13–14.

Notes to Pages 67–72   405

101. de' Giudici and Quaglioni, *Apologia Judaeorum*, 56.
102. de' Giudici and Quaglioni, *Apologia Judaeorum*, 146.
103. de' Giudici and Quaglioni, *Apologia Judaeorum*, 62, 64.
104. Letter of de' Giudici to Hinderbach from September 24, 1475, AST APV s.l. 69, doc. 20, 2r, published in de' Giudici and Quaglioni, *Apologia Judaeorum*, 130–134.
105. See also Hsia, *Trent 1475*, 75.
106. de' Giudici and Quaglioni, *Apologia Judaeorum*, 134.
107. de' Giudici and Quaglioni, *Apologia Judaeorum*, 58.
108. ASV, A. A. Arm. I–XVIII No. 6495, 120r; Esposito and Quaglioni, *Processi*, I: 414–415.
109. It was, for example, addressed in Benedetto Bonelli, *Dissertazione apologetica: sul martirio del Beato Simone da Trento nell'anno MCCCCLXXV da gli ebrei ucciso* (Trent: Per Gianbattista Parone Stampator Vescovile, 1747), 130–132.
110. de' Giudici and Quaglioni, *Apologia Judaeorum*, 56.
111. de' Giudici and Quaglioni, *Apologia Judaeorum*, 60.
112. de' Giudici and Quaglioni, *Apologia Judaeorum*, 62. See also, Quaglioni, "Il Procedimento Inquisitorio," 28.
113. de' Giudici and Quaglioni, *Apologia Judaeorum*, 76.
114. Laurie Nussdorfer, *Brokers of Public Trust: Notaries in Early Modern Rome* (Baltimore: Johns Hopkins University Press, 2009) and "Roman Notarial Records between Market and State," *Past & Present* 230, suppl. 11 (2016): 71.
115. de' Giudici and Quaglioni, *Apologia Judaeorum*, 76. A formal complaint against Raphael was filed by Antonius de Facinis before Battista dei Giudici, AST APV s.l. 69, doc. 167.
116. de' Giudici and Quaglioni, *Apologia Judaeorum*, 76.
117. AST APV s.l. 69, doc. 168.
118. de Pavinis, *Inquisitio et condemnatoria sententia*, 11r. On his personal copy Bishop Hinderbach drew a manicule (shape of a pointed hand) to draw attention to this point, AT APV s.l. 69, doc. 188.
119. See, for example, de Pavinis, *Inquisitio et condemnatoria sententia*, 11r.
120. AST APV s.l. 69, doc. 68.
121. On Paolo de Novara, see Esposito and Quaglioni, *Processi*, I: 98–100. Esposito and Quaglioni, *Processi* II: 21, n. 42. Treue, *Der Trienter Judenprozess*, 114–115. Vienna Cod. 5360. On the copy given to de' Giudici, see his trial AST APV s.l. 69, doc. 68, and Bonelli, *Dissertazione apologetica*, 130–131.
122. AST APV s.l. 69, doc. 68, e.g. 11r–12r, 23r–24v, 27v–31v, 39r, 41v.
123. AST APV s.lat. 69, doc. 106, a letter from Rottaler and Approvino to Hinderbach requesting copies of the protocols of trials against Jews and against Paolo de Novara, December 13, 1477.
124. AST APV s.lat. 69, doc. 74, 3v, 4v, 7r. Michele de Carcano was also known for promoting the monti di pietà and preaching against usury and also against Muslims. He was so famous that he was mentioned in Jacobus Philippus

Bergomensis, *Supplementvm supplementi de la chroniche* (Venice: Impresso per Ioanne Francischo & Ioanne Antonio fratelli di Rusconi, 1524), 329r. On Carcano, see Roberto Rusconi, "Carcano, Michele," in *Dizionario biografico degli Italiani* (Rome: Istituto della Enciclopedia Italiana, 1976), vol. 19, 742–744; and Evelyn S. Welch, *Art and Authority in Renaissance Milan* (New Haven: Yale University Press, 1995), 136–137.

125. AST APV s. s.l. 69, doc. 74, 10v–11r, in letter from October 31, 1476.
126. AST APV lat 69, docs. 79 and 81, request and receipt of trial records in January 1477. Again in December 1477, Rottaler and Approvino request that original records be sent to Rome (AST APV s.l. 69, doc. 106), which they report receiving on March 24, 1478 (AST APV s.l. 69, doc. 119).
127. AST APV s.l. 69, doc. 111.
128. AST APV s.l. 69, doc. 88, letter from Wilhemus Rottaler to Hinderbach mentioning that while the emperor received a copy of the trial records from Hinderbach, Jews sent another.
129. AST APV s.l. 69, docs. 94, 158. Esposito and Quaglioni, *Processi*, II: 4.
130. AST APV s.l. 69, doc. 20, 2r–v.
131. de' Giudici and Quaglioni, *Apologia Judaeorum*, 136. This should not have surprised Duke Sigismund, because on September 20, he had sent a letter directly to Hinderbach, dispatching his officers to Trent, and echoing what the pope had written in the mandate for de' Giudici that "innocents should not be taken for the guilty [*semper sumus inclinati adhori que innocent per nocentibus non habeantur*]," AST APV, s.l. 69, doc. 19.
132. Simonsohn, *The Apostolic See and the Jews, 1464–1521*, no. 986.
133. Simonsohn, *The Apostolic See and the Jews, 1464–1521*, nos. 987 and 988.
134. On the threat of excommunication to Jacobo de Sporo, see AST APV s.l. 69, doc. 39; on the excommunication of de Salis in 1475, see AST APV s.l. 69, doc. 50; on the lifting of the excommunication in July 1479, see Ludwig Schmugge, Michael Marsch, and Alessandra Mosciatti, eds., *Repertorium Poenitentiariae Germanicum: Sixtus IV (1471–1484)*, vol. 6.1 (Tubingen: Max Niemeyer Verlag, 2005), no. 2953. "Johannes de Salis de Brixia legum doct. [exponit], quod dudum cum esset pretor Trident. et pro homicidio in personam Simonis, qui ut nonnullorum testimoniis et pluribus coniecturis asserebatur, a Judeis interfectus fuerat, tam de mandato dom. ep. Trident. quam ex eius offficio realiter et personaliter contra Hebreos inquireret in fidei nostre augmentum, et illorum peniciem, ep. Ventimilien. commisarius et nuntius ap. in eo loco constitutes, prefato Johanni sub penis et censuris inhibuit ac mandavit non ulterius contra ipsos Judeos procedure aut in ea causa se ingerere; et quia frequens rumor erat et vox publ., quod dictus puer ab ipsis Hebreis trucidatus fuerat, quadam modo eorum aliqui comprobatur, non in contemptum sed. ap. sed ut veritatas patefieret similiter quod Hebreorum insidie contra christianos elucescerent, incoatum opus et iudicium media iustitia prosequi non destitit, quinimmo contra illos continue processit et nonnullos secundum eorum gravissimum scelus mulctavit et morte afferit; cum autem predictus Johannes propter eius inobedientiam excom. sent. Dubitet incurrisse, licet ea fidei zelo catholice perpetrasset: supplicat humiliter sanctitati vestre, ut postquam processus per eum facti et sent.

contra Hebreos late a commissariis in R. cur. super hoc deputatis comprobati fuerint, ex quo ipsum rite et sancte constat egisse, quatenus ipsum a sent. huiusmodi excom. et censuris, si quibus forte innodatus extitit, absolve misericorditer mandare dignemini. Rome apud s. Petrum, 26. Iul. 79." For the protocols of the interrogation of women, see Esposito and Quaglioni, *Processi*, II.

135. Esposito and Quaglioni, *Processi*, II: 235–237.
136. On October 12, 1475, Popes Sixtus IV ordered the release of the women; on April 3, 1476, the suspension of any action against them; Simonsohn, *The Apostolic See and the Jews, 1464–1521*, nos. 987, 989.
137. On Hinderbach's conciliarist sympathies, see Rando, *Dai margini la memoria*, 45–96.
138. AST APV s.l. 69, docs. 80 and 82. The two documents were published in Esposito and Quaglioni, *Processi*, II: 237–249. See also, Treue, *Der Trienter Judenprozess*, 126–127.
139. Esposito and Quaglioni, *Processi*, II: 239.
140. Esposito and Quaglioni, *Processi*, II: 246–247.
141. Esposito and Quaglioni, *Processi*, II: 248.
142. AST APV s.l. 69, doc. 84.
143. AST APV s.l. 69, doc. 85.
144. AST APV s.l. 69, doc. 87. On that legal point, see de Pavinis, *Inquisitio et condemnatoria sententia*, 9v.
145. Esposito and Quaglioni, *Processi*, II: 242. There was also a legal question whether the minors were legally baptized, but Hinderbach's allies used the conversions to attack the bishop of Ventimiglia, arguing that had the women and children been released they would not have been baptized and their souls would have perished; de Pavinis, *Inquisitio et condemnatoria sententia*, 10r.
146. Moses A. Shulvass, "Maqor 'ivri ḥadash le-toledot 'alilat ha-dam be-Trento," in *Minḥah li-yehudah: mugash le-harav Yehudah Leib Zlotnik*, ed. Simha Assaf, Yehudah Even-Shemuel, and Yehuda Leib Avida (Jerusalem: Mosad ha-Rav Kuk, 1949–1950), 193. Italian translation of the letter is in Emanuela Trevisan Semi, "Gli ḥaruge Trient (gli assassiati di Trento) e lo ḥerem di Trento nella tradizione ebraica," in *Il Principe Vescovo*, 411.
147. Rando, *Dai margini la memoria*, 484. Anna Esposito, "Vite delle donne: le ebree nel giudizio inquisitorio," in Esposito and Quaglioni, *Processi*, II: 44–45.
148. Rando, *Dai margini la memoria*, 413 n. 499. Esposito, "Vite di donne," 45.
149. Esposito, "Vite di donne," 45–46.
150. Esposito, "Vite di donne," 33.
151. Esposito, "Vite di donne," 33–34, n. 16.
152. Ubertinus Pusculus, *Vbertini Pusculi Brixien[sis] duo libri Symonidos: de iudeorum perfidia quo modo Ihesum [Christu]m crucifixerunt diuos Ricardu[m] Parisiensem Symone Tridentinu[m] afflixere martyrio supliciaq[ue] dedere* (Auguburg p[er] Johannem Otmar, 1511). The poem with an English translation was published in Bowd and Cullington, *"On Everyone's Lips,"* dating 31, Pusculo's verse epic, 116–213; on Brunetta, 207–211.

153. de' Giudici and Quaglioni, *Apologia Judaeorum*, 86; his bona fide, 110. On his qualifications, and the pope's confidence in Battista de' Giudici, see AST APV s.l. 69, doc. 29.
154. de' Giudici and Quaglioni, *Apologia Judaeorum*, 88.
155. de' Giudici and Quaglioni, *Apologia Judaeorum*, 90.
156. de' Giudici and Quaglioni, *Apologia Judaeorum*, 82.
157. Quaglioni, "Il procedimento inquisitorio," 25. On Hinderbach's service to the emperor, see Rando, *Dai margini la memoria*, 127–205. On his role as an imperial ambassador in Rome, see 156–165. On the makeup of the commission and Hinderbach's connections in Rome, see de' Giudici and Quaglioni, *Apologia Judaeorum*, 22, 35.
158. A letter from Hinderbach to an official in Innsbruck from fall 1475. Frumenzio Ghetta, "Fra Bernardino Tomitano da Feltre e gli Ebrei di Trento nel 1475," in *Contibuiti alla storia della regione Trentino-Alto Adige, Civis* (Trent: 1986).
159. Quaglioni, "Il procedimento inquisitorio," 44; Quaglioni, "Giustizia criminale e cultura giuridica," 402.
160. de' Giudici and Quaglioni, *Apologia Judaeorum*, 112.
161. de' Giudici and Quaglioni, *Apologia Judaeorum*, 88.
162. See, for example, the lengthy discussion of jurisdiction in de Pavinis, *Inquisitio et condemnatoria sententia*.
163. For example, AST APV s.l. 69, doc. 21; also in de' Giudici and Quaglioni, *Apologia Judaeorum*, 134–137.
164. de' Giudici and Quaglioni, *Apologia Judaeorum*, 88.
165. de' Giudici and Quaglioni, *Apologia Judaeorum*, 144.
166. On this, see de Pavinis, *Inquisitio et condemnatoria sententia*.
167. de' Giudici and Quaglioni, *Apologia Judaeorum*, 152. Also see Quaglioni, "Il procedimento inquisitorio," 29; and de Pavinis, *Inquisitio et condemnatoria sententia*, 7r ff.
168. de' Giudici and Quaglioni, *Apologia Judaeorum*, 140–141, also 142. Quaglioni, "Il Procedimento inquisitorio," 27.
169. Much of what follows is based on the excellent studies by Diego Quaglioni: "Il procedimento inquisitorio"; "Giustizia criminale e cultura giuridica"; and *La giustizia nel medioevo e nella prima età moderna* (Bologna: Il Mulino, 2008).
170. Quaglioni, "Il procedimento inquisitorio"; and "Giustizia criminale e cultura giuridica." See also, Edward Peters, *Torture*, expanded ed. (Philadelphia: University of Pennsylvania Press, 1999), 50.
171. Peters, *Torture*, 56.
172. Quaglioni, "La parola 'data' e la parola 'presa,'" 11–13.
173. de Pavinis, *Inquisitio et condemnatoria sententia*.
174. See for example, Hinderbach's justification from February 1476, AST APV s.l. 69, doc. 66. See also, Peters, *Torture*, ch. 2.
175. On the efforts of Hinderbach's agent, the Dominican Heinrich of Schlettstett, see AST APV s.l. 69, docs, 44, 45, 46, 48. On the use of Vincent de Beauvais's *Speculum Historiale*, see AST APV s.l. 69, doc. 11; and de Pavinis, *Inquisitio et condemnatoria sententia*, 12r. On Heinrich of Schlettstett, see also, Hsia, *Trent 1475*, 76–77.

176. Quaglioni, "Il procedimento inquisitorio," 32; and "Giustizia criminale e cultura giuridica," 398.
177. Quaglioni, "Il procedimento inquisitorio," 35–36.
178. Esposito and Quaglioni, *Processi*, II: 15.
179. Peters, *Torture*, 47.
180. "Mediocribus tormentis torti et minoribus quam Christianit eciam pro minori delicto torqueri consueverant"; de' Giudici and Quaglioni, *Apologia Judaeorum*, 140.
181. de Pavinis, *Inquisitio et condemnatoria sententia*.
182. Pusculus, *Symonidos*. The poem with an English translation was published in Bowd and Cullington, "*On Everyone's Lips*," 207–211.
183. Quaglioni, "Il procedimento inquisitorio," 48–49.
184. Quaglioni, "Il procedimento inquisitorio," 50, n. 125.
185. "Et hec que predicantur de Symone sunt ficta et mendaciis plena ac fabulosa et composita ad tantum scelus obtegendum sicut alia factum est in partibus Alemanie," AST APV s.l. 69, doc. 188, 4r; also discussed and extensively quoted in Quaglioni, "Il Procedimento inquisitorio," 50.
186. AST APV s.l. 69, doc. 188, 4v; for the quote in Jerome, J. P. Migne, ed. *Sancti Eusebii Hieronymi Stridonensis Presbyteri Opera Omnia*, vol. 7 (1845), 609–610.
187. He wrote "anti" before "Christi" in the traditional phrase at the beginning of letters, turning "In Christi nomine" into "In anti-Christi nomine." AST APV s.l. 69, doc. 188 1r; see also Quaglioni, "Il procedimento inquisitorio," 50.
188. Quaglioni, "Il procedimento inquisitorio," 42.
189. de Pavinis, *Inquisitio et condemnatoria sententia*, 12v ff.
190. Diego Quaglioni, "I giuristi medievali e gli ebrei: due "consultationes di G. F. Pavini (1478)," in *Ebrei e cristiani nell'Italia medievale e moderna: conversioni, scambi, contrasti*, ed. Michele Luzzati (Roma: Carucci, 1986), 66.
191. Quaglioni, "Il procedimento inquisitorio," 45–46; and "Giustizia Criminale e Cultura Giuridica," 402–403. AST APV s.l. 69, doc. 52.
192. Quaglioni, "Il procedimento inquisitorio," 46–47.
193. Quaglioni, "Il procedimento inquisitorio," 46, n. 116.
194. de Pavinis, *Inquisitio et condemnatoria sententia*, 1v: Septimo propter statutum loci imponens. There is a copy in Bayerische Staadtsbibliothek, 2 Inc. s.a. 961 m, and at AST APV s.l. 69, 188 (with Hinderbach's notes).
195. de' Giudici and Quaglioni, *Apologia Judaeorum*, especially, 68–74, 88–90.
196. de Pavinis, *Inquisitio et condemnatoria sententia*, 7r ff.
197. de Pavinis, *Inquisitio et condemnatoria sententia*, 9v.
198. AST APV s.l. 69, docs. 120, 123. On Regensburg, see Chapter 3 and R. Po-chia Hsia, *The Myth of Ritual Murder: Jews and Magic in Reformation Germany* (New Haven: Yale University Press, 1988), ch. 3. On Passau, see Miri Rubin, *Gentile Tales: The Narrative Assault on Late Medieval Jews* (New Haven: Yale University Press, 1999), 129–131, 174–175.
199. AST APV s.l. 69, doc. 17.
200. de Pavinis, *Inquisitio et condemnatoria sententia*, 6v.

201. Diego Quaglioni, "Propaganda antiebraica e polemiche di Curia," in *Un Pontificato ed Una Città: Sisto IV (1471–1484)*, ed. Massimo Miglio et al. (Rome: Istituto storico italiano per il Medio Evo and Scuola di Paleografia, Diplomatica, e Archivistica, 1986), 264–265.
202. Quaglioni, "Il procedimento inquisitorio," 40.
203. Latin text available in Simonsohn, *The Apostolic See and the Jews, 1464–1521*, no. 999, 1246–1247. Also both the Latin and the English translation by Kenneth Stow are presented in "Trent 1475: Responses of a Pope and a Jewish Chronicler" at the Early Modern Workshop in 2004, http://www.earlymodern.org.
204. Simonsohn, *The Apostolic See and the Jews, 1464–1521*, no. 999.
205. The relevant section of Canon 62 of the IV Lateran Council reads as follows: "And let no one presume to venerate publicly new [relics] unless they have been approved by the Roman pontiff. In the future prelates shall not permit those who come to their churches *causa venerationis* to be deceived by worthless fabrications or false documents as has been done in many places for the sake of gain."
206. The sentence—"quod nullus Christianus, premissorum vel alia occasione absque iudicio terrene potestatis, Iudeorum aliquem occidere, mutilare, aut vulenarare, sive ab eis pecunias indebite extoquere, sive eos quominus ritus suos a iure permissos continuare valeant, impedire presumant"—contains nearly verbatim language from *Sicut Iudaeis* (the version by Pope Innocent III differs, but in Gregory IX's *Decretales* the language reverted to the version attributed to Clemens III), which has "Nullus etiam Christianus eorum quemlibet sine judicio potestatis terrenae vulnerare vel occidere vel suas eis pecunias auferre presumant," Shlomo Simonsohn, *The Apostolic See and the Jews: Documents, 492–1404* (Toronto: Pontifical Institute of Mediaeval Studies, 1988), no. 49. Solomon Grayzel, "The Papal Bull *Sicut Judaeis*," in *Studies and Essays in Honor of Abraham A. Neuman*, ed. Meir Ben-Horin, Bernard D. Weinryb, and Solomon Zeitlin (Leiden: Brill, 1962), 244. The phrase "occidere, mutilare, aut vulnerare" differs from what is in the original *Sicut Iudaeis*, but it was used by Pope Paul II in his 1466 bull *Viros sanguineos*.
207. For example, AST APV s.l. 69, docs 10, 11, 15, 34.
208. AST APV s.l. 69, doc. 14.
209. Treue, *Der Trienter Judenprozess*, 113.
210. AST APV s.l. 69, doc. 20, 26, 27, 32. Doc. 20 was published in de' Giudici and Quaglioni, *Apologia Judaeorum*, 130–134.
211. For example, a letter from October 4, 1476, AST APV s.l. 69, 74, 13r.
212. For example, AST APV s.l. 69, doc. 56, 71, 104.
213. de' Giudici and Quaglioni, *Apologia Judaeorum*, 140.
214. For example, AST APV s.l. 69, doc. 37, 51, 56.
215. de' Giudici and Quaglioni, *Apologia Judaeorum*, 110.
216. AST APV s.l. 69, doc. 52 (on alms), docs. 100, 118, 122, 130 (on expenses).
217. AST APV s.l. 69, doc. 68.
218. Rando, *Dai margini la memoria*, especially, 471 ff.

219. E.g. AST APV s.l. 69, docs. 109, 110, 117.
220. E.g. AST APV s.l. 69, doc. 85.
221. Shulvass, "Maqor 'ivri"; Trevisan Semi, "Gli ḥaruge Trient," 411. On Jewish literary responses to blood libels, see Chapter 5.
222. AST APV s.l. 69, doc. 68, 25r–26v.
223. Shulvass, "Maqor 'ivri."
224. The lamentation *(qinah)* was first published in 1912 in David Frankel, "Qinah le-ḥarugei Trient," *Ha-zofeh le-ḥokhmat Yisrael* 2 (1912). An Italian translation was published by Trevisan Semi, "Gli ḥaruge Trient," and the English translation by Sylvia A. Herskowitz, *Medieval Justice: The Trial of the Jews of Trent* (New York: Yeshiva University Museum, 1989).
225. Shlomo Halevi, "Kinah: Lament for the Victims of Trent," in Herskowitz, *Medieval Justice*. Frankel, "Qinah le-ḥarugei Trient."
226. Shulvass expressed this surprise; Shulvass, "Maqor 'ivri."
227. See Stern et al., *The Monk's Haggadah* and Chapter 3.
228. It was in a German quarter, led by a German bishop, supported by evidence from German territories. Paolo de Novara said that "all in the castle were Germans," AST APV s.l. 69, doc 68, 45r.
229. Alexandra Walsham, "The Social History of the Archive: Record-Keeping in Early Modern Europe," *Past & Present* 230, suppl. 11 (2016): 47.
230. Walsham, "The Social History of the Archive," 32, 46.

3. Echoes of Simon of Trent in European Culture

1. Stephen D. Bowd and J. Donald Cullington, *"On Everyone's Lips": Humanists, Jews, and the Tale of Simon of Trent* (Tempe, AZ: Brepols, 2012), 122–123. I use this Latin-English edition to quote the text in English, unless otherwise noted.
2. R. Po-chia Hsia, "Atti del processo contro gli ebrei conservati alla Yeshiva University, New York," in *Il Principe Vescovo Johannes Hinderbach (1465–1486)*, ed. Iginio Rogger and Marco Bellabarba (Bologna: Edizioni Dehoniane, 1992), 427.
3. Bowd and Cullington, *"On Everyone's Lips,"* 6–15.
4. The Latin text with the English translation is in Bowd and Cullington, *"On Everyone's Lips,"* 40–57.
5. On the trial, see Chapter 2 and Rogger and Bellabarba, *Il Principe Vescovo*, 100–107; Bowd and Cullington, *"On Everyone's Lips."* The text is described by R. Po-Chia Hsia in his *Trent 1475: Stories of a Ritual Murder Trial* (New Haven: Yale University Press, 1992), 53–56.
6. *Hystorie von Simon zu Trient* (Trent: Albert Kunne, 1475); Johannes Mathias Tiberinus, *Relatio de Simone puero Tridentino* (Venice: Gabriele di Pietro, 1475); Johannes Matthias Tiberinus, *Passio Beati Simonis pueri Tridentini a p[er]fidis Judeis nup[er] occisi* (Rome: Bartholomaeus Guldinbeck, 1475); Johannes Mathias Tiberinus, *De infantulo in ciuitate Tridentina p[er] Iudeos rapto atq[ue] i[n] vilipendium [christianae] religionis post multas maximasq[ue]*

trucibationes [isic] ... crudelissme necato ac deinde in flume[n] cadauer edimerso hystoria feliciter incipit (Rome: Bartholomaeus Guldinbeck, June 19, 1475). Johannes Mathias Tiberinus, De infantulo in ciuitate Tridentina p[er] iudeos rapto atq[ue] i[n] vilipendium [christianae] religionis post multas maximasq[ue] trucibationes [isic] anno iubileo die parasceue crudelissme necato ac deinde in flume[n] cadauer edimerso hystoria feliciter incipit (Rome: Bartholomaeus Guldinbeck, July 24, 1475). Jean Bolland et al., Acta Sanctorum Martii (Antwerp: apud Iacobum Meursium, 1668), 494–502. On the scope of the literary impact of the trial, see the bibliography in Paul Oskar Kristeller, "The Alleged Ritual Murder of Simon of Trent (1475) and Its Literary Repercussions," Proceedings of the American Academy for Jewish Research 59 (1993).
7. Bowd and Cullington, "On Everyone's Lips," 44–47.
8. Bowd and Cullington, "On Everyone's Lips," 44–45.
9. Bowd and Cullington, "On Everyone's Lips," 46–47. This description is consistent with the idea of a ḥerem, a rabbinic ban, prohibiting social interaction with the person affected.
10. Bowd and Cullington, "On Everyone's Lips," 44–45.
11. Bowd and Cullington, "On Everyone's Lips," 42–43.
12. Tiberino's discussion of Jewish messianic calculations was not entirely inaccurate. As Israel Yuval has noted, "Producing calculations of the End is an ancient Jewish pastime," though admittedly one frequently condemned by rabbis. In Christian Europe, Jewish eschatological calculations were sometimes included in works of anti-Christian polemics. It would not have been unusual if Trent Jews shared the belief in an imminent messianic era. There is evidence that in the fifteenth century, some Ashkenazic Jews continued to expect the imminent arrival of the messianic era and were forced to revise their calculations when the expected date passed, Israel Jacob Yuval, Two Nations in Your Womb: Perceptions of Jews and Christians in Late Antiquity and the Middle Ages (Berkeley: University of California Press, 2006), ch. 6.
13. Epistola Raphaeli Zovenzonio, in Tiberinus, Relatio de Simone puero Tridentino. Reprinted with the English translation in Bowd and Cullington, "On Everyone's Lips," 36–41.
14. Bowd and Cullington, "On Everyone's Lips," 38–39.
15. Bowd and Cullington, "On Everyone's Lips," 40–41.
16. Bowd and Cullington, "On Everyone's Lips," 59–63.
17. Bowd and Cullington, "On Everyone's Lips," 58–59. The discussion of the form and meter of the poem is on 59, n. 2.
18. Bowd and Cullington, "On Everyone's Lips," 60–61.
19. Bowd and Cullington, "On Everyone's Lips," 62–63. See Matthew 11:5 and Luke 7:22.
20. Bowd and Cullington, "On Everyone's Lips," 62–63.
21. Bowd and Cullington, "On Everyone's Lips," 62–63.
22. See, for a most explicit example, Bowd and Cullington, "On Everyone's Lips," 74–75, 80–81, 106–107.
23. Bowd and Cullington, "On Everyone's Lips," 74–75. Incidentally, perhaps, the notion that Jews conducted a "war" against Christian is also found in the popular work of Alfonso de Espina, Fortalitium fidei, Book III.

24. Quote from Pusculo in Bowd and Cullington, "*On Everyone's Lips,*" 204–205. On this, see also Anna Esposito, "Il culto del 'beato' Simonino e la sua prima diffusione in Italia," in *Il Principe Vescovo*, 436–437; and Silvester de Balneoregio, *Conclusiones cum earum declaracionibus edite ... super canonisatione Simonis Tridentini quem impia gens hebrea incontemptum fidei cristiane crudeliter enecauit ad Reuerendissimum Episcopum et Tridentine civitatis principem dominum Johannem Hynderbach* (Trent: Albrecht Kunne, December 6, 1475).
25. Bowd and Cullington, "*On Everyone's Lips,*" 64–69. Tiberinus Johannes Matthias, *Hystoria Completa* (Tridenti: Hermanno Schindeleyp auctore, 1476).
26. Bowd and Cullington, "*On Everyone's Lips,*" 64–69.
27. Also see Bowd and Cullington, "*On Everyone's Lips,*" 72–73. For a full treatment of the Jews as dogs in Christian imagination, see Kenneth R. Stow, *Jewish Dogs: An Image and Its Interpreters* (Stanford: Stanford University Press, 2006).
28. Bowd and Cullington, "*On Everyone's Lips*", 68–73.
29. Bowd and Cullington, "*On Everyone's Lips,*" 68–69.
30. Bowd and Cullington, "*On Everyone's Lips,*" 70–71.
31. Bowd and Cullington, "*On Everyone's Lips,*" 76–77.
32. Bowd and Cullington, "*On Everyone's Lips,*" 74–75.
33. Pusculo's poem was written in 1482 but published in 1511. It is now available in Part III of Bowd and Cullington, "*On Everyone's Lips.*" Quote on 205.
34. Bowd and Cullington, "*On Everyone's Lips,*" 72–73.
35. Battista de' Giudici and Diego Quaglioni, *Apologia Judaeorum invectiva contra Platinam: Propaganda antiebraica e polemiche di curia durante il pontificato di Sisto IV (1471–1484)*, (Rome, 1987), 112.
36. R. Po-chia Hsia, *The Myth of Ritual Murder: Jews and Magic in Reformation Germany* (New Haven: Yale University Press, 1988), 42.
37. See Chapter 2. Latin text available in Shlomo Simonsohn, *The Apostolic See and the Jews: Documents, 1464–1521*, no. 999, p. 1246–1247. Both Latin and the English translation are in Kenneth Stow, "Trent 1475: Responses of a Pope and a Jewish Chronicler" at the Early Modern Workshop in 2004, http://www.earlymodern.org.
38. Fabiano Veraja, *La beatificazione: storia problemi prospettive* (Rome: S. Congregazione per le Cause dei Santi, 1983), 18–19, 26–28, 31.
39. Simonsohn, *The Apostolic See and the Jews, 1464–1521*, no. 999, pp. 1246–1247.
40. Bowd and Cullington, "*On Everyone's Lips,*" 73–74.
41. In one of his later letters, Giusto Approvino notified Bishop Hinderbach in 1478 of the printing cost of 300 copies of his *consultatio*, which amounted to 30 ducats; Diego Quaglioni, "Giustizia criminale e cultura giuridica: i giuristi trentini e i processi contro gli ebrei," in *Il Principe Vescovo*, 399; Esposito, "Il culto del 'Beato' Simonino," 436.
42. AST, APV, s.l. 69, n. 1, fasc. 1, 1r, record for April 23, 1475. Frumenzio Ghetta, "Johannes Hinderbach, amministratore: i registri delle offerte della Chiesa di S. Pietro a Trento," in *Il Principe Vescovo*, 207.
43. AST, ASV, s.l. 69, n. 1, fasc. 1, 3r. Ghetta, "Johannes Hinderbach, amministratore," 209.

44. AST, ASV, s.l. 69, n. 1, fasc. 1, 5v: "Item Stampher pro salario suo habuit libras 14, pro capsa plumbea facta. Ghetta, "Johannes Hinderbach, amministratore," 210.
45. See, for example, Tommaso Caliò, *La leggenda dell'ebreo assassino: percorsi di un racconto antiebraico dal medioevo ad oggi* (Rome: Viella, 2007), ch. 1; Dana E. Katz, *The Jew in the Art of the Italian Renaissance* (Philadelphia: University of Pennsylvania Press, 2008), ch. 5; Esposito, "Il Principe Vescovo."
46. Esposito, "Il culto del 'beato' Simonino," 440. Already in 1475, churches and clergy were asking for relics; see a letter from Gabriel Bertuci to Bishop Hinderbach from October 9, 1475, AST, ASV, s.l. 69, no. 31. See also letters regarding donations of relics in 1476, AST, ASV, s.l. 69, nos. 74, 77.
47. Salomone G. Radzik, *Portobuffolè* (Florence: Casa Editrice Giuntina, 1984), 20, n.13.
48. Letter from Battista di Campofrenoso, AST, ASV, s.l. 69, no. 139. On Simon's toe, see Michelangelo Mariani, *Il glorioso infante S. Simone: historia panegirica* (Trent: Zanetti Stampator Episcopale, 1668), 132; on the queen's visit to Trent, 194.
49. Hsia, *The Myth of Ritual Murder*, ch. 2.
50. Rando, *Dai margini la memoria*, 469–471. Wolfgang Treue, *Der Trienter Judenprozess: Voraussetzungen, Abläufe, Auswirkungen (1475–1588)* (Hannover: Hahn, 1996), 308–318.
51. Treue, *Der Trienter Judenprozess*, 308–312. Werner Rolevinck, *Fasciculus temporum* (Venice: cura impensisq[ue] Erhardi Ratdolt de Augusta, 1480 [November 24]), 65. Werner Rolevinck, *Fasciculus temporum* (Basel: Bernhardus Richel, 1482 [February 20]), 90r. For a more detailed discussion of the chronicles, see Chapter 4.
52. On the story of Simon in Schedel's chronicle, see Hsia, *The Myth of Ritual Murder*, 48. For the images of Simon's martyrdom in the Augsburg editions, Hartmann Schedel, *Liber chronicarum cum figuris et imaginis ab initio mundi usque nunc temporis* (Augsburg: Johann Schönsperger, 1497), 285v–286r; and *Das Buch der Croniken vnnd Geschichten mit Figuren vnd Pildnussen von Anbeginn der Welt bis auff dise vnsere Zeijt* (Augsburg: Johann Schönsperger, 1500), 286v–287r.
53. Mariani, *Il glorioso infante*, 171. Also, Esposito, "Il culto del 'Beato' Simonino," 442.
54. Esposito, "Il culto del 'beato' Simonino," 443. Laura Dal Prà, "L'immagine di Simonino nell'arte Trentina dal XV al XVIII secolo," in *Il Principe Vescovo*, 449.
55. Mariani, *Il Glorioso Infante*, 171–173. See also Treue, *Der Trienter Judenprozess*, 486–487.
56. Mariani, *Il Glorioso Infante*, 173.
57. Mariani, *Il Glorioso Infante*, 173–174.
58. Dal Prà, "L'immagine di Simonino," 449, n. 13.
59. Treue, *Der Trienter Judenprozess*, 481.
60. Treue, *Der Trienter Judenprozess*, 482.
61. Laurentius Surius, *De probatis sanctorum historiis: partim ex tomis Aloysii Lipomani partim etiam ex egregiis manuscriptis codicibus, quarum permultae*

antehàc numquàm in lucem prodiere, optima fide collectis (Cologne: apud Geruinum Calenium et haeredes Quentelios, 1571), 387–390.

62. Vol. 8: Luigi Lippomano, *Octauus tomus vitarum sanctorum priscorum patrum* (Rome: apud Antonium Bladum impressorem cam., 1560).

63. See especially vol. 7, which contains saints for March and April: Luigi Lippomano, *Septimus tomus vitarum sanctorum priscorum patrum* (Romae: Apud Antonium Bladum impressorem cam., 1558). On Lippomano and his role in the host desecration trial, see Magda Teter, *Sinners on Trial: Jews and Sacrilege after the Reformation* (Cambridge, MA: Harvard University Press, 2011), ch. 5.

64. Fidel Gonzalez Fernandez, "Prefazione," in *Le cause di canonizzazione nel primo periodo della Congregazione dei Riti (1588–1634)*, ed. Giovanni Papa (Roma: Urbaniana University Press, 2001), 1.

65. Fernandez, "Le cause di canonizzazione," 1.

66. Veraja, *La beatificazione*, 9.

67. Fernandez, "Le cause di canonizzazione," 4–5. For a detailed study of the reform of the canonization process, see Giovanni Papa, *Le cause di canonizzazione nel primo periodo della Congregazione dei Riti (1588–1634)* (Rome: Urbaniana University Press, 2001).

68. Papa, *Le cause di canonizzazione*, 15–26.

69. Veraja, *La beatificazione*, 5.

70. Veraja, *La beatificazione*, 12–13.

71. An example of such threats can be found regarding the cult of Charles of Blois, condemned by Pope Urban V in 1368; Veraja, *La beatificazione*, 14–15.

72. Ludovico Carbone, *Summæ summarum casuum conscientiæ siue totius theologiæ practicæ in tribus tomi [sic] distributa* (Venice: apud Robertum Meiettum, 1606), vol. 3, book 1, ch. 17, 41–44.

73. "[A]lii qui privatis in locis et a privatis personis in sanctorum certum esse creduntur, quos beatos vocantur," Carbone, *Summæ summarum casuum*, vol. 3, book 1, ch. 17, 41.

74. Fernandez, "Le cause di canonizzazione," 1. Simonsohn, *The Apostolic See and the Jews, 1464–1521*, no. 1041, p. 1277.

75. For the text of the letter, see Simonsohn, *The Apostolic See and the Jews, 1464–1521*, no. 986, p. 1231.

76. Veraja, *La beatificazione*, 26–27.

77. The text of the breve from August 1482 is in Veraja, *La beatificazione*, 27.

78. Veraja, *La beatificazione*, 19, 27–28.

79. Veraja, *La beatificazione*, 19, 33–34.

80. Veraja, *La beatificazione*, 5.

81. AST APV s. l. 69, docs. 183, 190.

82. On the reform of the procedures and the creation of the Congregation of Rites, see Papa, *Le cause di canonizzazione*.

83. Papa, *Le cause di canonizzazione*, 16–19. Session Twenty-Five, December 3–4, 1563.

84. Robert Bireley, "Early-Modern Catholicism as a Response to the Changing World of the Long Sixteenth Century," *Catholic Historical Review* 95, no. 2

(2009): 238; Natalia Nowakowska, "From Strassburg to Trent: Bishops, Printing and Liturgical Reform in the Fifteenth Century," *Past & Present* 213, no. 1 (2011): 7. For a musicological study of the liturgical reforms following the Council of Trent, see Theodore Karp, *An Introduction to the Post-Tridentine Mass Proper* (Middleton, WI: American Institute of Musicology, 2007).

85. Pio Paschini, "La riforma gregoriana del Martirologio romano," *La Scuola Cattolica* 51 (1923): 201–203.
86. Paschini, "La riforma gregoriana," 198.
87. Paschini, "La riforma gregoriana," 198–199.
88. Cesare Baronio, *Martyrologivm romanvm, ad novam kalendarii rationem, et ecclesiasticæ historiæ veritatem restitutum Gregorii XIII. Pont. Max. ivssv editvm. accesservnt notationes, atque tractatio de martyrologio romano. avctore Cæsare Baronio Sorano Congreg. Oratoij Presbyt* (Romæ: Ex Typographia Dominici Basae, 1586). On the stipend, see Paschini, "La riforma gregoriana," 200.
89. Paschini, "La riforma gregoriana," 207.
90. Paschini, "La riforma gregoriana," 209.
91. Paschini, "La riforma gregoriana," 274.
92. Paschini, "La riforma gregoriana," 274–275.
93. Baronio recounted his difficult job of making the call whether to retain or expunge someone in the *Martyrologium;* Paschini, "La riforma gregoriana," 276.
94. Prospero (Benedict XIV) Lambertini, *De servorum Dei beatificatione et beatorum canonizatione* (Bologna: Formis Longhi excusoris archiepiscopalis, 1734–1738), Lib IV, pars II, cap. XVII, no. 15.
95. *Martyrologium Romanvm Ad Nouam Kalendarij Rationem, & Ecclesiasticae Historiae Veritatem Reftitutum Gregorii XIII Pont. Max. Iussu Editum* (Rome: ex typographia Dominici Basae, 1583).
96. Baronio, *Martyrologivm romanvm (1586)*.
97. Baronio, *Martyrologivm romanvm (1586)*.
98. Papa, *Le cause di canonizzazione*, 21.
99. *Martyrologium romanum (1583)*, 66–67. Treue located the insertion in 1584, likely after the Bollandists; Treue, *Der Trienter Judenprozess*, 488.
100. Surius, *De probatis sanctorum historiis*, 387–390; Ioannes Molandus, *Usuardi martyrologium quo romana ecclesia ac permultae aliae utuntur* (Lovanii: apud Hieronymum Wellaum, 1573), 55v (misnumbered 53v). Earlier editions of Usuard's *Martyrologium* do not mention Simon either: Usuard, *Martyrologium* (Florence: Francesco Bonaccorsi, 1486) and *Martyrologium* (Venice: Jmpressum arte et impēsis Luceantonij de giunta, 1517).
101. Quaglioni, "Giustizia criminale e cultura giuridica," 405. See also, Dal Prà, "L'immagine di Simonino," 462. See Chapter 2.
102. Hsia, *The Myth of Ritual Murder*, ch. 2.
103. Hsia, *The Myth of Ritual Murder*, 36–41.
104. *Hystorie von Simon zu Trient;* Johannes M. Tiberinus, *Die Geschicht und Legend von dem seligen Kind und Marterer gennant Symon von den Juden zu Trent gemartet und gemortet*, trans. Ginther Zainer (Augsburg: Ginther Zainer, 1475).

105. Rochus von Liliencron, *Die historischen Volkslieder der Deutschen*, 5 vols. (Leipzig: Vogel, 1866–1869), vol. 2, 13–21, no. 128. See for example Kunig's description of Simon's torture and death, in Liliencron, 15, lines 103–125, 153–154, and compare with Tiberino; Bowd and Cullington, "On Everyone's Lips," 50–53. Lines 153–154 are taken nearly verbatim from Tiberino, who himself was evoking John 19:30: "He tilted his head to his right, and gave up his noble spirit" (Kunig) vs. "Bending his head he gave up his holy spirit to the Lord."
106. Hsia, *The Myth of Ritual Murder*, ch. 3.
107. On Israel/Wolfgang, see Hsia, *Trent 1475*, ch. 9.
108. See also, AST, ASV, s.l. 69, nos. 76, 161.
109. Hsia, *The Myth of Ritual Murder*, 74. The document with questions dated April 8, 1476, is published in Raphael Straus, *Urkunden und Aktenstücke zur Geschichte der Juden in Regensburg 1453–1738* (Munich: C. H. Beck'sche Verlagsbuchhandlung, 1960), 72–73, no. 230.
110. Hsia, *The Myth of Ritual Murder*, ch. 5.
111. Hsia, *The Myth of Ritual Murder*, 92.
112. Hsia, *The Myth of Ritual Murder*, 87.
113. On Sappenfeld, see Hsia, *The Myth of Ritual Murder*, 125–131; on Worms, see ch. 8.
114. Hsia, *The Myth of Ritual Murder*, ch. 7, esp. 148ff.
115. Piotr Skarga, *Żywoty Świętych Starego i Nowego Zakonu z Pisma Świętego i poważnych pisarzów i doktorow kościelnych wybranych* (Drukarnia Oświeconego Pana Mikołaja Christofa Radziwiłła, 1579), "Przedmowa do czytelnika." On the influence of Skarga's work in Poland, see Hanna Węgrzynek, *"Czarna legenda" żydów: procesy o rzekome mordy rytualne w dawnej Polsce* (Warsaw: Bellona: Wydawnictwo Fundacji Historia pro Futuro, 1995), 98.
116. Skarga, *Żywoty Świętych*, 279–281. Cf. Surius, *De probatis sanctorum historiis*, 356–359.
117. The Bollandists noted that a missal published in Venice in 1487 placed Simon's story on March 30. Later Wagenseil noted that as well, no doubt following the Bollandists, Johann Christoph Wagenseil, *D. Joh. Christoph. Wagenseils Benachrichtigungen wegen einiger die Judenschafft* (Leipzig: Heinichen, 1705), 195.
118. Skarga, *Żywoty Świętych*, 281. See also Węgrzynek, *"Czarna legenda" żydów*, 104.
119. Skarga, *Żywoty Świętych*, 281.
120. Skarga, *Żywoty Świętych*, 281.
121. For a list of publications with dates, see Treue, *Der Trienter Judenprozess*, 306–308.
122. *Li Horribili Tormenti del Beato Simone di Trento* (Treviso: Gerardus Lisa [Gerardo da Fiandra], 1475). There is no date in the paratext of this work, but the text itself refers to "this holy easter [*questa sancta pasca*]."
123. Thomas Pratus, *De immanitate judaeorum in Simonem infantum* (Treviso: Gerardus de Lisa de Flandria, 1475); Johannes Matthias Tiberinus, *De obitu Beati Simonis Tridentini: ad rectores et cives brixianos* (Tavri: GF, 1475); and *Passio Beati Simonis pueri tridentini* (Treviso: Gerardus de Lisa de Flandria, 1475).

124. *Li horribili tormenti (1475)*, 1r–v. The allusion to Mary is likely not accidental, because ritual murder and blood accusations against Jews were often linked to Marian devotion. March 25 is a feast of the Annunciation. Because March 25, 1475, was Good Friday, the feast would have been moved to after Easter. On the Marian connection, see also Chapter 1.
125. *Li horribili tormenti (1475)*. Kenneth Stow examined the metaphor of "Jewish dogs" in his *Jewish Dogs*.
126. *Li horribili tormenti (1475)*, 6r.
127. *Li horribili tormenti (1475)*, 7v.
128. *Li horribili tormenti (1475)*, 8r.
129. Documents related to the incident in Pavia, along with the final decree by the Sforzas, are found in Guidetti, Pro Judaeis, 280–294.
130. Guidetti, Pro Judaeis, 280–281. Donato's name is mentioned in the letter sent from Milan to Pavia on April 28, 1479, in Guidetti, Pro Judaeis, 285.
131. Guidetti, Pro Judaeis, no. 2, 281.
132. Letter from Giovanni Calzavacca to the Sforzas in Milan, April 22, 1479, in Guidetti, Pro Judaeis, 282.
133. Letter from dated April 22, 1479, from "Deputati officio provisionis comunis civitatis vestrae Pavie" to the Dukes of Milan, in Guidetti, Pro Judaeis, 282.
134. Guidetti, Pro Judaeis, 284.
135. Guidetti, Pro Judaeis, 285–287.
136. Guidetti, Pro Judaeis, 289–294.
137. Guidetti, Pro Judaeis, 290.
138. Guidetti, Pro Judaeis, 290.
139. Guidetti, Pro Judaeis, 291.
140. Guidetti, Pro Judaeis, 291.
141. Guidetti, Pro Judaeis, 291–292.
142. The dukes were mistaken in dating Jewish settlement in Rome to the destruction of the temple in 70 CE. There is evidence of a Jewish presence in Rome as early as the second century B.C.E.
143. Guidetti, Pro Judaeis, 293–294.
144. Giorgio Sommariva, *Martyrium Sebastiani Novelli trucidati a judaeis* (Tarvisii [Treviso]: Diligentia Bernardini Celerii de Luere, 1480). The copy of Sommariva's booklet at Biblioteca Angelica in Rome has a note: "B. Simon Trid. et alÿ a Iudaeis trucidati." No body was ever found though three Jews were executed in Venice. On this case, see also Radzik, *Portobuffolè*; Caliò, *La leggenda dell'ebreo assassino*, 33–35; and in passim, Esposito, "Il culto del 'Beato' Simonino."
145. Italo Cammarata and Ugo Rozzo, *Il Beato Giovannino patrono di Volpedo: Un fanciullo "martire" della fine del secolo XV* (Volpedo: Associazione "Pelizza da Volpedo," 1997).
146. Caliò, *La leggenda dell'ebreo assassino*, chap. 1.
147. Ambrogio Franco, *Martirio del Beato Simone trentino* (Trent: per li fratelli Gelmini da Sabbio, 1586). It was republished under a different title in 1608; see the later discussion.
148. Gesti, *Martirio di S. Simone*. On Gesti's description of the procession, see the later discussion in this chapter.

149. *Ristretto della vita e martirio di S. Simone fanciullo della Città di Trento* (Rome: Filippo Neri alle Muratte, 1594?). The date of the publication is questionable. On the one hand, the approbation says *reimprimatur,* or re-approbation, thereby implying an earlier edition. On the other, information within the book suggests that it was in fact published much later. The preface to *Ristretto* makes reference to Philippe de Berlaymont's *Paradisus puerorum,* first published in 1618 in Cologne and republished a year later. Berlaymont's book was certainly written earlier, because the approbations go back to 1616, but some examples in this book are from the seventeenth century. It is difficult to imagine how the author of *Ristretto* would have had access to Berlaymont's book before 1616 (in manuscript) or 1618 (in print). The named printer raises another question. This press did not produce anything but *Ristretto* and then another work in 1794. Filippo Neri was, of course, the founder of the Congregation of the Oratory and a close friend of Cesare Baronio and other prominent figures; he died in 1595, was beatified in 1615, and canonized in 1622. Neri and his disciples displaced a small group of nuns for following the rule of St. Claire, when Neri's congregation grew in size. The nuns were forced to move to a different monastery in the *Muratte.* Given the internal evidence within *Ristretto,* the date must be a typographical error, or, considering other issues, an attempt at willful deception. On the move of the nuns to the *Muratte,* see Alfonso Capecelatro, *La vita di S. Filippo Neri* (Naples: R. Stab. Tipografico del Comm. g. de Angelis e Figlio, 1879), vol. 2, 41.
150. *Ristretto,* 4.
151. On the term "ghetto," see Kenneth R. Stow, "The Consciousness of Closure: Roman Jewry and Its *Ghet,*" in *Essential Papers on Jewish Culture in Renaissance and Baroque Italy,* ed. David Ruderman (New York: New York University Press, 1992), 386–400; Benjamin Ravid, "From Geographical Realia to Historiographical Symbol: The Odyssey of the Word Ghetto," in *Essential Papers on Jewish Culture in Renaissance and Baroque Italy,* 373–385.
152. *Ristretto,* 6–8.
153. I left the spelling of the Hebrew words to retain the flavor of the original text. *Beresci* here likely refers to the Book of Genesis, known in Hebrew as *Be-reshit,* and "*scirascirim* of Solomon" is the Song of Songs; *Ristretto,* 7.
154. *Ristretto,* 7–8.
155. *Ristretto,* 7–8.
156. *Ristretto,* 10. Cf. Ambrogio Franco, *Martirio di S. Simone di Trento nel quale si tratta de la gran crudeltà che vsarono gli empi ebrei in martirizarlo. et come è stato posto nel cattalogo de' santi, & la solenne processione fatta nella sua prima festa, con molti miracoli fatti da esso santo* (Trent: Battista Gelmini, 1608 [1586]), 4.
157. Shlomo Simonsohn, *The Apostolic See and the Jews: Documents, 492–1404* (Toronto: Pontifical Institute of Mediaeval Studies, 1988), 198, no. 188.
158. *Ristretto,* 26.
159. *Ristretto,* 26.
160. *Ristretto,* 27–31.

161. Mariani, *Il glorioso infante*, 1.
162. Mariani, *Il glorioso infante*, 18.
163. Cf. Mariani, *Il glorioso infante*, 5. Bowd and Cullington, "*On Everyone's Lips*," 64.
164. Mariani, *Il glorioso infante*, 10.
165. Mariani, *Il glorioso infante*, 13.
166. Mariani, *Il glorioso infante*, 30.
167. Mariani, *Il glorioso infante*, 21.
168. Mariani, *Il glorioso infante*, 39.
169. Mariani, *Il glorioso infante*, 57. Cf. Luke 2:41–52.
170. If Mariani read this part of Simon's story in parallel with the episode in the Gospels, some preachers in Poland would do the opposite; they would read this part of the Gospels for its allusions to the cruelty of Jews and ritual murder accusations. In a sermon collection from 1758 of a Franciscan friar in Cracow, the preacher claimed that after Jesus was lost, Mary thought he was caught and killed by Jews. MS. 279 "O. Bernard, Reformata, Kazania misjonarskie, 1758," Archiwum OO. Franciszkanów-Reformatów w Krakowie, folio 17: "Pro Dominica infra Octavam Epiphaniae."
171. "Involuto nella porpora del proprio sangue," Mariani, *Il glorioso infante*, 65.
172. Mariani, *Il glorioso infante*, 191–192.
173. See David Biale, *Blood and Belief: The Circulation of a Symbol between Jews and Christians* (Berkeley: University of California Press, 2007), chap. 2, esp. 78; Yuval, *Two Nations*. Joshua Schwartz, "Treading the Grapes of Wrath: The Wine Press in Ancient Jewish and Christian Tradition," *Theologische Zeitschrift* 49 (1993): 218–219, 318–322.
174. NRSV, Matthew 27:28; also Mark 15:17, and John 19:2.
175. Mariani, *Il glorioso infante*, 43–44.
176. See also Biale, *Blood and Belief*, 48ff.
177. Mariani, *Il glorioso infante*, 61–62.
178. Also later in Würzburg, 1569–70; Hsia, *The Myth of Ritual Murder*, 202. In another case a body began to sweat in the presence of a murderer; Hsia, *The Myth of Ritual Murder*, 128. This would also be found in Poland; see Chapters 6 and 8.
179. Bowd and Cullington, "*On Everyone's Lips*," 9, 168–169.
180. Mariani, *Il glorioso infante*, 70–71.
181. Mariani, *Il glorioso infante*, 72–73.
182. Mariani, *Il glorioso infante*, 92–93.
183. Mariani, *Il glorioso infante*, 95.
184. Mariani, *Il glorioso infante*, 111–112.
185. For a similar argument in Poland regarding a host desecration legend, see Teter, *Sinners on Trial*, ch. 4.
186. Augustine, *City of God*, Book 18, ch. 46 on Psalm 59–10.
187. Mariani, *Il glorioso infante*, 122–124.
188. Mariani, *Il glorioso infante*, 123.
189. To be sure, this was not a new call. Ever since Christians realized that Jews did not solely follow the biblical precepts, such calls were voiced from time to time.

190. Mariani, *Il glorioso infante*, 2–3.
191. Mariani, *Il glorioso infante*, 47.
192. See, for example, Mariani, *Il glorioso infante*, 103–105, 150, 156, 201.
193. This was not the first time Simon's body was examined. It was examined in 1637, also under Guarinoni's direction; Marcin Zgliński, "Nagrobki i kult ofiar rzekomych żydowskich mordów rytualnych na historycznych ziemiach litewskich XVII–XIX wieku," in *Socialiniu Tapatumu Repreznetacijos: Lietuvos Didžiosios Kunigaikštystes Kulturoje* (Vilnius: 2010), 320, n. 62.
194. Mariani, *Il glorioso infante*, 132.
195. Mariani, *Il glorioso infante*, 138ff.
196. Mariani, *Il glorioso infante*, 139–145.
197. Some Christian writers claimed that Jesus sustained 5,490 wounds; Thomas Lentes, "Counting Piety in Late Middle Ages," in *Ordering Medieval Society: Perspectives on Intellectual and Practical Modes of Shaping Social Relations*, ed. Bernhard Jussen (Philadelphia: University of Pennsylvania Press, 2001), 58–59. Isaac Cardoso mentioned this tradition in *Las excelencias de los hebreos* (Amsterdam: David de Castro Tartas, 1679), 411.
198. Mariani, *Il glorioso infante*, 145–151.
199. Mariani, *Il glorioso infante*, 112–119.
200. Mariani, *Il glorioso infante*, 112.
201. Mariani, *Il glorioso infante*, 115.
202. See AST APV lat. 69, doc. 68.
203. Mariani, *Il glorioso infante*, 157–159.
204. Ghetta, "Johannes Hinderbach, amministratore."
205. AST, APV, s.l. Capsa 69, no. 1, 1r; published in Ghetta, "Johannes Hinderbach, amministratore," 207.
206. AST, APV, s.l. 69, no. 1, 11v, published in Ghetta, "Johannes Hinderbach, amministratore," 217.
207. Ghetta, "Johannes Hinderbach, amministratore," 248.
208. On this, see de' Giudici and Quaglioni, *Apologia Judaeorum*.
209. Mariani, *Il glorioso infante*, 184.
210. Mariani, *Il glorioso infante*, 132–133.
211. Mariani, *Il glorioso infante*, 133.
212. Mariani, *Il glorioso infante*, 153–154.
213. Mariani, *Il glorioso infante*, 206.
214. Mariani, *Il glorioso infante*, 193. See Chapter 1 for a similar question regarding William of Norwich.
215. Mariani, *Il glorioso infante*, 209–210.
216. Dominique Rigaux, "L'immagine di Simone di Trento," 488. The most comprehensive overview of Simonine iconography in northern Italy to date is Valentina Perini, *Il Simonino: geografia di un culto* (Trento: Società di studi trentini di scienze storiche, 2012). See also Treue, *Der Trienter Judenprozess*, 348–392; Magda Teter, "The Iconography of Blood Libel: A European Story," in *Blood: Uniting and Dividing*, edited by Małgorzata Stolarska-Fronia (Warsaw: POLIN Muzeum Historii Żydów Polskich, 2017), 120–149.
217. Ghetta, "Johannes Hinderbach, amministratore."
218. Ghetta, "Johannes Hinderbach, amministratore," 209.

219. Esposito, "Il culto del 'Beato' Simonino," 431–432; Dal Prà, "L'immagine di Simonino," 447.
220. Dal Prà, "L'immagine di Simonino," esp. 466–468. Treue, *Der Trienter Judenprozess*, 348–392.
221. Esposito, "Il culto del 'Beato' Simonino," 437. Schindeleyp is named in the 1476 *Hystoria completa* by Johannes Matthias Tiberino.
222. Lamberto Donati, *L'inizio della stampa a Trento ed il Beato Simone* (Trento: Centro culturale "Fratelli Bronzetti," 1968).
223. On the dissemination of images of Simon of Trent, including the chapbook published by Kunne in Trent, see David S. Areford, *The Viewer and the Printed Image in Late Medieval Europe* (Farnham, UK: Ashgate, 2010). The images of this work and others related to Simonine iconography have also been published in Magda Teter and Urszula Stępień, *Stosunki chrześcijańsko-żydowskie w historii, pamięci i sztuce: europejski kontekst obrazów sandomierskich* (Sandomierz: Wydawnictwo Diecezjalne, 2014).
224. On the emergence and evolution of the "Jewish hat" in Christian iconography, see Sara Lipton, *Dark Mirror: The Medieval Origins of Anti-Jewish Iconography* (New York: Metropolitan Books, 2014). See also her *Images of Intolerance: The Representation of Jews and Judaism in the Bible Moralise'e* (Berkeley: University of California Press, 1999), esp. ch. 1.
225. August Herzog Bibliothek Wolfenbüttel, 5 Xylogr. http://diglib.hab.de/inkunabeln/5-xylogr/start.htm.
226. See for example, Friedrich Zoller's image from 1442 in Bolzano, in which menacing Jews are circumcising baby Jesus; Perini, *Il Simonino*, fig. 17, p. 119. Also, the stained-glass circumcision of Christ from Cologne ca. 1460–1470, now in the Metropolitan Museum of Art, accession no. 2003.14. For the Italian examples, see images of the circumcision of Christ by Cosme' Tura (1470s), in the Isabella Garner Museum in Boston or by Fra Angelico, ca. 1450 in the Museo di San Marco in Florence. On Jewish women in Christian art, and a discussion of circumcision, see Lipton, *Dark Mirror*, ch. 6.
227. For example, "The Last Supper by the Mazarine Master," British Library, Egerton MS 1070, f. 113r.
228. See, for example, the fifteenth-century ivory "Last Supper" at the Metropolitan Museum of Art in New York, Friedsam Collection, Bequest of Michael Friedsam, 1931 (accession number 32.100.207), and Bernat Martorell (d. 1452), "Altarpiece of St Mary Magdalene" at the Museo Episcopal de Vic, Osona, Catalonia, Spain. Also, though later, Pedro Beruguette's "Last Supper" at LACMA, Gift of the Ahmanson Foundation (M.90.171).
229. Areford, *The Viewer and the Printed Image*, 178.
230. Tiberinus, *Die Geschicht und Legend von dem seligen Kind und Marterer gennant Symon*. For a comparison of these works, see Dal Prà, "L'immagine di Simonino," 451–453.
231. The same was true for most paintings in churches in northern Italy, where head coverings were not "Jewish" and Jews had to be marked by the round badge. For examples, see Perini, *Il Simonino*.

232. Treue, *Der Trienter Judenprozess*, 306–308, 348–392. A broadsheet in German depicting pilgrims visiting the bloodied body of Simon with *arma Simonis*, instruments of passion akin to *arma Christi*, has been preserved in the Bayerische Staatsbibliothek in Munich, Rar. 338. The 1476 German version of Tiberino's account published in Nuremberg contains the image of Simon's crucifixion; see fig. 7 in Dal Prà, "L'immagine di Simonino."
233. Areford, *The Viewer and the Printed Image*, ch. 4.
234. See Veraja, *La beatificazione*, 17–19.
235. Simonsohn, *The Apostolic See and the Jews, 1464–1521*, no. 986, p. 1231. See also Rigaux, "L'immagine di Simone di Trento," 486.
236. Quoted in Areford, *The Viewer and the Printed Image*, 167.
237. Treue, *Der Trienter Judenprozess*, 240, n. 55.
238. Esposito, "Il culto del 'Beato' Simonino," 433; Rigaux, "L'immagine di Simone di Trento," 492.
239. Rigaux, "L'immagine di Simone di Trento," 489–490. See also, Church S. Andrea in Malegno, in Katz, *The Jew in the Art of the Italian Renaissance*, 142–143. For Malegno, see Perini, *Il Simonino*, 258–260; for other examples, 213–214, 230–232.
240. Ghetta, "Johannes Hinderbach, Amministratore."
241. Perini, *Il Simonino*, 276–281.
242. An example of the narrative can be seen on the exterior wall of the parochial church Sant'Andrea in Malegno; see Katz, *The Jew in the Art of the Italian Renaissance*, 142–143, fig. 60.
243. Hsia, *The Myth of Ritual Murder*, fig. 14, 215. On Schedel's ownership of the broadsheets, see Areford, *The Viewer and the Printed Image*, ch. 4.
244. Miri Rubin, *Corpus Christi: The Eucharist in Late Medieval Culture* (Cambridge: Cambridge University Press, 2002), 304–310.
245. Dal Prà, "L'immagine di Simonino," 463, 465. Perini, *Il Simonino*, 240–241. The detail with Simon of Trent is on the cover of the book of Dana Katz's book, *The Jew in the Art of the Italian Renaissance*. Another example of the connection between Simon and Christ is a fresco in Povo in the Church of St. Pietro e Andrea; see Perini, *Il Simonino*, 141–142; and Katz, *The Jew in the Art of the Italian Renaissance*, 150, fig. 67.
246. So wrote Approvino degli Approvini in March 1478 to Bishop Hinderbach about the order of images he made; Treue, *Der Trienter Judenprozess*, 366. Esposito, "Il culto del 'Beato' Simonino," 438; Rigaux, "L'immagine di Simone di Trento," 489, n. 26. See also, Katz, *The Jew in the Art of the Italian Renaissance*, chap. 5.
247. For images of Christ after the resurrection, holding a similar banner, see, for an early example, Giotto's depiction in Capella Scrovegni in Padua. For nearly contemporary fifteenth-century examples, see Fra Angelico, "Resurrection of Christ and Women at the Tomb" (1440–1442) in Cell 8 in Convento di San Marco, Florence; Master of the Osservanza, "The Resurrection" (c. 1445), Institute of Arts, Detroit; Piero della Francesca, "Resurrection" (1463–1465) in Pinacoteca Comunale, Sansepolcro; Giovanni Bellini "Resurrection of Christ" (1475–1479) in Gemäldegalerie der Staatlichen

Museen, Berlin; Alvise Vivarini, "Resurrection" (1497–1498) in San Giovanni in Bragora, Venice; and Master of the Housebook, "Resurrection" (1480–1485) in Städelsches Kunstinstitut, Frankfurt.

248. The estimates are based on the catalog by Perini, *Il Simonino*. For maps of the distribution, see www.thebloodlibeltrail.org.
249. Perini, *Il Simonino*, 196–198.
250. Rigaux, "L'immagine di Simone di Trento," fig. 7 and 493. Perini, *Il Simonino*, 196–198.
251. For other examples, see Areford, *The Viewer and the Printed Image*, ch. 4; and Perini, *Il Simonino*, 114, fig. 16, and other examples of Simon Triumphant. An image of Simon Triumphant from monastery of San Ponziano in Spoleto can be seen at http://www.pprg.infoteca.it/easyne2/LYT.aspx?IDLYT=3550&Code=cemir&ST=SQL&SQL=ID_Documento=3547; and Perini, *Il Simonino*, 327–329. Also see Mario Sensi, Mario Tosti, and Corrado Fratini, *Santuari nel territorio della provincia di Perugia* (Perugia: Quattroemme, 2002), 57.
252. Pusculus, *Vbertini Pusculi brixien[sis] duo libri Symonidos*. Perini, *Il Simonino*, 141–142. According to the survey of Simonine art by Valentina Perini, there are only about six instances of this iconography, and most of them come from the first decades of the sixteenth century. Only two, from Bressarone and Cavareno, can be dated to the period before 1500; the other examples are in Cunevo, Cloz, Mechel, and Provaglio d'Iseo.
253. For another example, see Mariani, *Il glorioso infante*.
254. A scanned copy of the book from Bayerische Staatsbibliothek is available for view on Google books.
255. *Martyrologium romanum (1583)*, 66–67. Gesti, *Martirio di S. Simone di Trento* (1589), 21; Gesti, *Martirio di S. Simone di Trento* (1593), 20. Even the title of Antonio Gesti's work underscores the importance of inclusion of Simon in "the catalogue of the saints."
256. *Officia propria Sancti Vigilii Episcopi, et B. Simonis innocentis martyrum, ac Sanctae Maxentiae viduae* (Tridenti: Apud Ioan. Baptistam, et Iacobum fratres de Gelminis de Sabbio, 1588); Gesti, *Martirio di S. Simone* (1589); Franco, *Martirio di S. Simone di Trento* (1608).
257. *Officium proprium S. Simonis innocentis, et martyris tridentini: per totam dioecesin trid. a secularibus, & regularibus die XXIIII martii celebrandum*, (Tridenti: Ex typographia episcopale, 1655). The same image had been used on the frontispiece of Franco, *Martirio del Beato Simone trentino* (1586).
258. Dal Prà, "L'immagine di Simonino," figs. 20–22, 28, 30, 36; Mariani, *Il glorioso infante*.
259. Quoted in Laura Dal Prà, "Ancora su Hinderbach e la sua creazione iconografica, con la scoperta del ciclo Simoniniano di S. Maria Della Misericordia di Trento," in Perini, *Il Simonino: Geografia di un culto*, 27–30. For expenses related to converting Samuel's house and Simon's home into chapels, see Ghetta, "Johannes Hinderbach, Amministratore," 240, 243, 245, 246.
260. Dal Prà, "Ancora su Hinderbach," 22.
261. Gesti, *Martirio di S. Simone*.

262. Gesti, *Martirio di S. Simone* (1589), 21r.
263. Gesti, *Martirio di S. Simone* (1589), 21; Gesti, *Martirio di S. Simone* (1593), 20.
264. Gesti, *Martirio di S. Simone* (1589), fol. 21r.
265. Gesti, *Martirio di S. Simone* (1589), fol. 21 r–v.
266. Gesti, *Martirio di S. Simone* (1589), 21r–v.
267. Gesti, *Martirio di S. Simone* (1589), 22r.
268. Gesti, *Martirio di S. Simone* (1589), 22r–v. For an eighteenth-century representation of the procession, see Dal Prà, "L'immagine di Simonino," il. 31.
269. Gesti, *Martirio di S. Simone* (1589), 23r.
270. Mariani, *Il glorioso infante*, 186. A 1724 print shows a catafalque with a baldachin carried in the procession; Dal Prà, "L'immagine di Simonino," il. 31. For images of the relics, see Giuseppe Divina, *Storia del Beato Simone da Trento* (Trent: Artigianelli, 1902), ch. 13, a plate after 32; ch. 18, a plate after 176; and ch. 22, plates after 304 and 320. Divina also recounts the ebbs and flows of the processions. The 1724 print, according to Divina, was produced to celebrate the reformation of the procession, perhaps indeed the decision to carry the body. The procession was then suspended and only reinstated in 1835 in five-year intervals. But it was suspended again, to be reinstated on the 400th anniversary of Simon's birth in 1872. In 1875, on the 400th anniversary of Simon's death, another celebration was to be held, but "bad weather impeded the procession." That year it was established that the procession was to take place every ten years, but the next procession did not take place until 1887. Divina published his book in 1902, and for him the last such procession had taken place in 1895, Divina, *Storia del Beato Simone da Trento*, 329. The last known procession was in 1955. In 1965 the cult was abolished.
271. Mariani, *Il glorioso infante*, 125.
272. Mariani, *Il glorioso infante*, 125–126. Also, Dal Prà, "L'immagine di Simonino," 461.
273. Mariani, *Il glorioso infante*, 125–126. The removed frescoes had been moved to the Museum of Castel Buonconsiglio and are not available for view. But a photograph was published by Antonio Morsassi in 1934. Morassi, *Storia della pittura nella Venezia tridentina: dalle origini alle fine del quattrocento* (Rome: La libreria dello stato, 1934), 366, fig. 235. Also, Dal Prà, "L'immagine di Simonino," figs. 10–11.
274. Mariani, *Il glorioso infante*, 136.
275. Mariani, *Il glorioso infante*, 137.
276. Dal Prà, "L'immagine di Simonino," 461. The list of what was preserved in the Church of St. Peter's in Trent is in Mariani, *Il glorioso infante*, 133–135.
277. Mariani, *Il glorioso infante*, 167.
278. Although the date may be a result of a typographical error, Mariani also claimed that Ferdinand IV was her brother—yet he was her son. Mariani, *Il glorioso infante*, 194.
279. Mariani, *Il glorioso infante*, 196, 198–199. The list of dignitaries visiting Trent is found on 194–199.

280. Mariani, *Il glorioso infante*, 204.
281. Dal Prà, "L'immagine di Simonino," 469, Figs. 20–21.
282. Now at the Jagiellonian library in Cracow, Biblioteka Klasztoru Kamedułów na Bielanach, BJ Cam. C. I. 27
283. On the trials of the Jews in Poland, see Chapter 6. On the iconography in Poland, see most recently, Magda Teter, "The Sandomierz Paintings of Ritual Murder as *Lieux De Mémoire*," in *Ritual Murder in Russia, Eastern Europe, and Beyond*, ed. Eugene M. Avrutin, Jonathan Dekel-Chen, and Robert Weinberg (Bloomington: Indiana University Press, 2017), 253–277; and "The Iconography of Blood Libel: A European Story."
284. The quote comes from Johann Christoph Wagenseil. Allison Coudert, "Seventeenth-Century Christian Hebraists: Philosemites or Antisemites?" in *Judaeo-Christian Intellectual Culture in the Seventeenth Century: A Celebration of the Library of Narcissus Marsh (1638–1713)*, ed. Allison Coudert et al. (Dordrecht: Kluwer Academic Publisher, 1999), 55.
285. Stefan Żuchowski, *Process kryminalny of niewinne dziecie Jerzego Krasnowskiego iuz to trzecie, roku 1710 dnia 18 sierpnia w Sendomirzu okrutnie od zydow zamordowane. dla odkrycia iawnych kryminalow zydowskich, dla przykladu sprawiedliwosci potomnym wiekom* (Sandomierz: after 1720), 88.
286. Archiwum Kapituły Kolegiackiej i Katedralnej w Sandomierzu (henceforth AKKiKS), 742, fols. 23–24.
287. For the most recent and most comprehensive discussion of the Sandomierz paintings of the calendar, see Teter and Stępień, eds., *Stosunki chrześcijańsko-żydowskie*.
288. On these paintings, including images, see Magda Teter, "Stosunki chrześcijańsko-żydowskie z perspektywy historii oraz czasu: sandomierskie obrazy w ikonograffi europejskiej," in *Stosunki chrześcijańsko-żydowskie*, esp. 42–51, figs. 19–23.
289. Jan Wiśniewski, *Dekanat sandomierski* (Radom: Jan Kanty Trzebiński, 1915), 177.
290. There was a Tuvia (Tobias) in Różana (now, Ruzhany, Belarus), where a blood libel took place in 1659. Meir Sokolowsky and Joseph Abramovitsch, *Rozana: A Memorial to the Ruzhinoy Jewish Community* (New York: JewishGen, 2012), 10–28.
291. *Officium proprium S. Simonis innocentis*, 7.
292. *Officium proprium S. Simonis innocentis*.
293. *Officium proprium S. Simonis innocentis*. See also, on p. 9: "Dixerunt impii Judaei in contumeliam Iesu, quem Christiani Deum colunt, huius pueri sanguinem exhauriamus." For a direct comparison between the inscriptions in St. Paul's Church and *Officium proprium S. Simonis innocentis*, see Teter, "The Sandomierz Paintings of Ritual Murder as 'Lieux De Mémoire,'" 265.
294. The transcription provided in Wiśniewski's book contains errors; they may be errors of transcription or typographical errors made by the printer. But what is on the frame may also be errors of memory that were the responsibility of the painter. Wiśniewski, *Dekanat sandomierski*, 177.
295. *Officium proprium S. Simonis innocentis*, 14.

Notes to Pages 144–148   427

296. Or errors of transcription by Wiśniewski.
297. A copy of the broadside dedicated to Aliprando Madruzzo is at the Wolfegg Castle in the Wolfegger Kabinett; a reproduction is published in Capriotti, *Lo scorpione sul petto*, 150, fig. 60; another version is in Zgliński, "Nagrobki i kult ofiar," 311.
298. On Pietromartino di Anversa, see Francesco Federico Mancini, *Miniatura a Perugia tra cinquecento e seicento* (Perugia: Electa; Editori Umbri Associati, 1987), 122, n. 45.
299. Teter, "Stosunki chrześcijańsko-żydowskie"; for images, see the appendix, especially fig. 20. Francesco Santi, *Dipinti, sculture e oggetti dei secoli XV–XVI* (Rome: Libreria dello Stato, 1989), 221–222. Perini, *Il Simonino*, 339. But the most comprehensive study of the work and the artist is Capriotti, *Lo scorpione sul petto*, 141–157. Capriotti dates the painting to 1597, based on a faint signature, 151.
300. Images in Teter and Stępień, *Stosunki chrześcijańsko-żydowskie*.
301. Mariani, *Il glorioso infante*, 43–44. The imagery of the resurrected Christ often included a red tunic; Dieric Bouts the Elder, "Resurrection" (1450–1460), Norton Simon Museum of Art, Pasadena, CA; Piero della Francesca, "Resurrection" (1463–1465), Museo Civico, Sansepolcro; Michael Wolgemut, "Resurrection" (c. 1485), Alte Pinakothek, Munich. For imagery of Simon, see Perini, *Il Simonino*.
302. See a reproduction in Capriotti, *Lo scorpione sul petto*, 150; Zgliński, "Nagrobki i kult ofiar," 311.
303. I thank Francesca Bregoli for asking a question about the hat and putting me in touch with Fabrizio Lelli, who in turn pointed to the marrano iconography. Private communication, March 14, 2014. For an example of a representation of marranos in iconography as dressed in black and wearing hats, see "Chaferiz d'el-Rei in the Alfama District," Lisbon, ca. 1560–80, oil on panel, 36 5/8 × 64 3/16 in. (93 × 163 cm), Bernardo Collection, Lisbon. It was on display in the exhibition, "Revealing the African Presence in Renaissance Europe," at the Walters Art Museum in Baltimore from October 14, 2012, to January 21, 2013.
304. Wiśniewski, *Dekanat sandomierski*, 177. Also quoted in Jolanta Żyndul, *Kłamstwo krwi: legenda mordu rytualnego na ziemiach polskich w XIX i XX wieku* (Warsaw: Wydawnictwo Cyklady, 2011), 241.
305. Żyndul, *Kłamstwo krwi*, 241.
306. Piotr Skarga, *Żywoty Świętych Starego i Nowego Zakonu z Pisma świętego i poważnych pisarzów i doktorow kościelnych wybranych* (Drukarnia Oświeconego Pana Mikołaja Christofa Radziwiłła, 1579), 280. Skarga's mention of stuffing the child's body in a barrel, along with the prominent presence of barrels in the painting by Pietromartino di Anversa, as well as in many other Simonine paintings, may help explain the barrel motif in the Sandomierz paintings. However, a much closer parallel, mentioning nails in a barrel, can be found in Solomon ibn Verga's *Shevet Yehudah*; see Chapter 5. On the iconography of the barrel, see Teter, "The Sandomierz Paintings of Ritual Murder as *Lieux De Mémoire*," 263.
307. AKKiKS, 741, 68.

308. Żyndul, *Kłamstwo krwi*, 256, 260–264. The painting is mentioned in David Jakubowicz, ed. *Sefer zikaron kehilot Wadowice, Andrychow, Kalwaria, Meslenice, Sucha* (Jerusalem: Masada Publishing,1967), 346; and Gemma Volli, *I "processi tridentini" e il culto del Beato Simone da Trento* (Florence: La Nuova Italia, 1963). Volli mistakenly located, after what appears to be a Nazi description, the painting in Góra Kalwaria near Warsaw.
309. A rather poor image of the painting can be found in Volli, *I "processi tridentini,"* fig. 4. This is the only known photograph of this now-lost painting. A painting clearly based on that in Kalwaria Zebrzydowska is now at the museum in Jarosław, published in color, Żyndul, *Kłamstwo krwi*, fig. 20.
310. The inscription is visible in Gemma Volli's reproduction of the painting, Volli, *I "processi tridentini."* A German translation of the inscription, not without errors, is in Joseph Samuel Bloch, *Israel und die Völker: nach jüdischer Lehre* (Berlin: Verlag Benjamin Harz, 1922), 753–754.
311. Żyndul, *Kłamstwo krwi*, 261. See Chapter 8.
312. Perini, *Il Simonino*, 332. See, more extensively, Ghetta, "Fra Bernardino," 129–177.
313. Żyndul, *Kłamstwo krwi*, chap. VIII, and figs. 22–23, 26. Zgliński, "Nagrobki i kult ofiar."
314. The founding of Kalwaria Zebrzydowska was inspired by Christian van Adrichem's book on Jerusalem during the times of Christ; see Augustyn Chadam, *Zarys dziejów Kalwarii Zebrzydowskiej* (Kalwaria Zebrzydowska: Wydawnictwo Calvariarum, 1984), 4; Hieronim Eug. Wyczawski, *Dzieje Kalwarii Zebrzydowskiej* (Cracow: Nakładem Prowincjałatu OO. Bernarynów, 1947), V.

4. Blood Libels and Cultures of Knowledge in Early Modern Europe

1. There is a vast literature on Christian Hebraism in German lands and Italy; see, for example, Aaron L. Katchen, *Christian Hebraists and Dutch Rabbis: Seventeenth Century Apologetics and the Study of Maimonides' Mishneh Torah* (Cambridge, MA: Harvard University Press, 1984); Allison Coudert and Jeffrey S. Shoulson, *Hebraica Veritas? Christian Hebraists and the Study of Judaism in Early Modern Europe* (Philadelphia: University of Pennsylvania Press, 2004); and the following by Stephen G. Burnett: *From Christian Hebraism to Jewish Studies: Johannes Buxtorf (1564–1629) and Hebrew Learning in the Seventeenth Century* (Leiden: Brill, 1996); "Distorted Mirrors: Antonius Margaritha, Johann Buxtorff and Christian Enthographies of the Jews," *Sixteenth Century Journal* 25 (1994); "Calvin's Jewish Interlocutor: Christian Hebraism and Anti-Jewish Polemics during the Reformation," *Bibliotheque d'Humanisme et Renaissance* 55 (1993); and *Christian Hebraism in the Reformation Era (1500–1660): Authors, Books, and the Transmission of Jewish Learning* (Leiden: Brill, 2012). On Jewish converts to Christianity and their work, see Elisheva Carlebach, *Divided Souls: Converts from Judaism in Early Modern*

Notes to Pages 153–160   429

German Lands, 1500–1750 (New Haven: Yale University Press, 2001); and Yaacov Deutsch, *Judaism in Christian Eyes: Ethnographic Descriptions of Jews and Judaism in Early Modern Europe* (Oxford: New York, 2011).

2. Schmidt quoted in Judith Pollmann, "Archiving the Present and Chronicling for the Future in Early Modern Europe," *Past & Present* 230, suppl. 11 (2016); 233, 249, 250.

3. To be sure, Jews sometimes convert and become good Christians, like Petrus Alphonsus, but sometimes they revert to Judaism and deserve death; for example, Hartmann Schedel, *Liber chronicarum* (Nuremberg: Anton Koberger, 1493), 198r.

4. Schedel, *Liber chronicarum,* 149v.

5. Schedel, *Liber chronicarum,* 201v.

6. Schedel, *Liber chronicarum,* 220v, 230v, 257v.

7. Hartmann Schedel, *Liber chronicarum cum figuris et imaginis ab initio mundi usque nunc temporis* (Augsburg: Johann Schönsperger, 1497), 168v, 225r, 247v, 258v, 285v, 289v.

8. For example, the 1337 Deckendorff and the 1492 Sternberg host desecrations appear only in Schedel until the post-Reformation era when some Catholic chroniclers included them in their works. Schedel is also the only chronicler to mention the 1298 persecution and the attack on the Jews of Prague.

9. This point is made in a different context by Anthony Grafton, *What Was History?: The Art of History in Early Modern Europe* (New York: Cambridge University Press, 2007), 124.

10. On Werner Rolevinck's *Fasciculus temporum,* see Margaret Bingham Stillwell, "The *Fasciculus Temporum*: A Genealogical Survey of Editions before 1480," in *Bibliographical Essays: A Tribute to Wilberforce Eames,* ed. Bruce Rogers (Cambridge, MA: Harvard University Press, 1924): 409–440.

11. Vincent de Beauvais, *Speculum historiale* (Strasbourg: Johann Mentelin, 1473), lib. 28, LXXIII–LXXIIII; lib. 30, XXV, LIII.

12. See for example, Werner Rolevinck, *Fasciculus temporum omnes antiquorum chronicas complectens* (Venice: Goergius Walch, 1479), 37r, 40r, 56v, 57r, 58v, 59v, 60r, 61r.

13. Daniela Rando, *Dai margini la memoria: Johannes Hinderbach (1418–1486)* (Bologna: Il Mulino, 2003), 243–244, 469. Rando refers to a copy in Biblioteca Communale di Trento, F b 64.

14. See also Wolfgang Treue, *Der Trienter Judenprozess: Voraussetzungen, Abläufe, Auswirkungen (1475–1588)* (Hannover: Hahn, 1996), 308–311.

15. Werner Rolevinck, *Fasciculus temporum* (Cologne: Nicolaus Götz, 1478), 64r.

16. See p. 90r in these editions by Werner Rolevinck: *Fasciculus temporum* (Basel: Bernhardus Richel, 1482 [February 20]); *Fasciculus temporum* (Strassburg: Johann Prüss, 1488); and *Fasciculus temporum* (Strassburg: Johann Prüss, 1490).

17. Werner Rolevinck, *Dat boek dat men hiet fasciculus temporum mit beig* (Utrecht: Johann Veldener, 1480) and his *Fasciculus temporum, le fardelet hystorial* (Genf: Drucker des Fardelet du temps, 1495).

18. "Iudei etiam quidam furati puerulum quendam in ciuitate tridentina nomine Symonem: fecerunt in eum mysteria quodammodo passionis ad similitudinem

domini nostri iesu christi," Werner Rolevinck, *Fasciculus temporum* (Venice: cura impensisq[ue] Erhardi Ratdolt de Augusta, 1480 [November 24]), 65. See also, for example, the 1485 Venice edition, fol. 64v; 1524, 316v.

19. See, for example, Joannes Sichardus, ed. *En damus chronicon divinum plane opus eruditissimorum autorum: repetitum ab ipso mundi initio, ad annum usque salutis M.D. XII* (Basel: Henricus Petrus, 1529), 144v.

20. Treue, *Der Trienter Judenprozess*, 312. For example, Jacobus Philippus Foresti Bergomensis, *Supplementum chronicarum* (Brescia: Boninus de Boninis, 1485 [December 1]), 347v–348r; Jacobus Philippus Foresti Bergomensis, *Supplementum chronicarum* (Venice: Bernardinus Ricius de Novaria, 1492), 249r.

21. "Cum xpianum non haberent imolandum cuius sanguine in azimis suis uti possent," in Bergomensis. Bergomensis, *Supplementum chronicarum* (1492), 248v.

22. Jacobus Philippus Foresti Bergomensis, *Supplementum chronicarum* (Venice: Bernardino Rizzo, 1491), 288v.

23. Treue, *Der Trienter Judenprozess*, 312.

24. Alexandra Kess, *Johann Sleidan and the Protestant Vision of History* (Oxon, UK: Routledge, 2016), 106.

25. The Polish chronicler Marcin Bielski also framed his universal history within the four empires; his chronicle was first published in 1551 and republished numerous times. Bielski, *Kronika. Tho Iesth, Historya swiata na szesc wiekow, a czterzy monarchie, rozdzielona* (Cracow: Mateusz Siebeneycher, 1564).

26. Kess, *Johann Sleidan*, 109–110.

27. Laurentius Surius, *Commentarius breuis rerum in orbe gestarum: ab anno salutis millesimo quingentesimo, vsq[ue] ad annum LXVI* (Cologne: apud haeredes Ioannis Quentel & Geruinum Calenium, 1566), 67–68 (Lisbon massacre), 84–86 (1510 host desecration), 551–553 (1556, Sochaczew). Laurentius Surius, *Commentarius breuis rerum in orbe gestarum: ab anno salutis M.D. vsque in annum M.D. LXXIIII* (Cologne: apud Geruinum Calenium, & haeredes Ioannis Quentelij, 1574), 50–51 (Lisbon massacre), 63–64 (1510 host desecratio), 487–488 (1556, Sochaczew). On the Lisbon massacre, see Yosef Hayim Yerushalmi, *The Lisbon Massacre of 1506 and the Royal Image in the Shebet Yehudah* (Cincinnati: Hebrew Union College-JIR, 1976). On Sochaczew, see Magda Teter, *Sinners on Trial: Jews and Sacrilege after the Reformation* (Cambridge, MA: Harvard University Press, 2011), ch. 5. On communion and Eucharist in Protestantism, see Lee Palmer Wandel, *The Eucharist in the Reformation: Incarnation and Liturgy* (Cambridge; New York: Cambridge University Press, 2006).

28. Johann Mayr, *Epitome cronicorum seculi modernidas ist: kurzter begriff und inhalt aller gedenckwürdigen sachen, so von 1500 biß zu dem 1604. jar Christi* (Munich: N. Henricus, 1604), 38r and 335r (Regensburg), 181v (1591, Pressburg).

29. Stefania Tutino, "'For the Sake of the Truth of History and of the Catholic Doctrines': History, Documents, and Dogma in Cesare Baronio's *Annales Ecclesiastici*," *Journal of Early Modern History* 17 (2013): 130–131. See also Anthony Grafton, "Church History in Early Modern Europe: Tradition and In-

novation," and Giuseppe Antonio Guazzelli, "Cesare Baronio and the Roman Catholic Vision of the Early Church," in *Sacred History: Uses of the Christian Past in the Renaissance World,* ed. Katherine Van Liere, Simon Ditchfield, and Howard Louthan (Oxford: Oxford University Press, 2012), 3–26 and 52–70.

30. Grafton, "Church History in Early Modern Europe," 23. For a more detailed study on Baronio and Casaubon's critique, see Anthony Grafton and Joanna Weinberg, "*I Have Always Loved the Holy Tongue*": *Isaac Casaubon, the Jews, and a Forgotten Chapter in Renaissance Scholarship* (Cambridge, MA: Belknap Press, 2011).
31. Tutino, "'For the Sake of the Truth,'" 144.
32. Cesare Baronio, *Annales ecclesiastici* (Venice: Apud Stephanum Monti, 1738–1740), vol. 7, cols. 392 (504 legislation), 723–724 (Gregory I against violence), vol. 398, cols. 544–545 (VIII Council of Toledo).
33. Baronio, *Annales ecclesiastici,* vol. 12, cols. 389–390.
34. Tutino, "'For the Sake of the Truth,'" 152–153, n. 59.
35. Abraham Bzowski, *Annalium ecclesiasticorum post Illustriss. et Revedend. Dominum D. Caesare Baronium S.R.E cardinalem Bibliothecarem Tomus XIII rerum in orbe christiano an anno domini 1198 usque annum dom. 1299 gestarum narrationem complectens.* (Cologne: Agrippinae apud Antonium Boetzerum, 1616). Henceforth, Bzowski, *Annalium,* vol. 13.
36. Bzowski, *Annalium,* vol. 13, col. 443, under 1234.19.
37. Hugh of Lincoln, Bzowski, *Annalium,* vol. 13, col. 638–639, under 1255.12.
38. Other blood libel stories included in Bzowski, *Annalium* vol. 13 were of Wissenburg (1252.16) and Prague (1287.9).
39. Bzowski, *Annalium,* vol. 13, col. 464.
40. Christian Wurtisen, *Germaniae historicorum illustrium, quorum pleriq[ue] ab henrico IIII imperatore vsque ad annum Christi, M. CCCC* (Frankfurt a.M: Apud haeredes Andreae Wecheli, 1585), vol. 2, part "Fragmentum historicum incerti auctoris," 91 verse 14 under 1236.
41. See, for example, Bzovius, in his vol. 15 covering the years 1378–1431 and published in 1622; when describing the 1399 story of host desecration in Poznań, copied verbatim a book about it recently published in 1609 by a Polish writer, Tomasz Treter, Abraham Bzovius, *Annalium ecclesiasticorum post Illutriss. et Reverenidss. D.D. Caesarem Baronium. Tomus XV rerum in orbe christiano ab Anno Domini 1378 usque as Annum Domini 1431* (Cologne, 1622), 188–208, under 1399.13 On the Poznań story, see Teter, *Sinners on Trial,* ch. 4.
42. Odoricus Rinaldi, *Annales ecclesiastici ab anno quo desinit Card. Caes. Baronius MCXCVIII usque ad annum MDXXXIV Continuati, Tomus XIII* (Cologne: Sumptibus Ioannis Wilhelmi Friessem, 1692). *Sicut Iudaeis* on 37 under 1199.54 and 425, under 1235.20; *Lachrymabilem* on 441–442, under 1236.48; and the 1247 bull on 581, under 1247.83–84. These documents are in Shlomo Simonsohn, *The Apostolic See and the Jews: Documents,* 492–1404 (Toronto: Pontifical Institute of Mediaeval Studies, 1988), nos. 79, 144, 185.
43. This apologetic statement follows the full text of *Sicut Iudaeis* under 1235.20.
44. On the concept of "traveling facts," see Mary S. Morgan, "Travelling Facts," in *How Well Do Facts Travel? The Dissemination of Reliable Knowledge,* ed. Peter

Howlett and Mary S. Morgan (Cambridge: Cambridge University Press, 2011), 3–39.
45. Marquardus de Susannis, *Tractatus de iudaeis et aliis infidelibus* (Venice: apud Cominum de Tridino Montisferrati, 1558), section 2 of ch. 7, 25r–26r.
46. Mathew Adam McLean, *The Cosmographia of Sebastian Münster: Describing the World in the Reformation* (Aldershot, UK: Ashgate, 2007), 151.
47. McLean, *Cosmographia*, esp. 16–26.
48. Sebastian Münster, *Cosmographia: Beschreibung aller Lender durch Sebastianum Munsterum* (Basel: Getruckt durch Henrichum Petri, 1544), 38; Sebastian Münster, *Cosmographiae uniuersalis lib. VI* (Basel: apud Henrichum Petri, 1550), 46; Sebastian Münster, *Sei libri della cosmografia* (Basel: Stampato a spese di Henrigo Pietro Basiliense, 1558), 52. Henceforth, *Cosmographia (1544)*, *Cosmographia (1550)*, and *Cosmografia (1558)*, respectively.
49. Palmieri under 1492: "Expulsa sunt Hispania tota, centum et viginti-quatuor milla familiarum Iudaicarum." Johannes Sichardt, ed. *Habes opt. lector chronicon opus felicissime renatum* (Basel: Excudebat Henricus Petrus,1536), 152v. In Münster, in the first German edition of *Cosmographia (1544)*, 50.
50. For example, Münster, *Cosmographia (1544)*, 86; Münster, *Cosmographia (1550)*, 132; Münster, *Cosmografia (1558)*, 150.
51. Münster, *Cosmographia (1544)*, 129; Münster, *Cosmographia (1550)*, 230; Münster, *Cosmografia (1558)*, 258–259.
52. "Omnium maleficiorum auctores." Münster, *Cosmographia (1550)*, 457–458. See also, for example, the story of Rufach in 1298 in Münster, *Cosmographia (1550)*, 444–445; Münster, *Cosmografia (1558)*, 506.
53. This concept was developed by Augustine built on the idea of the six-day creation of the world that was followed by the day of rest. Similarly, there were six ages of the world, followed by seventh, when Jesus would return ushering a messianic era.
54. On Münster's predecessors, see McLean, *Cosmographia*, ch. 2.
55. McLean, *Cosmographia*, 144–145.
56. Quoted in McLean, *Cosmographia*, 148.
57. McLean, *Cosmographia*, 161, 200.
58. Münster, *Cosmographia (1550)*, 444–445; Münster, *Cosmografia (1558)*, 506. This story does not enter the German editions until 1561.
59. On the differences between editions, see McLean, *Cosmographia*, 173–188.
60. McLean, *Cosmographia*, 170, 173.
61. Joseph Ha-Kohen and Karin Almbladh, *Sefer Emeq Ha-Bakha (The Vale of Tears) with the Chronicle of the Anonymous Corrector* (Uppsala: Uppsala University, 1981). See Chapter 6.
62. Georg Braun, *Civitates orbis terrarvm liber primvs* (Cologne: Apud Godefridum Kempensem, 1582), no. 14.
63. Braun, *Civitates Orbis,* 48.
64. "Creditum autem est vulgo eam a Iudaeis infectis veneno fontibus effectam esse." Kromer in Johann Pistorius, ed. *Polonicae historiae corpus: hoc est polonicarum rerum latini recentiores & veteres scriptores, quotquot extant, uno*

volumine compraehensi omnes, & in aliquot distributi tomos (Basel: Per Sebastianum Henricpetri, 1582), 603.

65. On the Esterke story and its legacy in Polish and Yiddish literature, see Chone Shmeruk, *The Esterke Story in Yiddish and Polish Literature: A Case Study in the Mutual Relations of Two Cultural Traditions* (Jerusalem: Zalman Shazar, 1985). On Długosz, see Piotr Dymmel, *Tradycja rekopiśmienna roczników Jana Długosza* (Warsaw: Wydawictwo Naukowe PWN, 1992).
66. For example, see Jan Herburt, *Chronica, sive historiae polonicae compendiosa: ad per certa librorum capita ad facilem memoriam recens facta descriptio* (Basel: Ex Officina Oporiniana, 1571), 180. Maciej Miechowita in Pistorius, *Polonicae historiae corpus*, 165.
67. Teter, *Sinners on Trial*, ch. 4.
68. Pistorius, *Polonicae historiae corpus*, 202. Marcin Bielski and Joachim Bielski, *Kronika polska Marcina Bielskiego* (Sanok: K. Pollak, 1856), 508. Bielski, *Kronika. Tho iesth, historya świata*, 385r. On sixteenth-century Polish historiography, see Agnieszka Dziuba, *Wczesnorenesansowa historiografia polsko-łacińska* (Lublin: Katolicki Uniwersytet Lubelski, 2000), esp, chap. 1.
69. Bielski, *Kronika*, fol. 279.
70. Bielski, *Kronika*, fol. 283.
71. Bielski, *Kronika*, fol. 283v–284r.
72. Bielski, *Kronika*, 287r.
73. Bielski, *Kronika*, 385r, 424r.
74. Bielski, *Kronika*, 462v–466r.
75. Bielski, *Kronika*, 465v.
76. Václav Hájek of Libočan, *Böhmische Chronica Vvenceslai Hagecii* (Prague: Gedruckt durch Nicolaum Straus, Jnn Verlegung Andreaszen Weidlichs, 1596). On the chronicle, see Zdenek V. David, "Hajek, Dubravius, and the Jews: A Contrast in Sixteenth-Century Czech Historiography," *Sixteenth-Century Journal* 27, no. 4 (1996): 997–1013.
77. David, "Hajek, Dubravius, and the Jews," 1000.
78. Hájek of Libočan, *Böhmische Chronica*, 156.
79. Although readers could also encounter Jews in genres not explicitly devoted to them, such as chronicles, cosmographies, and even rather technical books, including chronographies, not all Christian writers automatically jumped at the opportunity to retell those tales. A book on calendars by Jeronimo Chaves's *Chronographia*, for example, compared the Jewish calendar with others, pointing to Jewish errors in the calendar. Still, though Jews are often described with derogatory vocabulary, such as "obstinate" or "adulterers," and are shown to follow erroneous beliefs, Chaves's *Chronographia* did not mention anti-Jewish stories related to Passover. Chaves, *Chronographia o reportorio de los tiempos el mas copioso y preciso que hasta ahora ha salido a luz* (Sevilla: Alonso Escriuano, 1572), 152r–153r.
80. Alisa Meyuhas Ginio, "'The Fortress of Faith'—at the End of the West: Alfonso de Espina and His 'Fortalitium Fidei,'" in *Contra Judaeos: Ancient and Medieval Polemics between Christians and Jews*, ed. Ora Limor (Tubingen: Mohr, 1996), 215.

81. Alfonso de Espina, *Fortalitium fidei* (Nuremberg: Anton Koberger, 1485), Lib. 3, cons. 7 "de iudaeorum crudelitatibus."
82. *Pharetra fidei catholice siue ydonea disputatio inter christianos et judeos* (Cologne: Heinrich Quentel, 1494); *Pharetra catholice fidei* (Landschut: Per Joannem Weyssenburger, 1514).
83. R. Po-chia Hsia, "Christian Ethnographies of the Jews in Early Modern Germany," in *Expulsion of the Jews: 1492 and After*, ed. Raymond B. Waddington and Arthur Williamson (London: Garland Publishing, 1994), 223.
84. Carlebach, *Divided Souls*, esp. chs. 9 and 10; see Deutsch, *Judaism in Christian Eyes*, esp. 65–76.
85. Hsia, "Christian Ethnographies," 224–226; and *Trent 1475*. On von Pappenheim, see David Stern, Christoph Markschies, and Sarit Shalev-Eyni, *The Monk's Haggadah: A Fifteenth-Century Illuminated Codex from the Monastery of Tegernsee, with a Prologue by the Friar Erhard Von Pappenheim* (University Park: Pennsylvania State University Press, 2015), 8–10, 73, 85.
86. Stern et al., *The Monk's Haggadah*, 116–117.
87. Carlebach, *Divided Souls*, 174.
88. Carlebach, *Divided Souls*, 174ff, section "Minhag Literature in the Culture of Ashkenaz." What follows is based on that section.
89. Carlebach, *Divided Souls*, 177–179. An English translation is now available of Johann Pfefferkorn, *The Jews' Mirror*, trans. Ruth I. Cape (Tempe, AZ: ACMRS, 2011). Von Carben was not forgotten, however; see, for example, references to his work in Conrad Huser and Marcus Lombardus, *Tractatus de imposturis et ceremoniis judaeorum nostri temporis ab autore germanice editus nunc vero in gratiam reipublicae christianae latine redditus a Conrado Husero Tigurino* (Basel: Per P. Pernam, 1575), 3, 8. On von Carben, see Carola Maria Werhahn, *Die Stiftung des Victor Von Carben (1423–1515) im Kolner Dom: Glaubenspropaganda zwischen Judentum und Christentum in Text und Bild* (Munich: Herbert Utz Verlag, 2013).
90. Johannes Pfefferkorn, *Ich heyss eyn Buchlijn der Iuden beicht.* (Cologne: Johann Landen, 1508). The two copies I consulted, one at the New York Public Library and one from the Bayerische Staadtbibliothek, have the images bound in different order.
91. Johann Pfefferkorn, *In hoc libello coparatur absoluta explicatio, quomı ceci illi iudei suu pascha servet* (Cologne: Per Henricum in nussia, 1509); Johann Pfefferkorn, *In disem Buchlein vindet jer ain entlichenn furtrag wie die blinden Juden yr Ostern halten unnd besunderlich wie das abentmal gessen wirt, weiter wurdt aussgetruckt das die Juden ketzer seyn des alten und des Newenn Testaments* (Cologne: Landen, 1509).
92. On Pfefferkorn's book on Passover, see also David Price, *Johannes Reuchlin and the Campaign to Destroy Jewish Books* (Oxford: Oxford University Press, 2010), 104–106.
93. On this most recently, see Price, *Johannes Reuchlin*.
94. Thomas Murner, *Hukat ha-pesah: ritus et celebratio phase iudeorum cum orationibus eorum et benedictionibus menses ad litteram interpretatis cum omni observatione uti soliti sunt suum pasca extra terram promissionis sine*

esu agni pascalis celebrare (Frankfurt a.M: Beatus Murner, 1512). On Murner's Haggadah, see Yosef Hayim Yerushalmi, *Haggadah and History* (Philadelphia: Jewish Publication Society, 2005), 27–30, and plates 6–7.
95. Lawrence A. Hoffman, "The Passover Meal in Jewish Tradition," *Passover and Easter: Origin and History of Modern Times*, ed. Paul F. Bradshaw and Lawrence A. Hoffman (Notre Dame: University of Notre Dame Press, 2002), 22–23. Richard I. Cohen, *Jewish Icons: Art and Society in Modern Europe* (Berkeley: University of California Press, 1998), 21–22. See also Hans-Martin Kirn, *Das Bild vom Juden in Deutschland des Fruehen 16. Jahrhunderts* (Tubingen: J. C. B. Mohr, 1989), 50–51.
96. Pfefferkorn, *Jews' Mirror*, 90–93.
97. Martin Luther, *Das Jhesus Christus eyn geborner Jude sey* (Wittemberg: Melchior Lotter, 1523), second to last paragraph.
98. First printing, Martin Luther, *Von den Juden und iren Lugen. D. M. Luth. zum andernmal gedruckt, und mehr dazu gethan. M. D. XLIII* (Wittemberg: durch Hans Lufft, 1543), S, g ii verso–g iii.
99. Carlebach, *Divided Souls*, 179. Antonius Margaritha, *Der gantz Jüdisch Glaub* (Augsburg: Heynrich Steyner, 1530).
100. Carlebach, *Divided Souls*, 174.
101. Margaritha, *Der gantz Jüdisch Glaub*.
102. Burnett, "Distorted Mirrors," 276–277.
103. Carlebach, *Divided Souls*, 180.
104. Carlebach, *Divided Souls*, 181.
105. Maria Diemling, "Anthonius Margaritha on the 'Whole Jewish Faith': A Sixteenth-Century Convert from Judaism and His Depiction of Jewish Religion," in *Jews, Judaism, and the Reformation in Sixteenth-Century Germany*, ed. Dean Phillip Bell and Stephen G. Burnett (Leiden: Brill, 2006), 305–306. Elisheva Carlebach, "Jewish Responses to Christianity in Reformation Germany," in *Jews, Judaism, and the Reformation*, 460. Michael Thomson Walton, "Anthonius Margaritha: Honest Reporter?," *Sixteenth Century Journal* 36, no. 1 (2005): 129–130. Also see Chava Fraenkel-Goldschmidt, ed. *The Historical Writings of Joseph of Rosheim: Leader of Jewry in Early Modern Germany* (Leiden: Brill, 2006), 176–187, 321–322, 372–373.
106. Luther, *Von den Juden und iren Lugen*, c verso. See also Burnett, "Distorted Mirrors," 278. See Huser and Lombardus, *Tractatus de imposturis*, 18, and Polish works based on Lombardus.
107. "Brauchen dazu weder saltz noch schmaltz nur wasser und mel." Antonius Margaritha, *Der gantz Judisch Glaub* (Leipzig: Melchior Lotther, 1531). Carlebach, *Divided Souls*, 198–199.
108. Andreas Osiander, *Ob es war und glaublich sey, daß die Juden der Christen Kinder Heymlich erwürgen, vnd jr Blut gebrauchen: ein treffenliche Schrifft, auff eines yeden Vrteyl gestelt* (Nuremberg: Petreius, 1530). Osiander's essay is discussed in detail in R. Po-chia Hsia, *The Myth of Ritual Murder*, 136–143. See Joy Kammerling, "Andreas Ossiander, the Jews, and Judaism," in *Jews, Judaism, and the Reformation*.

109. Osiander, *Ob es war und glaublich sey,* bv–b2; Carlebach, *Divided Souls,* 199; and Kirn, *Das Bild vom Juden,* 51, n.157.
110. Ernst Ferdinand Hess, *Flagellvm ivdeorvm, Juden Geissel* (1598); Carlebach, *Divided Souls,* 199.
111. Quoted in Allison Coudert, "Seventeenth-Century Christian Hebraists: Philosemites or Antisemites?" in *Judaeo-Christian Intellectual Culture in the Seventeenth Century: A Celebration of the Library of Narcissus Marsh (1638–1713),* ed. Allison Coudert et al. (Dordrecht: Kluwer Academic Publisher, 1999), 54–55.
112. Johann Buxtorf, *Synagoga judaica, hoc est schola judaeorum* (Hanau: Typis Petri Antoni Impensis J. Stöckle, 1622), "Praefatio ad lectorem." On Buxtorf, see Burnett, *From Christian Hebraism to Jewish Studies.*
113. Burnett, *From Christian Hebraism to Jewish Studies,* 55, 63–65.
114. Buxtorf, *Synagoga judaica,* chap. 12, 325.
115. Buxtorf, *Synagoga judaica,* ch. 13, esp. 331.
116. Buxtorf, *Synagoga judaica,* 333–334.
117. Buxtorf, *Synagoga judaica,* chs. 26–27.
118. Friedrich Albrecht Christiani, *Der Jüden Glaube und Aberglaube* (Leipzig: Lanckisch, 1705), fig. VII, 102.
119. Bernard Picart and Jean-Frèdèric Bernard, *Cèrèmonies et coutumes religieuses de tous les peuples du monde: reprèsentèes par des figures* (Amsterdam: Chez J. F. Bernard, 1723). On Picart and the Jews, see Samantha Baskind, "Judging a Book by Its Cover," *Journal of Modern Jewish Studies* 15, no. 1 (2016).
120. On Picart's *Ceremonies,* see Lynn Hunt, Margaret Jacob, and Wijnand Mijnhardt, *Bernard Picart and the First Global Vision of Religion* (Los Angeles: Getty Research Institute, 2010); Lynn Hunt, Margaret C. Jacob, and Wijnand Mijnhardt, *The Book that Changed Europe: Picart and Bernard's Religious Ceremonies of the World* (Cambridge, MA: Belknap Press, 2010).
121. Joannes Boemus, *Omnivm gentivm mores leges et ritvs ex mvltis clarissimis rervm scriptoribus* (Augusta: Excusa in officina Sigismundi Grimm medici, ac Marci Vuirsung, 1520); Claude Fleury, *Les moeurs des Israèlites* (Paris: Veuve G. Clouzier, 1681). Fleury's book became a bestseller; it was quickly republished and translated into many European languages, including English (1683), German (1709), Italian (1712), and even Polish (1783).
122. Baskind, "Judging a Book by Its Cover."
123. Neither the 1723 French edition nor the 1731 English has the image of *malkot,* flagellation, but the 1741 Paris edition (available through Hathi trust) does. Picart and Bernard, *Cèrèmonies et coutumes (1723);* Jean-Frèdèric Bernard and Bernard Picart, *Histoire gènèrale des cèrèmonies, moeurs et coutumes religieuses de tous les peuples du monde* (Paris: Rollin Fils, 1741), image between pp. 164 and 165. For the image of *malkot* from Calmet's *Dictionnaire historique,* see Deutsch, *Judaism in Christian Eyes,* 92.
124. Some of the images are reproduced in Cohen, *Jewish Icons,* ch. 1.
125. Hsia, "Christian Ethnographies," 228.
126. Christiani, *Der Jüden Glaube und Aberglaube,* 182.

127. Bernard Picart, *The Religious Ceremonies and Customs of the Several Nations of the Known World* (London: Printed for Nicholas Prevost, 1733), vol. I: 50–51 (meat), 173ff ("Crimes laid to the charge of the Jews").
128. For a study of Slonik's work and an English translation of the Yiddish text, see Edward Fram, *My Dear Daughter: Rabbi Benjamin Slonik and the Education of Jewish Women in Sixteenth-Century Poland* (Cincinnati: Hebrew Union College Press, 2007). Benjamin Aaron Slonik, *Precetti da esser imparati dalle donne hebree*, trans. Jacob Halpron (Venice: G. Sarzina, 1616). Girolamo Allè, *I convinti e confusi hebrei* (Ferrara: Nella stamparia camerale, 1619), Latin preface. For examples of Yiddish *minhag* books in Italy, see Chava Turnyanski and Erika Timm, *Yiddish in Italia: Yiddish Manuscripts and Printed Books from the 15th to the 17th Century* (Milan: Associazione Italiana Amici dell' Univ. di Gerusalemme, 2003).
129. Pietro Galatino, *Opus toti christian[a]e reipublic[a]e maxime utile de arcanis catholic[a]e ueritatis contra obstinatissimam iud[a]eoru[m] nostr[a]e tempestatis p[er]fidiam* (Ortona: Summa cum diligentia per Hieronymum Suncinum [Gersom b. Moshe Soncino], 1518). On Galatino, see Alba Paladini, *Il de arcanis di Pietro Galatino: Traditio giudaica e nuove istanze filologiche* (Lecce: Congedo Editore, 2004); Cesare Vasoli, "Giorgio B. Salviati, Pietro Galatino e la edizione di Ortona—1518—del 'De arcanis catholicae fidei,'" in *Cultura umanistica nel meridione e la stampa in Abruzzo* (L'Aquila: Deputazione Abruzzese di storia patria, 1984); Grafton and Weinberg, "*I Have Always Loved the Holy Tongue.*"
130. Carlebach, *Divided Souls*, 174. See also Lucia Raspe, "Minhag and Migration: A Yiddish Custom Book from Venice, 1553," *Early Modern Workshop: Jewish History Resources*, 2010, available at www.earlymodern.org.
131. On Christian Kabbalah, see Francois Secret, *I cabbalisti cristiani del Rinascimento* (Rome: Arkeios, 2001). Originally published in French in 1985.
132. Cited in Paladini, *Il de arcanis di Pietro Galatino*, 13.
133. On censorship, see, for example, Amnon Raz-Krakotzkin, *The Censor, the Editor, and the Text: The Catholic Church and the Shaping of the Jewish Canon in the Sixteenth Century* (Philadelphia: University of Pennsylvania Press, 2007); Federica Francesconi, "'This Passage Can Also Be Read Differently . . .:' How Jews and Christians Censored Hebrew Texts in Early Modern Modena," *Jewish History* 26 (2012): 139–160.
134. On Galatino and *De arcanis*, see Vasoli, "Giorgio B. Salviati."
135. On charges of plagiarism against Galatino, see Paladini, *Il de arcanis di Pietro Galatino*, 14–19. Grafton and Weinberg, "*I Have Always Loved the Holy Tongue.*" Yaacob Dweck has argued that Galatino "demonstrated a considerably greater knowledge of Hebrew sources and Jewish culture" than Raymond Martini. Dweck, *Scandal of Kabbalah: Leon Modena, Jewish Mysticism, Early Modern Venice* (Princeton, NJ: Princeton University Press, 2013), 156. Indeed, Paladini argued that the Italian manuscripts of works that Galatino used had no Hebrew in them; the Hebrew in his book was his own. On *Pugio*'s importance, see Secret, *I cabbalisti cristiani*, 35–40; Jeremy Cohen, *The Friars and the Jews: A Study in the Development of Medieval Anti-Judaism*

(Ithaca: Cornell University Press, 1982), ch. 6; Robert Chazan, *Daggers of Faith: Thirteenth-Century Christian Missionizing and Jewish Response* (Berkeley: University of California Press, 1989), ch. 7.

136. Ora Limor, "The Epistle of Rabbi Samuel of Morocco: A Best-Seller in the World of Polemics," in *Contra Judaeos: Ancient and Medieval Polemics between Christians and Jews* (Tubingen: Mohr, 1996), 178.

137. In 1651 and 1653 (Paris), 1687 with an introduction of Benedict Carpzov (Leipzig), and in 1744.

138. See, for example, Isidore of Seville, *Liber Ysidori contra iudeos* (Rome, 1485). On Isidore and his book, along with a Spanish translation, see Isidore of Seville, Eva Marìa Castro Caridad, and Francisco Peña Fernández, *Isidoro de Sevilla: sobre la fe catolica contra los judìos* (Sevilla: Universidad de Sevilla, 2014), esp. 13–41.

139. Dweck, *Scandal of Kabbalah*, 156; Paladini, *Il de arcanis di Pietro Galatino*, 28; Secret, *I cabbalisti cristiani*, 112–114.

140. I examined the first 1518, the 1550, the 1561, and the last 1672 editions; Galatino, *De arcanis catholicae ueritatis*; Pietro Galatino, *Petri Galatini de arcanis catholicae veritatis, Libri XII* (Frankfurt a.M: Sumptibus Jacobi Godofredi Seyler, 1672). For medieval polemic, see, for example, the issues raised in works against Jews by Isidore of Seville, *De fide catholica contra judaeos* (Rome, 1485).

141. Paladini, *Il De arcanis di Pietro Galatino*, 102, 108. On Reuchlin, see Erika Rummel, *The Case against Johann Reuchlin: Religious and Social Controversy in Sixteenth-Century Germany* (Toronto: University of Toronto Press, 2002); Johannes Reuchlin, *Recommendation whether to Confiscate, Destroy and Burn All Jewish Books: A Classic Treatise against Anti-Semitism* (New York: Paulist Press, 2000); Price, *Johannes Reuchlin*.

142. Galatino, *De arcanis catholicae ueritatis*, Lib. I cap. VII. For a list of sources cited by Galatino, see Paladini, *Il De arcanis di Pietro Galatino*, 64–68.

143. Secret, *I cabbalisti cristiani*, 79, 114. Raz-Krakotzkin, *The Censor, the Editor, and the Text*, 40.

144. Fabiano Fioghi, *Dialogo fra il cathecumino et il padre cathechizante* (Rome: Per gli heredi d'Antonio Blado stampatori camerali, 1582). On Fioghi, briefly, see Kenneth R. Stow, *Jewish Life in Early Modern Rome* (Burlington, VT: Ashgate, 2007), I, 17–18.

145. Fioghi, *Dialogo*, chs. 29 and 49.

146. Pietro Pichi, *Trattato della passione e morte del Messia contra gli Ebrei* (Rome: Nella stamperia dello Spada appresso Stefano Paolino, 1618), 120–121, 186.

147. Pichi, *Trattato della passione*, 184.

148. Pichi, *Trattato della passione*, 203. Pietro Pichi, *Epistola a gli ebrei d'Italia nella quale si dimostra la vanità della loro penitenza* (Rome: Guglielmo Facciotto, 1622), 1, 20, 87, 88. Fioghi also called Jews "brothers," but he himself was a convert, Fioghi, *Dialogo*.

149. Interpreting Isaiah (1:4, 15) as punishment for that *role*; Pichi, *Trattato della passione*, 105, 176, 222.

150. The first quote is from Thomaso Bell'Haver, *Dottrina facile et breve per ridurre l'hebreo al conoscimento del Vero Messia, & Salvator del Mondo* (Venice: i Farri, 1608), a3. Antonino Stabili, *Fascicolo delle vanità giudaiche* (Ancona: Appresso Francesco Saluioni, 1583), 304r, 305v. On Stabili, see Martina Mampieri, "'The Jews and Their Doubts': Anti-Jewish Polemics in the Fascicolo Delle Vanità Giudaiche (1583) by Antonino Stabili," *Yearbook of the Maimonides Centre for Advanced Studies* (2016).
151. Pietro Pichi, *Le stolte dottrine de gli ebrei con la loro confutatione* (Rome: Apresso Manelfo Manelfi, 1640), 1, 4. First published in 1625.
152. Pichi, *Le stolte dottrine*, 110ff, 120, 141.
153. Pichi, *Le stolte dottrine*, 153.
154. Pichi, *Le stolte dottrine*, 141.
155. Francesco Carboni, *Le piaghe dell'hebraismo* (Venice: Appresso Stefano Curti, 1674), ch. 15.
156. Carboni, *Le piaghe dell'hebraismo*, book II, 4.
157. Carboni, *Le piaghe dell'hebraismo*, 130–132.
158. Carboni, *Le piaghe dell'hebraismo*, 336–337. Carboni did not acknowledge Jeronimo de Santa Fe as his source, but Giovanni Pietro Pinamonti made the same argument, explicitly citing this fifteenth-century Iberian polemicist. Pinamonti, *La Sinagoga disingannata* (Bologna: Longhi, 1694), 57–58. See also Jeronimo de Santa Fe, *Contra iudaeos Hieronymi de Sancta Fide, iudaei, ad christianismum conuersi, libri* (Tiguri: apud Andream Gesnerum F. & Rodolphum Vuissenbachium, 1552).
159. Kenneth Stow, "The Catholic Church and the Jews," in *The Cambridge History of Judaism: The Early Modern World*, ed. Jonathan Karp and Adam Sutcliffe (Cambridge: Cambridge University Press, 2018), 26.
160. Stow, *Jewish Life in Early Modern Rome*, I, 8; Stow, "Catholic Church and the Jews," 31–38. On Catholic conversionary policies in the early modern period in the Papal States, see the following by Kenneth R. Stow: *Catholic Thought and Papal Jewry Policy, 1555–1593* (New York: Jewish Theological Seminary of America, 1977); "The Papacy and the Jews: Catholic Reformation and Beyond," *Jewish History* 6, no. 1–2 (1992); and "Church, Conversion and Tradition: The Problem of Jews Conversion in Sixteenth Century Italy," *Dimensioni e problemi della ricerca storica* (1996).
161. Bell'Haver, *Dottrina facile*, both in the dedication to the bishop of Rimini and his own preface.
162. Pinamonti, *La sinagoga disingannata*, 15 and chaps. VIII, XVIII, and XXIV.
163. Pinamonti, *La sinagoga disingannata*, 23.
164. Pinamonti, *La sinagoga disingannata*, 286–288.
165. Pinamonti, *La sinagoga disingannata*, 289–291.
166. Pinamonti, *La sinagoga disingannata*, 360. On Jesus in the Talmud, see Schäfer, *Jesus in the Talmud*.
167. Pinamonti, *La sinagoga disingannata*, chap. XIX, esp. 392, 397.
168. Pinamonti, *La sinagoga disingannata*, 36–37. The book ends (464–468) with the summary in Italian "of the privileges conceded to Jews who become Christians" and then the full text in Latin of the 1542 bull by Pope Paul III

Cupientes Iudaeos, dealing with issues of inheritance and assets—allowing, as John O'Malley put it, "Jewish converts to retain property, even that obtained by usury," thereby hoping to remove "a major obstacle to conversion," O'Malley, *The First Jesuits* (Cambridge, MA: Harvard University Press, 1993), 190.

169. Giovanni Pietro Vitti, *Memorie storico-cronologiche di varj bambini ed altri fanciulli martirizzati, in odio di nostra fede, da gli ebrei* (Venice: G. Zerletti, 1761).
170. Vitti, *Memorie,* xvi–xvii.
171. Vitti, *Memorie,* 139–183.
172. Vitti, *Memorie,* xi, xv, xxxiv, 183.
173. Vitti, *Memorie,* xii.
174. The phrases come from Hsia, "Christian Ethnographies," 226.
175. On Jews in Polish sources, see Janusz Tazbir, "Obraz żyda w opinii polskiej XVI–XVIII w," in *Mity i stereotypy w dziejach Polski* (Warsaw: Interpress, 1991), 64–98; Magdalena Teter, "Jews in the Legislation and Teachings of the Catholic Church in Poland 1648–1772" (PhD diss., Columbia University, 2000), ch. 3. Also, though not without errors, see Judith Kalik, "The Attitudes towards the Jews in the Christian Polemic Literature in Poland in the 16–18th Centuries," *Jews and Slavs* 11 (2003): 58–78. On Hebrew and Hebraism in Poland, also not without errors, see Rajmund Pietkiewicz, *W poszukiwaniu "szczyrego słowa bożego": recepcja zachodnioeuropejskiej hebraistyki w studiach chrześcijańskich w Rzeczypospolitej doby renesansu* (Wrocław: Papieski Wydział Teologiczny, 2011).
176. Samuel Marochitanus, *Epistola albo list Rabi Samuela ku drugiemu Rabi Isaakowi Żidowi posłany* (Cracow: Ungler, 1536), verso of the title page, and 43r; Samuel Marochitanus, *Epistola albo list Rabi Samuela ku drugiemu Rabi Isaakowi Żidowi posłany* (Cracow: Ungler, 1538), verso of the title page, and 43r. Other images of Jews are found in works associated with the story of host miracles in Poznań; see Teter, *Sinners on Trial,* ch. 4.
177. Limor, "Epistle of Rabbi Samuel," 178, 180.
178. Limor, "Epistle of Rabbi Samuel," 184.
179. For example, Marcin Czechowic, *Odpis Jakoba Żyda z Bełżyc na Dyalogi Marcina Czechowica, na ktory zaś odpowieda Jakobowi Żydowi tenże Marcin Czechowic* (Lublin, 1581); Marek Korona, *Rozmowa theologa katholickiego z rabinem zydowskim, przy aryaninie nieprawym chrześcianinie* (Lwów: W Drukarni Coll: Soc: Iesu u Sebastyana Nowogorskiego, 1645). Both works concern anti-Trinitarianism. Czechowic, an anti-Trinitarian himself, defended it, and Korona polemicized against it. Both used the Jewish character to their end. On Czechowic, see Judah M. Rosenthal, "Marcin Czechowic and Jacob of Belzyce Arian-Jewish Encounters in Sixteenth-Century Poland," *Proceedings of the American Academy for Jewish Research* 34 (1966); Magdalena Łuszczyńska, "'Odpis Jakoba Żyda' ... by Marcin Czechowic: A Study of Jewish-Arian Encounters in the Sixteenth-Century Poland" (PhD diss., Hebrew University, 2016).
180. Jakub Górski, *Index errorum aliquot, ex innumeris stultitiis blasphemiis, et impietatibus, talmudici operis collectus* (Cracow: Łazarz Andrysowic, 1569).

Senensis Sixtus, *Bibliotheca sancta* (Venice: apud Franciscum Franciscium Senense et Ioan Gryphius excudebat, 1566). I used the second edition, Senensis Sixtus, *Bibliotheca sancta* (Cologne: apud Maternum Maternus Cholinum, 1576). The "errors" are on pp. 133–136.

181. "Blasphemiae quae impii Iudaei in Christum Deum nostrum emittunt" vs. "Bluźniestwo ktorymi śmierdzący Naród Żydowski pana Krystusa szpeci," Sixtus, *Bibliotheca sancta*, 133. Górski, *Index Errorum*, Aiii.

182. For example, Sebastyan Miczyński, *Zwierciadło Korony Polskiey urazy ciężkie, y utrapienia wielkie ktore ponosi od Żydow wyrażaiące synom Koronnym w Roku Pańskim 1618* (1648 [1618]), 7, 19, 20, 24.

183. Przecław Mojecki, *Żydowskie okrucieństwa, mordy, y zabobony* (Cracow: W Drukarni Jak. Sibeneychera, 1598).

184. As examples of works continuing to address theological issues, see *List Michaela Żyda ochrzczonego,* (Cracow: Drukarnia Andrzeja Piotrowczyka, 1584). Jakub Radliński, *Prawda Chrzesciańska od nieprzyiaciela swego zeznana* (Lublin: Typis Societatis Jesu, 1733).

185. Mojecki, *Żydowskie okrucieństwa,* 8r–v.

186. Mojecki, *Żydowskie okrucieństwa,* unnumbered, in his dedication to Prince Janusz Ostrogski.

187. Mojecki, *Żydowskie okrucieństwa,* 1r–3r.

188. Mojecki, *Żydowskie okrucieństwa,* 4v.

189. Mojecki, *Żydowskie okrucieństwa,* 19v. This contrast between Poland and Italy would be drawn in the eighteeenth century, but in the exact mirror image.

190. Mojecki, *Żydowskie Okrucieństwa,* 5r–v.

191. See Hanna Węgrzynek, *"Czarna legenda" żydów: procesy o rzekome mordy rytualne w dawnej Polsce* (Warsaw: Bellona, 1995). Teter, *Sinners on Trial.*

192. Węgrzynek, *"Czarna legenda" żydów,* 99ff.

193. Węgrzynek, *"Czarna legenda" żydów,* 99. Teodor Wierzbowski and Jakub Sawicki, *Matricularum Regni Poloniae summaria, excussis codicibus* (Warsaw: Typis Officinae C. Kowalewski, 1905–), vol. 4, part 1, no. 7945. "Decretum regium in causa inter consules et iudaeos Revenses necis et tormentorum pueri christiani inculpates prorogaturs ad duas septimanas post causae inquisitionem, quae Ioanni de Trczyana capitaneo et Ioanni de Radzyeiowycze vexillifero Ravensibus, uti commissariis regiis specialibus committitur." Both Węgrzynek and Wijaczka give an erroneous number of the record.

194. Szymon Hubicki, *Żydowskie okrucieństwa nad naświętszym sakramentem y dziatkami* (Cracow: W Drukarni Mikołaja Szarffenbergera, 1602). Zenon Guldon and Jacek Wijaczka, *Procesy o mordy rytualne w Polsce w XVI–XVIII wieku* (Kielce: DCF, 1995), 96.

195. Hanna Węgrzynek, and Zenon Guldon and Jacek Wijaczka tallied the accusations, their sources, and, in Guldon and Wijaczka's work, the outcomes as well; Węgrzynek, *"Czarna legenda" żydów;* Guldon and Wijaczka, *Procesy o mordy rytualne;* Zenon Guldon and Jacek Wijaczka, "The Accusation of Ritual Murder in Poland, 1500–1800," *Polin: Studies in Polish Jewry* 10 (1997). See the map based on these sources at www.thebloodlibeltrail.org.

196. On these trials, see Chapter 6. Węgrzynek, *Polin: Studies in Polish Jewry* 115–117, 186–188. The exception of two cases from 1595 are documented by the surviving records of the Council of Four Lands, Israel Halpern, ed., *Pinkas va'ad arb'a arazot* (Jerusalem: Mosad Bialik, 1945), 8–10, nos. 22, 28, 30.
197. Mojecki, *Żydowskie okrucieństwa*, 8v.
198. Mojecki, *Żydowskie okrucieństwa*, 9r–10r.
199. Mojecki, *Żydowskie okrucieństwa*, 20v–21r.
200. Mojecki, *Żydowskie okrucieństwa*, 22r–v.
201. Hubicki, *Żydowskie okrucieństwa*, Preface "To the Reader." Halpern, *Pinkas va'ad arb'a arazot*, 8–10.
202. Some scholars refer to this village inaccurately as Świniary. On Świniarów, see Chapter 6.
203. Hubicki, *Żydowskie okrucieństwa*, 1v–2v.
204. For a discussion of host desecration trials in Poland, see Węgrzynek, "*Czarna Legenda*" *Żydów*, 31–90. And more recently, Teter, *Sinners on Trial*, ch. 6 focuses on Bochnia.
205. Hubicki, *Żydowskie okrucieństwa*, 15r.
206. Hubicki, *Żydowskie okrucieństwa*, 10v–11r.
207. Hubicki, *Żydowskie okrucieństwa*, 21v.
208. Hubicki, *Żydowskie okrucieństwa*, 22r.
209. Hubicki, *Żydowskie okrucieństwa*, 22r–v. Elsewhere, he also used Johannes Eckius's response to Andreas Osiander's defense of Jews against blood accusations, a work not available in Latin.
210. Hubicki, *Żydowskie okrucieństwa*, 22v–25v.
211. Sebastian Śleszkowski, *Odkrycie zdrad, złośliwych ceremoniy, taiemnych rad, praktyk szkodliwych Rzeczypospolitey y wszystkich zamysłów żydowskich, takze wytknienie niektórych pomocnikow żydowskich* (Brunsbergae: In Officina typographica Georgij Schonfels, 1621), ch. 23, list of adjectives by Jan Dantyszek.
212. Mojecki, *Żydowskie okrucieństwa*, 7r, no. 27; Hubicki, *Żydowskie okrucieństwa*, 17v ff.
213. In a letter from Ludovicus Hoffman to D. Papebroch, sent from Cracow on July 18, 1671, Hoffman promised more information about "Albertus Martyrium," the child whose death prompted the Świniarów trial; the 1675 volume of *Acta Sanctorum* also mentions that Hoffman provided a summary of Hubicki's work. Société des Bollandistes, Brussels, Ms. Boll. 246, f. 216. I thank the Reverend Robert Godding for his help.
214. Godefroid Henschen and Daniel Van Papenbroeck, *Acta Sanctorum Aprilis Collecta, Digesta, Illustrata Tomus II* (Antwerp: apud Michaelem Cnobarum, 1675), 838–839.
215. *Der Stürmer*, May 1, 1934, "Zusammenstellung jüdischen Ritualmorde aus der Zeit vor Christus bis 1932."
216. Compare their work with Stefan Żuchowski, *Process kryminalny* (Sandomierz, after 1720).
217. Szymon (Syrenius) Syreński, *Zielnik, herbarzem z ięzyka lacinskiego zowią* (Cracow: W drukarni Bazylego Skalskiego, 1613), 1536–1539.

218. Sebastian Miczynski, *Zwierciadło Korony Polskiey* (Cracow: Máciej Jedrzeiowczyk, 1618). Śleszkowski, *Odkrycie zdrad*.
219. Miczyński, *Zwierciadło Korony*, 1. Miczyński attributed the passage to Genesis 21:10, but, significantly, quoted it as transmitted through Paul Galatians 4:30.
220. Miczyński, *Zwierciadło Korony*, 98–101.
221. Miczyński, *Zwierciadło Korony*, 3.
222. Miczyński, *Zwierciadło Korony*, 102–105.
223. Miczyński, *Zwierciadło Korony*, 106–107.
224. Śleszkowski, *Odkrycie zdrad*.
225. Śleszkowski, *Odkrycie zdrad*, chap. XXVII and XXXII.
226. Śleszkowski, *Odkrycie zdrad*, unnumbered, V3 verso.
227. Śleszkowski, *Odkrycie zdrad*, unnumbered, page before Xr.
228. Śleszkowski, *Odkrycie zdrad*, X2v–X3r.
229. Stefano Quaranta, *Summa bullarii* (Venice: apud Juntas, 1609).
230. Śleszkowski, *Odkrycie zdrad*, X3r–v.
231. Quaranta, *Summa bullarii*, dedicatory letter from Prosper de Augustino and a note to reader by Quaranta; for laws concerning Jews, see 512.
232. In daily life it continued through the eighteenth century, Magda Teter, *Jews and Heretics in Catholic Poland: A Beleaguered Church in the Post-Reformation Era* (Cambridge: Cambridge University Press, 2006), esp. ch. 4.
233. Śleszkowski, *Odkrycie zdrad*, unnumbered folio before Cc.
234. Śleszkowski, *Odkrycie zdrad*, unnumbered, second page of the text, marked:)()(.
235. Huser and Lombardus, *Tractatus de imposturis*. On Lombardus, see Dean Phillip Bell, "Polemics of Confessionalization: Depiction of Jews and Jesuits in Early Modern Germany," in *"The Tragic Couple": Encounters between Jews and Jesuits*, ed. James Bernauer and Robert Maryks (Leiden: Brill, 2013), 80–82. Also see Salo Wittmayer Baron, *A Social and Religious History of the Jews* (New York: Columbia University Press, 1969), vol. XIII, 429, n. 26.
236. Śleszkowski, *Odkrycie zdrad*, e.g., chs, I, II, III, VII. Huser and Lombardus, *Tractatus de Imposturis*, e.g., 11, 21–22, 57–58, 59–60.
237. Śleszkowski, *Odkrycie zdrad*, ch. IX. Huser and Lombardus, *Tractatus de Imposturis*, 39–40.
238. Śleszkowski, *Odkrycie zdrad*, ch. XXXII.
239. Huser and Lombardus, *Tractatus de imposturis*, 56–57. This may also be the case more broadly with his list of sources. Some of the writers Śleszkowski listed as his sources had appeared in *De imposturis*, so it is not clear that Śleszkowski necessarily read them all.
240. Czechowic, *Odpis*, 28–29.
241. Miczyński, *Zwierciadło Korony*, 69.
242. R. Po-Chia Hsia in *Myth of Ritual Murder* credited the disenchantment with magic for the decline of blood accusations in the German lands.
243. Miczyński, *Zwierciadło Korony*, 74–75.
244. Śleszkowski, *Odkrycie zdrad*, chap. XXI. For similar examples, see Teter, *Jews and Heretics*, esp. ch. 4; Teter, *Sinners on Trial*, especially 95–97.

5. Ashkenazi and Sephardic Jews Respond to Blood Libels

1. Yosef Hayim Yerushalmi noted some of these Jewish polemical works, including defense of Jewish doctors, in *From Spanish Court to Italian Ghetto: Isaac Cardoso, a Study in Seventeenth-Century Marranism and Jewish Apologetics* (Seattle: University of Washington Press, 1981), 455–456, n. 98.
2. The work is in the Bodleian Library at Oxford, *Seyfer geules Isroel,* Opp80894 (2). The Poznań story was also included in *Seyfer mayseh ha-shem,* Opp Add 80 IV 41. I thank Joshua Teplitsky, then a fellow at Oxford, now a faculty member at SUNY Stony Brook, for finding these books for me. The story was discussed in Max Weinreich, *Shturemvint bilder fun dem yidisher geshikhte in 17tn yorhundert* (Vilna: Farlag "Totor," 1927), 190–199.
3. See also Yerushalmi, *From Spanish Court,* 455–456, n.98.
4. Weinreich, *Shturemvint Bilder,* 168.
5. Yosef Hayim Yerushalmi, *Zakhor: Jewish History and Jewish Memory* (New York: Schocken, 1989).
6. On this, see most recently, Rachel L. Greenblatt, *To Tell Their Children: Jewish Communal Memory in Early Modern Prague* (Stanford: Stanford University Press, 2014).
7. For a concise overview of early modern Jewish historical writings, see Yerushalmi, *Zakhor,* ch. 3. Azariah dei Rossi, *The Light of the Eyes,* ed. and trans. by Joanna Weinberg (New Haven: Yale University Press, 2001). David Gans divided his chronology into a Jewish and non-Jewish history. The part devoted to Jewish history focuses on rabbis and their works with mentions of calamities, such as the 1348 persecutions, accusations against Jews of well poisoning, and the expulsions from France. But his entries are generally short. David ben Solomon Gans, *Sefer Tsemaḥ David* (Prague: Solomon ha-Kohen, 1592).
8. Samuel Usque, *Consolation for the Tribulations of Israel* (Consolaçam Ás Tribulaçoens De Israel), tran. Martin A. Cohen (Philadelphia: Jewish Publication Society of America, 1965). Joseph Ha-Kohen's *Emek ha-bakha* was derived from his published chronicle, *Sefer divre ha-yamim le-malkhe ẓarefat u-malkhe beit otoman ha-tugar* (Chronicle of the Kingdoms of France and Ottoman Turkey). The edition used here is Joseph Ha-Kohen and Karin Almbladh, *Sefer Emeq Ha-Bakha (The Vale of Tears) with the Chronicle of the Anonymous Corrector* (Uppsala: Uppsala University, 1981).
9. Usque, *Consolation,* 30. Original edition, *Consolaçam às tribulaçoens de Israel* (Ferrara, 1553); a facsimile edition was published in 1989 in Lisbon by the Fundação Calouste Gulbenkian. A later edition, closely resembling the first one, was published in Amsterdam, Cohen, *Consolation,* 32.
10. Alfonso de Espina, *Fortalitium fidei* (Strasbourg: Johannes Mentelin, 1462). Written between 1458 and 1460, *Fortalitium* was first published in 1462 in Strasbourg and republished nine times before 1525. This book by an Iberian writer with a very heavy Iberian focus was mostly printed north of the Alps—in Strasbourg, Basel, and Nuremberg—with three separate editions also appearing in Lyons (1487, 1511, and 1525). The third part of *Fortalitium fidei,* "Liber tertius," included a section "De Judaeorum crudelitatibus" (Of the Cru-

elties of Jews). See, for example, the works by Polish writers in the seventeenth and eighteenth century who used *Fortalitium fidei,* discussed in Chapters 4 and 6.

11. Isaac Cardoso, *Las excelencias de los hebreos* (Amsterdam: David de Castro Tartas, 1679), 381; "fiction of history," 413. The quote from p. 381 is available in English in Yerushalmi, *From Spanish Court to Italian Ghetto,* 441.

12. See, for example, the account of violence in Toledo in 714, which *Fortalitium fidei* describes as "the first cruelty" of Jews, and Usque's account of the same event; Usque, *Consolation,* 169–170.

13. Usque, *Consolation,* 171–172.

14. The story is described as the "third cruelty of the Jews" in the section "Incipit consideration septima de iudeorum crudelitatibus" in *Fortalitium fidei* (Lugudi, 1487). The fact that the story is also found in Vincent de Beauvais's *Speculum historiale* is noted in Yerushalmi, *From Spanish Court to Italian Ghetto,* 457.

15. Usque, *Consolation,* 195–196. Cf. *Fortalitium fidei,* "Liber tertius," "Undecima crudelitas iudeorum."

16. Usque, *Consolation,* 196.

17. Ha-Kohen and Almbladh, *Sefer emeq ha-bakha,* 17–18, 27. For examples of a story taken from *Fortalitium* by Usque and found in Ha-Kohen, see 30–31, 48 (in the Hebrew section).

18. On Sebastian Münster's *Cosmographia,* see Mathew Adam McLean, *The Cosmographia of Sebastian Münster: Describing the World in the Reformation* (Aldershot, UK: Ashgate, 2007).

19. Ha-Kohen and Almbladh, *Sefer emeq ha-bakha,* 41 (Hebrew). And cf. Sebastian Münster, *Cosmographia universalis* (Basel: apud Henricum Petri, 1550), 380 (1554 edition). Ha-Kohen used the Latin edition.

20. Ha-Kohen and Almbladh, *Sefer emeq ha-bakha,* 41 (Hebrew). Cf. Münster, *Cosmographia universalis (1550),* 738. The story about the Jews in the privy is also found in Matthew Paris.

21. Ha-Kohen and Almbladh, *Sefer emeq ha-bakha,* 49 (Hebrew).

22. Ha-Kohen and Almbladh, *Sefer emeq ha-bakha,* 48–49 (Hebrew section). Cf. Münster, *Cosmographia universalis,* 458. "Cremati sunt in multis locis Iudaei, et cu[m] euadere se no[n] posse uidere[n]t, incluseru[n]t se in domibus et seipsos cremuerunt una cu[m] locis vicinis. Dicitur Moguntiae hinc ta[n]tum excitatum ignem, ut magna campana in ecclesia sancti Quintini ex igne defluxerit. Scribit[ur] etiam, quod inuenti fuerint sacculi in fonti[bus] ueneno pleni: quapropter fonts et putei obstrubebant[ur] et loco aquae putealis homines uteban[ur] aqua fluuiali et pluuiali. Multi etiam ex Iudaeis utriusque sexus baptisati sunt, pauc amore Dei sed potius timore poenae. Civitates imperiales diruerunt domos Iudaeorum et ex lapidib[us] earum atque coemiterioru[m] ipsorum co[n]struxerunt torres et muros. In summa omnia plena errant tumultib[us] propter Iudaeos." This section was preceded by a discussion of poisoning of wells and other Jewish "crimes," including the killing of children and falsifying credit documents and coins.

23. Münster, *Cosmographia universalis,* 230.

24. Ha-Kohen and Almbladh, *Sefer emeq ha-bakha,* 47–48 (Hebrew). For an English translation, see Kenneth Stow, "Trent 1475: Responses of a Pope and a Jewish Chronicler," http://www.earlymodern.org.

25. Stow, "Trent 1475."
26. Ha-Kohen and Almbladh, *Sefer emeq ha-bakha*, 68. And yet, Joseph Ha-Kohen did not mention the 1540 *breve* by Pope Paul III, the last papal condemnation of blood accusations against Jews to be issued by a pope until the abolition of the cult of Simon of Trent in 1965. For the text of Paul III's bull, see Shlomo Simonsohn, *The Apostolic See and the Jews: Documents, 1539–1545* (Toronto: Pontifical Institute of Mediaeval Studies, 1990), no. 1973.
27. Stephen D. Bowd and J. Donald Cullington, *"On Everyone's Lips": Humanists, Jews, and the Tale of Simon of Trent* (Tempe, AZ: Brepols, 2012), 194–195, 200–201.
28. For sources about funds spent on embalming Simon, see Frumenzio Ghetta, "Johannes Hinderbach, amministratore: i registri delle offerte della chiesa di S. Pietro a Trento," in Iginio Rogger and Marco Bellabarba, *Il Principe Vescovo Johannes Hinderbach (1465–1486)* (Bologna: Edizioni Dehoniane, 1992), 207
29. Cardoso, *Las excelencias de los hebreos*. The best discussion of Cardoso's work, with extensive quotes in English, is Yerushalmi, *From Spanish Court to Italian Ghetto*.
30. Yosef Hayim Yerushalmi showed that Cardoso used more than 100 Christian works throughout *Las excelencias*—not all, of course, in the context of anti-Jewish accusations. But Yerushalmi was unable to identify Surius and Bergomensis as Cardoso's sources for Simon of Trent. Yerushalmi, *From Spanish Court to Italian Ghetto*, 360–361, 457, n. 104.
31. Cardoso, *Las excelencias de los hebreos*, 410.
32. Cardoso, *Las excelencias de los hebreos*, 413. Tiberino's Trent account is in Laurentius Surius, *De probatis sanctorum historiis* (Cologne: apud Geruinum Calenium et haeredes Quentelios, 1571), 387–390. Jacobus Philipus Foresti's *Supplementum chronicarum* was first published in 1483, and in 1486 it was published with woodcut illustrations. The 1485 edition, included Simon's story, Jacob Philip Foresti, *Supplementum chronicarum* (Brescia: Boninus de Boninis, 1485 [December 1]), 347v–348r. The book became a source for Hartmann Schedel's famous *Liber chronicarum* published in Nuremberg in 1493. See also above, chapter 4.
33. Michelangelo Mariani, *Il glorioso infante S. Simone: historia panegirica* (Trent: Zanetti Stampator Episcopale, 1668), 18.
34. Mariani, *Il glorioso infante*, 154–155.
35. Mariani, *Il glorioso infante*, 76, 132, 138–152. Polish writers described Simon's body as "shriveled."
36. Yerushalmi, *From Spanish Court to Italian Ghetto*, 352–358. Shelomoh Zevi, *Yudisher teriyok* (Hanau: n.p., 1615). Both Brenz's work and Hirsch's apologetic response were re-published in Johann Wülfer et al., *Theriaca judaica ad examen revocata* (Norimbergae: Andreas Knorzius, 1681).
37. Most recently on *Shevet Yehudah*, see Jeremy Cohen, "The Blood Libel in Solomon ibn Verga's *Shevet Yehudah*," in *Jewish Blood: Reality and Metaphor in History, Religion and Culture*, ed. Mitchell B. Hart (London: Routledge, 2009), 116–135, and *A Historian in Exile: Solomon Ibn Verga, Shevet Yehudah, and*

the Jewish-Christian Encounter (Philadelphia: University of Pennsylvania Press, 2016).

38. Michael Stanislawski, "A Study in 'Ashenization' of a Spanish-Jewish Classic," in *Jewish History and Jewish Memory: Essays in Honor of Yosef Hayim Yerushalmi*, ed. Elisheva Carlebach, John M. Efron, and David N. Myers (Hanover, NH: University Press of New England, 1998), 134–149. Also see the later discussion.
39. Numerous editions in Hebrew, Yiddish, Latin, and Spanish were printed in the sixteenth through eighteenth centuries. In his study of early modern Jewish historiography, Yosef Hayim Yerushalmi consulted the nineteen edition; Yerushalmi, *Zakhor*, 68.
40. Chapters 7, 8, 12, 16, 17, 29, 61, and two parts of 64. For a succinct summary of these tales, see Cohen, "The Blood Libel in Solomon ibn Verga's *Shevet Yehudah*."
41. Solomon ibn Verga, *Sefer Shevet Yehudah*, ed. Meir Wiener, 2 vols. (Hannover: Sumptibus C. Rumpleri, 1856), 7. This edition is used here.
42. Ibn Verga, *Sefer Shevet Yehudah*, 7.
43. This is a very similar take to that in the Blois Hebrew letters.
44. Ibn Verga, *Sefer Shevet Yehudah*, 10.
45. Ibn Verga, *Sefer Shevet Yehudah*, 9.
46. This is an interesting statement given the discussion of cannibalism in the New World by Spanish Iberian writers, although it might suggest that ibn Verga was familiar with the 1236 imperial decree in defense of Jews.
47. The question of human blood, including bleeding gums, was discussed in rabbinic sources as well. See, for example, BT Ketubot 60a and BT Kerithot 21b–22a.
48. Ibn Verga, *Sefer Shevet Yehudah*, 10. The king and Thomas discussed the question of belief in the Trinity, which was excised from the 1640 Spanish translation, but was retained in the 1651 Latin translation by Georg Gentius, who based it on a copy of *Shevet Yehudah* owned by Buxtorf; Solomon ibn Verga, *La vara de Juda*. Amsterdam: por Mosseh d'Abraham Pretto Henriq: en la officina de Jan de Wolf, 1744; Salomon ibn Verga and Georg Gentius. *Historia judaica: res judaeorum ab eversa aede Hierosoymitana ad haec fere tempora usque complexa* (Amsterdam: apud Petrum Niellium, 1651).
49. Ibn Verga, *Sefer Shevet Yehudah*, 11.
50. "Liber Tertius" in de Espina's *Fortalitium fidei*. The scheme of the advice also seems to echo that received by King Philip Augustus, according to the French chronicler Rigord, from the hermit Bernardus following an accusation that Jews killed Christian children; see Chapter 1; Robert Chazan, *Church, State, and Jew in the Middle Ages* (New York: Behrman House, 1980), 288–289; and Stow, *Jewish Dogs*, 183–184.
51. Ibn Verga, *Sefer Shevet Yehudah*, 12–13.
52. This is consistent with some medieval pushes against usury; for example, Thomas Aquinas's letter to the Duchess of Brabant. See the English translation reprinted in Chazan, *Church, State, and Jew*, 200–201.
53. Ibn Verga, *Sefer Shevet Yehudah*, 25–29.

54. In the seventeenth century, Nathan Nata Hanover also noted that the role Jews played in the economy and the power they had in society contributed to resentment and violence against them.
55. William Prynne, *A Short Demurrer to the Jewes Long Discontinued Remitter into England* (London: for Edward Thomas dwelling in Green-Arbor, 1656), 4 (unnumbered) in the preface "To the Christian Reader."
56. Menasseh ben Israel, *Vindiciae Judaeorum, or, a Letter in Answer to Certain Questions Propounded by a Noble and Learned Gentleman* (London: R. D. [Roger Daniel], 1656), "The First Section," 2–4.
57. Israel, *Vindiciae Judaeorum*, 15. Menasseh ben Israel mentioned, by name, *Shevet Yehudah:* "This with many such like relations we may read in the book called Scebet Iehuda, how sundry times, when our nation was at the very brink of destruction, for such forged slanders, the truth hath discovered it self for their deliverance."
58. Israel, *Vindiciae Judaeorum*, 14. About Tertulian's "Advesus Judaeos," see http://www.tertullian.org/works/adversus_judaeos.htm.
59. Israel, *Vindiciae Judaeorum*, 6.
60. Prynne, *A Short Demurrer*, 19. Matthew Paris wrote, "About this time [1240 in the account but should be 1144], the Jews circumcised a Christian boy at Norwich, and after he was circumcised they called him Jurnin; they then kept him to crucify him, in contempt of the crucifixion of Jesus Christ." Paris, *Matthew Paris's English History: From the Year 1235 to 1273*, trans. J. A. Giles (London: George Bell and Sons, 1889), vol. 1, 277. Other medieval chroniclers also misdated the Norwich case; on this, see Chapter 1 and John M. McCulloh, "Jewish Ritual Murder: William of Norwich, Thomas of Monmouth, and the Early Dissemination of the Myth," *Speculum* 72, no. 3 (1997).
61. Israel, *Vindiciae Judaeorum*, 7.
62. Israel, *Vindiciae Judaeorum*, 9. See Johannes Hoornbeeck, *Teshuvat Yehudah, sive, pro convincendis et convertendis judaeis, libri octo* (Lugduni Batavorum: Ex officina Petri Leffen, 1655), 26.
63. Israel, *Vindiciae Judaeorum*, 8–9.
64. Reference to the very same passage in Hoornbeek would be included in Isaac Viva's *Vindex sanguinis* published in 1681. Viva may have had access to the Latin translation of Menasseh ben Israel's *Vindiciae Judaeorum*, but he also may have used Hoornbeek's work; Isaacus Viva, *Vindex sanguinis, sive vindiciae secundam veritatem, quibus judaei ab infanticidiis et victima humana contra Jacobum Geusium, vindicantur per Isaacum Vivam* (Amsterdam: Typis Adami Jongbloet, 1681), 10, 14. On his *Vindex sanguinis*, see Cristiana Facchini, "Il Vindex Sanguinis di Isaac Viva. Di una polemica sull'accusa di omicidio rituale," *Annali di storia dell'eseges* 16, no. 2 (1999) and *Infamati dicerie: la prima autodifesa ebraica dall'accusa del sangue* (Bologna: Edizioni Dehoniane Bologna, 2014).
65. Solomon Grayzel, *The Church and the Jews in the XIIIth Century: A Study of Their Relations during the Years 1198–1254* (Philadelphia: Dropsie College, 1933), 268–271 and 274–275.
66. Israel, *Vindiciae Judaeorum*, 10–12.

67. John H. Langbein, *Prosecuting Crime in the Renaissance England, Gernany, France* (Cambridge, MA: Harvard University Press, 1974), 206, n. 155. Also see Edward Peters, *Torture*, expanded ed. (Philadelphia: University of Pennsylvania Press, 1996), 58–59, 70.
68. Hoornbeeck, *Teshuvat Yehudah*, 26.
69. Cardoso, *Las excelencias de los hebreos*, 408–431.
70. Cardoso, *Las excelencias de los hebreos*, 409.
71. Cardoso, *Las excelencias de los hebreos*, 425–430.
72. On Metz, most recently, see Pierre Birnbaum, *Un récit de meurtre rituel au grand siècle: l'affaire Raphaël Lévy, Metz, 1669* (Paris: Fayard, 2008) and *A Tale of Ritual Murder in the Age of Louis XIV: The Trial of Raphaël Lévy, 1669* (Stanford: Stanford University Press, 2012).
73. Richard Simon, "Factum servant de réponse au livre intitulé abrégé du procès fait aux juifs de Metz," *Archives Israelites de France* 3, December (1842 [1670]): 678, 680. The decrees by Charles V and Frederick III were also mentioned in Johann Wülfer's 1681 commentaries and the Latin translation of Shlomo Zvi Ufhoyzen's *Yudisher teriyak*; see Wülfer et al., *Theriaca Judaica*, 82–84, in the Latin translation that follows the Yiddish version. The papal and imperial privileges are noted without details in 1615, in Zevi, *Yudisher teriyak*, ch. I, n. 16. Wülfer also addressed the blood accusation. *Theriaca judaica*, 76 ff.
74. Viva, *Vindex sanguinis*. Wülfer also published *Vindex sanguinis* in his *Theriaca judaica*.
75. ASCER, 1Va fasc. 13 coll. 2 inf. 2, in Italian, and in Latin, in Tranquillo Vita Corcos, *Alla Sagra Consvlta Illustriss. e Reuerendiss. Monsig. Ghezzi Ponente per l'vniuersità degl'hebrei di Roma. Sommario* (Rome: Nella stamperia della Rev. Camera apostolica, 1706), no. 3. Corrado Guidetti, *Pro Judæis: riflessioni e documenti* (Roux e Favale, 1884), 303–304.
76. Cardoso, *Las excelencias de los hebreos*, 418.
77. Cardoso, *Las excelencias de los hebreos*, 423. Ulpian in *Digest* 47.10.15.41: "tormenta et corporis dolorem ad eruendam veritatem"; see Anna Bellodi Ansaloni, *Ad eruendam veritatem: profili metodologici e processuali della question per tormenta* (Bologna: Bononia University Press, 2011). Ulpian's reservations are in *Digest* 48.18.1.23; *Digest* 48.18.1.21–24; English translation in Peters, *Torture*, 217.
78. Viva, *Vindex sanguinis*, 14–15. On this, see also Facchini, *Infamati dicerie*, 91–94.
79. On this, see Peters, *Torture*; John H. Langbein, *Torture and the Law of Proof: Europe in the Ancien Régime* (Chicago: University of Chicago Press, 2006); Laura Stokes, "Experiments in Pain: Reason and the Development of Judicial Torture," in *Ideas and Cultural Margins in Early Modern Germany*, ed. Marjorie Elizabeth Plummer and Robin Barnes (Farnham, UK: Ashgate, 2009), 239–254.
80. Lisa Silverman, *Tortured Subjects: Pain, Truth, and the Body in Early Modern France* (Chicago: University of Chicago Press, 2001), 64; Stokes, "Experiments in Pain," 240.
81. Augustine, *City of God*, XIX.6. Also excerpted in Peters, *Torture*, 229–230.

82. I thank W. David Myers of Fordham University for drawing my attention to Juan Luis Vives's commentary on Augustine's *City of God*. Augustine and Juan Luis Vives, *Tomus V Operum D. Aurelii Augustini Hipponensis Episcopi, De Civitate Dei libros XXII ad priscae uenerandae* (Basel: Ex officina Frobeniana, 1569), column 1156. Henceforth Augustine and Vives, *De Civitate Dei*.
83. Malcolm Smith, *Montaigne and the Roman Censors* (Geneva: Droz, 1981), 84.
84. Johann Wülfer also made that connection in his comments on Solomon Zvi Hirsch's *Yudisher teriyak*, which he translated into Latin; Wülfer et al., *Theriaca judaica*, 88, of the Latin translation that follows the Yiddish version.
85. Ibn Verga, *Sefer Shevet Yehudah*, 27.
86. Cohen, "The Blood Libel in Solomon ibn Verga's *Shevet Yehudah*," 122.
87. Ibn Verga, *Sefer Shevet Yehudah*, 40.
88. Ibn Verga, *Sefer Shevet Yehudah*, 41.
89. Ibn Verga, *Sefer Shevet Yehudah*, 42.
90. The most famous representation of this kind of execution is the story of Roman consul Marcus Atilius Regulus (d. 250 B.C.E.), executed so in Carthage. The story was pictorially rendered in the sixteenth and seventeenth centuries in prints by Sebald Beham (ca. 1518–1530), Georg Pencz (1535), Antonio Fantuzzi (1540–1545), Diana Scultori (after Giulio Romano's work in Palazzo Te' in Mantua, 1547–1612), Salvator Rosa (1661–1663), at the British Library, available online: http://www.britishmuseum.org/research/collection_online/search.aspx?people=24510&peoA=24510-1-7. I thank Haya Bar Itzhak from Haifa University for pointing me in this direction. See also Magda Teter, "The Sandomierz Paintings of Ritual Murder as *Lieux De Mémoire*," in *Ritual Murder in Russia, Eastern Europe, and Beyond: New Histories of an Old Accusation*, ed. Eugene M. Avrutin, Jonathan Dekel-Chen, and Robert Weinberg (Bloomington: Indiana University Press, 2017), 253–277.
91. Ibn Verga, *Sefer Shevet Yehudah*, 48–49.
92. Ibn Verga, *Sefer Shevet Yehudah*, 49.
93. Prynne, *Short Demurrer*.
94. Some of them have been discussed in Chava Turniansky, "Yiddish 'Historical' Songs as Sources for the History of the Jews," *Polin* 4 (1989), 42–52; Weinreich, *Shturemvint Bilder*.
95. Turniansky, "Yiddish 'Historical' Songs," 140.
96. I used the 1724 Fürth edition: Solomon ibn Verga, *Sefer Shevet Yehudah val far taitsht* (Fyorda/Fürth: Avraham Beng u-Boneft Sheneur, 1724).
97. See Tale Eight and Eleven (twelve in Hebrew versions), for example, in ibn Verga, *Sefer Shevet Yehudah val far taitsht*. In Tale Ten, God's agency is also emphasized.
98. Stanislawski, "The Yiddish *Shevet Yehudah*," 142.
99. Anonymous, *Sefer kedoshim k"k Vilne*, vol. Bodleian Library Opp 80 556 (7) (Amsterdam, after 1691).
100. See *Sefer kedoshim k"k Vilne*.
101. For example, Hillel of Bonn, in his poem "Emunei shelumei Israel," discussed by Susan Einbinder, evoked Psalm 2:2: "The kings and princes of the earth

were unmoved" when he commemorated the suffering and execution of the Jews in Blois. Susan Einbinder, *Beautiful Death: Jewish Poetry and Martyrdom in Medieval France* (Princeton, NJ: Princeton University Press, 2002), 28, also 48–49.

102. The most explicit example of this rhetoric is a pamphlet devoted to three named male victims and one anonymous female victim of accusations of host desecration and blasphemy; Anonymous, *Kidush ha-shem shel Reb Matis ve-Reb Pinhas ve-Reb Abraham zekhutam ya`amod lanu bi-medinat Polin* (no date). For example, "and they became as the sacrifices prepared for an sacrificial altar" [un zenen gevorn az di korbones oyf den mizbeykh ongebreyt]. Also in the story of the three *kedoshim* from Wilno, *Sefer kedoshim k"k Vilne*.

103. Bartłomiej Groicki, *Ten postępek wybran iest z praw cesarskich który Karolus V Cesarz wydać po wszystkich swoich państwiech* (Cracow, 1559 [1954]). See also Witold Maisel, "Miejskie prawo karne," in *Historia państwa i prawa Polski* (Warsaw: PWN, 1968), vol. II, 343–362. On Jews and the crime of sacrilege in Poland, see Teter, *Sinners on Trial*.

104. Shmuel Auerbach, *Min ha-kadosh hr"r Shlomoh be-nigun El Male Raḥamim*, vol. Opp 8to 627, Bodleian Library (Amsterdam (?): after 1692). I thank Joshua Teplitsky for finding this song for me.

105. Auerbach, *Min ha-kadosh*, unnumbered 3.

106. This motif reappears in almost all of the songs. For a discussion of the status of martyrs in the Ashkenazi world, see Edward Fram and Verena Kasper-Marienberg, "Jewish Martyrdom without Persecution: The Murder of Gumpert May, Frankfurt am Main, 1781," *AJS Review* 39, no. 2 (2015): 267–301.

107. The story is discussed in Haya Bar-Itzhak, "Women and Blood Libel: The Legend of Adil Kikinesh of Drohobycz," *Western Folklore* 71, no. 3–4 (2012): 279–290. The short Hebrew version is published in Gabriel ben Naftali Hirts Sochostow, *Matsevet kodesh, hu zikaron tsadikim: sefer zikaron le-khol ha-ge'onim veha-kedoshim sare ha-torah, asher le-mishmeret li-fene h' be-vet ha-mo'ed le-khol ḥai ha-yashan poh 'ir Lvov* (Lemberg: Kugel, Lewin, 1860). The Yiddish version of the story can be found in Leo Finkelstein, *Megiles Poyln: Toyre, hasides un shtayger-kultur in yidishn Poyln* (Buenos Aires: Tsentralfarband fun Poylishe Yidn in Argentine, 1947), 230–231.

108. Finkelstein, *Megiles Poyln*, 231. David Einsiedler, the founding member of the Jewish Genealogical Society of Los Angeles, who was born in Drohobycz in 1919, recalled the story in his piece, "I Remember Drohobycz," http://www.geshergalicia.org/wp-content/uploads/2014/07/I-Remember-Drohobycz.pdf. The Adil Kikenish story was used by Yitzhak Leybush Peretz in his short story, "Three Gifts" (for the second gift). Her story may well have been inspired by a story of an anonymous woman, who did not confess but also did not convert, and died as a result of a "false accusation," protecting her nakedness. The woman is part of the story of R. Abraham in Anonymous, *Kidush ha-shem shel Reb Matis*. Max Weinreich suggested that the story of the anonymous woman in this pamphlet may have been Peretz's inspiration. Weinreich, *Shturemvint Bilder*, 173, n. 1.

109. Finkelstein, *Megiles Poyln*, 231.
110. Bar-Itzhak, "Women and Blood Libel," 283.
111. Miriam Bodian, *Dying in the Law of Moses: Crypto-Jewish Martyrdom in the Iberian World* (Bloomington: Indiana University Press, 2007), 186.
112. One of the most detailed studies is Einbinder, *Beautiful Death*. See also Chapter 1.
113. Einbinder, *Beautiful Death*, 59.
114. Both works are in the Bodleian Library at Oxford: *Seyfer geules Isroel*, Opp80894 (2), and *Seyfer mayseh ha-shem*, Opp Add 80 IV 41. I again thank Joshua Teplitsky for these books. The story was discussed in Weinreich, *Shturemvint Bilder*, 190–199.
115. *Sefer geulat Israel* (ca. 1696) = *Seyfer geules Isroel*.
116. Anonymous, *Sefer geulat Israel*. On Rogoźno, see *Słownik geograficzny Królestwa Polskiego i innych krajów Słowiańskich* (Warsaw: Wydawnictwa Artsytyczne i Filmowe, 1975 [1880]), vol. IX, 677–681.
117. Augustine and Vives, *De civitate Dei*, col. 1156.
118. On medieval literature of martyrdom as evidence of acculturation, see Einbinder, *Beautiful Death*.
119. Joel F. Harrington, *The Faithful Executioner: Life and Death, Honor and Shame in the Turbulent Sixteenth Century* (New York: Picador, 2014).
120. Silverman, *Tortured Subjects*, 64, 128.
121. Laura Kounine, "Conscience, Confession, and Selfhood in a Lutheran Witch Trial," paper presented at the Sixteenth Century Studies Conference, New Orleans, October 2014. I thank Laura Kounine for generously sharing with me her written paper, as well as her unpublished work. See also Laura Kounine, "'The Devil Used Her Sins': Despair, Confession and Salvation in Seventeenth-Century Witch Trial," https://www.history-of-emotions.mpg.de/en/texte/the-devil-used-her-sins-despair-confession-and-salvation-in-a-seventeenth-century-witch-trial; and "The Gendering of Witchcraft: Defence Strategies of Men and Women in German Witchcraft Trials," *German History* 31, no. 3 (2014).
122. Laura Kounine, "Witch-Hunting and Attitudes to Gender in Counter-Reformation Wuerzburg" (M.Phil thesis, Cambridge University, 2007), 59. I thank Kounine for sharing her unpublished thesis with me.
123. Einbinder, *Beautiful Death*, esp. ch. 2.
124. For example, in Andechs, Wilsnack, Poznań, and elsewhere; see Miri Rubin, *Gentile Tales: The Narrative Assault on Late Medieval Jews* (Philadelphia: University of Pennsylvania Press, 2004); Teter, *Sinners on Trial*, ch. 4.
125. Einbinder, *Beautiful Death*, ch. 5.
126. See, for example, Mitchell B. Merback, *The Thief, the Cross, and the Wheel: Pain and the Spectacle of Punishment in Medieval and Renaissance Europe* (Chicago: University of Chicago Press, 1999).
127. See, for example, Maharam of Rothenburg's argument that once someone decided to die for the sanctification of God, he will not feel any pain; *Sh"ut Maharam mi-Rotenburg*, no. 517; also reiterated in Samson ben Zadok, *Sefer tashbez: ha-mekhuneh: tashbez katan, pesakim, minhagim u-teshuvot*

me-et ha-Maharam mi-Rotenburg (Jerusalem: Mif'al Torat Hakhme Ashkenaz, Mekhon Yerushalayim, 2010), no. 415.

128. Brad S. Gregory, *Salvation at Stake: Christian Martyrdom in Early Modern Europe* (Cambridge, MA: Harvard University Press, 1999), 7.

129. Gregory, *Salvation at Stake.*

130. "Trep op fun deiner emuneh, viln mir dir makhn raikh, mit di greste hern verstu zany glaykh." Anonymous, *Sefer kedoshim k"k Vilne.* A more readable version was published in Weinreich, *Shturemvint Bilder,* 210–220, quote on 216.

131. Gregory, *Salvation at Stake,* 7. The trope of going to death like a wedding appears in almost all these Yiddish songs and can be found in Christian sources as well. For Poland, see, for example, the story of Katarzyna Malcherowa, executed for Judaizing in 1539 in Cracow. Teter, *Jews and Heretics,* 42–44.

132. Anonymous, *Kidush ha-shem shel Reb Matis,* unnumbered second to last page.

133. Bodian, *Dying in the Law of Moses,* esp. 4–7. Also see Abraham Gross, *Struggling with Tradition: Reservations about Active Martyrdom in the Middle Ages* (Leiden: Brill, 2004), and an earlier debate, in 1995, between Abraham Gross and Ram ben Shalom in the Hebrew-language journal *Tarbiz.*

134. Bodian, *Dying in the Law of Moses,* 8.

135. Bodian, *Dying in the Law of Moses,* especially ch. 7.

136. Bodian, *Dying in the Law of Moses,* 189.

137. One interesting example is a song *"Des kadosh fun Heneh zayn lid"* at Oxford's Bodleian Library set as the last prayer of the *kadosh* calling, among other things, on the community to repent. Anonymous, *Des kadosh fun Heneh zayn lid,* vol. Bodleian Library Opp 8 to 556 (3) (date and publisher unknown).

138. This is especially true for host desecration accusations, but it was also evident in the Simon of Trent story. On the host desecration accusation in this context, see Teter, *Sinners on Trial.*

6. "Who Should One Believe, the Rabbis or the Doctors of the Church?"

1. R. Po-chia Hsia, *The Myth of Ritual Murder: Jews and Magic in Reformation Germany* (New Haven: Yale University Press, 1988).

2. On this trial most recently, see Pierre Birnbaum, *Un récit de meurtre rituel au grand siècle: l'affaire Raphaël Lévy, Metz, 1669* (Paris: Fayard, 2008); and *A Tale of Ritual Murder in the Age of Louis XIV: The Trial of Raphaël Lévy, 1669* (Stanford: Stanford University Press, 2012). See the later discussion in this chapter.

3. In 1899 in a polemical response to a Lwów rabbi, historian Aleksander Czołowski repeated arguments undermining the validity and applicability of both papal bulls and royal privileges defending Jews against blood accusations. Czołowski, *Odpowiedź rabinowi lwowskiemu Dr. Jecheskielowi Caro w sprawie "mordu rytualnego"* (Lwów: Nakładem autora, 1899), 13ff.

See also Stanisław Salmonowicz, "Niemiecki erudyta barokowy W. E. Tenzel a wyrok Trybunału Koronnego Z 1598 R.: Przyczynek do dziejów procesów o tak zwane mordy rytualne w dawnej Polsce," *Odrodzenie i Reformacja w Polsce* 33 (1988): 257, n. 11.

4. Some scholars refer to this village inaccurately as Świniary. The place is Świniarów, some 3.3 kilometers (2 miles) from Łosice, 2.6 kilometers from Woźniki, and 26 kilometers from Mielnik, where the first part of the trial took place.

5. Some sources say the boy was lost on March 25; others claim "feria quinta post festa sollennia Paschae" or Thursday after Easter, which would make it March 26. Szymon Hubicki, *Żydowskie okrucieństwa nad naświętszym sakramentem y dziatkami chrześciańskimi* (Cracow: W Drukarni Mikołaja Szarffenbergera, 1602), 18. Sebastian Śleszkowski, *Odkrycie zdrad* (Brunsbergae: In Officina typographica Georgij Schonfels, 1621), unnumbered page following T3. See also Hanna Węgrzynek, *"Czarna legenda" żydów: procesy o rzekome mordy rytualne w dawnej Polsce* (Warsaw: Bellona, 1995), 117–118.

6. The decree is dated "Sabbato ante Festum S. Margarithae Virginis," 1598 (July 19, 1598). Śleszkowski directed readers to the court records dated July 5, 1598, the beginning of the proceedings in Lublin, when Jews were brought in from Mielnik. Śleszkowski, *Odkrycie zdrad,* ch. IX.

7. Stefan Żuchowski, *Ogłos processow* (1700), appendix. Jakub Radliński, *Prawda chrześciańska od nieprzyiaciela swego zeznana* (Lublin: Typis Societatis Jesu, 1733), 533–546. Also later in German, see Salmonowicz, "Niemiecki erudyta," 268–272.

8. Hubicki, *Żydowskie okrucieństwa,* 18. Śleszkowski, *Odkrycie zdrad,* ch. IX.

9. "Ratione fori, iuridicas controuersias, ad iudicium praesens generale Tribunalis Regni ad disiudicandum easdem remissis," Śleszkowski, *Odkrycie zdrad,* unnumbered in the excerpt from the decree, which starts on one folio after the one marked T3.

10. "In ulteriori vero Processu huius causae, quamvis praedicti Iudaei hoc scelus suum nefandum omnino negantes, eiusdemque nullatenus se reos esse allegantes, dilationem ad deducendum scrutinium suamque innocentiam ostendendam, sibi a Iudicio praesenti concede postulabant." Śleszkowski, *Odkrycie zdrad,* fol. marked V, and, earlier, ch. IX.

11. Śleszkowski, *Odkrycie zdrad,* V verso.

12. Hubicki, *Żydowskie okrucieństwa,* 19. Salmonowicz, "Niemiecki Erudyta," 270.

13. *Shulḥan 'Arukh,* OH 422:5.

14. Hubicki, *Żydowskie okrucieństwa,* 20v.

15. "Sponte," "benevole": Śleszkowski, *Odkrycie zdrad.*

16. Śleszkowski, *Odkrycie zdrad,* ch. X verso.

17. On the use of these privileges by Jews, see also Modekhai Nadav, "Ma'aseh alimut ha-dadiyyim bein yehudim le-lo-yehudim be-Lita lifney 1648," *Gal-Ed* 7–8 (1985): 3.

18. Śleszkowski, *Odkrycie zdrad,* ch. IX.

19. Żuchowski, *Process kryminalny,* 148. On Żuchowski and the two trials, see the later discussion.
20. I. D. Kuzmin, *Materialy k voprosu ob obvineniakh evreev be ritualnykh prestupleniakh* (St. Petersburg, 1913), 35–41.
21. Węgrzynek, *"Czarna legenda" żydów,* 101, 186. The town is referred to as Wojnia, in the text, but *Słownik geograficzny Królestwa Polskiego* (Warsaw, 1977 [1893]), vol. 13, does not list such a town in the Brest region. Other possibilities are towns with names related to Wojnia in the same area: Wojnicz and Wojnówka, a small village. S. A. Bershadskii claims that there were only two Jewish homeowners in Wojnia, or Wojnicz in 1566, yet he also gives names of two Jewish butchers in town, one of whom was a woman. It is unlikely that there would be two Jewish butchers with virtually no Jewish families. Either more Jews settled there by 1566 and were simply not homeowners, or he was mistaken in assuming that these two butchers were kosher butchers. Sergei Aleksandrovich Bershadskii, ed. *Dokumenty i regesty k istorii litovskikh evreev,* 3 vols. (St. Petersburg, 1882), 2: 155–156.
22. *Akty izdavaemye vilenskoiu kommisieiu dla razbora drevnikh aktov,* vol. 5 (Vilna, 1871), 4–6. Henceforth *AIVK*. Kuzmin, *Materialy,* 43–45.
23. *AIVK*, vol. V, 4–5.
24. On the Crown Tribunal, most recently, see Waldemar Bednaruk, *Trybunał Koronny: szlachecki sąd najwyższy w latach 1578–1794* (Lublin: KUL, 2008).
25. Gombin, *Trybunał Koronny ceremonial i sztuka* (Lublin: KUL 2013), 7, 35.
26. Gombin, *Trybunał Koronny ceremonial i sztuka,* esp. ch. 2.
27. See also Krzysztof Gombin, *Trybunał Koronny ceremonial i sztuka;* Antoni Debinski, Waldemar Bednaruk, and Marzena Lipska, eds., *Trybunał Koronny w kulturze prawnej Rzeczypospolitej szlacheckiej* (Lublin: KUL, 2008); Bednaruk, *Trybunał Koronny.*
28. On the status of the Jews in Poland and the role of the Council of Four Lands, see Israel Halpern and Israel Bartal, eds., *Pinkas va`ad arb`a arazot* (Jerusalem: 1989 [1945]), "Introduction"; Israel Halpern, ed. *Pinkas va`ad arb`a arazot* (Jerusalem: Mosad Bialik,1945); Shmuel Ettinger, "The Council of Four Lands," in *The Jews in Old Poland, 1000–1795,* ed. Antony Polonsky, Jakub Basista, and Andrzej Link-Lenczowski (London: I. B. Tauris, 1993), 93–109; Adam Teller, "Some Comparative Perspectives on the Jews' Legal Status in the Polish-Lithuanian Commonwealth and the Holy Roman Empire," in *Social and Cultural Boundaries in Pre-Modern Poland,* ed. Adam Teller, Magda Teter, and Antony Polonsky (Oxford: Littmann Library of Jewish Civilization, 2010), 109–141; Moshe Rosman, "The Authority of the Council of Four Lands outside of Poland," in *Social and Religious Boundaries in Pre-Modern Poland,* 83–108.
29. Węgrzynek summarizes some of the local context of the 1598 accusation in *"Czarna legenda" żydów,* 120.
30. Węgrzynek, *"Czarna legenda" żydów,* 112–113. On the outcomes, see Zenon Guldon and Jacek Wijaczka, *Procesy o mordy rytualne w Polsce w XVI–XVIII wieku* (Kielce: DCF, 1995), 96–101. See also a map on a website accompanying this book, on www.thebloodlibeltrail.com.

31. Halpern, ed. *Pinkas va'ad arb'a arazot*, no. 22, 27, 28 under year '355 (1595).
32. Przecław Mojecki, *Żydowskie okrucieństwa, mordy, y zabobony* (Cracow: W Drukarni Jak. Sibeneychera, 1598), 17. See Chapter 4.
33. ARSI, Polonia 50: "Annuae et Historiae Poloniae 1555–1600, 171r, published with some redactions in *Annuae Litterae Societatis Iesu, Anni 1598. Ad patres, ac fratres eiusdem societatis* (Lugundi: ex typographia Iacobi Roussin,1607).
34. ARSI Polonia 51 I, 156v.
35. The *litterae annuae* for 1598 mention that they received donations, including a silver crucifix, but nothing about the body, ARSI Polonia 50, 171v. This note was omitted from the published version of the reports.
36. ARSI Polonia 51 I, 156v. Bernard Maciejowski, in fact, is the one who donated the silver crucifix mentioned in the 1598 report. *Annuae Litterae Societatis Iesu 1605*, (Duaci: Ex officina Viduae Laurentii Kellami, 1618), 907–908.
37. The Bollandists cite Hubicki's work as the book sent to Rome.
38. Godefroid Henschen and Daniel Van Papenbroeck, *Acta Sanctorum Aprilis collecta, digesta, illustrata tomus II. quo medii XI dies continentur. praeponitur illis propylaeum antiquarium, circa veri falsique discrimen in vetustis monumentis, praesertim diplomatis, observandum. subjunguntur acta graeca* (Antwerp: apud Michaelem Cnobarum, 1675), 837. See also a letter sent from Cracow by Ludovicus Hoffman, SJ to Daniel van Papenbroech from July 18, 1671, Société des Bollandistes, Brussels (Belgium), Ms. Boll. 246, 216r.
39. Bibliothèque royale de Belgique, Collectanea Bollandiana, Ms. 8030–32, February 27, 1616, "De sanctis Poloniae," 101v, no. 15.
40. Hubicki, *Żydowskie okrucieństwa*, 16. On Kyrilis, see Kuzmin, *Materiały*, 45–46. On other tombstones and shrines devoted to purported child victims of Jews, see Zgliński, "Nagrobki i kult ofiar rzekomych żydowskich morgów rytualnych na historycznych ziemiach litewskich XVII-XIX wieku" in *Socialiniu Tapatumu Repreznetacijos: Lietuvos Didžiosios Kunigaikštystes Kulturoje* (Vilnius: Lietuvos Kultūros Tyrimų Institutas, 2010), 302–341; and Jolanta Żyndul, *Kłamstwo krwi: legenda mordu rytualnego na ziemiach polskich w XIX i XX wieku* (Warsaw: Wydawnictwo Cyklady, 2011). In Staszów, a child was said to have been "entombed" in a local church following a charge that Jews killed him in 1610 or 1611. Sebastian Miczyński, *Zwierciadło Korony Polskiey* (Cracow: Máciej Jedrzeiowczyk, 1618), 17, and 17–18 (in 1648).
41. Węgrzynek, *"Czarna legenda" żydów*, 120–124. Węgrzynek also provides a chart of accusations. She does not distinguish between formal and informal accusations, nor between convictions and acquittals; 112–113. For outcomes, see Guldon and Wijaczka, *Procesy o mordy rytualne*, 96–101. See also maps at www.thebloodlibeltrail.org.
42. Archiwum Państwowe w Lublinie (APwL), Akta m. Lublina "Acta maleficorum" 141, 394–413v, 418v–422v. The trials are discussed in Meir Bałaban, "Hugo Grotius and the Blood Libel Trials in Lublin, 1636," in *Social and Cultural Boundaries in Pre-Modern Poland*, 47–67; Węgrzynek, *"Czarna legenda" żydów*, 125–128; Guldon and Wijaczka, *Procesy o mordy rytualne*, 34–35. Bałaban should be used with caution. In a manner that appears like a transcript of archival sources, he creatively reconstructed the proceedings of

Notes to Pages 244–248   457

the trials. But the appendix contains two valuable letters between Jerzy Słupecki, a Polish Protestant present at the trial, and Hugo Grotius. On the problems with Bałaban's reconstruction, see Teller and Teter, *Social and Cultural Boundaries in Pre-Modern Poland*, 42–43. Guldon and Wijaczka published the records of both trials, though with some differences in the original. Guldon and Wijaczka, *Procesy o mordy rytualne*, 102–122.

43. Guldon and Wijaczka, *Procesy o mordy rytualne*, 105.
44. Guldon and Wijaczka, *Procesy o mordy rytualne*, 107.
45. Guldon and Wijaczka, *Procesy o mordy rytualne*, 107.
46. Guldon and Wijaczka, *Procesy o mordy rytualne*, 108–110.
47. Guldon and Wijaczka, *Procesy o mordy rytualne*, 104.
48. Guldon and Wijaczka, *Procesy o mordy rytualne*, 110.
49. Guldon and Wijaczka, *Procesy o mordy rytualne*, 113.
50. Guldon and Wijaczka, *Procesy o mordy rytualne*, 114–115.
51. Guldon and Wijaczka, *Procesy o mordy rytualne*, 111–112.
52. Guldon and Wijaczka, *Procesy o mordy rytualne*, 112–113.
53. Bałaban, "Hugo Grotius and the Blood Libel Trials," 58. Żuchowski argued that the Jews' release was thanks to perjury, Żuchowski, *Process kryminalny*, 153.
54. Bałaban, "Hugo Grotius and the Blood Libel Trials," 50, 63. Bałaban seems to argue that the original decree was rescinded and the Jews were executed.
55. Bałaban, "Hugo Grotius and the Blood Libel Trials," 52.
56. APwL, Akta m. Lublina, 141, 394v. See also Guldon and Wijaczka, *Procesy o mordy rytualne*, 102. Psalm 52:3ff.
57. Guldon and Wijaczka, *Procesy o mordy rytualne*, 106, 113.
58. AP w Lublinie, Akta m. Lublina, Acta Maleficorum 141, 418v–422v, printed in Guldon and Wijaczka, *Procesy o mordy rytualne*, 115–122. See also Bałaban, "Hugo Grotius and the Blood Libel Trials," 59–63, and Węgrzynek, *"Czarna legenda" żydow*, 127–128.
59. Guldon and Wijaczka, *Procesy o mordy rytualne*, 116.
60. Guldon and Wijaczka, *Procesy o mordy rytualne*, 117.
61. Guldon and Wijaczka, *Procesy o mordy rytualne*, 120.
62. Sebastyan Śleszkowski, *Jasne dowody o doktorach żydowskich* (1623). It was then republished in 1649 and 1758.
63. Żuchowski, *Ogłos processów,* in source appendix. The 1639 case is briefly discussed by Węgrzynek, *"Czarna legenda" żydów*, 126. Interrogation records are preserved in AP in Lublin, Akta m. Lublina, Acta maleficorum 142, 65v–80v and published in Guldon and Wijaczka, *Procesy o mordy rytualne*, 122–129. The decree is printed also in Kuzmin, *Materiały*, 80–92.
64. Bałaban, "Hugo Grotius and the Blood Libel Trials," 64–65.
65. Edwin Rabbie, "Hugo Grotius and Judaism," in *Hugo Grotius, Theologian*, ed. Henk J. M. Nellen and Edwin Rabbie (Leiden: Brill, 1994), 109.
66. Bałaban, "Hugo Grotius and the Blood Libel Trials," 66.
67. Tyrnau or Tyrnavia, now Trnava in Slovakia, was the site of a 1494 accusation in which Jews confessed to using blood and listed reasons for their doing so. The story entered many chronicles and was widely used to support the accusation.

First it appears to have been mentioned in Antonius Bonfinius, *Rerum ungaricum* (Hannover: typis Wechel, 1606), 718. Szymon Syreniusz included it in the appendix to his *Zielnik* in 1613, and Abraham Bzovius, after Bonfinius, included it in 1627 in his *Annales ecclesiastici* in vol. 18 covering the years 1472–1503.

68. On leprosy and the blood cure, see Irven M. Resnick, *Marks of Distinction: Christian Perceptions of Jews in the High Middle Ages* (Washington, DC: Catholic University of America Press, 2012), especially 95–97. Note 12 on p. 95 provides Christian sources for this belief. Jews also had a legend that Pharaoh ordered the slaughter of Israelite children to cure leprosy; David Malkiel, "Infanticide in Passover Iconography," *Journal of Warburg and Courtland Institutes* 56 (1993); Ephraim Shoham-Steiner, "Pharaoh's Bloodbath: Medieval Jewish Thoughts about Leprosy, Disease, and Blood Therapy," in *Jewish Blood: Reality and Metaphor in History, Religion and Culture*, ed. Mitchell B. Hart (London: Routledge, 2009), 99–115.
69. Bałaban, "Hugo Grotius and the Blood Libel Trials," 66–67.
70. Bałaban, "Hugo Grotius and the Blood Libel Trials," 66.
71. Hugo Grotius, *Hugonis Grotii Reginae Regnique Sueciae Consiliarii et apud Regem Christianissimum legati etc. epistolae quotquot reperiri* (Amsterdam: ex typographia P. & I. Blaev: prostant apud Wolfgang, Waasberge, Boom a Someren & Goethals, 1687), 286.
72. APwL, Akta m. Lublina 140, 159r–163v.
73. This trial is discussed in Teter, *Sinners on Trial*, 207–209. For the court summary of the case, see *AIVK*, vol. 28: *Akty o evreiakh* (Vilna, 1901), 392–395.
74. In Polish, "pospólstwo."
75. The dossier of the trial is in the Archives departementales de la Moselle in Metz, B 2144 (henceforth ADMM). The trial came into focus in the aftermath of the Damascus affair in 1840, when *Archive Israelite* published a contemporary Jewish account of it translated from Yiddish into French. A few decades later, Joseph Reinach published a monograph with some sources, including Richard Simon. Joseph Reinach, *Une erreur judiciaire sous Louis XIV: Raphaël Levy* (Paris: Delagrave, 1898).
76. Didier's disappearance in a forest and his red bonnet uncannily resemble the folk tale of Little Red Riding Hood, whose origins can be traced to the early modern period. Robert Darnton, *The Great Cat Massacre and Other Episodes in French Cultural History* (New York: Vintage Books, 1985), ch. 1.
77. See, for example, ADMM, B 2144, supplication from January 8, 1670, and "Deffences par attenuation" from January 15, 1670. A fragment of the January 8 document was translated in Birnbaum, *A Tale of Ritual Murder*, 106.
78. For Raphaël Levy as "a foreign Jew," see Reinach, *Une erreur judiciaire*, 41.
79. Reinach, *Une erreur judiciaire*, 31.
80. Reinach, *Une erreur judiciaire*, 153.
81. The original Yiddish account does not seem to have survived; only the 1840s French translation has. Reinach, *Une erreur judiciaire*, 153.

82. The file in ADMM, B 2144, consists of disorganized loose documents. It is not a formal dossier. Perhaps the imperial decree still exists somewhere in the archive, perhaps it never was filed, or perhaps it has been lost.
83. The decree was published in a bilingual French-German issue, *Gerichtlicher Proceß und Urtheil deß Parlaments zu Metz eines Jude[n] Raphael Levi genandt wegen eines von ihme den 23. Septembr. 1669 geraubten und hingerichteten drey jährigen Kindes: Auß dem zu Metz gedrucktem frantzösischen Exemplar ins teutscheübersetzt* (1670).
84. Roger Clèment, *La condition des juifs de Metz dans L'ancien règime* (Paris: Imprimerie Henri Jouve, 1903), 19–25.
85. Reinach, *Une erreur judiciaire*, 9–11; Clèment, *La condition*, 34–37.
86. On the Jews in Bordeaux, see the classic work by Frances Malino, *The Sephardic Jews of Bordeaux: Assimilation and Emancipation in Revolutionary and Napoleonic France* (Tuscaloosa: University of Alabama Press, 1978).
87. For Metz, albeit in the eighteenth century, see Jay R. Berkovitz, *Rites and Passages: The Beginnings of Modern Jewish Culture in France, 1650–1860* (Philadelphia: University of Pennsylvania Press, 2011) and his *Protocols of Justice: The Pinkas of the Metz Rabbinic Court 1771–1789*, vol. 1 (Leiden: Brill, 2014).
88. Abraham-Nicolas Amelot de La Houssaie, *Abregé dv procés fait aux Juifs de Mets* (Paris: Chez Frederic Leonard, imprimeur ordin. du roy, ruë Saint Jacques, à l'Escu de Venise, 1670). Also published in Reinach, *Une erreur judiciaire*.
89. Reinach, *Une erreur judiciaire*, 73–74; Amelot de La Houssaie, *Abregé dv procés*, 4–6.
90. Schedel's *Liber chronicarum*, known as the "Nuremberg Chronicle," includes more than three stories. They are William of Norwich, Richard of Pontoise, Simon of Trent, and Forli (Motta Castello). Simon's story is incorrectly dated to 1472; perhaps this is a typographical error made by the printer.
91. The Yiddish originals, if they existed, have not survived.
92. Reinach, *Une erreur judiciaire*, 84; Amelot de La Houssaie, *Abregé dv procés*, 25–26.
93. Reinach, *Une erreur judiciaire*, 103–105; Amelot de La Houssaie, *Abregé dv procés*, 66–68.
94. Reinach, *Une erreur judiciaire*, 37ff.
95. Richard Simon's response was published in 1709 in a collection of letters and more recently in Reinach, *Une erreur judiciaire*, 120–135.
96. Reinach, *Une erreur judiciaire*, 121.
97. Simon uses the verb "plagiaire" in the sense it had in Roman law, describing a "plagiarist" as someone who stole the children of others. *Dictionnaire de la langue française (Littré)* (1873), http://artfl-project.uchicago.edu/node/17.
98. Reinach, *Une erreur judiciaire*, 122–123.
99. Reinach, *Une erreur judiciaire*, 123–124. Cesare Baronio, *Annales Ecclesiastici* (Moguntia: Sumptibus Ioannis Gymnici et Antonii Hierati Coloniensi, 1608), vol. XII: 1146.XVII–XIX.
100. Reinach, *Une erreur judiciaire*, 124–125.

101. Reinach, *Une erreur judiciaire*, 125–129.
102. Reinach, *Une erreur judiciaire*, 129.
103. Reinach, *Une erreur judiciaire*, 62–66.
104. *Maximi fructus monitum* (Fürth: Abraham von Werth, 1699). Archiwum Kapituły Kolegiackiej i Katedralnej w Sandomierzu (henceforth, AKKKS), MS. 740, 121r–124v, 126v. *Maximi fructus monitum* would later be mentioned in Cardinal Lorenzo Ganganelli's report; see Cecil Roth, *The Ritual Murder Libel and the Jew* (London: Woburn Press, 1935), 52.
105. Żuchowski's two books were *Process kryminalny* and *Ogłos processów*. On Żuchowski and the Sandomierz trials, see Waldemar Kowalski, "W obronie wiary: Ks. Stefan Żuchowski—między wzniosłością a okrucieństwem," in *Żydzi wsród chrześcijan w dobie szlacheckiej Rzeczypospolitej* (Kielce: Akademia Świętokrzyska, 1996), 221–233; Feliks Kiryk, "Ksiądz Stefan Żuchowski Archidiakon Sandomierski—próba portretu" in *Stosunki chrześcijańsko-żydowskie w historii, pamięci i sztuce: europejski kontekst dzieł w katedrze sandomierskiej*, ed. Magda Teter and Urszula Stępień (Sandomierz: Wydawnictwo diecezjalne, 2013); Teter, "Stosunki chrześcijańsko-żydowskie." For the long-term legacy of the trials and the work of art, see Anna Landau-Czajka, "The Last Controversy over Ritual Murder? The Debate over the Paintings in Sandomierz Cathedral," *Polin: Studies in Polish Jewry* 16 (2003); Teter, "The Sandomierz Paintings of Ritual Murder as *Lieux De Mémoire*"; and in fiction, Zygmunt Miłoszewski, *Ziarno prawdy* (Warsaw: Wydawn. W.A.B., 2011).
106. On Żuchowski most recently, see Kiryk, "Ksiądz Stefan Żuchowski." For examples of Żuchowski's cases in the Crown Tribunal, see the registry of cases in Archiwum Państwowe w Lublinie (AP Lublin): Akta Trybunału Koronnego 254, Acta Arianismi.
107. Achivum Romanum Societatis Iesu (ARSI), FG.1592/Collegia 207 Sendomir, fols. 33–274; fols. 275–778 contain supplementary evidence in the case. See also AKKKS 742, fols 4r–5v.
108. AKKKS 742, 6r–8v. She was baptized on June 23, 1695.
109. Although in the Catholic liturgical calendar, the first Sunday after Easter is called "dominica in albis" (Sunday in white), in the early modern period in Poland, the fifth Sunday of Lent or the last one before Palm Sunday, was also popularly called "white Sunday." Żuchowski seems to be trying to eliminate this confusion by both placing the plot to kill the girl on March 13 and stating that the girl died on the Sunday "called by the Church as the Sunday of Christ suffering, but popularly called white," Żuchowski, *Ogłos processów*, 11v. The Sunday of the Octave of Easter (i.e. the *dominica in albis*) would have been on April 6; the Sunday before Palm Sunday, or the fifth Sunday of Lent, would have been on March 16.
110. AKKKS 742, 7v.
111. AKKKS 742, 8v.
112. Żuchowski, *Ogłos processów*, [14r], [74v]. Unnumbered pages; the folio numbers provided here refer to pages of the *Ogłos*, including the dedication.

113. Żuchowski, *Ogłos processów,* [12r]. For this claim in Śleszkowski, see Śleszkowski, *Odkrycie zdrad,* V3.
114. AKKKS 742, 9r–v.
115. AKKKS 742, 10r.
116. AKKKS 742, [15r].
117. Żuchowski, *Ogłos processów,* [17r].
118. Żuchowski, *Ogłos processów,* [21r], [76r]; on the bishop's support, [16r], [43v]; on the laudum of the noble's dietine, see Kowalski, "W obronie wiary," 225. For the texts of the lauda, see Polska Akademia Umiejętności (PAU), Teki Pawińskiego 8338, 864r (April 28, 1698), 867 (September 22, 1698).
119. AKKKS 742, 16r, a letter from Bp. Jan Małachowski to Stefan Żuchowski, May 26, 1698.
120. Żuchowski, *Ogłos processów,* [19v].
121. AKKKS 742, 6r–22v.
122. Żuchowski, *Ogłos processów.* On Żuchowski's role in the trial and his accounts of them, see Kowalski, "W obronie wiary." See also, with caution, Daniel Tollet, "Le goupillon, le prétoire et la plume: Stefan Żuchowski et l'accusation de crimes rituels en Pologne a la fin du XVII siécle et au début du XVIII siécle," in *Żydzi wśród chrześcijan w dobie szlacheckiej Rzeczypospolitej,* portions of which were published in Daniel Tollet, *Accuser pour convertir* (Paris: Presses universitaires de France, 2000).
123. Żuchowski, *Ogłos processów,* e.g. [22r], [46r–47r], [56r]. Jews may have hoped that August II would be their ally because he was inclined to support Jews in other matters—leasing salt mines to them and allowing some Jews, especially German Jews, to stay in Warsaw despite legal exclusion of Jews from Mazovia, ASV Sec. Stato Polonia 119, fols. 313 and 325. On tensions following that support in Warsaw, see ASV Sec. Stato Polonia 119, fol. 438.
124. Żuchowski, *Ogłos processów,* [17v–18v], [25r–v], [46v–47r], [54v–56v], [59v–60r], [75r].
125. Żuchowski, *Ogłos processów,* [60v].
126. Żuchowski, *Ogłos processów,* [31r–v].
127. Żuchowski, *Ogłos processów,* [29v].
128. Żuchowski, *Ogłos processów,* [30r], [31r].
129. Żuchowski, *Ogłos processów,* [33v].
130. Żuchowski, *Ogłos processów,* [76v].
131. Żuchowski, *Ogłos processów,* [34r].
132. Żuchowski, *Ogłos processów,* [41v–42r].
133. Żuchowski, *Ogłos processów,* [44r].
134. Żuchowski, *Ogłos processów,* [67r].
135. Żuchowski, *Ogłos processów,* [46r].
136. Żuchowski, *Ogłos processów,* [44v–45r], [50v].
137. Kowalski, "W obronie wiary," 230; Żuchowski, *Ogłos processów,* [50v]. The 1598 trial is mentioned as a precedent in the final court decree from July 1698. Żuchowski, *Ogłos processów,* 63r. The papal nuncio also alluded to it in his dispatch on August 23, 1698, saying that "in these parts, Jews are

accused of similar cruelties, with many such cases described"; ASV Sec. Stato Polonia 119, fol. 463v.
138. Żuchowski, *Ogłos processów,* [55r.]
139. Żuchowski, *Ogłos processów,* [56r].
140. ASV Sec. Stato Polonia 119, fol. 469, and ASV Seg. Stato Polonia 120, fol. 235r–v, 238r–v.
141. Żuchowski, *Ogłos processów,* [60v–61r].
142. Żuchowski, *Ogłos processów,* [61v].
143. Żuchowski, *Ogłos processów,* [62r–72v].
144. AKKKS 742, 16r.
145. AKKKS, 742, fols. 23–24.
146. Żuchowski, *Process kryminalny,* 279.
147. AKKKS 741, fols. 122–152, a plan for twenty-four paintings representing "Historiae Crudelitatis Judaicae in Christianos Infantes exeritae ex classicis authoribus collectae et iconibus expressae." An additional series of paintings was planned based on stories collected from Polish books; a fragmentary description of paintings five through twelve is on fol. 59.
148. The image is on the cover of Teter, *Jews and Heretics,* and is published in black and white in Teter, "The Sandomierz Paintings of Ritual Murder as *Lieux de Mémoire,*" and in color in Teter and Stępień, *Stosunki chrześcijańsko-żydowskie.*
149. The trial has been described in Zenon Guldon, "Proces of Mord Rytualny w Sandomierzu w Latach 1710–1713," *Notatnik Sandomierski* 6 (1994). This article gives a good outline of chronology; however, it should be used with caution, because Guldon often took Żuchowski's text at face value.
150. AKKKS 740, fol. 13r, 16v.
151. Żuchowski, *Process kryminalny,* 281.
152. AKKKS 740, fol. 38r–v, 40r–45v; Żuchowski, *Process kryminalny,* 4–5, 282, 285.
153. Żuchowski, *Process kryminalny,* 283. Guldon, "Proces," 11.
154. AKKKS 740, 46r–51v; Żuchowski, *Process kryminalny,* 286.
155. AKKKS 740, 47r–v.
156. AKKKS 740, 49v–50r.
157. AKKKS 740, 50r–51r.
158. Żuchowski, *Process kryminalny,* 286–287.
159. Żuchowski, *Process kryminalny,* 287.
160. AKKKS 740, 54r–63r.
161. Żuchowski, *Process kryminalny,* 289–290. Żuchowski refers to him as Mazowiecki, but on the list of deputies to the Crown Tribunal for 1710, such a name does not appear. But there were two deputies from Mazovia: Paulus (Paweł) Przeradowski and Josephu (Józef) Zembrzyński. AKKKS 740, 34r–v.
162. AKKKS 740, 56v–63r.
163. AKKKS 740, 70r–v, 71r–72r.
164. AKKKS 740, 73r. Tymiński's first name is unknown.
165. Żuchowski's letter to King August II, asking the king to expel Jews from Sandomierz on account of "the blood spilled from the three children mar-

tyred by the merciless and cruel Jews in the City of Sandomierz," AKKKS 740, 102r.

166. Żuchowski, *Process kryminalny,* 301–302, 307. For example, AKKKS 740, 180r–181r, 235r, 491r–492v. The nuncio communicated, without directly mentioning the trial, the issue of the bishop of Cracow's permission for clergy to engage in criminal trials and the bishop's request to have a bull by Gregory XIII of 1572 reissued, ASV Sec. Stato Polonia 137, 796r–807v. The nuncio also reported about his contacts with Żuchowski, but they concerned questions related to ecclesiastical property or the court dispute between the Jesuits in Sandomierz and Żuchowski, ASV Sec. Stato Polonia 138, fol. 76v–77r, 187r–189r. On Jews' appeal to the nuncio, see AKKKS 740, 147v.

167. AKKKS 740, 103r–v. Żuchowski, *Process kryminalny,* 307.

168. In June 1711 he wrote to the king to request an edict of expulsion of Jews from Sandomierz, AKKKS 740, 102r–v.

169. The papal nuncio reported the spread of plague from the east westward and to Lublin, ASV Sec. Stato Polonia 135, 754r, 783v, 812r–v.

170. One of these converts was the enigmatic figure of Jan Serafinowicz. Paweł Maciejko, "Christian Accusations of Jewish Human Sacrifice in Early Modern Poland: The Case of Jan Serafinowicz," *Gal-`Ed* 22 (2010).

171. Kowalski, "W obronie wiary."

172. Żuchowski, *Process kryminalny,* 322; the forty reasons are on 322–330.

173. Żuchowski, *Process kryminalny,* 339.

174. Żuchowski, *Process kryminalny,* 12–62.

175. Żuchowski, *Process kryminalny,* 76–100.

176. Żuchowski, *Process kryminalny,* 100–148.

177. AKKKS 740, 127r–128v.

178. Halpern, *Pinkas va`ad arb`a arazot,* 277, n. 1.

179. AKKKS 740, 127r–v.

180. AKKKS 740, 129r–130v.

181. 2 Maccabees 6:18ff. *Maximi fructus monitum,* 12–15.

182. *Maximi fructus monitum,* 16–17.

183. Żuchowski, *Process kryminalny,* 190.

184. Żuchowski, *Process kryminalny,* 190–191. On the 1670 expulsion from Vienna, see Mordechai Breuer and Michael Graetz, *German-Jewish History in Modern Times: Tradition and Enlightenment, 1600–1780,* ed. Michael Brenner and Michael A. Meyer (New York: Columbia University Press, 1996), 100–101.

185. Żuchowski, *Process kryminalny,* 191. The two works mentioned are Stefano Quaranta, *Summa bullarii earum que summorum pontificum constitutionum quae ad communem Ecclesiae usum post volumina juris canonici usquë ad Paulum V. Emanrunt, authore Stephano Quaranta, cum additionibus Prosperi de Augustino* (Venice: apud Juntas, 1609) and Lorenzo Brancati, *Epitome canonum Omnium qui in conciliis generalibus ac prouincialibus, in decreto Gratiani, in decretalibus, in epistolis & constitutionibus romanorum pontificum vsque ad sanctiss. D. N. Alexandri VII annum quartum continentur* (Rome: Typis Mascardi, 1649). On Śleszkowski's argument, see Chapter 4.

186. Żuchowski, *Process kryminalny*, 192.
187. Żuchowski, *Process kryminalny*, 116–117.
188. Żuchowski, *Process kryminalny*, 192–193.
189. AKKKS 741, 5v–6r. ASV Arm. XLI, vol. 17, 255r–256r, published in Shlomo Simonsohn, *The Apostolic See and the Jews: Documents, 1539–1545*, no. 1973, 2174–2175.
190. Radliński, *Prawda chrześcianska*, e.g., 464, 470–472, 483, 549ff. For a list of accusations, see Guldon and Wijaczka, *Procesy o mordy rytualne*, 100.
191. Lippmann Hirsch Loewenstein, *Damascia die Judenverfolgung zu Damaskus und ihre Wirkung auf die öffentliche Meinung nebst Nnachweisungen über den Ursprung der gegen die Juden wiederholten Beschuldigung, als bedienten sie sich des Menschenblutes bei Rituellen Zeremonien* (Frankfurt a.M: Loewenstein, 1841), 352–362. The report was first published in 1751 in Christian Friedrich Börner, *Auserlesene Bedenken der Theologischen Fakultät zu Leipzig in Drey Theile verfasset* (Leipzig: Bernhard Christoph Breitkopf, 1751), 613–622. On the report, see Jakub Goldberg, "Leipziger Theologen gegen die Ritualmordprozesse: Das Gutachten vom Jahre 1714," *Herbergen der Christenheit: Jahrbuch für deutsche Kirchengeschichte* 23 (1999); Nicola Cusumano, *Ebrei e accusa di omicidio rituale nel settecento: il carteggio tra Girolamo Tartarotti e Benedetto Bonelli, 1740–1748* (Milan: UNICOPLI, 2012), 44; Jan Doktór, "Konwertyta mimo woli: sprawa rabina ziemskiego litwy Samuela Ben Jaakowa (Jana Serafinowicza)," *Kwartalnik Historii Żydów*, no. 3 (2007): 280.
192. Loewenstein, *Damascia*, 352–353.
193. Loewenstein, *Damascia*, 354.
194. This refers to the renewal of *Sicut Iudaeis* on May 3, 1235.
195. Loewenstein, *Damascia*, 354–356.
196. On *Shevet Yehudah* and blood libel, see Chapter 5 and the literature cited there.
197. Hsia, *The Myth of Ritual Murder*, 216–217.
198. Johann Andreas Eisenmenger, *Endecktes Judenthum* (Frankfurt, 1700), part II, 220–224. Eisenmenger discussed the blood accusation in the lengthy chapter 3 of part II.
199. Loewenstein, *Damascia*, 356.
200. Loewenstein, *Damascia*, 356–357. Eisenmenger, *Endecktes Judenthum*, part II: 225–227.
201. Loewenstein, *Damascia*, 357.
202. Loewenstein, *Damascia*, 358.
203. Loewenstein, *Damascia*, 359–362.
204. Börner, *Auserlesene Bedenken*, 613–622.
205. For example, ASV Segr. Stato Polonia 139, and Polonia 190.
206. Archiwum Państwowe w Poznaniu, Akta m. Poznania I 2258, 1–9 (henceforth APP, AmP).
207. APP, AmP I 2258, 2, also 8.
208. "Zamordowane y umęczone." Although "umęczone" can also be translated as "tortured," a Latin phrase later uses the phrase "cruentis martyris corpori suprascripti," AmP I 2258, 3.

209. APP, AmP I 2258, 11.
210. APP, AmP I 2258, 12. On the Przemyśl trial and the resulting 1633 law, see Teter, *Sinners on Trial*, ch. 7.
211. The letter from the Dominican general was cited in Italian defenses of Jews; see Chapter 7. An Italian version of the letter is found in ASCER, 1Va, fasc. 13, coll. 2 inf. 2. The Latin document and its German translation are published in Moritz Stern, *Die Päpstlichen Bullen über die Blutbeschuldigung* (Munich: August Schupp, 1900), 134–137. A draft in Italian of Naftali's appeal is in ASCER 1Ql fasc. 11.
212. ACDF St. St. TT 2c "Hebraei."
213. In chapter 3 of *Ma'akhalot asurot*, Maimonides actually discusses only blood spots in eggs.
214. For a summary of this case, see Guldon and Wijaczka, *Procesy o mordy rytualne*, 69–70. Also, to be used with great caution, Majer Bałaban, "Arje Lejb Kalahora (Do przyczynku procesu Poznańskiego w latach 1736–1740," in *Studia Historyczne* (Warsaw: Korona, 1927). On the Jews of Poznań, most recently, see Adam Teller, Ḥayim be-zavta: ha-rov`a ha-yehudi shel Poznan ba-maḥazit ha-rishonah shel ha-me'ah ha-shev`a 'esreh (Jerusalem: Magnes Press, 2003).
215. ASV Segr. Stato Polonia 167, 458r–v.
216. ASV Segr. Stato Polonia 249, 447v.
217. ASV, Segr. Stato Polonia 167, 488v.
218. ASV, Segr. Stato Polonia 168, 46v–47r.
219. ASV, Segr. Stato Polonia 228, 281v.
220. ASV Segr. Stato Polonia 168, 254r.
221. APP, AmP Gr 1238.
222. ASV Segr. Stato Polonia 168, 141r.
223. Dispatch from March 1737, ASV Segr. Stato Polonia 168, 182r. Several converts were mentioned in a 1738 letter from August III calling on them, as well as others, to stand before the commission as witnesses, APP, AmP Gr 1238, 299v–300r.
224. APP, AmP I 2258, 56. On the request, see ASV Segr. Stato Polonia 168, 254r.
225. Guldon and Wijaczka, *Procesy o mordy rytualne*, 70.
226. For example, APP, AmP I 2258, 51 (August 1739).
227. ACDF St. St. TT 2c "Hebraei"; ASV Segr. Stato Polonia 170, 178r.
228. ACDF St. St. TT 2c "Hebraei."
229. ASV Segr. Stato Polonia 170, 178r.
230. ASV Segr. Stato Polonia 228, 374r–375r. For the deliberations of the Holy Office, see ACDF St. St. TT 2c "Hebraei."
231. The issue is raised by the Holy Office and the Secretary of State; ACDF St. St. TT 2c "Hebraei"; ASV Segr. Stato Polonia 234, 78v–80v, 369, 377–378, 392; ASV Segr. Stato Polonia 235, 7r–8v; ASV Segr. Stato Polonia 253, 184r–186v.
232. ASV Segr. Stato Polonia 255A (unnumbered). Israel Halpern located Solomon Zalman "the shtadlan" of Poznań at the end of the seventeenth century, but the Vatican document suggests that he was alive and active during the Poznań trial. Halpern, *Pinkas va`ad arb`a arazot*, 498, n. 4.

233. ASV Segr. Stato Polonia 231, letter from July 27, 1743.
234. On business relations between Jews and the clergy in Poland, see, in particular, Jakub Goldberg, "Jak ksiądz z żydem zakładali manufakturę żelazną w Wielkopolsce," in *The Jews in Poland,* ed. Andrzej Paluch (Cracow: Jagiellonian University, 1992), 146–160; Yehudit Kalik, "Patterns of Contact between the Catholic Church and the Jews in the Polish-Lithuanian Commonwealth: Jewish Debts," in *Studies in the History of the Jews in Old Poland in Honor of Jacob Goldberg,* ed. Adam Teller (Jerusalem: Magnes Press, 1998), 102–122. On the question of debts and insolvency of the Jewish community in Rome, see Mario Rosa, "La Santa Sede e gli ebrei nel settecento," *Storia d'Italia: Annali* "Gli ebrei in Italia" 11, no. 2 (1997): 1072. On the status of the Jews in Poland and the reasons why it outraged the Church officials, see Magda Teter, *Jews and Heretics in Catholic Poland: A Beleaguered Church in the Post-Reformation Era* (Cambridge: Cambridge University Press, 2006).
235. ASV Segr. Stato Polonia 255A, unnumbered, after the memorandum.
236. ASV Segr. Stato Polonia 231, letter from August 31, 1743.
237. AGAD, "Xięga Czarna. Krzemieniec (1747–1764)," 3–27. The document was published in Anna Michałowska, "Protokół procesu o mord rytualny: Fragment Czarnej Księgi Krzemienieckiej z 1747 roku," *Biuletyn Żydowskiego Instytutu Historycznego,* no. 3 (1995): 107–120. Also see Teter, *Sinners on Trial,* 211 ff.
238. The verdict was translated in Teter, *Sinners on Trial,* 212–213.
239. AGAD, "Xięga Czarna. Krzemieniecka (1747–1764)," 27. Michałowska, "Protokół Procesu," 120.
240. Jan Tysowski, *Dekret na żydow morderców y zaboyców pewnego katolika* (after April 17, 1747); *Dekret w sprawie o zamordowanie okrutne przez żydów chrześcianina Antoniego pod Zasławiem ferowany w Zamku Zasławskim dnia 17 kwietnia Roku Pańskiego 1747* (after April 17, 1747). See copies at the Biblioteka Narodowa, mf 76629 and mf 76167, respectively.
241. Archiwum Państwowe w Krakowie-Oddział na Wawelu (APK, Wawel) Akta XX. Sanguszków, Teka 5/27, 39, 41. The full text of the letter was "For information, lest there be any doubt about the Zasław decree against Jews accused of killing a Christian, published this year. That is why herewith is printed a copy of a letter from His Highness Duke Lubartowicz Sanguszko, the Grand Marshal of the Grand Duchy of Lithuania addressed to a certain correspondent from Zasław, dated 5th September, 1747."
242. ASV Segr. Stato Polonia, 233, 234, 235, 376.
243. Published in Hebrew in I. Galant, "Zhertvy ritualnogo obvinenya ve Zaslave v 1747 g: po aktam Kievskago Tsentralnago Arkhiva," *Evreiskaia starina* 5, no. 2 (1912): 217.

7. "Jews Are Deemed Innocent in the Tribunals of Italy"

1. On the report, see Chapter 9. For the text of the report in Italian and English, see Cecil Roth, *The Ritual Murder Libel and the Jew* (London: Woburn Press, 1935).

2. On the eighteenth-century trials in Italy and the relationship between them and polemical literature, see Tommaso Caliò, "L'omicidio rituale nell'Italia del settecento tra polemica antigiudaica ed erudizione agiografica," *Rivista di storia e letteratura religiosa* 38, no. 2 (2002). This article later became a chapter in Tommaso Caliò, *La leggenda dell'ebreo assassino: percorsi di un racconto antiebraico dal medioevo ad oggi* (Rome: Viella, 2007).
3. There is a good deal of literature on this subject; the most recent and extraordinarily useful work in English is Irene Fosi, *Papal Justice: Subjects and Courts in the Papal State, 1500–1750* (Washington, DC: Catholic University of America Press, 2011).
4. The text is published in Tranquillo Vita Corcos, *Alla Sagra Consvlta Illustriss. e Reuerendiss. Monsig. Ghezzi Ponente per l'vniuersità degl'hebrei di Roma. Sommario* (Rome: Nella stamperia della Rev. Camera apostolica, 1706), doc. no. 6. Henceforth, Corcos, *Sommario*.
5. The full text of the April 22, 1475, decree was published in Corrado Guidetti, *Pro Judæis: Riflessioni e documenti* (Roux e Favale, 1884), 278–280.
6. For a brief article about the case, see Nello Pavoncello, "Una 'accusa del sangue' a Viterbo nel 1705," *Lunario Romano* (1981): 223–234. See also Marina Caffiero, "Alle origini dell'antisemitismo politico: L'accusa di omicidio rituale nel sei-settecento tra autordifesa degli ebrei e pronunciamenti papali," in *Les racines chrétiennes de l'antisemitisme politique (fin XIXe–XXe siècle)* (Rome: Ecole française de Rome, 2003), 39. Shlomo Simonsohn, *History of the Jews in the Duchy of Mantua* (Jerusalem: Kiryath Sepher, 1977), 437–440.
7. Pavoncello, "Una 'accusa del sangue' a Viterbo," 224. Pietro Ioly Zorattini and Marcello Massenzio, *I nomi degli altri: conversioni a Venezia e nel Friuli Veneto in età moderna* (Leo S. Olschki, 2008), 46. The text of the bull can be found in Laerzio Cherubini and Angelo Maria Cherubini, *Magnum Bullarium Romanum, a Clemente VIII Vsque Ad Gregorium XV* (Lugundi: sumptib. Philippi Borde, Laur. Arnaud & Cl. Rigaud, 1655), vol. 3, 23–25, no. XIX.
8. On the Jews' presence in Viterbo at the end of the seventeenth century, see a case of a Jewish convert from 1698, in whose trial before the Inquisition Roman Jews visiting the town for fairs were summoned as witnesses, Fosi, *Papal Justice*, 137–138.
9. In 1601, Pope Clement VIII established that the fair in the spring was to begin on a Wednesday before the Pentecost and end eight days after Corpus Christi. In 1705, Pentecost was on Sunday, May 31, and Corpus Christi was on Thursday, June 11. Archivio Santa Maria della Quercia, pergamena no. 73, in "I Papi devoti della Madonna della Quercia," http://www.madonnadellaquercia .it/I%20PAPI%20%20DEVOTI%20della%20Madonna%20della%20 Quercia.pdf.
10. Archivio della Congregazione per la Dottrina della Fede (henceforth, ACDF), St. St. TT-4-C, fasc. 4, unnumbered, following the report about the contents of archives of the Jewish community in Rome dated September 18, 1731.
11. ACDF, St. St. TT-4-C, fasc. 4.
12. The names of the signatories of the letter are Pellegrino Acarelli, Tranquillo Volterra, Sabbato Tarni, Emanuel Tedesco, Moise del Monte, Abram Abaot, Angelo

Coen, Angelo Terni, Haarone [?] Alpron, and Ezechia Ambron, ACDF, St. St. TT-4-C fasc. 4.
13. ACDF, St. St. TT-4-C, fasc. 4
14. ACDF, St. St. UV53, 410r–412v.
15. The hardships were often exaggerated in supplications; see Fosi, *Papal Justice*, 207.
16. ACDF, St. St. UV53, 411r–v.
17. On the Jews' trust in the Holy Office, see, for example, Marina Caffiero, *Battesimi forzati: Storie di ebrei, cristiani e convertiti nella Roma dei papi* (Rome: Viella, 2004), esp. 30–31. On the moderating effect of the Holy Office, see also Fosi, *Papal Justice*, ch. 7.
18. ACDF, St. St. UV53, 410r, 411r–412r.
19. ACDF, St. St. TT-4-C, fasc. 4. In 1728, Jews requested a copy of the document. For information about the timeline, see ASCER, 1Qc fasc. 10, coll. 1 inf. 4.
20. On Tranquillo Vita Corcos, see Abraham Berliner, *Geschichte der Juden in Rom von der ältesten Zeit bis zur gegenwart: zwei Bände in einem Band* (Georg Olms, 1893), II: 69–82.
21. On the Sacra Consulta, see Fosi, *Papal Justice*, 184–187.
22. Tranquillo Vita Corcos, *Alla Sacra Consvlta Illustriss., e Reuerendiss. Monsig. Ghezzi Ponente per l'vniuersità degl'hebrei di Roma. Memoriale* (Rome: Stamperia della Reu. Cam. Apostolica 1705), Ar. Henceforth, Corcos, *Memoriale 1705*.
23. The *Memoriale* has September 9, 1236, with the year added by hand. See the copy at Houghton Library at Harvard University, IC7.C8116.705m.
24. Shlomo Simonsohn, *The Apostolic See and the Jews: Documents, 492–1404* (Toronto: Pontifical Institute of Mediaeval Studies, 1988), 165, no. 155.
25. Solomon Grayzel, *The Church and the Jews in the XIIIth Century: A Study of Their Relations during the Years 1198–1254* (Philadelphia: Dropsie College, 1933), 268–271.
26. ASCER, 1Ql fasc. 11 coll. 1 inf. 5, unnumbered pages. On Jacob ben Naftali's mission, see Majer Bałaban, *Le-toledot ha-tenu`ah ha-frankit* (Tel-Aviv: Dvir, 1934–1935), 130.
27. The manuscript of the Italian translation of the general's letter to Poland, ASCER 1Va fasc. 13, coll. 2 inf. 2. The Latin document and its German translation are published in Moritz Stern, *Die Päpstlichen Bullen über die Blutbeschuldigung* (Munich: August Schupp, 1900), 134–137.
28. Corcos, *Sommario*.
29. Corcos, *Memoriale 1705*, Av.
30. Isaac Cardoso, *Las excelencias de los hebreos* (Amsterdam: David de Castro Tartas, 1679), 426–429; on Simon of Trent, 410, 413. On Cardoso's *Las excelencias*, see Yosef Hayim Yerushalmi, *From Spanish Court to Italian Ghetto: Isaac Cardoso, a Study in Seventeenth-Century Marranism and Jewish Apologetics* (Seattle: University of Washington Press, 1981).
31. Corcos, *Memoriale 1705*, Av–A2v. For an earlier use of this argument, see Grayzel, *The Church and the Jews*, fragment quoted on 274–275.

32. Thomas Aquinas, *Summa theologica*, I-IIae Q. 102, Art. 3, response to objection 8.
33. Corcos, *Memoriale 1705*, A2r–A3v. Cf. Thomas Aquinas, *Summa theologica*, Prima Secundae, Question 102, Art. 3, response to objection 8.
34. Corcos, *Memoriale 1705*, A3v. See Chapter 5 and a discussion of this argument in Solomon ibn Verga's *Shevet Yehudah*. For rabbinic sources of this teaching, see BT Ketubot 60a and BT Kerithot 21b–22a.
35. Corcos, *Memoriale 1705*, verso of a page following A3v.
36. Corcos, *Memoriale 1705*.
37. Corcos, *Memoriale 1705*, second to last page.
38. Tranquillo Vita Corcos, *Alla Sagra Consvlta Illustriss. e Reverendiss. Monsignor Ghezzi Ponente per l'vniuersità degli ebrei. Memoriale additionale ad altro dato li 26. settembre 1705* (Rome: Nella stamperia della Rev. Cam. apostolica, 1706); Henceforth, Corcos, *Memoriale Additionale*. For the manuscript version of the *Sommario*, see ASCER, 1 Va fasc. 13 coll 2 inf 2.
39. Corcos, *Sommario*; Corcos, *Memoriale Additionale*.
40. Corcos, *Memoriale Additionale*, A2r.
41. Corcos's rabbinic sources included Maimonides' *Mishneh Torah*, Jacob ben Asher's *Arba'a Turim*, Joseph Caro's *Shulḥan 'Arukh*, and several other works; Corcos, *Memoriale Additionale*, A2r–v.
42. Corcos, *Memoriale Additionale*, A3v–A4r.
43. Corcos, *Memoriale Additionale*, two pages from the end.
44. The bull of February 1, 1589, granting Paolo Blado the office of the Official Apostolic Printer specified what the press would be responsible for publishing; Valentino Romani, "Per lo Stato e per la Chiesa: La Tipografia della Reverenda Camera Apostolica e le altre tipografie pontificie (Secc. XVI–XVIII)," *Il Bibliotecario* 2 (1998): 177.
45. Romani, "Per lo Stato e per la Chiesa," 183.
46. Corcos, *Memoriale 1705*. Based on the specific note in the expanded version of this text published in 1706, this document was written or published on September 26, 1705. Copies of Corcos's publications can also be found in ASV, Fondo Garampi 259. On Corcos and his treatises, see Caffiero, "Alle origini dell'antisemitismo politico," 33–36, 39–41; and her *Battesimi forzati*, 46–47.
47. Giovanni Pastrizio's correspondence and notes related to his study of Jewish books, including from 1681 a series of letters about Jewish customs with Giulio Morosini—a Jewish convert to Christianity and the author of *Via della Fede* published in 1683 in Rome—are preserved in the ASV; his correspondence with Jewish book dealers reveals much about the early modern Hebrew book trade. Biblioteca Apostolica Vaticana (henceforth BAV), Borg. Lat 481, esp. 172r–174r, commentaries on the famous singer Melchiore Pallantrotti's (Palantrotti) anti-Jewish songs; 336r–360r, 448r–466r, 472r–477r on Jewish books and calendars. For his correspondence with Giulio Morosini, see BAV Borg. Lat. 503, 27r–38r, 40r–62v.
48. For an example of such an opinion, see ASV, Archivio Nunziatura Varsavia 94.

49. Andreas Alberettus, *Sacra Consulta sive Illustriss. Et Revedendiss. D. Ghezzio Ponente Viterben. calumniae super praetensa attentata iugulatione pro Gioiello de Core et Iosepho Samen haebreis contra fiscum et illi adhaeren. restrictus Facti et iuris* (Rome: Typis Reverendae Camerae Apostolicae, 1706), A1r-v.
50. Alberettus, *Sacra Consulta*, A1v–A2v.
51. Alberettus, *Sacra Consulta*, A4r.
52. Alberettus, *Sacra Consulta*, A5v. See also *Sacra Consulta sive illustriss. et revedendiss. D. Ghezzio Ponente Viterben. calumniae super praetensa attentata Iugulatione pro Gioiello de Core et Iosepho Samen Haebreis. Summarium* (Rome: Typis Reverendae Camerae Apostolicae, 1706). Henceforth, *Summarium*. A copy can be found in ASCER, 2Vi fasc. 9 coll. 10 sup. 2.
53. Alberettus, *Sacra Consulta*, A3v.
54. Alberettus, *Sacra Consulta*, 11 unnumbered. The last two pages contain a summary of all the inconsistencies in nine points.
55. Alberettus, *Sacra Consulta*, 13ff unnumbered. A lengthy discussion of the two questionable witnesses and the ramifications of their testimonies follows.
56. Alberettus, *Sacra Consulta*, unnumbered.
57. Alberettus, *Sacra Consulta*, unnumbered second to last page.
58. ASCER 2Vi fasc. 9, coll. 10 sup. 2.
59. *Summarium*, in ASCER 2Vi fasc. 9, coll. 10 sup. 2.
60. *Summarium*, unnumbered 17.
61. *Summarium*, unnumbered 17–18.
62. *Summarium*, unnumbered 19–20.
63. ASCER, 1Qc fasc. 10 coll. 1 inf. 4.
64. ASCER, 1Qc fasc. 10 coll. 1 inf. 4.
65. *Alla Sagra Consulta per Gioiello di Core. Memoriale* (Rome: Stamperia della Rev. Camera Apostolica, 1706) (henceforth, *Memoriale per Gioiello di Core*). A copy can be found in ASCER, 1Qc fasc. 10. coll. 1 inf. 4.
66. *Memoriale per Gioiello di Core*, 1r. On this, see also Antonio Pertile, *Storia del diritto italiano: dalla caduta dell'Impero Romano alla codificazione*, ed. Pasquale del Giudice (Torino: Unione tipografico-editrice, 1902), 152–153.
67. The quote from the Statute of Rome—"Ex eorum [senator vel judex] pro innocentia investigare et indagare testes de veritate informatos per quoscumque aliorum notitiam deducantur, examinare teneantur, et debeant, et non praeterire testem, et testium dicta pro innocentia deponents"—can be found in *Memoriale per Gioiello di Core*, 1v.
68. *Memoriale per Gioiello di Core*, 2r.
69. Pavoncello, "Una 'accusa del sangue' a Viterbo nel 1705," 227, 232–233. The financial weight of the affair was also noted in *Memoriale per Gioiello di Core*.
70. ACDF, St. St. TT-4-C, fasc. 4: Florence contributed 150.55 scudi, Mantova, 95, Reggio 52, Ancona 80, Venice 33.20, Livorno 125, Ferrara 70, Lugo 35, Cento 23.50, Verona 29.20, Fiorenzola and Piacenza together 41, Modena 40, Pesaro 40, Casale 33.32, Senigalia 20, and Siena 122.91. Mantua initially offered 50 scudi, Simonsohn, *History of the Jews in the Duchy of Mantua*, 438.

71. ASCER, 1Va fasc. 13, coll. 2 inf. 2, in Italian, and in Latin, in Corcos, *Sommario*, no. 3. Guidetti, *Pro Judaeis*, 303–304.
72. Guidetti, *Pro Judaeis*, 290–291. On the case that prompted the decree, see Chapter 3.
73. The dukes mistakenly dated Jewish settlement in Rome to the destruction of the temple in 70 CE. There is evidence of a Jewish presence in Rome as early as the second century B.C.E.
74. Corcos, *Sommario*, no. 4. Guidetti, *Pro Judaeis*, 295–298.
75. Many unbound copies are still preserved at the ASCER.
76. Copies of the supplication to the Pope Clement XI and the Holy Office, with a short summary of events can be found in ASV, Fondo Garampi 259, fasc. 6; ACDF St. St. BB 3f, fasc. 1. But a full record of the interrogations and testimonies is in Trinity College in Dublin, ms. 1260, 35r–106v (henceforth TCD 1260).
77. TCD 1260, 35r.
78. TCD 1260, 35v, and cf. Corcos, *Memoriale 1705*; Corcos, *Memoriale Additionale*.
79. The supplication preserved at the ASV contains only the printed copies of Corcos's treatises. The same is held in ACDF. But the records of the Holy Office, now preserved in Dublin, contain manuscript copies of the texts of the mentioned decrees along with Corcos's printed works, TCD 1260, 36r–67v. For example, the Trinity College file contains the full text of the emperors' decree, whereas Corcos's *Sommario* contains only the section directly addressing blood accusations.
80. TCD 1260, 69r.
81. TCD 1260, 70r–72v.
82. See another copy of the letter: TCD 1260, 78v–79v.
83. TCD 1260, 71v.
84. TCD 1260, 72r.
85. TCD 1260, 73r–74r and also 79v–80v.
86. TCD 1260, 73v–74r.
87. On June 3, the Holy Office approved the decision, and on June 6, a letter forwarding a copy of the letter to Ancona was composed and signed by Cardinal Marescotti. It seems to have reached Ancona on June 10. TCD 1260, 75v, 76v, 78r.
88. Letter from Ancona to the Holy Office in Rome from June 21, 1711, TCD 1260, 77r.
89. TCD 1260, 80v–81v.
90. He later said they fit the older daughter but "they did not go on the younger daughter's feet."
91. TCD 1260, 83r–84r.
92. TCD 1260, 84r–85v.
93. TCD 1260, 86r–88r.
94. TCD 1260, 88r–92r.
95. TCD 1260, 93r.
96. The cover letter attached to the testimony is on TCD 1260, 95r; the testimony is on 96r–97v.

97. *The Historical Register*, no. XXIV (1721), 347–348.
98. Caliò, "L'omicidio rituale nell'Italia del settecento," esp. 478–479; Caliò, *La leggenda dell'ebreo assassino*, esp. 85.
99. IV Lateran Council, Canon 18. Norman P. Tanner, *Decrees of the Ecumenical Councils* (Washington, DC: Georgetown University Press, 1990).
100. Fosi, *Papal Justice*, 2.
101. By the middle of the eighteenth century, there was a saying that championed the weakness of the Polish state: "Polska nierządem stoi" (Poland stands by the lack of government [anarchy]). On this topic in English, see Jerzy Lukowski, *Disorderly Liberty: The Political Culture of the Polish-Lithuanian Commonwealth in the Eighteenth Century* (London: Bloomsbury, 2010).

8. The "Enlightenment" Pope Benedict XIV and the Blood Accusation

1. A classic example of this adulation is Renée Haynes, *Philosopher King: The Humanist Pope Benedict XIV* (London: Weidenfeld and Nicolson, 1970). For the most recent example, see Rebecca Marie Messbarger, Christopher M. S. Johns, and Philip Gavitt, eds., *Benedict XIV and the Enlightenment: Art, Science, and Spirituality* (Toronto: University of Toronto Press, 2016). Typically, and still strikingly, not a single chapter in this volume is devoted to Jews, a topic that would have tarnished the premise of the book.
2. For example, Mario Rosa, "La Santa Sede e gli ebrei nel settecento," *Storia d'Italia: Annali* 11–12, no. Gli ebrei in Italia (1997): 1069–1087; Marina Caffiero, *Battesimi forzati: storie di ebrei, cristiani e convertiti nella Roma dei papi* (Forced Baptisms] (Rome: Viella, 2004); Nicola Cusumano, "I papi e le accuse di omicidio rituale: Benedetto XIV e la bolla 'Beatus Andreas,'" *Dimensioni e problemi della ricerca storica* 1 (2002): 7–35; Nicola Cusumano, *Ebrei e accusa di omicidio rituale nel settecento: il carteggio tra Girolamo Tartarotti e Benedetto Bonelli, 1740–1748* (Milan: UNICOPLI, 2012).
3. The work consists of four volumes, *libri*, in five tomes; Prospero (Benedict XIV) Lambertini, *De servorum Dei beatificatione et beatorum canonizatione* (Bologna: Formis Longhi excusoris archiepiscopalis, 1734–1738). The first volume of a modern bilingual Latin-Italian edition appeared in 2010, with the rest to follow; Pope Benedict XIV, *De servorum Dei beatificatione et beatorum canonizatione* (Vatican City: Libreria editrice vaticana, 2010–).
4. Benedict XIV, *De servorum Dei*, I/1, 302. Lib. I, cap. XIII, no. 9.
5. Benedict XIV, *De servorum Dei*, vol. III/1, 161. Lib. III, cap. VII. no. 2. A full chapter devoted to *Promotor Fidei* is in Lib. I, cap. XVIII.
6. Benedict XIV, *De servorum Dei*, I/1. Lib. I. cap. V.
7. Benedict XIV, *De servorum Dei*, I/1, 119. Lib. I, cap. II, no. 7.
8. Benedict XIV, *De servorum Dei*, III/1. Lib. III. caps. XI–XVIII.
9. Benedict XIV, *De servorum Dei*, I/1, 320. Lib I, cap. XIV, no. 1.
10. Benedict XIV, *De servorum Dei*, I/1, 322–323. Lib. I, cap. XIV, no. 3.
11. Benedict XIV, *De servorum Dei*, III/1.Lib. III, cap. XIV.

12. Benedict XIV, *De servorum Dei*, I/1, 324–325. Lib. I, cap. XIV, no. 4.
13. Benedict XIV, *De servorum Dei*, I/1, 325–329. Lib. I, cap. XIV, nos. 4–5. This erroneous date is also in the 1734 edition.
14. Benedict XIV, *De servorum Dei*, I/1, 329. Lib. I, cap. XIV, no. 5.
15. Benedict XIV, *De servorum Dei*, I/1, 303. Lib. I, cap. XIII, no. 10.
16. Benedict XIV, *De servorum Dei*, III/1, 375, 377, 381. Lib. III, cap. XV, no. 4, 5, 6.
17. Benedict XIV, *De servorum Dei*, III/1, 380. Lib. III, cap. XV, no. 6. Lambertini referred here to ASV, A.A. Arm I–XVIII 6495, "Processus et sentential contra quosdam Hebraeos qui in Civitate Tridentina immanter occiderun puerum duorum annorum Christianum nomine Simonem, die veneris sancti die 24 Martii 1475," discussed in Chapter 2.
18. Benedict XIV, *De servorum Dei*, III/1, 380. Lib. III, cap. XV, no. 6.
19. Benedict XIV, *De servorum Dei*, I/2, 95–100. Lib. I, cap. XLII, nos. 8–10.
20. Lambertini, *De servorum Dei*, vol. IV, part II, 153. Lib. IV, pars Secunda, cap. XVII, no. 15.
21. Maria Pia Donato, "Reorder and Restore: Benedict XIV, the Index, and the Holy Office," in *Benedict XIV and the Enlightenment* (Toronto: University of Toronto Press, 2016), 227–252; Maria Pia Donato, "Gli "strumenti" della politica di Benedetto XIV: Il 'Giornale De' Letterati' (1742–1759)," *Dimensioni e problemi della ricerca storica*, no. 1 (1997): 39–61. Also see Caffiero, *Forced Baptisms*, 4. Lambertini's historical overview of the development of formal procedures was also designed to show that, even in the earliest days of the Christian Church, information about candidates for sainthood was sent to the bishop of Rome, the pope, "because decisions of the individual bishops about the veneration of martyrs and confessors could not have authority in the universal Church." Benedict XIV, *De servorum Dei*, on I/1, 196. Lib. I, cap. VII, no. 1, also cap. IV.
22. Benedict XIV, *De servorum Dei*, III/1, 380. Lib. III, cap. XV, no. 6.
23. Benedict XIV, *De servorum Dei*, I/1, 612–613. Lib. I, cap. XXIX, no. 13.
24. Cusumano, *Ebrei e accusa di omicidio rituale*.
25. On Abeles, see Elisheva Carlebach, *The Death of Simon Abeles: Jewish-Christian Tension in Seventeenth Century Prague* (New York: Center for Jewish Studies, City Universiy of New York, 2001); Howard Louthan, *Converting Bohemia: Force and Persuasion in the Catholic Reformation* (Cambridge: Cambridge University Press, 2011), 301–316; Rachel L. Greenblatt, *To Tell Their Children: Jewish Communal Memory in Early Modern Prague* (Stanford: Stanford University Press, 2014), 161–165.
26. Their reports were published in Joannes Eder, *Virilis constantia pueri duodennis Simonis Abeles in odium fidei ‡ judaeo parente Lazaro Abeles: Pragae crudeliter occisi 21 februarij anno 1694* (Prague: Typis Universitatis Carolo-Ferdinandeae, 1696), 37–38, 39–40, 44–47; Joannes Eder and Paolo Medici, *Patimenti e morte di Simone Abeles*, trans. Paolo Medici (Firenze: Piero Martini, 1705), 62, 65–66, 73–77.
27. Eder, *Virilis Constantia*, ch. XVII; Eder and Medici, *Patimenti*, ch. XVII. ARSI, Boh 108-I, 273–276, 466–467. See also Louthan, *Converting Bohemia*, 303.
28. Carlebach, *The Death of Simon Abeles*, 37. Greenblatt, *To Tell Their Children*, 162–164.

29. On this, see Louthan, *Converting Bohemia*, 305–310. For example, *Crudelis judaeorum perfidia amabili christianae fidei constantia ab hebraeo adolescente Simone Abeles superata, pro theatro exhibita ab infima grammatices classe, Collegii Academici Societatis Jesu, Olomucii Anno M.DCC.XXXVI*, (Prague, 1736). See also Marcin Zgliński, "Nagrobki i kult ofiar rzekomych żydowskich morgów rytualnych na historycznych ziemiach litewskich XVII-XIX wieku," in *Socialiniu Tapatumu Represnetacijos: Lietuvos Didžiosios Kunigaikštystes Kulturoje* (Vilnius: 2010), 321–327.
30. The judicial narrative was *Processus inquisitorius* (Prague: Endter, 1696). The narrative focusing on Simon Abeles's "martyrdom" and apotheosis was authored by the Jesuit Eder, *Virilis constantia;* Eder and Medici, *Patimenti*.
31. Carlebach, *The Death of Simon Abeles*, 33–34.
32. Rachel Greenblatt discusses this song in detail, Greenblatt, *To Tell Their Children*, 162–165.
33. On the medieval tropes of martyrdom and sacrifice in Judaism, see Israel Jacob Yuval, *Two Nations in Your Womb: Perceptions of Jews and Christians in Late Antiquity and the Middle Ages* (Berkeley: University of California Press, 2006); Jeremy Cohen, *Sanctifying the Name of God: Jewish Martyrs and Jewish Memories of the First Crusade* (Philadelphia: University of Pennsylvania Press, 2006).
34. On *Maximi fructus monitum,* see Chapter 6. Cardinal Ganganelli mentioned it in 1759 in his report; Cecil Roth, *The Ritual Murder Libel and the Jew* (London: Woburn Press, 1935), 52.
35. See Chapter 6.
36. Johann Christoph Wagenseil, *Benachrichtigungen wegen einiger die Judenschafft angehenden wichtigen Sachen* (Leipzig: Heinichen, 1705), 28ff. On Wagenseil and Sulzbach, see R. Po-chia Hsia, *The Myth of Ritual Murder: Jews and Magic in Reformation Germany* (New Haven: Yale University Press, 1988), 216.
37. Wagenseil, *Benachrichtigungen*. Part two starts on p. 127.
38. Wagenseil, *Benachrichtigungen*, 166–173, 191–192.
39. Wagenseil, *Benachrichtigungen*, 150–152, 172–196.
40. Wagenseil, *Benachrichtigungen*, 189ff. I discuss the role of Tiberino's narrative above in Chapter 2.
41. Wagenseil, *Benachrichtigungen*, 182.
42. Jacques Basnage, *Histoire des juifs 9,2 (13)* (La Haye: Scheurleer, 1716), ch. XIII, no. XVII, 371–393. Also see Jacques Basnage, *Histoire des juifs 9,3* (La Haye: Scheurleer, 1716), 914–915; Adam Sutcliffe, *Judaism and Enlightenment* (Cambridge: Cambridge University Press, 2004), 84.
43. Basnage, *Histoire des juifs 9,2 (13)*, 371–372.
44. Basnage, *Histoire des juifs*, 374.
45. Basnage, *Histoire des juifs*, 375.
46. Basnage, *Histoire des juifs*, 375–378. Hugh in Lincoln in 1255 was the first such case, according to Basnage.
47. Basnage, *Histoire des juifs*, 376.
48. Although enmity and political and economic goals might have been behind the murder accusations, theological benefits motivated host desecration accusa-

tions. Basnage asked, "But of what utility was this crime to the Jews, who thereby exposed themselves most surely to the most cruel tortures? It seems that the Jews have fallen into such excesses, only to give the Transubstantiers an opportunity to persecute them." Basnage, *Histoire des juifs* 9,2 *(13)*, 381. Recently Mitchell Merback argued that stories of host desecration were frequently manufactured postfactum to justify anti-Jewish violence; Mitchell B. Merback, *Pilgrimage & Pogrom: Violence, Memory, and Visual Culture at the Host-Miracle Shrines of Germany and Austria* (Chicago: University of Chicago Press, 2012).

49. Eder and Medici, *Patimenti*. On the events of 1705, see Chapter 7.
50. Paolo Sebastiano Medici, *Riti e costumi degli ebrei confutati* (Madrid: Luc'Antonio de Bedmar, 1737), 82–83. I use the 1737 edition, because it is also the one used by Benedetto Bonelli in his work on Simon of Trent. On Medici and Abeles, see Marina Caffiero, "Alle origini dell'antisemitismo politico: L'accusa di omicidio rituale nel sei-settecento tra autodifesa degli ebrei e pronunciamenti papali," in *Les racines chrétiennes de l'antisemitisme politique (fin XIXe–XXe siècle)* (Rome: Ecole française de Rome, 2003), 30–32.
51. Medici, *Riti e costumi* (1737), 323.
52. Giulio Morosini, *Via della fede mostrata agli ebrei* (Rome: Nella Stamparia della Sacra Congregazione de Propaganda Fide, 1683), 1394–1403, esp. 1398. Although Morosini denied blood accusations, he did not deny the killing *in odio*.
53. "La morale giudaica e il mistero di sangue," *La civiltà cattolica* V (1893): 273.
54. Benedetto Bonelli, *Dissertazione apologetica: sul martirio del Beato Simone da Trento nell'anno MCCCCLXXV da gli ebrei ucciso* (Trent: Per Gianbattista Parone Stampator vescovile, 1747). Medici's statement is on p. 19; On Bonelli, see Cusumano, *Ebrei e accusa di omicidio rituale*.
55. Bonelli devoted only one chapter of just over forty pages to Basnage, but nearly two hundred pages to Wagenseil.
56. Some of this effort is described in Bonelli's correspondence with the learned Girolamo Trattarotti, published in the source appendix in Cusumano, *Ebrei e accusa di omicidio rituale*.
57. Cusumano, *Ebrei e accusa di omicidio rituale*, 221.
58. Cusumano, *Ebrei e accusa di omicidio rituale*, 222.
59. Bonelli, *Dissertazione apologetica*, 36–37.
60. Bonelli, *Dissertazione apologetica*, 31.
61. Bonelli, *Dissertazione apologetica*, 179 ff.
62. Bonelli, *Dissertazione apologetica*, 187–188.
63. Bonelli, *Dissertazione apologetica*, 179–180, also in a different context, 207–211.
64. Bernhard Fresacher, *Anderl von Rinn: Ritualmordkult und Neuorientierung in Judenstein 1945–1995* (Innsbruck-Wien: Tyrolia-Verlag, 1998), 19. M. A. Katritzky, *Healing, Performance and Ceremony in the Writings of Three Early Modern Physicians: Hippolytus Guarinonius and the Brothers Felix and Thomas Platter* (Farnham, UK: Ashgate, 2012), 90.
65. Katritzky, *Healing*, 91. See also Zgliński, "Nagrobki i kult ofiar," 318–322. Georg R. Schroubek, "The Question of Historicity of Andrew of Rinn," in

Ritual Murder: Legend in European History, ed. Susanna Buttaroni and Stanisław Musiał (Cracow: Association for Cultural Initiatives, 2003), 159–180.
66. Ignatius Zach, *Ausführliche Beschreibung der Marter, eines heiligen und unschuldigen Kinds Andreae, von Rinn, in Tyrol, und bistumb Brixen: Welches von denen Juden aus angebohrnem Hass gegen Christum, und gesambten seiner Christenheit Grausam Gequälet und ermordet worden* (Augsburg: Verlag Matthias Wolff, 1724).
67. Benedict XIV, *De servorum Dei*, III/1, 378. Lib. III, cap. XV, no. 6.
68. The image of the killing was covered up when the cult was abolished in 1989; for the remaining three images, see Fresacher, *Anderl von Rinn*, 11, 15, 16.
69. Hadrian Kembter, *Acta pro veritate martyrii corporis & cultus publici B. Andreae Rinnensis pueruli anno MCCCCLXII Die 12. Julii in odium fidei occisi, collecta, variis notis illustrata & proposita ab Adriano Kembter* (Oeniponti: Wagner, 1745).
70. Benedict XIV, *De servorum Dei*, III/1, 378. Lib. III, cap. XV, no. 6.
71. He discussed it in his letter *Beatus Andreas;* Pope Benedict XIV, *Benedicti XIV Pont. Opt. Max. olim prosperi cardinalis de Lambertinis bullarium*, 17 vols., vol. 3/2 (Prati: Typographia Aldina, 1847), 213–225. In Italian, Pope Benedict XIV, *Lettera della Santità di Nostro Signore Benedetto Papa XIV a Monsignore Benedetto Veterani Avvocato Concistoriale e Promotore della Fede* ([S.l.]: [s.n.], 1755).
72. "Beatus Andreas," § 4, in Benedict XIV, *Bullarium* 3/2, 214. The date in the Roman calendar is "decimo octavo kalendii Ianuarii 1753." The Italian version has a Gregorian date, Benedict XIV, *Lettera*, 7. The decree was printed in Rome; Pope Benedict XIV, *Officium proprium Beati Andreae innocentis, et martyris Rinnensis: a clero seculari, & regulari Diocesis Brixinensis die XII Julii recitandum/juxta S. D. N. Benedicti XIV decretum.* (Rome: ex Typographia Reverendae Camerae Apostolicae, 1754).
73. On *Beatus Andreas,* see Cusumano, *Ebrei e accusa di omicidio rituale;* Cusumano, "I papi e le accuse." On the cult of Andreas of Rinn, see Fresacher, *Anderl von Rinn*.
74. *Beatus Andreas* § 1, 5, 8, 13, 29, also less explicitly, § 10, 20, 23, 25,
75. Rosa, "La Santa Sede e gli ebrei nel settecento," 1072.
76. Rosa, "La Santa Sede e gli ebrei nel settecento," 1073. On this concern in Poland, see Magda Teter, *Jews and Heretics in Catholic Poland: A Beleaguered Church in the Post-Reformation Era* (New York: Cambridge University Press, 2006)
77. Rosa, "La Santa Sede e gli ebrei nel settecento," 1074–1077. See also Caffiero, "Alle origini dell'antisemitismo politico." On the conversionary tendencies, see also Caffiero, *Forced Baptisms*.
78. On the jubilee of 1750, see Stefania Nanni, "Anno di rinnovazione e di penitenza: anno di riconciliazione e di grazia: il giubileo del 1750," *Roma moderna e contemporanea* 5, nos. 2/3 (1997): 553–587.
79. ASV Segr. Stato Polonia 236, 5r–v, 30v; ASV Segr. Stato Polonia 263, 5; ASV Segr. Stato Polonia 379, 73r.

Notes to Pages 316–318   477

80. The encyclical from June 26, 1749, Pope Benedict XIV, *Benedicti XIV Pont. Opt. Max. olim Prosperi Cardinalis de Lambertinis bullarium*, 17 vols., vol. 3/1 (Prati: Typographia Aldina, 1847), § 16, 27, 29. pp. 118–132. On views of the Jews in Poland by nuncios, see for example, Henryk Damian Wojtyska, ed. *Aloisius Lippomano (1555–1557)*, vol. 3/1, 276–277.
81. Rosa, "La Santa Sede e gli ebrei nel settecento," 1077–1080. For the release of the encyclical, see ASV Segr. Stato Polonia 380, 231r, 227r–330v. *A Quo Primum* is discussed in Gershon David Hundert, *Jews in Poland-Lithuania in the Eighteenth Century: A Genealogy of Modernity* (Berkeley: University of California Press, 2004), 59–63; Teter, *Jews and Heretics*, 89–90. The dispatch from Rome contained two other communications from Benedict XIV, one regarding private prayer houses in home and another on an creation of two archbishoprics; ASV Segr. Stato Polonia 380, 213ff; for the encyclical against private prayer houses, see Benedict XIV, *Bullarium* 3/1, 286–296.
82. Benedict XIV, *Bullarium* 3/1, 298.
83. Benedict XIV, *Bullarium* 3/1, § 4–5 on 298–299.
84. "Contro la mente di Papa e il tenore della Pontificia nota lettera circolare," ASV Segr. Stato Polonia 368, 104v. For example, in 1752, a legal fight erupted over rebuilding a synagogue in Piotrków, ASV Segr. Stato Polonia 267, 101r–102v, 143r–144r
85. I. Galant, "Zhertvy ritualnogo obvinenya be Zaslave v 1747 g: po aktam Kievskago Tsentralnago Arkhiva," *Evreiskaia starina* 5, no. 2 (1912); I. Galant, "Ritual'nyi protsess v Dunaigorod'e 1748 godu," *Evreiskaia starina* 4 (1911). Also see Magda Teter, *Sinners on Trial: Sacrilege after the Reformation* (Cambridge, MA: Harvard University Press, 2011), 211ff.
86. Odoricus Rinaldi, *Annales ecclesiastici ab anno quo desinit Card. Caes. Baronius MCXCVIII usque ad annum MDXXXIV Tomus XIII* (Cologne: Sumptibus Ioannis Wilhelmi Friessem, 1692). *Sicut Iudaeis* is on 37 under 1199.54 and on 425 under 1235.20; *Lachrymabilem* on 441–442 under 1236.48; and the 1247 bull on 581 under 1247.83–84.
87. Kajetan Sołtyk et al., *Dekret o zamęczenie przez żydów dziecięcia katolickiego, ferowany w grodzie żytomirskim. a naprzod kopia listu I. W. Imci Xiędz Kaietana Sołtyka, Biskupa emauseńskiego, koadiutora kiiowskiego, do J. O. Xiążęcia Imci Arcybiskupa lwowskiego, z żytomierza; list do arcybiskupa lwowskiego* (1753). The text was more recently published in Zenon Guldon and Jacek Wijaczka, *Procesy o mordy rytualne w Polsce w XVI–XVIII Wieku* (Kielce: DCF, 1995). See also Hanna Węgrzynek, "Deputacje żydów polskich do stolicy apostolskiej w drugiej polowie XVIII w.," *Kwartalnik historii żydów*, no. 3 (2001): 320–321; Zgliński, "Nagrobki i kult ofiar," 329–330; Jolanta Żyndul, *Kłamstwo Krwi: Legenda Mordu Rytualnego Na Ziemiach Polskich w XIX i XX Wieku* (Warsaw: Wydawnictwo Cyklady, 2011), 42–43; Paweł Maciejko, *The Mixed Multitude: Jacob Frank and the Frankist Movement, 1755–1816* (Philadelphia: University of Pennsylvania Press, 2011), 103–104.
88. Sołtyk et al., *Dekret o zamęczenie,*]a[verso.
89. "w pień wyciąć" on]a[verso.
90. Sołtyk and al., *Dekret o zamęczenie,*]a[verso.

91. Sołtyk and al., *Dekret o zamęczenie*, Bv.
92. Sołtyk and al., *Dekret o zamęczenie*, "Relacya o exekucyi tegoż dekretu."
93. Zgliński, "Nagrobki i kult ofiar," 329–330. Żyndul, *Kłamstwo krwi*, 42–43, 261–262, and images following 262.
94. On Jewish reactions to this and other trials in the middle of the eighteenth century, see Węgrzynek, "Deputacje żydów polskich."
95. Letter from the Amsterdam Sephardic Jewish Community to the Sephardic community in Ferrara, July 16, 1753, translated by Evelyne Oliel Grausz, "Communication and Community: Multiplex Networks in the 18th Century Sephardi Diaspora," *Early Modern Workshop* 7 (2010), http://www.earlymodern.org.
96. Letter to the Sephardic community in Ferrara, July 16, 1753, in Oliel Grausz, "Communication and Community."
97. Letter to the Sephardic community in Ferrara, 14 Tammuz, 5513 (July 16, 1753), in Oliel Grausz, "Communication and Community."
98. ASV, Segr. Stato Polonia 382, 274r. For the text of the *memoriale*, see ASV Segr. Stato Polonia 266, 217r–v.
99. ASV Segr. Stato Polonia 266, 217r–v.
100. ASV SEgr. Stato Polonia 369, 230v; ASV Segr. Stato Polonia 266, 216r–v.
101. ASV, Segr. Stato Polonia 368, 53r–v.
102. ASV, Segr. Stato Polonia 369, 230v–231r.
103. ASV, Segr. Stato Polonia 370, 489r–v, also ASV, Segr. Stato Polonia 266, 226r.
104. ASV, Segr. Stato Polonia 382, 362r.
105. Benedict XIV, *De servorum Dei*, III/1, 378. Lib. III, cap. XV, no. 6.
106. ASV Nunziatura Varsavia 94, 24–32. Israel's name is spelled as "Isdrael."

9. Cardinal Ganganelli's Secret Report

1. Zelig's name appears differently in non-Jewish sources, Jacob Zelig, Selek, Zelikowicz, etc., but in Hebrew sources his name is consistently spelled as Eliyakim ben Asher Zelig.
2. Paweł Maciejko, *The Mixed Multitude: Jacob Frank and the Frankist Movement, 1755–1816* (Philadelphia: University of Pennsylvania Press, 2011), 103. The letters Zelig wrote from Rome in the spring and fall of 1758 are in Israel Halpern, ed., *Pinkas va'ad arb'a arazot* (Jerusalem: Mosad Bialik, 1945), 424–428, nos. 759–761. Although Majer Bałaban's account is not without errors, he seems to have understood that Jacob Eliyakim Zelig did not receive an audience with the pope; instead Jews in Italy were able to help him reach influential cardinals who helped pass this supplication along, Majer Bałaban, *Le-toledot ha-tenu`ah ha-frankit* (Tel-Aviv: Dvir, 1934–1935), 127–133. Still, the romantic idea that Zelig received an audience with the pope was embraced by others in Jewish historiography. Yet, as Irene Fosi has shown, the pope was removed from the process of hearing the petitions, a task that was entrusted to the curial officials, with "precise rules, ceremonies, and symbolic actions, all in the curia," Irene Fosi, *Papal Justice: Subjects and*

Courts in the Papal State, 1500–1750 (Washington, DC: Catholic University of America Press, 2011), 212.

3. For a letter of recommendation on behalf of Eliyakim ben Asher Zelig sent by Elia ben Raphael, the rabbi of Alexandria, from Baron Pier Guidobono Cavalchini Garofoli to Cardinal Guidobono Cavalchini, the prefect of the Congregation of the Bishops, see Umberto Cassuto, "Una lettera di racommandazione per un inviato degli ebrei polacchi al papa (1758)," *Rivista israelitica* (1904): 25–27.
4. ACDF, St.St. CC-5-R. Other copies of documentation related to Jacob Eliyakim Zelig's mission can also be found in ACDF, St. St. TT-2-D; St. St. TT-2-M, fasc. 3.
5. On Benedict XIV and *Beatus Andreas* see Chapter 8 and Nicola Cusumano, "I papi e le accuse di omicidio rituale: Benedetto XIV e la bolla 'Beatus Andreas,'" *Dimensioni e problemi della ricerca storica* 1 (2002).
6. The report was approved by the pope on January 10, 1760. See a letter of the papal nuncio in Poland, dated April 8, 1761, recounting the conversation, in ACDF, St. St. TT-2-D.
7. See Chapter 7.
8. ACDF, St. St. CC-5-R.
9. ACDF, St. St. CC-5-R. On the Viterbo case, see Chapter 7.
10. ACDF, St. St. CC-5-R.
11. On the 1711 Ancona case, see Chapter 7, and ACDF, St. St. BB-3-F. The records of the trial are in Trinity College Library, Dublin, Ms. 1260.
12. ACDF, St. St. CC-5-R.
13. ACDF, St. St. CC-5-R.
14. Pope Benedict XIV, *Benedicti XIV Bullarium*, 3/1, vol. III, part 2, 213.
15. ACDF, St. St. CC-5-R.
16. See an inserted sheet in ACDF, St. St. CC-5-R.
17. ACDF, St. St. T-2-D, document A.
18. ACDF, St. St. T-2-D, document B.
19. Prince Radziwiłł's order dated May 25, 1756, to investigate the case is found in AGAD, Archiwum Radziwiłłowskie XXIX, 9, fol. 83. I thank Adam Teller from Brown University for pointing me to this source. An account of the case in Italian is in ASV, Archivio Nunziatura di Varsovia 94, fols. 19r–21r. Some scholars mistakenly claimed that the Jampol case involved a child. Maciejko, *Mixed Multitude*, 103.
20. ACDF, St. St. T-2-D, document C.
21. On the role of the clergy in "blood" cases, see canon 18 in the IV Lateran Council. See also Chapter 6.
22. ACDF, St. St. T-2-D, document C.
23. For Bishop Sołtyk's gambling problem, see Maciejko, *Mixed Multitude*, 103; Majer Bałaban, "Studien und quellen zur Frankistichen Bewegung in Polen," in *Livre d'hommage a la memoire du Dr. Samuel Poznański (1864–1921)* (Warsaw: Otto Harrassowitz, 1927), 44.
24. ACDF, St. St. T-2-D, document C.
25. ACDF, St. St. T-2-D, document C.

26. ASV, Nunziatura di Varsovia 94, fols. 24r–27v.
27. ACDF, St. St. T-2-D, document D. The document can be found in three versions: the Polish original, one Latin translation made in Poland, and one copy of the Latin transcribed by the same scribe who prepared the rest of the documents. The Polish copy has Hebrew writing on it, which says that the document contains evidence against libels against Jews. Another transcript of the affair, made by the apostolic notary in Warsaw, Joseph Augustynowicz, can be found in ASV, Archivio Nunziatura di Varsovia 94, fols. 30r–32r.
28. ACDF, St. St. T-2-D, document dated on top, September 24, 1759.
29. For the most recent study of Frankism, see Maciejko, *Mixed Multitude;* chapter 4 addresses the question of the blood libel and Frankism. See also Bałaban, *Le-toledot ha-tenu`ah ha-frankit,* esp. 241–275, 282–292. The Talmud was condemned in a 1240 disputation in Paris and then in 1553 in Rome; see Kenneth R. Stow, *Jewish Life in Early Modern Rome: Challenge, Conversion, and Private Life* (Burlington, VT: Ashgate, 2007), ch. 1. For primary sources regarding the Paris disputation, see Robert Chazan, Jean Hoff, and John Friedman, *The Trial of the Talmud: Paris, 1240* (Toronto: Pontifical Institute of Mediaeval Studies, 2012).
30. On this, see Maciejko, *Mixed Multitude,* chs. 1–2.
31. Gaudenty Pikulski, *Złość żydowska przeciwko Bogu i bliźniemu prawdzie y sumieniu na obwinienie Talmudystow na dowód ich zaślepienia y religii dalekiey od prawa bożego przez Moyżesza danego* (Lwów: Jan Szlichtyn, 1760), 142.
32. Maciejko, *Mixed Multitude,* 66.
33. ASV, Segr. Stato Polonia 271, 66r–80v. On the debate in Kamieniec and its aftermath, see Maciejko, *Mixed Multitude,* ch. 3; Bałaban, *Le-toledot ha-tenu`ah ha-frankit,* 137–151.
34. ASV, Segr. Stato Polonia 271, 70v–71r, 72v–73r.
35. ASV, Segr. Stato Polonia 271, 75r–v. Marquardus de Susannis, *Tractatus de iudaeis et aliis infidelibus* (Venice: apud Cominum de Tridino Montisferrati, 1558), part I, chapter 7, no. 2, on 25. The first expulsion of Jews from France was in 1182.
36. ASV Segr. Stato Polonia 271, 75v.
37. ASV Segr. Stato Polonia 271, 76r–v.
38. ASV Segr. Stato Polonia 271, 77r–78v.
39. On the mission of Barukh Mi-Ereẓ Yavan to Nuncio Serra in Warsaw, see Maciejko, *Mixed Multitude,* 31; Paweł Maciejko, "Baruch Yavan and the Frankist Movement: Intercession in an Age of Upheaval," *Yearbook of the Simon Dubnow Institute* 4 (2005). The petition is in ASV, Acta Nunziatura Varsavia, 94, 153r–v, published in Maciejko, "Baruch Yavan," 353–354. No mention of this contact can be found in the 1757 dispatches, see ASV Segr. Stato Polonia 270.
40. ASV, Segr. Stato Polonia 271, 66r–80v.
41. Pikulski, *Złość żydowska,* part I, ch. IX. ASV, Segr. Stato Polonia 271, 322r–324v.
42. Pikulski, *Złość żydowska,* 148–149.
43. Supplication to the King, Pikulski, *Złość żydowska,* 153.

44. ASV, Segr. Stato Polonia 271, 322r–324v. Karaite Jews were a sect that emerged in the ninth century and rejected the teachings of the Talmud.
45. *Supplex libellus: a iudaeis Fidem Catholicam amplectentibus et baptismum expetentibus, Illustrissimo et Reverendissimo D. D. Łubieński Archi-Episcopo Leopoliensi, nunc celsissimo nominato principi primati porrectus* (1759). ASV, Segr. Stato Polonia 271, 324r.
46. ASV Segr Stato Polonia 237, 61v–62r.
47. Copies of the supplication of May 16, 1759, in French and Italian are in ASV, Segr. Stato Polonia 272, 35r–42v. The sectarians were referred to as anti-Talmudists by both Jews and Christians. Bałaban, *Le-toledot ha-tenu`ah ha-frankit,* 252.
48. The Polish text was published in Pikulski, *Złość żydowska,* 158–169. A printed Latin copy of *Manifestatio judaeorum cathechumenorum ex consistorii Leopol: extracta* (1759), in ASV Segr. Stato Polonia 272, 56r–59v. See also Maciejko, *Mixed Multitude,* 107–126.
49. ASV Segr. Stato Polonia 272, 59r, and Pikulski, *Złość żydowska,* 167–168. The seven points are summarized in Maciejko, *Mixed Multitude,* 108, and his "Frankism," *YIVO Encyclopedia.*
50. ASV Segr. Stato Polonia 272, 92r–93v. See also Augustin Theiner, *Vetera monumenta Poloniae et Lithuaniae gentiumque finitimarum historiam illustrantia maximam partem nondum,* 4 vols. (Rome: Typis Vaticanis, 1860–1864), 4: 155. This was also the amount mentioned in a later account by Ber of Bolechów, in which he said that a deal was reached between Stanisław Mikulski, the administrator of the Lwów diocese and the moderator of the debate, and the Jewish leaders represented by the chief rabbi of Lwów, Hayyim Cohen Rapoport. Ber of Bolechów, however, implied that the money was used to soften Mikulski to be favorable to Jews during the debate, Bałaban, *Le-toledot ha-tenu`ah ha-frankit,* 251–252.
51. ASV Segr. Stato Polonia 272, 93r–v.
52. See the letter of Stanisław Mikulski informing the nuncio about the July debate and the letter from Nuncio Serra to Secretary of State Torrigiani dated August 15, 1759, ASV Segr. Stato Polonia 272, 60r–61v, 106r.
53. Pikulski, *Złość żydowska,* 268–269.
54. ASV Segr. Stato Polonia 272, 107r.
55. Pikulski, *Złość żydowska,* 296–314. On the Jews' choice to use Christian authorities in defense, see Bałaban, *Le-toledot ha-tenu`ah ha-frankit,* 253. On Grotius, see Chapter 6.
56. Pikulski, *Złość żydowska,* 303.
57. Serra's dispatches of September 12, September 19, and September 26, 1759. The following dispatches from October and November only report on Jacob Frank and his followers. ASV Segr. Stato Polonia 272.
58. ASV Segr. Stato Polonia 237, 74v.
59. ASV Segr. Stato Polonia 272, 230r–v. Cf., Maciejko, *Mixed Multitude,* 114.
60. Pikulski, *Złość żydowska,* part I, ch. X.
61. ASV Segr. Stato Polonia 272, 237r. The troubling documents regarding the new converts included a Latin translation of a letter that some of Gaudenty Pikulski's

informants about Frank and his followers gave to Pikulski. ASV Segr. Stato Polonia 272, 239r–240v. For the Polish texts, see Pikulski, *Złość żydowska*, 327–333.
62. ASV Segr. Stato Polonia 272, 259v. See Maciejko, *Mixed Multitude*, esp. chs. 5–6.
63. Roth, *Ritual Murder*, 42, cf. 70. Vincenzo Manzini, *L'omicidio rituale e i sacrifici umani con particolare riguardo alle accuse contro gli ebrei: ricerche storiche-sociologiche* (Torino: Fratelli Bocca, 1925), 234.
64. Roth, *Ritual Murder*, 62.
65. Roth, *Ritual Murder*, 89.
66. My translation of the Italian. Roth mistranslated the sentence, *Ritual Murder*, 59, cf. 89.
67. "Memoriale del padre Virgulti," in Domenico Rocciolo, "Documenti sui catecumeni e neofiti a roma nel seicento e settecento," *Ricerche per la storia religiosa di Roma* 10 (1998): 428–432.
68. See for example, Antonius Pagius, *Critica historico-chronologica in universos annales ecclesiasticos emminentissimi et reverendissimi Caesaris Cardinalis Baronii in qua rerum narratio defenditur, illustratur, suppletur, ordo temporum corrigitur, innovatur, et periodo graeco-romana, nunc primum concinnata munitur* (Cologne: Allobrogum sumptibus Fratrum de Tournes, 1727); Abraham Bzowski, *Annalium ecclesiasticorum post Illustriss. et Reverend. Dominum D. Caesare Baronium . . . Tomus XIII* (Cologne: Agrippinae apud Antonium Boetzerum, 1616); Abraham Bzowski, *Annalium ecclesiasticorum tomus XIV* (Cologne: Agrippinae apud Antonium Boetzerum 1618). See Chapter 4.
69. On this most recently, see Caffiero, *Battesimi forzati*; in English, Caffiero, *Forced Baptisms*.
70. Roth, *Ritual Murder*, 45, 73.
71. Roth, *Ritual Murder*, 45.
72. Roth, *Ritual Murder*, 43, 71–72.
73. Roth, *Ritual Murder*, 45, 73.
74. Tranquillo Vita Corcos, *Alla Sagra Consvlta Illustriss. e Reverendiss. Monsignor Ghezzi Ponente per l'vniuersità degli ebrei. Memoriale additionale ad altro dato li 26. settembre 1705* (Rome: Nella stamperia della Rev. Cam. apostolica, 1706).
75. Roth, *Ritual Murder*, 46, 74.
76. Roth, *Ritual Murder*, 56, 85.
77. Roth, *Ritual* Murder, 46, 74–75.
78. Ganganelli quoted here the decree from Verona 1603; Roth, *Ritual Murder*, 49, 78.
79. Roth, *Ritual Murder*, 48–49, 77–78.
80. Ganganelli here referred to Tranquillo Vita Corcos's treatises of 1705 and 1706, which, having been printed by the official Vatican printing house, were also in the possession of the Holy Office.
81. Roth, *Ritual Murder*, 52, 81.
82. Roth, *Ritual Murder*, 53, 82. Ganganelli used very similar wording to that used by Corcos and quoted the same passage Corcos provided in his 1706 *Memoriale additionale*, unnumbered 17.

Notes to Pages 340–343   483

83. Roth, *Ritual Murder*, 55, 83.
84. Roth, *Ritual Murder*, 55, slightly different English, 85.
85. Roth, *Ritual Murder*, 55, 84.
86. Roth, *Ritual Murder*, 54, 83.
87. For a reference to *Beatus Andreas* in a letter from 1900 denying help to Jews, see Caffiero, *Battesimi Forzati*, 50–53; Caffiero, *Forced Baptisms*, 34–36.
88. For the text of Paul III's bull, see Shlomo Simonsohn, *The Apostolic See and the Jews: Documents, 1539–1545* (Toronto: Pontifical Institute of Mediaeval Studies, 1990), no. 1973.
89. Roth, *Ritual Murder*, 90.
90. Roth, *Ritual Murder*, 60, slightly different English on 90.
91. Roth, *Ritual Murder*, 64, 94.
92. On this, see Kenneth R. Stow, *Catholic Thought and Papal Jewry Policy, 1555–1593* (New York: Jewish Theological Seminary, 1977), and other works by this author.
93. See, for example, ASV, Segr. Stato, Polonia 230, two printed copies of an encyclical from the newly elected Benedict XIV, following a letter dated January 28, 1741, and a printed copy of "Allocutio Sanctissimi Domini Nostri Papae Benedicti XIV" after a letter from the secretary of the state dated March 11, 1741.
94. See, for example, ACDF, St. St. P-4-H.
95. The significance of Corcos's work being printed by the official pontifical printing house was also appreciated by the Jews, who saved many copies of the printed work for future use. See, for example, ASCER, 1Qc fasc. 10 coll. 1 inf. 4; 1Ql fasc. 11 inf 5; 1Rb fasc 8 coll. 1 inf 5; 1Va fasc. 12 coll. 12 inf. 2; 1Va fasc. 13 coll. 2 inf. 2; 2Vi fasc. 9 coll. 10 sup. 2.
96. Today the historical archive of the Jewish community in Rome does possess a copy, and a copy can be found at the Yeshiva Museum in New York City; in the nineteenth century the Jewish community in Mantua had a copy as well. Majer Bałaban suggested that copies were given to the Roman Jews, but they decided to withhold them from Zelig. This scenario is highly unlikely. There is no indication anywhere that the report was known to Jews until it was first noted in the 1860s. But even if Jews had had access to the cardinal's report, the fact that it gave credence to Simon of Trent and Andreas of Rinn and ended with a hope for Jewish conversions would have likely been enough for Jews to decide against publishing it.
97. ACDF, St. St. TT-2-D, decree of the Holy Office signed by B. Veterani, assessor, dated January 10, 1760; also, ACDF St. St. CC-5-R, fasc. 12.
98. ACDF, St. St. TT-2-D, decree of the Holy Office signed by B. Veterani, assessor, dated January 10, 1760; also, ACDF St. St. CC-5-R, fasc. 12.
99. Two copies, one a draft with a note that the letter was to be open and one clean copy, in ACDF, St. St. T-2-D (unnumbered).
100. ASV, Nunziatura di Varsavia 94, 75r–v.
101. By the time Ganganelli's report was voted on by the Holy Office, it had already been known that Antonio Eugenio Visconti, a newly appointed titular archbishop of Ephesus, was to succeed Bishop Niccolò Serra in February 1760.

Serra was notified about his successor in a dispatch from Rome on November 24, 1759. ASV, Segr. Stato Polonia 237, 75r.
102. ASV, Nunziatura di Varsavia 94, 18r.
103. ASV, Nunziatura di Varsavia 94, 76r.
104. Cf. Maciejko, *Mixed Multitude*, 125–126.
105. On the earlier Jewish missions to Rome, see Bałaban, *Le-toledot ha-tenu`ah ha-frankit*, 127–133.

10. Calculated Pragmatism and the Waning of Accusations

1. ASV, Nunziatura di Varsavia 94, 38r–39r.
2. See, for example, the privilege given by King Sigismund III in 1671, in *Documenta judaeos in Polonia concernentia, ad Acta Metrices Regni suscepta, et ex iis fideliter iterum descripta et extradita* (Warsaw, 1763).
3. On this, see Paweł Maciejko, *The Mixed Multitude: Jacob Frank and the Frankist Movement, 1755–1816* (Philadelphia: University of Pennsylvania Press, 2011), 124–125. ACDF, St. St. TT-2-D, unnumbered documents, both the printed court records in Latin and a shorter description of the execution in Polish; it also includes a Latin translation of the Polish sections of the printed materials (descriptions of the wounds on the child's body and the execution). See also ASV, Nunziatura di Varsavia 94, 35r–36r (summary of points made by Szloma Pliskowski, one of the implicated Jews), 40r–41r (Latin translations of the material printed in Polish), and 48r–57r (the Latin and Polish printed materials).
4. See Chapter 9.
5. ASV Nunziatura di Varsavia 94, 65r-v and 67r-v (Polish), and 66 r-v (Latin translation).
6. Maciejko, *Mixed Multitude*, 77.
7. Gaudenty Pikulski (?), *Błędy talmutowe od samychże żydow uznane. Y przez nową sektę siapwscieciuchow, czyli contra talmudystow wyiawione* (Lwów: Jan Szlichtyn, 1758).
8. See the published texts of rabbis' responses to Frankists in part I, ch. X of Gaudenty Pikulski, *Złość żydowska przeciwko bogu i bliźniemu prawdzie y sumieniu na obwinienie talmudystow na dowód ich zaślepienia y religii dalekiey od prawa bożego przez Moyżesza danego* (Lwów: Jan Szlichtyn, 1760). For examples of direct parallels and verbatim phrases in Pikulski's *Złość żydowska* and *Błędy Talmutowe*, see Pikulski, *Złość żydowska*, part III, ch. IX, esp. 759 and Pikulski (?), *Błędy Talmutowe*, "MARZEC po hebraysku nazywa sie OODER."
9. Pikulski, *Złość żydowska*, part III, especially chs. VIII–X.
10. *Processus judiciarius in causa patrati cruenti infanticidii per infideles judaeos* (1761). The printed material was included by Nuncio Visconti in his letter from August 26, 1762, to Cardinal Corsini at the Holy Office, ACDF St. St. TT-2-D; a draft of the letter can also be found in ASV Segr. Stato Polonia 388, "Sant'Offizio." The Wojsławice material was then republished

Notes to Pages 348–352   485

in Polish translation in a work attributed to Kajetan Sołtyk and titled *Złość żydowska* in 1761 and in 1774, and, most recently, in Zenon Guldon and Jacek Wijaczka, *Procesy o mordy rytualne w Polsce w XVI–XVIII Wieku* (Kielce: DCF, 1995), 146–151.

11. *Złosc żydowska w zamęczeniu dzieci katolickich przez list nastepuiący y dekreta grodzkie wydana. List J. O. Xcia Jmci Kaietana Sołtyka Biskupa Krakowskiego, Na Ten Czas Biskupa Emuaseńskiego, Koadjutora Kijowskiego, Do J. W. Jmci X. Biskupa Lwowskiego z Żytomierza pisany* (after 1761); *Złosc żydowska w zamęczeniu dzieci katolickich przez list nastepuiący y dekreta grodzkie wydana. list J. O. Xcia Jmci Kaietana Sołtyka Biskupa Krakowskiego* (Lublin: Drukarnia J. K. M. y Rzeczypospolitey, 1774). Some scholars have attributed the publication of these documents to Bishop Kajetan Sołtyk. Yet the only evidence in support of that contention is that the booklet includes Sołtyk's decree of 1753. The booklet was first published in the aftermath of the trial in Wojsławice in 1761.

12. ASV, Nunziatura di Varsavia 94, 35r–36r, 40r–41r. See also Maciejko, *Mixed Multitude*, 124–125 and literature cited there.

13. ASV, Nunziatura di Varsavia 94, 35v.

14. ASV, Nunziatura di Varsavia 94, 61r.

15. ASV, Nunziatura di Varsavia 94, 61r.

16. For the letter in French, see ASV, Segr. Stato Polonia 388, fascicolo C, 20. For the Italian version, ACDF, St. St. TT-2-D, letter from Visconti to Corsini dated April 9, 1761.

17. ACDF, St. St. TT-2-D, letter from Visconti to Corsini, April 9, 1761.

18. ASV, Segr. Stato, Polonia 388, fasc. C, 31–32.

19. ACDF, St. St. TT-2-D, document A, dated May 16, 1761. A copy is also in ASV, Nunziatura di Varsavia 94, 80r–v.

20. ASV, Segr. Stato, Polonia 388, fasc. C, 63–64.

21. ASV, Segr. Stato, Polonia 388, fasc. C, 64–65.

22. The letter of the "syndic" of the Council of Four Lands (*Syndicus Generalis Synagogae Totius Regni Poloniae*) to Nuncio Visconti, ASV, Segr. Stato, Nunziatura di Varsavia 94, 43r–v (copy), 44r (original).

23. ASV, Segr. Stato, Polonia 388, fasc. E, 88; fasc. F, 12; also fasc. G.

24. See, for example, ASV, Segr. Stato, Polonia 237, where among many dispatches regarding Frank, the majority deal with other matters; for letters about war activities and international relations, see the ciphered dispatches, Segr. Stato, Polonia 238 (1759–1768); see also Segr Stato, Polonia 385, "Minute delle lettere della Segretaria 1760–1763"; Segr. Stato, Polonia add 9, "Varia 1734–35, 1760–1761." On the preoccupation with "heretics," see, for example, ASV, Segr. Stato, Polonia 273.

25. ASV, Segr. Stato, Polonia 388, fasc. C, 68.

26. ACDF, St. St. T-2-R, "Polonia 1762."

27. I want to thank my colleague and friend, Federica Francesconi, for disentangling this sentence.

28. Letters dated April 16, 1761, from Bishop Wężyk of Chełm and Felix Potocki to Visconti, ASV, Nunziatura di Varsavia 94, 68r and 69r.

29. ACDF, St. St. T-2-R, "Polonia 1762."
30. ACDF, St. St. T-2-R, "Polonia 1762." *Processus judiciarius in causa patrati cruenti infanticidii per infideles judaeos* (1761), last page. For the text in Polish, see *Złość żydowska (1774)*, page preceeding C.
31. Irene Fosi, *Papal Justice: Subjects and Courts in the Papal State, 1500–1750* (Washington, DC: Catholic University of America Press, 2011), ch. 10, esp. 178–183.
32. ACDF, St. St. T-2-R, "Polonia 1762."
33. ACDF, St. St. T-2-R, "Polonia 1762."
34. See ACDF, St. St. TT-2-D, section 3; and ASV, Nunziatura di Varsavia 94, 4r–16v.
35. On this, see also Maciejko, *Mixed Multitude*, 119–121. Jean-Baptiste de Ladvocat, a known Hebraist and author of books on Hebrew and biblical criticism, was also an author of a celebrated *Dictionnaire geographique*; see also Andrew S. Curran, *The Anatomy of Blackness: Science & Slavery in an Age of Enlightenment* (Baltimore: Johns Hopkins University Press, 2011), 152.
36. ASV, Nunziatura di Varsavia 94, 4r–v.
37. ACDF, St. St. TT-2-D, report dated "Feria 2ª die 20 Septembris, 1762," signed by Benedetto Veterani, the assessor of the Holy Office, and, on the same page, votum dated September 22, also signed by Veterani.
38. The draft, ACDF, St. St. T-2-D, document "AA" following the above votum. A clean copy can be found in ASV, Nunziatura di Varsavia 94, 81r–v.
39. ASV, Nunziatura di Varsavia 94, 84r–v, letter from Count Heinrich von Brühl to Nuncio Visconti dated March 18, 1763.
40. Paweł Maciejko, "Baruch Yavan and the Frankist Movement: Intercession in an Age of Upheaval," *Yearbook of the Simon Dubnow Institute* 4 (2005): 337.
41. The text of the apparent response, dated March 21, 1763, is preserved in ASV, Segr. Stato Polonia 388, fasc. G, 36. The notarized Polish translation was published in 1763, *Documenta judaeos in Polonia concernentia*, 41–42.
42. *Documenta judaeos in Polonia concernentia*. ASV Archivio Nunziatura di Varsovia 94, 86r–92.
43. Israel Halpern, ed., *Pinkas va`ad arb`a arazot* (Jerusalem: Mosad Bialik, 1945), 438 no. 820, 445 no. 837. See also Majer Bałaban, "Studien und Quellen zur Frankistichen Bewegung in Polen," in *Livre d'hommage a la memoire du Dr. Samuel Poznański (1864–1921)* (Warsaw: Otto Harrassowitz, 1927), 45–47; Majer Bałaban, *Le-toledot ha-tenu`ah ha-frankit* (Tel-Aviv: Dvir, 1934–1935), 290–292.
44. ASV, Nunziatura di Varsavia 94, 94r. Also, ACDF, St. St. T-2-D.
45. ACDF, St. St. T-2-D, unnumbered, copy of Kleczewski's letter and the votum of the Congregation. For the letter sent to Visconti, see ASV, Nunziatura di Varsavia 94, 85r.
46. ASV, Nunziatura di Varsavia 94, 97r.
47. ASV, Nunziatura di Varsavia 94, 85r–98v.
48. Maciejko, *Mixed Multitude*, 125.
49. See, for example, ASV, Segr. Stato Polonia 275 and 277.
50. See, especially, ASV, Segr. Stato Polonia 238, for late 1763 and 1764, esp. 58v.

51. ASV, Nunziatura di Varsavia 94, 99r–103v, images on 100v and 101r, text of the postmortem examination on 102r.
52. On the trial in Zasław, see Magda Teter, *Sinners on Trial: Sacrilege after the Reformation* (Cambridge, MA: Harvard University Press, 2011), 211–213, also 300 n. 243; I. Galant, "Zhertvy ritualnogo obvinenya be Zaslave v 1747 g," *Evreiskaia starina* 5, no. 2 (1912). On Żytomierz, see Chapter 8 and records published in Zenon Guldon and Jacek Wijaczka, *Procesy o Mordy Rytualne w Polsce w XVI–XVIII Wieku* (Kielce: DCF, 1995), 141–146.
53. Mariani, Michelangelo. *Il glorioso infante S. Simone: historia panegirica* (Trent: Zanetti Stampator Episcopale, 1668), 72–73.
54. ASV, Segr. Stato Polonia 238, 96r.
55. ASV, Segr. Stato Polonia 238, 97r–v, letter from Cardinal Torrigiani to Nuncio Visconti, October 25, 1766.
56. ASV, Segr. Stato Polonia 238, 99r, letter from Cardinal Torrigiani to Nuncio Visconti, November 22, 1766.
57. Halpern, *Pinkas va'ad arb'a arazot*, expenses, 433–434, no. 793; the commission's resolution, LXXXV. Bałaban, "Studien und Quellen," 45–47; Bałaban, *Le-toledot ha-tenu'ah ha-frankit*, 290–292. In 1760, one red złoty was the equivalent of 18 Polish złoty. Pikulski, *Złość żydowska*, 84. For example, in 1765–1766, one ox cost just over 10 "red złoty," a gallon of wine cost 3.5, a gallon of vodka cost 0.5, and a gallon of beer cost 0.03.Władysław Adamczyk, *Ceny w Lublinie od XVI do końca XVIII wieku. Les prix à Lublin dès le XVIe siècle jusquaaà la fin du XVIIIe siècle* (Lwów: Kasa im. Mianowskiego, 1935), 73, 79–80.
58. See, for example, the instructions prepared for the newly appointed nuncio to Poland, Angelo Maria Durini, who replaced Visconti in 1767, which focused on preventing reforms that would end laws prohibiting mixed marriages, holding offices by non-Catholics, equating conversion from Catholicism to non-Catholic denominations with apostasy, "crimes committed against the Church, the clergy, and the Catholic religion," and many others, ASV, Segr. Stato Polonia 238, 125v–144v.
59. ASV, Nunziatura di Varsavia 94, 104r–130r. AGAD, Zbiór Popielów 303, 47–71. For the summary of the trial, see Guldon and Wijaczka, *Procesy o mordy rytualne*, 87–88. François Guesnet is currently working on a study focusing on this case.
60. ASV, Nunziatura di Varsavia 94, 104r.
61. ASV, Nunziatura di Varsavia 94, 104v, and the Jewish supplication on 108r. AGAD, Zbiór Popielów 303, Jews' supplication in Warsaw, 50–53.
62. ASV, Nunziatura di Varsavia 94, 104v.
63. ASV, Nunziatura di Varsavia 94, 104v.
64. ASV, Nunziatura di Varsavia 94, 105r.
65. ASV, Nunziatura di Varsavia 94, 105v.
66. Guldon and Wijaczka, *Procesy o Mordy Rytualne*, 88.
67. AGAD, Zbiór Popielów 303, 50–53; a poetic appeal, 50; a description, dated April 11, of the affair submitted by Jews, 51–53.
68. AGAD, Zbiór Popielów 303, 55–59.

69. ASV, Nunziatura di Varsavia 94, 108r–110v.
70. ASV, Nunziatura di Varsavia 94, 108v.
71. ASV, Nunziatura di Varsavia 94, 109r. On Garampi's views of Poland, see Larry Wolff, *The Vatican and Poland in the Age of the Partitions* (New York: Columbia University Press, 1988), 88–89.
72. ASV, Nunziatura di Varsavia 94, 109r.
73. ASV, Nunziatura di Varsavia 94, 110r.
74. See the excellent study by Wolff, *The Vatican and Poland*.
75. ASV, Nunziatura di Varsavia 94, 112r.
76. The Polish original can be found in ASV, Nunziatura di Varsavia 94, 126r–130r; Latin translation sent to Rome, 114r–125r. The Polish text has also been published in Guldon and Wijaczka, *Procesy o mordy rytualne*, 151–159. More broadly on European debates about torture and the move away from its use, see John H. Langbein, *Torture and the Law of Proof: Europe in the Ancien Régime* (Chicago: University of Chicago Press, 2006).
77. Guldon and Wijaczka, *Procesy o mordy rytualne*, 151.
78. "Żadną miarą naturalnie być nie mogło." Guldon and Wijaczka, *Procesy o mordy rytualne*, 152.
79. Guldon and Wijaczka, *Procesy o mordy rytualne*, 152.
80. Żuchowski, *Process kryminalny*, 199.
81. Pikulski, *Złość żydowska*, 773.
82. Israel Jacob Yuval, *Two Nations in Your Womb: Perceptions of Jews and Christians in Late Antiquity and the Middle Ages* (Berkeley: University of California Press, 2006), 236–239.
83. Guldon and Wijaczka, *Procesy o mordy rytualne*, 153. On Serafinowicz, see Paweł Maciejko, "Christian Accusations of Jewish Human Sacrifice in Early Modern Poland: The Case of Jan Serafinowicz," *Gal-Ed* 23 (2010): 15–66.
84. Guldon and Wijaczka, *Procesy o mordy rytualne*, 153.
85. Guldon and Wijaczka, *Procesy o mordy rytualne*, 155.
86. Guldon and Wijaczka, *Procesy o mordy rytualne*, 155.
87. "To zdanie Ojca świętego i Stolicy Apostolskiej moc stałego wyroku mające."
88. Guldon and Wijaczka, *Procesy o mordy rytualne*, 156.
89. Guldon and Wijaczka, *Procesy o mordy rytualne*, 88.
90. Article IV in Bartłomiej Groicki, *Ten postępek wybran iest z praw cesarskich który Karolus V Cesarz wydać po wszystkich swoich państwiech, ktorym się nauka daie, iako w tych sądziech a sprawach około karania na gardle abo na zdrowiu sędziowie y każdy rząd ma sie zachować y postępować wedle boiaźni bożey sprawiedliwie, pobożnie, roztropnie y nieskwapliwie* (Cracow, 1559 [1954]). See also Groicki, *Porządek Sądow i Spraw Miejskich Prawa Majdeburskiego w Koronie Polskiej* (Warsaw: Wydawnictwa Prawnicze, 1953 [1559]), 191.
91. Article IV, Groicki, *Ten postępek*. Also see Langbein, *Torture and the Law of Proof*, 8–10.
92. Guldon and Wijaczka, *Procesy o mordy rytualne*, 159.
93. ASV Nunziatura di Varsavia 94, 133r–135v. Commissions established by the noble courts were routine at the highest level, and many were established during

the 1773–1775 Sejm; see, for example, *Konstytucye publiczne seymu extraordynaryinego warszawskiego pod węzłem Generalney Konfederacyi Oboyga Narodów, trwaiącego roku 1773, dnia 19. kwietnia zaczętego, a z limity y sześciu prorogacyi w roku 1775* (Warsaw: Drukarnia J. K. Mci Rzeczypospolitey u XX. Scholarum Piarum, 1775), 2: 3–287. On the role of Młodziejowski in suppressing the Jesuit order in Poland, see Wolff, *The Vatican and Poland*, 90.

94. ASV Nunziatura di Varsavia 94, 134v–135r.
95. "Gazeta Warszawska," no. 55, July 12, 1775, 1–2. A Latin translation of the article was sent to Rome, ASV Nunziatura di Varsavia 94, 132r–v.
96. The importance of the Grabie trial was noted by Stanisław Waltoś in his book discussing the most impactful trials and events on law in Europe. Waltoś, *Owoce zatrutego drzewa: procesy i wydarzenia, które wstrząsnęły prawem* (Cracow: Wydawnictwo Literackie, 1978).
97. Adam Lityński, "Problem kary śmierci w Polsce 1764–1794: Z badań nad historią polskiej myśli prawniczej," *Czasopismo prawno-historyczne* 40, no. 2 (1988); Mariusz Affek, "Il pensiero giuridico di Cesare Beccaria e di Giacinto Dragonetti nella Polonia del settecento," *Studi Storici* 31, no. 1 (1991); Małgorzata Pilaszek, "W poszukiwaniu prawdy: O działalności sądów w Koronie XVI–XVIII w.," *Przegląd historyczny* 89, no. 3 (1998): 366, 372.
98. See, for example, Pilaszek, "W poszukiwaniu prawdy."
99. Groicki, *Porządek sądow,* 131.
100. Article IV, Groicki, *Ten postępek.*
101. Article XVI, Groicki, *Ten postępek.*
102. Article XVII, Groicki, *Ten postępek.*
103. Article XVII, Groicki, *Ten postępek.*
104. Articles XVII–XVIII, Groicki, *Ten postępek.*
105. Pilaszek, "W poszukiwaniu prawdy," 374, 379.
106. See these works by Bartłomiej Groicki: *Porządek sądów y spraw mieyskich* (Przemyśl: Drukarnia Societatis Jesu, 1760); *Postępek wybrany iest z praw cesarskich* (Przemyśl: Drukarnia Societatis Jesu, 1760); and *Tytuły Práwá Maydeburskiego* (Przemyśl: Drukarnia Societatis Jesu, 1760).
107. Pilaszek, "W poszukiwaniu prawdy," 379.
108. Affek, "Il pensiero giuridico," 111–120.
109. Fosi, *Papal Justice*, chs. 7 and 10, 180–183.
110. Lityński, "Problem kary śmierci w Polsce."
111. Wolff, *The Vatican and Poland*, 23, 64.
112. Stanisław Wodzicki, *Wspomnienia z przeszłości od roku 1768 do roku 1840* (Cracow: Drukarnia Leona Paszkowskiego, 1873), 198–204, quote on 203. The cases are briefly discussed in Guldon and Wijaczka, *Procesy o mordy rytualne:* 40 (Chrzanów), 41 (Olkusz), 79–80, and 159–162 (Izbica Kujawska).
113. For example, Helmut Walser Smith, *The Butcher's Tale: Murder and Anti-Semitism in a German Town* (New York: W. W. Norton, 2003), 111.
114. There were a small number in the first half of the nineteenth century, but a resurgence of accusations took place mostly after 1880. For an excellent study

of accusations in this period in Poland see Żyndul, *Kłamstwo krwi*. For Germany, see Smith, *The Butcher's Tale*, 112–133.

115. For example, Lippmann Hirsch Loewenstein, *Damascia die Judenverfolgung zu Damaskus und ihre Wirkung auf die öffentliche Meinung nebst Nnachweisungen über den Ursprung der gegen die Juden wiederholten Beschuldigung, als bedienten sie sich des Menschenblutes bei Rituellen Zeremonien* (Frankfurt a.M: Loewenstein, 1841); Corrado Guidetti, *Pro Judæis: Riflessioni e Documenti* (Roux e Favale, 1884); Moritz Stern, *Die Päpstlichen Bullen über die Blutbeschuldigung* (Munich: August Schupp, 1900).
116. Caffiero, *Battesimi*, 19–20; Caffiero, *Forced Baptisms*, 7.
117. It was published in German translation in 1888 by A. Berliner as *Gutachen Ganganelli's—Clemens XIV—Angelengenheit der Blutbeschuldigung der Juden* (Berlin: Ph. Deutch, 1888); then in the original by Loeb, "Un memoire de Laurent Ganganelli sur la calomnie du meurtre rituel" in *Revue des études juives* (1889), 179–211; and then with additional materials, by Moritz Stern in his *Die Päpstlichen Bullen*.

Epilogue

1. Żuchowski, *Process Kryminalny* (after 1720), 116–117.
2. See Eugene M. Avrutin, *The Velizh Affair: Blood Libel in a Russian Town* (New York: Oxford University Press, 2018).
3. Hillel J. Kieval, "Representation and Knowledge in Medieval and Modern Accounts of Jewish Ritual Murder," *Jewish Social Studies* 1, no. 1 (1994): 52–72. See, for example, Sergei Aleksandrovich Bershadskii, ed., *Dokumenty i Regesty K Istorii Litovskikh Evreev* (St. Petersburg, 1882); Auguste Molinier, *Enquête sur un meurtre imputé aux Juifs de Valréas* (Paris: H. Champion, 1883); Corrado Guidetti, *Pro Judæis: Riflessioni e documenti* (Roux e Favale, 1884); P. Ghinzoni, "Simone di Trento: nuovi documenti," *Archivio Veneto* 19, no. 37 (1889); Henri de Grézes, *Saint Vernier (Verny, Werner, Garnier), martyr, patron des vignerons en auvergne, en Bourgogne et en Franche-Comte, sa vie, son martyre et son culte* (Clermont-Ferrand: L. Brustel, 1889); Adolf Neubauer and Moritz, *Hebräische Berichte über die Judenverfolgungen während der Kreuzzüge* (Berlin: Simion 1892); "La morale giudaica e il mistero di sangue," *La Civiltà cattolica* V (1893); Jacobs, "St. William of Norwich," *The Jewish Quarterly Review*, no. 4 (1897): 748–755; Joseph Reinach, *Une erreur judiciaire sous Louis XIV: Raphaël Levy* (Paris: Delagrave, 1898); Moritz Stern, *Die Päpstlichen Bullen über die Blutbeschuldigung* (Munich: August Schupp, 1900); Guiseppe Divina, *Storia del Beato Simone da Trento* (Trent: Artigianelli, 1902.); Menestrina, "Gli ebrei a Trento," *Tridentum* (1903); Umberto Cassuto, "Una lettera di racommandazione per un inviato degli ebrei polacchi al papa (1758)." *Rivista israelitica* (1904): 25–27; Galant, "Ritual'nyi protsess v Dunaigorod'e 1748 godu," *Evreiskaia starina* 4 (1911); Galant, "Zhertvy ritualnogo obvinenya," *Evreiskaia starina* 5, no. 2 (1912); Kuzmin, *Materialy k Voprosu ob obvineniakh evreev* (1913); Giorgio Zaviziano, *Un raggio di luce: la persecuzione degli ebrei nella storia* (Corfu: Tip. Corai, 1891).

4. Grèzes, *Saint Vernier.*
5. Cecil Roth, *The Ritual Murder Libel and the Jew* (London: Woburn Press, 1935), 106–109.
6. "Christians and Jews: Towards Better Understanding," *Wiener Library Bulletin* 13, no. 3–4 (1959): 60.
7. Roth, *Ritual Murder.*
8. On the Beilis affair, see Ezekiel Leikin, *The Beilis Transcripts : The Anti-Semitic Trial That Shook the World* (Northvale, NJ: Jason Aronson, 1993); Robert Weinberg, *Blood Libel in Late Imperial Russia: The Ritual Murder Trial of Mendel Beilis* (Bloomington, Indiana: Indiana University Press, 2014).
9. Jill Lepore, "Hard News: The State of Journalism." *New Yorker,* January 28, 2019, 24.

ARCHIVAL AND PRINTED PRIMARY SOURCES

Archival Sources

Akademia Umiejętności (PAU, Kraków):

Teki Pawińskiego 8338

Archives departementales de la Moselle in Metz, France (ADMM):

B 2144

Archivio della Congregazione per la Dottrina della Fede (ACDF, Vatican City):

St. St. BB 3f, fasc. 1
St. St. CC-5-R
St. St. P-4-H
St. St. TT 2c "Hebraei"
St. St. TT-2-D
St. St. TT-2-M, fasc. 3
St. St. TT-4-C, fasc. 4
St. St. UV 53

Archivio Segreto Vaticano (ASV, Vatican City):

Archivi Arcis Arm. I-XVIII No. 6495
Arm. XLI, vol. 17
Fondo Garampi 259
Nunziatura Varsavia 94
Sec. Stato Polonia add 9, 119, 120, 135, 138, 139, 167, 168, 170, 190, 228, 230, 231, 233, 234, 235, 236, 237, 238, 249, 253, 255A, 263, 266, 267, 270, 271, 272, 275, 277, 368, 369, 370, 376, 379, 382, 388

Archivio di Stato di Trento (AST, Trent, Italy):

Archivio Principesco Vescovile (APV), Sezione Latina (sl), Capsa 69

Archivio Storico della Comunità Ebraica di Roma (ASCER, Rome, Italy):

1Qc fasc. 10 coll. 1 inf 4
1Ql fasc. 11 inf 5
1Rb fasc 8 coll. 1 inf 5
1Va fasc. 12 coll. 12 inf 2
1Va fasc 13 coll 2 inf 2
2Vi fasc. 9 coll. 10 sup. 2

Archivum Romanum Societatis Iesu (ARSI, Vatican City):

Polonia 50
Polonia 51 I
FG.1592/Collegia 207 Sendomir

Archiwum Główne Akt Dawnych (AGAD, Warsaw, Poland):

Archiwum Radziwiłłowskie XXIX
Księgi Miejskie Krzemienieckie, Nabytki Nie-dokumentowe oddziału I, Nr. 58 "Xięga Czarna. Krzemieniec (1747–1764)"
Zbiór Popielów 303

Archiwum Kapituły Kolegiackiej i Katedralnej w Sandomierzu (AKKiKS, Sandomierz, Poland):

740, 741, 742

Archiwum OO. Franciszkanów-Reformatów w Krakowie (Cracow, Poland):

MS. 279 "O. Bernard, Reformata, Kazania misjonarskie, 1758"

Archiwum Państwowe w Krakowie-Oddział na Wawelu (APK, Wawel, Cracow, Poland):

Akta XX. Sanguszków, Teka 5/27

Archiwum Państwowe w Lublinie (APwL, Lublin, Poland):

Akta m. Lublina "Acta maleficorum" 141
Akta Trybunału Koronnego 254, Acta Arianismi

Archiwum Państwowe w Poznaniu (APP, Poznań, Poland):

Akta m. Poznania: I 2258; Gr 1238

Biblioteca Apostolica Vaticana (BAV, Vatican City):

Borg. Lat 481
Borg. Lat. 503
Pal.lat 858

Bibliothèque royale de Belgique (Brussels, Belgium):

Collectanea Bollandiana, Ms. 8030–32

Österreichische Nationalbibliothek (ÖNB, Vienna, Austria):

MS: Cod. 5360: Processus inquisitionis contra Iudaeos Tridentinos propter occisum puellum Simonem de Tridento

Société des Bollandistes, Brussels, Belgium:

Ms. Boll. 246

Trinity College in Dublin (TCD, Dublin, Ireland):

Ms. 1260

Yeshiva University Museum (YUM, New York, U.S.A.):

YUM 1988.001
YUM 1989.257

Printed Primary Sources

Akty izdavaemye vilenskoiu kommisieiu dla razbora drevnikh aktov (AIVK). Vol. 5. Vilna, 1871.

Akty izdavaemye vilenskoiu kommisieiu dla razbora drevnikh aktov: Akty o Evreiakh, vol. 28. Vilna, 1901.

Alberettus, Andreas. *Sacra Consulta Sive Illustriss. et Revedendiss. D. Ghezzio Ponente Viterben. calumniae super praetensa attentata iugulatione pro Gioiello de Core et Iosepho Samen haebreis contra fiscum et illi adhaeren. restrictus facti et iuris.* Rome: Typis Reverendae Camerae Apostolicae, 1706.

Alla Sagra Consulta per Gioiello di Core. Memoriale. Rome: Stamperia della Rev. Camera Apostolica, 1706.

Allè, Girolamo. *I convinti e confusi hebrei opera del M. R. P. M. Girolamo Allè Bolognese, dell Ordine di S. Girolamo di Fiesole, divisa in alcune prediche da lui predicate nell antico et gia patriarca tempio di San Silvestro di Venetia: aggiunavi con altre la predica fatta da lui in S. Marco la domenica delle palme, alla presenza del Sereniss. Principe, Eccelentissimi Ambasciadori del Papa, Francia, Savoia, et altri Illustriss. Senatori.* Ferrara: Nella stamparia camerale, 1619.

Amelot de La Houssaie, Abraham-Nicolas. *Abregé dv procés fait aux juifs de Mets. Avec trois arrests du parlement qui les declarent convaincus de plusieurs crimes, & particulierement Rahaël [Sic] Levi d'avoir enlevé sur le grand chemin de Mets à Boulay, un enfant chrestien âgé de trois ans: pour reparation de quoy il a esté brûlé vif le 17. janvier 1670.* Paris: Chez Frederic Leonard, imprimeur ordin. du roy, rüe Saint Jacques, à l'Escu de Venise, 1670.

"Annales Erphordienses." In *Monumenta Germaniae Historica,* edited by Georg Heinrich Pertz. Hannover: Hahn, 1859.

"Annales Merbacenses." In *Monumenta Germaniae Historica,* edited by Georg Heinrich Pertz. Hannover: Hahn, 1861.

Anonymous. *Des kadosh fun Heneh zayn lid.* Vol. Bodleian Library Opp 8 to 556 (3). Publisher and date unknown.

Anonymous. *Kidush ha-shem shel Reb Matis ve-Reb Pinhas ve-Reb Abraham zekhutam ya'amod lanu bi-medinat Polin.* Publisher and date unknown.

Anonymus. *Sefer Geulat Israel.* s.l.: s.n., ca. 1696.

Anonymous. *Sefer Kedoshim K"K Vilne.* Bodleian Library Opp 80 556 (7). Amsterdam: after 1691.

Anonymous. *Seyfer mayseh ha-shem,* Bodleian Library Opp Add 80 IV 41.

Annuae litterae Societatis Iesu 1605. Duaci: Ex officina Viduae Laurentii Kellami, 1618.

Annuae litterae Societatis Iesu, Anni 1598. ad patres, ac fratres eiusdem societatis. Lugundi: ex typographia Iacobi Roussin, 1607.

Auerbach, Shmuel. *Min ha-kadosh hr"r Shlomoh be-nigun el male raḥamim.* Vol. Opp 8 to 627, Bodleian Library. Amsterdam (?)after 1692.

Augustine and Juan Luis Vives. *Tomus V operum D. Aurelii Augustini Hipponensis Episcopi, De Civitate Dei libros xxii ad priscae uenerandae que uetustatis exemplaria iam iterum post uirum undequaque doctissimum ioannem lodovicum vivem summo studio collatos ac eiusdem commentariiis erudissimis illustratos continens.* Basel: Ex officina Frobeniana, 1569.

Balneoregio, Silvester de. *Conclusiones cum earum declaracionibus edite a reverendo sacre thelogogie magistro Siluestro de Baleoregio Ordinis Fratrum Heremitarum Sancti Augustini: super canonisatione Simonis Tridentini quem impia gens hebrea incontemptum fidei cristiane crudeliter enecauit ad Reuerendissimum Episcopum et Tridentine civitatis principem dominum Johannem Hynderbach.* Trent: Albrecht Kunne, December 6, 1475.

Baronio, Cesare. *Annales ecclesiastici.* Moguntia: Sumptibus Ioannis Gymnici et Antonii Hierati Coloniensi, 1608.

Baronio, Cesare. *Annales ecclesiastici.* Venice: apud Stephanum Monti, 1738–1740.

Baronio, Cesare. *Martyrologivm romanvm, ad novam kalendarii rationem, et ecclesiasticæ historiæ veritatem restitutum Gregorii XIII. Pont. Max. ivssv editvm. accesservnt notationes, atque tractatio de martyrologio romano. avctore Cæsare Baronio sorano congreg. oratoij presbyt.* Rome: Ex Typographia Dominici Basae, 1586.

Basnage, Jacques. *Histoire des juifs 9,2 (13).* La Haye: Scheurleer, 1716.

Basnage, Jacques. *Histoire des juifs 9,3.* La Haye: Scheurleer, 1716.

Bell'Haver, Thomaso. *Dottrina facile et breve per ridurre l'hebreo al conoscimento del vero Messia, & Salvator del mondo/del R.P. Thomaso Bell'hauer ... divisa in otto trattati.* Venice: Appresso i Farri, 1608.

Benedict XIV, Pope. *Benedicti XIV Pont. Opt. Max. olim Prosperi Cardinalis de Lambertinis Bullarium.* 17 vols. Vol. 3/1 and Vol 3/2. Prati: Typographia Aldina, 1847.

Benedict XIV, Pope. *Lettera della santità di nostro signore Benedetto Papa XIV a monsignore Benedetto Veterani Avvocato Concistoriale e Promotore della Fede.* [S.l.]: [s.n.], 1755.

Benedict XIV, Pope. *Officium proprium Beati Andreae innocentis, et martyris rinnensis: a clero seculari, & regulari diocesis Brixinensis die XII Julii recitandum/juxta S. D. N. Benedicti XIV Decretum.* Rome: ex Typographia Reverendae Camerae Apostolicae, 1754.

Bergomensis, Jacobus Philippus Foresti. *Supplementum chronicarum.* Brescia: Boninus de Boninis, 1485 (12.01.)

Bergomensis, Jacobus Philippus Foresti. *Supplementum chronicarum.* Venice: Bernardino Rizzo, 1491.

Bergomensis, Jacobus Philippus Foresti. *Supplementum chronicarum.* Venice: Bernardinus Ricius de Novaria, 1492.

Bergomensis, Jacobus Philippus Foresti. *Supplementum chronicarum.* Venice: Impressum Opere & impensa Georgii de Rusconibus, 1506.

Bergomensis, Jacobus Philippus Foresti. *Supplementum chronicarum.* Venice: Opere & īpensa Georgii de Rusconibus, 1513.

Bergomensis, Jacobus Philippus Foresti. *Supplementvm supplementi de la chroniche.* Venice: Impresso per Ioanne Francischo & Ioanne Antonio fratelli di Rusconi, 1524.

Bergomensis, Jacobus Philippus Foresti. *Supplementum chronicarum.* Paris: apud Simonem Colineum, 1535.

Bergomensis, Jacobus Philippus Foresti. *Svpplementvm svpplementi delle croniche.* Venice: B. Bindone, 1535.

Bernard, Jean-Frèdèric, and Bernard Picart. *Histoire gènèrale des cèrèmonies, moeurs et coutumes religieuses de tous les peuples du monde.* Paris: Rollin Fils, 1741.

Bershadskii, Sergei Aleksandrovich, ed. *Dokumenty i regesty k istorii litovskikh evreev.* 3 vols. St. Petersburg, 1882.

Bielski, Marcin. *Kronika. Tho iesth, historya swiata na szesc wiekow, a czterzy monarchie, rozdzielona z rozmaitych historykow, tak w swietym pismie krzescijanskim zydowskim, iako y poganskim, wybierana y na polski iezyk wypisana dosthatheczniey niz pierwey, s przydanim wiele rzeczy nowych: od poczatku swiata, az do tego roku, ktory sie pisze 1564. s figurami ochedoznymi y wlasnymi.* Cracow: Mateusz Siebeneycher, 1564.

Bielski, Marcin, and Joachim Bielski. *Kronika polska Marcina Bielskiego.* Sanok: K. Pollak, 1856.

Boemus, Joannes. *Omnivm gentivm mores leges et ritvs ex mvltis clarissimis rervm scriptoribus.* Augusta: Excusa in officina Sigismundi Grimm medici, ac Marci Vuirsung, 1520.

Bolland, Jean, Godefroy Henschen, Abraham van Diepenbeeck, and Daniel van Papenbroeck *Acta Sanctorum Martii.* Antwerp: apud Iacobum Meursium, 1668.

Bonelli, Benedetto. *Dissertazione apologetica : sul martirio del Beato Simone da Trento nell'anno MCCCCLXXV da gli ebrei ucciso.* Trent: Per Gianbattista Parone Stampator vescovile, 1747.

Bonfinius, Antonius, and Joannes Sambucus. *Antonii Bonficii rerum ungaricarum decades IV cum demidia: his acc. Jo Sambuci aliquot appendicis et alia: una cum priscorum regum ungariae decretis, seu constitutionibus.* Hannover: typis Wechel, 1606.

Börner, Christian Friedrich. *Auserlesene Bedenken der theologischen Fakultät zu Leipzig in drey Theile verfasset.* Leipzig: Bernhard Christoph Breitkopf, 1751.

Bowd, Stephen D., and J. Donald Cullington. *"On Everyone's Lips": Humanists, Jews, and the Tale of Simon of Trent.* Tempe, AZ: Brepols, Arizona Center for Medieval and Renaissance Studies, 2012.

Brancati, Lorenzo. *Epitome canonum omnium qui in conciliis generalibus ac prouincialibus, in decreto Gratiani, in decretalibus, in epistolis & constitutionibus romanorum Pontificum vsque ad Sanctiss. D. N. Alexandri VII annum quartum continentur.* Rome: Typis Mascardi, 1649.

Braun, Georg. *Civitates orbis terrarvm liber primvs.* Cologne: apud Godefridum Kempensem, sumptibus auctorum, 1582.

Buxtorf, Johann. *Synagoga judaica, hoc est schola judaeorum, in qua nativitas, institutio, religio, vita, mors sepulturaque ipsorum, e libris eorundem, a M. Johanne Buxdorfio, descripta est. addita est mox per eundem judaei cum christiano disputatio de messia nostro. quae utraque germanica nunc latine reddita sunt, opera ... M. Hermanni Germbergii. accessit Ludovici Carreti Epistola de conversione ejus ad christum, per eundem ex hebraeo latine conversa.* Hanau: Typis Petri Antoni Impensis J. Stöckle, 1622.

Bzovius (Bzowski), Abraham. *Annalium ecclesiasticorum post Illustriss. et Revedend. Dominum D. Caesare Baronium S.R.E Cardinalem Bibliothecarem*

Tomus XIII rerum in orbe christiano an anno domini 1198 usque annum dom. 1299 gestarum narrationem complectens. Cologne: Agrippinae apud Antonium Boetzerum, 1616.

Bzovius (Bzowski), Abraham. *Annalium ecclesiasticorum post Illustriss. et Revedend. Dominum D. Caesare Baronium S.R.E Cardinalem Bibliothecarem Tomus XIV rerum in orbe christiano an anno domini 1300 usque annum dom. 1378 gestarum narrationem complectens.* Cologne: Agrippinae apud Antonium Boetzerum, 1618.

Bzovius (Bzowski), Abraham. *Annalium ecclesiasticorum post Illustriss. et Revedend. Dominum D. Caesare Baronium S.R.E Cardinalem Bibliothecarem. Tomus XV rerum in orbe christiano ab anno domini 1378 usque as annum domini 1431.* Cologne, 1622.

Carbone, Ludovico. *Summæ summarum casuum conscientiæ siue totius theologiæ practicæ in tribus tomi [sic] distributa: per quam ad alias in praesens vsque editas omnes summas de casibus conscientiae inscriptas facilis aditus & introductio quaedam paratur.* Venice: apud Robertum Meiettum, 1606.

Carboni, Francesco. *Le piaghe dell'hebraismo, scoperte nuouamente da Francesco Carboni . . . col lume delle più pretiose dottrine d'antichi scrittori cattolici, hebrei, e gentili.* Venice: Appresso Stefano Curti, 1674.

Cardoso, Isaac. *Las excelencias de los hebreos.* Amsterdam: David de Castro Tartas, 1679.

Cassuto, Umberto. "Una lettera di racommandazione per un inviato degli ebrei polacchi al papa (1758)." *Rivista israelitica* (1904): 25–27.

Chazan, Robert, Jean Hoff, and John Friedman. *The Trial of the Talmud: Paris, 1240.* Toronto: Pontifical Institute of Mediaeval Studies, 2012.

Cherubini, Laerzio, and Angelo Maria Cherubini. *Magnum bullarium romanum, a Clemente VIII usque ad Gregorium XV.* 4 vols, Magnum Bullarium Romanum. Lugundi: sumptib. Philippi Borde, Laur. Arnaud & Cl. Rigaud, 1655.

Christiani, Friedrich Albrecht. *Der Jüden Glaube und Aberglaube.* Leipzig: Lanckisch, 1705.

Corcos, Tranquillo Vita. *Alla Sacra Consvlta Illustriss. e Reuerendiss. Monsig. Ghezzi Ponente per l'vniuersità degl'hebrei di Roma. Memoriale.* Rome: Stamperia della Reu. Cam. Apostolica 1705.

Corcos, Tranquillo Vita. *Alla Sagra Consvlta Illustriss. e Reuerendiss. Monsig. Ghezzi Ponente per l'vniuersità degl'hebrei di Roma. Sommario.* Rome: Nella stamperia della Rev. Camera apostolica, 1706.

Corcos, Tranquillo Vita. *Alla Sagra Consvlta Illustriss. e Reuerendiss. Monsignor Ghezzi Ponente per l'vniuersità degli ebrei. Memoriale additionale ad altro dato li 26. settembre 1705.* Rome: Nella stamperia della Rev. Cam. apostolica, 1706.

Crudelis judaeorum perfidia amabili christianae fidei constantia ab hebraeo adolescente Simone Abeles superata, pro theatro exhibita ab infima grammatices classe, Collegii Academici Societatis Jesu, Olomucii anno M.DCC.XXXVI. Prague, 1736.

Czechowic, Marcin. *Odpis Jakoba żyda z Bełżyc na dyalogi Marcina Czechowica, na ktory zaś odpowieda Jakobowi żydowi tenże Marcin Czechowic.* Lublin, 1581.

Czołowski, Aleksander. *Odpowiedź rabinowi lwowskiemu Dr. Jecheskielowi Caro w sprawie "mordu rytualnego."* Lwów: Nakładem autora, 1899.

de Beauvais, Vincent. *Speculum historiale*. Strasbourg: Johann Mentelin, 1473.
de Espina, Alfonso. *Fortalitium fidei*. Strasbourg: Johannes Mentelin, 1462.
de Espina, Alfonso. *Fortalitium fidei*. Nuremberg: Anton Koberger, 1485.
de' Giudici, Battista, and Diego Quaglioni. *Apologia judaeorum invectiva contra Platinam: propaganda antiebraica e polemiche di curia durante il pontificato di Sisto IV (1471–1484)*. Rome, 1987.
de Pavinis, Johannes Franciscus. *Inquisitio et condemnatoria sententia contra judaeos tridentinos*. Rome: apud Sanctum Marcum, 1478.
de Santa Fe, Jeronimo. *Contra iudaeos Hieronymi de Sancta Fide, iudaei, ad christianismum conuersi, libri duo: quorum prior fidem & religione[m] eorum impugnat, alter uero Talmuth: ad mandatum Domini Papae Benedicti XIII, facta relatione, Anno Domini 1412, mense augusto in Hispania*. Tiguri: apud Andream Gesnerum F. & Rodolphum Vuissenbachium, 1552.
de Susannis, Marquardus. *Tractatus de iudaeis et aliis infidelibus: circa concernentia originem, contractuum, ... eorum conversationes ad fidem*. Venice: apud Cominum de Tridino Montisferrati, 1558.
de Torigni, Robert. *The Chronicles of Robert De Monte*. London: Llanerch Publishers, 1856.
Dekret w sprawie o zamordowanie okrutne przez zydow chrześcianina Antoniego pod Zasławiem ferowany w zamku zasławskim dnia 17 kwietnia roku pańskiego 1747. After April 17, 1747.
Delaborde, Henri F., ed., *Œuvres de Rigord et de Guillaume le Breton, historiens de Philippe-Auguste: Chroniques de Rigord et de Guillaume le Breton*. Paris: Librairie Renouard, 1882.
Divina, Giuseppe. *Storia del Beato Simone da Trento*. Trent: Artigianelli, 1902.
Documenta judaeos in Polonia concernentia, ad Acta Metrices Regni Suscepta, et ex iis fideliter iterum descripta et extradita. Warsaw, 1763.
Eder, Joannes. *Virilis constantia pueri duodennis Simonis Abeles in odium fidei ‡ judaeo parente Lazaro Abeles: Pragae crudeliter occisi 21 februarij anno 1694*. Prague: Typis Universitatis Carolo-Ferdinandeae, in Collegio Societatis Jesu ad S. Clementem, 1696.
Eder, Joannes, and Paolo Medici. *Patimenti e morte di Simone Abeles*. Translated by Paolo Medici. Firenze: Piero Martini, 1705.
Eisenmenger, Johann Andreas. *Endecktes Judenthum*. Frankfurt a.M, 1700.
Esposito, Anna, and Diego Quaglioni. *Processi contro gli ebrei di Trento (1475–1478)*, Vol. 1. Padova: CEDAM, 1990.
Esposito, Anna, and Diego Quaglioni. *Processi contro gli Ebrei di Trento: I Processi Alle Donne (1475–1476)*, Vol. 2. Padova: CEDAM, 2008.
Finkelstein, Leo. *Megiles Poyln: Toyre, hasides un shtayger-kultur in yidishn Poyln, Dos Poylishe Yidntum*. Buenos Aires: Tsentral-farband fun Poylishe Yidn in Argentine, 1947.
Fioghi, Fabiano. *Dialogo Fra il cathecumino et il padre cathechizante, composto per Fabiano Fioghi dal Monte Santo Sauino, lettore della lingua hebrea nel collegio dei neophiti. nel quale si risoluono moltij dubij, li quali sogliono far li hebrei, contro la uerità della santa fede christiana, con efficacissime ragioni, & per li santi profeti, & per li rabini*. Rome: Per gli heredi d'Antonio Blado stampatori camerali, 1582.

Fleury, Claude. *Les moeurs des israèlites.* Paris: Veuve G. Clouzier, 1681.
Franco, Ambrogio. *Martirio del Beato Simone Trentino.* Trent: per li fratelli Gelmini da Sabbio, 1586.
Franco, Ambrogio. *Martirio di S. Simone di Trento nel quale si tratta de la gran crudeltà che vsarono gli empi ebrei in martirizarlo. et come è stato posto nel cattalogo de' santi, & la solenne processione fatta nella sua prima festa, con molti miracoli fatti da esso santo.* Trent: Battista Gelmini, 1608.
Frankel, David. "Qinah le-Ḥarugei Trient." *Ha-ẓofeh le-ḥokhmat Yisrael* 2 (1912): 19–20.
Galant, I. "Ritual'nyi protsess v Dunaigorod'e 1748 godu." *Evreiskaia starina* 4, (1911): 268–285.
Galant, I. "Zhertvy ritualnogo obvinenya v Zaslave v 1747 g: po aktam Kievskago Tsentralnago Arkhiva." *Evreiskaia starina* 5, no. 2 (1912): 202–218.
Galatino, Pietro. *Opus toti christin[a]e reipublic[a]e maxime utile de arcanis catholic[a]e ueritatis contra obstinatissimam iud[a]eoru[m] nostr[a]e tempestatis p[er]fidiam : ex Talmud aliisq[ue] hebraicis libris nuper excerptum.* Ortona: Summa cum diligentia per Hieronymum Suncinum (Gersom b. Moshe Soncino), 1518.
Galatino, Pietro. *Petri Galatini de arcanis catholicae veritatis, libri xii : qvibvs pleraqve religionis christianae capita contra ivdaeos, tam ex scripturis veteris testamenti authenticis, qŭm ex talmudicorum commentariis, confirmare & illustrare conatus est. : item, iohannis revchlini : phorcensis, de cabala, sev de symbolica receptione, dialogus tribus libris absolutus.* Frankfurt a.M: Sumptibus Jacobi Godofredi Seyler, 1672.
Gans, David ben Solomon. *Sefer tsemaḥ David.* Prague: Solomon ha-Kohen, 1592.
Gazeta Warszawska, no. 55, July 12, 1775.
Gerichtlicher Proceß und Urtheil deß Parlaments zu Metz eines Jude[n] Raphael Levi genandt wegen eines von ihme den 23. Septembr. 1669 geraubten und hingerichteten drey jährigen Kindes: Auß dem zu Metz gedrucktem frantzösischen exemplar ins teutscheübersetzt. 1670.
Gesti, Antonio. *Martirio di S. Simone di Trento nel quale si tratta de la gran crudeltà che usarono gli empi ebrei in martirizarlo, et come è stato posto nel cattalogo de santi e la solenne processione fatta nella sua prima festa con molti miracoli fatti da esso santo.* Trent: Per i fratelli de Gelmini, 1589.
Gesti, Antonio. *Martirio di S. Simone di Trento nel quale si tratta de la gran crudeltà che usarono gli empi ebrei in martirizarlo, et come è stato posto nel cattalogo de santi e la solenne processione fatta nella sua prima festa con molti miracoli fatti da esso santo.* Trento: Per Gio[vanni] Battista Gelmini da Sabbio, 1593.
Górski, Jakub. *Index errorum aliquot, ex innumeris stultitiis blasphemiis, et impietatibus, talmudici operis collectus. ex secundo libro bibliothecae sanctae sixti senensis extractus. Okazanie kilka błędów z Talmuda żydowskiego zebranych.* Cracow: Łazarz Andrysowic, 1569.
Gottardi, Alessandro Maria. "Notificazione circa il culto al piccolo Simone da Trento." *Rivista diocesana tridentina* XCI, October (1965): 595–596.
Groicki, Bartłomiej. *Porządek sądow i spraw miejskich prawa majdeburskiego w Koronie Polskiej.* Warsaw: Wydawnictwa Prawnicze, 1953 [1559].

Groicki, Bartłomiej. *Porządek Sądów Y Spraw Mieyskich Prawa Maydeburskiego w Koronie Polskiey w Krakowie Drukowany Roku Pańskiego 1616. Teraz Znowu Z Pozwoleniem Starszych Przedrukowany.* Przemyśl: Drukarnia Societatis Jesu, 1760.

Groicki, Bartłomiej. *Postępek wybrany iest z praw cesarskich, ktory Karolus V Cesarz kazał wydać po wszystkich swoich państwach, którym się nauka daie, iako w tych sądach á sprawach, około karania na gardle álbo na zdrowiu, sędziowie, y każdy urząd ma się zachować y postępować wedle boiaźni bożey, spráwiedliwie, pobożnie, rostropnie y nieskwapliwie. cum gratia & privilegio S. R. M. w Krakowie drukowany roku pańskiego 1616. a teraz znowu, z pozwoleniem starszych przedrukowany.* Przemyśl: Drukarnia Societatis Jesu, 1760.

Groicki, Bartłomiej. *Ten postępek wybran iest z praw cesarskich który Karolus V Cesarz wydać po wszystkich swoich państwiech, ktorym się nauka daie, iako w tych sądziech a sprawach około karania na gardle abo na zdrowiu sędziowie y każdy rząd ma sie zachować y postępować wedle boiaźni bożey sprawiedliwie, pobożnie, roztropnie y nieskwapliwie.* Cracow, 1559 [1954].

Groicki, Bartłomiej. *Tytuły práwá maydeburskiego, do porządku y do artykułow, pierwey po polsku wydanych. w sprawach tego czasu naywięcey kłopotnych, z tegoż prawa maydeburskiego przydane. W Krakowie drukowane Roku Pańskiego 1616. Co się teraz nad pierwszą edicyą przyczyniło, summa tytułow naprzód położona, á koniec tych kśiążek pokaże. teraz znowu, z pozwoleniem starszych przedrukowane.* Przemyśl: Drukarnia Societatis Jesu, 1760.

Grotius, Hugo. *Hugonis Grotii Reginae Regnique Sueciae Consiliarii et apud Regem Christianissimum legati etc. epistolae quotquot reperiri potuerunt, in quibus praeter hactenus editas, plurimae theologici, iuridici, philologici, historici et politici argumenti occurrunt.* Amsterdam: ex typographia P. & I. Blaev : prostant apud Wolfgang, Waasberge, Boom a Someren & Goethals, 1687.

Guidetti, Corrado. *Pro judæis: riflessioni e documenti:* Roux e Favale, 1884.

Ha-Kohen, Joseph. *El valle del llanto [emeq ha-bakha]: cronica hebrea del siglo XVI*, Biblioteca Nueva Sefarad. Barcelona: Riopiedras Ediciones, 1989.

Ha-Kohen, Joseph. *'Emeq ha-bakha de Yosef Ha-Kohen.* Translated by Pilar Leon Tello, Biblioteca Hebraico-Espanola. Madrid: Consejo Superior de Investigaciones Cientìficas, Instituto Arias Montano, 1964.

Ha-Kohen, Joseph. *La valle' des pleurs: chronique des souffrances d'israel depuis sa dispersion jusqu'a nos jours*, Les Chroniques Juives. Paris: Chez le traducteur, 1881.

Ha-Kohen, Joseph. *Sefer divre ha-yamim le-malkhe tsarefat u-malkhe bet otoman ha-tugar.* Jerusalem: Mosad Bialik, 1955.

Ha-Kohen, Joseph. *The Vale of Tears.* Translated by Harry S. May. The Hague: M. Nijhoff, 1971.

Ha-Kohen, Joseph, and Karin Almbladh. *Sefer Emeq Ha-Bakha (the Vale of Tears) with the Chronicle of the Anonymous Corrector*, Acta Universitatis Upsaliensis. Studia Semitica Upsaliensia. Uppsala: Uppsala University, 1981.

Hájek of Libočan, Václav. *Böhmische Chronica Vvenceslai Hagecii. Von Ursprung der Böhmen von irer Hertzogen und Konige, Graffen, Adels und Geschlechter Ankunfft ... jetzt aus böhmischer in die deutsche Sprache.* Prague: Gedruckt durch Nicolaum Straus, Jnn Verlegung Andreaszen Weidlichs, 1596.

Halevi, Shlomo. "Kinah: Lament for the Victims of Trent." In *Medieval Justice: The Trial of the Jews of Trent.* New York: Yeshiva University Museum, 1989 [1475].

Halpern, Israel, ed. *Pinkas va'ad arb'a arazot.* Jerusalem: Mosad Bialik, 1945.

Halpern, Israel, and Israel Bartal, eds. *Pinkas va'ad arb'a arazot.* Jerusalem, 1989 [1945].

Henschen, Godefroid, and Daniel Van Papenbroeck. *Acta Sanctorum aprilis collecta, digesta, illustrata tomus II. Quo medii XI dies continentur. praeponitur illis propylaeum antiquarium, circa veri falsique discrimen in vetustis monumentis, praesertim diplomatis, observandum. subjunguntur acta graeca.* Antwerp: apud Michaelem Cnobarum, 1675.

Herburt, Jan. *Chronica, sive historiae polonicae compendiosa: ad per certa librorum capita ad facilem memoriam recens facta descriptio.* Basel: Ex Officina Oporiniana, 1571.

Hess, Ernst Ferdinand. *Flagellum Iudeorum: Juden Geissel, Das ist: Ein Neuwe sehr nütze vnd grundliche Erweisung, dass Iesus Christus, Gottes vnd der H. Jungkfrauwen Marien Sohn, der wahre vergeissene vnd gesandte Messias sey. Wider alle . . . Juden, deren . . . Messias noch kommen . . . soll. Darbey auch angehengt von des Machomets vn[d] aller Türken vrsprung, Glaub[n] vnd Gottsdienst . . . Mit allerley Exempeln, lustigen Historien vnd Jüdischen Fabelwerck . . . Auss langweiliger erfahrung zusammen gebracht* s.l.: s.l., 1598.

The Historical Register, XXIV (1721): 347–348.

Hoornbeeck, Johannes. *Teshuvat yehudah, sive, pro convincendis et convertendis judaeis, libri octo.* Lugduni Batavorum: Ex officina Petri Leffen, 1655.

Hubicki, Szymon. *Żydowskie okrucieństwa nad naświętszym sakramentem y dziatkami chrześciańskimi ku temu przydana iest tychże zdrayców zbrodnia w Świniarowie pod Łosicami popełniona którą sądzono na trybunale lubelskim roku pańskiego 1598.* Cracow: W Drukarni Mikołaja Szarffenbergera, 1602.

Huser, Conrad, and Marcus Lombardus. *tractatus de imposturis et ceremoniis judaeorum nostri temporis ab autore germanice editus nunc vero in gratiam reipublicae christianae latine redditus a Conrado Husero Tigurino.* Basel: Per P. Pernam, 1575.

Hystorie von Simon zu Trient. Trent: Albert Kunne, 1475.

Ibn Verga, Salomon, and Georg Gentius. *Historia judaica: res judaeorum ab eversa aede hierosolymitana ad haec fere tempora usque complexa.* Amsterdam: apud Petrum Niellium, 1651.

Ibn Verga, Salomon, and Georg Gentius. *Shevet Yehudah = Tribus Judae Salomonis Fil. Virgae complectens varias calamitates, martyria, dispersiones, accusationes, ejectiones, aliasque res judaeorum ab euerso hierosolymorum templo ad haec ferë tempora . . . de hebraeo in latinum versa ‡ Georgio Gentio.* Amsterdam: apud Henricum Wetstenium, 1680.

Ibn Verga, Solomon. *La vara de Juda.* Amsterdam: por Mosseh d'Abraham Pretto Henriq: en la officina de Jan de Wolf, 1744.

Ibn Verga, Solomon. *Sefer Shevet Yehuda.* Adrianople, 1554.

Ibn Verga, Solomon. *Sefer Shevet Yehuda.* Adrianople (?)/Sabionetta, 1567.

Ibn Verga, Solomon. *Shevet Yehuda.* Cracow, 1591.

Ibn Verga, Solomon. *Shevet Yehudah*. Horodna, 1793.
Ibn Verga, Solomon. *Shevet Yehudah*. Adrianople, 1564.
Ibn Verga, Solomon. *Shevet Yehuda*. Amsterdam, 1648.
Ibn Verga, Solomon. *Sefer Shevet Yehudah*. Edited by Meir Wiener. 2 vols. Hannover: Sumptibus C. Rumpleri, 1856.
Ibn Verga, Solomon. *Sefer Shevet Yehudah val far taitsht*. Fyorda/Fürth: Avraham Beng u-Boneft Sheneur, 1724.
Ibn Verga, Solomon. *Shevet Yehuda*. Prague: Gershom ben Yosef Betsalel Kats, 1608.
Ibn Verga, Solomon. *Sefer Shevet Yehudah: val far taytsht*. Zultsbakh: Bi-defus ha-mehokek Aharon ben Uri Lipman Mevin, 1700.
Ibn Verga, Solomon. *Vara de Ivda*. Amsterdam: Imanvel Benbeniste, 1640.
Ibn Verga, Solomon, and Joseph ibn Verga. *Sefer Shevet Yehudah: zeh sefer toldot yisrael mi-meora'ot ve-zarot ve-telaot*. 1550.
Israel, Menasseh ben. *Vindiciae Judaeorum, or, a Letter in Answer to Certain Questions Propounded by a Noble and Learned Gentleman: Touching the Reproaches Cast on the Nation of the Jevves; Wherein All Objections Are Candidly and yet Fully Cleared*. London: R. D. [Roger Daniel], 1656.
Isadore of Seville. *De fide catholica contra judaeos*. Rome, 1485.
Isadore of Seville. *Liber Ysidori contra iudeos*. Rome, 1485.
Kembter, Hadrian. *Acta pro veritate martyrii corporis & cultus publici B. Andreae Rinnensis pueruli anno MCCCCLXII die 12. julii in odium fidei occisi, collecta, variis notis illustrata & proposita ab Adriano Kembter*. Oeniponti: Wagner, 1745.
Konstytucye publiczne seymu extraordynaryinego warszawskiego pod węzłem generalney konfederacyi oboyga narodów, trwaiącego roku 1773, dnia 19. kwietnia zaczętego, a z limity y sześciu prorogacyi w roku 1775. Warsaw: Drukarnia J. K. Mci Rzeczypospolitey u XX. Scholarum Piarum, 1775.
Korona, Marek. *Rozmowa theologa katholickiego z rabinem zydowskim, przy aryaninie nieprawym chrześcianinie*. Lwów: W Drukarni Coll: Soc: Iesu u Sebastyana Nowogorskiego, 1645.
Kuzmin, I. D. *Materialy k voprosu ob obvineniakh evreev be ritualnykh prestupleniakh*. St. Petersburg, 1913.
Lambertini, Prospero (Benedict XIV). *De servorum dei beatificatione et beatorum canonizatione*. Bologna: Formis Longhi excusoris archiepiscopalis, 1734–1738.
"La morale giudaica e il mistero di sangue." *La Civiltà cattolica* V (1893).
Li horribili tormenti del Beato Simone di Trento. Treviso: Gerardo da Fiandra, 1475.
Lippomano, Luigi. *Octauus tomus vitarum sanctorum priscorum patrum*. Rome: apud Antonium Bladum impressorem cam., 1560.
Lippomano, Luigi. *Septimus tomus vitarum sanctorum priscorum patrum*. Rome: apud Antonium Bladum impressorem cam., 1558.
List Michaela żyda ochrzczonego. Cracow: Drukarnia Andrzeja Piotrowczyka, 1584.
Loewenstein, Lippmann Hirsch. *Damascia die Judenverfolgung zu Damaskus und ihre Wirkung auf die öffentliche Meinung nebst nachweisungen über den Ursprung der gegen die Juden wiederholten Beschuldigung, als bedienten sie sich des Menschenblutes bei Rituellen Zeremonien*. Frankfurt a.M: Loewenstein, 1841.

Luther, Martin. *Das Jhesus Christus eyn geborner Jude sey.* Wittenberg: Melchior Lotter, 1523.
Luther, Martin. *Von den Juden und iren Lugen. D. M. Luth. zum andernmal gedruckt, und mehr dazu gethan. M.D. XLIII.* Wittenberg: durch Hans Lufft, 1543.
Manifestatio judaeorum cathechumenorum ex consistorii leopol: extracta. 1759.
Margaritha, Antonius. *Der gantz judisch Glaub.* Leipzig: Melchior Lotther, 1531.
Margaritha, Antonius. *Der gantz judisch Glaub.* Augsburg: Heynrich Steyner, 1530.
Mariani, Michelangelo. *Il glorioso infante S. Simone: historia panegirica.* Trent: Zanetti Stampator Episcopale, 1668.
Martyrologium romanvm ad nouam kalendarij rationem, & ecclesiasticae historiae veritatem reftitutum Gregorii XIII Pont. Max. iussu editum. Rome: ex typographia Dominici Basae, 1583.
Maximi fructus monitum, quoad nuperas vehementiores in cohortem judæorum factas graffationes, ad doctrinam St. Pauli, nos autem scientes timoren domini: placide & moderate illos ferendos esse, ubi simul de stirpe eorum, post Abrahami tempora florentissima, ut & veteri eorum republ. hic, ut & in textu germanico latè agitur: nec non firmissimis rationibus, argumentis, & attestatis publicis ostenditur: falsissimè illos olim hodieque, infanticidi puerulorum christianorum, & usus sanguinis christianorum in variis rebus argui. Fürth: Abraham von Werth, 1699.
Mayr, Johann. *Epitome cronicorum seculi modernidas ist: kurzter Begriff und Inhalt aller gedenckw‚Rdigen Sachen, so von 1500 bifl zu dem 1604. Jar Christi auf dem gantzen erdenkreiss sich verlaufen : sampt erzelung viler lander und nationen seltzamer sitten und gebrauchen.* Munich: N. Henricus, 1604.
Medici, Paolo Sebastiano. *Riti e costumi degli ebrei confutati dal dottore Paolo Medici sacerdote fiorentino coll'aggiunta in questa seconda edizione di una lettera all'universale del giudaismo, compilata colle riflessioni di Niccolò Stratta gia rabbino, e poi cattolico romano.* Madrid: Luc'Antonio de Bedmar, 1737.
Miczyński, Sebastian. *Zwierciadlo Korony Polskiey: urázy ciezkie y utrapienia wielkie, ktore ponosi od zydow wyrazaiace synom koronnym ná seym walny w roku panskim 1618.* Cracow: Máciej Jedrzeiowczyk, 1618.
Miczyński, Sebastian. *Zwierciadło Korony Polskiey urazy ciężkie, y utrapienia wielkie ktore ponosi od żydow wyrażaiące synom koronnym w roku pańskim 1618 . . . teraz znowu przydatkiem y dostateczniey wydane roku 1648. adige seruum ad opus, quod officium eius postulat.* 1648 [1618].
Mojecki, Przecław. *Żydowskie okrucieństwa, mordy, y zabobony.* Cracow: W Drukarni Jak. Sibeneychera, 1598.
Molandus, Ioannes. *Usuardi martyrologium quo romana ecclesia ac permultae aliae utuntur.* Lovanii: apud Hieronymum Wellaum, 1573.
Monmouth, Thomas of, and Miri Rubin. *The Life and Passion of William of Norwich.* Translated by Miri Rubin. London: Penguin Books, 2014.
Morosini, Giulio. *Via della fede mostrata a'gli ebrei da Giulio Morosini Venetiano. Diuisa in tre parti. Nella prima si pruoua, che non deuono osseruare la legge mosaica. Nella seconda si mostrano tutte le cerimonie. Nella terza si palesa, che në meno osseruano i precetti del decalogo.* Rome: Nella Stamparia della Sacra Congregazione de Propaganda Fide, 1683.

Münster, Sebastian. *Cosmographei, Oder Beschreibung Aller Lander, Herrschafften, Fernemsten Stetten, Geschichten*. Basel: Durch Henrichum Petri, 1561.Münster, Sebastian. *Cosmographey Oder Beschreibung Aller Lander, Herrschafften, Fernem[b]sten Stetten, Geschichten, Gebre‚Che[n], Handtierungen*. Basel: Henri Petri, 1567.

Münster, Sebastian. *Cosmographia: Beschreibung aller Lender durch Sebastianum Munsterum in welcher begriffen, aller Volcker, Herrschafften, Stetten, und namhafftiger Flecken, Herkommen : Sitten, Gebreuch, Ordnung, Glauben, Secten, Und Hantierung, durch die gantze Welt, und fernemlich teutscher Nation: ulas auch besunders in iedem Landt gefunden, und darin beschehen sey*. Basel: Getruckt durch Henrichum Petri, 1544.

Münster, Sebastian. *Cosmographia. Beschreibug aller Lender, etc. aller Volcker, Herrschafften, Stetten, etc. durch die gantze Welt, und fernemlich teutscher Nation. . . . allesmMit Figuren undt schonen Landt Tafeln erklart, etc. allenthalben fast seer gemeret und gebessert, etc*. Basel: Henri Petri, 1545.

Münster, Sebastian. *Cosmographia, Beschreibu[n]g aller Lender durch Sebastianum Munsterum*. Basel: Henri Petri, 1548.

Münster, Sebastian. *Cosmographia universalis*. Basileae: apud Henricum Petri, 1554.

Münster, Sebastian. *Cosmographiae uniuersalis Lib. VI: In quibus, iuxta certioris fidei scriptorum traditionem describuntur, omniu[m] habitalbilis orbis partiu[m] situs p[ro]priaeq[ue] dotes, regionum topographicae effigies, terrae ingenia, quibus sit ut tam differe[n]tes & uarias specie res, & animatas & inanimatas, ferat, animalium peregrinorum naturae & picturae, nobiliorum ciuitatum icones & descriptiones, regnorum initia, incrementa & translationes, omnium gentiu[m] mores, leges, religio, res gestae, mutationes, item regum & principium genealogiae*. Basel: apud Henrichum Petri, 1550.

Münster, Sebastian. *cosmographiae uniuersalis lib. vi in quibus, iuxta certioris fidei scriptorum traditionem describuntur: omniu[m] habitabilis orbis partiu[m] situs, propriae[que] dotes: regionum topographicae effigies : terrae ingenia, quibus fit ut tam differentes & uarias specie res, & animatas & inanimatas, ferat : animalium peregrinorum naturae & picturae: nobiliorum ciuitatum icones & descriptiones: regnorum initia, incrementa & translationes: omnium gentium mores, leges, religio, res gestae, mutationes : item regum & principum genealogiae*. Basel: apud Henrichum Petri, 1552.

Münster, Sebastian. *Cosmographiae universalis lib. vi. in quibus iuxta certioris fidei scriptorum traditionem describuntur, omnium habitabilis orbis partium situs, pro priaeque dotes. regionum topographicae effigies. terrae ingenia, quibus sit ut tam differentes & uarias specie res, & animatas, & inanimatas, ferat. animalium peregrinorum naturae & picturae. nobiliorum ciuitatum icones & descriptiones. regnorum initia, incrementa & translationes. regum & principum genealogiae. item onmium gentium mores, leges, religio, mutationes: atq. memorabilium in hunc usque annum 1559. gestarum rerum historia*. Basel: Henri Petri, 1559.

Münster, Sebastian. *La cosmographie universelle, contenant la situation de toutes les parties du monde, auec leurs proprietez & apartenances : la description des pays & regions d'iceluy*. Basel: Laquelle a este acheuèe d'imprimer, aux despens de Henry Pierre, 1568.

Münster, Sebastian. *Sei libri della cosmografia vniuersale: ne quali secondo che n'hanno parlatto i piu ueraci scrittori son disegnati: i siti de tutte le parti del mondo habitabile & le proprie doti, le tauole topographice delle regioni, le natural qualita del terreno, on de nascono tante diferenze, & uarieta dicose, & animate & non animate, le nature, & le dipinture degli animali pellegrini, l'imagini, & descrittioni delle citta piu nobili, i principij de regni, glia accrescimenti, tramutamenti, i costumi di tutte le genti, le leggi, la religione, i fatti, le mutationi, le genealogie altresi de re, de principi.* Basel: Stampato a spese di Henrigo Pietro Basiliense, 1558.

Murner, Thomas. *Hukat ha-pesah: ritus et celebratio phase iudeorum cum orationibus eorum et benedictionibus menses ad litteram interpretatis cum omni observatione uti soliti sunt suum pasca extra terram promissionis sine esu agni pascalis celebrare.* Frankfurt a.M: Beatus Murner, 1512.

Neubauer, Adolf, and Moritz Stern. *Hebräische Berichte über die Judenverfolgungen während der Kreuzzüge.* Berlin: Simion, 1892.

Officia propria Sancti Vigilii episcopi, et B. Simonis Innocentis Martyrum, ac Sanctae Maxentiae Viduae, ab omnibus ecclesiasticis in tridentina dioecesi statutis diebus recitanda et ad commodiorem usum cum psalmis congesta. Tridenti: Apud Ioan. Baptistam, et Iacobum fratres de Gelminis de Sabbio, 1588.

Officium proprium S. simonis innocentis, et martyris tridentini: per totam dioecesin trid. a secularibus, & regularibus die XXIIII martii celebrandum. Tridenti: Ex typographia episcopale, 1655.

Osiander, Andreas. *Ob Es War vn[d] Glaublich Sey, Daß die Juden der Christen Kinder Heymlich Erwürgen, vnd Jr Blut Gebrauchen: Ein Treffenliche Schrifft, auff eines yeden vrteyl gestelt.* Nuremberg: Petreius, 1530.

Pagius, Antonius. *Critica historico-chronologica in universos annales ecclesiasticos emminentissimi et reverendissimi Caesaris Cardinalis baronii in qua rerum narratio defenditur, illustratur, suppletur, ordo temporum corrigitur, innovatur, et periodo graeco-romana, nunc primum concinnata munitur.* Cologne: Allobrogum sumptibus Fratrum de Tournes, 1727.

Paris, Matthew. *Matthew Paris's English History: From the Year 1235 to 1273.* Translated by J. A. Giles. London: George Bell and Sons, 1889.

Pfefferkorn, Johann. *Ich Heyss Eyn Buchlijn der Iuden Beicht. Jn Allen Orten Vint Man Mich Leicht Vill Neuwe Meren Synt Myr Wall Bekant Jch Will Mich Spreyden in Alle Landt Wer Mich Lyst Den Wuschen Ich Heyl Doch Das Ich Den Iuden Nit Werde Tzu Deyl.* Cologne: Johann Landen, 1508.

Pfefferkorn, Johann. *In Disem Buchlein Vindet Jer Ain Entlichenn Furtrag Wie Die Blinden Juden Yr Ostern Halten Unnd Besunderlich Wie Das Abentmal Gessen Wirt, Weiter Wurdt Aussgetruckt Das Die Juden Ketzer Seyn Des Alten Und Des Newenn Testaments, Etc.* Cologne: Landen, 1509.

Pfefferkorn, Johann. *In hoc libello coparatur absoluta explicatio, quomi ceci illi iudei suu pascha servet, etc.* G.L. Cologne: Per Henricum in nussia, 1509.

Pharetra fidei catholice siue ydonea disputatio inter christianos et judeos. in qua perpulchra tanguntur media et rationes. quibus quiuis christifidelis tam ex prophetis suis proprijs q[uam] ex nostris eorum erroribus faciliter poterit obuiare. Cologne: Heinrich Quentel, 1494.

Pharetra catholice fidei sive ydonea disputatio inter christianos et judeos in qua perpulchra tanguntur media et rationes quibus quivis christifidelis tam ex prophetis suis proprijs quam ex nostris eorum erroribus faciliter poterit obviare. Landschut: Per Joannem Weyssenburger, 1514.

Picart, Bernard. *The Religious Ceremonies and Customs of the Several Nations of the Known World : Represented in above an Hundred Copper-Plates, Designed by the Famous Picart, Together with Historical Explanations, and Several Curious Dissertations.* London: Printed for Nicholas Prevost, 1733.

Picart, Bernard, and Jean-Frèdèric Bernard. *Cèrèmonies et coutumes religieuses de tous les peuples du monde : reprèsentèes par des figures.* Amsterdam: Chez J. F. Bernard, 1723.

Pichi, Pietro. *Epistola a gli ebrei d'Italia nella quale si dimostra la vanità della loro penitenza. del p. maestro f. Pietro Pichi da Trievi Dominicano, predicatore de gli ebrei in Roma.* Rome: appresso Guglielmo Facciotto, 1622.

Pichi, Pietro. *Le stolte dottrine de gli ebrei con la loro confutatione.* Rome: Apresso Manelfo Manelfi, 1640.

Pichi, Pietro. *Trattato della passione e morte del messia contra gli ebrei.* Rome: Nella stamperia dello Spada appresso Stefano Paolino, 1618.

Pikulski (?), Gaudenty. *Błędy talmutowe od samychże żydow uznane. y przez nową sektę siapwscieciuchow, czyli contra talmudystow wyiawione.* Lwów: Jan Szlichtyn, 1758.

Pikulski, Gaudenty. *Złość żydowska przeciwko bogu i bliźniemu prawdzie y sumieniu na obwinienie talmudystow na dowód ich zaślepienia y religii dalekiey od prawa bożego przez Moyżesza danego.* Lwów: Jan Szlichtyn, 1760.

Pinamonti, Giovanni Pietro. *La sinagoga disingannata, overo, via facile à mostrare à qualunque ebreo la falsità della sua setta, e la verità della legge christiana.* Bologna: Longhi, 1694.

Pistorius, Johann, ed. *Polonicae historiae corpus: hoc est polonicarum rerum latini recentiores & veteres scriptores, quotquot extant, uno volumine compraehensi omnes, & in aliquot distributi tomos.* Basel: Per Sebastianum Henricpetri, 1582.

Pius X, Pope. *Codex iuris canonici.* Vol. IX pars II, Acta Apostolicae Sedis Commentarium Officiale. Rome: Typis Polyglotis Vaticanis, 1917.

Pratus, Thomas. *De immanitate judaeorum in Simonem infantum.* Treviso: Gerardus de Lisa de Flandria, 1475.

"Privilegium et sententia in favorem iudaeorum." In *Monumenta Germaniae Historica,* edited by Ludwig Weiland, Jakob Schwalm and Margarete Kuhn. Hannover: Hahn, 1896.

Processus Inquisitorius, Welcher in Der Königl. Böhm. Residenz-Stadt Prag/Von Dem Hochlöbl. Königl. Appellations-Tribunal . . . Im Jahr 1694. Wider Beyde Prager-Juden Lazar Abeles Und Löbl Kurtzhandl/Wegen Des/Ex Odio Christianae Fidei, Von Ihnen Juden/Ermordeten zwölffjährigen jüdischen Knabens/Simon Abeles/Als Leiblichen Sohn Des Erstern/verführet; und zu mehrern Erhöhung des Christlichen Glaubens . . . Samt Denen Dienlichen Haubt-Inquisitions-Acten/ . . . In Offenen Druck Gestellet Worden. Prague: Endter, 1696.

Processus judiciarius in causa patrati cruenti infanticidii per infideles judaeos. 1761.

Prynne, William. *A Short Demurrer to the Jewes Long Discontinued Remitter into England. Comprising an Exact Chronological Relation of Their First Admission into, Their Ill Deportment, Misdemeanors, Condition, Sufferings, Oppressions, Slaughters, Plunders, by Popular Insurrections, and Regal Exactions in; and Their Total, Final Banishment by Judgment and Edict of Parliament, out of England, Never to Return Again: Collected out of the Best Historians. With a Brief Collection of Such English Laws, Scriptures, as Seem Strongly to Plead, and Conclude against Their Readmission into England, Especially at This Season, and against the General Calling of the Jewish Nation. With an Answer to the Chief Allegations for Their Introduction. By William Prynne Esq; a Bencher of Lincolnes-Inne.* London: Printed for Edward Thomas, dwelling in Green-Arbor, 1656.

Pusculus, Ubertinus. *Vbertini Pusculi Brixien[Sis] duo libri symonidos: de iudeorum perfidia quo modo Ihesum [Christu]m crucifixerunt diuos Ricardu[m] Parisiensem Symone Tridentinu[m] afflixere martyrio supliciaq[ue] dedere.* Augsburg: Johannem Otmar, 1511.

Quaranta, Stefano. *Summa bullarii earum que summorum pontificum constitutionum quae ad communem ecclesiae usum post volumina juris canonici usquë ad Paulum V. Eman, Runt, Authore Stephano Quaranta, cum additionibus Prosperi De Augustino.* Venice: apud Juntas, 1609.

Radliński, Jakub. *Prawda chrześciańska od nieprzyiaciela swego zeznana: to iest traktat rabina samuela pokazuiacy błędy żydowskie około zachowania prawa moyżeszowego y przyiscia messyaszowego, którego żydzi czekaią.* Lublin: Typis Societatis Jesu, 1733.

Rinaldi, Odoricus. *Annales ecclesiastici ab anno quo desinit Card. Caes. Baronius MCXCVIII usque ad annum MDXXXIV continuati, ex regestis pontificum, et literis auctoritate publica fideque muntis: antiquissimis S. Sedis Apostolicae scriniis & amplissimis Vaticanae potissimum, aliarumque bibliothecarum archivis confirmati: imperatorum, regum ac principum diplomatibus, epistolis, & manuscriptis codicibus, aliisq[ue] qua publicis qua privatis monumentis: probatissimorum denique & antiquissimorum auctorum, testium saepe ocularium libris ac scriptis copiose illustrati tomus XIII.* Cologne: Sumptibus Ioannis Wilhelmi Friessem, 1692.

Ristretto della vita e martirio di S. Simone fanciullo della città di Trento. Rome: Filippo Neri alle Muratte, 1594?

Rolevinck, Werner. *Fasciculus temporum.* Basel: Bernhardus Richel, 1482 (February 20).

Rolevinck, Werner. *Fasciculus temporum.* Venice: cura impensisq[ue] Erhardi Ratdolt de Augusta, 1480 (November 24).

Rolevinck, Werner. *Fasciculus temporum.* Strassbourg: Johann Prüss, 1488.

Rolevinck, Werner. *Fasciculus temporum.* Strassbourg: Johann Prüss, 1490.

Rolevinck, Werner. *Fasciculus temporum.* Cologne: Nicolaus Götz, 1478.

Rolevinck, Werner. *Fasciculus temporum. Le Fardelet Hystorial.* Genf: Drucker des Fardelet du temps, 1495,

Rolevinck, Werner. *Fasciculus temporum omnes antiquorum chronicas complectens.* Venice: Goergius Walch, 1479.

Rolevinck, Werner. *Dat Boek dat men hiet fasciculus temporum mit beig.* Utrecht: Johann Veldener, 1480.

Rossi, Azariah dei, and Joanna Weinberg. *The Light of the Eyes.* New Haven: Yale University Press, 2001.

Sacra Consulta sive Illustriss. et Revedendiss. D. Ghezzio Ponente Viterben. calumniae super praetensa attentata iugulatione pro Gioiello de Core et Iosepho Samen haebreis. Summarium. Rome: Typis Reverendae Camerae Apostolicae, 1706.

Samuel, Marochitanus. *Epistola albo list Rabi Samuela ku drugiemu Rabi Isaakowi Żidowi Posłany, że Jezus nazarenski prawdziwem iest messiaszem y wszego świata zbawicielem, a że żydowie próżno innego messiasza oczekiwają. ksiąźki wszem krześcianom barzo użyteczne. item przeniesienie barzo skrytey tajemnice żydowskiey od żyda Theodorego o Panu Jesu Kriscie iż on był Synem Bożim Prawdziwym.* Cracow: Ungler, 1536.

Samuel, Marochitanus. *Epistola albo list Rabi Samuela ku drugiemu Rabi Isaakowi Żidowi Posłany, że Jezus nazarenski prawdziwem iest messiaszem y wszego świata zbawicielem, a że żydowie próżno innego messiasza oczekiwają. ksiąźki wszem krześcianom barzo użyteczne. item przeniesienie barzo skrytey tajemnice żydowskiey od żyda Theodorego o Panu Jesu Kriscie iż on był Synem Bożim Prawdziwym.* Cracow: Ungler, 1538.

Schedel, Hartmann. *Das Buch der Croniken unnd Geschichten mit Figuren und Pildnussen von Anbeginn der Welt bis auff dise vnsere Zeijt* [Weltchronik]. Augsburg: Johann Schönsperger, 1500.

Schedel, Hartmann. *Liber chronicarum.* Nuremberg: Anton Koberger, 1493.

Schedel, Hartmann. *Liber chronicarum cum figuris et imaginis ab initio mundi usque nunc temporis.* Augsburg: Johann Schönsperger, 1497.

Shulvass, Moses A. "Maqor 'ivri ḥadash le-toledot 'alilat ha-dam be-Trento." In *Minḥah li-Yehudah: mugash le-harav Yehudah Leib Zlotnik*, edited by Simha Assaf, Yehudah Even-Shemuel, and Yehuda Leib Avida, 189–196. Jerusalem: Mosad ha-Rav Kuk, 1949–1950.

Sichardt, Johannes, ed. *Habes opt. lector chronicon opus felicissime renatum : infinitis membris emendatis exactiusq[ue] conformatis, & adiectis multis quibus anteh‡c caruerat annis, perfectum: omnibus omnium, quas uocant, facultatum professoribus non solum utilissimum, sed & maxime necessarium, in quo diuinitus est scriptum, & plusquam humano iudicio distributum quicquid magnum & memorabile per deum opt. maximum rerum omnium rectorem, & per miseros mortales cum mortalibus, ‡ mundo creato usque ad hunc annum, est gestum.* Basil: Excudebat Henricus Petrus, 1536.

Sichardus, Joannes, ed. *En damus chronicon divinum plane opus eruditissimorum autorum: repetitum ab ipso mundi initio, ad annum usque salutis M.D. XII.* Basel: Henricus Petrus, 1529.

Simon, Richard. "Factum servant de réponse au livre intitulé abrégé du procès fait aux juifs de metz." *Archives Israelites de France* 3, no. December (1842 [1670]): 675–685.

Simonsohn, Shlomo. *The Apostolic See and the Jews: Documents, 492–1404.* Vol. 94, Studies and Texts. Toronto: Pontifical Institute of Mediaeval Studies, 1988.

Simonsohn, Shlomo. *The Apostolic See and the Jews: Documents, 1464–1521*. Vol. 99, Studies and Texts. Toronto: Pontifical Institute of Mediaeval Studies, 1990.
Simonsohn, Shlomo. *The Apostolic See and the Jews: Documents, 1539–1545*. Vol. 105, Studies and Texts. Toronto: Pontifical Institute of Mediaeval Studies, 1990.
Simonsohn, Shlomo. *History of the Jews in the Duchy of Mantua*. Jerusalem: Kiryath Sepher, 1977.
Sixtus, Senensis. *Bibliotheca sancta*. Venice: apud Franciscum Franciscium Senense et Ioan Gryphius excudebat, 1566.
Sixtus, Senensis. *Bibliotheca sancta*. Cologne: apud Maternum Maternus Cholinum, 1576.
Skarga, Piotr. *Żywoty Świętych Starego i Nowego Zakonu z Pisma Świętego i poważnych pisarzów i doktorow kościelnych wybranych*. Drukarnia Oświeconego Pana Mikołaja Christofa Radziwiłła, 1579.
Śleszkowski, Sebastian. *Odkrycie zdrad, złośliwych ceremoniy, taiemnych rad, praktyk szkodliwych rzeczypospolitey y wszystkich zamysłów żydowskich, takze wytknienie niektórych pomocnikow żydowskich. przytym zdrowa rada, jako zdradom praktykom y przedsięwzięciom żydowskim ieśli chcemy w cale bydź przed czasem zabiegać mamy z siedmidziesiąt y ośmi nie omylnych autorów y z samego doświadczenia teraz nowo na przestrogę wszystkim stanom Królestwa Polskiego z pilnością wydane*. Brunsbergae: In Officina typographica Georgij Schonfels, 1621.
Śleszkowski, Sebastian. *Jasne dowody o doktorach żydowskich, że nie tylko dusze ale y ciało swoie w niebiespieczeństwo zginienia wiecznego wdaią, ktorzy Żydow, Tatarow y innych niewiernych, przeciwko zakazaniu kościoła świetego powszechnego za lekarzów używaia*. 1623.
Slonik, Benjamin Aaron. *Precetti da esser imparati dalle donne hebree*. Translated by Jacob Halpron. Venice: G. Sarzina, 1616.
Sochostow, Gabriel ben Naftali Hirts. *Matsevet kodesh, hu zikaron tsadikim: sefer zikaron le-khol ha-ge'onim veha-kedoshim sare ha-torah, asher le-mishmeret li-fene h' be-vet ha-mo'ed le-khol ḥai ha-yashan poh 'ir Lvov*. Lemberg: Kugel, Lewin, 1860.
Sokolowsky, Meir, and Joseph Abramovitsch. *Rozana: A Memorial to the Ruzhinoy Jewish Community*. New York: JewishGen, 2012.
Sołtyk, Kajetan et al. *Dekret o zamęczenie przez zydow dziecięcia katolickiego, ferowany w grodzie żytomirskim. a naprzod kopia listu I. W. Imci Xiędz Kaietana Sołtyka, Biskupa Emauseńskiego, Koadiutora Kiiowskiego, Do J. O. Xiążęcia Imci Arcybiskupa Lwowskiego, z Zytomierza; list do Arcybiskupa Lwowskiego*. 1753.
Sommariva, Giorgio. *Martyrium Sebastiani Novelli trucidati a judaeis*. Treviso: Diligentia Bernardini Celerii de Luere, 1480.
Stabili, Antonino. *Fascicolo delle vanità giudaiche, composto per Il R.P.F. Antonino Stabili da S. Angelo a Fasanella, Dell'ordine De' Predicatori. Giornate Sedici, nelle quali si discorre sopra la Scrittura Vecchia, & Noua, et si proua la venuta del vero Messia Christo, Giesu, Signore, & Redentor Nostro. Con Due Tauole, L'una De Gl'autori Citati Nell'opera, L'altra De Gl'argomenti in Ciascuna Giornata*. Ancona: Appresso Francesco Saluioni, 1583.

Supplex libellus: a iudaeis fidem catholicam amplectentibus et baptismum expetentibus, Illustrissimo et Reverendissimo D. D. Łubieński Archi-Episcopo Leopoliensi, nunc celsissimo nominato principi primati porrectus, 1759.

Surius, Laurentius. *Commentarius breuis rerum in orbe gestarum: ab anno salutis millesimo quingentesimo, vsq[ue] ad annum LXVI.* Cologne: apud haeredes Ioannis Quentel & Geruinum Calenium, 1566.

Surius, Laurentius. *Commentarius breuis rerum in orbe gestarum: ab anno salutis M.D. vsque in annum M.D. LXXIIII ex optimis quibusque scriptoribus congestus, & nunc recens non parum auctus & locupletatus.* Cologne: apud Geruinum Calenium, & haeredes Ioannis Quentelij, 1574.

Surius, Laurentius. *De probatis sanctorum historiis: partim ex tomis Aloysii lipomani partim etiam ex egregiis manuscriptis codicibus, quarum permultae antehàc numquàm in lucem prodiere, optima fide collectis.* Cologne: apud Geruinum Calenium et haeredes Quentelios, 1571.

Surius, Laurentius. *De probatis sanctorum historiis: partim ex tomis Aloysii Lipomani, doctissimi episcopi, partim etiam ex egregiis manvscriptis codicibvs, qvarvm permultae antehunc nunquam in lucem prodire. complectens sanctos mensium martii et aprilis.* Coloniae Agrippinae: Calenius & Quentel, 1578.

Surius, Laurentius. *Tomus VII de probatis sanctorum historiis: in quem ordine mensium obseruato relatae sunt cum omnes illae historiae, quae ad secundam sex tomorum editionem accesserunt.* Coloniae Agrippinae: apud Geruinum Calenium et haeredes Quentelios, 1581.

Syreński, Szymon (Syrenius). *Zielnik, herbarzem z ięzyka lacinskiego zowią, to iest opisanie własne imion, kształtu ... y mocy ziół wszelakich drzew ... takze trunków, syropów ... przytym o ziemiach y glinkach roznych, o kruscach, perlach y drogich kamieniach, tez o zwierzetach ... od dioscorida, z przydaniem y dostatecznym dokladem z wielu innych tey materiey pisacych ... polskiem iezykiem zebrany y na viii ksiag rozlozony ... przez D. Simona Syrenniusa.* Cracow: W drukarni Bazylego Skalskiego, 1613.

Tiberinus, Johannes Mathias. *Die Geschicht und Legend von dem seligen Kind und Marterer gennant Symon von den Juden zu Trent gemartet und gemortet.* Translated by Ginther Zainer. Augsburg: Ginther Zainer, 1475.

Tiberinus, Johannes Mathias. *De infantulo in ciuitate Tridentina p[er] iudeos rapto atq[ue] i[n] vilipendium [christianae] religionis post multas maximasq[ue] trucibationes [isic] ... crudelissme necato ac deinde in flume[n] cadauer edimerso hystoria feliciter incipit.* Rome: Bartholomaeus Guldinbeck, June 19, 1475.

Tiberinus, Johannes Mathias. *Hystoria Completa.* Tridenti: Hermanno Schindeleyp auctore, 1476.

Tiberinus, Johannes Mathias. *De infantulo in ciuitate Tridentina p[er] iudeos rapto atq[ue] i[n] vilipendium [christianae] religionis post multas maximasq[ue] trucibationes [isic] anno iubileo die parasceue crudelissme necato ac deinde in flume[n] cadauer edimerso hystoria feliciter incipit.* Rome: Bartholomaeus Guldinbeck, July 24, 1475.

Tiberinus, Johannes Mathias. *De obitu Beati Simonis Tridentini: ad rectores et cives Brixianos.* Tavri: GF, 1475.

Tiberinus, Johannes Mathias. *Passio Beati simonis pueri tridentini a p[er]fidis judeis nup[er] occisi.* Rome: Bartholomaeus Guldinbeck, 1475.
Tiberinus, Johannes Mathias. *Passio Beati Simonis pueri tridentini.* Treviso: Gerardus de Lisa de Flandria, 1475.
Tiberinus, Johannes Mathias. *Relatio de Simone puero tridentino.* Venice: Gabriele di Pietro, 1475.
Theiner, Augustin. *Vetera monumenta Poloniae et Lithuaniae gentiumque finitimarum historiam illustrantia maximam partem nondum.* 4 vols. Rome: Typis Vaticanis, 1860–1864.
Tynemouth, John of, and John Capgrave. *Explicit (noua lege[n]da Anglie).* London: Wynkyn de Worde, 1516.
Tysowski, Jan. *Dekret na zydow mordercow y zaboycow pewnego katolika. działo się to na zamku zasławskim w dobrach dziedzicznych Jaśnie Oświeconego Xiążęcia Jmci Pawła . . . Lubartowicza Sanguszka.* After April 17, 1747.
Usque, Samuel, and Martin A. Cohen. *Consolation for the Tribulations of Israel (Consolaçam Ás Tribulaçoens De Israel).* Philadelphia: Jewish Publication Society of America, 1965.
Vitti, Giovanni Pietro. *Memorie storico-cronologiche di varj bambini ed altri fanciulli martirizzati, in odio di nostra fede, da gli ebrei.* Venice: G. Zerletti, 1761.
Viva, Isaacus. *Vindex sanguinis, sive vindiciae secundum veritatem, quibus judaei ab infanticidiis et victima humana contra Jacobum Geusium, vindicantur per Isaacum Vivam.* Amsterdam: Typis Adami Jongbloet, 1681.
von Liliencron, Rochus. *Die historischen Volkslieder der Deutschen.* 5 vols. Leipzig: Vogel, 1866–1869.
Voragine, Jacques de. *Hystorie plurimorum sanctorum noviter e laboriose ex diversis libris in unum collecte.* Lavanii: Johannis de Westfalia, 1485.
Wagenseil, Johann Christoph. *D. Joh. Christoph. Wagenseils Benachrichtigungen wegen einiger die Judenschafft angehenden wichtigen Sachen erster Theil worinnen I. Die Hoffnung Der Erlösung Israelis oder Klarer Beweiß Der . . . Herannahenden Juden-Bekehrung . . . II. Wiederlegung der Unwarheit daß die Juden zu ihrer Bedürfniß Christen-Blut haben müssen. III. Anzeigung, Wie leicht es dahin zu bringen, daß die Juden forthin abstehen müssen, die Christen mit Wuchern und Schinden zu Plagen.* Leipzig: Heinichen, 1705.
Wierzbowski, Teodor, and Jakub Sawicki. *Matricularum Regni Poloniae summaria, excussis codicibus.* Warsaw: Typis Officinae C. Kowalewski, 1905–.
Wojtyska, Henryk Damian, ed. *Aloisius Lippomano (1555–1557).* Vol. 3/1, Acta Nuntiaturae Polonae. Rome: Institutum Historicum Polonicum Romae, 1993.
Wülfer, Johann, Shlomo Zalman Ufhoyzen, Samuel Friedrich Brenz, Hirsch Solomon Zebi, and Isaacus Viva. *Theriaca judaica ad examen revocata, sive scripta amoibaea Samuelis Friderici Brenzii, conversi judaei, & Salomonis Zevi, apellae astutissimi.* Nuremberg: Sumt. Autoris Excudit Andreas Knorzius, 1681.
Wurtisen, Christian. *Germaniae historicorum illustrium, quorum pleriq[ue] ab Henrico IIII Imperatore vsque ad annum christi, M. CCCC, ex ijs quidem septem nunquam antea editi, gentis eius res gestas memoriae consecrarunt.* Frankfurt a.M: apud haeredes Andreae Wecheli, 1585.

Zach, Ignatius. *Ausführliche Beschreibung der Marter, eines heiligen und unschuldigen Kinds Andreae, Von Rinn, in Tyrol, und Bistumb Brixen: welches von denen Juden aus angebohrnem Hass gegen Christum, und gesambten seiner Christenheit grausam gequälet und ermordet worden*. Augsburg: in Verlag Matthias Wolff, 1724.

Zadok, Samson ben. *Sefer tashbez: ha-mekhuneh: tashbez katan, pesakim, minhagim u-teshuvot me-et ha-Maharam mi-Rotenburg*. Jerusalem: Mif'al Torat Hakhme Ashkenaz, Mekhon Yerushalayim, 2010.

Zaviziano, Giorgio A. *Un raggio di luce: la persecuzione degli ebrei nella storia*. Corfu: Tip. Corai, 1891.

Zevi, Shelomoh. *Yudisher teriyak das iz ayn refueh di damit sikh al gemayne yuden unt yudins gegen den kristen mit varhayt purgiren un ver-antverten, aukh mit bevweys der toreh u-neviim ... das mumer Samoel vridrikh prents ... in seynem ney gedrukten sefer der yudishe shlangen-balg ... velshlikh bezikhtigt*. Hanau, 1615.

Złosc żydowska w zamęczeniu dzieci katolickich przez list nastepuiący y dekreta grodzkie wydana. List J. O. Xcia Jmci Kaietana Sołtyka Biskupa Krakowskiego, na ten czas Biskupa Emuaseńskiego, Koadjutora Kijowskiego, Do J. W. Jmci X. Biskupa Lwowskiego [Mikołaja Gerarda Wyżyckiego] z Żytomierza pisany. After 1761.

Złosc żydowska w zamęczeniu dzieci katolickich przez list nastepuiący y dekreta grodzkie wydana. List J. O. Xcia Jmci Kaietana Sołtyka Biskupa Krakowskiego, na ten czas Biskupa Emuaseńskiego, Koadjutora Kijowskiego, Do J. W. Jmci X. Biskupa Lwowskiego [Mikołaja Gerarda Wyżyckiego] z Żytomierza pisany. A teraz powtornie przedrukowany za pozwoleniem starszych. Lublin: Drukarnia J. K. M. y Rzeczypospolitey, 1774.

Żuchowski, Stefan. *Oglos processow criminalnych na zydach o rozne excessy, takze morderstwo dzieci, osobliwie w Sandomierzu roku 1698 przeswiadczone. w przeswietnym Trybunale Koronnym przewiedzionych dla dobra pospolitego wydany od X. Stephana Zuchowskiego oboyga prawa doktora*. 1700.

Żuchowski, Stefan. *Process kryminalny of niewinne dziecie Jerzego Krasnowskiego iuz to trzecie, roku 1710 dnia 18 sierpnia w Sendomirzu okrutnie od zydow zamordowane. dla odkrycia iawnych kryminalow zydowskich, dla przykladu sprawiedliwosci potomnym wiekom*. Sandomierz: after 1720.

ACKNOWLEDGMENTS

When I began this project in 2011, the book idea was more contained—it was to be a comparative study of blood libels in Poland and Italy. But as I followed the paper trail, I ended up on a tour of Europe, learning about each region's intellectual, religious, cultural, and legal histories. For that reason, *Blood Libel* is indebted to scholars before me who studied and wrote about some of the aspects of that long and complicated story. I also would not have been able to complete the work without the effort of many librarians, archivists, and IT professionals who have digitized holdings and made them available on their own digital platforms, Hathi Trust, and through Google Books. Their efforts make it easier for scholars to compare different copies and different editions without having to travel to different countries.

But even in this digital era, there is nothing like working in libraries and archives. In fact, this book would have been very different without the systematic work with physical books that I was able to do at the New York Public Library (NYPL) as a fellow at the Cullman Center for Scholars and Writers. This allowed me to examine methodically books published in Europe from the late fifteenth century on, one after another, page by page, and experience what contemporary readers might have felt when reading these books. I am grateful to the NYPL and the Cullman Center for giving me this opportunity and thereby making this book so much richer, as well as to the staff at the Dorot Jewish Division and the Rare Book Division of the NYPL for their assistance and patience.

Blood Libel is based on archival materials from archives in eight countries, including the Vatican City. It was these sometimes hitherto unknown documents that helped illuminate processes not visible and known in printed records. I thank the staff at the Archivio Segreto Vaticano in the Vatican City for giving me access to hundreds of volumes of diplomatic correspondence between Rome and the papal nuncios residing in Poland covering more than two centuries. I am also grateful to Monsignor Alejandro Cifres and Dr. Daniel Ponziani of the Archivio della Congregazione per la Dottrina della Fede (Archive of the Congregation for the Doctrine of Faith; ACDF). Their holdings were fundamental in clarifying the events surrounding the wave of accusations experienced by Jews in the eighteenth century. And I am grateful to the late Anne Jacobson Schutte and Adriano Prosperi for helping me with access, and Stefania Pastore for advice on the holdings.

Equally fundamental were the materials in Archiwum Kapituły Kolegiackiej i Katedralnej w Sandomierzu. I am enormously grateful to Bishop Krzysztof Nitkiewicz and Rev. Dr. Piotr Tylec for permitting me to work in the archive and for welcoming me to Sandomierz. Indeed, my work with Bishop Nitkiewicz has had a profound impact on this project, especially my exploration of the blood libel iconography in Sandomierz and tracing it back to Trent. The Sandomierz paintings have often raised controversy, but until 2013 they had never been examined fully from a broader historical perspective. I am grateful to Bishop Nitkiewicz for creating an opportunity to see Sandomierz as a stop made by this story along a long European path.

Staff at other archives were also incredibly helpful. Robert Godding of the Société des Bollandistes provided scans of specific documents and assistance in identifying the location of others. Staff members at the Archivio di Stato di Trento scanned the crucial body of archival documents related to the trial at Trent (APV s.l. capsa 69), making this massive body available to me remotely. Staff at the Archives departementales de la Moselle (ADMM in Metz, France), Bibliothèque royale de Belgique (Brussels), and Trinity College (TCD) in Dublin also scanned archival materials relevant for this book. I am grateful to Yeshiva University Museum (New York) for allowing me to examine some of their holdings physically. Robert Danieluk and especially Mauro Brunello from the Archivum Romanum Societatis Iesu (Roman Archive of the Society of Jesus; ARSI) made it a pleasure for me to work at the archive and to obtain specific documents, when I could not make it there. Dr. Elzbieta Knapek of the Polska Akademia Umiejętności (Polish Academy of Sciences, PAU) was helpful in her capacity both at the PAU and previously at the Archiwum Kurii Metropolitalnej w Krakowie. The staff members at the Bayerische Staadtsbibliothek were most helpful in providing scans of books not available elsewhere.

Research at these many libraries and archives would not have been possible without generous fellowships and grants I received. My deepest gratitude to the Harry Frank Guggenheim Foundation and the John Simon Guggenheim Foundation for their support of this book at an early stage.

As I look back at the community of friends and scholars who helped in this process and have left their own imprints on it in one way or another, I am thankful for the wisdom and, more importantly, the friendship of Debra Kaplan, Sara Lipton, and Josh Teplitsky: they not only read significant parts of the book but also gave me their ears and their minds while I was trying to answer big and small questions that emerged from the research. Brainstorming sessions about titles were a lot of fun, because they forced me to think about the essence of the book.

I am also grateful to everyone who read chapters and proposals, invited me to give talks on early versions of the book, and wrote letters of recommendation for me as I was applying for grants and fellowships that allowed me to travel and take time off from teaching to write. Hence my gratitude to David Biale, Miriam Bodian, Judith Brown, Hillel Kieval, Brian Porter-Szűcs, and Larry Wolff. I am particularly grateful to Elisheva Carlebach for all of the above and also for being a partner in making the Early Modern Workshop (EMW) a vibrant community in New York. Indeed, our discussions about archives during the EMW 2016–2017 were critical for understanding and rethinking the Trent trial and other court and archival records. And in 2017–2018, my fellow Cullmanites at the NYPL's Cullman Center for Scholars and Writers made that year unforgettable. I want to particularly thank Blake Gopnik for listening to and giving me suggestions and advice on sixteenth-century Italian art; Ava Chin and Joan Acocella for great conversations; Salvatore Scibona, Lauren Goldman, and Paul Delaverdac for making "the Cullman year" so meaningful; and Georgi Gospodinov and Nellie Herman for their books, which took me off my path but enriched my mind.

My gratitude also to Andrzej Kamiński, Peter Kracht, and Kathleen McDermott for including me in a book manuscript workshop in June 2017 in Warsaw. I thank Waldemar Kowalski and Hanna Węgrzynek for reading and commenting on several chapters of the manuscript in progress.

I want to thank my former institutional home, Wesleyan University, for the generous sabbatical policy that allowed me to jumpstart the project, as well as former colleagues who were also supportive and helpful, especially by critiquing the early proposals and reading early chapters: Ruth Nisse, Laurie Nussdorfer, and Victoria Smolkin. And big thanks to Jennifer Tucker for suggestions of books I would have not considered and for good cheer, and to Jeremy and Vicky Zwelling, whose friendship and support over my fifteen years at Wesleyan and beyond are some of the most valuable treasures of my life. I was very proud to hold the Jeremy Zwelling Chair in Jewish Studies at Wesleyan.

I am grateful to my new intellectual home, Fordham University, for welcoming me as a colleague. I am happy to have such a wonderful community of scholars and friends in the History Department and in Jewish Studies, especially Orit Avishai, Doron Ben-Atar, Ayala Fader, Emanuel Fiano, Sarit Kattan Gribetz, Anne Hoffman, David Myers, Nicholas Paul, Daniel Soyer, Kirsten Swinth, and Ebru Turan. Fordham's terrific undergraduate students in two seminars on the history of antisemitism have read and discussed chapters of this book in progress. I am thankful to them for serving as an early sounding board.

And there are others who make me grateful for being at Fordham. I want to thank Eva Badovska, Jonathan Crystal, Ellen Fahey-Smith, and the Reverend Joseph McShane, SJ, for their support of me as a scholar and of Jewish Studies at Fordham. Fordham's Jewish Studies community, which has nourished me in the last few years, has been made possible thanks to the foresight and generosity of Eugene Shvidler; it has flourished thanks to the trust and belief in us by Henry Miller, Joel Pickett, and Bruce Taragin. I am grateful to all.

The question "Have you finished?" that my parents, Alina and Zdzisław Teter, would ask each time I called kept me wanting to reach the finish line. As did the love and support of Shawn Hill, my best friend and life partner, who has contributed even more to this project than to my previous books. His love and patience have steadied me for decades, but his professional trajectory as a specialist in digital humanities helped me see my stories in a new way. Without him there would be no maps and no website, www.thebloodlibeltrail.org.

As I was following the paper trail that these anti-Jewish accusations produced, I realized my intellectual debt to the late Yosef Hayim Yerushalmi. His scholarship on Isaac Cardoso and a graduate seminar decades ago on Solomon ibn Verga's *Shevet Yehudah* proved invaluable. The late Jeannette Hopkins suggested I embark on this trail; I only hope she would be proud of where it ended. As I was writing I found myself missing her incisive criticisms and tried to imagine what she would have said. I also wish I could have shared the joy of finishing this book and seeing it in print with Stephen Freedman, the late provost of Fordham University and a good friend, who was instrumental in bringing me to Fordham and whose cheer and encouragement I truly miss.

INDEX

Page numbers in *italics* indicate illustrations. Titles of works will be found under the author's name, unless anonymous, in which case they are alphabetized by title.

Abeles, Simon and Lazar, 306–307, 309
Abramino, Giuseppe (Verona), 221, 291
Abramovich, Nachum (an accused in 1577), 241
Abravanel, Isaac, 271
Abregé du procés fait aux Juifs de Mets (1670), 252–256
Acta Sanctorum, 10, 25–26, 27, 41–42, 92, 166, 191, 200, 243, 244, 269, 303, 305, 312, 340, 380, 393n60, 417n117
Aelred of Rievaulx, 22
Aelwerd (in William of Norwich story), 21
Æthelberht (saint), 21
Æthelberht of Hereford (saint), 21
Æthelred of Ramsey (saint), 21
afikomen, 245, 264, 368
Aimar (prior, in William of Norwich story), 25
Alberettus (Alberetti), Andreas, 287–288
Albert I of Germany (Duke of Austria and Styria), 154, 255
Albert of Świniarów. *See* Świniarów blood libel
Alexander III (pope), 24, 101
Allè, Girolamo, 182
Ambrose, Adrienne Nock, 19

Amelot de La Houssaie, Abraham-Nicolas, *Abregé du procés fait aux Juifs de Mets* (1670), 252–256
Ancona blood libel (1711), 293–298, 325–326
Andreas (father of Simon of Trent), 46, 49, 53–54, 57, *120*
Andreas Oxner of Rinn: *Beatus Andreas* (papal bull, 1755), 127, 301, 313–314, 315, 323, 324, 327, 340, 353, 378, 483n87; Benedict XIV and, 11, 311–314, 322, 476n68; cult of, 11, 22, 123–124, 191, 311–314, *313*; in Ganganelli report, 11, 339–341; modern unofficial persistence of cult, 383; in *Der Stürmer,* 380
Angelini, Giuseppe and Maddalena (of Ancona), 294
Angelo/Engel (in Simon of Trent narrative), 47, 50, 53, 54, 56, 57, 58, 71, 92, 117, 129, 401n34, 402n56
Anna (in Simon of Trent narrative), 51, 71, 74
Annales ecclesiastici (by Baronio and continuators), 91–92, 100, 104, 162–166, 203, 254, 269, 271, 317, 380
Anselm of Canterbury, 19

Anti-Defamation League, 1
anti-Talmudists. *See* Frankists
anti-Trinitarianism, 204, 440n179
Antoniano, Silvio (canon of St. Peter's), 103
Antonius (in Ancona blood libel), 297
Approvino degli Approvini, 69, 73, 83, 405n123, 406n126, 413n41, 423n246
A quo primum (papal encyclical, 1751), 316–317, 327, 330, 332, 358
archives and archival records, 10, 11, 44, 98–99, 123–127, 163, 194, 195, 207, 221, 229, 236, 243, 269, 310, 352, 375, 456n42; chronicles as, 153; Church, 269, 303, 324, 359; Jewish archives, 283, 284, 375, 483n96; memory and, 236, 243, 249, 322, 380;
Areford, David, 131, 136
arma Simonis, 137, 140, 423n232
Aron/Gromek (in Świniarów blood libel), 238, 239
art and iconography of Simon of Trent, 7, 8, 44, 89, 91, 97, 98, 121, 126, 127–137, 129–134, 140–149, 141, 144–146, 150
Astrucas (accused in Valréas case), 35
Audivimus (papal bull, 1179), 24
August II (king of Poland-Lithuania), 259, 265, 269, 461n123, 462–463n165
August III (king of Poland-Lithuania), 272, 276, 359, 465n223
Augustine of Hippo, 122–123, 264, 432n53; *City of God*, 223
Augustynowicz, Joseph (apostolic notary), 322, 330, 480n27
Azemar (Franciscan friar in Valréas case), 35

Bałaban, Majer (or Meir), 456–457n42, 457n54, 478n2
Bale, Anthony, 394n67
Bandino, Giambattista, 103
Baronio, Camillo, 104
Baronio, Cesare, 91, 100, 104–106, 114, 119, 162–163, 165, 166, 169, 203, 206, 254, 271, 317, 336, 380, 416n93
Basnage, Jacques, *History of the Jews* (1716), 271, 308, 310, 474–475n48
Batory, Cardinal Andrzej, 202
Batory, King Stefan, 195, 241, 242
Battista di Campofregoso (duke of Genoa), 98
beatification process, 7, 101–103, 301–302, 303–305, 378

Beatus Andreas (papal bull, 1755), 127, 301, 313–314, 315, 323, 324, 327, 340, 353, 378, 483n87
Beccaria, Cesare, *On Crimes and Punishments* (1764), 374
Beham, Sebald, 450n90
Beilis, Menachem Mendel, and Beilis affair (1911–1913), 11, 375–376, 382
Belhomo (in Pavia blood libel), 111, 112
Bella (in Simon of Trent narrative), 71, 74
Bellarmino, Roberto (Cardinal), 103
Bell'Haver Crucifero, Thomaso, *Dottrina facile et breveper ridurre l'hebreo* (1608), 188
Benedictines, in child martyr cults, 394n67
Benedict XII (pope), 255
Benedict XIV (pope; formerly Prospero Lambertini), 11, 300–322; Andreas Oxner cult, recognition of, 124, 127, 301, 311–314, 313, 322, 324; *A quo primum* (papal encyclical, 1751), 316–317, 327, 330, 332, 358; *Beatus Andreas* (papal bull, 1755), 127, 301, 313–314, 315, 323, 324, 327, 340, 353, 378, 483n87; Bonelli and, 310–311, 358; on children martyred by Jews, in *De servorum Dei*, 302–305; death of, 324, 336; debates over blood libel in lifetime of, 305–311; *De servorum Dei beatificatione et beatorum canonizatione* (1734–1738), 301–302, 305, 311, 312, 314, 315, 340, 472n3; Enlightenment reputation of, 300–301, 472n1; Ganganelli report and, 324, 325, 327, 332, 335, 336, 340–341, 382; on *Martyrologium romanum*, 104; official condemnation, 18th-century Polish Jews' efforts to elicit, 355; Poland/Poland-Lithuania and, 276, 300, 314–322, 325; as *Promotor Fidei* (Devil's Advocate), 302; Roman Jewish community and, 315, 320–321; Vitti and, 191; on Werner of Oberwesel, 42
Benedig (accused in Valréas case), 35
Berek Alexander (accused in Sandomierz), 258–261
Bergamo, church of San Bartolomeo, painted sequence of Simon of Trent narrative, 135
Bergomensis, Jacobus Philippus, *See* Foresti, Jacob Philip of Bergamo
Berko (later Michael; Jewish child in Grabie blood libel), 364–371
Berlaymont, Philippe de, 419n149

Berlin, host desecration (1510), 162
Bernardino da Feltre, 122, 149
Bernard of Clairvaux, 163, 189, 254, 270, 316–317, 326, 337–338, 341
Berne blood libel (1287), 168, 171, 211, 248
Ber of Bolechów, 481n50
Bershadskii, S. A., 455n21
Beruguette, Pedro, 422n228
Biale, David, 397–398n141
Bidermann, Ernest, 312
Bielski, Marcin, 170–171, 430n25
Bieniasz (in Lublin blood libel), 244, 245, 246
Binia/Dina (later Barbara; Jewish child in Grabie blood libel), 364–371
Bishop, Jennifer, 44
Black Death, 154, 172, 264, 265
Blado, Paolo, 469n44
Błędy Talmutowe (1758), 347–348
Blois massacre (1171), 27–32, 33, 34, 229, 450n101
blood, discussions of Jewish attitudes toward/use of: Benedict XIV and, 307, 308, 320–321; cultures of knowledge and, 161, 171, 189–190, 199, 204–205; in emerging medieval blood libel narrative, 34–35, 36, 38–39; in ethnographic/cultural texts, 175, 176, 177–178, 180, 182; Frankists on, 331–335, 354; Ganganelli report on, 323–324, 338, 340–341; in Italian blood libel cases, 282, 283–285, 292; in Jewish responses, 210–211, 215–216, 217, 218–219, 221; legacy of Simon of Trent and, 107, 112–113; modern (19th and 20th century) blood libel accusations, 489–490n114; official condemnation, 18th-century Polish Jews' efforts to elicit, 349, 350, 353–355, 378–379; in Polish/Polish-Lithuanian blood libel cases, 239–240, 244–246, 248, 260, 263, 264, 269–271, 273, 364, 365, 368, 369; in Simon of Trent narratives, 51, 55, 57, 81–82, 92–93, 117–118, 121, 122–123
blood cure for leprosy, 39, 248, 392n39, 457n68
blood libel, 1–13, 377–384; attraction of far right, fascist, and white supremacist groups to, 1–4, 3, 380–383, 381, 398n156; Benedict XIV and, 11, 300–322 (*See also* Benedict XIV); cultures of knowledge and, 9–10, 152–207 (*See also* cultures of knowledge); defined, 4; emergence in medieval Europe, 4–9, 14–42 (*See also* medieval emergence of blood libel); "facts," becoming, 166–170, 199, 377; Ganganelli report on, 10–11, 323–344 (*See also* Ganganelli report); Jewish responses to, 10, 208–235 (*See also* Jewish responses); modern (19th and 20th century) instances of, 377, 379–383, 489–490n114; official condemnations of, 11–12, 378–379 (*See also* official condemnations and protections); viewed as singular crime *versus* serial occurrence, 92–93, 116, 190. *See also* Simon of Trent, *and other specific blood libels; specific locations and countries*
blood piety, Christian, 39, 41
blood/sweat flowing from corpse in presence of murderers, 121, 361, 420n178
Blurton, Heather, 23
Bodenschatz, Johann Christian, *Kirchliche Verfassung*, 181
Bodian, Miriam, 234
Boemus, Joannes, 180
Boener, Johann Alexander, 181
Bolesław the Pious (Prince of Great Poland), 196, 201
Bollandists, *Acta Sanctorum*, 10, 25–26, 27, 41–42, 92, 166, 191, 200, 243, 244, 269, 303, 305, 312, 340, 380, 393n60, 417n117
Bomberg, Daniel, 184
Bona (in Simon of Trent narrative), 71, 74, 85, 270
Bona of Savoy (duchess of Milan), 111, 112, 221, 284, 292, 293, 380
Bonafortuna, Antonio Valentino, 294–298
Bonafortuna, Giuseppe, 294–298
Bonanzi, Paolo, 281
Bonaventura (of Trent), *See* Seligman
Bonelli, Benedetto, *Dissertazione apologetica* (1747), 190, 310–311, 340, 358, 475n50
Bonfinius, Antonius, 248, 457n67
Bono, Giovanni, 97, 103
Börner, Christian Friedrich, 271
Botero, Giovanni, 204
Brancato de Lauraea, Cardinal Laurentio, 268
Braun, Georg, *Civitates orbis terrarum*, 169
Brenz, Samuel Friedrich, 215
Bretorio, Bernardino, 221, 291

British Movement, 1–2
broadsheets (also broadside), 6, 44, 45, 77, 98, 99, 132, 135, 144, 145, 147, 261, 262, 306, 320, 423n232, 423n243, 427n297
Brunetta (Engel's mother, in Simon of Trent narrative), 76
Brunetta (Samuel's wife, in Simon of Trent narrative), 46, 49, 51–52, 56, 59, 73–76, 77, 81
Budek (in Cracow blood libel), 170–171
Burcellas (accused in Valréas case), 35
Burnett, Stephen, 179
Buxtorf, Johannes, *Synagoga judaica*, 178–180, 182, 286
Bynum, Caroline, 39, 41
Bzovius, Abraham, 100, 163–164, 165, 166, 169, 189, 206, 271, 431n41, 458n68

Caeca et obdurata Hebraeorum perfidia (papal bull, 1593), 280
Calas, Jean, 374
Calfurnio, Giovanni (Johannes Calphurnius), 95
Caliò, Tommaso, 299
Calmet, August, *Dictionnaire historique* (1722), 181
Calzavacca (Calzavacha), Giovanni, 111–112
Canizza (in Ancona blood libel), 294, 295, 297
cannibalism, 4, 37–38, 48, 190, 388n11, 447n46
canonization/beatification process, 7, 101–103, 138, 301–302, 303–305, 378, 473n21
Canons/canon law, on saints and saint-making, 12, 24, 84, 410n205
Capgrave, John, 25
Capistrano, Giovanni, 97, 149
capital punishment, *See* death penalty
Capodilista, Antonio, 81–82
Capriolo, Elia, 135
Carbone, Ludovico, *Summa summarum casuum* (1606), 102
Carboni, Francesco, 186–187, 189, 439n158
Cardoso, Isaac, *Las excelencias de los hebreos* (1679), 210, 214, 221–223, 234, 270, 284, 308, 421n197, 446n30
Carlebach, Elisheva, 173, 177, 178
Carolina (law code of Charles V), 223, 372, 373

Carthage, Fifth Council of (401), 24
Carus, Joannes Baptista, 287
Casimir the Great (king of Poland), 170, 196, 201
Catani/Catanei, Giovanni (of Ancona), 294–298
Catherine the Great, 359
Catherine of Sweden (saint), 102–103
Catholic Counter-Reformation and Protestant Reformation, 5, 100, 101, 103, 161–172, 173, 177, 191, 379
Cavalchini, Guidobono (Cardinal), 479n3
Celsus (saint), 22
Cerveno, St. Martin's church, fresco of Simon of Trent, 136
Cesidio (saint), 104
Charles of Blois, cult of, 415n71
Charles of Parma, 276
Charles V (Holy Roman Emperor), 221, 223, 256, 267, 284, 286, 291, 292, 293, 380, 449n73
Chaucer, Geoffrey, "Prioress's Tale" (*Canterbury Tales*), 1, 26
Chaves, Heronimo, *Chronographia* (1572), 433n79
Choroduski, Alan, 341
Christian Hebraism, 152–153, 168–169, 175, 179, 183–184, 187, 188, 191, 206–207, 287
Christiani, Friedrich Albrecht, *Der Jüden Glaube und Aberglaube* (1705), 180, 181–182
Christina Alexandra (queen of Sweden), 140
Christological imagery: blood libel narratives using, 18–20, 59, 94, 96–97, 111, 119–120, 127, 129–131, 135–136, 147, 149, 421n197, 422n226, 423n245, 423n247; in Jewish responses, 232–234
Chronicle of the Monastery of St. Peter's (late 14th/early 15th century), 26
chronicles, 152, 153–172; early modern post-Reformation texts, 161–172; "facts" about Jews in, 166–170, 199; Jewish chronicles, rarity of, 208–209; Leipzig report on, 271; medieval texts, 154–161; on official condemnations and protections, 165–166; Polish chronicles, 170–172; printed editions of medieval texts, 164–165. *See also Liber chronicarum*, and other specific chronicles
Cipolletta, Giuseppe (of Ancona, rabbi), 294

Clement III (pope), 410n206
Clement V (pope), 184
Clement VIII (pope), 103, 280, 332, 468n9
Clement XI (pope), 293, 326, 471n76
Clement XIII (pope), 293, 324, 326, 335, 342, 343, 355, 357–358, 366, 382
Clement XIV (pope). *See* Ganganelli, Lorenzo; Ganganelli report
cognitive bias, 383
Cohen, Jeffrey, 18
Cohen, Jeremy, 224
Colmar Annals, 380
conciliarism, 74
condemnations of blood libel narratives. *See* official condemnations and protections
Conditi, Don Donato (of Ancona, priest), 294
confirmation bias, 4, 383
Constantine (Roman emperor), 39
converts and conversion from Judaism: Abeles, Simon, death of, 306–307, 309; accusations against Jews, converts making, 309, 310, 339; in chronicles and texts about Jews, 157, 165, 173, 174, 178, 182, 185–188, 206, 429n3; *Cupientes Iudaeos* (papal bull, 1542), 439–440n168; of Frankists, 332–333, 335, 342; Ganganelli report on, 178, 339, 341–342, 347; Grabie blood libel and, 371; information sources, converts as, 34; Jewish responses and, 215; kidnapping of Jewish children for purposes of conversion, Polish rumors of, 330; as official Catholic policy, 187–188, 299, 336–337; Polish converts alleging persecution from Jews in Poland, 315; Sandomierz blood libels and, 265, 463n170; Simon of Trent and, 50–51, 74–76, 107, 109, 118; Wagenseil's polemic against blood libel and, 308; Wojsławice blood libel and, 346–347; in Zytomierz/Markowa Wolica blood libel, 319–320
Corcos, Tranquillo Vita (rabbi), *Memoriale* (1705) and *Memoriale additionale* (1706), 222, 282–287, 292–293, 324, 335, 341, 342, 469n46, 482n80, 482n82, 483n95
Corsini, Cardinal Andrea, 343, 349–350, 352, 355–358, 366, 369
Counter-Reformation, Catholic, and Protestant Reformation, 5, 100, 101, 103, 161–172, 173, 177, 191, 379
counter-Talmudists. *See* Frankists

Cracow blood libel (1406/7), 170–171
Crassino of Novara (in Simon of Trent story), 71, 85
Crescas (accused in Valréas case), 35
Crescas, Hasdai, 234
Crusades and Crusaders, 33, 163, 189, 229, 270, 337
cult of Simon of Trent: abolition of (1965), 12–13, 446n26; Albert of Świniarów compared to Simon, 244; *arma Simonis*, 137, 140, 423n232; *beatus*/saint designation and, 7, 101–103, 114, 138, 213, 311, 378, 392n33; corpse of Simon, 66, 72, 74–75, 93–94, 98, 100, 123–124, 125, 139, 214, 421n193, 423n232; Council of Trent and, 99–100, 103; devotional spaces and procession routes in Trent, 137–140, 141, 425n270; Hinderbach and, 7, 44, 64, 73, 88, 99, 103, 138, 140; in Italy, 279, 299; lives of the saints/*Martyrologum romanum*, inclusion of Simon in, 7, 8, 100, 104–106, 108, 114, 118, 137, 213; Mariani publication written to raise funds for, 125–126; in *Martyrologium romanum*, 7, 8, 104–106, 108, 114, 118, 137, 213, 302, 303, 304, 378, 379; modern unofficial persistence of, 383; official condemnations of, 7, 9, 12–13, 43, 83–84, 118–119, 124–125, 132–135; *officium* for, 97, 103, 105, 137, 138, 143, 144; path to papal recognition of, 100–106, 118, 137, 268–269, 378; in Poland/Poland-Lithuania, 142–151, 144–146, 150, 194, 198, 205, 320; popularity of, 139, 140, 279; publications about Simon and, 97–98; relics, 43, 45, 98, 99, 100, 101, 135, 138, 140, 142, 261, 340, 414n46, 425n270; trial of Jews for death of Simon and, 44, 62–65, 73, 84, 88
cultures of knowledge, 9–10, 152–207; Bollandists' *Acta Sanctorum*, authoritativeness of, 200; ethnographic/cultural texts, 173–182, 176; "facts," blood libels becoming, 166–170, 199, 377; in Germany, 172, 173–182, 191, 206–207; Hebraism, Christian, 152–153, 168–169, 175, 179, 183–184, 187, 188, 191, 206–207, 287; Hinderbach and Simon of Trent case, 88; impact of, 203–205, 383–384; Internet and confirmation bias, 4; in Italy, 172, 173, 182–191, 206–207;

cultures of knowledge (*continued*)
  Jews, Christian knowledge about,
  152–153; in Poland/Poland-Lithuania,
  172–173, 191–207; regional epistemologies, 172–173, 206–207; theological
  texts, 172–173, 182–183, 184, 187,
  191–192. *See also* chronicles
Cum nimis absurdum (papal bull, 1555), 187
Cupientes iudaeos (papal bull, 1542),
  439–440n168
Cusumano, Nicola, 305
Czechowic, Marcin, *Odpis* (1581),
  204–205, 206, 440n179
Czołowski, Aleksander, 453n3

Dainessius (in Simon of Trent narrative), 46
Damascus affair (1840), 375, 458n75
David (in Simon of Trent narrative), 117, 118
David, Zdenek, 171
dead bodies, Jewish rules on touching, 38,
  397n132
death penalty/capital punishment, 278,
  299, 329, 355, 367, 371, 372, 373–374
de Espina, Alfonso, *Fortalitium fidei*, 170,
  172, 190, 193, 206, 210, 211, 214,
  216–217, 248, 271, 380, 412n23,
  444–445n10
de Facinis, Antonius, 405n115
de Franchi, Curzio, 104
de Fundo, Giovanni, 71
de Gara, Giovanni, *Sefer minhagim* (1589),
  182
de Giglis, Giovanni, 82
de' Giudici, Battista (bishop of Ventimiglia),
  59, 60, 64–71, 73–74, 76–83, 85, 87,
  96–97, 107, 125, 128, 161, 213; *Apologia
  iudaeorum invectiva contra Platinam*,
  213
del Prà, Laura, 135
del Val, Cardinal Rafael Merry, 382, 383
de Malefaratis, Petrus, 70
de Marinis, Giovanni Battista (or de'
  Marini), 341, 382
Dembowski, Mikołaj (bishop), 332
de Prevo, Carlo, 144, 147, 263
de Salis, Giovanni (podestà), 46, 50, 51, 52,
  53, 55, 61, 68, 70, 74, 161, 194, 406n134
de Spina, Alfonso, *See* de Espina
de Sporo, Jacobo, 73–74, 406n134
de Susannis, Marquardus, *De Iudaeis et
  aliis infidelibus* (1558), 166, 332
de Vaschetis (Guaschetta), Giovanni
  Antonio, 82

de Zaulis, Dominicus, 287
Decretales, 24, 101, 410n206
Decretum (Gratian's), 24,
Didier (in Metz blood libel), 250–251,
  458n76
La difesa della razza (1942), 4
Dina/Binia (later Barbara; Jewish child in
  Grabie blood libel), 364–371
Divina, Giuseppe, 425n270
Długosz, Jan, 170
Documenta judaeos in Polonia concernentia
  (1763), 357–359, 362
dog metaphors for Jews, 110–111, 148,
  180, 240, 413n27
Dominican Order, chronicles, 32, 167;
  Cologne 174, 184; relations with Jews
  and, 275, 336; Jews/blood libels and, 61,
  80, 185; letter from head of, 174, 273,
  284, 326, 341, 344, 382; Pfefferkorn/
  Reuchlin affair, 174, 184
Donato (in Pavia blood libel), 111, 418n130
Dragonet de Montauban, 35, 37
Dulceta (in Simon of Trent narrative), 71, 74
Durand/Durantus (accused in Valréas case),
  35, 36
Durini, Angelo Maria, 487n58
Dweck, Yaacob, 437n135

Eckius, Johannes, 197, 199, 442n209
economic role of Jews, in Christian society,
  49, 109, 151, 199, 201, 216–218, 253,
  275–277, 329–330, 448n54
Eder, Johannes (Jesuit), 306, 309
Edward the Martyr (saint), 21
Einbinder, Susan, 28, 229
Einsiedler, David, 451n108
Eisenmenger, Johann Andreas, *Endecktes
  Judenthum* (1700), 270–271, 307,
  464n198
Ela (in Żytomierz/Markowa Wolica blood
  libel), 319
Eli ben Raphael, 479n3
Ems, Gregorius, 84
Endingen blood libel (1470), 80, 98, 106,
  107, 221, 380
Engel/Angelo (in Simon of Trent narrative),
  47, 50, 53, 54, 56, 57, 58, 71, 92, 117,
  129, 401n34, 402n56
England: 25–27, 164 (*See also* Hugh of
  Lincoln; William of Norwich); expulsion
  of Jews from, 26; *Der Stürmer* blood libel
  issue, reaction to, 380–382
Ephraim bar Jacob of Bonn, 30, 31, 395n91

epistemology/epistemologies: 255; blood libel and, 262, 268–269; epistemological communities, 380; epistemological trajectories, 152; new era, 123, 180, 370; regional, 9, 172–207, 208. *See also* cultures of knowledge

Epistle of Rabbi Samuel Maroccanus, 191–192

Erfurt chronicle *(Annales erphordienses)*, 32–33

Esposito, Anna, 75, 403n66

ethnographic/cultural texts about Jews, 173–182, *176*

Etsi Judaeos (papal bull), 201

Eucharist and Eucharistic practices, beliefs, and imagery, 38, 41, 154, 165, 171, 186, 187, 194, 232, 233, 240, 246, 283, 353,

Everard (bishop, in William of Norwich story), 24–25

Exodus Rabbah, 39

expulsions of Jews: blood libel publications calling for, 84, 110, 111; from England, 26, 218–220; "facts" about Jews justifying, 166; from France, 15, 31, 157, 164, 167, 252, 317, 332, 480n35; Hubicki on, 199; from Papal States, 196, 268, 280; from Rawa, Poland, 195; from Regensburg (1519), 162; from Sandomierz, 265; from Spain, 171, 212, 332; from Trent, 49; from Vienna, 268

Facebook, "Jewish ritual murder" page, 1

Fantuzzi, Antonio, 450n90

Fegella (Feigele; in Lublin blood libel), 245

Ferdinand III (Holy Roman Emperor), 140

Ferdinand IV of Hungary, 140, 425n278

Fiani, Shabbatai (rabbi), 323

Filipino, Morganti (Ancona), 296

Fino, Adriano, 190

Fioghi, Fabiano, *Dialogo fra il cathecumino et il padre catechizante* (1582), 185, 438n148

Fleury, Claude, 180, 436n121

Foresti, Jacob Philip, of Bergamo, *Supplementum chronicarum,* 98–99, 157, 160–161, 193, 206, 214, 405–406n124, 446n32

Forli, *See* Motta

Fortis, Isaac, 267, 268

Fosi, Irene, 299, 478n2

Fra Angelico, 422n226

France: blood libels in, 15, 27, 164, 167, 210, 250–256; expulsions of Jews from, 15, 31, 157, 164, 167, 252, 317, 332, 480n35; official pronouncements of French Kings about Jews, effectiveness of, 396n100

Franciscans: blood libel/child murder cases and, 35, 72, 75, 98, 119, 122, 148–149, 310, 331, 420n170; Moroccan martyrs, 97, 102

Franco, Ambrogio, *Martirio del Beato Simone Tridentino* (1586), 114, 137, 138, 142, 418n147, 424n257

Frank, Jacob, 331, 335, 342, 350, 485n24

Frankfurt Brückenturm, mural of Simon of Trent on, 5, 6, 135, 253, 307

Frankists, 333, 354, 366, 481n44 331–335, 337, 339, 342, 347–349, 353, 354, 366, 481n44

Frederick I Barbarossa (Holy Roman Emperor), 34

Frederick II (Holy Roman Emperor), 5, 32–34, 94, 178, 283

Frederick III (Holy Roman Emperor), 45, 71, 221, 256, 270, 284, 291, 292, 293, 380, 449n73

Freiburg blood libel (1502), 98, 107–108

Fridenheim, Caspar Joseph, *Mikve Israel-Die Hoffnung Israel* (1769), 364

Frising, Otto, *De gestis Friderici,* 163, 254

Fulda blood libel (1235), 5–6, 32–34, 36, 39, 40, 42, 86, 164, 178, 283

Gaguin, Robert, 27

Galatino, Pietro, *De arcanis catholicae veritatis* (1518), 182, 183–185, 188, 205, 437n135

Gallerani, Girolamo Antonio (Viterbo), 281, 288–290

Ganganelli, Cardinal Lorenzo (later Clement XIV), 10, 222, 293, 324, 343

Ganganelli report (1759), 10–11, 323–344; acceptance of preliminary report, 327; approval of final report, 342; Benedict XIV and, 324, 325, 327, 332, 335, 336, 340–341, 382; blood, on Jewish attitudes toward/use of, 323–324, 338, 340–341; comparing Polish and Italian court cases, 279, 298; contents and argument of preliminary report, 324–327; on converts and conversion, 178, 339, 341–342, 349; final report, 335–344; Frankists and, 331–335, 337, 339, 342; as internal document not released to public, 342–344, 350, 379, 483n96; Jewish

Ganganelli report (*continued*)
  sources used by, 222, 293, 324, 335, 482n80, 482n82; modern (19th and 20th century) use of, 375–376, 380, 382; Poland, evidence collected from, 328–331; publication of, 375–376, 379, 382–383, 389n19; on Simon of Trent and Andreas of Rinn, 339–341
Gans, David, *Tsemaḥ David* (1592), 214, 444n7
Garampi, Giuseppe, 364–367, 369, 371, 374
Garani, Carlo, 275
Gasparro Baldassare Nicolò (in Ancona blood libel), 294
Gavanto, Bartolomeo (a Barnabite), 104
Genebrand, Gilbert, *Chronography*, 271
Gentilotti, Giovanni Benedetto (of Trent), 119
Gerardo da Fiandra (Gerardus Lisa), 110
Germany: blood libel cases, medieval and early modern, 80, 106; cultures of knowledge and blood libel in, 172, 173–182, 191, 206–207; Nazis' *Der Stürmer*, blood libel in, 2–4, *3*, 200, 380–382, *381*; Simon of Trent and, 106–108, 380–382, *381*; William of Norwich in German martyrology, 27; witch trials in, 232. *See also specific blood libels, by location or name*
Gesti, Antonio (of Trent) and *Martirio di S. Simone di Trento* (1589), 114, *115*, 137, 138, 139, 424n255
Ghezzi, Placido Eustachio, 282, 284, 286, 290
Ghisleri, Michele, 103–104
Gioiello di Core (Viterbo), 281, 288, 290, 291
Giovanni da Feltre, 50–51, 53, 54, 80
Giovanni da Padova, *Martirio crudele dato da gli ebrei a S. Simone innocente da Trento* (1690), 142, 261
Giovanni de Gara (printer), 182
Giovannino di Volpedo, 114
Godwin (priest, in William of Norwich story), 24
Gonzaga, Eleanora, 140
Gonzalez-Fernandez, Fidel, 101
Górski, Jan, *Index errorum* (1569), 192
Gostynin blood libel (1595), 195, 242
Gottardi, Alessandro Maria, 12–13
Gottfried, Johann Ludwig, *Historische Kronyck* (1698), *150*

Götz, Nicolaus, 160
Grabie blood libel (1774), 363–374
Gratian, 24, 154
Grayzel, Solomon, 397n114
Gregory, Brad, 233
Gregory I (pope), 431n32
Gregory IX (pope), 24, 101, 255, 270, 283, 332, 336, 341, 410n206
Gregory X (pope), 43, 83
Gregory XIII (pope), 11, 103, 104–105, 118, 137, 138, 303, 304, 324, 332, 378, 463n166
Grèzes, Henri de, 42, 398n147
Groicki, Bartłomiej, 370; on torture 372–373
Gromek/Aron (in Świniarów blood libel), 238, 239
Grotius, Hugo, 334, 370; blood libel and, 247–249
Guarinoni, Hippolytus, 123–124, 311–312, 421n193
Guillem Chaste (Franciscan friar in Valréas case), 35
Guldinbeck, Bartholomeus, 64
Guldon, Zenon, 441n195

Hájek, Václav, of Libočan, *Bohemian Chronicle* (1541/1596), 171–182, 193, 206
Ha-Kohen, Joseph (or Yosef), 169, 210, 211–213; *Emek ha-bakha*, 209, 211, 226, 444n8, 446n12; *Sefer divrei ha-yamim*, 211
Halpern, Israel, 465n232
Halpron, Jacob, 182
Hanover, Nathan Nata, 448n54
Harff, Arnold von, 99
Harold of Gloucester, 26
Harrington, Joel, 231
Hayward, Paul A., 21
Hebraism, Christian, 152–153, 168–169, 175, 179, 183–184, 187, 188, 191, 206–207, 287
Heinrich IV of Absberg (bishop of Regensburg), 107
Heinrich of Schlettstett, 80, 408n175
Helżbieta/Kalżuchna (child in Punia blood libel), 109
Henri III (king of France), 251–252
Henry III (king of England), 26
Henry (archbishop of Mainz), 337
Henry (count, in Richard of Pontoise narrative), 31

Herc, Abraham, 263, 264–265
Herc, Jacob, 261–263
Hess, Ernst Ferdinand, 178
Hildegard of Bingen, 154
Hillel of Bonn, 450–451n101
Hinderbach, Johannes (prince-bishop of Trent), 7, 88, 377–378; art and iconography of Simon of Trent promoted by, 91, 97, 98, 127–128, 135; Bonelli using archive of, 310; bull partially exonerating, 97–98; chronicles used by, 160, 170; conciliarism of, 74; confrontation with pope over appointment as bishop, 45–46; cult of Simon of Trent and, 7, 44, 64, 73, 88, 99, 103, 138, 140; death of, 99–100, 114; Endingen blood libel, knowledge of, 106; Foresti's chronicle on, 161; historical consciousness of, 88; initial disappearance of Simon reported to, 46; Jewish responses to, 72, 85, 86, 124; legality of trial defended by, 78–84; preservation of Simon's body, expenditures on, 125; publications about Simon of Trent and, 93–98, 131; records of Simon of Trent case and, 44, 59–62, 65, 123, 403n80, 405n118; Regensburg blood libel and, 107; resistance to ducal and papal interventions, 63–70, 73–78; Tiberino narrative and, 49; truthfulness and authenticity of records, issues regarding, 70–73; vernacular Italian blood libel literature and, 110; Werner of Oberwesel, interest in, 42
Hirsch, Solomon Zvi, 446n36, 450n84; *Yudisher teryok*, 214–215
Hoffman, Ludovicus (Jesuit), 200, 442n213
Holy Innocents, cult of, 22, 23, 27, 100, 126–127, 243, 302, 314, 392n39
holy innocents of Pharaoh, Jewish counternarrative of, 39, 392n39, 458n68
Honorius Augustodunensis, *Sigillum Beatae Mariae*, 19
Hoogstraten, Johannes, 184
Hoornbeek, Johannes, 220, 223, 448n64
Li horribili tormenti del beato Simone di Trento, 110–111
host desecrations: Berlin (1510), 162; conflation with blood libel, 42; Deckendorff (1337), 154, 429n8; official condemnation, 18th-century Polish Jews' efforts to elicit, 353; Passau (1478), 83; in Poland, 100, 170–171, 172, 194, 198, 272; in post-Reformation chronicles, 162, 164, 169, 170–171, 172; Poznań (1399), 170, 189, 431n41; Sternberg (1492), 429n8; theolgoical motivations for accusations of, 453n138, 474–475n48
Hsia, R. Po-Chia, 7, 60, 89, 97, 106, 107, 108, 173, 237, 400–401n19, 403n66, 443n242
Hubicki, Szymon, *Żydowskie okrucieństwa nad Naświętszym Sakramentem y dziatkami chrześciańskimi* (1602), 195, 197–200, 203, 238, 244
Hugh of Lincoln (Little Hugh), 1–2, 25–27, 382, 383, 393n60, 474n46
Hussites, 40
Hystorie von Simon zu Trient (Kunne chapbook; 1475), 66, 66–69, 128–131, 129–133, 135, 137

ibn Verga, Solomon, *Shevet Yehudah*, 29, 215–218, 223–227, 229, 270–271, 447n46, 447n48, 448n57
iconography and art of Simon of Trent, 7, 8, 44, 89, 91, 97, 98, 126, 127–137, 129–134, 140–149, 141, 144–146, 150
imperial condemnations. *See* official condemnations and protections; *specific emperors*
Innocent III (pope), 317, 410n206
Innocent IV (pope): Beilis affair and, 382; Benedict XIV and, 311, 317; Ganganelli report and, 326, 327, 336, 338, 341; Jewish responses and, 211, 220, 221; letters and reissuance of *Sicut Iudaeis* by (1247), 5–6, 11, 32, 34–38, 43, 255, 270, 283; Simon of Trent and, 83, 118, 203
Inquisition (or Holy Office): archival evidence from, 11; Jewish responses to blood libel and, 220, 223; Jews' confidence in, 298, Poland's lack of, 325, 326; Polish blood libel cases and, 220, 273, 275, 315, 323ff; Spanish Inquisition, 223, 231; torture, use of, 231; Viterbo, Ancona, and Senigaglia blood libels, involvement in, 295, 309. *See also* Ganganelli report
Ioannetto of Cologne, 303
Isaac (in Simon of Trent narrative), 51, 57, 58
Isaac (in Świniarów blood libel), 238
Isidore of Seville, 184
Isotta (in Ancona blood libel), 296
Israel (later Wolfgang, in Simon of Trent narrative), 46, 53, 56, 107, 117, 129, 401n34, 402n59

Italy, 279–299; blood libel cases in, 111–114, 280–291, 293–299; cultures of knowledge and blood libel in, 172, 173, 182–191, 206–207; vernacular pamphlets about Simon in, 110–111, 114, 114–127. *See also specific blood libels, by location or name*
R. Itzhak (in Richard of Pontoise narrative), 29
Iwaszkiewicz, Jarosław, 147
Izbica Kujawska blood libel (1779), 374

Jabłonowicz, Wojciech (Albertus, Poznań blood libel 1736), 272
Jachim (in Świniarów blood libel), 238–239
Jacob ben Naftali of Gniezno (or Naftali of Gniezno), 272, 283, 284, 285
Jacob of Brescia, 85
Jacob of Riva, 85
Jacques de Voragine, *Golden Legend*, 41
Jampol blood libel (1756), 323, 324, 328
Jankowski, Thomas (in the Grabie case), 363
Jean de Bernin (archbishop of Vienne), 36, 38
Jenson, Nicholas, 91
Jerome (saint), 81
Jeronimo de Santa Fe, 187, 439n158
Jesuits: Abeles, Simon, death of, 306–307; Andreas of Rinn and, 312–313; Guarignoni, Hyppolitus and, 312; Jews and, 275, Lublin, 243–244; Sandomierz, 257, 271; suppression of order in Poland, 366–367, 371; Świniarów blood libel and, 243–244; Wojsławice blood libel and, 346–348; see also Bollandists; Pinamonti, Giovanni Piero; Skarga, Piotr;
Jewish responses, 10, 208–235; Abeles, Simon, death of, 306–307; Ashkenazi responses, 10, 28, 32, 87, 208–209, 214–215, 226–229, 231–232, 234–235; to Beilis affair, 375–376; Benedict XIV and, 306–307; to Blois massacre, 28–31; Christian/non-Jewish sources, appropriation of, 209–215; Christological imagery in, 232–234; consolidation of blueprint for, 291–293; diplomacy, 5, 10, 39, 87, 148, 383; to Fulda, 34; to Hinderbach, 72, 85, 86, 124; holy innocents of Pharaoh, Jewish counternarrative of, 39, 392n39, 458n68; to Italian blood libels, 280, 281–287, 290–293; kidnapping of Jewish children for purposes of conversion, Polish rumors of, 330; legal strategies and tools, 221–222; martyrs/*kadoshim*, accused Jews as, 10, 227–234, 260, 451n102, 453n137; to Metz blood libel, 251–252, 253–256; to modern (19th and 20th century) cases, 382–383; to Mojeki's *Żydowskie okrucieństwa*, 197; official condemnations and protections, citing, 221–222, 255–256, 267, 283–284, 291–292, 320, 366, 369–370; to persecution, ill treatment, and deaths of Jews, 220, 222–234; polemical treatises, Sephardic, 215–220; to Polish blood libels, 240–242, 259, 265, 266–269, 272–274, 320–322, 364–371, 461n123; publication of documents, 356–359, 383; public condemnation of blood libels, 18th-century Polish Jews seeking, 345–356; Sephardic responses, 10, 32, 208, 209–214, 215–220, 223, 226–227, 231–232, 234, 235; to Simon of Trent case, 63, 69–70, 72, 73, 84–88, 118, 124–125, 212–214, 221; torture, discussions about use of, 220, 222–227, 231–232; to Valréas, 36, 39; to Werner of Oberwesel, 40
Jewish ritual murder. *See* blood libel
Jews: earliest visual representations of, 15, 16, 17, 157, 390n4; economic role of, in Christian society, 49, 109, 151, 199, 201, 216–218, 253, 275–277, 329–330, 448n54; eschatological/messianic calculations by, 92, 412n12; forced to listen to sermons, 109–110, 188, 315; Frankists, 331–335, 337, 339, 342; Karaite Jews, 333, 354, 366, 481n44; marranos, 147, 427n303; *minhag* literature, 173–174, 182, 183. *See also* blood, discussions of Jewish attitudes toward/use of; blood libel; converts and conversion from Judaism; expulsions of Jews; official condemnations and protections; Roman Jewish community
Johannes Petrus of Padua (preacher), 72
John of Tynemouth, 25, 26, 393n60
Jopin (in Hugh of Lincoln story), 2
Josel of Rosheim, 177
Joseph (biblical), 253
Joseph (in Lublin blood libel, 1636), 245–246
Joseph (in Verona blood libel), 256
Joseph I (Holy Roman Emperor), 267, 268
Josephus, 154

Józefowicz, Jakub, 363, 364, 367
judicial issues. *See* legal issues
Julius III (pope), 326, 332
Juzefowicz, Israel Iser, 322

Kabbalah and Kabbalists, 116, 183, 205, 206, 331; Christian Kabbalah, 183–184; seen as superstition, 205,
kadoshim / martyrs, accused Jews viewed as, 10, 227–234, 260, 451n102, 453n137
Kakhna (in Wojnia blood libel), 241
Kalisz, Moses, 276
Kalisz blood libel (1763), 358–359
Kaluski, Reverend (in Sandomierz blood libel), 259–260
Kalwaria Zebrzydowska, painting (now lost) in Bernardine monastery, 148–149, 428n314, 428nn308–309
Kalżuchna / Helżbieta (child in Punia blood libel), 109
Kamieński, Hieronym, 363
Kammermeister, Sebastian, 14
kapparot, 174, 180, 181, 199, 228
Karaites, *See* Frankists
Karwicki, Andrzej Dunin, 258
Kazimierz (near Cracow), 203
Kazimierz the Great (king of Poland, see Casimir the Great)
Kembter, Hadrian, *Acta* (1745), 312
Kemp, E. W., 24
Kidush ha-shem shel Reb Matis, 451n102, 451n108
kiddush ha-shem (martyrdom), 10, 28, 227, 229
Kielce pogrom (1946), 377
Kierelis, Szymon (or Kyrilis, Wilno), 149, 244
Kikinesh, Adil, of Drohobycz, 228–229, 451n108
Kimhi, David, 186
Kirchner, Paul Christian, *Jüdisches Ceremoniel*, 181
Kleczkowski, Stanislaus, 357–358
Koberger, Anton, 14, 170
Korona, Marek, 440n179
Korpiska, Joannes (in Lublin), 246
Kossakowska, Katarzyna, 348
Kowalski, Waldemar, 260, 266
Krasnowski, Jerzy, 147, 256, 261–263
Kromer, Martin, 170
Krzemieniec blood libel (1753), 322, 330–331
Kubarka, Agnieszka, 272

Kunig, Matthias, 107, 417n105
Kunne, Albrecht (or Albert), chapbook produced by, 66, 66–69, 128–131, 129–133, 135, 137
Kurtzhandel, Löbl (Levi), 306

Lachman (in Lublin blood libel, 1636), 244–245
Lachrymabilem Iudaeorum in Regno Francie (1236), 165, 283
Ladvocat, Jean-Baptiste de, 354, 486n35
Lambertini, Prospero. *See* Benedict XIV
Landschut blood libel case (1440), 50–51
Langmuir, Gavin, 18, 22, 391n13
Lateran IV, Council, 84, 410n205
Lazarus / Lazzaro (in Simon of Trent narrative), 56, 60, 61–62, 92, 117, 118
League of Cambrai, 99
legacy of Simon of Trent in European culture, 89–151; Andreas of Rinn and, 312, 314; in art and iconography, 7, 8, 44, 89, 91, 97, 98, 126, 127–137, 129–134, 140–149, 141, 144–146, 150; blood libel accusations in Italy, 111–114; Council of Trent and, 99–100; cultures of knowledge and, 160, 167–168, 169, 190, 194, 195, 198, 204, 205, 271; interest in Jewish rituals and culture, 173; Latin publications about Simon, 90, 91–99, 100; liminality and, 89, 101; Metz blood libel and, 252–253; Nazis' *Der Stürmer*, 380–382, 381; north of the Alps, 106–110 (*See also* Germany; Poland); Sandomierz blood libels and, 142–143, 144, 145, 261, 264, 270, 427n306; as singular crime *versus* part of serial occurrence, 92–93, 116, 190; vernacular pamphlets about Simon in Italy, 110–111, 114, 114–127, 137; Viterbo blood libel and, 281, 284. *See also* cult of Simon of Trent
legal issues: cultures / practices, 43, 51, 78ff, 278, 299, 301, 352–353, 372–374; Jewish legal strategies and tools, 221–222; judicial / legal reforms in Europe, 370–374; Simon of Trent trial, legality of, 58, 59, 78–84, 87–88, 97
Leipzig report by Ollearius (1714), 270–271, 380
Leopold I (Holy Roman Emperor), 268
Leopold (brother of Holy Roman Emperor), 312
Leo X (pope), 103, 184

leprosy, blood cure for, 39, 248, 392n39, 457n68
Leusden, Jean, *Philologus Hebraeo-Mixtus* (1663), 364
Lévy, Raphaël, of Boulay, and Metz blood libel (1669–1670), 222, 237, 250–256
Leyzorowicz, Merch, 330
Liber chronicarum (also Nuremberg Chronicle or *Weltchronik*): framework of world in, 168; Jews, Christian knowledge about, 154–157, *155*, *156*; medieval emergence of blood libel narrative and, 14–15, *16*, *17*, 27, 41; Metz blood libel pamphlet referring to, 252; pirated editions, 90, 91, 99, 157; Schedel's publication (1493), 14–15, *16*, *17*, 27, 41, 91, 99, 132, 135, 154–157, *155*, *156*, 168, 170, 380, *381*, 459n90; Simon of Trent in, *17*, 91, 99, 132, 135, 154.15, 459n90; *Der Stürmer* using, 380, *381*
Limor, Ora, 184
Lincoln Cathedral, 1–2, 26, 382
Lindanus, William Damasus, 105
Lippomano, Luigi, 100, 108
Lisbon massacre (1506), 162, 212, 430n27
Little Red Riding Hood, 458n76
liturgy: blood libel and, 23, 31, 38, 58, 94, 193; Council of Trent and revision of, 103–104; *officium* for Simon of Trent, 97, 103, 105, 137, 138, 143, 144. *See also qinah*
Litwinianka, Maryan Janowa and her son Demian, 249–250
Lombardus, Marcus, and Conrad Huser, *De Imposturis*, 204, 206, 434n89
Łomski, Jerzy, 249–250
Lorenzino da Marostica, 114
Louis III (Elector Palatine and Duke of Bavaria), 40
Louis VII (king of France), 316–317
Louis XIII (king of France), 252, 253
Louis XIV (king of France), 251, 252
Łubieński, Kazimierz (bishop), 263, 265
Łubieński, Władysław (archbishop), 332
Lublin blood libels (1636/1659), 244–249
Lucatelli, Bartholomeo, 297–298
Lucius (accused in Valréas case), 35–36
Luther, Martin, 174, 204; *Jesus Was Born a Jew* (1523), 176; *On Jews and Their Lies* (1543), 176, 177, 178
Lutherans and Lutheranism, 99, 247, 264

Maciej Kazimierz (child in Poznań), 272
Maciejko, Paweł, 331

Maciejowski, Cardinal Bernard, 243, 456n36
MacLehose, William F., 392n33
Madruzzo, Aliprando, 145, 427n297
Madruzzo, Cristoforo, 100
Madruzzo, Cardinal Ludovico, 104, 140
Magdeburg Centuries, 162
Maharam of Rothenburg, 452–453n127
Maimonides, used in arguments against blood libel 163, 273, 285, 397n132, 465n213 469n41
Mainz, Council of (813), 24
Małachowski, Jan (bishop of Cracow), 258, 261
Malcherowa, Katarzyna, 453n131
malkot, 174, 181, 436n123
Malvicino, Antonio, 111, 112
Marbach chronicle *(Annales marbecenses)*, 32, 33, 34, 396n109
Marcucci (physician in Viterbo blood libel), 289
Marcus Atilius Regulus, 450n90
Marek (in Świniarów blood libel), 239, 243, 246–247
Margareta Gelbegret, 53, 54, 62, 80
Margaritha, Antonius, *Der gantz Judisch Glaub* (1530 and later editions), 173–174, 177–178, 180, 181, 199; blood accusation and, 177–178
Maria Amalia of Saxony, 276
Maria Anna (queen of Spain), 98, 123, 140
Marian associations in blood libel stories, 19, 23, 120, 418n124, 420n170
Mariani, Michelangelo, *Il glorioso infante S. Simone* (1668), 99–100, 119–127, *126*, 136–137, 139–140, 142, 214, 361, 420n170
Marianna (in Grabie blood libel), 363, 368, 371
Marina (in Wojnia blood libel), 241
Markowa Wolica/Żytomierz blood libel (1753), 148–149, 318–322, 323, 325, 328–330, 348, 361
marranos, 147, 427n303
Martini, Raymondo, *Pugio fidei* (13th century/1643), 183–184, 437n135
Martin V (pope), 40–41, 267, 398n154
martyrdom: child martyrs, 15, 21–22, 23, 302–305, 392n33, 394n67; *kadoshim/* martyrs, accused Jews viewed as, 10, 227–234, 260, 451n102, 453n137. *See also* saints and saint-making
Martyrologium romanum: Andreas of Rinn excluded from, 314; Simon of Trent in, 7,

8, 104–106, 108, 114, 118, 137, 213, 302, 303, 304, 378, 379
Mary (Jesus's mother), 19–20, 23, 48, 75, 96, 110, 111, 120, 130, 136, 164, 288, 318, 418n124, 420n170
Mary (Simon's mother), 96, 120
Mary Magdalene, 130
Mathias (in Lublin blood libel), 244, 246
Matthew Paris, 2, 25, 26, 164, 165, 219, 380, 448n60
Maximi fructus monitum (1699), 256–257, 267–268, 307
Maximilian I (Holy Roman Emperor), 107
Maximilian II (Holy Roman Emperor), 221, 256, 284, 291, 292, 293, 380
Mayer/Mohar (in Simon of Trent narrative), 57, 58, 117
Mayr, Johann, 162
Mazarine, Master, 422n227
McCulloh, John, 18, 23
Medici, Paolo Sebastiano, *Riti e costumi degli ebrei confutati* (1736), 182, 309–310
medieval emergence of blood libel, 4–9, 14–42; Fulda and Valréas cases, 5–6, 32–39, 40, 42, 86, 398n146; Harold of Gloucester, 26; Hugh of Lincoln, 1–2, 25–27, 393n60; in *Liber chronicarum* (1493), 14–15, 16, 17, 27, 41; Richard of Pontoise and Blois massacre, 15, 27–32, 33; Robert of Bury St. Edmunds, 26; saints and saint-making, 7, 8, 15, 20–22, 23–27, 40–42, 398n146; Werner of Oberwesel, 15, 40–42, 398n154; William of Norwich, 4, 7–8, 15, 16, 18–27, 40, 395n103. *See also* Simon of Trent
Meilla (dead child in Valréas case), 35
Meir of Dubno, 362
memory: 8, 9, 15, 25, 26 32, 44, 47, 87, 91, 101, 125, 144, 152, 191, 212, 214, 236, 238, 243, 247, 256, 277, 280, 379; grammars of, 153–172; local, 263; memory trail, 5, 18, 26, 27–32, 119, 247, 383
Menasseh ben Israel: *Hope of Israel*, 234; *Vindiciae judaeorum* (1656), 218–221, 222, 223, 226, 448n57
Menchey, Giovanni, 69
Merback, Mitchell, 475n48
Meshorer, Itzḥak bar Ḥayim, 229
Metz blood libel (1669–1670), 222, 237, 250–256, 458n76
Michele de Carcano (Michele of Milan), 72, 75, 405–406n124

Miczyński, Sebastian, 200–202, 203, 204, 205, 206, 266, 443n219
Middle East, blood libel in, 2
Miechowita, Maciej, 170
Mikulski, Stanisław, 481n50, 481n52
Milan, official condemnation of duke of, 111–114, 221, 256, 270, 284, 291, 292, 293, 326, 380
Mildorfer, Josef Ignaz, 312
minhag literature, 173–174, 182, 183
Młodziejowski, Andrzej Stanisław, 371
Mocenigo, Pietro (doge of Venice), 133–135, 221, 255, 270, 280, 284, 291, 307, 326, 380
Modena, 291
Modena, Leone, 182, 184, 309, 339
modern (19th and 20th century) blood libel accusations, 377, 379–383, 489–490n114
Mohar/Mayer (in Simon of Trent narrative), 57, 58, 117
Mojecki, Przecław, *Żydowskie okrucieństwa, mordy, y zabobony* (1598), 192–197, 198, 199, 200, 201, 203, 237, 241, 242, 257, 310
Molanus, Joannes, *Usuardi martyrologium* (1568/1573), 106, 416n100
Molkho, Shlomo, 212
Montaigne, Michel de, 223
Monumenta Germaniae Historica, 164–165
Morgan, Mary S., 166
Morosini, Giulio, 182, 310, 339, 469n47
Mortara, Marco, 375
Moses (in Simon of Trent narrative), 47–49, 54, 55, 57, 58, 62, 68, 86, 87, 92, 110, 116–117, 129, 130, 401n34
Moszko (in Wojsławice blood libel), 348
Motta blood libel (or Forli, 15th century), 160
Mroczkowiczowa, Maragaretha and Catherina (in Sandomierz blood libel), 257–261
Münster, Sebastian, *Cosmographia* (1567), 157, 158–159, 167–169, 171, 204, 211–212, 445n22
Murner, Thomas, *Hukat ha-pesaḥ* (1512), 175, 176, 177
Murschel, Anna, 232

Naftali of Gniezno (see Jacob ben Naftali of Gniezno)
Naftolowicz, Samuel Szmulko, 322
Napoleon, 375
Nardini, Cardinal Stephano, 65

Nastaska (in Świniarów blood libel), 238, 239
Navagerio, Luca, 135
Nazis and blood libel, 2–4, 3, 200, 380–382, *381*
Neander, Michael, 248
Neri, Filippo, 419n149
Neta of Mantua, 362
Nicolas of Lyra, 113, 285, 339
Noahide laws, 30, 395n94
Nodkowicz, Jakub (in Grabie), 363, 364, 367
Norwich, 4, 15, 18, 24, 40, 164, 166, 219. *See also* William of Norwich
Nostra Aetate (1963), 12
notaries, authority and trustworthiness of, 71
Novello, Sebastiano (Portobuffolè), 114
Novi (Novi Ligure) blood libel (1513), 213
Nuremberg Chronicle. *See Liber chronicarum*
Nussdorfer, Laurie, 71

Odoricus de Brezio, 74
official condemnations and protections, 11–12, 378–379; ambivalence regarding, 11–12; Bonelli on, 310–311; chronicles mentioning, 165–166; first medieval imperial and papal condemnations (for Fulda and Valréas), 5–6, 32, 33–39, 86; in Freiburg, Sappenfeld, and Worms blood libels, 107–108; French kings, effectiveness of official pronouncements about Jews by, 396n100; importance of, 384; Jewish responses citing, 221–222, 255–256, 267, 283–284, 291–292, 320, 366, 369–370; at Lincoln Cathedral, 1–2; modern (19th and 20th century) use of, 380, 382–383; in Pavia blood libel, 112–114; Pinamonti on, 189; in Poland/Poland-Lithuania, 195–196, 200–203, 205, 206, 266–270, 272–274, 276–277; public condemnation of blood libels, 18th-century Polish Jews seeking, 345–356; in Richard of Pontoise narrative, 30–31, 34; Rothschild letter from Vatican, 11, 375–376, 382–383; of Simon of Trent cult, 7, 9, 12–13, 43, 83–84, 118–119, 124–125; to Werner of Oberwesel persecutions, 40; William of Norwich and, 395n103. *See also* Ganganelli report, *and other specific documents*

Olkusz blood libel (1787), 374–375
Ollearius, Gottfried, 270–271
O'Malley, John, 440n168
ordeal by water, 29, 395n90
"Orleans Letter," 28–31. *See also* Blois massacre
Osiander, Andreas, *Whether It Was True or Believable*... (1529), 178

Paladini, Alba, 437n135
Pallantrotti, Mechiore, 469n47
Pallotta, Antonio, 294
Palmieri, Mattia, of Pisa, 160
Pancras (saint), 22
Pantaleon (saint), 22
Paolo de Novara, 71–72, 85–86, 125
papal bulls: *Audivimus*, 24; *Beatus Andreas*, 127, 301, 313–314, 315, 323, 324, 327, 340, 353, 378, 483n87; *Caeca et obdurata Hebraeorum perfidia*, 280; *Sancta Mater Ecclesia* (1584), 187–188; *Sicut Iudaeis*, 84, 165, 317; *Vices eius nos*, 109–110; *Vineam sorec*, 188. *See* specific bulls and popes.
papal condemnations and protections. *See* official condemnations and protections; specific popes
Parone, Giovanni, 262
Passover seder/Last Supper imagery, 129, 130, 422nn227–228
Pastrizio, Giovanni (Ivan Paštric), 287, 335, 469n47
Paszka, Nicolas and Ignacy, 359–361, *360*
Paul II (pope), 410n206
Paul III (pope), 267, 268, 269, 326, 341, 353, 378, 439–440n168, 446n26, 483n80
Paul IV (pope), 342
Paul V (pope), 185
Paul VI (pope), 12
Paul (apostle), 113
Paul of Burgos, 175, 285, 339
Paul (monk in Lublin), 246–247
Pavia blood libel (1479), 111–114
Pavini, Giovanni Francesco, 61, 71, 82–83
Pellikan, Konrad, 168–169
Peñaforte, Raymondo de, *Decretalium* (1234), 204
Pencz, Georg, 450n90
Peretz, Yitzhak Leybush, 451n108
Perini, Valentina, 424n252
persecution, ill treatment, and deaths of Jews, 2, 22; accused Jews as martyrs/*kadoshim*, 227–234, 260, 451n102,

453n137; Basnage on, 308; Blois massacre (1171), 27–32, 33, 34; efficacy of torture, discussions about, 220, 222–227, 231–232, 307–308, 365, 370–371, 373–374; at Fulda, 32–33; in Grabie blood libel, 365, 371; Hugh of Lincoln and, 26; Jewish responses to, 220, 222–234; in Lublin blood libels, 249; Poway shootings (2019), 2; in Poznań blood libel, 274–275; in Sandomierz blood libels, 259, 260, 264, 265; in Simon of Trent case, 6, 52–59, 61, 62, 63, 72, 74, 75–76, 80–81; in Valréas case, 35, 36, 37; Werner of Oberwesel and, 40; William of Norwich, no association with, 2; in Zytomierz/Markowa Wolica blood libel, 318, 319

Pete, Istavan, 243
Peter Comestor, 154
Peter Lombard, 154
Peter the Venerable, 163
Petrus Alphonsus, 429n3
Petrus Bernardus, 35
Pfefferkorn, Johannes, 174–176, 178, 180, 181, 204, 270, 271; blood accusation and, 174; *Ich heyss eyn Buchlijn* (1508), 174–175; *Der Juden Spiegel* (*The Jews' Mirror,* 1507), 174, 175
Pforzheim blood libel (1271), 121
Pharaoh, Jewish counternarrative of holy innocents of, 39, 392n39, 458n68
Pharetra fidei (1490s/1514), 173
Philip II Augustus (king of France), 15, 27, 164, 447n50
Picart, Bernard, *Cèrèmonies et coutumes religieuses de tous les peuples du monde* (1723), 180–181, 182
Pichi, Pietro (Dominican), 185–186
Pietromartino di Anversa (Pier Martino Fiammingo), "San Simonino da Trento" (painting, 1597), 145–147, 146, 427n306
Pikulski, Gaudenty, *Złość żydowska* (1760), 331, 334, 347–348, 481–482n61
Pinamonti, Giovanni Piero, *La sinagoga disingannata* (1694), 188–190, 191, 439–440n168, 439n158
Pistorius, Johannes, 204
Pius V (pope), 196, 268, 332
plague. *See* Black Death
Planctus Mariae, 23
Pliny, *Historia naturalis,* 39, 168
Pliskowski, Szloma, 248

pointed hats, as iconographic markers for Jews, 128, *129, 131, 132, 133*
poisoning, Jews accused/suspected of: church officials, 71, 86; food, 239; wells/water, 2, 86, 124–125, 154, 157, 165–166, 170, 172, 189, 212, 336, 376, 444n7, 445n22
Poland/Poland-Lithuania, 236–278, 323–344; Benedict XIV and, 276, 300, 314–322, 325; blood libel cases in, 5, 9, 10, 92, 93, 100, 108–110, 142–143, 147–149, 194–195, 197–198, 237–250, 256–278, 318–322, 328–331, 345–353, 358–361, *360,* 363–375, 377; chronicles about, 170–172; Council of the Four Lands in, 197, 242, 267, 348, 362, 442n196; Crown Tribunal in, 197–198, 237–238, 240–242, 258, 260, 263–264, 272, 352; cult of Simon of Trent in, 142–151, *144–146, 150,* 194, 198; cultures of knowledge and blood libel in, 172–173, 191–207; Frankists in, 331–335, 337, 339, 342, 347–349, 353, 354; Ganganelli report, evidence collected for, 328–331 (*See also* Ganganelli report); Inquisition, lack of, 325, 326; kidnapping of Jewish children for purposes of conversion, rumors of, 330; knowledge about Jews in, 153; legal reforms in, 370–374; Leipzig report of Ollearius, 270–271, 380; modern (19th and 20th century) blood libel accusations, 377, 379–383, 489–490n114; partitioning of Poland, 362–363, 366–367; publication of documents by 18th-century Polish Jews, 356–359; public condemnation of blood libels, 18th-century Polish Jews seeking, 345–356; status of Jews in, anxieties about, 275–277, 315–317; turmoil, reform, and a decrease in accusations, 359–376, 489–490n114; Visconti's efforts in, 348–362, *360,* 366, 369, 483–484n101, 484n10, 487n58. *See also specific blood libels, by location or name*
Pollmann, Judith, 153
Poniatowski, Stanisław August (Stanisław II August of Poland), 359, 364, 374
Portobuffolè (1480), 114, 418n144
Portugal. *See* Spain and Portugal
Pösing blood libel (1529), 178
Potocki, Feliks Wincenty, 349–350, 352, 356

Poway shooting (2019), 2
Poznań, blood libel (story), 209, 229–231, 235; (blood libel 1736–1740), 272–278, 300, 315, 321, 344; host desecration (1399), 170, 189, 431n41
Pranaitis, Justinius Elisejevitch, 376
Processus judiciarium (1761), 348
protections for Jews. *See* official condemnations and protections
Protestant Reformation and Catholic Counter-Reformation, 5, 100, 101, 103, 161–172, 173, 177, 191, 379
Prynne, William, *A Short Demurrer to the Jews Long Discontinued Remitter into England* (1655), 218–221, 226
Przeradowski, Paulus (Paweł), 462n161
Ptolemy, 168
Publilius Syrus, 223
Pucellina (in Richard of Pontoise narrative), 28, 29
Punia blood libel (1574), 108–109, 194
Pusculo, Ubertino, *Symonides* (1482/1511), 76, 81, 89, 95, 96, 121, 136, 213, 413n33

qinah for the killed Jews in Trent, 86–87
Quaglioni, Diego, 79, 82, 403n66
Quaranta, Stefano, *Summa bullarii* (1608 and later editions), 202–203, 268
Quentell, Heinrich, 160

Rader, Matthaeus, *Bavaria Sancta*, 380
Radliński, Jakub, 238
Radulph (monk attacking Jews, reactions), 163, 254–255, 270, 316, 317, 326, 337–338, 341
Radziwiłł, Prince Michał Kazimierz, 312, 328, 479n19
Ragusa (Dubrovnik), 220
Raimondo, Francesco, 98
Raphael (notary in Simon of Trent case), 71, 405n115
Rapoport, Hayyim Cohen, 481n50
Rashi, 402n60
Rawa blood libel (1547), 195
red bonnet of Didier (in Metz blood libel), 251, 458n76
red tunic, Simon of Trent depicted in, 120, 136, 147, 427n301
Regensburg: blood libel (1476), 83, 107; expulsion of Jews from (1519), 162
Regina (in Kalisz blood libel), 358–359
relics: of Albert of Świniarów, 243; of Andreas of Rinn, 313; Lublin blood libel and, 246; Canons and Councils on, 12, 24, 101, 103, 410n205; Hinderbach's interest in, 44; of Simon of Trent, 43, 45, 98, 99, 100, 101, 135, 138, 140, 142, 261, 340, 414n46, 425n270; of Werner of Oberwesel, 41
Replika na powództwo instygatora sądowego i jego donosicielów (1774), 367
Reuchlin, Johannes, 175, 183, 184
Richard of Pontoise (Richard of Paris), 15, 27–32, 157, 169, 268, 303
Ricius, Paul, 178
Rigord (French chronicler), 27, 447n50
Rinaldi, Odorico, 91–92, 100, 163, 165, 166, 169, 189, 203, 255, 317, 336, 337, 382
Ristretto della vita e martirio di S. Simone fanciullo della citta di Trento (1594?), 114–118, 419n149
ritual murder. *See* blood libel
Robert of Bury St. Edmunds, 26
Robert of Torigni, 28, 163, 395n80
Rolevinck, Werner, *Fasciculus temporum* (1474 and later editions), 41, 98, 100, 157–160, 168, 170, 171
Roman Jewish community: Benedict XIV's crackdown on, 315; Ganganelli report and, 323; on Viterbo blood libel, 325; on Żytomierz/Markowa Wolica blood libel, 320–321
Romano, Giulio, 450n90
Roper the Tailor (in Simon of Trent narrative), 51
Rosa, Salvator, 450n90
rose, symbolism, 19
Roth, Cecil, 382–383
Rothschild, Baron Nathaniel Mayer, 11, 375–376, 382–383
Rottaler, Wilhelm, 72, 406n126, 406n128
royal condemnations and protections. *See* official condemnations and protections; *specific rulers*
Różana blood libel (1659), 426n290
Rozmarynowski, Franciszek, 345–346
Rudolph II (Holy Roman Emperor), 40
Rufach, 168–169, 432n52

Sabbatianism, 331
Sacra Consulta, 282–284, 286, 288, 290–291, 309, 325
saints and saint-making: Albert of Świniarów, 243–244; Andreas of Rinn,

11, 22, 123–124, 191, 311–314, 313; Benedict XIV (as Prospero Lambertini), on child martyrs, 302–305; canonization/beatification process, 7, 101–103, 138, 301–302, 303–305, 378, 473n21; Canons and Councils on, 12, 24, 84, 101, 410n205; Catherine of Sweden, 102–103; Charles of Blois, cult of, 415n71; child martyrs, 15, 21–22, 23, 302–305, 392n33, 394n67; Holy Innocents, cult of, 22, 23, 27, 100, 126–127, 243, 302, 314, 392n39; liturgical revisions to calendar after Council of Trent, 103–104; medieval emergence of blood libel narratives and, 7, 8, 15, 20–22, 23–27, 40–42, 398n146; "private" cults, 101–102. *See also* cult of Simon of Trent; relics
Sales, Francesco de, 101
Salvador, Jona, 253
Salvert, Lucas de Toux de, 364
Samen, Josef, 281, 288, 290, 291
Samuel (in Simon of Trent narrative), 46, 47, 49, 50, 51, 53–57, 61, 63, 86, 92, 117, 129, 142, 401n34, 402n56
Sancta Mater Ecclesia (papal bull, 1584), 187–188
Sandomierz: blood libels (1698/1710–1713), 142–143, 147–148, 247, 256–271, 427n306, 461–462n137; Simon of Trent and infanticide murals, St. Paul's Church, 142–148, *144, 145,* 261, 427n306, 462n147
Sanguszko, Aleksander, 351
Sanguszko, Duke Paweł, 277, 466n241
Sansone, Francesco (Francesco Nani), 72
Sappenfeld blood libel (1540), 108
Sara (in Simon of Trent narrative), 74
Sawina/Sawin blood libel (1595), 195, 242
Saya di Piacenza, 111
Schario, Jakub, 263
Schedel, Hartmann. *See Liber chronicarum*
Schmidt, Heinrich, 153
Schreyer, Sebald, 14
Schweitzer (in Simon of Trent narrative), 53–54, 72
Scultori, Diana, 450n90
Second Crusade, 163, 189, 337
Sedlnicki, Karol Józef, 349
Sefer geulat Israel (ca. 1696), 208–209
Sefer ma'aseh ha-shem, 229
Seligman/Bonaventura son of Mayer (in Simon of Trent narrative), 52–58, 64, 80, 403n64

Seligman/Bonaventura the cook (in Simon of Trent narrative), 51–53, 56, 58, 64
Senensis, Sixtus, *Bibliotheca sancta* (1566), 192, 204
Senigalia blood libel (1721), 291, 293, 298, 320
Sephardic Jews and blood libel, 209, 210–211, 215–226, 445n12; literary responses and torture, 220, 222–227. *See also Shevet Yehudah* and Jewish responses
Serafinowicz, Jan, 368, 463n170
Serbelloni (papal nuncio in Poland), 276–278, 463n166
Serra, Niccolò, 327–328, 332–335
Seven Years War, 351
Sforza, Giovanni Galeazzo (duke of Milan), 111–114, 221, 256, 270, 284, 291, 292, 293, 326, 380
Shevet Yehudah by Solomon ibn Verga, 29, 215, 227, 229, 270, 271, 427n306; popularity, 218; Menasseh ben Israel and, 223; torture in, 223–227; in Yiddish 215, 226–227
Shlomo bar Shimson, 31
Shoham-Steiner, Efraim (also Ephraim), 39
Sichardus, Joannes, *En damus chronicon* (1529), 160
Sicut Iudaeis (papal bull), 84, 165, 317; blood libel and, 34–35, 37, 40, 97, 203, 317, 396–397n115, 410n206
Sigismund III (king of Poland), 366
Sigismund August (king of Poland-Lithuania), 108, 353
Sigismund (duke of Austria and Tyrol), 58, 63, 73, 84, 93, 95, 406n131
Simḥah, Solomon, "Shaḥar avi todah," 232–233
Simon, Richard, *FACTUM servant de réponse au livre intitulé Abrégé*... (1670), 222, 250, 253–257, 270, 284, 338, 383
Simon of Trent, 6–9, 43–88; abolition of the cult, 12–13; in *Acta Sanctorum,* 41; Benedict XIV (as Prospero Lambertini) on, 302–304; body of, 66, 72, 74–75; Bonelli on, 310, 311, 475n50; documentation of, 44, 56, 59–60, 70, 123; executions of Jews accused of killing, 58–59; in Ganganelli report, 11, 339–341; Holy Innocents, cult of, 22, 126–127; influence/power struggles in Trent and, 44–46, 62–63, 81–83, 87–88; initial

Simon of Trent (*continued*)
disappearance, discovery/autopsy of body, and arrests of Jews, 43, 46–47, 49–50, 79; interrogations of witnesses and suspects, 50–58; interventions in case, ducal and papal, 44–45, 58, 59, 63–70, 73–78; Jewish responses to, 63, 69–70, 72, 73, 84–88, 118, 124–125, 212–214, 221; Jewish women and children imprisoned over, 6, 59, 60, 61, 62, 65, 71, 72–75, 84, 85, 407n136, 407n145; Kunne chapbook, 66, 66–69, 128–131, *129–133*, 135, *137*; late-sixteenth-century painting of, 7, *8*; legality of trial, 58, 59, 78–84, 87–88, 97; in *Liber chronicarum* (1493), 17, 91, 99, 132, 135, 154.15; modern attempts to revive cult of, 2; persecution, ill treatment, and deaths of Jews, 6, 52–59, 61, 62, 63, 72, 74, 75–76, 80–81; relationship of witness statements to Tiberino narrative, 53, 54, 55–59, 402nn55–56, 403n64; representations of, 5, 6, 7, 8, 45, 90, *115*, *126*, *129–134*; Richard of Pontoise narrative by Gaguin and, 27; in Rolevinck's *Fasciculus temporum*, 160; significance of case of, 42; suspensions of trials, 58, 59, 63, 64, 93, 404n83; Tiberino narrative, 45, 46–49, 53, 54, 55, 62–64, 77, 80, 83, 106, 149, 400n12; trial records, order and narrative of, 59–63; truthfulness and authenticity, issues regarding, 70–73, 76–77; as turning point in history of blood libel, 377–378, 379; Wagenseil on, 307–308, 310, 311; wounds on body, 50, 124, 421n197. *See also* cult of Simon of Trent; Hinderbach, Johannes; legacy of Simon of Trent in European culture
Simonsohn, Shlomo, 397n114
"Simon Triumphant" iconography, *115*, *126*, 135–137, 140, *141*, 149, 424n251
Simon *victima* iconography, 6, 17, 45, *128*, 135–136
Sixth Crusade, 33
Sixtus IV (pope): Simon of Trent and, 7, 59, 61, 63, 64, 65, 73, 83, 84, 86, 91, 94, 96, 97, 102–103, 124–125, 132–133, 268, 303, 340, 378, 407n136; Foresti's chronicle on, 161
Sixtus V (pope), 7, 11, 97, 105, 114, 118, 137, 138, 149, 300, 303, 305, 314, 324, 340, 378

Skarga, Piotr, *Lives of Saints* (1579), 108–110, 142, 194, 195, 204, 205, 237, 427n306
Skowieski (in Świniarów blood libel), 242–243
Sleidanus, Johannes, 161–162
Śleszkowski, Sebastian, 200, 202–204, 206, 207, 237–240, 243, 247, 258, 266, 268, 443n239
Śliwicki, Piotr Hiacynt, 354
Sloman (Solomon; in Simon of Trent case), 85
Slonik, Benjamin, *Seder mizvot nashim* (1577/1616), 182
Słupecki, Jerzy, 247–249
Smerlowicz, Joachim, 108–109
Smith (in Lublin blood libel), 247
Sołtyk, Kajetan (bishop), 148–149, 479n23; Markowa Wolica blood libel, 318–322, 328–330, 348; Ganganelli and, 336; Grabie accusation and 370; publications and, 485n11
Sommariva, Giorgio, 114, 418n144
Soncino, Gershom, 184
Sowińska, Helena and Rosa, 272, 275
Spain and Portugal: expulsion of Jews from, 171, 212, 332; Lisbon massacre (1506), 162, 212; Sephardic Jewish responses to blood libels, 10, 32, 208, 209–214, 215–220, 223, 226–227, 231–232, 234, 235; Simon of Trent's toe given to queen of Spain, 98, 123, 140; Toledo, violence against Jews in (714), 445n12
Spanish Inquisition, 223, 231. *See also* Inquisition.
Spondanus, Henri (continuator of *Annales ecclesiastici*), 163, 189, 206
Stadnicki, Adam, 197–198, 240
Stanisław II August Poniatowski (king of Poland), 359, 364, 374
Stanislawski, Michael, 215, 226
Staszów blood libel (1610/1611), 456n40
Stefan Batory (king of Poland-Lithuania), 195, 241
Stern, David, 60
Stow, Kenneth, 31–32, 395–396nn98–99, 398n147
Strabi, 168
Streicher, Julius, 200, 380
Studziński, Stefan and Adam, 318, 328
Stumphius, 248
Der Stürmer, blood libel in, 2–4, *3*, 200, 380–382, *381*

Sulzbach blood libel (1699), 307
Super non cultu (papal decree, 1625), 103
Surius, Laurentius (Lorenz Sauer), 191, 206; *Commentarius brevis in orbe gestarum* (1566), 161–162; *Lives of Saints*, 41, 100, 106, 108, 119, 194, 213, 214, 399n160, 446n32
Świniarów blood libel (1598), 197–198, 199, 200, 237–244, 561–562n137
Sylvester (saint), 39
Syrenius, Szymon (also Syreniusz and Syreński), 200, 457n67
Szembek, Fryderyk, 243–244
Szmer (in Sandomierz blood libels), 264
Szmuyłowicz, Zelman, 267
Szydłów blood libel (1597), 193, 242

Talmud, Frankist rejection of. See Frankists
Taranto, Giovanni Giacomo Giovani da, 119–120
Teofilowicz, Marcin (Martino Telofilo Polacco), 142
Tertullian, 219
theological texts about Jews and Judaism, 172–173, 182–183, 184, 187, 191–192
Thibaut (count, in Richard of Pontoise narrative), 28, 29, 30, 31
Thomas Aquinas, *Summa Theologica*, 284–285, 447n42
Thomas of Canterbury, 220
Thomas of Monmouth, *The Life and Passion of William of Norwich* (1172–1174), 18–27, 302, 396n103
Tiberino, Giovanni Matthia (Johannes Matthias Tiberinus): at autopsy on Simon of Trent, 50, 303; chronicles influenced by Simon narrative of, 166; Germany, influence of Simon narrative in, 106–107; *Hystoria completa* (1476), 95, 422n221; "I Am the Boy Simon" (1476), 95–96, 107; Italian translations of Simon narrative, 110; Italy, influence of Simon narrative in, 110, 111, 116, 119, 123; Kunne pamphlet and Simon narrative of, 129; narrative on Simon of Trent, 45, 46–49, 53, 54, 55, 62–64, 77, 80, 83, 106, 149, 303, 400n12; preservation of Simon's body, expenditures on, 125; publications of Simon narrative, 91–93, 95; "Salve, Sancte Simone" (1478), 97–98; Simonian epigrams, 1482 collection of, 95, 96–97; Wagenseil's doubts about Simon narrative of, 307; witness narratives and story of, 53, 54, 55–59, 402nn55–56, 403n64
Tinkle, Teresa, 23
Tobias (in Simon of Trent narrative), 46, 47, 49, 50, 52–54, 56–58, 67, 92, 128, 140, 144, 145, 146, 147, 401n34, 402nn55–56
Tobias/Tuvia (Rożana blood libel), 426n290
Toledo, violence against Jews in (714), 445n12
toleration of Jews in Christendom: efforts to undermine, 110, 113, 123, 193–194, 201, 290; *Etsi Judaeos* on, 201; *Sicut Iudaeis* calling for, 34–35, 37, 40, 84, 97, 396–397n115, 410n206; as traditional policy, 110, 201, 282–283, 290
Tomassini, Luca, 289–290
Torres, Lodovico, 103
Torrigiani, Cardinal Ludovico Maria, 334, 361–362
torture: discussions about efficacy of, 220, 222–227, 231–232, 307–308, 365, 370–371, 373–374. See also persecution, ill treatment, and deaths of Jews
Trattarotti, Girolamo, 310, 475n56
Trent, trial of Jews in: archival documentation and records, 44, 59–63, 70–73, 89, 123; duke of Austria and, 58, 63, 73, 84, 93, 95, 406n131; literary narratives, 47–49; papal intervention in, 59, 64–65, 73–75; validity of, 70–73, 75, 78–84. See also de' Giudici, and Simon of Trent.
Trent, Council of, 99–100, 101, 103
trial of the Talmud (1240), 38
Trithemius, Johannes, *Chronicon*, 164, 380
Troyes, Jewish martyrs of (1288), 232–233
Trulli, Giovanni, 289–290
Tryndoch, Andrzej, 368–369
Tura, Cosme', 422n226
Turluru (in Pavia blood libel), 111, 112
Tutino, Stefania, 162
Tuvia/Tobias (Rożana blood libel), 426n290
Tyczyn blood libel (1764), 359–361, 360
Tyrnau/Tyrnavia blood libel (1494), 457–458n67

Ulpian, 222–223
Urban V (pope), 415n71
Urban VIII (pope), approval of cults, 314; *Super non cultu* (1625), 103
Urszula of Lublin, 109

Usque, Samuel, *Consolation for the Tribulatio of Israel* (1553), 209, 210–211, 226, 445n12
usury, 47, 49, 109, 163, 165, 196, 197, 199, 210, 216–217, 223–224, 307, 317, 405n124, 440n168, 447n52

Valenti Gonzaga, Cardinal Silvio, 276, 277
Valréas blood libel (1247), 5–6, 35–39, 40, 42, 86, 211, 398n146
Vauchez, André, 24, 42, 398n142
Venice: Mocenigo, Pietro, condemnation of blood libel by (1475), 133–135, 221, 255, 270, 280, 284, 291, 307, 326, 380; Rialto Bridge display of blood libel painting (1705), 280, 282, 285–286, 291, 309, 326
Vernier/Verny. *See* Werner of Bachrach
Verona, 68, 110, 291, 470n70; archives, 221, Cardoso, Isaac and, 214, 221; blood libel (1603), 221, 256, 279, 284, 291–292, 293; Ganganelli report and blood libel in, 326, 338, 482n78; use of the blood libel decree from, 380
Veterani, Benedetto (Officer at the Holy Office), 313, 343, 483nn97–98, 486n37
Vices eius nos (papal bull, 1577), 109–110
Vienna expulsion of Jews (1670), 268
Vincent de Beauvais, *Speculum historiale*, 154, 157, 210, 445n14; Hinderbach and, 75, 80
Vineam sorec (papal bull, 13th century), 188
Virgulti, Lorenzo, 336
Visconti, Antonio Eugenio (papal nuncio), 324, 343, 344, 348–362, 366, 369, 483–484n101, 484n10, 487n58
Vital[e] (in Simon of Trent narrative), 53, 55–56, 58, 403n34
Viterbo blood libel (1705–1706), 222, 279, 280–291, 298, 309; as defense blueprint, 291–293, 309, 325, 342; Ganganelli and, 324–325
Vitti, Giovanni Pietro, 190–191, 200
Viva Cantarini, Isaac, *Vindeo sanguinis* (1681), 222, 223, 270, 284, 448n64
Vives, Juan Luis, 223
Volpedo blood libel (1482), 114
Volpini, Antonio, 281
von Brühl, Count Heinrich, 356, 357, 358, 366

von Carben, Victor, 174, 434n89
von Pappenheim, Erhard, 61, 62, 173, 175
von Sonnenfels, Ludwig, 339

Wagenseil, Johann Christoph, *Benachrichtigungen* (1705), 178, 270, 271, 307–308, 310, 311, 417n117
Waldensians, 248
Walsham, Alexandra, 88
Wasilyw, Patricia Healy, 22
Węgrzynek, Hanna, 195, 241, 242, 441n195, 456n21
Weinreich, Max, 209, 451n108
Weißenohe blood libel (1303), 193–194
Weltchronik. *See Liber chronicarum*
Werner of Bachrach (also Werner of Oberwesel or Vernier/Verny) 15, 40–42, 157, 168, 305, 380, 398n154
Wężyk, Walenty, 350–351, 352, 359
white supremacy, 1–2, 383
Wijaczka, Jacek, 441n195
William of Norwich: Benedict XIV on, 303; in chronicles, 154, 157, 163–164, 166, 172, 448n60; Frankist debates and, 332; Jewish responses to, 219–220; medieval emergence of blood libel and, 4, 7–8, 15, 16, 18–27, 40, 395n103; Pinamonti on, 189; in Roth's preface to Ganganelli report, 382
winemakers, Werner/Vernier of Oberwesel as patron saint of, 41, 42
witches, witchcraft, and witch trials, 75, 205, 231–232, 245, 310, 374
Wodzicki, Stanisław, 374–375
Wohyń/Brześć blood libel (1663), 249–250
Wojnia blood libel (1577), 241, 455n21
Wojsławice blood libel (1761), 346–352, 356, 364, 484–485nn10–11
Wolfhart, Konrad, 168–169
Wołłowicz, Antoni Erazm, 328, 336
Wolodkowicz, Philip Felician, 352
Worms blood libel (1540), 108
Wulfer, Johann, 450n84
Wurtisen, Christian, 164

Yavan, Barukh Mi-Erez (Polish Jewish emissary), 332, 356
Yiddish songs and tales about blood libels, 10, 209, 215, 226–235, 240, 306, 365; Christian imagery in, 233–234; martyrdom in, 234–235; torture in, 231–232, 235, 365. *See also* Jewish responses

Yerushalmi, Yosef Hayim, 215, 444n1, 446n30
Yushchinsky, Andrei, 382
Yuval, Israel, 29, 412n12

Zainer, Ginther, *Die Geschicht und Legend von . . . Symon von de Juden au Trent* (1475), 131–132, 134
Zainer, Johann, 107
Zalman, Solomon, 276, 465n232
Zamparinus (in Viterbo blood libel), 288
Zanvil, Shlomo, of Krzeszów (in a Yiddish song), 228
Zasław blood libel (1747), 277–278, 300, 320, 361, 466n241
Zelig, Eliyakim ben Asher, of Jampol (Jacob Selig or Zelik), 323–324, 334, 335, 342–344, 345, 349, 356, 357, 362, 369, 383n96, 478–479nn1–3
Zembrzyński, Joseph (Józef), 462n161
Zeno, Jacopo, 72
Zoller, Friedrich, 422n226
Zovenzoni, Rafaele, 46, 63, 93–95, 119, 128, 400n12
Żuchowski, Stefan, 142–143, 148, 238, 241, 247, 257–269, 271, 272, 310, 368, 460n109, 462–463n165
Żyndul, Jolanta, 148
Żytomierz/Markowa Wolica blood libel (1753), 148–149, 318–322, 323, 325, 328–330, 348, 361